Lecture Notes in Computer Science **15746**

The series Lecture Notes in Computer Science (LNCS), including its subseries Lecture Notes in Artificial Intelligence (LNAI) and Lecture Notes in Bioinformatics (LNBI), has established itself as a medium for the publication of new developments in computer science and information technology research, teaching, and education.

LNCS enjoys close cooperation with the computer science R & D community, the series counts many renowned academics among its volume editors and paper authors, and collaborates with prestigious societies. Its mission is to serve this international community by providing an invaluable service, mainly focused on the publication of conference and workshop proceedings and postproceedings. LNCS commenced publication in 1973.

Yuan Zhou · Sin G. Teo · Xiaofei Xie ·
Zuohua Ding · Yang Liu
Editors

Engineering of Complex Computer Systems

29th International Conference, ICECCS 2025
Hangzhou, China, July 2–4, 2025
Proceedings

Springer

Editors
Yuan Zhou
Zhejiang Sci-Tech University
Hangzhou, China

Xiaofei Xie
Singapore Management University
Singapore, Singapore

Yang Liu
Nanyang Technological University
Singapore, Singapore

Sin G. Teo
Agency for Science Technology
and Research (A*STAR)
Singapore, Singapore

Zuohua Ding
Zhejiang Sci-Tech University
Hangzhou, China

ISSN 0302-9743 ISSN 1611-3349 (electronic)
Lecture Notes in Computer Science
ISBN 978-3-032-00827-5 ISBN 978-3-032-00828-2 (eBook)
https://doi.org/10.1007/978-3-032-00828-2

This Springer imprint is published by the registered company Springer Nature Switzerland AG
The registered company address is: Gewerbestrasse 11, 6330 Cham, Switzerland

Preface

Welcome to the 29th International Conference on Engineering of Complex Computer Systems (ICECCS 2025), held in Hangzhou, China, from July 2nd to July 4th. This edition was part of the well-established event that has been held around the world for the past 28 years. The goal of this conference is to bring together industrial, academic, and government experts from a variety of application domains and software disciplines, to discuss how the disciplines' problems and solution techniques interact within the whole system.

This year the conference expanded beyond the traditional focus on complex computer systems to include new topics regarding complex intelligent systems, such as embodied systems, that leverage emerging artificial intelligence (AI), large language models, and machine learning techniques.

We invited three recognized researchers in the field to give keynote addresses: Tsong Yueh Chen is an IEEE fellow and a professor in software engineering at Swinburne University of Technology in Australia, Tianwei Zhang is an associate professor at College of Computing and Data Science, Nanyang Technological University, Singapore, and Lei Ma is an associate professor with The University of Tokyo and University of Alberta. Professor Chen delivered a keynote talk on failure-based testing, Professor Zhang delivered a keynote talk on security and trustworthiness of Vision-Language Model-driven agent systems, and Professor Ma delivered a keynote talk on Trustworthiness Assurance of Intelligent Software Systems in the Age of Generative AI.

We received 70 submissions, and each of them underwent rigorous single-blind review by at least three reviewers, followed by in-depth discussions among reviewers and a Program Committee co-chair. The Program and General Chairs eventually selected 21 regular papers and 3 short papers for presentation during the conference and publication in the conference proceedings (around 30% acceptance rate for regular papers and 34% overall acceptance rate). With the rapid development of large language methods (LLMs), we organized a position paper track, focused on the positioning and trajectory of LLMs, facilitating discussions on current developments, future research directions, and their applications in complex software systems. We thank the authors for submitting their inspiring work to us, and the Program Committee members and their external reviewers for providing their valuable and timely reviews. The success of ICECCS 2025 was largely due to the support of the Steering Committee and the hard work of the Organization Committee. We hope that all the participants enjoyed ICECCS 2025!

May 2025

Yuan Zhou
Sin G. Teo
Xiaofei Xie

Organization

General Chair

Zuohua Ding	Zhejiang Sci-Tech University, China
Yang Liu	Nanyang Technological University, Singapore

Program Committee Chairs

Yuan Zhou	Zhejiang Sci-Tech University, China
Sin G. Teo	A*Star, Singapore
Xiaofei Xie	Singapore Management University, Singapore

Steering Committee

Jin Song Dong	National University of Singapore, Singapore
Mike Hinchey (Chair)	University of Limerick, Ireland
Xiaohong Li	Tianjin University, China
Shaoying Liu	Hiroshima University, Japan
Mauro Pezze	University of Lugano, Switzerland
Roy Sterritt	Ulster University, UK
Jing Sun	University of Auckland, New Zealand
Yamine Aït-Ameur	IRIT, France

Program Committee

Yamine Aït-Ameur	IRIT/INPT-ENSEEIHT, France
Étienne André	Université Sorbonne Paris Nord, France
Cyrille Artho	KTH Royal Institute of Technology, Sweden
Christian Attiogbé	L2N - Université de Nantes, France
Guangdong Bai	University of Queensland, Australia
Bihuan Chen	Fudan University, China
Xiang Chen	Nantong University, China
Yuting Chen	Shanghai Jiao Tong University, China
Florin Craciun	Babeș-Bolyai University, Romania
Juergen Dingel	Queen's University, Canada

Ruitao Feng	Southern Cross University, Australia
Qian Fu	CSIRO's Data61, Australia
Ning Ge	Beihang University, China
Sudipto Ghosh	Colorado State University, USA
Brahim Hamid	IRIT-CNRS, Université of Toulouse, France
Xingshuo Han	Nanyang Technological University, Singapore
Hiroshi Hosobe	Hosei University, Japan
Zhe Hou	Griffith University, Australia
Qiang Hu	Tianjin University, China
Fuyuki Ishikawa	National Institute of Informatics, Japan
Riheng Jia	Zhejiang Normal University, China
Mingyue Jiang	Zhejiang Sci-Tech University, China
Yu Jiang	Tsinghua University, China
Ferhat Khendek	Concordia University, Canada
Scott Uk-Jin Lee	Hanyang University, South Korea
Yi Li	Nanyang Technological University, Singapore
Yuekang Li	University of New South Wales, Australia
Feilong Lin	Zhejiang Normal University, China
Wang Lin	Zhejiang Sci-Tech University, China
Shangqing Liu	Nanjing University, China
Ye Liu	Singapore Management University, Singapore
Gerald Lüttgen	University of Bamberg, Germany
Yixing Luo	Beijing Institute of Control Engineering, China
Frédéric Mallet	Université Côte d'Azur, France
Guozhu Meng	Chinese Academy of Sciences, China
Dominique Méry	Université de Lorraine, France
Shin Nakajima	National Institute of Informatics, Japan
Helen Paik	University of New South Wales, Australia
Fethi Rabhi	University of New South Wales, Australia
Neeraj Kumar Singh	IRIT-ENSEEIHT Toulouse, France
Ting Su	East China Normal University, China
Yulei Sui	University of New South Wales, Australia
Jing Sun	University of Auckland, New Zealand
Meng Sun	Peking University, China
Wenbing Tang	Nanyang Technological University, Singapore
Haijun Wang	Xi'an Jiaotong University, China
Limin Wang	Nanjing University, China
Shi Lin Wang	Shanghai Jiao Tong University, China
Hironori Washizaki	Waseda University, Japan
Tingting Wu	Zhejiang Sci-Tech University, China
Dongming Xiang	Zhejiang Sci-Tech University, China
Zhiwu Xu	Shenzhen University, China

Cen Zhang	Georgia Tech, USA
Peixin Zhang	Singapore Management University, Singapore
Xiao-Yi Zhang	Beijing University of Science and Technology, China
Jianjun Zhao	Kyushu University, Japan
Yangyang Zhao	Zhejiang Sci-Tech University, China
Yongwang Zhao	Zhejiang University, China
Junjun Zheng	Osaka University, Japan
Changjun Zhou	Zhejiang Normal University, China

Additional Reviewers

Abdelhakim Baouya
Rong Cong
Junchen Ding
Ziqi Ding
Han Fu
Weigang He
Kerstin Jacob
Shuo Li
Xueyang Li
Jingjing LiangBernhard Luedtke
Stephan Merz
Jerome Rocheteau
Mingsi Wang
Youcheng Wang
Xiuheng Wu
Fan Xiang
Feng Xu
Zihao Xu
Tingwei Zhu

Contents

Edge Computing Systems

Large Language Models Empowered Software Engineering

Formal Methods

Position Papers: Software Engineering for Large Language Models

Position Papers: Large Language Models for Software Engineering

Machine Learning for Complex Systems

Runtime Anomaly Detection for Drones: An Integrated Rule-Mining and Unsupervised-Learning Approach

Ivan Tan(✉), Wei Minn, Christopher M. Poskitt, Lwin Khin Shar, and Lingxiao Jiang

Singapore Management University, Singapore, Singapore
{ivantan,wei.minn.2023,cposkitt,lkshar,lxjiang}@smu.edu.sg

Abstract. Unmanned Aerial Vehicles (UAVs), commonly referred to as drones, have witnessed a remarkable surge in popularity due to their versatile applications. These cyber-physical systems depend on multiple sensor inputs, such as cameras, GPS receivers, accelerometers, and gyroscopes, with faults potentially leading to physical instability and serious safety concerns. To mitigate such risks, anomaly detection has emerged as a crucial safeguarding mechanism, capable of identifying the physical manifestations of emerging issues and allowing operators to take preemptive action at runtime. Recent anomaly detection methods based on LSTM neural networks have shown promising results, but three challenges persist: the need for models that can generalise across the diverse mission profiles of drones; the need for interpretability, enabling operators to understand the nature of detected problems; and the need for capturing domain knowledge that is difficult to infer solely from log data. Motivated by these challenges, this paper introduces `RADD`, an integrated approach to anomaly detection in drones that combines rule mining and unsupervised learning. In particular, we leverage rules (or invariants) to capture expected relationships between sensors and actuators during missions, and utilise unsupervised learning techniques to cover more subtle relationships that the rules may have missed. We implement this approach using the ArduPilot drone software in the Gazebo simulator, utilising 44 rules derived across the main phases of drone missions, in conjunction with an ensemble of five unsupervised learning models. We find that our integrated approach successfully detects 93.84% of anomalies over six types of faults with a low false positive rate (2.33%), and can be deployed effectively at runtime. Furthermore, `RADD` outperforms a state-of-the-art LSTM-based method in detecting the different types of faults evaluated in our study.

Keywords: Anomaly detection · Rule mining · Unsupervised learning

1 Introduction

In recent years, Unmanned Aerial Vehicles (UAVs), commonly known as drones, have surged in popularity owing to their use in areas as diverse as aerial photog-

Y. Zhou et al. (Eds.): ICECCS 2025, LNCS 15746, pp. 3–23, 2026.
https://doi.org/10.1007/978-3-032-00828-2_1

raphy, construction inspection, and product delivery. These sophisticated and complex cyber-physical systems (CPSs) are operated remotely with the help of inputs from multiple sensors, including cameras, GPS receivers, accelerometers, and gyroscopes, all of which the control software uses to determine appropriate motor actuations. Failures in sensors and actuators (e.g. due to intentional sound noise attacks [32]), and even environmental factors (e.g. strong wind [29]) can impact the stability of a drone's operation, which can lead to serious and sometimes life-threatening hazards. Detecting and diagnosing these faults accurately and promptly is thus crucial to ensuring the safety and success of the drone and its mission.

One approach for achieving this is *anomaly detection*, a commonly used technique for identifying behaviours that deviate significantly from the norm. In this context, behaviours are inferred from logs of timestamped sensor readings and actuator states, with anomalies defined as abnormal data points or sequences within these logs. Anomaly detection systems for CPSs can be built in a number of different ways, but a particularly popular approach is to train a machine learning (ML) model on historical data from the system. If labelled data is available, then supervised learning approaches like SVM can be used to train a model that classifies new data points as normal or anomalous [8]. However, in drone anomaly detection, labelled data is often unavailable due to the volatile nature of anomalies and the substantial manual effort required for labelling, even when anomalies are known. In the absence of labelled data, unsupervised approaches like clustering [19], local outlier factor [16], and one-class SVM [17] can be used to learn a decision boundary that encapsulates the normal data points. Deep learning approaches, in which neural networks learn the complex non-linear patterns in data sets, can also be used for anomaly detection by serving as time series predictors, with the anomaly alarm raised when predicted physical states differ significantly from the ones eventually observed [13,20,21]. Anomalies can also be detected by evaluating data points against rules (or invariants), in which expected relationships between sensors and actuators are extracted from data sets [12], control programs and the laws of physics [9], or alternatively, are defined based on *a priori* knowledge [4,34].

DronLomaly [30] has taken some first steps towards applying anomaly detection techniques to drones, specifically, by utilising LSTM netural networks to predict future sensor/actuator states and marking anomalies when the actually observed states diverge. Despite some promising results for three sets of flight logs, there remain a number of challenges that are particularly pertinent to drones. First is the risk of overfitting to the training data from sample flying logs. Models must be able to *generalise*, as no two missions are the same: flying in an open field is different to flying in a crowded city, not to mention the differences that arise due to weather. Second, some existing methods, such as LSTM-based ones, lack *interpretability*, making it difficult for operators to understand the nature of an anomaly and to decide what the appropriate action is to take. Finally, drones are often required to satisfy properties that are simple to define with *domain knowledge* but may not always be easily inferred from log data. For example, regulations concerning speed and height restrictions, or acceptable lag between an operator issuing a command and the drone enacting it. Therefore, we are motivated to explore alternative anomaly detection approaches that overcome these specific challenges for drones.

In this paper, we propose RADD *(Runtime Anomaly Detection for Drones)*, an integrated approach to anomaly detection for drones that combines rule-checking and unsupervised-based methods. First, we leverage rules (or invariants) to capture expected relationships between sensors and actuators throughout the main phases of drone missions. Our rule sets are automatically mined from log data using the Apriori algorithm, then complemented with additional custom rules based on domain knowledge (e.g. acceptable latency). Second, we utilise an ensemble of unsupervised models in order to be able to identify more subtle deviations that the rules may have missed. If a rule is violated or (a majority of) the ensemble reports an anomaly, then an anomaly is reported. By eschewing deep neural networks for an integrated rule- and unsupervised-based approach, RADD identifies anomalies across a wide range of missions and reports them alongside the human-readable rules used for their detection, making the results more understandable to users than in previous approaches.

We implemented RADD for the ArduPilot drone software [2] in the Gazebo simulator [1], utilising 44 rules mined across the five main phases of generic drone missions, as well as an ensemble of five unsupervised models (k-means, DBSCAN, OPTICS, LOF, and SVM) that operate by majority vote. We evaluated the approach against multiple datasets covering normal flights as well as multiple faults, such as engine failures, sensor failures, and heavy wind. We found that our integrated approach was able to detect an average of 93.84% of anomalies over six types of faults with a low rate of false positives. RADD's detection rate rises to over 99% of anomalies for the specific cases of heavy wind and various sensor faults. Furthermore, we found that RADD outperformed the baseline of DronLomaly's LSTM model [30], and in an ablation study, observed that our approach requires *both* the rule- and unsupervised-based components to maintain its high accuracy across missions in general. Finally, we observed that RADD was efficient enough to be deployed at runtime and detect anomalies during missions.

The main contributions of our work include:

- The first anomaly detection technique for drones based on the integration of rule-mining and unsupervised learning.
- An implementation for ArduPilot, including 44 rules defined over several mission phases, and an ensemble of five unsupervised models.
- An experimental evaluation in which 93.84% of anomalies over six types of faults (rising to over 99% for heavy wind and sensor faults) with a false positive rate of 2.33%.
- An interpretability study evaluating RADD, where it achieved 6.6 out of 7 on a Likert scale rating as compared to raw data (3.2) in terms of understanding anomalies identified.
- A demonstration of the feasibility of verifying the absence of drone anomalies at runtime using RADD.

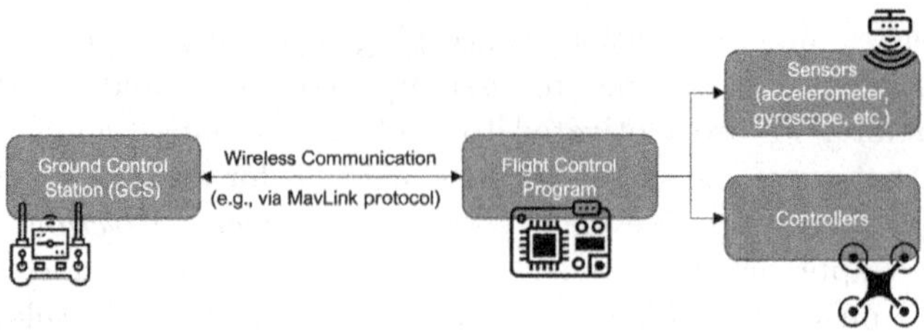

Fig. 1. Overview of a typical drone system

- Source code and datasets used for RADD, available at [3].

RADD's integration of rules and unsupervised models addresses the challenges of generalising across missions and capturing domain knowledge, while ensuring that detected anomalies are accompanied by human-readable rules–enhancing interpretability compared to state-of-the-art LSTM methods [30].

The rest of the paper is organised as follows. Section 2 provides background on drones and the components of the simulation environment we used. Section 3 presents our approach. Section 4 presents our research questions, experiments, and results. Section 5 discusses the related works on anomaly detection techniques for drones and other cyber-physical systems. Finally, Sect. 6 concludes the paper and discusses future work.

2 Background

In this section, we present some background on the structure of a typical drone system, its logs, and our simulation environment.

Drone Setup and Logs. Typically, a drone system consists of a ground control station (GCS), flight control program, sensors, and controllers. Figure 1 shows a block diagram of a drone system.

The flight control program can be embedded in a small computing device such as a Raspberry Pi. It is the heart of the system that controls the drone's movements and operations. It may operate autonomously through an autopilot function for accomplishing a mission (e.g. flying along a preset flight path with multiple waypoints) or by dynamic commands sent from the GCS via a communication protocol, e.g. via a MavLink (Micro Air Vehicle Link) message. It reads data from sensors, such as the Global Positioning System (GPS), barometers, accelerometers, gyroscopes, and thermometers, to detect the physical states of the drone, and sends actuator commands to the physical controllers according to the pre-programmed flight mission or the dynamic commands sent by the user via the GCS. It may control multiple physical controllers, e.g. the z-axis controller for movement along vertical direction, the x-axis and y-axis controllers for movement along horizontal directions, and roll, pitch, and yaw controllers for rotation.

Drones are subjected to extreme conditions including vibration, noise, and environmental stresses. Ideally, sensors/actuators in drones should have high shock survival capability and be fast enough to capture/withstand vibrations, and sensors should be able to filter noise such as GPS signal interference. The performance of sensors and actuators should not vary with changes in environment parameters such as temperature and humidity. When this is not the case, failures or anomalies are said to occur. It is important to detect them in real time so that an operator can take a corrective action promptly.

A majority of drones, especially industrial drones, log flight data during missions. This data typically includes the flight status, sensor readings, actuator outputs, and other information such as configuration parameter values. Behaviours of the drone including anomalies can be inferred from such logs. These logs can be accessed by a program embedded in the drone or in the GCS during runtime[1].

Simulation Environment. To simulate the drones' missions and gather the log data, we used a combination of Ardupilot, Pymavlink, and Gazebo. Ardupilot is an open-source control program for drones and other unmanned vehicles that provides a range of features for controlling the flight of the vehicle, including waypoint navigation, automated takeoff and landing, stabilisation, and various flight modes. Pymavlink is a Python implementation of the MavLink communication protocol, which is a lightweight messaging protocol designed for communication between unmanned vehicles and their ground control stations. The protocol provides a set of Python modules for encoding and decoding these MAVLink messages, as well as tools for working with MavLink logs and performing simulations. The Gazebo Simulator is an open-source 3D robotics simulation software widely used for testing and developing robotics algorithms and systems. It provides a high-fidelity physics engine that simulates the dynamics and kinematics of robots and other objects in a virtual environment.

3 Our Approach

In this section, we present `RADD` *(Runtime Anomaly Detection for Drones)*, a new approach that integrates rule mining and unsupervised learning techniques to detect and interpret anomalies across different drone mission profiles. First, we propose segmenting generic drone missions into several key phases, which is essential, as rule associations may differ across the phases. Second, we describe our rule mining approach for drones, based on the Apriori algorithm. These rules are complemented with additional custom rules based on domain knowledge (e.g. acceptable latency between issuing a command and the drone acting on it). Finally, we propose an ensemble of five unsupervised models to cover the gaps missed by our rules, and explain how the rules and models can be used together to check anomalies at runtime.

[1] As a proof-of-concept and for our experiments, we developed a C/C++ program for DJI drones and embedded it in a Raspberry Pi device attached to a DJI drone.

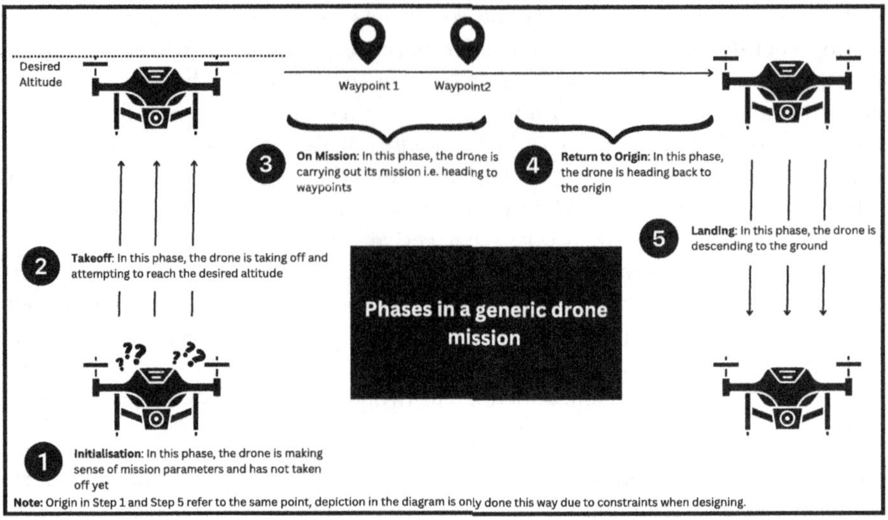

Fig. 2. Phases in a generic drone mission

Deriving the Mission Phases. Segmenting missions into general phases is important for rule mining, because certain relationships between values in the data logs only hold during certain parts of the mission.

For the case of ArduPilot, throttle while the drone is initialising (i.e. setting up and registering the given parameters) would always be expected to be 0. Unfortunately, phases are not defined in the logs of Ardupilot-controlled drones, other than for a column called 'MODE' which has three possible values: Stabilise, Auto and RTL (Return to Launch).

Thus, we propose five phases of a generic drone mission that can be inferred from indicators in the logs. After observing a multitude of missions, we identified five key phases that took place across all of them: Initialisation, Takeoff, On Mission, Return to Origin, and Landing. A depiction of these phases can be seen in Fig. 2.

In the **Initialisation** phase, there is a period of time in which the drone receives commands before taking off or starting a new mission from an airborne point. During this time, the drone is essentially trying to make sense of the mission parameters and waypoints it was given. Thus, we expect the same behaviour in this phase regardless of the particular mission, i.e. no climbing, and no throttle, and thus an invariant range of values.

The **Takeoff** phase begins right after the mission parameters and configurations have been set. The drone will attempt to take off from the starting position and reach the desired altitude of the mission. Once the desired altitude is reached, the **On Mission** phase begins, in which the drone carries out most of its mission, i.e. travelling via some set waypoints.

Table 1. Methodology used for deriving mission phases

Phase	Conditions to check
INITIALISATION	"MODE" in original drone logs is STABILISE
TAKEOFF	"MODE" has changed to AUTO
ON MISSION	Desired takeoff altitude has been reached
RETURN TO ORIGIN	Last waypoint has been reached
LANDING	Original/Desired Coordinates have been reached

Upon completing the mission, the drone moves into the **Return to Origin** phase, in which it attempts to navigate back to its initial position, in the fastest and most linear way possible. Finally, once its original position has been reached, it will enter the **Landing** phase, in which it tries to safely descend to the ground.

Note that these phases are intended to be generic across different types of drones and missions, and we cannot assume that the current phase is given directly in the drone logs. Rather, the current phase is derived according to some key indicators that are likely to be present. For example, we use the relative altitude values to determine whether the drone is ready to transition from Takeoff to On Mission. The indicators for each phase can be seen in Table 1.

Rule Construction. We implemented a form of association rule mining, the outcome of which can be transformed into rules that can be checked at runtime (i.e. Boolean expressions over sensor and actuator values). We classify these mined rules into two types: universal rules, which should hold at any point of the drone's mission, and phase-specific rules, which should hold throughout one of the five mission phases that were previously discussed. Finally, we complement these with domain-specific rules based on domain expertise that may not be implicit from logs.

For CPS logs, specifically drones, rules usually involve a certain kind of range, due to the volatility of the values. We define these ranges based on the minimum and maximum values in our datasets. For example, during takeoff, the roll (rotation along front-back axis) value of the drone would be an abstract raw number like -0.00030842. After considering the data points from the relevant timestamps within a phase and processing it into a range, we would have a lower bound and upper bound. We then used the Apriori algorithm to find transactions that happened frequently during each phase—in our experiments, across a total of 30 datasets (Sect. 4). The algorithm removes infrequent transactions, and uses a minimum support threshold to retain frequent transactions. These transactions are then translated into association rules which would eventually end up as our rules for checking.

Universal Rules. Universal rules refer to the straightforward associations that the algorithm picked up without any changes to the input parameters. These are rules that hold throughout the missions without violation. As missions differ, there are not many of these rules, and they mostly had to do with sensors such as the GPS or Barometer. Barring any faults, these would have constant values throughout a mission.

Phase-Specific Rules. Phase-specific rules refer to those that the algorithm picked up for each of the specific phases only. These rules only hold throughout that particular phase. After mining the phase rules, we observed that there were some rules that might not necessarily hold true at all times in a phase due to possible instabilities. This does not mean that they should not be rules though. By setting a threshold of 99% (100% would be too rigid as there is the possibility of slight deviations due to the volatile nature of drones), we were able to find frequent relationships that held true except for certain minority data points. For example, in a scenario where the expected throttle is between 0 and 80, but one of the observations has a throttle value of 80.12. If not for this one data point, the range would hold. Then, we would examine the minority points, to see if they were negligible or explainable enough for us to still accept the rule or perhaps modify it. In the case of the throttle, we modified the rule to incorporate this value, as it was a negligible amount.

Domain-Specific Rules. We discussed with a few domain experts from the drone industry and gathered some domain-specific rules, with respect to acceptable latency between the remote controller issuing a command and the drone acting upon it. For their specific use cases, drones are required to conduct long range missions, where drones may be affected by conditions like signal interference and obstacles like buildings and trees, which may result in delays in responding to the commands or signal lost. In such cases, since the drone may be visually out of sight, it is difficult to determine whether there is an anomaly or not. Even though the drone documentation may provide a specification of distances where a drone can safely operate in, it is often not clear what would be the acceptable latency. Therefore, we worked with the domain experts to conduct physical experiments with DJI drones and establish rules for determining anomalous latency issues. For example, from our experiments, we observed that the worst possible latency under normal circumstances is approximately 2 s for the DJI drones we tested and any latency more than 2 s should be considered an anomaly.

Unsupervised Learning. While rules can help us define boundaries to catch anomalies that we expect, there are bound to be anomalies that our rules are unable to catch. This is where unsupervised learning comes in to fill the gap, allowing us to capture unexpected or unseen anomalies. Unsupervised learning also focuses on patterns rather than domain-knowledge, complementary to the rule-checking. We propose an ensemble of five models (K-Means, DBSCAN, OPTICS, LOF and SVM), to tap on their respective strengths to detect anomalies, by using a majority vote approach.

Identifying Anomalies by Voting. We then propose a voting ensemble based on the five models to finalise anomaly detection results, as each model has its own strengths in terms of anomaly detection. This is later confirmed in Sect. 4, where we observe that k-means is effective in detecting anomalies from significantly more obvious anomalies, while SVM is effective for anomalies from datasets which are not too severe. We use the majority vote as a decision maker for whether a particular data point is deemed an anomaly or not.

Integrating Rules and Unsupervised Models. We combine rule-based and unsupervised methods through a decision matrix, as shown in Table 2. At runtime, both approaches independently check for anomalies. If an alert is triggered, the user receives a specific explanation—either identifying the violated rule or indicating that the unsupervised model has classified the point as anomalous. Within a sliding window, voting is performed on a per-timestamp basis, with each timestamp's result treated independently. In practice, based on the drone type, mission, and operator knowledge, alerts can be configured to trigger only when the proportion of anomalous timestamps within the window exceeds a specified threshold.

Table 2. Decision matrix for combining the two methods

Rule-Based Method	Clustering Ensemble Method	Decision
Rule(s) Broken	Majority Voted as Anomaly	Anomaly
No Rule(s) Broken	Majority Voted as Anomaly	Anomaly
Rule(s) Broken	Majority Voted as Non-Anomaly	Anomaly
No Rule(s) Broken	Majority Voted as Non-Anomaly	Non-Anomaly

4 Evaluation

In this section, we present the design and results of our experiments to assess the efficacy of RADD at detecting anomalies at runtime. Our experiments are designed to answer the following Research Questions (RQs):

- **RQ1.** How effective is our approach at detecting anomalies in drone missions?
- **RQ2.** Is there a requirement for both parts of the approach?
- **RQ3.** How does RADD compare against the state-of-the-art?
- **RQ4.** Are the results produced by RADD more interpretable?
- **RQ5.** Can RADD be deployed at runtime?

4.1 Datasets Used

Using the simulation environment mentioned in Sect. 2, we generated representative datasets to train and validate our models, as well as datasets with anomalies for evaluation of our approach. The datasets generated were designed to cover a range of 'normal' drone logs with no anomalies (which acted as the base of our training when evaluating our own validation datasets), as well as logs that are representative of several types of anomalies, ranging from harsh environmental conditions to different kinds of drone faults. Table 3 shows the statistics of each dataset.

Table 3. Statistics of our datasets

Dataset	#Entries	Anomalies?
Base	450	No Anomalies
Random	278	No Anomalies
Windy I	674	Anomalous Winds
Windy II	424	Anomalous Winds
Actuator	470	Faulty actuator
Sensor I (Roll)	213	Faulty sensor
Sensor II (Baro)	356	Faulty sensor

Base Dataset Generation. For the base datasets that we used in our models for training, we used the Ardupilot autopilot software, along with *pymavlink* protocol and Gazebo simulator to run missions and collect log data from the drone missions. For the base dataset, we set four waypoints to complete a loop (simulating a real mission, using the same ones every time), and had the drone fly to each of them before returning to the origin.

Validation Datasets Generation. The simulations are configured differently to make sure each of the validation datasets was not identical to the base dataset. Some were created by injecting wind, engine faults, or manually injected sensor faults either throughout the whole mission or at certain periods throughout a mission. We then took note of when these faults were present, and labelled these timestamps as anomalies in these datasets. We then extracted *only* the anomalous segments of the missions to have a 100% anomalous dataset. We first created validation datasets of random missions, which were created in scenarios where we randomised the parameters such as the number of waypoints and mission coordinates, to ensure that they were significantly different from the datasets we used for training.

Simulating Harsh Environmental Conditions. We leveraged on the simulator's ability to simulate winds at user-desired speeds and directions. In cases of sensor or actuator faults, instability would be caused in the drone for various reasons. By applying a strong wind condition to the environment, we aimed to recreate this instability caused by these faults, to create a reflective simulation of them. These datasets had strong winds throughout the whole mission, to simulate sensor or actuator faults throughout. For these missions, there are severe instabilities throughout, and the drone did not manage to complete the mission by returning to the origin. We also created another dataset with respect to wind. As the strong wind that we simulated was too strong for the drone to complete the mission, we lowered the wind speeds minimally (at around 25% of the strong wind's value) such that it could now do so. The instabilities caused in this simulation would still affect the drone heavily, with the only difference that the mission could be completed.

Simulating Actuator Faults. The simulator also had an option to cause faults in the drone's actuator. We could tweak a parameter, to have it only operating at a certain capacity. By setting it to lower values, the drone would not even be able to takeoff. We set the capacity to 0.7, which gave the drone enough to carry out the mission, but with many instabilities along the way. As the value was set throughout the mission, the drone had instabilities throughout as well, even during takeoff and landing.

Table 4. Overall anomaly detection rates achieved by `RADD` (%). Random dataset contains no anomalies and therefore, we do not present *Recall*. All other datasets are entirely anomalous and therefore, we do not present *False Positives* or *Precision*.

	Recall	False Positives
Random (No Anomalies)	N.A	2.33
Windy I (Mission not Completed)	99.40	N.A
Windy II (Mission Completed)	96.93	N.A
Actuator	68.08	N.A
Sensor I (Roll)	100.0	N.A
Sensor II (Baro)	100.0	N.A
Crash	98.64	N.A

Manual Injections to Simulate Sensor Failures. For these type of faults, we simulated sensor failures using manual injection. In many cases, when a sensor is faulty or malfunctioning, it will be 'stuck', and will only display a certain value. A very common sensor fault involves values being stuck either at the minimum or maximum possible value. To simulate this, we chose a random mission and set one of the columns to its maximum possible value according to the simulator's documentation, and used the dataset as one with sensor failure. Specifically, we set the 'roll' column to π, as that was the maximum possible value. We also created another dataset where we assumed the barometer was broken, showing 0 at all times.

Hard Engine Failure Resulting in Crash. For the last type of fault, we wanted to simulate a drone during a crash. Similar to the actuator faults mentioned above, this time, instead of tweaking the capacity parameter by a little bit, we shut it off mid-flight to cause the drone to crash and not complete its mission. We then took the timestamps of when we injected the crash and extracted that part of the dataset for analysis.

4.2 Results

Effectiveness of Anomaly Detection (RQ1). We applied RADD to the logs within all of the aforementioned datasets, and present our results in Table 4.

For the various kinds of anomalies, our approach averaged an anomaly detection rate of 93.84%, rising above 96% for five of the faults. For actuator faults, the rate is lower (68%), which we believe is because the throttle loss induced was not severe enough to be detected as anomalous during all parts of the mission. As for the other faults, they were severe enough to be almost fully detected. Particularly for Windy I, where the wind speeds were so strong that the drone was unable to complete the mission based on the parameters and coordinates that were set. Due to the strong winds, the drone was unstable throughout the mission, and ended up crashing eventually. These occurrences were severe enough for RADD to almost fully detect them. In terms of false positives, RADD kept this down to 2.33%. We observed that the false positives were mostly isolated rows rather than sustained sequences, which means that they can actually be eliminated by having the system only alerting the operator when a sustained sequence of a few points (according to a threshold) are anomalous. Usually, these isolated rows could be due to the volatile nature of drones, where slight deviations or drifts can occur which causes the particular point to be slightly different from its neighbouring points. These detection and false positive rates suggest that RADD may be suitable and practical for anomaly detection in drones.

Table 5. Anomaly detection rates of the rule-checking component only (%)

	Recall	False Positives
Random (No Anomalies)	N.A	2.33
Windy I (Mission not Completed)	99.40	N.A
Windy II (Mission Completed)	96.93	N.A
Actuator	28.08	N.A
Sensor I (Roll)	100.0	N.A
Sensor II (Baro)	100.0	N.A
Crash	98.64	N.A

Table 6. Anomaly detection rates of individual models and the ensemble (%)

	K-Means	DBSCAN	OPTICS	LOF	SVM	Ensemble Recall	Ensemble False Positives
Random (No Anomalies)	0.0	0.58	0.0	87.13	15.2	N.A	0.58
Windy I (Mission not Completed)	55.34	3.1	76.56	97.03	84.42	75.07	N.A
Windy II (Mission Completed)	0.0	3.1	50.0	96.11	1.65	1.17	N.A
Actuator	59.78	0.85	74.89	99.57	75.1	64.25	N.A
Sensor I (Roll)	100.0	2.83	75.94	100.0	100.0	100.0	N.A
Sensor II (Baro)	0.0	0.84	24.43	69.66	3.65	2.52	N.A
Crash	91.89	20.2	0.0	98.6	91.89	91.89	N.A

Ablation Study (RQ2). To prove the effectiveness and need for our approach to combine rules and unsupervised learning, we performed an ablation study, where we isolated the methods and ran the experiment with them solely, to find out the performance without the other method being involved.

Rule-Checking. In terms of false positives, rule-checking alone fared well, with a false positive rate of 2.33%. As for the various faults, it was able to detect anomalies effectively for five of the faults, with only 28.08% for the Actuator dataset, as the throttle loss induced was not severe enough to trigger any breaking of the rules, which resulted in most of the points not being regarded as anomalies. More results can be seen in Table 5.

Unsupervised Learning. Table 6 shows the results for the unsupervised learning portion of the approach. In terms of false positives, unsupervised learning alone fared very well, with a rate of only 0.58. Out of the five models, three had very low scores for false positives, and with a voting ensemble, this percentage was kept low. As for the anomaly detection rates for the various faults, the ensemble had a generally good performance for four of them, but had very low detection rates for Windy II and Sensor II specifically, which we elaborate on below.

Windy I vs Windy II. In the scenario where we simulated heavy wind and the drone eventually crashed, the winds were so strong that the drone failed to complete its mission. Needless to say, these anomalies were caught almost fully by the rule-checking, and mostly by the unsupervised learning. We investigated and found that in the unsupervised learning check, the anomalies that were not caught belonged to a certain period, where the drone was trying to go the wind, and there were certain data points which were very similar in nature. Upon comparison, we found that they were similar to the normal 'On Mission' data points, which could be why they were not flagged out.

As for the scenario where the wind was heavy, but not heavy enough to make the drone fail the mission, while rule-checking was able to flag out almost all the anomalies, unsupervised learning had a very low percentage. This could be because while there are instabilities now, they are constant instabilities, so the models are still able to cluster the points, and the points are not different enough to be recognised as anomalies.

A diagram depicting the two scenarios during takeoff can be seen in Fig. 3.

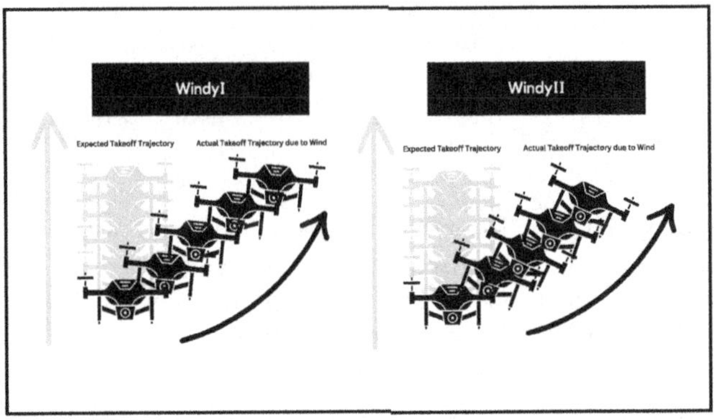

Fig. 3. Comparison between Windy I and Windy II

Actuator. For the scenario where we simulated actuator faults, unsupervised learning performed a lot better than rule-checking. Upon investigation, we noticed that this is because to simulate the actuator faults, we adjusted their performance to 70%. This caused slight instabilities, but not enough for rules to be broken. However, unsupervised learning was able to pick these instabilities up. This scenario shows an example where anomalies are only caught by unsupervised learning, and not by rule-checking.

Sensor (Roll). In this scenario, the Roll value was set to π. While it is a possible value according to the documentation, it is unlikely that the Roll of a drone will ever be that high. Thus, both our unsupervised learning and rule-checking methods detected it at full accuracy.

Sensor (Baro). In this scenario, the Barometer status remained at 0 throughout the entire mission. For the unsupervised learning model, this was not a significant anomaly, as the absence of sudden changes made it difficult to detect—the model primarily identifies deviations rather than constant incorrect values. However, our rule-based checking explicitly requires the Barometer status to be 1, allowing it to successfully detect the anomaly in this case.

Crash. For the crash scenario, as the drone was spiraling towards crashing, the instabilities were very obvious in most of the data points, explaining the high accuracy for both methods.

Comparison to Baseline (RQ3). With respect to RQ3, we evaluated our approach with a baseline comparison against the LSTM model used in DronLomaly [30]. Using the same implementation of LSTM, we compared the performance with regards to our test datasets. Table 7 shows the performance of the LSTM implementation, for 2, 2.5 and 3 standard deviations. Our approach fared better for all the type of faults in terms of detecting anomalies, and was able to achieve a lower false positive rate. In terms of cost, our approach also fared better than LSTM, due to the lesser training time required. The amount of data required for training was also significantly less than what was required for LSTM, with some of our base datasets only having about 500 data points.

Table 7. Recall metrics for the DronLomaly LSTM detector

	2σ	2.5σ	3σ	RADD
Random (No Anomalies)	0.3784	0.1779	0.1301	0.0292
Windy I (Mission not Completed)	0.8352	0.0534	0.046	0.9940
Windy II (Mission Completed)	0.314	0.1362	0.0589	0.9693
Actuator	0.3662	0.3342	0.1572	0.6808
Sensor I (Roll)	1.0	1.0	1.0	1.0
Sensor II (Baro)	0.2643	0.1519	0.1038	1.0
Crash	0.9452	0.2577	0.0532	0.9864

Interpretability (RQ4). We designed a user study to evaluate the interpretability of our approach, i.e. whether RADD allows drone operators to identify what exactly is anomalous about the drone's behaviour. We recruited 20 computer science undergraduates with varying levels of experience in drone operations and data analysis. The participants were first given a briefing on drones, their missions, and the various attributes and parameters that would be involved. We did not, however, show examples of what anomalous data looked like. This was to prevent them from forming ideas of what to look out for. Then, they were presented with anomalous drone missions generated through our simulations. They were then asked to assess and interpret the anomalies using both results: from rules generated by RADD and from just raw data. Feedback indicated that our approach was much easier to analyse (averaging a 6.6 out of 7 on the Likert scale compared to the 3.2 scored by the raw data, with 7 being the easiest), with participants reporting a more intuitive understanding of the anomalies. In terms of actually identifying the anomalies, using our approach, 18 of the 20 participants were able to accurately determine what the anomalous behaviour was. As for the raw data, only 3 participants were able to identify the anomaly. This was achieved through the transparent presentation of rules broken, which allowed users to identify anomalous behaviors more quickly and confidently. In contrast, the raw data often required more time and led to uncertainty in decision-making. The study highlights the potential of our approach to enhance operational workflows by improving anomaly detection accuracy, especially in critical situations where swift identification of issues is essential to maintaining drone safety and performance. More details of the study can be found online[2].

Deploying at Runtime (RQ5). To test runtime deployment of our approach, we deployed it on a Raspberry Pi 4 Model B with 8 GB memory, which can actually be used to control/fly a drone. On the device, we then ran the approach and predicted each observation entry in the random validation dataset, one at a time to simulate an actual log pipeline feeding it data. As the predictions were being made one at a time, we collected the time taken for each prediction for analysis. The results for K-Means, DBSCAN, LOF and SVM can be seen in Fig. 4. The results for OPTICS can be seen in Fig. 5. We can see that k-means, DBSCAN, and LOF are very lightweight, taking about 10 ms (0.01 s) for each prediction on average, whereas LOF is a little bit heavier, taking about 20 ms (0.02 s) for each prediction on average. OPTICS, on the other hand, requires more time as it has to re-fit the training data along with the new data to make a prediction. This makes the average timing significantly higher than the rest, at about 1250 ms (1.25 s). As for the rule checking, the time in milliseconds was almost negligible. Adding all the timings together, it would take about 1.3 s to analyse each data point. Taking into account the amount of time it takes for a drone to actually crash to the ground as well as how long it would take for the user to read an alert and make a decision, this timing is reasonable for deployment at runtime.

Threats to Validity. *(1) Lack of variety in simulator-generated datasets.* As the simulator has limited environment variables for us to experiment with, the simulation data is not comprehensive enough to cover all possible real scenarios. Many faults–such as those caused by human error, which can occur in countless unpredictable ways–remain beyond our reach. As a result, while we can confidently say that our simulations test certain aspects, we cannot generalise the models to all possible fault conditions in drones. A potential mitigation strategy for future work is to incorporate real-world flight log data and adapt it to create more realistic, domain-specific scenarios.
(2) Running the analyses on raw data. We chose not to standardise the data because the selected features–representing the drone's position, speed, and angles–are critical absolute values that are inherently sensitive to changes. Applying a scaler could have distorted these values and compromised their true meaning, potentially affecting the accuracy of anomaly detection.

[2] https://sites.google.com/view/raddstudy/home.

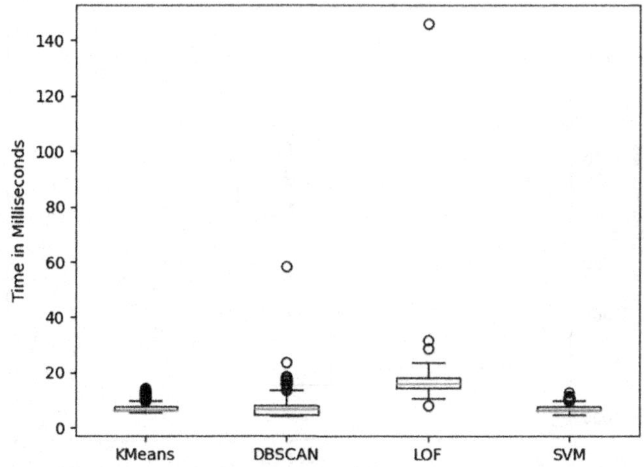

Fig. 4. Boxplot of prediction times for unsupervised models

5 Related Work

Our study is closely related to anomaly detection for CPSs, which typically involves profiling behaviours or patterns from observations such as sensor readings and actuator outputs, and identifying those that differ significantly from the expected behaviour. In general, these approaches can be broadly categorised into rule-based approaches, supervised learning-based approaches, and unsupervised learning-based approaches.

Log-Based Defence Mechanisms for CPSs. Anomalies can be detected by evaluating data points against rules (or invariants), in which expected relationships between sensors and actuators are extracted from data sets [12], control programs and the laws of physics [9], or alternatively, are defined based on *a priori* knowledge [4,34]. To our knowledge, rules for detecting anomalies in drone systems have not been explored. Therefore, in this work, we define some domain specific rules for drones and also propose a rule mining algorithm on the drone logs to automatically derive a specific rule set.

If labelled data is available, then supervised learning approaches like SVM can be used to train a model that classifies new data points as normal or anomalous [8]. However, it may be hard to gather labeled anomaly data, especially since anomalies are often unknown or unpredictable for complex systems like CPSs. In this case, unsupervised approaches like clustering [19], local outlier factor [16], and one-class SVM [17] can be used to learn a decision boundary that encapsulates the normal data points. *Clustering* approaches have been reviewed by Aghabozorgi et al. [5] and Alqahtani et al. [6]. According to these surveys, there is a considerable focus on using clustering to detect patterns in CPSs, for example, for detecting spatial patterns in Silicon wafers [23], for detecting

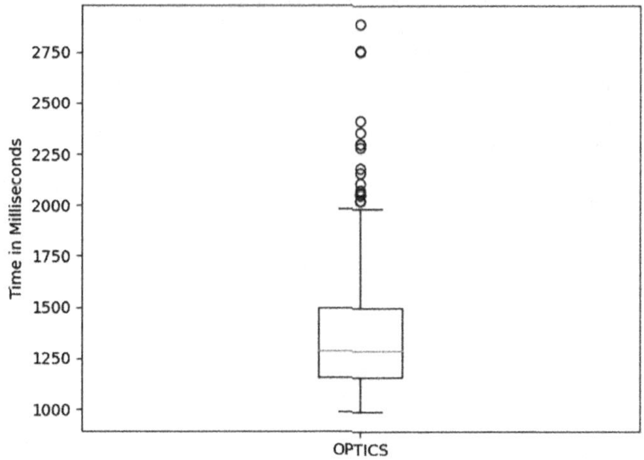

Fig. 5. Boxplot of Prediction Times for OPTICS on Raspberry Pi

machine wear and predictive maintenance [7], and for detecting anomalies in traffic data [27]. Outlier detection algorithms such as One-Class SVM [25] and Local Outlier Factor (LOF) [24] have also been applied for anomaly detection on CPS log data and achieved promising results. But, to our knowledge, these approaches have not been applied in the context of anomaly detection for drone systems. A recent work [31] also focuses on the severity being a key factor in separating critical anomalies and less severe ones. Drone anomalies might not always be critical or severe, so this is an important motivation for us to consider as well.

Deep learning approaches, in which neural networks learn the complex non-linear patterns in data sets, can be used as time series predictors, with the anomaly alarm raised when predicted physical states differ significantly from the ones eventually observed. For example, in [11,13,20,21], LSTM, RNN, and CNN were used to detect anomalies or cyber attacks to industry control systems. DronLomaly [30] has taken some first steps towards applying anomaly detection techniques to drones, specifically, by utilising LSTM netural networks to predict future sensor/actuator states and marking anomalies when the actually observed states diverge. However, DronLomaly has the risk of overfitting to the training data from sample flying logs as its model is trained from a specific mission log and is used to detect anomalies when the drone is conducting the same mission. Models must be able to *generalise*, as no two missions are the same: flying in an open field is different to flying in a crowded city, not to mention the differences that arise due to weather. Generally, deep learning approaches lack *interpretability*. In the context of drone missions, this makes it difficult for drone operators to understand the nature of an anomaly and decide what appropriate action to take, in time. Furthermore, drones are often required to satisfy properties that are simple to define with *domain knowledge* such as acceptable latency, but may not always be easily learnt from log data. These findings motivated us to explore alternative anomaly detection approaches that overcome the specific challenges for drones.

Defence and Analysis Techniques for Drones. In [22,26,28], forensics frameworks for examining the drone's activities via its logs, upon the occurrence of an incident, have been presented. These approaches deal with after-the-fact drone forensics analyses, e.g. to find evidence for the court of law. Drone-specific fuzzing approaches such as PGFuzz [18] and LGDFuzzer [15] have been proposed to detect bugs in drone control programs. These approaches execute a given drone mission with perturbed drone control parameters and detect if the drone violates safety constraints such as crashes. Such approaches are useful at detecting input validation and semantic bugs in drone control programs but are not designed for detecting anomalies such as sensor/actuator failures during runtime.

There are also approaches for detecting cyber attacks on drones at runtime. For example, [14] describes a Moving Target Defense approach focusing on communication network security and intrusion detection, [35] proposes algorithms at the network layer to secure wireless channels used in drones to ground communication in 5G networks, and [10] discusses anomaly detection techniques focusing on distributed denial of service attacks in drone networks. [33] talked about compilating the features and patterns of anomalies in drone logs. Our work in this paper on log-based runtime detection of anomalies in drones can complement such existing defence approaches which have been focusing more on the network and communication layer of drone systems.

6 Conclusion and Future Work

This paper presents RADD, an anomaly detection approach for drones based on the integration of rule-checking and unsupervised learning. The combination of these methods allows RADD to generalise to a diversity of weather conditions and scenarios, while ensuring that detected anomalies are also more interpretable than those caught by deep neural networks. We have implemented RADD for the ArduPilot drone software in the Gazebo simulator, mining 44 rules across five derived mission phases, and training an ensemble of five unsupervised models. We have evaluated RADD with various drone log datasets and found that it is able to detect an average of 93.84% of anomalies over six types of faults (rising to 99% for heavy wind and sensor faults) with a low false positive rate (2.33%), and exceed the performance of a widely-used LSTM-based detector for drones. Finally, in an ablation study we have observed that the integration of approaches exceeds the performance of any one part, and that they are efficient enough to be deployed as runtime checkers.

There are a number of interesting directions of future work. First, we would like to explore whether the ensemble can be improved, e.g. by exploring weighted voting mechanisms based on the level of 'trust' in individual models. Currently, only a basic voting system is used, which can be improved to give us more information about the anomaly if weights were involved. Second, we would like to extend the study to datasets in which multiple types of anomalies are happening at once (or in an interleaved manner). Third, we want to explore incremental rule updates during missions and their phases to adapt to unforeseen scenarios. Finally, we would be interested in exploring strategies for automatically recovering from anomalies once they have been identified by RADD.

References

1. Simulator (ArduPilot Dev Team) (2025). https://ardupilot.org/dev/docs/-simulator-software-in-the-loop.html
2. Ardupilot documentation (2025). https://ardupilot.org/dev/docs
3. RADD repository (2025). https://github.com/ivantanweihan/RADD
4. Adepu, S., Mathur, A.: Using process invariants to detect cyber attacks on a water treatment system. In: Hoepman, J.-H., Katzenbeisser, S. (eds.) SEC 2016. IAICT, vol. 471, pp. 91–104. Springer, Cham (2016). https://doi.org/10.1007/978-3-319-33630-5_7
5. Aghabozorgi, S.R., Shirkhorshidi, A.S., Teh, Y.W.: Time-series clustering - a decade review. Inf. Syst. **53**, 16–38 (2015)
6. Alqahtani, A., Ali, M., Xie, X., Jones, M.W.: Deep time-series clustering: a review. Electronics **10**(23), 3001 (2021)
7. Amruthnath, N., Gupta, T.: A research study on unsupervised machine learning algorithms for early fault detection in predictive maintenance. In: ICIEA, pp. 355–361. IEEE (2018)
8. Chen, Y., Poskitt, C.M., Sun, J.: Learning from mutants: using code mutation to learn and monitor invariants of a cyber-physical system. In: IEEE Symposium on Security and Privacy, pp. 648–660. IEEE Computer Society (2018)
9. Choi, H., et al.: Detecting attacks against robotic vehicles: a control invariant approach. In: CCS, pp. 801–816. ACM (2018)
10. Condomines, J.P., Zhang, R., Larrieu, N.: Network intrusion detection system for uav ad-hoc communication: from methodology design to real test validation. Ad Hoc Netw. **90**, 101759 (2019)
11. Feng, C., Li, T., Chana, D.: Multi-level anomaly detection in industrial control systems via package signatures and LSTM networks. In: DSN, pp. 261–272. IEEE Computer Society (2017)
12. Feng, C., Palleti, V.R., Mathur, A., Chana, D.: A systematic framework to generate invariants for anomaly detection in industrial control systems. In: NDSS. The Internet Society (2019)
13. Goh, J., Adepu, S., Tan, M., Lee, Z.S.: Anomaly detection in cyber physical systems using recurrent neural networks. In: HASE, pp. 140–145. IEEE Computer Society (2017)
14. Gudla, C., Rana, M.S., Sung, A.H.: Defense techniques against cyber attacks on unmanned aerial vehicles. In: ESCS, pp. 110–116 (2018)
15. Han, R., Yang, C., Ma, S., Ma, J., Sun, C., Li, J., Bertino, E.: Control parameters considered harmful: Detecting range specification bugs in drone configuration modules via learning-guided search. In: ICSE, pp. 462–473. ACM (2022)

16. Harada, Y., Yamagata, Y., Mizuno, O., Choi, E.: Log-based anomaly detection of CPS using a statistical method. In: IWESEP, pp. 1–6. IEEE Computer Society (2017)
17. Inoue, J., Yamagata, Y., Chen, Y., Poskitt, C.M., Sun, J.: Anomaly detection for a water treatment system using unsupervised machine learning. In: ICDM Workshops, pp. 1058–1065. IEEE Computer Society (2017)
18. Kim, H., Ozmen, M.O., Bianchi, A., Celik, Z.B., Xu, D.: PGFUZZ: policy-guided fuzzing for robotic vehicles. In: NDSS. The Internet Society (2021)
19. Kiss, I., Genge, B., Haller, P.: A clustering-based approach to detect cyber attacks in process control systems. In: INDIN, pp. 142–148. IEEE (2015)
20. Kravchik, M., Shabtai, A.: Detecting cyber attacks in industrial control systems using convolutional neural networks. In: CPS-SPC@CCS, pp. 72–83. ACM (2018)
21. Kravchik, M., Shabtai, A.: Efficient cyber attack detection in industrial control systems using lightweight neural networks and PCA. IEEE Trans. Dependable Secur. Comput. **19**(4), 2179–2197 (2022)
22. Kumar, R., Agrawal, A.K.: Drone GPS data analysis for flight path reconstruction: a study on DJI, Parrot & Yuneec make drones. Forensic Sci. Int. Dig. Investigat. **38**, 301182 (2021)
23. Liukkonen, M., Hiltunen, Y.: Recognition of systematic spatial patterns in silicon wafers based on SOM and k-means. IFAC-PapersOnLine **51**(2), 439–444 (2018)
24. Ma, M.X., Ngan, H.Y., Liu, W.: Density-based outlier detection by local outlier factor on largescale traffic data. Electron. Imaging **2016**(14), 1–4 (2016)
25. Manevitz, L.M., Yousef, M.: One-class SVMs for document classification. J. Mach. Learn. Res. **2**, 139–154 (2001)
26. Mekala, S.H., Baig, Z.: Digital forensics for drone data – intelligent clustering using self organising maps. In: Doss, R., Piramuthu, S., Zhou, W. (eds.) FNSS 2019. CCIS, vol. 1113, pp. 172–189. Springer, Cham (2019). https://doi.org/10.1007/978-3-030-34353-8_13
27. Münz, G., Li, S., Carle, G.: Traffic anomaly detection using k-means clustering. In: GI/ITG Workshop MMBnet, vol. 7 (2007)
28. Renduchintala, A.L.S., Albehadili, A., Javaid, A.Y.: Drone forensics: digital flight log examination framework for micro drones. In: CSCI, pp. 91–96. IEEE (2017)
29. Shankland, S.: Facebook drone investigation: Wind gust led to broken wing (2016). https://www.cnet.com/tech/services-and-software/facebook-drone-investigation-wind-gust-led-to-broken-wing
30. Shar, L.K., Minn, W., Duong, T.N.B., Fan, J., Jiang, L., Kiat, D.L.W.: DronLomaly: runtime detection of anomalous drone behaviors via log analysis and deep learning. In: APSEC, pp. 119–128. IEEE (2022)
31. Silalahi, S., Ahmad, T., Studiawan, H., Anthi, E., Williams, L.: Severity-oriented multiclass drone flight logs anomaly detection. IEEE Access (2024)
32. Son, Y., et al.: Rocking drones with intentional sound noise on gyroscopic sensors. In: 24th USENIX Security Symposium (USENIX Security 15), pp. 881–896 (2015)
33. Wang, D., et al.: An exploratory investigation of log anomalies in unmanned aerial vehicles. In: ICSE, pp. 210:1–210:13. ACM (2024)
34. Yoong, C.H., Palleti, V.R., Maiti, R.R., Silva, A., Poskitt, C.M.: Deriving invariant checkers for critical infrastructure using axiomatic design principles. Cybersecurity **4**(1), 1–24 (2021). https://doi.org/10.1186/s42400-021-00069-7
35. Zhang, G., Wu, Q., Cui, M., Zhang, R.: Securing UAV communications via joint trajectory and power control. IEEE Trans. Wirel. Commun. **18**(2), 1376–1389 (2019)

FinPTA: An Effective Model for Financial Sentiment Analysis

Chen Yang[1,2], Xiao Yi[1,2], Guisheng Fan[1,2](✉), Huiqun Yu[1,2], and Hengrun Zhang[1,2]

[1] East China University of Science and Technology, Shanghai, China
{yangchen0716,yixiao}@mail.ecust.edu.cn,
{gsfan,yhq,zhanghengrun}@ecust.edu.cn
[2] Shanghai Engineering Research Center of Smart Energy, Shanghai, China

Abstract. Financial sentiment analysis is crucial for market insights and investment strategies. While pre-trained language models (PLMs) have demonstrated significant advancements in general domains, they struggle with the unique linguistic characteristics of financial texts. Financial PLMs improve financial feature extraction but are hindered by limited and uniform training data, restricting their ability to capture contextual and semantic nuances. To address these challenges, this work proposes ***FinPTA*** a novel framework for financial sentiment analysis. Specifically, FinPTA leverages FiLM (Financial Language Model) for domain-specific feature extraction, capturing intricate semantic features embedded in financial texts. After that, the tTransformer, an enhanced transformer encoding model, is employed to better capture contextual relationships within financial texts. Finally, to further enhance robustness and generalization, we incorporate adversarial training, enabling the model to withstand perturbations and ambiguities inherent in financial texts. Experimental results demonstrate that FinPTA achieves state-of-the-art performance across multiple financial datasets, providing a robust and reliable solution for financial sentiment analysis tasks.

Keywords: Financial Text · Sentiment Analysis · PLMs · Transformer · Adversarial Training

1 Introduction

The financial industry has traditionally relied on structured data such as stock prices and economic indicators. Recently, the emergence of unstructured data, including financial news, social media content, and corporate announcements, has introduced an additional dimension to analysis: financial sentiment. Financial sentiment captures the emotions of market participants and significantly influences short-term price fluctuations and broader market trends. Analyzing financial sentiment has become critical for tasks such as market forecasting, risk management, and investment decision-making. By extracting sentiment signals

Y. Zhou et al. (Eds.): ICECCS 2025, LNCS 15746, pp. 24–37, 2026.
https://doi.org/10.1007/978-3-032-00828-2_2

from various textual sources, firms can better predict stock movements and optimize portfolio strategies accordingly.

Despite its potential, financial sentiment analysis presents several challenges, such as the use of domain-specific terminology and inconsistent data quality. Accurate sentiment interpretation necessitates advanced techniques capable of capturing the linguistic complexity inherent in financial texts. Early lexicon-based approaches relied on static dictionaries, which restricted their adaptability to evolving language usage. Supervised machine learning methods improved classification performance but required labor-intensive manual annotation. PLMs provide richer semantic representations. However, they often fail to effectively capture finance-specific terminology. Although domain-adapted financial PLMs have been developed to address this gap, they remain constrained by limited domain-specific corpora and susceptibility to adversarial perturbations.

To overcome these challenges, we propose FinPTA, a framework for financial sentiment analysis. Our contributions lie in three aspects:

- We propose FinPTA, a novel framework for financial sentiment analysis that leverages financial PLMs for domain-specific feature extraction, integrates tTransformer for contextual relationship modeling, and enhances model robustness through adversarial training.
- To further improve the contextual understanding of financial texts, we introduce a post-processing model, tTransformer, which applies transposed self-attention learning to financial features. By incorporating future-sentence prediction as an auxiliary task, the model refines the extracted features to achieve more accurate sentiment classification.
- Experimentally, FinPTA achieves state-of-the-art performance across financial benchmark datasets, providing an effective approach for financial sentiment analysis tasks. We conduct extensive analyses of architectural choices and generality of the tTransformer, effectively demonstrating the feasibility of combining PLMs with time-series models for financial sentiment analysis.

2 Related Work

2.1 Financial Sentiment

Financial sentiment reflects the emotions and attitudes of market participants toward financial markets, companies, or stocks, influencing market behavior and investment decisions [4]. Sentiment classification is commonly divided into three dimensions: polarity-based (positive, negative, neutral), emotion-based (happy, sad, hopeful), and dimensional approaches (continuous numerical values). These methods are widely applied in predicting market trends, assessing risks, and informing investment strategies by analyzing sentiment in financial news, social media, and analyst reports [6].

2.2 Methods of Financial Sentiment

Machine Learning. Sentiment analysis frequently combines machine learning and lexicon-based approaches, framing the task as a classification problem. Loughran proposed a financial sentiment dictionary, which has become a foundational work in the field [17]. Bollen [3] leveraged Twitter sentiment to predict the Dow Jones using Support Vector Machines, while Amrani [1] applied Random Forests to Amazon reviews, achieving superior performance. However, these approaches require extensive manual annotation, which is time-consuming and costly [8].

Deep Learning. Deep learning excels in financial sentiment analysis by automatically extracting complex features and eliminating the need for manual feature engineering. Hybrid models like CNN-LSTM have demonstrated high accuracy in sentiment analysis tasks [10]. Jangid [12] applied multi-channel CNN and BiLSTM for sentiment analysis and ranked among the top performers in the FiQA 2018 challenge.

Pre-trained Language Models. PLMs are pre-trained on large-scale corpora via self-supervised learning objectives, producing high-quality sentence representations. BERT [7] pre-trained on extensive unlabeled text for rich embeddings, excelling in various tasks. XLNet [24] improves on BERT by capturing bidirectional context. However, general PLMs struggle with financial terminology. FinBERT [2], trained on financial texts, more effectively captures financial semantics. FiLM [5], trained on a broader financial corpus, outperforms both financial and generic PLMs in financial tasks.

Adversarial Training. Adversarial training, a concept introduced by GAN [9], improves model robustness by incorporating perturbation-based adversarial examples. BERT Adversarial Training [13] applies the approach to aspect-based sentiment analysis, enhancing BERT's ability to capture nuanced sentiments.

3 Method

This section provides a detailed overview of FinPTA. The overall architecture, illustrated in Fig. 1, consists of three main modules: FiLM, tTransformer, and Adversarial Training. The input financial text first undergoes tokenization, where it is segmented and special markers are added. Subsequently, the text is processed by FiLM for feature extraction, effectively capturing the semantic features of the financial text. Perturbations are introduced at the embedding layer of FiLM to enhance the model's robustness. Finally, the features are transposed and fed into a tTransformer, which deeply explores the contextual relationships within the text from a different perspective.

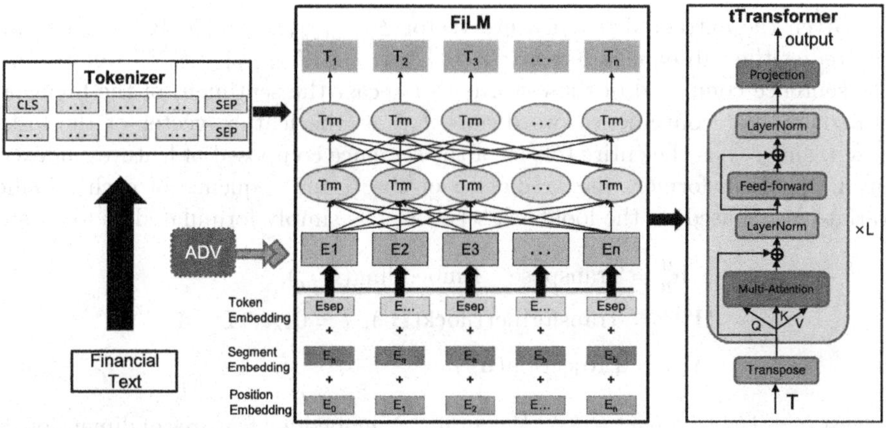

Fig. 1. The overall structure of FinPTA.Trm represents the transformer block.

3.1 FiLM for Feature Extraction

FiLM is a RoBERTa-based language model trained on diverse financial texts, effectively capturing domain-specific terminology and context. It outperforms other PLMs on six financial tasks, showing superior semantic and representational capabilities. Our work utilizes FiLM to extract features from financial text, effectively capturing the co-occurrence relationships between financial terms and phrases. Given a financial text of length t, denoted as $T = \{T_1, T_2, \ldots, T_t\}$, where T_i represents the i-th word or symbol, the raw input is first processed using a tokenizer. This process step includes tokenization, stop-word removal, and the insertion of special tokens for segment separation. After this step, we obtain $X = \{Input\_ids, Token\_type\_ids, Attention\_mask\} \in \mathbb{R}^{3\times M}$, where M is the maximum sentence length. Subsequently, the encoded input X is fed into the FiLM model for feature extraction, as follows:

$$F = \text{FiLM}(X),$$

where $F = \{f_1, f_2, f_3, \ldots, f_M\}$, and each $f_i \in \mathbb{R}^N$ represents the N-dimensional feature vector of the i-th token. These vectors correspond to the output of the last hidden layer in FiLM and capture the semantic and contextual information of the financial text.

3.2 tTransformer for Contextual Exploration

Structure Overview. The tTransformer (transpose Transformer) is composed of a transposed embedding layer, L Transformer blocks, and a final projection layer. The embedding layer transposes feature vectors, while each Transformer block consists of self-attention, layer normalization, and feed-forward networks. Finally, the projection layer aggregates features using Max Pooling, followed by a Multilayer Perceptron (MLP) to perform financial sentiment classification.

Given the extracted text feature vector $F = \{f_1, ..., f_M\} \in \mathbb{R}^{M \times N}$, we aim to predict the subsequent S words $Y = \{X_{M+1}, ..., X_{M+S}\} \in \mathbb{R}^{S \times N}$ and utilize the sentence composed of these words to forecast the sentiment of the financial statement. For convenience, we denote $f_{m,:}$ as the feature vector of the m-th token, and $f_{:,n}$ as the entire tokens of the sentence composed of features indexed by n. In tTransformer, the prediction of the future sequence of each specific variate $\hat{\mathbf{Y}}_{:,n}$ based on the lookback series $\mathbf{F}_{:,n}$ is simply formulated as follows:

$$\begin{aligned} \mathbf{h}_n^0 &= \text{Transpose\_Embedding}(\mathbf{F}_{:,n}), \\ \mathbf{H}^{l+1} &= \text{TransformerBlock}(\mathbf{H}^l), \ l = 0, \ldots, L-1, \\ \hat{\mathbf{Y}}_{:,n} &= \text{Projection}(\mathbf{h}_n^L), \end{aligned} \tag{1}$$

where $H = \{h_1, \ldots, h_N\} \in \mathbb{R}^{N \times D}$ contains N embedded features of dimension D and the superscript denotes the layer index. Transpose_Embedding : $\mathbb{R}^{M \times N} \mapsto \mathbb{R}^{N \times M} \mapsto \mathbb{R}^{N \times D}$ and Projection : $\mathbb{R}^{N \times D} \mapsto \mathbb{R}^{D \times N} \mapsto \mathbb{R}^{S \times N}$ are both implemented through a combination of transposition and an MLP. The embedded features interact with one another through self-attention mechanisms and are independently processed by a feed-forward network within each TransformerBlock.

TransformerBlock. tTransformer comprises L stacked TransformerBlock layers, each containing self-attention, layer normalization, and feed-forward networks, which are integral to the architecture.

Layer Normalization. This method normalizes neuron activations within each sample, improving convergence and training stability in deep models. Standard layer normalization in Transformer architectures may weaken word distinctions by normalizing across all token features. To improve this, we normalize each word independently across feature dimensions, enhancing word salience, robustness, and overall performance.

Feed-Forward Network. In the transformerBlock, each layer consists of a feed-forward network (FFN) with two linear layers, a GEGLU activation function, and a Dropout layer. GEGLU enhances pattern recognition by combining the non-linearity of GeLU with the gating mechanism of GLU, while Dropout mitigates overfitting. The tTransformer processes transposed feature sequences through the FFN, enabling better capture of complex financial sentiment features.

Self-attention. We propose transposing the input by treating the sequence of sentences corresponding to a single feature as input tokens for the attention mechanism. This allows the model to more effectively capture inter-sentence dependencies and semantic relationships. The transposed self-attention mechanism captures the contextual relevance of financial terms, integrating sentiment cues with domain knowledge, thereby enhancing representation learning, as shown in Eq. 2.

$$\text{Attention}(Q, K, V) = \text{softmax}(\frac{QK^T}{\sqrt{d_k}})V \tag{2}$$

Specifically, for the representations obtained after transpose embedding $H = \{h_0, \ldots, h_N\} \in \mathbb{R}^{N \times D}$, the self-attention module applies linear projections to obtain the queries, keys, and values denoted as $Q, K, V \in \mathbb{R}^{N \times d_k}$, where d_k represents the projected dimension.Let $q_i, k_j \in \mathbb{R}^{d_k}$ represent any two query and key vectors with respect to the feature. The term $A_{i,j} = (QK^\top/\sqrt{d_k})_{i,j} \propto q_i^\top k_j$ reveals the value retrieved from q_i using k_j. The generalized matrix $A \in \mathbb{R}^{N \times N}$ captures relationships among all features. Through the subsequent softmax operation, highly correlated features are assigned larger weights, enhancing their interaction with V and strengthening feature associations.

3.3 Adversarial Training for Robustness

To improve model robustness and enhance the effectiveness of sentiment classification, we introduced adversarial perturbations into the word embedding layer of the FiLM. These adversarial examples are generated using Eq. 4, which is based on the gradient of the loss function to compute the perturbations [15].

The adversarial perturbation $\mathbf{r}_{\text{adv}}$ is obtained by solving the following optimization problem:

$$\mathbf{r}_{\text{adv}} = \arg \min_{\mathbf{r}, \|\mathbf{r}\| \leq \epsilon} \log p(\mathbf{y}|\mathbf{x} + \mathbf{r}; \hat{\boldsymbol{\theta}}), \tag{3}$$

where $\mathbf{x}$ represents the original input, $\mathbf{y}$ is the ground truth label, $p(\mathbf{y}|\mathbf{x} + \mathbf{r}; \hat{\boldsymbol{\theta}})$ is the model's predicted probability for $\mathbf{y}$ given perturbed input $\mathbf{x}+\mathbf{r}$, $\hat{\boldsymbol{\theta}}$ denotes the fixed model parameters during perturbation generation, and ϵ controls the magnitude of the perturbation $\mathbf{r}$.

The perturbation $\mathbf{r}_{\text{adv}}$ is approximated using the gradient of the loss function with respect to the input, as follows:

$$\mathbf{r}_{\text{adv}} = \frac{\epsilon \mathbf{g}}{\|\mathbf{g}\|_2}, \tag{4}$$

where $\mathbf{g} = \nabla_{\mathbf{x}} \mathcal{L}(\hat{\boldsymbol{\theta}})$ is the gradient of the loss function $\mathcal{L}$ with respect to the input $\mathbf{x}$, and $\|\cdot\|_2$ represents the ℓ_2-norm. This formulation ensures that the perturbation has a bounded magnitude, making it a small but effective modification to the input embeddings.

4 Experiment

Comparative Experiment. To comprehensively evaluate the model, we selected four English sentiment analysis benchmark datasets(FPB, SS, TFS, FOMC) and one Chinese financial dataset(CD), all of which are publicly available online. Also, Accuracy(ACC) and F1-Score(F1) are used as the metrics to evaluate the model's performance. We selected comparative models as baselines from three distinct categories. Traditional Deep Learning Models: BiLSTM [11] and TextCNN [25]. General PLMs: BERT [7], RoBERTa [16], and XLNet [24]. Financial PLMs: FinBERT [2], FLANG-BERT&FLANG-RoBERTa [22], and SECBERT [18].

Table 1 presents the comprehensive prediction results, with the best results in blue and the second underlined. Higher ACC and F1 scores indicate better model performance. The detailed experimental setup is provided in Appendix A.

Table 1. The Results of Comparative Experiment.

Models	FinPTA		BiLSTM		TextCNN		BERT		RoBERTa		XLNet		FinBERT		FLANG-BERT		FLANG-RoBERTa		SEC-BERT	
Metric(%)	ACC	F1	ACC	F1	ACC	F1	ACC	F1	ACC	F1	ACC	F1	ACC	F1	ACC	F1	ACC	F1	ACC	F1
FPB	***88.33***	***88.06***	58.16	24.52	70.87	57.65	85.85	84.93	85.64	85.33	85.64	85	**87.19**	**86.26**	86.05	85.31	86.67	85.55	85.98	84.81
FOMC	***68.75***	***66.38***	49.4	22.04	59.16	44.85	60.89	57.73	**67.95**	**66**	65.32	61.21	60.89	57.50	63.31	31.28	65.32	64.31	65.93	63.82
TFS	**62**	**56.20**	52	22.81	56	38.09	56	49.94	60.4	51.89	54.4	49.7	56.4	44.22	58.4	50.27	**60.4**	**53.05**	56	46.10
CD	***89.01***	***89.01***	50.71	37.10	65.33	51.10	83.68	83.65	**88.67**	**88.67**	77.01	77.01	83.56	83.54	83.47	83.44	77.98	77.87	75.21	75.10
SS	***82.59***	***77.32***	72.86	42.15	75.50	59.92	77.44	72.46	**81.06**	**75.63**	79.34	72.44	78.17	70.73	79.11	71.66	80.57	74.81	74.55	67.71

FinPTA significantly outperforms traditional deep learning methods like BiLSTM and TextCNN in ACC and F1 scores across five datasets. TextCNN focuses on local features, while BiLSTM captures sequential dependencies, but both struggle with global context modeling, limiting their performance.

PLMs, pre-trained on large-scale corpora and fine-tuned on task-specific datasets, extract deep, context-rich representations, enhancing generalization and efficiency compared to traditional methods. However, general-purpose PLMs often struggle on financial tasks due to mismatched pre-training corpora. Our model improves F1 scores by 1âĂŞ3% points over the best-performing general PLMs by leveraging a financial PLM tailored to financial texts. FiLM captures financial terminology and context intricacies, enabling accurate sentiment extraction.

Compared to financial PLMs, our model also achieves notable improvements. While financial PLMs understand terminology, limited training data restricts their ability to fully capture contextual relationships. FinPTA addresses this limitation by integrating FiLM for domain-aware feature extraction and employing tTransformer to enhance contextual dependency modeling, thereby improving representation quality and overall performance.

Ablation Study. To evaluate the effectiveness of each module in the model, an ablation study was conducted, as illustrated in Fig. 2. The detailed configurations of the models are as follows: FiLM, a financial PLM. FiLM + tTransformer, which integrates the tTransformer module into downstream tasks. FiLM + Adversarial Training, which introduces adversarial training to the FiLM model. Finally, FinPTA, the proposed model in this paper. The ablation study demonstrates that each module plays a critical role in improving the overall performance.

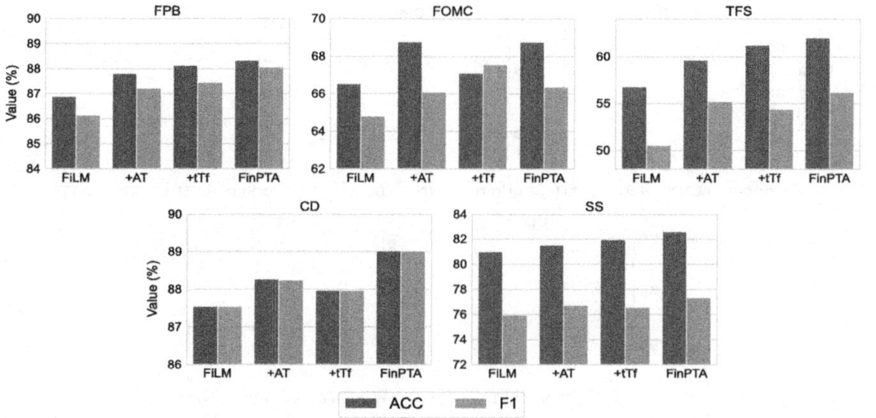

Fig. 2. The ablation study results. AT is abbreviation for Adversarial Training and tTf is abbreviation for tTransformer.

The FiLM + tTransformer model combines FiLM for financial text feature extraction with tTransformer for enhanced contextual modeling in sentiment classification. It improves F1 scores by 3 points on small datasets, 1.3 points on medium datasets, and shows minimal gains on large datasets. FiLM struggles with complex features on small datasets, while tTransformer enhances contextual modeling. On medium and large datasets, FiLM effectively captures semantic dependencies, limiting tTransformer's benefits and risking overfitting on larger datasets.

FiLM with adversarial training significantly improves F1 scores on small datasets by enhancing noise suppression, addressing challenges of limited sample size and diversity. On larger datasets, its impact diminishes due to sufficient data volume. Finally, FinPTA integrates FiLM for semantic extraction, tTransformer for contextual modeling, and adversarial training for robustness, achieving F1 score improvements of 5 points on small datasets and 1.5–2 points on medium and large datasets, demonstrating its effectiveness.

tTransformer Generality. To further investigate the effectiveness of tTransformer, we conducted experiments by applying two common post-processing models, CNN [14] and BiLSTM [11], to BERT [7], FinBERT [2], and FiLM [5]. The experimental results are presented in Fig. 3.

Our experiments show that using tTransformer consistently enhances the F1 score, whether with general PLMs like BERT or financial PLMs like FinBERT and FiLM. However, switching FiLM's post-processing model to CNN and BiLSTM can lead to unstable performance, sometimes worse than using the PLMs alone. CNN excels at extracting local features but struggles with global dependencies. BiLSTM captures sequential information but faces challenges with long sequences. Both models have limited generalization, risking overfitting and performance degradation when test data deviates from the training distribution. In contrast, tTransformer uses transposed attention mechanisms to extract token-

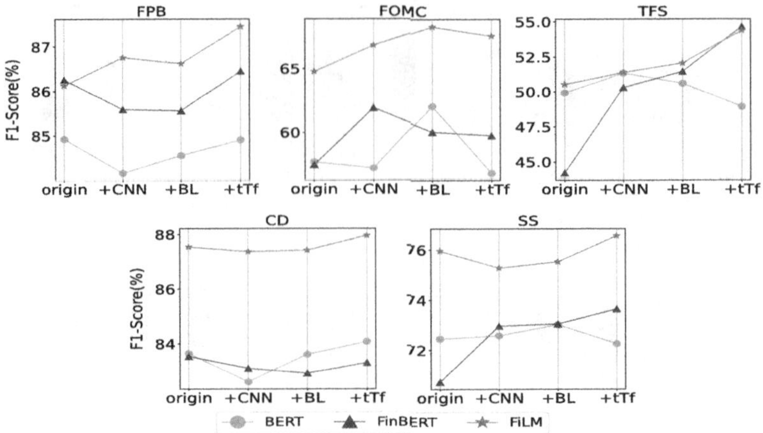

Fig. 3. Results of generality experiment. BL represents the BiLSTM.

level features from entire sentences, effectively capturing long-range dependencies and improving performance across datasets.

5 Conclusions

This paper points out that, due to the specificity of financial terminology, existing general PLMs struggle with sentiment analysis tasks. The scarcity and limited diversity of training data in the financial domain hinder financial PLMs from effectively capturing contextual relationships and nuanced semantic information, thereby constraining their accuracy and generalization performance.

To address these challenges, this paper proposes a novel financial sentiment analysis model–FinPTA. FinPTA leverages FiLM to extract financial text features, thereby uncovering deep semantic dependencies within the texts. Subsequently, the model incorporates tTransformer, which utilizes transposition operations to treat specific features of entire sentences as tokens, further enhancing contextual understanding and enriching features relevant to sentiment analysis. Finally, to improve the model's robustness and generalization capability, perturbations are introduced into the word embedding layer of FiLM. Experimental results on multiple financial datasets demonstrate that FinPTA achieves state-of-the-art performance, showcasing its effectiveness and superiority in financial sentiment analysis tasks.

However, FinPTA has certain limitations. First, insufficient attention to numerical data during FiLM's training reduces the model's sensitivity to numerical information. Second, its complex architecture demands substantial computational resources for training. Future research should focus on developing efficient numerical annotation techniques to improve numerical sensitivity and on designing simplified model architectures that reduce resource consumption without compromising performance.

Acknowledgments. This work was partially supported by the National Natural Science Foundation of China (No. 62372174) and the Computational Biology Program of Shanghai Science and Technology Commission (No. 23JS1400600).

Disclosure of Interests. The authors have no competing interests to declare that are relevant to the content of this article.

A Experiment Setup

Preparation. The experiments were conducted using the PyTorch framework, with model training performed on an NVIDIA GeForce RTX 3090 GPU. During training, we used the AdamW optimizer. The detailed model parameters are outlined in Table 2. The batch_size = {16, 32, 64} depending on the dataset size. The larger the dataset, the larger the batch size. The parameter experiments are detailed in Appendix B.

Table 2. Parameters for the Experiments

ALL Models			FinPTA						
learning_rate	num_epoch	batch_size	max_seq_length	variate	dim	depth	heads	drop_out	pre_length
2e-5	30	{16,32,64}	64	768	256	6	8	0.5	1

Dataset. To conduct a comprehensive evaluation of the model, we selected four English-language benchmark datasets for sentiment analysis in the financial domain, along with one open-source Chinese financial dataset. These datasets include both social media content and financial news, ensuring a diverse and robust assessment of the proposed FinPTA. After data cleaning, the splits for training, validation, and testing sets are detailed in Table 3. The datasets used are as follows:

- Financial Phrase Bank (FPB) [19]: This dataset, derived from financial news articles, contains sentences labeled as positive, neutral, or negative. It is divided into subsets based on annotator agreement. In this study, we use the FPB-50% subset, which includes 4,846 instances with at least 50% annotator consistency.
- StockSen(SS) [23]: This dataset consists of 20,675 financial tweets from the StockTwits platform, collected between June and August 2019. Each tweet is labeled with either a positive or negative sentiment.
- TweetFinSent(TFS) [20]: This dataset is constructed from financial tweets and contains 2,113 sentences, annotated as positive, neutral, or negative.
- Federal Open Market Committee(FOMC) [21]: This dataset, the largest annotated collection of FOMC speeches, minutes, and press conferences, is designed to analyze the impact of monetary policy on financial markets. It includes fields such as Date, Content, and Political Stance ("Hawkish," Neutral, or "Dovish"). Collected by October 15, 2022, the dataset consists of 2,480 instances, with 1,984 for training and 496 for testing.

- GitHub Chinese Sentiment Analysis Dataset(CD)[1] This dataset is sourced from financial news headlines on the Chinese Xueqiu website. After data cleaning, the dataset comprises 15,561 news items, including six fields: Date, Company, Code, Sentiment (Positive/Negative), Title, and Content.

Finally, in this paper, based on the differences in dataset sizes, we define FPB as a medium-scale dataset, SS and CD as large-scale datasets, and FOMC and TFS as small-scale datasets.

Table 3. Split Datasets

	FPB	SS	TFS	FOMC	CD
Training set	3291	10256	1013	1554	10677
Validation set	581	3500	250	389	2500
Test set	968	5992	250	496	2384

B Parameter Experiments

To determine the optimal length of predicted sentences for sentiment classification, we conducted a series of parameter experiments, testing sentence lengths of 1, 16, 32, and 64. As shown in Fig. 4, the best performance was achieved with a predicted sentence length of 1. This can be attributed to the inherent locality of sentiment classification tasks, where shorter sentences are more effective at

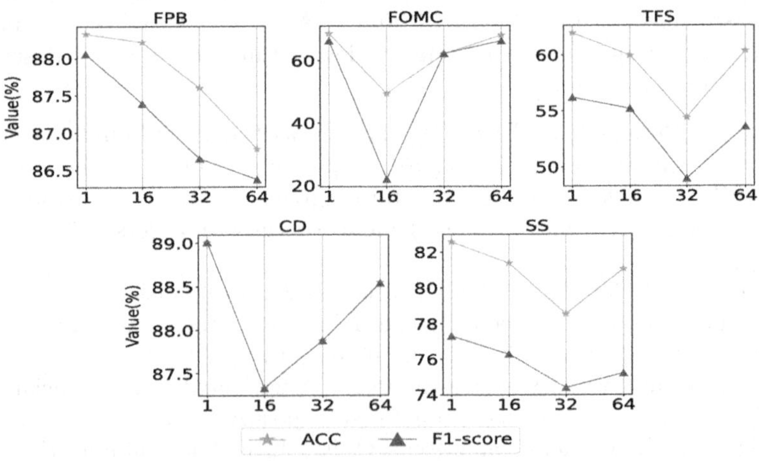

Fig. 4. The Result of Parameters Experiment.

[1] The dataset can be found at https://github.com/wwwxmu/Dataset-of-financial-news-sentiment-classification.

capturing sentiment signals while minimizing irrelevant information and noise. Moreover, shorter lengths reduce model complexity and mitigate the risk of overfitting, which is crucial in financial sentiment analysis where both precision and efficiency are paramount.

C Overall Architecture

Algorithm 1. FinPTA- Overall Architecture.

Require: Input financial text $\mathbf{T} \in \mathbb{R}^{W}$; text length W; max sequence length M; FiLM last hidden state N; predicted sentence length S; tTransformer token dimension D; tTransformer block number L; classification of sentiment P.

$\mathbf{X} = \texttt{tokenizer}(\mathbf{T})$ ▷ $\mathbf{X} \in \mathbb{R}^{3\times M}$

$\mathbf{F} = \texttt{FiLM}(\mathbf{X})$ ▷ $\mathbf{F} \in \mathbb{R}^{M\times N}$

▷ Transpose_Embedding layer transpose the features of the word tokens and embed word tokens into tTransformer tokens.

$\mathbf{F} = \mathbf{F}.\texttt{transpose}$ ▷ $\mathbf{F} \in \mathbb{R}^{N\times M}$

$\mathbf{H}^0 = \texttt{MLP}(\mathbf{F})$ ▷ $\mathbf{H}^0 \in \mathbb{R}^{N\times D}$

for l **in** $\{1, \dots, L\}$**:** ▷ Run through tTransformer blocks.

  ▷ Self-attention is employed between each Transformer tokens to capture dependencies between any two words in a sentence.

  $\mathbf{H}^{l-1} = \texttt{LayerNorm}(\mathbf{H}^{l-1} + \texttt{Self-Attn}(\mathbf{H}^{l-1}))$ ▷ $\mathbf{H}^{l-1} \in \mathbb{R}^{N\times D}$

  ▷ Feed-forward network processes the entire sequence representation and broadcasts it to each token.

  $\mathbf{H}^{l} = \texttt{LayerNorm}(\mathbf{H}^{l-1} + \texttt{Feed-Forward}(\mathbf{H}^{l-1}))$ ▷ $\mathbf{H}^{l} \in \mathbb{R}^{N\times D}$

  ▷ LayerNorm is applied to the entire sequence representation to mitigate token discrepancies.

End for

▷ Projection layer generates the predicted sentence representation and integrates features to produce the final sentiment classification by using max_pooling.

$\mathbf{Y} = \texttt{MLP}(\mathbf{H}^L)$ ▷ $\mathbf{Y} \in \mathbb{R}^{N\times S}$

$\mathbf{Y} = \mathbf{Y}.\texttt{transpose}$ ▷ $\mathbf{Y} \in \mathbb{R}^{S\times N}$

$\mathbf{Y} = \texttt{Max\_pooling}(\mathbf{Y})$ ▷ $\mathbf{Y} \in \mathbb{R}^{N}$

$\hat{\mathbf{Y}} = \texttt{MLP}(\mathbf{Y})$ ▷ $\hat{\mathbf{Y}} \in \mathbb{R}^{P}$

Return $\hat{\mathbf{Y}}$ ▷ Return the result $\hat{\mathbf{Y}}$

References

1. Al Amrani, Y., Lazaar, M., Kadiri, K.E.: Random forest and support vector machine based hybrid approach to sentiment analysis. Procedia Comput. Sci. **127**, 511–520 (2018). https://doi.org/10.1016/j.procs.2018.01.150
2. Araci, D.: Finbert: financial sentiment analysis with pre-trained language models. ArXiv arxiv:1908.10063 (2019)

3. Bollen, J., Mao, H., Zeng, X.: Twitter mood predicts the stock market. J. Comput. Sci. **2**, 1–8 (2011). https://doi.org/10.1016/j.jocs.2010.12.007
4. Bourezk, H., Raji, A., Acha, N., Barka, H.: Analyzing Moroccan stock market using machine learning and sentiment analysis. In: IRASET (2020). https://doi.org/10.1109/IRASET48871.2020.9092304
5. Choe, J., Noh, K., Kim, N., Ahn, S., Jung, W.: Exploring the impact of corpus diversity on financial pretrained language models. In: EMNLP, pp. 2101–2112 (2023). https://doi.org/10.18653/v1/2023.findings-emnlp.138
6. De Carosia, A.E., Coelho, G.P., Da Silva, A.E.: The influence of tweets and news on the Brazilian stock market through sentiment analysis. In: WebMedia, pp. 385–392 (2019). https://doi.org/10.1145/3323503.3349564
7. Devlin, J., Chang, M.W., Lee, K., Toutanova, K.: BERT: pre-training of deep bidirectional transformers for language understanding. In: NAACL, pp. 4171–4186 (2019). https://doi.org/10.18653/v1/N19-1423
8. Dong, S., Liu, C.: Sentiment classification for financial texts based on deep learning. Comput. Intell. Neurosci. **2021** (2021). https://doi.org/10.1155/2021/9524705
9. Goodfellow, I., et al.: Generative adversarial networks. Commun. ACM **63**, 139–144 (2020). https://doi.org/10.1145/3422622
10. Hota, H., Sharma, D.K., Verma, N.: Integration of deep learning techniques for sentiment and emotion analysis of social media data. IJISTA **21**(1), 1–20 (2023). https://doi.org/10.1504/IJISTA.2023.130552
11. Huang, Z., Xu, W., Yu, K.: Bidirectional lstm-crf models for sequence tagging. ArXiv arxiv:1508.01991 (2015)
12. Jangid, H., Singhal, S., Shah, R.R., Zimmermann, R.: Aspect-based financial sentiment analysis using deep learning. In: Companion Proceedings of the Web Conference 2018, pp. 1961–1966 (2018). https://doi.org/10.1145/3184558.3191827
13. Karimi, A., Rossi, L., Prati, A.: Adversarial training for aspect-based sentiment analysis with bert. In: ICPR, pp. 8797–8803 (2020). https://doi.org/10.1109/ICPR48806.2021.9412167
14. Krizhevsky, A., Sutskever, I., Hinton, G.E.: Imagenet classification with deep convolutional neural networks. Commun. ACM **60**, 84–90 (2017). https://doi.org/10.1145/3065386
15. Liu, X., Dai, S., Fiumara, G., Meo, P.: An adversarial training method for text classification. J. King Saud Univ. Comput. Inf. Sci. **35**, 101697 (2023). https://doi.org/10.1016/j.jksuci.2023.101697
16. Liu, Y., et al.: Roberta: a robustly optimized bert pretraining approach. ArXiv arxiv:1907.11692 (2019)
17. Loughran, T., McDonald, B.: When is a liability not a liability? Textual analysis, dictionaries, and 10-ks. J. Finan. **66**, 35–65 (2011). https://doi.org/10.1111/j.1540-6261.2010.01625.x
18. Loukas, L., et al.: Finer: financial numeric entity recognition for xbrl tagging. In: Proceedings of the 60th Annual Meeting of the Association for Computational Linguistics (2022). https://doi.org/10.18653/v1/2022.acl-long.303
19. Malo, P., Sinha, A., Korhonen, P., Wallenius, J., Takala, P.: Good debt or bad debt: detecting semantic orientations in economic texts. JASIST **65**, 782–796 (2014). https://doi.org/10.1002/asi.23062
20. Pei, Y., et al.: TweetFinSent: a dataset of stock sentiments on Twitter. In: FinNLP, pp. 37–47 (2022). https://doi.org/10.18653/v1/2022.finnlp-1.5
21. Shah, A., Paturi, S., Chava, S.: Trillion dollar words: a new financial dataset, task & market analysis. In: Proceedings of the 61st Annual Meeting of the Association

for Computational Linguistics, pp. 6664–6679 (2023). https://doi.org/10.18653/v1/2023.acl-long.368
22. Shah, R., et al.: When FLUE meets FLANG: benchmarks and large pretrained language model for financial domain. In: EMNLP, pp. 2322–2335 (2022). https://doi.org/10.18653/v1/2022.emnlp-main.148
23. Xing, F., Malandri, L., Zhang, Y., Cambria, E.: Financial sentiment analysis: an investigation into common mistakes and silver bullets. In: COLING, pp. 978–987 (2020). https://doi.org/10.18653/v1/2020.coling-main.85
24. Yang, Z., Dai, Z., Yang, Y., Carbonell, J.G., Salakhutdinov, R., Le, Q.V.: Xlnet: generalized autoregressive pretraining for language understanding. In: NeurIPS (2019)
25. Zhang, Y., Wallace, B.C.: A sensitivity analysis of (and practitioners' guide to) convolutional neural networks for sentence classification. ArXiv arxiv:1510.03820 (2015)

Single Image Defocus Deblurring in Photography Systems

He Zhao[1], Shenggui Ling[1,2(✉)], Hongmin Zhan[1], and Rui Shi[1]

[1] School of Computer Science and Engineering, Sichuan University of Science and Engineering, Zigong, China
{324085406138,323085406134}@stu.suse.edu.cn, {lingsg,shirui}@suse.edu.cn
[2] Key Laboratory of Higher Education of Sichuan Province for Enterprise Informationalization and Internet of Things, Sichuan University of Science and Engineering, Zigong, China

Abstract. Defocus deblurring aims to reconstruct a high-quality image from its degraded counterpart, playing significant roles in many intelligent systems. However, current methods for processing defocused images have deficiencies in perceiving and enhancing the frequency information of images, resulting in the loss of image details. In view of this, we innovatively propose the Frequency-Aware Encoding Block (FAEB), aiming to strengthen the encoder's ability to extract high-frequency information. In addition, areas with a high degree of blurring in the image often result in many artifacts during the processing. To solve this problem, we also propose the Lightweight Artifact Removal Module (LARM), which is applied in the decoding process to effectively handle the large number of artifacts that appear in the image. Experimental results show that our proposed Artifact Removal Frequency-Aware Network (ArFaNet) outperforms the state-of-the-art algorithms in terms of objective metrics on the popular Dual-Pixel Defocus Deblurring (DPDD) and Real Depth of Field (RealDOF) datasets.

Keywords: defocus deblurring · defocus image · out-of-focus deblurring · blur image · image restoration

1 Introduction

When taking photos, objects within the focal range usually present clear images, while objects outside the focal range lose details and become blurry. This blurring phenomenon is called defocusing blur, which is influenced by aperture shape, lens design, scene depth, and camera parameters [1]. This affects many computer vision tasks such as object detection and text recognition. Therefore, restoring full-focus images is a valuable research.

S. Ling—This research was supported by the Key Laboratory of Higher Education of Sichuan Province for Enterprise Informationalization and Internet of Things (2024WZJ01).

Y. Zhou et al. (Eds.): ICECCS 2025, LNCS 15746, pp. 38–48, 2026.
https://doi.org/10.1007/978-3-032-00828-2_3

Traditional defocus deblurring methods simulate blur by applying predefined convolution kernels (e.g., Gaussian or disk) to all-in-focus images [2–5]. These approaches typically construct a blur model, estimate per-pixel kernels, and then perform non-blind deconvolution. However, they often rely on simplified assumptions that fail to process the complex real-world blur. In real-world camera systems, defocus blur often stems from inaccurate focusing and affects critical high-frequency regions, degrading downstream tasks like detection and recognition. Despite progress in defocus deblurring, challenges remain in extracting high-frequency information and removing artifacts. To address this, we introduce a Frequency-Aware Encoding Block that enhances the restoration of such regions. Additionally, to mitigate visual artifacts (e.g., ringing, noise) common in lightweight networks, we propose a Lightweight Artifact Removal Module, which effectively balances visual quality and computational cost. These components enable our method to surpass existing approaches in four metrics and deliver superior visual results. Our main contributions are as follows:

- Firstly, an innovative Frequency-Aware Encoding Block (FAEB) is proposed, which aims to improve the network's ability to extract high-frequency information by focusing on the features of different frequencies.
- Secondly, we propose a Lightweight Artifact Removal Module (LARM), which aims to effectively remove artifacts that may be generated during the deblurring through a lightweight design, while further enhancing the ability to restore image details.
- Finally, we present a novel single image defocus deblurring algorithm. Qualitative and quantitative experimental results show that the proposed method outperforms the state-of-the-art methods in image quality.

2 Related Work

In recent years, deep learning has significantly promoted progress in the field of defocused image restoration. Abuolaim et al. [6] first released the DPDD dataset and developed an end-to-end deep learning deblurring framework. Abuolaim et al. [7] proposed a dual-pixel synthetic data generation approach and developed the Recurrent Convolutional Network architecture. Pan et al. [8] jointly estimated depth and performed deblurring from dual-pixel images, while developing a DP image simulator for training data generation. Abuolaim et al. [9] proposed a multi-task deblurring approach through joint dual-pixel view prediction. Lee et al. [10] proposed IFAN achieving SOTA performance in defocus deblurring. Ruan et al. [11] enhanced deblurring performance via a domain-adaptive three-module architecture and light-field synthesized data. Son et al. [1] achieved high-quality deblurring by efficiently modeling inverse kernel invariance through kernel sharing and scale attention. Quan et al. [12] proposed an end-to-end method that combines Gaussian kernel mixture modeling with a scale-recurrent network. Ruan et al. [13] proposed a deep network that combines light field pre-training with dual-lens fine-tuning. Zamir et al. [14] proposed an efficient Transformer architecture, Restormer, suitable for image restoration tasks. Quan et al. [15] proposed a physics-driven network based on recursive kernel representation (RKR). Cui et al. [16] incorporated a dual-domain channel attention mechanism into image restoration. Liang et al. [17] proposed a hierarchical model based on the vision transformer. Cui et al. [18] improved the performance of image restoration tasks through spatial and frequency strip attention units. Cui et al. [19] improve image restoration tasks through multi-scale representation learning and a three-branch design. Ling et al. [20] proposed an efficient multi-module architecture for single image defocus deblurring. Although previous methods have achieved good results in image defocus deblurring, their performance is limited when the defocused image contains large blurry regions.

3 Proposed Method

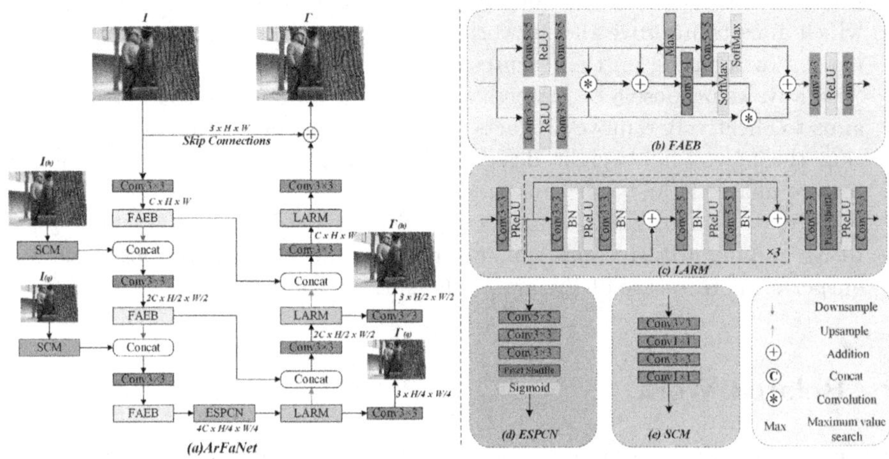

Fig. 1. The architecture of ArFaNet.

This section begins with a systematic exposition of the overall architecture and details of our proposed ArFaNet framework. We then provide an in-depth analysis of two core components: the Frequency-Aware Encoding Block (FAEB) and the Lightweight Artifact Removal Module (LARM). Finally, we elaborate on the design of loss functions employed during the training.

3.1 Overview of the Proposed Architecture

Figure 1 (a) illustrates the overall architecture of ArFaNet, which adopts a Multi-input Multi-output (MIMO) framework [21]. Specifically, the network takes the original blurry image $I \in \mathbb{R}^{3\times H\times W}$, along with its 1/2 and 1/4 downscaled versions $I_{\rm h} \in \mathbb{R}^{3\times H/2\times W/2}$ and $I_{\rm q} \in \mathbb{R}^{3\times H/4\times W/4}$, as inputs. When the original image I enters the pipeline, it first undergoes preliminary feature extraction through the 3×3 convolution $f_{3\times3}^{c}$. Meanwhile, the 1/2-scaled image and 1/4-scaled image obtained by performing scaling operations on the original image will respectively undergo more in-depth feature extraction through Shallow Convolutional Module (SCM) S_c. Compared with ordinary convolution, S_c contains multiple layers of convolution, so it can extract features of the scaled images more deeply. The formulas are as follows:

$$F = f_{3\times3}^{c}(I), F_h = S_c(I_h), F_q = S_c(I_q). \tag{1}$$

After initial processing, the feature map F is fed into the FAEB module to extract high-frequency information from defocused images. The enhanced features are then concatenated with F_h, as expressed by:

$$F_{ca}^{1} = Concat(FAEB(F), F_h). \tag{2}$$

After convolution and FAEB processing, F_{ca}^{1} is concatenated with F_q, incorporating 1/4-resolution features to enrich representation and support high-quality image generation:

$$F_{ca}^{2} = Concat(FAEB(f_{3\times3}^{c}(F_{ca}^{1})), F_q). \tag{3}$$

F_{ca}^{2} undergoes convolution, FAEB refinement, detail enhancement via ESPCN, partial restoration through LARM, and a final convolution to produce a 1/4-scale restored image:

$$I_q' = f_{3\times3}^{c}(LARM(ESPCN(FAEB(f_{3\times3}^{c}(F_{ca}^{2}))))). \tag{4}$$

In decoding, the first LARM output is concatenated with the second FAEB output to fuse multi-scale, multi-depth features, enhancing representation for higher-resolution output:

$$F_{ca}^{3} = Concat(LARM(ESPCN(FAEB(f_{3\times3}^{c}(F_{ca}^{2})))), FAEB(f_{3\times3}^{c}(F_{ca}^{1}))). \tag{5}$$

After the concatenation, F_{ca}^{3} is first convolved once and then fed into the second LARM in the decoding. Next, the result of the LARM is deconvolved once and the result I_h' of the LARM is outputted. The detailed formula is as follows:

$$I_h' = f_{3\times3}^{c}(LARM(f_{3\times3}^{c}(F_{ca}^{3}))). \tag{6}$$

Next, the upsampled result with the result of the first FAEB is concatenated. By fully integrating information from different stages and resolutions, this step provides rich features for generating the final full-resolution output. The corresponding formula is as follows:

$$F_{ca}^{4} = Concat(LARM(f_{3\times3}^{c}(F_{ca}^{3})), FAEB(F)). \tag{7}$$

Finally, F_{ca}^{4} is refined by a convolution and LARM module, followed by another convolution. The result is added to the original image I to produce the final output I', effectively combining restored details with the original.

$$I' = I + f_{3\times3}^{c}(LARM(f_{3\times3}^{c}(F_{ca}^{4}))). \tag{8}$$

3.2 Frequency-Aware Encoding Block

To improve frequency information capture and feature representation, we designed the Frequency-Aware Encoding Block (FAEB). As shown in Fig. 1 (b), FAEB leverages multi-scale characteristics via multi-path processing. The upper path uses two 5×5 convolutions with ReLU activation, while the lower path applies 3×3 convolutions to capture features at different scales. The outputs of both paths are element-wise multiplied to enhance feature richness in the frequency domain. This product is then added to the upper path output, passed through a 1×1 convolution for channel integration, and normalized via SoftMax for channel weighting. The result is multiplied by the output of the lower 3×3 convolution to enhance feature extraction. A maximum value search is performed on the output of upper 5×5 convolution to extract key features, which are then passed through a 5×5 convolution and SoftMax for normalization. These features are added to the lower path multiplication result, integrating information at different scales. The final features undergo a 3×3 convolution, followed by ReLU, and another 3×3 convolution to complete FAEB.

3.3 Lightweight Artifact Removal Module

Based on the work of Ling et al. [20], we propose the Lightweight Artifact Removal Module (LARM) to eliminate artifacts caused by defocus deblurring and enhance image detail restoration. As illustrated in Fig. 1(c), the module first performs feature extraction via a 3×3 convolution followed by PReLU activation. It then refines the features through two sets of 3×3 convolutions (PReLU activation is attached after the first convolutions) and two normalization operations, with the results added back to the input via skip connections to preserve fundamental information. Subsequently, another set of 5×5 convolutions (also combined with PReLU and normalization) is applied, and the output is further added to the previous results to improve feature stability and effectiveness. This cascaded processing is repeated three times, each employing different convolutional layer configurations and normalization operations to progressively remove artifacts and restore image details. Such a layer-wise enhancement mechanism enables LARM to effectively suppress artifacts and enhance image clarity. Finally, the features are optimized through a 3×3 convolution, upsampled via Pixel Shuffle to increase resolution, nonlinearly transformed with PReLU, and processed by another 3×3 convolution to complete the entire LARM computation.

3.4 Loss Functions

We adopt the spectral L1 loss to accentuate the useful frequency. Just as in the work of [22], we use a multi-input multi-output method, so when calculating the loss, we also perform comparisons on multiple prediction results and blurred images to obtain the loss. We use two losses in both spatial and frequency domains to optimize our deblurring network, and they are denoted as $\mathcal{L}_{\text{concent}}$ and $\mathcal{L}_{\text{fft}}$ respectively. The dual-domain loss functions are as follows:

$$\mathcal{L}_{concent} = \sum_{j=1}^{3} \frac{1}{C_j} \left\| \hat{p}_j - l_j \right\|_1, \tag{9}$$

$$\mathcal{L}_{fft} = \sum_{j=1}^{3} \frac{1}{C_j} \left\| F(\hat{p}_j) - F(l_j) \right\|_1, \tag{10}$$

where j is the index of multiple outputs, and $\hat{p}_j$ is the j-th output of the model. $\hat{p}_j$ and l_j respectively denote the predicted image and the real image. C_j is the total number of elements in the j-th image and is used for normalization. $F(\cdot)$ represents the Fast Fourier Transform, and $\hat{p}_j$ and l_j are the results obtained by performing a 2D Fourier Transform and then stacking the real part and the imaginary part.

$$\mathcal{L}_{total} = \mathcal{L}_{concent} + \lambda \mathcal{L}_{fft}. \tag{11}$$

Among them, $\lambda = 0.23$ is used to balance the training in the spatial domain and the frequency domain.

4 Experiments

During training, we use the AdamW [23] optimizer with an initial learning rate of 1×10^{-4}, which is gradually reduced to 1×10^{-6} using cosine annealing. The optimizer parameters are set as follows: $\beta_1 = 0.9$, $\beta_2 = 0.999$, $\epsilon = 1 \times 10^{-8}$ and weight decay $= 1 \times 10^{-4}$ to prevent overfitting. We set the batch size to 2 and apply random horizontal flipping and random cropping as data augmentation. All models are trained and evaluated on an NVIDIA 1080 Ti GPU.

4.1 Evaluation on the DPDD

Table 1 shows the evaluation on the DPDD dataset. While our model has slightly higher parameters and slower speed, it outperforms others in key metrics. In the Combined scenario, it achieves 27.15 dB PSNR, 0.823 SSIM (Structural Similarity), 0.035 MAE, and 0.171 LPIPS (Learned Perceptual Image Patch Similarity) – surpassing DSANet by 0.84 dB in PSNR and ChaIR by 0.007 in SSIM, demonstrating superior deblurring performance.

Figure 2 presents visual comparisons on DPDD. Cropped results (Cols. 3âĂŞ6) highlight differences, with the red box in Col. 1 indicating the region of interest. Compared to other methods, our method better restores step textures and preserves fine details, such as the house outside the window.

4.2 Evaluation on the RealDOF

To assess generalization, we evaluated our model on RealDOF (Table 2). It outperforms others in PSNR (25.20 dB), SSIM (0.775), and LPIPS (0.280), surpassing NRKNet, OKNet, and Restormer. These results confirm the effectiveness of our FAEM and LARM modules.

Table 1. Quantitative comparisons of different defocus deblurring methods on the DPDD [6] test set. We use red and blue to indicate the best and the second-best. ↑ indicates that the larger is better. ↓ means that the smaller is better. '+' indicates the method is trained with extra data.

Method	Venue	Indoor Scenes			Outdoor Scenes			Combined				Model	
		PSNR↑	SSIM↑	MAE↓	PSNR↑	SSIM↑	MAE↓	PSNR↑	SSIM↑	MAE↓	LPIPS↓	Params (M) ↓	FLOPs (G)↓
Input	–	26.16	0.816	0.035	21.73	0.665	0.059	23.89	0.738	0.047	0.315	–	–
DPDNet [6]	*ECCV'20*	27.48	0.849	0.029	22.90	0.726	0.052	25.13	0.786	0.041	0.223	32.25	3150
RDPD+ [7]	*ICCV'20*	28.10	0.843	0.027	22.82	0.704	0.053	25.39	0.772	0.040	0.255	24.28	901
DDDNet [8]	*CVPR'20*	27.57	0.833	0.030	23.28	0.708	0.050	25.36	0.768	0.041	0.197	6.04	1661
MDPNet [9]	*WACV'21*	–	–	–	–	–	–	25.34	0.763	0.040	0.268	46.86	1898
IFAN [10]	*CVPR'21*	28.66	0.868	0.025	23.46	0.743	0.049	25.99	0.804	0.037	0.207	10.48	794
AIFNet [11]	*TCI'21*	–	–	–	–	–	–	25.53	0.798	–	0.247	41.55	–
KPAC [1]	*ICCV'21*	27.97	0.852	0.026	22.62	0.701	0.053	25.22	0.774	0.040	0.227	2.06	113
GKMNet [12]	*NeurIPS'21*	–	–	–	–	–	–	25.46	0.789	–	0.306	1.4	603.5
DRBNet+ [13]	*CVPR'22*	–	–	–	–	–	–	25.46	0.792	0.039	0.254	11.69	1273
Restormer [14]	*CVPR'22*	28.87	0.882	0.025	23.24	0.743	0.050	25.98	0.811	0.038	0.178	26.13	4458
NRKNet [15]	*CVPR'23*	28.66	0.873	0.025	23.69	0.752	0.048	26.11	0.811	0.037	0.255	6.1	–
IRNeXt [22]	*ICML'23*	29.22	0.879	0.024	23.53	0.752	0.049	26.30	0.814	0.037	0.206	5.46	41
ChaIR [24]	*KBS'23*	29.21	0.881	0.023	23.52	0.755	0.049	26.29	0.816	0.036	0.193	8.78	–
SANet [16]	*IJCAI'23*	29.30	0.878	0.024	23.43	0.748	0.049	26.29	0.811	0.037	0.196	–	–
SFNet [25]	*ICLR'23*	29.16	0.878	0.023	23.45	0.747	0.049	26.23	0.811	0.037	0.207	–	–
ViT-B [17]	*TCM'24*	–	–	–	–	–	–	26.11	0.814	–	0.201	113.34	111.83
CSNet [26]	*IJCAI'24*	29.20	0.881	0.023	23.45	0.752	0.049	26.25	0.815	0.037	0.178	–	–
DSANet [18]	*NN'24*	29.27	0.881	0.024	23.50	0.749	0.049	26.31	0.813	0.036	0.195	13.16	1757.13
OKNet [19]	*AAAI'24*	28.99	0.877	0.024	23.51	0.751	0.049	26.18	0.812	0.037	0.206	2.40	17.86
Ours (ArFaNet)	–	29.80	0.885	0.023	23.98	0.762	0.047	27.15	0.823	0.035	0.171	7.88	71.75

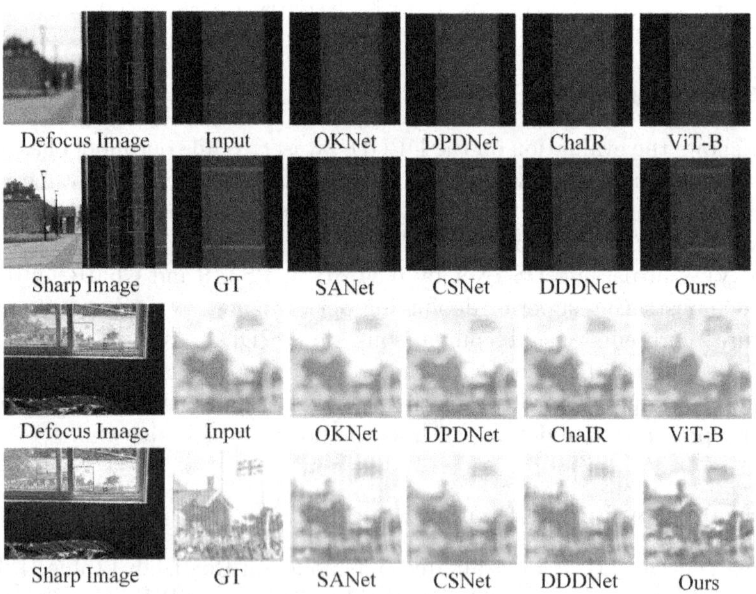

Fig. 2. Visual comparisons of ours and the latest methods on the DPDD.

Table 2. Quantitative results of the RealDOF [10]. The best and second-best are shown in red and blue, respectively. ↑ indicates that the larger is better. ↓ means that the smaller is better. '+' indicates the method is trained with extra data.

Method	Venue	PSNR↑	SSIM↑	LPIPS↓	Params (M) ↓	FLOPs (G)↓
Input	–	22.45	0.657	0.450	–	–
DDDNet [8]	*CVPR'20*	22.87	0.670	0.425	6.04	–
DPDNet [6]	*ECCV'20*	22.87	0.670	0.425	32.25	3150
RDPD+ [7]	*ICCV'20*	23.22	0.693	0.451	24.28	901
AIFNet [11]	*TCI'21*	23.09	0.680	0.413	41.55	–
MDPNet [9]	*WACV'21*	23.50	0.681	0.444	46.86	1898
KPAC [1]	*ICCV'21*	23.98	0.762	0.338	2.06	113
IFAN [10]	*CVPR'21*	24.71	0.748	0.306	10.48	794
GKMNet [12]	*NeurIPS'21*	24.25	0.732	0.392	1.4	603.5
DRBNet+ [13]	*CVPR'22*	24.88	0.751	0.376	11.69	1273
Restormer [14]	*CVPR'22*	25.09	0.762	0.285	26.13	4458
NRKNet [15]	*CVPR'23*	25.14	0.768	0.361	6.1	–
ChaIR [24]	*KBS'23*	23.97	0.721	0.391	8.78	–
SANet [16]	*IJCAI'23*	23.84	0.707	0.423	–	–
SFNet [25]	*ICLR'23*	24.08	0.719	0.405	–	–
DSANet [18]	*NN'24*	23.63	0.701	0.431	13.16	1757.13
CSNet [26]	*IJCAI'24*	25.00	0.764	0.341	–	–
ViT-B [17]	*TCM'24*	24.57	0.743	0.337	113.34	111.83
OKNet [19]	*AAAI'24*	24.43	0.769	0.327	2.40	17.86
Ours (ArFaNet)	–	25.20	0.775	0.280	7.88	71.75

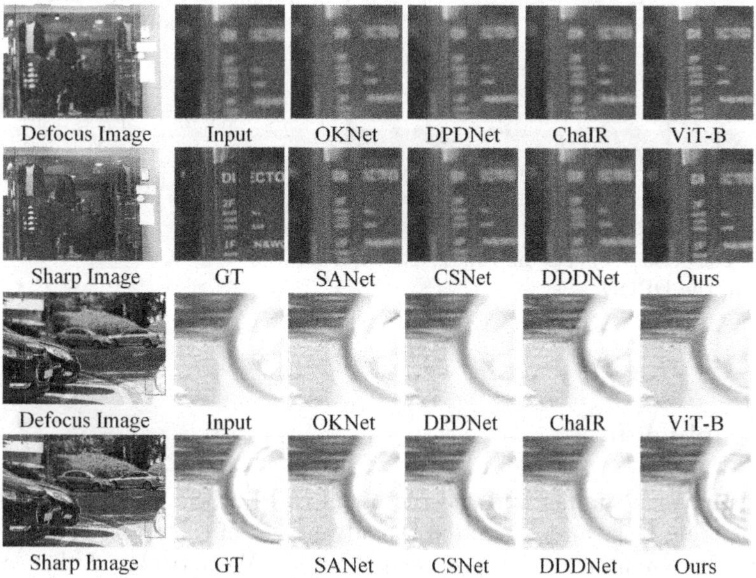

Fig. 3. Visual comparison of ours and latest methods on the RealDOF [10]. All results are tested on the model trained on the DPDD [6].

The visual comparison of different methods on the RealDOF dataset is shown in Fig. 3. The compared methods include DPDNet, ChaIR, ViT-B, SANet, CSNet, DDDNet and OKNet. Compared with the GT, in the first photo, our method performs more clearly in restoring the text on the signage; in the second photo, our method can restore the outline of the car light more clear than others.

4.3 Ablation Studies

We evaluated the effectiveness of FAEB and LARM by modifying the network with different modules (Table 3). The baseline model achieves 26.30 dB PSNR, 0.792 SSIM, and 0.206 LPIPS. Adding FAEB or LARM improves performance, with the best results obtained when both modules are used together.

Figure 4 shows visualization results from the ablation study on the DPDD. The baseline model produces blurry results with insufficient detail restoration. Adding FAEB improves image quality while adding LARM further enhances details and removes artifacts. When both modules are combined, the best visual results are achieved–letters like "GE CANADA" become clear, and blurry areas are nearly eliminated.

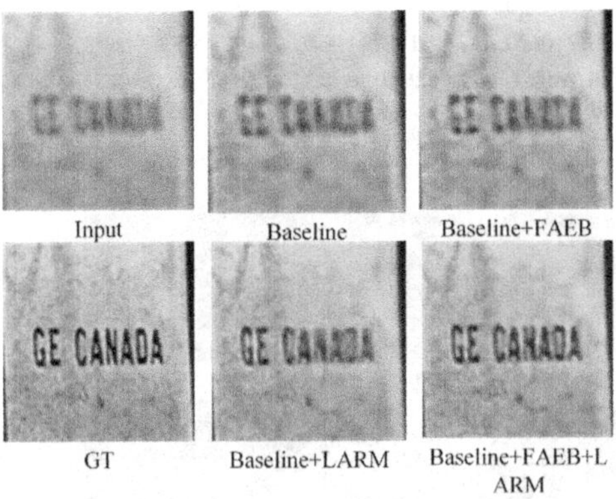

Fig. 4. The visual effects of the FAEB and LARM on the DPDD.

Table 3. Ablation experiments of the proposed method on DPDD. ↑ indicates that the larger is better. ↓ means that the smaller is better. ✓ indicates adding a module on the baseline.

No.	FAEB	LARM	PSNR↑	SSIM↑	LPIPS↓
1			26.30	0.792	0.206
2	✓		26.73	0.809	0.193
3		✓	26.92	0.819	0.181
4	✓	✓	27.15	0.823	0.171

5 Conclusion

In this study, we summarized the successful cases in the previous image defocus deblurring tasks and integrated the advantages of existing methods to fully unleash the potential of our proposed modules. We introduced the ArFaNet model for defocus deblurring. Specifically, we proposed the Frequency-Aware Encoding Block (FAEB) to perceive the high-frequency information for restoring the details in the blurred regions. Subsequently, to remove the artifacts in the defocused images, we proposed the LARM module. In addition, we used a Multiple-Input Multiple-Output (MIMO) framework for multi-scale input and hierarchical feature extraction. ArFaNet extracts deep features and generates sharp results at multiple resolutions. Experiments show that our method outperforms the state-of-the-art algorithms in 4 metrics, demonstrating its performance.

References

1. Son, H., Lee, J., Cho, S., Lee, S.: Single image defocus deblurring using kernel-sharing parallel atrous convolutions. In: 18th International Conference on Computer Vision (ICCV), pp. 2622–2630. IEEE, Montreal (2021)
2. Ali, K., Cláudio, R.J.: Edge-based defocus blur estimation with adaptive scale selection. IEEE Trans. Image Process. **27**, 1126–1137 (2018)
3. Cho, S., Lee, S.: Convergence analysis of map based blur kernel estimation. In: 17th International Conference on Computer Vision (ICCV), pp. 4818–4826. IEEE, Venice (2017)
4. D'Andrés, L., Salvador, J., Kochale, A., Süsstrunk, S.: Non-parametric blur map regression for depth of field extension. IEEE Trans. Image Process. **25**, 1660–1673 (2016)
5. Liu, Y.Q., Du, X., Shen, H.L., Chen, S.J.: Estimating generalized gaussian blur kernels for out-of-focus image deblurring. IEEE Trans. Circ. Syst. Video Technol. **31**, 829–843 (2020)
6. Abuolaim, A., Brown, M.S.: Defocus deblurring using dual-pixel data. In: Vedaldi, A., Bischof, H., Brox, T., Frahm, J.-M. (eds.) ECCV 2020. LNCS, vol. 12355, pp. 111–126. Springer, Cham (2020). https://doi.org/10.1007/978-3-030-58607-2_7
7. Abuolaim, A., Delbracio, M., Kelly, D., Brown, M.S., Milanfar, P.: Learning to reduce defocus blur by realistically modeling dual-pixel data. In: 18th International Conference on Computer Vision (ICCV), pp. 2269–2278. IEEE, Montreal (2020)
8. Pan, L., Chowdhury, S., Hartley, R., Liu, M., Zhang, H., Li, H.: Dual pixel exploration: simultaneous depth estimation and image restoration. In: 34th Conference on Computer Vision and Pattern Recognition (CVPR), pp. 4338–4347. IEEE, Nashville (2021)
9. Abuolaim, A., Afifi, M., Brown, M.S.: Improving single-image defocus deblurring: How dual-pixel images help through multi-task learning. In: 15th Winter Conference on Applications of Computer Vision (WACV), Kauai, pp. 82–90. IEEE, Hawaii (2022)
10. Lee, J., Son, H., Rim, J., Cho, S., Lee, S.: Iterative filter adaptive network for single image defocus deblurring. In: 34th Conference on Computer Vision and Pattern Recognition (CVPR), pp. 2034–2042. IEEE, Nashville (2021)
11. Ruan, L., Chen, B., Li, J., Lam, M.L.: Aifnet: all-in-focus image restoration network using a light field-based dataset. IEEE Trans. Comput. Imaging **7**, 675–688 (2021)
12. Quan, Y., Wu, Z., Ji, H.: Gaussian kernel mixture network for single image defocus deblurring. In: 35th Neural Information Processing Systems. OpenReview, New Orleans (2021)
13. Ruan, L., Chen, B., Li, J., Lam, M.: Learning to deblur using light field generated and real defocus images. In: 35th Conference on Computer Vision and Pattern Recognition (CVPR), pp. 16283–16292. IEEE, New Orleans (2022)

14. Zamir, S.W., Arora, A., Khan, S., Hayat, M., Khan, F.S., Yang, M.H.: Restormer: efficient transformer for high-resolution image restoration. In: 35th Conference on Computer Vision and Pattern Recognition (CVPR), pp. 5718–5729. IEEE, New Orleans (2022)
15. Quan, Y., Wu, Z., Ji, H.: Neumann network with recursive kernels for single image defocus deblurring. In: 36th Conference on Computer Vision and Pattern Recognition (CVPR), pp. 5754–5763. IEEE, Honolulu (2023)
16. Cui, Y., Tao, Y., Jing, L., Knoll, A.: Strip attention for image restoration. In: 32th International Joint Conference on Artificial Intelligence. AAAI Press, Busan (2023)
17. Liang, P., Jiang, J., Liu, X., Ma, J.: Decoupling image deblurring into twofold: a hierarchical model for defocus deblurring. IEEE Trans. Comput. Imaging **10**, 1207–1220 (2024)
18. Cui, Y., Knoll, A.: Dual-domain strip attention for image restoration. Neural Netw. Off. J. Int. Neural Netw. Soc. **171**, 429–439 (2023)
19. Cui, Y., Ren, W., Knoll, A.: Omni-kernel network for image restoration. In: 38th Conference on Artificial Intelligence. AAAI Press, Honolulu (2024)
20. Ling, S., Zhan, H., Cao, L.: SIDGAN: efficient multi-module architecture for single image defocus deblurring. Electronics **13**(12), 2265–2288 (2024)
21. Cho, S.J., Ji, S.W., Hong, J.P., Jung, S.W., Ko, S.J.: Rethinking coarse-to-fine approach in single image deblurring. In: 18th International Conference on Computer Vision (ICCV), pp. 4621–4630. IEEE, Montreal (2021)
22. Cui, Y., Ren, W., Yang, S., Cao, X., Knoll, A.: Irnext: rethinking convolutional network design for image restoration. In: 40th International Conference on Machine Learning. PMLR, Honolulu (2023)
23. Ilya, L., Frank, H.: Decoupled weight decay regularization. In: ICLR (2017)
24. Cui, Y., Knoll, A.: Exploring the potential of channel interactions for image restoration. Knowl.-Based Syst. **282**, 111–156 (2023)
25. Cui, Y., et al.: Selective frequency network for image restoration. In: 11th International Conference on Learning Representations. OpenReview, Miami (2023)
26. Cui, Y., Liu, M., Ren, W., Knoll, A.: Hybrid frequency modulation network for image restoration. In: 33th International Joint Conference on Artificial Intelligence. AAAI Press, Vancouver (2024)

AMF-GCN: An Adaptive Graph Convolution Network for Pull-up Evaluation

Xianglong Cao[1], Xin Li[2], and Jijun Tong[1](✉)

[1] School of Information Science and Engineering, Zhejiang Sci-Tech University, Hangzhou 310018, China
jijuntong@zstu.edu.cn
[2] Zhejiang Cancer Hospital, Hangzhou 310018, China

Abstract. Traditional pull-up assessments are typically conducted manually, a process that lacks objectivity and is both time-consuming and labor-intensive. To overcome these limitations, it is essential to develop an automated model for evaluating the correctness of pull-up movements. However, due to the absence of publicly available datasets, we constructed a custom pull-up action dataset consisting of videos recorded from both professional athletes and regular college students. In response to the limitations of existing action recognition models, this paper proposes an Adaptive Multi-dimensional Fusion Graph Convolutional Network (AMF-GCN), which comprises two key components: an Adaptive Graph Convolutional Module (AGCN) and a Multi-dimensional Fusion Module (MF). The AGCN module adaptively modifies the graph topology based on sample-specific data, enabling it to capture complex relationships among various joints. The MF module fuses information from multiple feature dimensions, thereby enhancing the model's flexibility and generalization capability. Extensive experimental comparisons demonstrate that our method achieves an accuracy of 97.33%, significantly outperforming several state-of-the-art action recognition models, thus validating its superior performance and effectiveness.

Keywords: Graph convolutional network · Action recognition · Pull-up

1 Introduction

Pull-ups, as a multijoint compound exercise, require the body to remain straight throughout the movement, avoiding swinging or using momentum for assistance [1]. With the rapid development of deep learning, numerous datasets have been proposed for action recognition tasks [2–4]. However, there is a notable lack of datasets specifically designed for evaluating pull-up performance, particularly in terms of determining whether the movement meets standard criteria. To address this gap, we propose a dedicated dataset for the strict evaluation of pull-up movement standards and use it to assess the effectiveness of our method.

Y. Zhou et al. (Eds.): ICECCS 2025, LNCS 15746, pp. 49–59, 2026.
https://doi.org/10.1007/978-3-032-00828-2_4

Human actions can be recognized through various modalities, such as sequential RGB images, depth maps, optical flow, and skeletal data. Skeletal data provides an efficient representation of human motion. In skeleton-based action recognition tasks, the first step involves extracting skeletal information of the human body, followed by using an action recognition model to infer whether the performed movement meets the standard. To the best of our knowledge, although several skeleton-based models for evaluating pull-up movements have been proposed, existing methods still face several challenges. Due to common issues such as estimation errors or missing data in skeletal information, Ke et al. [5] and Wang et al. [6] proposed Boolean-based evaluation methods using only a few joint coordinates, which suffer from limited robustness. Liu et al. [7] adopted an ST-GCN [8]-based model to extract high-dimensional features; however, ST-GCN is limited by its inability to learn the graph topology adaptively from the data.

To address the aforementioned issues, this paper proposes an Adaptive Multi-dimensional Fusion Graph Convolutional Network (AMF-GCN), which consists of two modules: the Adaptive Graph Convolutional Module (AGCN) and the Multi-dimensional Fusion Module (MF).1. The AGCN module first uses an attention mechanism to learn high-dimensional features from the data, then generates corresponding graphs based on different features, and adaptively modifies the graph structure, overcoming the limitations of physical connections.2. The MF module integrates information across the time, spatial, and channel dimensions of human skeleton sequences, enabling the network to more easily extract high-dimensional features.

To evaluate the effectiveness of the proposed AMF-GCN model, we conducted extensive experiments on our self-built pull-up dataset.

In summary, the three main contributions of our work are as follows:

- The proposed AGCN module extracts high-dimensional features from human skeleton data using an attention mechanism, and then generates different graphs for different action samples. This significantly enhances the model's adaptability and effectively improves the network's learning ability, enabling it to learn joint relationships that are not physically connected.
- The proposed MF module integrates multi-dimensional information across the channel, spatial, and temporal dimensions of action data using simple 1×1 convolutions, addressing the issue of previous action recognition methods failing to fuse spatiotemporal information.
- We have proposed a pull-up action standard judgment dataset, and multiple experiments conducted on this dataset demonstrate that our proposed AMF-GCN model outperforms previous methods.

2 Related Works

Due to the time-consuming, labor-intensive, and subjective nature of manual pull-up counting, several automatic pull-up counting methods have been proposed at this stage. Liu et al. [9] used infrared sensors for chin detection, which can accurately determine whether the chin has passed the bar. However, it does not address whether the tester fails to fully extend their arms or performs swinging motions, which are violations of the standard. Zhao et al. [10] proposed a depth image-based method that relies on the Kinect depth camera [11], which is costly and susceptible to environmental influences. Huang et al. [12] proposed a computer vision-based method that calculates the centroid coordinates of the hand and face using Haar features, and then compares the changes in centroid coordinates with thresholds to determine the standard of the action. This method records the video first and processes it later, which results in poor real-time performance. It also does not consider issues such as the tester's body swinging. Liu et al. [7] used deep learning methods to extract human joint coordinates and then applied an ST-GCN-based model [8] for action recognition. This method can effectively judge pull-up actions, but the ST-GCN model [8] still has significant room for improvement.

Skeleton-based action recognition is a computer vision technique that understands and classifies human actions by analyzing human skeletal data. Skeletal data has been widely used in the field of action recognition due to its efficiency in representing motion data. Traditional skeleton-based action recognition methods typically design handcrafted features to model the human body [11,13]. However, handcrafted features are limited in their ability to account for all parameters simultaneously. With the development of deep learning, data-driven methods have become mainstream, primarily categorized into RNN-based methods, CNN-based methods, and GCN-based methods. However, RNNs and CNNs cannot fully represent the structure of skeletal data, as skeletal data is inherently embedded in graph form rather than as vector sequences or two-dimensional grids. Recently, Yan et al. [8] proposed a spatiotemporal graph convolutional network (ST-GCN), which directly models skeletal data as a graph structure. It eliminates the need to design handcrafted conversion rules to transform skeletal data into vector sequences or pseudo-images, thereby achieving better performance.

3 Method

We propose the AMF-GCN model, the overall architecture of which is shown in Fig. 1. In this model, BN represents batch normalization, GAP denotes global average pooling, and Softmax refers to the normalized exponential function. Layers L1 to L10 consist of ten identical adaptive graph convolutional blocks, with each layer specified by three numbers representing the input channels, output channels, and stride, respectively.

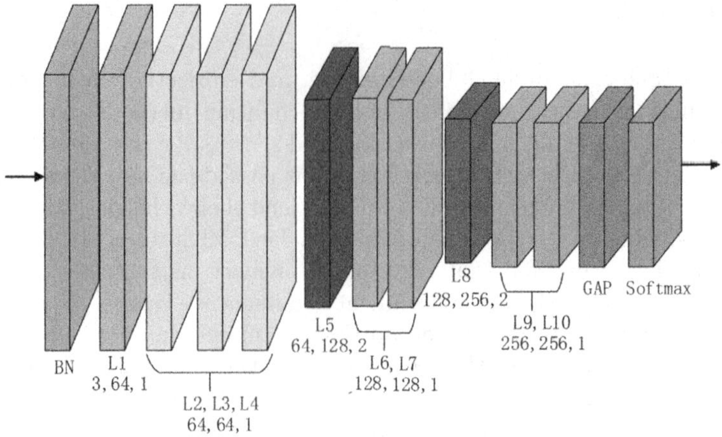

Fig. 1. AMF-GCN Network Structure

3.1 Adaptive Graph Convolution Block

As shown in Fig. 1, the Adaptive Multi-dimensional Fusion Graph Convolutional Network (AMF-GCN) is composed of multiple stacked graph convolutional operation blocks. Each graph convolutional operation block consists of an Adaptive Graph Convolutional Module (AGCN) and a Multi-dimensional Fusion Module (MF). To better capture the temporal dimension of skeleton data, we adopt MS-TCN [14] as the temporal graph convolutional model.

Graph convolution cannot be directly computed using conventional convolutional neural networks. In the spatial dimension, to implement graph convolution in programming, the spatial graph convolution operation can be expressed as Eq. 1.

$$f_{out} = \sum_{k}^{Kv} W_k \left(f_{in} A_k \right) \tag{1}$$

Here, $f_{\text{in}} \in \mathbb{R}^{C_{\text{in}} \times T \times N}$ represents the input features, and $f_{\text{out}} \in \mathbb{R}^{C_{\text{out}} \times T \times N}$ represents the output features. T and N denote the number of frames and joints in the action sample, respectively, while C_{in} and C_{out} denote the input and output channels, respectively. The adjacency matrix A_k represents the physical connections of the human body.

To enable the model to generate corresponding graphs for each sample, we improved the additive attention mechanism proposed by Shaker et al. [15]. We propose an Adaptive Graph Convolutional Network (AGCN) module. This module can construct different graphs for different samples to better adapt to action recognition tasks. The module's structure is shown in Fig. 2.

The Additive Attention Module is employed to capture global contextual information using an additive attention mechanism. This global context is then

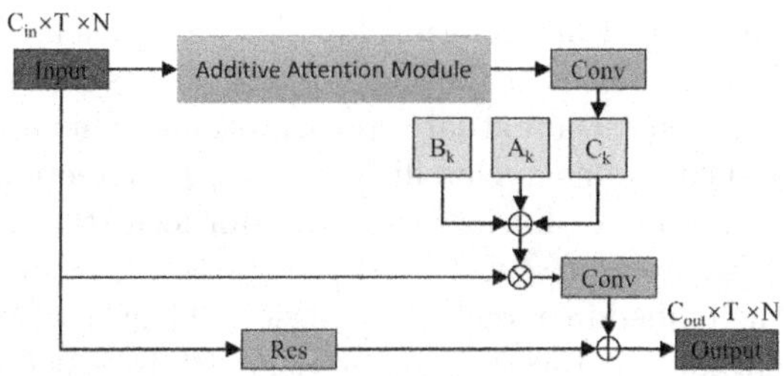

Fig. 2. AGCN Network Structure

utilized to extract a sample-adaptive graph structure for each input. The detailed architecture of the Additive Attention Module is illustrated in Fig. 3.

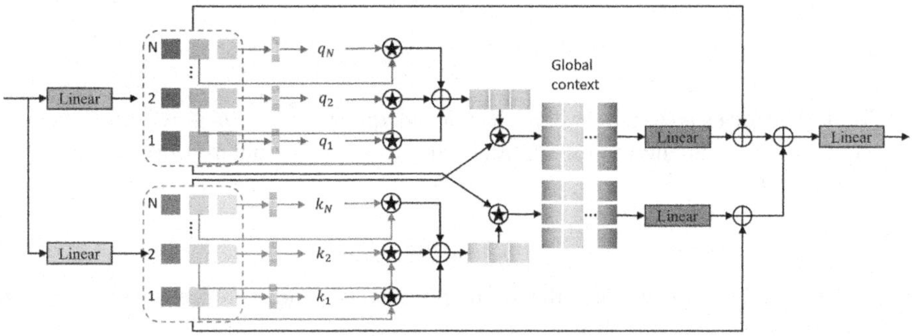

Fig. 3. Additive Attention Module Structure

Specifically, we utilize the additive attention mechanism to obtain global contextual information, which is then used to extract an adaptive graph for each sample. The final adaptive graph is obtained by combining the physical connections of the human skeleton with the global adaptive graph, enabling the model to better capture the differences between samples. By modifying Eq. 1, our operation can be expressed as Eq. 2.

$$f_{\text{out}} = \sum_{k}^{K_v} W_k f_{\text{in}} \left(A_k + B_k + C_k\right) \tag{2}$$

The key difference between Eq. 1 and Eq. 2 lies in the composition of the adjacency matrix. In Eq. 2, the adjacency matrix is divided into three parts: A_k, B_k, and C_k.

The parameters of B_k are trainable and are learned from the entire training dataset. Unlike B_k, which shares parameters across all samples, C_k learns a unique graph structure for each individual sample. Shaker et al. [15] demonstrated that key-value interactions can be omitted without sacrificing performance, focusing instead on efficiently encoding query-key interactions through linear projection layers to learn relationships between tokens. They referred to this method as efficient additive attention, which achieves faster inference speeds and produces more robust contextual representations. This approach has been validated in tasks such as image classification, object detection, and segmentation. Additive attention uses linear layers to transform the input into queries (Q) and keys (K), where $Q, K \in \mathbb{R}^{n\times d}$, $W_q, W_k \in \mathbb{R}^{d\times d}$, n represents the token length, and d is the embedding vector dimension. Then, the query matrix Q is multiplied by a learnable parameter vector $W_a \in \mathbb{R}^d$ to learn attention weights for the query, resulting in the globally attended query vector $\alpha \in \mathbb{R}^n$:

$$\alpha = Q \cdot \frac{W_a}{\sqrt{d}} \tag{3}$$

Then, the query matrix is pooled according to the learned attention weights to obtain a single global query vector $q \in \mathbb{R}^d$:

$$q = \sum_{i=1}^{n} \alpha_i * Q_i \tag{4}$$

Next, the interaction between the global query vector $q \in \mathbb{R}^d$ and the key matrix $K \in \mathbb{R}^{n\times d}$ is encoded using an element-wise product to obtain the global context $\hat{x} \in \mathbb{R}^{n\times d}$:

$$\hat{x} = \hat{Q} + \tau(K * q) \tag{5}$$

where $\hat{Q}$ represents the normalized query matrix, and τ represents the linear transformation.

Additive attention has proven its effectiveness in extracting contextual information in tasks such as image classification, but since human skeletal data are not spatially adjacent, it cannot be directly applied to action recognition tasks. To address this issue, we have improved additive attention to better capture the similarity between joints, rather than just contextual information. Inspired by Shi et al. [16], we do not distinguish between queries and keys, meaning the operations on queries and keys are the same, resulting in a symmetric additive attention, as shown in Fig. ??. The formula for joint similarity calculation can be expressed as follows:

$$C_k = W\left(\hat{Q} + \hat{K} + \tau(K * q) + \tau(Q * k)\right) \tag{6}$$

Here, $\hat{Q}$ and q are consistent with those in the additive attention, and the computation steps for $\hat{K}$ and k are the same as those for $\hat{Q}$ and q.W is a 1×1 convolution, which results in a matrix of size $N \times N$. The overall structure of the adaptive graph convolution is shown in Fig. 4.

3.2 Multidimensional Fusion

There are many methods for feature dimension fusion [17–19]. Through extensive experiments, we propose a multi-dimensional fusion module, as shown in Fig. 4.

To fuse information across different dimensions of the input features, we use the dot product for information interaction between dimensions. Specifically, given an input size of $C \times T \times N$, we first use a 1×1 convolution to aggregate the input feature's channel dimension information, and then use two separate 1×1 convolutions to aggregate the time and spatial dimension information. Then, we multiply them to obtain a feature weight of size $1 \times T \times N$, and finally multiply the input features with the feature weights to obtain the multi-dimensional fused features.

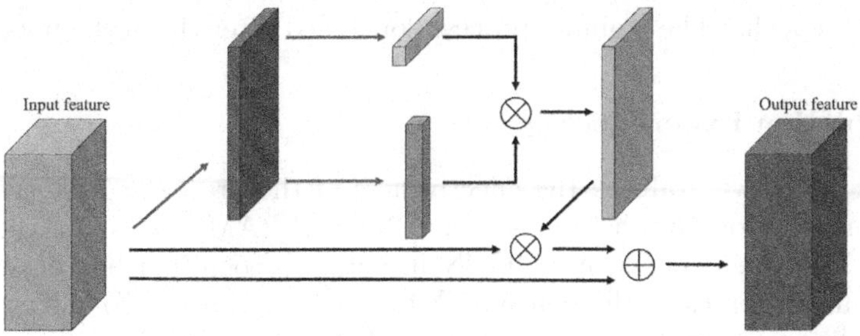

Fig. 4. Spatiotemporal Graph

4 Experiment

To validate the effectiveness of the proposed method, we created a custom pull-up dataset and conducted extensive experiments on it. We compared our method with several state-of-the-art models in the field of action recognition on this dataset and conducted detailed ablation studies to verify the effectiveness of the model components proposed based on recognition performance. The joints and their natural connections we used are defined as shown in Fig. 3, which includes 13 human body keypoints, capturing subtle variations in body part positions during the pull-up motion.

4.1 Dataset

Due to the lack of publicly available pull-up action datasets, we created a custom pull-up dataset. The dataset consists of 379 pull-up videos performed by both professional athletes and regular college students, including 135 standard movements and 244 non-standard movements, and is used for binary classification of pull-up performance. We used a pose estimation method [20] to extract human pose skeleton information from each pull-up action video. To ensure label accuracy, the dataset labels were strictly determined by professional sports teachers according to the pull-up action standards [1].

4.2 Training Details

All experiments were conducted using the Pytorch 2.1.0 deep learning framework [21]. The optimization strategy used was stochastic gradient descent (SGD) with a Nesterov momentum of 0.9. The batch size was set to 16. Cross-entropy was chosen as the loss function for backpropagating the gradients. Weight decay was set to 0.0005. Since the length of each action video varied, we standardized the maximum number of frames per sample to 160. For samples with fewer than 160 frames, we performed repeat sampling until reaching 160 frames. The initial learning rate was set to 0.1, and starting from the 10th epoch, it was divided by 10 every 5 epochs. The training process concluded after the 30th epoch.

4.3 Ablation Experiment

In this section, we evaluate the effectiveness of the proposed Adaptive Multi-dimensional Fusion Graph Convolutional Network (AMF-GCN) on the pull-up dataset. The effectiveness of ST-GCN in action recognition has been demonstrated, and it serves as the benchmark for our experiments.To better evaluate the model's performance, we use a Softmax layer to classify the features and use accuracy and precision as evaluation metrics.

Contrast Experiment. In this section, we compare our model with state-of-the-art methods in the field of action recognition on the pull-up dataset. The experimental results are shown in Table 1. Many outstanding methods in action recognition adopt multi-stream fusion approaches. To improve efficiency and ensure fairness, all the methods we use take only skeleton data as input. The experimental results demonstrate that our model achieves state-of-the-art performance on the pull-up dataset, attaining the highest accuracy and precision, which validates the superiority of our approach.

Table 1. Comparisons with the state-of-the-art methods on Pull-up dataset

Methods	Accuracy (%)	Precision (%)
STGCN [8]	90.67	80.00
PB-GCN [22]	90.67	82.61
MADT-GCN [23]	92.00	90.00
TE-GCN [24]	93.33	86.96
AAGCN [25]	93.33	86.96
AMF-GCN(ours)	97.33	95.45

The Effect of Adaptive Graph Convolution Module. We use STGCN as the baseline method.The proposed adaptive graph convolution consists of three subgraphs, as described in Sect. 3.2. We test the performance of each graph individually and then measure the performance of different combinations of them. The experimental results show that the two designed graphs significantly improve the performance of the pull-up action recognition task. The model achieves the best performance when the two graphs are combined. The experimental results are shown in Table 2. Where A represents the human physical connection graph, B represents the global graph, and C represents the individual sample graph

Table 2. Comparison of the accuracy of different combinations of adaptive graph convolution subgraphs for the pull-up action recognition task

Methods	Accuracy (%)	Precision (%)
STGCN	90.67	80.00
AGCN-B	92.00	80.77
AGCN-C	92.00	80.77
AGCN-BC	94.67	81.48
AGCN-ABC	96.00	91.30

The Effect of Multidimensional Fusion Module. In this section, we validate the effectiveness of the multi-dimensional fusion module (MF) proposed in Sect. 3.3, with the experimental results shown in Table 3. We use STGCN as the baseline model and test the performance of our module as well as the combination of STGCN and the MF module. AMF-GCN represents AGCN combined with the MF module. Experimental results show that the MF module contributes to improving the system's performance. Notably, the improvement brought by the multi-dimensional fusion module to AGCN (+1.33%) is less significant compared to STGCN (+2.66%). We believe this is because AGCN is already powerful and achieves high accuracy, limiting the enhancement effect of the multi-dimensional fusion module.

Table 3. The influence of multidimensional fusion module on recognition accuracy

Methods	Accuracy (%)	Precision (%)
STGCN	90.67	80.00
STGCN-MF	93.33	90.48
AGCN	96.00	91.30
AMF-GCN	97.33	95.45

5 Conclusion

This paper presents a novel AMF-GCN model specifically designed for the pull-up recognition task, leveraging advances in action recognition technology. The proposed model consists of two key modules: the AGCN module and the MF module. The AGCN module learns a more informative and adaptive adjacency matrix by employing an attention mechanism. The MF module utilizes simple 1×1 convolutions and matrix multiplication to fuse multi-dimensional feature information, thereby enhancing the model's feature extraction capability. Experimental results validate the effectiveness of the proposed AMF-GCN model. To improve the inference speed of the network, future research will focus on model lightweighting.

Acknowledgment. This study was funded by Zhejiang Provincial Natural Science Foundation (grant number LY22H170001).

Disclosure of Interests. The authors declare that they have no known competing financial interests or personal relationships that could have appeared to influence the work reported in this paper.

References

1. Ronai, P., Scibek, E.: The pull-up. Strength Cond. J. **36**(3), 88–90 (2014)
2. Shahroudy, A., Liu, J., Ng, T.-T., Wang, G.: Ntu rgb+ d: a large scale dataset for 3d human activity analysis. In: Proceedings of the IEEE Conference on Computer Vision and Pattern Recognition, pp. 1010–1019 (2016)
3. Liu, J., Shahroudy, A., Perez, M., Wang, G., Duan, L.-Y., Kot, A.C.: Ntu rgb+ d 120: a large-scale benchmark for 3d human activity understanding. IEEE Trans. Pattern Anal. Mach. Intell. **42**(10), 2684–2701 (2019)
4. Kay, W., et al.: The kinetics human action video dataset. arXiv preprint arXiv:1705.06950 (2017)
5. Ke, M., Tang, H., Zhu, H., Li, M.: Image vision-based pull-up recognition. In: 2023 3rd International Conference on Electronic Information Engineering and Computer Science (EIECS), pp. 872–876. IEEE (2023)
6. Wang, L., Chen, Y., Duan, W.: Monocular keypoint based pull-ups measurement on strict pull-ups benchmark. In: Proceedings of the 4th International Conference on Computer Science and Software Engineering, pp. 307–311 (2021)
7. Liu, Z., Gao, F., Song, K., Xiao, J.: Automated evaluation system for pull-up exercises in physical fitness testing scenarios. In: 2023 3rd International Conference on Information Technology and Contemporary Sports (TCS), pp. 11–15. IEEE (2023)
8. Yan, S., Xiong, Y., Lin, D.: Spatial temporal graph convolutional networks for skeleton-based action recognition. In: Proceedings of the AAAI Conference on Artificial Intelligence, vol. 32, no. 1 (2018)
9. Zhaopeng, L., Zhikun, W.: Automatic pull-up counting device. Hebei Agric. Mach. **1**, 60–60 (2018). (in Chinese)
10. Sufang, Z.: Research and development of automatic pull-up test system combined with depth image. Master's thesis, Wuyi University (2014). (in Chinese)

11. Zhang, Z.: Microsoft kinect sensor and its effect. IEEE Multimedia **19**(2), 4–10 (2012)
12. Zhichao, H., Wenming, Z., Huarong, Z., Deye, J.: A pull-up counting method based on machine vision. Video Eng. **42**(01), 77–83 (2018). (in Chinese)
13. Vemulapalli, R., Arrate, F., Chellappa, R.: Human action recognition by representing 3d skeletons as points in a lie group. In: Proceedings of the IEEE Conference on Computer Vision and Pattern Recognition, pp. 588–595 (2014)
14. Liu, Z., Zhang, H., Chen, Z., Wang, Z., Ouyang, W.: Disentangling and unifying graph convolutions for skeleton-based action recognition. In: Proceedings of the IEEE/CVF Conference on Computer Vision and Pattern Recognition, pp. 143–152 (2020)
15. A. Shaker, M. Maaz, H. Rasheed, S. Khan, M.-H. Yang, and F. S. Khan, "Swiftformer: Efficient additive attention for transformer-based real-time mobile vision applications," in *Proceedings of the IEEE/CVF International Conference on Computer Vision*, 2023, pp. 17 425–17 436
16. Shi, L., Zhang, Y., Cheng, J., Lu, H.: Two-stream adaptive graph convolutional networks for skeleton-based action recognition. In: Proceedings of the IEEE/CVF Conference on Computer Vision and Pattern Recognition, pp. 12 026–12 035 (2019)
17. Ma, X., et al.: Stnet: spatial and temporal feature fusion network for change detection in remote sensing images. In: 2023 IEEE International Conference on Multimedia and Expo (ICME), pp. 2195–2200. IEEE (2023)
18. Jia, Y., Lin, Y., Hao, X., Lin, Y., Guo, S., Wan, H.: Witran: water-wave information transmission and recurrent acceleration network for long-range time series forecasting. Adv. Neural Inf. Process. Syst. **36** (2024)
19. Chen, L., Fu, Y., Gu, L., Yan, C., Harada, T., Huang, G.: Frequency-aware feature fusion for dense image prediction. IEEE Trans. Pattern Anal. Mach. Intell. **46**, 10763–10780 (2024)
20. Zheng, C., et al.: Deep learning-based human pose estimation: a survey. ACM Comput. Surv. **56**(1), 1–37 (2023)
21. Paszke, A., et al.: Automatic differentiation in pytorch (2017)
22. Thakkar, K., Narayanan, P.: Part-based graph convolutional network for action recognition. arXiv preprint arXiv:1809.04983 (2018)
23. Xia, Y., Gao, Q., Wu, W., Cao, Y.: Skeleton-based action recognition based on multidimensional adaptive dynamic temporal graph convolutional network. Eng. Appl. Artif. Intell. **127**, 107210 (2024)
24. Xie, Y., Zhang, Y., Ren, F.: Temporal-enhanced graph convolution network for skeleton-based action recognition. IET Comput. Vision **16**(3), 266–279 (2022)
25. Shi, L., Zhang, Y., Cheng, J., Lu, H.: Skeleton-based action recognition with multi-stream adaptive graph convolutional networks. IEEE Trans. Image Process. **29**, 9532–9545 (2020)

A Q-Learning-Driven Multi-crossover NSGA-II Framework for Energy-Efficient Hybrid Flow Shop Scheduling

Jiale Wang[1], Mingyue Jiang[1], Hongyun Huang[2], Rui Xie[3], and Zuohua Ding[1(✉)]

[1] Faculty of Computer Science and Technology, Zhejiang Sci-Tech University, Hangzhou, Zhejiang, China
zuohuading@zstu.edu.cn

[2] Center of Library Big Data Processing and Analysis, Zhejiang Sci-Tech University, Hangzhou, Zhejiang, China

[3] Zhejiang Petroleum Comprehensive Energy Sales Co., Ltd., Hangzhou, Zhejiang, China

Abstract. In recent years, the energy-efficient hybrid flow shop scheduling problem (EHFSP) has gained significant attention in both academia and industry. However, most existing studies focus solely on either energy supply or demand strategies, which leads to suboptimal overall system efficiency and energy waste. To address this challenge, this paper proposes a novel multi-objective mixed-integer nonlinear model that integrates time-of-use pricing with machine power-down strategy, achieving a coordinated optimization of production efficiency and energy costs. To solve the proposed model, we develop a Q-learning-driven multi-crossover operator non-dominated sorting genetic algorithm II (QMCO-NSGA-II). By embedding Q-learning into the multi-crossover operator framework, the algorithm adaptively selects crossover operators, effectively balancing solution diversity and convergence. Additionally, an improved Nawaz-Enscore-Ham heuristic is introduced to generate high-quality initial solutions, enhancing both the convergence speed and solution quality. Extensive experiments on standard EHFSP datasets demonstrate that QMCO-NSGA-II significantly outperforms four state-of-the-art multi-objective algorithms in terms of convergence and solution diversity, showcasing its practical applicability to complex industrial scenarios.

Keywords: Energy-efficient scheduling · Q-learning · Multiobjective

1 Introduction

The hybrid flow shop scheduling problem (HFSP) is a well-known combinatorial optimization problem widely encountered in industries such as electronics [25], steel [8], and glass manufacturing [23]. HFSP consists of multiple sequential processing stages, each with several parallel machines, where tasks must follow a

Y. Zhou et al. (Eds.): ICECCS 2025, LNCS 15746, pp. 60–78, 2026.
https://doi.org/10.1007/978-3-032-00828-2_5

predefined order. Its flexibility makes it highly suitable for multi-variety, small-batch production systems [11]. However, HFSP is inherently complex due to its combinatorial nature and various constraints, which pose significant challenges to both researchers and practitioners.

Over the years, extensive studies on HFSP have primarily focused on improving production efficiency, such as minimizing makespan, reducing delays, and enhancing throughput [16]. While these objectives are critical, they often neglect environmental sustainability and energy efficiency, which are becoming increasingly important in manufacturing. The industrial sector, responsible for approximately 64.8% of China's electricity consumption [15], plays a pivotal role in reducing energy use and mitigating environmental impacts. Consequently, energy-efficient scheduling has emerged as a critical research area, giving rise to the energy-efficient hybrid flow shop scheduling problem (EHFSP) [12].

The research on EHFSP has explored various energy-efficient strategies (EES), including energy-supply approaches such as time-of-use (TOU) pricing [1], and energy-demand approaches such as power-down strategy that shut off idle machines [2]. These strategies have been proven effective in reducing energy costs without compromising production efficiency. However, most existing approaches fail to consider TOU pricing and power-down strategy simultaneously, thereby reducing their adaptability and flexibility in achieving higher energy savings in complex manufacturing environments.

Currently, algorithms for solving the EHFSP can be categorized into two main types: exact methods and metaheuristic approaches. Exact methods are capable of solving small-scale problems, while metaheuristic algorithms are designed to provide near-optimal solutions for larger-scale problems within limited time frames [10]. Among metaheuristics, the non-dominated sorting genetic algorithm II (NSGA-II) [3] is one of the most widely used algorithms and has demonstrated strong performance. However, as a genetic algorithm, the effectiveness of NSGA-II is significantly influenced by the crossover strategy and it is prone to getting trapped in local optima, thus requiring enhancements to improve both search efficiency and solution quality. In recent years, Q-learning [24] has shown great potential in complex optimization problems due to its ability to optimize decision-making strategies through interaction with the environment without the need for large amounts of labeled data. Through a trial-and-error mechanism, Q-learning can continuously adjust scheduling strategies, enabling the algorithm to adapt effectively in dynamic environments.

Despite these advancements, significant gaps remain in leveraging Q-learning to enhance metaheuristic algorithms for EHFSP. Additionally, EES that integrate both TOU pricing and power-down strategy have been insufficiently explored. To address these issues, this paper constructs a mathematical model for EHFSP, optimizing the makespan, total delay time, and total energy cost, while considering both TOU pricing and power-down strategy. Furthermore, a Q-learning-driven multi-crossover operator framework is proposed to effectively solve the EHFSP.

The main contributions of this paper are as follows:

- A mathematical model is proposed to solve the EHFSP by simultaneously considering EES based on TOU pricing and power-down strategy, aiming to minimize energy costs while ensuring production efficiency.
- The proposed method utilizes an improved Nawaz-Enscore-Ham (INEH) heuristic for population initialization to generate high-quality initial solutions, thereby enhancing both convergence speed and solution quality. Additionally, Q-learning is integrated into the multi-crossover operator framework, enabling the algorithm to adaptively select crossover operators and effectively balance solution diversity with convergence speed.
- The QMCO-NSGA-II algorithm is evaluated against four state-of-the-art multi-objective algorithms using standard EHFSP datasets. Experimental results demonstrate that QMCO-NSGA-II outperforms the existing methods in terms of both convergence and solution diversity.

2 Problem Formulation and Modeling

2.1 Problem Formulation

In the EHFSP, the workshop consists of multiple stages, with each stage equipped with a set of parallel machines for processing jobs. Each job must sequentially pass through all stages and select an appropriate machine for processing at each stage. The scheduling should consider the processing order, machine selection, and fluctuations in TOU pricing to optimize electricity costs, while also strategically managing machine idle times through a power-down strategy to reduce energy costs and maintain production efficiency [21].

2.2 Mathematical Model

The multiple objectives for minimizing the EHFSP are as follows (Table 1):

- Makespan ($C_{\max}$):

$$f_1 = \max(C_{js}) \tag{1}$$

- Total tardiness (TT):

$$f_2 = \sum_{j \in J} \max\{0, C_{js} - d_j\} \tag{2}$$

- Total energy cost (TEC):

$$f_3 = \sum_{t \in N} f(t) \sum_{k \in S} \sum_{i \in M_k} E_{ik}^t \tag{3}$$

All feasible solutions to this problem must satisfy the following constraints:

$$\sum_{k \in S} \sum_{i \in M_k} \sum_{j \in J} a_{ikj}^t \leq 1, t \in N. \tag{4}$$

Table 1. Notation definitions for EHFSP

Notation	Definition
J	Number of jobs, $j \in J$
S	Number of stages, $k \in S$
M_k	Number of machines at stage k, $m_{ik} \in M_k$
d_j	Delivery time of job j
C_{js}	Completion time of job j at the final stage
t	Time
N	Set of time period t
$f(t)$	TOU pricing function (CNY/MWh)
pe_{ik}	Energy consumption of machine m_{ik} during processing at stage k
se_{ik}	Energy consumption of machine m_{ik} during idle at stage k
t_{reset}	Reset time of machine m_{ik}
re_{ik}	Energy consumption of machine m_{ik} during reset
E^t_{ik}	Total energy consumption of machine m_{ik} during period t
a^t_{ikj}	1 if job j is processed on machine m_{ik} at stage k, 0 otherwise
b^t_{ikj}	1 if job j starts on machine m_{ik} at stage k, 0 otherwise
χ_{ikjh}	1 if job j precedes job h on machine m_{ik}, 0 otherwise ($j \neq h$, $h \in J$)
χ^t_{ik}	1 if machine m_{ik} is in standby mode, 0 otherwise

$$\sum_{t \in N} \sum_{i \in M_k} b^t_{ikj} = 1, j \in J, k \in S. \tag{5}$$

$$\sum_{h \in J \cup \{0\}} \chi_{ikjh} = \sum_{t \in N} b^t_{ikj}, i \in M_k, j \neq h, j \in J. \tag{6}$$

$$\sum_{j \in J \cup \{0\}} \chi_{ikjh} = \sum_{t \in N} b^t_{ikh}, i \in M_k, j \neq h, h \in J. \tag{7}$$

$$C_{jk} \leq S_{j(k+1)}, j \in J, k \in S. \tag{8}$$

Equation (4): Ensure that each machine can process only one job at a time. Equation (5): Guarantee that each operation can only start once. Equation (6): Each job can have only one predecessor job. Equation (7): Each job can have only one successor job. Equation (8): The successor operation cannot start before the preceding operation is completed. EHFSP is a combinatorial optimization problem. Since multi-objective optimization problems do not have a single optimal solution, the goal is to find the pareto optimal solutions for EHFSP.

3 The QMCO-NSGA-II Algorithm

3.1 Population Initialization

The NEH algorithm proposed by Nawaz et al. [14] is widely regarded as one of the most successful heuristic methods for the HFSP. Inspired by their work, we have developed an INEH heuristic for the EHFSP to initialize the population. Algorithm 1 outlines the INEH algorithm, ensures rapid convergence while maintaining diversity.

Algorithm 1. INEH Algorithm

Input: number of jobs n.
Output: a feasible schedule π.
Sort jobs by processing time in descending order to generate job sequence π_r.
Select the first two jobs and schedule them in π by minimizing a specific objective (e.g., f_1 value)
for $i = 3$ **to** n **do**
    Take job $\pi_r(i)$ and insert it into all possible positions in the current schedule.
    Calculate objective f_1, f_2, and f_3 values for the new sequence.
    // Update schedule π to the sequence with the smallest f_1 value.
    if multiple sequences have the same f_1 value **then** compare the f_2 value.
    end if
    if multiple sequences have the same f_1 and f_2 values **then** compare the f_3 value.
    end if
    if multiple sequences have the same f_1, f_2 and f_3 values **then** randomly select one from these sequences.
    end if
end for
return a feasible schedule π.

3.2 Q-Learning for Multi-crossover Operator Framework

In the crossover phase, the algorithm selects one crossover operator from multi-crossover operator (MCO) framework, including a novel crossover operator (SX [7]) and five classical crossover operators (PBX, OX, PMX, LOX and OBX [6,9,17]). To optimize selection, Q-learning dynamically adjusts the probabilities. The probability of selecting the novel operator is $(1 - p)$, while the probability of choosing one of the classical operators is p. Through continuous learning, Q-learning adapts the crossover strategy to enhance performance at different optimization stages.

States and Actions. In Q-MCONSGA-II, the main task of the Q-learning algorithm is to dynamically adjust the most suitable multi-crossover operator selection probabilities at each iteration. The Q-learning algorithm performs addition or subtraction operations on the multi-crossover operator selection probabilities to find the most appropriate selection probability within a given range. The mathematical expression for this operation is shown in Eq. 9, where +0.05 and -0.05 represent the increase and decrease operations on the current selection probability, respectively, while 0 indicates that the current selection probability remains unchanged. All actions are selected based on feedback from the current environmental state.

$$A = \{-0.05, 0, +0.05\} \tag{9}$$

During the training process, the action set is defined as the addition and subtraction operations on the multi-crossover operator selection probabilities. Therefore, the state in the algorithm is represented by the new selection probability value obtained after selecting an action, which typically falls within the range [0, 1] and is expressed with two decimal places.

Reward Function. After each training step, each action receives a feedback reward value, which is primarily determined based on the objectives of the problem. This study uses two evaluation metrics to calculate the reward value for each action. One metric is the best fitness of all solutions, representing the local improvement made by the action on the population; the other is the average fitness of the population, representing the global improvement of the population due to the action. Compared to the basic reward mechanism, using these two evaluation metrics to calculate the reward value not only increases the probability of obtaining better solutions but also maximizes the retention of the optimal population. The specific steps of the reward and penalty mechanism are described in Algorithm 2.

Algorithm 2. Reward Function

Input: $maxGen, f_1, f_2, f_3$
Output: Q $value$

$gen = 0$
while $gen < maxGen$ **do**
  $f^{norm} = \frac{f - \min(f)}{\max(f) - \min(f)}$ // Normalize the fitness values
  $\omega fit = \omega_1 f_1^{norm} + \omega_2 f_2^{norm} + (1 - \omega_1 - \omega_2) f_3^{norm}$ // Compute the weighted sum of normalized fitness
  $bestfit = \min(\omega fit), meanfit = mean(\omega fit)$
  if $gen = 0$ **then**
    $f_{best} = bestfit$, $f_{mean} = meanfit$, $reward = 0$
  else
    if $bestfit < f_{\text{best}}$ && $meanfit < f_{\text{mean}}$ **then** reward $= 16$
    else if $bestfit < f_{\text{best}}$ && $meanfit \geq f_{\text{mean}}$ **then** reward $= 6$
    else if $bestfit \geq f_{\text{best}}$ && $meanfit < f_{\text{mean}}$ **then** reward $= 3$
    else if $bestfit \geq f_{\text{best}}$ && $meanfit \geq f_{\text{mean}}$ **then** reward $= -10$
    end if
  end if
  $update(f_{best}, f_{mean})$
  $gen = gen + 1$
end while
return Q $value$

The detailed design of the reward function during the learning process is divided into four cases based on the changes in the individual's best fitness and the population's average fitness: (1) Both the individual's best fitness and the population's average fitness decrease. (2) The individual's best fitness decreases, while the population's average fitness increases. (3) The individual's best fitness increases, but the population's average fitness decreases. (4) Both the individual's best fitness and the population's average fitness increase.

Process of Q-Learning. Q-learning is an off-policy RL algorithm, meaning it evaluates action policies differently from on-policy methods. The action policy follows an ε-greedy approach, while the evaluation method adopts a greedy approach. Using the action-value function Q, the Q-learning update is expressed in Eq. 10.

$$Q\left(s,a\right)=Q\left(s,a\right)+\alpha[r+\gamma max_{a'}Q\left(s',a'\right)-Q(s,a)] \tag{10}$$

Exploration and exploitation are crucial in Q-learning for achieving optimal solutions. Consistently choosing the action with the highest value increases the use of acquired knowledge but may lead to getting trapped in local optima. To address this, the ε-greedy approach introduces a probability to explore other actions, as represented in Eq. 11.

$$a=\begin{Bmatrix} argmaxQ(s,a) \\ any\ action\ in\ A \end{Bmatrix} \tag{11}$$

RL is an iterative process of experimentation aimed at optimizing the long-term expected total reward. Balancing exploration and exploitation when selecting actions is a key factor in the training process. The detailed steps are provided in Algorithm 3.

Algorithm 3. Q - learning

Input: $\epsilon, \alpha, \gamma, a \in A, s \in S, maxGen$
Output: Q, s', a'
gen $= 0, p_{\text{rand}} = \text{rand}(S)$
while $gen < maxGen$ **do**
  $r = reward(\omega\text{fit}, bestfit, meanfit)$
  if gen $= 0$ **then**
    $s = p_{rand}, a = rand(A), p_{temp} = update(s,a)$
  else
    $s' = p_{temp}$
  end if
  $Q(s,a) = Q(s,a) + \alpha[r + \gamma \max_{a'} Q(s',a') - Q(s,a)]$
  if rand $< \epsilon$ **then**
    $a' = randomaction(A)$
  else
    $a' = arg\ maxQ(s',a')$
  end if
  $p_{temp} = update(s',a'),\ gen = gen + 1$
end while
return Q, s', a'

3.3 Power-Down Strategy

Figure 1 illustrates the machine switching strategy using a Gantt chart. The gray dashed box represents the standby state of the machine between processing two jobs, while the green dashed box indicates the machine's shutdown and restart state. In the figure, the machine power-down strategy causes the machine to shut down for a period, reducing electricity costs without affecting the delay time. The strategy determines whether to shut down the machine to save power costs or keep it in standby mode. Additionally, if there is no available time for resetting, the machine will not be shut down. The power-down strategy dynamically adjusts the machine's state to reduce energy consumption.

The inter-arrival time between two consecutive jobs on a machine, denoted as RT_{ik}, is computed as:

$$\mathrm{RT}_{ik\sigma_{ik}(q)\sigma_{ik}(q+1)} = C_{\sigma_{ik}(q+1)k} - \frac{p_{\sigma_{ik}(q+1)k}}{v_{ik}} - C_{\sigma_{ik}(q)k}, i \in M_k, k \in S \quad (12)$$

where C represents the completion time, p is the processing time, and v is the speed of the machine. The break-even time for shutting down a machine, BT_{ik}, is defined as:

$$\mathrm{BT}_{ik} = \frac{t_{reset} e^{r}_{ik}}{e^{S}_{ik}}, i \in M_k, k \in S \quad (13)$$

A machine m_{ik} is power-down if $\mathrm{RT}_{ik} > \mathrm{BT}_{ik}$. Otherwise, it remains in standby mode, as the energy consumed during the idle state is lower than the reset cost.

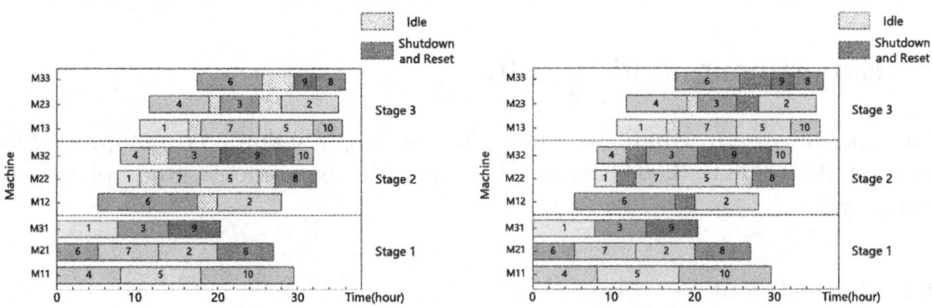

(a) NO power-down. (b) After power-down.

Fig. 1. The effect of power down strategy.

3.4 Flow Chart of the QMCO-NSGA-II

The framework of the proposed QMCO-NSGA-II algorithm is illustrated in Fig. 2.

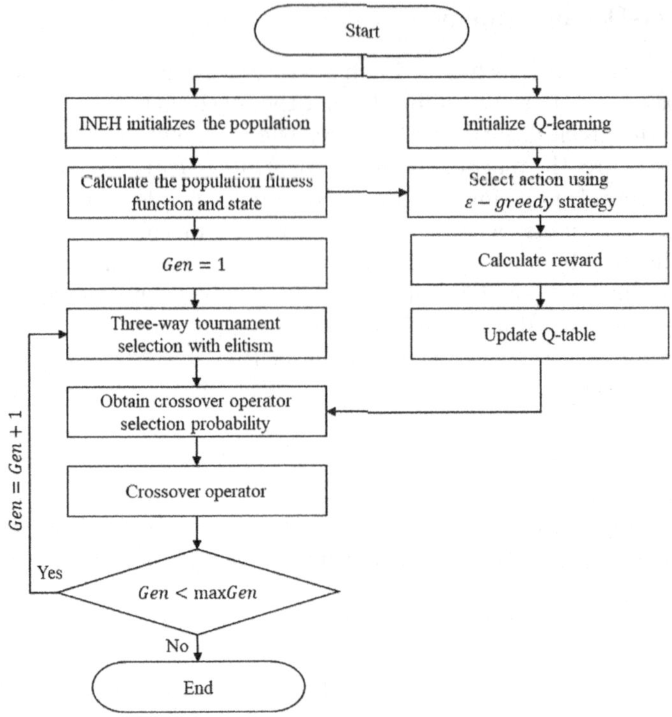

Fig. 2. Flow chart of the QMCO-NSGA-II.

4 Experiments and Results

All experiments are conducted on a PC running Windows 11, equipped with an Intel i9-13900KF, 3.00 GHz, 32 GB RAM. The experiments are implemented using Python.

4.1 Experiment Settings

Due to the lack of previous studies on benchmark instances for the EHFSP, test instances are generated based on the guidelines provided by Li et al. [13], with detailed specifications given in Table 2.

(i)The delivery time d_j is determined by Eq. 14:

$$d_j = \max\left(0, U\left[p\left(1-\tau-\frac{R}{2}\right), p\left(1-\tau+\frac{R}{2}\right)\right]\right) \tag{14}$$

where p is the lower bound of the makespan, $\tau \in \{0.2, 0.4\}$ is the tardiness factor, and $R \in \{0.6, 1.0\}$ is due date factor. $U[a, b]$ denotes a uniform random number in $[a, b]$, and the due date is rounded to the nearest integer.

(ii)The TOU pricing are based on the actual industrial electricity usage data from Zhejiang Province during the spring and autumn seasons. The price function is represented as:

$$f(t) = \begin{cases} 0.287 & 24n \leq t < 24n + 8 \\ 1.055 & 24n + 8 \leq t < 24n + 11 \\ 0.287 & 24n + 11 \leq t < 24n + 13 \\ 1.055 & 24n + 13 \leq t < 24n + 17 \\ 0.639 & 24n + 17 \leq t < 24n + 24 \end{cases} \quad (\text{CNY/kWh}),\ n \in \{0, 1, 2, \dots\} \tag{15}$$

Table 2. Test instance parameter settings.

Factors	Levels
Number of jobs	10, 20, 50
Number of stages	3, 5
Number of machines at each stage	3, 4, 6
Processing time of each operation	U[5, 10] (hour)
Power of machine	U[5, 10] (kw)
Processing speed	1.2, 1.0, 0.8
Conversion rate	1.5, 1.0, 0.6
Standby power of machine	2 kw
Reset power of machine	4 kw

The quality of multi-objective algorithms is assessed using the following performance indicators:

1. Coverage Metric (CM) [5]: CM is a binary measure for comparing two solution sets, A and B. The value of $C(A, B)$ is calculated as:

$$C(A, B) = \frac{|\{b \in B | \exists a \in A : a \succ b \text{ or } a = b\}|}{|B|} \tag{16}$$

Here, $a \succ b$ indicates that a dominates b. It holds that $C(A, B) + C(B, A) \leq 1$. A larger $C(A, B)$ indicates that A dominates B more effectively.

2. Spacing Metric (SM) [22]: SM measures the diversity of solutions along the Pareto front. A lower SM indicates better uniformity. It is computed as:

$$\text{SM} = \sqrt{\frac{\sum_{i=1}^{|A|} \left(d_i - \bar{d}\right)^2}{|A|}} \tag{17}$$

where d_i is the minimum sum of normalized objective value differences between the i-th solution and all others in the non-dominated set A, and $\bar{d}$ is the average value of d_i.

4.2 Parameter Calibration

QMCO-NSGA-II includes five important parameters: population size P_s, crossover rate P_c, mutation rate P_m, stop condition of Q-learning Q_{iter}, and CPU time ($CT \times n \times m$). Here, CT represents cycle time, and n and m are the number of jobs and stages, respectively. The "20-3-3" medium-scale instance is used for the Taguchi method [18] experiments on these parameters. Each parameter is treated as a factor, with three levels for each factor. Table 3 lists the orthogonal array, which contains five factors, each with three levels. Under the assumption of generality, the following parameters are set: maximum iteration number $maxGen = 100$, learning rate $\alpha = 0.1$, greedy probability $\varepsilon = 0.86$, discount factor $\gamma = 0.9$, and initial crossover operator selection probability $p = 0.5$. The performance metric SM is used as the response indicator.

Table 3. Parameters and levels.

Parameter	Level		
	1	2	3
P_s	80	100	120
P_c	0.7	0.8	0.9
P_m	0.1	0.2	0.3
Q_{iter}	3	5	8
CT	0.8	1.2	1.5

The main effect plot of the parameters is shown in Fig. 3. It can be observed that the points with the lowest SM response values in these five modules repre-

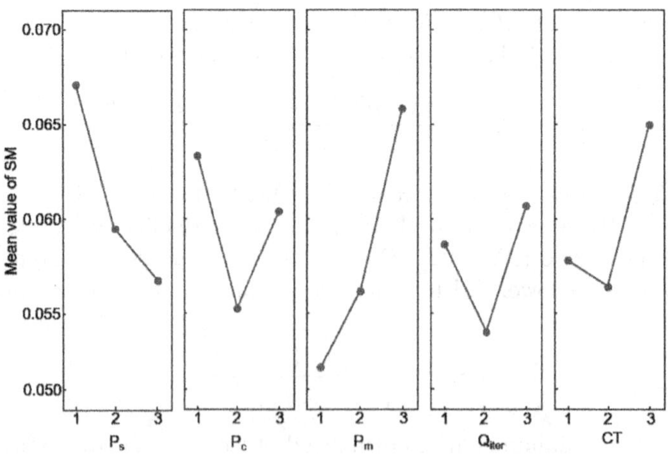

Fig. 3. Main effect plot of each parameter on SM values.

sent the optimal levels for each parameter. The parameter settings for QMCO-NSGA-II are: $P_s = 120$, $P_c = 0.8$, $P_m = 0.1$, $Q_{iter} = 5$, and $CT = 1.2$.

4.3 Impact of the Enhancements on QMCO-NSGA-II

This section evaluates the impact of two key improvements made to the Q-MCONSGA-II algorithm. To verify the effectiveness of these enhancements, two algorithm variants are designed for comparison: (1)N1: This variant adopts the improved initialization strategy (INEH) but does not use Q-learning for adaptive crossover operator selection during the crossover phase. Instead, a fixed crossover operator is applied. (2)N2: This variant employs Q-learning for adaptive crossover operator selection but does not use the INEH strategy for initialization. Instead, the initial population is generated randomly.

The performance metric SM is used to evaluate solution quality. The results in Table 4 show that Q-MCONSGA-II achieved the best performance in 15 out of 18 instances, significantly outperforming the other two variants. This indicates that Q-MCONSGA-II exhibits clear advantages in both convergence and solution diversity, validating the effectiveness of the improved initialization strategy and Q-learning-based adaptive crossover selection. These improvements work synergistically to enhance the algorithm's capability in solving the EHFSP, enabling it to generate a more uniformly distributed and higher-quality Pareto front, thereby improving optimization stability and robustness.

Table 4. Comparing the effectiveness of algorithm improvements using SM performance metrics.

Instance	QMCO-NSGA-II		N1		N2	
	mean	std	mean	std	mean	std
10-3-3	**9.27E-2**	2.15E-3	1.51E-1	3.21E-3	9.34E-2	1.98E-3
10-3-4	**6.38E-2**	1.97E-3	2.15E-1	4.12E-3	7.28E-2	2.45E-3
10-3-6	6.34E-2	1.75E-3	1.14E-1	2.98E-3	**6.27E-2**	1.12E-3
10-5-3	**6.43E-2**	1.88E-3	1.71E-1	4.18E-3	7.74E-2	2.39E-3
10-5-4	7.98E-2	2.14E-3	1.10E-1	2.97E-3	**7.24E-2**	1.68E-3
10-5-6	5.11E-2	1.54E-3	**5.03E-2**	1.22E-3	5.22E-2	1.88E-3
20-3-3	**5.36E-2**	1.88E-3	1.39E-1	3.79E-3	7.96E-2	2.68E-3
20-3-4	**4.72E-2**	1.61E-3	1.20E-1	3.45E-3	6.00E-2	2.21E-3
20-3-6	**5.65E-2**	1.79E-3	1.13E-1	3.52E-3	5.90E-2	1.98E-3
20-5-3	**6.34E-2**	1.92E-3	1.66E-1	4.21E-3	1.06E-1	2.85E-3
20-5-4	**4.77E-2**	1.43E-3	1.07E-1	2.98E-3	5.82E-2	1.79E-3
20-5-6	**4.84E-2**	1.76E-3	1.54E-1	3.92E-3	7.92E-2	2.45E-3
50-3-3	**5.15E-2**	1.82E-3	1.42E-1	3.64E-3	7.02E-2	2.01E-3
50-3-4	**6.10E-2**	2.12E-3	1.92E-1	4.53E-3	9.15E-2	2.68E-3
50-3-6	**4.50E-2**	1.52E-3	1.70E-1	4.12E-3	6.07E-2	2.15E-3
50-5-3	**6.28E-2**	2.13E-3	2.56E-1	5.28E-3	9.31E-2	3.14E-3
50-5-4	**4.98E-2**	1.76E-3	2.24E-1	4.37E-3	5.14E-2	1.98E-3
50-5-6	**5.77E-2**	1.16E-3	1.24E-1	2.18E-3	6.23E-2	2.06E-3
Hit rate	**15/18**		1/18		2/18	

4.4 Comparison with the Other Algorithms

In this section, we compare the proposed QMCO-NSGA-II approach with several leading algorithms: the classical NSGA-II [4], the improved Jaya algorithm [18], the multi-objective evolutionary algorithm based on decomposition (MOEA/D) [20], and the enhanced multi-objective artificial bee colony algorithm (MOABC) [19].

Each algorithm is executed with identical stopping criteria to ensure a fair comparison. Specifically, the CPU time allocated to each algorithm is proportional to the number of jobs and stages in the corresponding problem instance. This setup ensures a controlled and consistent evaluation of the algorithms across different instances. Each algorithm is run ten times, and the average values along with standard deviations are reported to ensure statistical reliability.

Table 5. Comparison results of CM.

Instance	C(Q,N)		C(N,Q)		C(Q, J)		C(J ,Q)		C(Q,M)		C(M,Q)		C(Q,A)		C(A,Q)	
	mean	std	mean	std	mean	std	mean	std	mean	std	mean	std	mean	std	mean	std
10-3-3	**0.87**	0.11	0.00	0.00	**1.00**	0.00	0.00	0.00	**1.00**	0.00	0.00	0.00	**1.00**	0.00	0.00	0.00
10-3-4	**0.89**	0.05	0.00	0.00	**0.98**	0.03	0.00	0.00	**1.00**	0.00	0.00	0.00	**1.00**	0.00	0.00	0.00
10-3-6	**0.97**	0.07	0.00	0.00	**0.99**	0.01	0.00	0.00	**1.00**	0.00	0.00	0.00	**1.00**	0.00	0.00	0.00
10-5-3	**0.96**	0.16	0.00	0.00	**1.00**	0.00	0.00	0.00	**1.00**	0.00	0.00	0.00	**1.00**	0.00	0.00	0.00
10-5-4	**0.89**	0.04	0.00	0.00	**1.00**	0.00	0.00	0.00	**1.00**	0.00	0.00	0.00	**1.00**	0.00	0.00	0.00
10-5-6	**0.86**	0.12	0.00	0.00	**1.00**	0.00	0.00	0.00	**0.98**	0.03	0.00	0.00	**1.00**	0.00	0.00	0.00
20-3-3	**0.82**	0.23	0.00	0.00	**1.00**	0.00	0.00	0.00	**1.00**	0.00	0.00	0.00	**1.00**	0.00	0.00	0.00
20-3-4	**0.88**	0.08	0.00	0.00	**1.00**	0.00	0.00	0.00	**1.00**	0.00	0.00	0.00	**1.00**	0.00	0.00	0.00
20-3-6	**0.91**	0.05	0.00	0.00	**1.00**	0.00	0.00	0.00	**1.00**	0.00	0.00	0.00	**1.00**	0.00	0.00	0.00
20-5-3	**0.90**	0.11	0.00	0.00	**1.00**	0.00	0.00	0.00	**1.00**	0.00	0.00	0.00	**1.00**	0.00	0.00	0.00
20-5-4	**0.88**	0.12	0.00	0.00	**1.00**	0.00	0.00	0.00	**1.00**	0.00	0.00	0.00	**1.00**	0.00	0.00	0.00
20-5-6	**0.92**	0.10	0.00	0.00	**1.00**	0.00	0.00	0.00	**1.00**	0.00	0.00	0.00	**1.00**	0.00	0.00	0.00
50-3-3	**0.90**	0.07	0.00	0.00	**1.00**	0.00	0.00	0.00	**1.00**	0.00	0.00	0.00	**1.00**	0.00	0.00	0.00
50-3-4	**0.89**	0.02	0.00	0.00	**1.00**	0.00	0.00	0.00	**1.00**	0.00	0.00	0.00	**1.00**	0.00	0.00	0.00
50-3-6	**0.95**	0.05	0.00	0.00	**1.00**	0.00	0.00	0.00	**1.00**	0.00	0.00	0.00	**1.00**	0.00	0.00	0.00
50-5-3	**0.94**	0.13	0.00	0.00	**1.00**	0.00	0.00	0.00	**1.00**	0.00	0.00	0.00	**1.00**	0.00	0.00	0.00
50-5-4	**0.92**	0.06	0.00	0.00	**1.00**	0.00	0.00	0.00	**1.00**	0.00	0.00	0.00	**1.00**	0.00	0.00	0.00
50-5-6	**0.89**	0.03	0.00	0.00	**1.00**	0.00	0.00	0.00	**1.00**	0.00	0.00	0.00	**1.00**	0.00	0.00	0.00
Hit rate	**18/18**		0/18		**18/18**		0/18		**18/18**		0/18		**18/18**		0/18	

Table 5 presents the CM results for all algorithms. For simplicity, each algorithm is represented by a single letter (Q for QMCO-NSGA-II, N for NSGA-II, J for Jaya, M for MOEA/D, and A for MOABC). For example, C(Q, NSGAII) represents QMCO-NSGA-II and NSGA-II. The CM values are calculated by comparing the sets of solutions obtained by each algorithm, with the objective of determining how well each algorithm's Pareto front dominates the others. In this comparison, QMCO-NSGA-II consistently dominates all other algorithms across all instances, as indicated by its higher CM values, demonstrating its superior performance.

The results strongly support that QMCO-NSGA-II outperforms all other algorithms in terms of convergence and robustness. Its superior performance in terms of CM is attributed to its effective exploration of promising solution spaces, driven by the synergy of INEH and Q-learning. The consistently high CM values across all instances further emphasize the algorithm's robustness and its capacity to identify high-quality solutions in various problem instances. This consistent performance reinforces the algorithm's potential as a reliable and efficient approach for optimization problems.

Finally, Table 6 presents the SM comparison results for all five algorithms. The SM metric evaluates the distribution of solutions along the Pareto front, with lower values indicating a more balanced and uniform distribution. QMCO-NSGA-II performs exceptionally well, achieving the lowest SM values in 15 out of 18 instances, which demonstrates its ability to produce solutions that are more evenly distributed along the Pareto front.

4.5 Cost Saving Analysis of Scheduling Strategies

In this experiment, we aimed to validate the impact of the EES strategy on scheduling results. We selected the 20-5-6 instance, which closely reflects the factory's production needs, and conducted four sets of experiments. These included: (1) the standard scheduling strategy without any EES strategy, (2) the power-down strategy without considering TOU pricing, (3) the TOU pricing without considering the power-down strategy, and (4) a combined strategy considering both TOU pricing and the power-down strategy. The experimental results are presented in Table 7.

The results indicate that all EES effectively reduce the TEC compared to the standard scheduling approach. Specifically, the power-down strategy alone achieves a 19.61% cost saving, the TOU pricing strategy saves 22.46%, and the combined TOU + power-down strategy offers the best savings, reducing the energy cost by 24.15%. These results demonstrate that the introduction of EES strategies significantly lowers energy costs, with the combined use of the power-down and TOU pricing strategies yielding the most optimal energy savings.

Furthermore, Fig. 4 presents 3D scatter plots of the Pareto fronts generated by the five algorithms. The axes represent the three objective functions: C_{max}, TT, and TEC. These plots, using examples from medium- and large-scale cases such as 10-3-6, 20-5-4, 50-3-6, and 50-5-3, show the Pareto fronts in 3D space. From the figure, it is clear that the solutions produced by QMCO-

Table 6. Comparison results of SM.

Instance	QMCO-NSGA-II		NSGA-II		Jaya		MOEA/D		MOABC	
	mean	std	mean	std	mean	std	mean	std	mean	std
10-3-3	8.57E-02	1.45E-3	**8.04E-02**	2.12E-3	1.23E-01	1.33E-3	2.15E-01	2.21E-3	3.01E-01	1.44E-3
10-3-4	**5.38E-02**	1.08E-3	7.34E-02	1.04E-3	2.08E-01	1.56E-3	2.22E-01	2.31E-3	1.19E-01	1.38E-3
10-3-6	6.04E-02	1.14E-3	6.13E-02	1.02E-3	1.03E-01	1.23E-3	**5.43E-02**	0.96E-3	1.46E-01	1.72E-3
10-5-3	**6.26E-02**	1.30E-3	7.34E-02	1.26E-3	1.53E-01	1.15E-3	1.43E-01	1.39E-3	2.52E-01	1.89E-3
10-5-4	7.66E-02	1.51E-3	**7.12E-02**	1.45E-3	1.08E-01	1.21E-3	2.23E-01	2.14E-3	2.88E-01	1.76E-3
10-5-6	**5.01E-02**	1.08E-3	5.32E-02	1.16E-3	7.63E-02	1.39E-3	2.26E-01	1.56E-3	3.13E-01	2.02E-3
20-3-3	**5.45E-02**	1.09E-3	7.36E-02	1.23E-3	1.19E-01	1.43E-3	1.03E-01	1.21E-3	1.22E-01	1.56E-3
20-3-4	**4.52E-02**	1.02E-3	6.06E-02	1.07E-3	1.34E-01	1.15E-3	1.18E-01	1.21E-3	1.32E-01	1.24E-3
20-3-6	**5.34E-02**	1.16E-3	5.56E-02	1.14E-3	1.28E-01	1.26E-3	1.92E-01	1.36E-3	1.29E-01	1.48E-3
20-5-3	**6.01E-02**	1.40E-3	1.02E-01	1.41E-3	1.33E-01	1.57E-3	2.14E-01	1.61E-3	2.87E-01	1.93E-3
20-5-4	**4.49E-02**	1.18E-3	5.69E-02	1.26E-3	1.01E-01	1.24E-3	1.13E-01	1.31E-3	1.23E-01	1.35E-3
20-5-6	**4.76E-02**	1.10E-3	7.86E-02	1.30E-3	1.35E-01	1.29E-3	1.21E-01	1.39E-3	1.09E-01	1.32E-3
50-3-3	**5.05E-02**	1.23E-3	6.82E-02	1.32E-3	1.22E-01	1.48E-3	7.03E-02	1.41E-3	9.74E-02	1.56E-3
50-3-4	**5.21E-02**	1.26E-3	8.68E-02	1.49E-3	1.96E-01	1.62E-3	6.44E-02	1.52E-3	7.97E-02	1.53E-3
50-3-6	**4.57E-02**	1.12E-3	6.18E-02	1.19E-3	1.48E-01	1.51E-3	9.09E-02	1.40E-3	6.81E-02	1.44E-3
50-5-3	**6.32E-02**	1.34E-3	9.47E-02	1.47E-3	2.32E-01	1.83E-3	1.39E-01	1.65E-3	1.18E-01	1.71E-3
50-5-4	**4.67E-02**	1.10E-3	5.49E-02	1.20E-3	2.54E-01	1.92E-3	1.58E-01	1.80E-3	1.92E-01	2.02E-3
50-5-6	**5.09E-02**	1.16E-3	5.47E-02	1.18E-3	1.22E-01	1.22E-3	1.43E-01	1.35E-3	9.91E-02	1.42E-3
Hit rate	**15/18**		2/18		0/18		1/18		0/18	

Table 7. Cost saving analysis.

Experiment	EES	Total enery cost (CNY)	Cost saving (%)
1	standard scheduling	4758.11	–
2	power-down strategy	3824.71	19.61 %
3	TOU pricing	3690.17	22.46 %
4	TOU + power-down strategy	3608.08	**24.15** %

NSGA-II significantly outperform those of the other algorithms. The scatter points of QMCO-NSGA-II are more concentrated near the coordinate origin, visually indicating better convergence towards the ideal solution set.

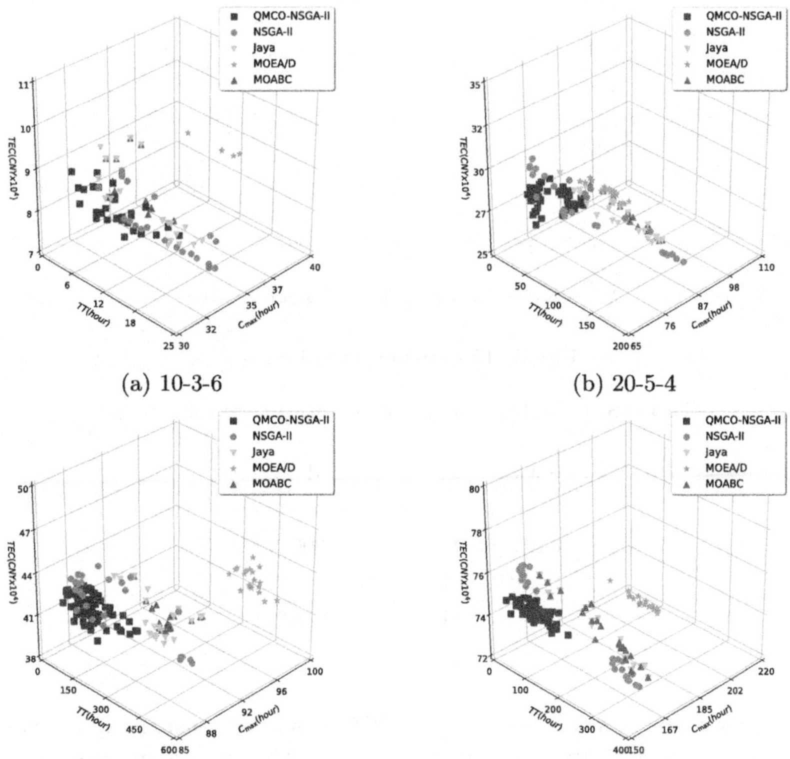

(a) 10-3-6

(b) 20-5-4

(c) 50-3-6

(d) 50-5-3

Fig. 4. Pareto results of the four instances.

4.6 Statistical Significance Testing

The boxplot of SM values for each algorithm, shown in Fig. 5, further confirms the superior performance of QMCO-NSGA-II. The boxplot reveals that the spread of SM values for QMCO-NSGA-II is consistently narrower compared to the other algorithms, indicating less variation and more consistent performance across different problem instances.

To ensure the robustness of the results, we conducted statistical significance tests, such as paired-sample t-tests [5], across all performance metrics (CM, SM) for each algorithm. The results in Table 8 show that QMCO-NSGA-II significantly outperforms the other algorithms in all comparisons ($p < 0.05$), validating the observed performance improvements. For the CM metric, the t-test evaluates the disparity between $C(A, B)$ and $C(B, A)$, such as $C(Q, \text{NSGA-II})$ for QMCO-NSGA-II and NSGA-II.

The results of the CM, SM comparisons clearly demonstrate that the proposed QMCO-NSGA-II algorithm outperforms the other four algorithms in terms of solution quality, convergence, and distribution. This is particularly true

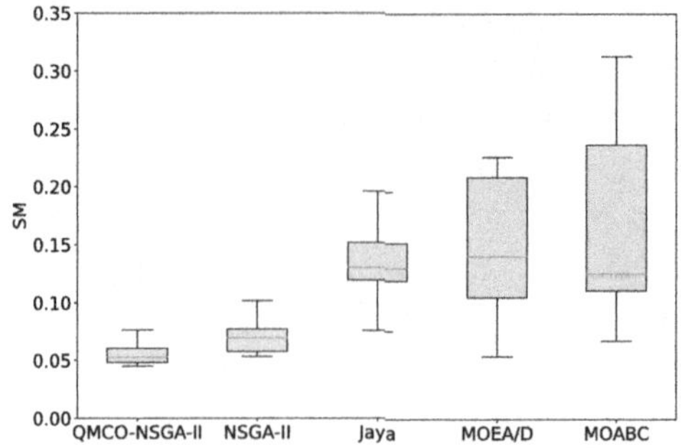

Fig. 5. The boxplot of SM results.

Table 8. Paired-sample t-tests for statistical robustness.

t-test(A, B)	CM	SM
t-test(Q, NSGA-II)	0.000	0.003
t-test(Q, Jaya)	0.000	0.000
t-test(Q, MOEA/D)	0.000	0.000
t-test(Q, MOABC)	0.000	0.000

for complex problem instances, where QMCO-NSGA-II consistently provides the best results across all twoperformance metrics. The success of QMCO-NSGA-II can be attributed to its combination of the INEH heuristic, which generates high-quality initial solutions, and the Q-learning-driven MCO framework, which allows the algorithm to effectively balance exploration and exploitation during the optimization process. These features enable QMCO-NSGA-II to efficiently explore the solution space and identify better solutions, leading to superior performance in multi-objective optimization tasks such as the EHFSP.

5 Conclusion

The QMCO-NSGA-II algorithm proposed in this study integrates time-of-use (TOU) pricing and a power-down strategy to address the Energy-Efficient Hybrid Flow Shop Problem (EHFSP), optimizing the balance between production efficiency and energy costs. By incorporating an improved Nawaz-Enscore-Ham heuristic for initial population generation, the algorithm accelerates convergence and enhances solution quality. Additionally, integrating Q-learning into the multi-crossover operator framework enables adaptive crossover selection, improving the trade-off between diversity and convergence. Experimental results on standard EHFSP datasets demonstrate that the proposed QMCO-NSGA-II algorithm significantly outperforms four state-of-the-art metaheuristics in terms of both convergence speed and solution diversity.

In EHFSP, only TOU pricing and power down strategy constraints were considered. Future research could incorporate more complex constraints, such as urgent orders, machine failures, material inventory levels, and others, to make the problem more aligned with real-world production scenarios. Future work could focus on extending this approach to other complex optimization challenges and improving the algorithm's scalability in dynamic environments.

References

1. Cui, W., Lu, B.: Energy-aware operations management for flow shops under tou electricity tariff. Comput. Ind. Eng. **151**, 106942 (2021)
2. Dai, M., Tang, D., Giret, A., Salido, M.A., Li, W.D.: Energy-efficient scheduling for a flexible flow shop using an improved genetic-simulated annealing algorithm. Rob. Comput.-Integrat. Manuf. **29**(5), 418–429 (2013)
3. Deb, K., Agrawal, S., Pratap, A., Meyarivan, T.: A fast elitist non-dominated sorting genetic algorithm for multi-objective optimization: NSGA-II. In: Schoenauer, M., et al. (eds.) PPSN 2000. LNCS, vol. 1917, pp. 849–858. Springer, Heidelberg (2000). https://doi.org/10.1007/3-540-45356-3_83
4. Deb, K., Pratap, A., Agarwal, S., Meyarivan, T.: A fast and elitist multiobjective genetic algorithm: NSGA-II. IEEE Trans. Evol. Comput. **6**(2), 182–197 (2002)
5. Ding, J.Y., Song, S., Wu, C.: Carbon-efficient scheduling of flow shops by multi-objective optimization. Eur. J. Oper. Res. **248**(3), 758–771 (2016)
6. Engin, O., Ceran, G., Yilmaz, M.K.: An efficient genetic algorithm for hybrid flow shop scheduling with multiprocessor task problems. Appl. Soft Comput. **11**(3), 3056–3065 (2011)
7. Guan, Y., et al.: Hybrid flow-shop scheduling in collaborative manufacturing with a multi-crossover-operator genetic algorithm. J. Ind. Inf. Integr. **36**, 100514 (2023)
8. Jiang, S.L., Xu, C., Zhang, L., Ma, Y.: A decomposition-based two-stage online scheduling approach and its integrated system in the hybrid flow shop of steel industry. Expert Syst. Appl. **213**, 119200 (2023)
9. Kahraman, C., Engin, O., Kaya, I., Yilmaz, M.K.: An application of effective genetic algorithms for solving hybrid flow shop scheduling problems. Int. J. Comput. Intell. Syst. **1**(2), 134–147 (2008)
10. Kurdi, M.: Ant colony system with a novel non-daemonactions procedure for multiprocessor task scheduling in multistage hybrid flow shop. Swarm Evol. Comput. **44**, 987–1002 (2019)
11. Li, C., Han, Y., Zhang, B., Wang, Y., Li, J., Gao, K.: A novel collaborative iterative greedy algorithm for hybrid flowshop scheduling problem with batch processing machines and variable sublots. Int. J. Prod. Res. **62**(11), 4076–4096 (2024)
12. Li, J.Q., Sang, H.Y., Han, Y.Y., Wang, C.G., Gao, K.Z.: Efficient multi-objective optimization algorithm for hybrid flow shop scheduling problems with setup energy consumptions. J. Clean. Prod. **181**, 584–598 (2018)
13. Li, P., Xue, Q., Zhang, Z., Chen, J., Zhou, D.: Multi-objective energy-efficient hybrid flow shop scheduling using q-learning and GVNs driven NSGA-II. Comput. Oper. Res. **159**, 106360 (2023)
14. Nawaz, M., Enscore, E.E., Jr., Ham, I.: A heuristic algorithm for the m-machine, n-job flow-shop sequencing problem. Omega **11**(1), 91–95 (1983)
15. Network, T.C.P.: China's power industry statistics (2023). http://mm.chinapower.com.cn/sj/ndsj/20230202/186101.html

16. Neufeld, J.S., Schulz, S., Buscher, U.: A systematic review of multi-objective hybrid flow shop scheduling. Eur. J. Oper. Res. **309**(1), 1–23 (2023)
17. Ouz, C., Ercan, M.F.: A genetic algorithm for hybrid flow-shop scheduling with multiprocessor tasks. J. Sched. **8**, 323–351 (2005)
18. Pan, Y., Gao, K., Li, Z., Wu, N.: Solving biobjective distributed flow-shop scheduling problems with lot-streaming using an improved jaya algorithm. IEEE Trans. Cybern. **53**(6), 3818–3828 (2022)
19. Sassi, J., Alaya, I., Borne, P., Tagina, M.: A decomposition-based artificial bee colony algorithm for the multi-objective flexible jobshop scheduling problem. Eng. Optim. **54**(3), 524–538 (2022)
20. Tang, Y., Li, H., Shui, Y., Sun, J.: A modified moea/d based on guided search directions for large-scale multiobjective optimization. 2023 IEEE Congress on Evolutionary Computation (CEC), pp. 1–8 (2023)
21. Utama, D.M., Primayesti, M.D., Umamy, S.Z., Kholifa, B.M.N., Yasa, A.D.: A systematic literature review on energy-efficient hybrid flow shop scheduling. Cogent Eng. **10**(1), 2206074 (2023)
22. Wang, H., Fu, Y., Huang, M., Huang, G.Q., Wang, J.: A NSGA-II based memetic algorithm for multiobjective parallel flowshop scheduling problem. Comput. Ind. Eng. **113**, 185–194 (2017)
23. Wang, S., Wang, X., Chu, F., Yu, J.: An energy-efficient two-stage hybrid flow shop scheduling problem in a glass production. Int. J. Prod. Res. **58**(8), 2283–2314 (2020)
24. Yang, Y., et al.: Advancements in q-learning meta-heuristic optimization algorithms: a survey. Wiley Interdisc. Rev. Data Min. Knowl. Disc. **14**(6), e1548 (2024)
25. Yue, L., Wang, H., Mumtaz, J., Rauf, M., Li, Z.: Energy-efficient scheduling of a two-stage flexible printed circuit board flow shop using a hybrid pareto spider monkey optimisation algorithm. J. Ind. Inf. Integr. **31**, 100412 (2023)

MixRecLGB: Language-Enhanced Mixed Attention for Temporal Context Modeling in Time Series Forecasting

Yuxin Mei, Luxi Zhang, Li Han, and Jing Liu(✉)

East China Normal University, Shanghai 200062, China
{51265902146,51265s902164}@stu.ecnu.edu.cn, {hanli,jliu}@sei.ecnu.edu.cn

Abstract. Accurate time series forecasting demands effective integration of temporal dynamics and contextual semantics. While existing attention mechanisms capture numerical patterns effectively, they often neglect domain-specific temporal knowledge. We propose MixRecLGB, a novel framework that synergizes LightGBM with a language-enhanced mixed attention mechanism. Our key contributions include: 1) A recursive VAE architecture (RecLGB) that compresses long historical sequences into hierarchical memory features through progressive latent space learning; 2) A temporal-semantic fusion mechanism that injects frozen language model embeddings into both static linear attention and dynamic self-attention components, preserving temporal order while incorporating contextual knowledge; 3) A parameter-efficient integration strategy that enhances attention computation through adaptive bias injection and feature fusion, requiring minimal architectural modifications. Evaluated on five real-world datasets, MixRecLGB reduces forecasting errors while maintaining computational efficiency. This work establishes a new paradigm for combining deep temporal modeling with efficient gradient boosting, particularly effective for long-term forecasting scenarios.

Keywords: LightGBM · time series forecasting · VAE

1 Introduction

Time series forecasting serves as a critical component in modern intelligent systems, powering decision-making processes across finance, energy management, and smart cities. While deep learning approaches have advanced temporal pattern recognition, fundamental challenges persist in balancing computational efficiency with long-term dependency modeling. Traditional statistical methods like ARIMA and exponential smoothing struggle with nonlinear patterns, whereas deep neural networks (RNNs, Transformers) often suffer from computational overhead and temporal order distortion. This efficiency-accuracy tradeoff becomes particularly acute in long-horizon forecasting scenarios requiring both sequence-aware modeling and real-time inference capabilities.

Y. Zhou et al. (Eds.): ICECCS 2025, LNCS 15746, pp. 79–97, 2026.
https://doi.org/10.1007/978-3-032-00828-2_6

Recent advancements reveal two complementary research directions: Transformer-based models achieve remarkable sequence modeling through self-attention mechanisms yet face quadratic complexity constraints, while gradient boosting methods (e.g., LightGBM) offer computational efficiency but lack inherent temporal awareness. The emerging paradigm of hybrid architectures attempts to bridge this gap, but existing solutions either introduce excessive complexity or fail to preserve essential temporal semantics. Particularly, the integration of semantic understanding with numerical pattern recognition remains underexplored in time series analysis.

To address these challenges, we propose **MixRecLGB**, a novel framework that synergizes LightGBM's efficiency with deep temporal modeling. LightGBM is selected as our base predictor due to its demonstrated efficiency in handling large-scale time-series data through gradient-based one-side sampling and exclusive feature bundling [20]. Compared to deep learning architectures, LightGBM provides superior training speed while maintaining competitive accuracy. The Variational Autoencoder (VAE) component addresses the latent feature disentanglement problem through its evidence lower bound (ELBO) optimization framework [22], offering more stable latent space learning compared to conventional autoencoders.

The framework incorporates three fundamental innovations: First, we develop a recursive Variational Autoencoder (RecLGB) that progressively compresses historical sequences into hierarchical memory features via latent space learning. This architecture enables efficient long-range dependency capture while maintaining linear computational complexity. Second, we introduce a language-enhanced mixed attention mechanism that injects temporal semantics through frozen language model embeddings, combining static linear attention for order preservation and dynamic self-attention for pattern adaptation. Third, our parameter-efficient integration strategy establishes a new paradigm for combining deep sequence modeling with gradient boosted trees, requiring minimal architectural modifications to LightGBM while achieving substantial performance gains.

The principal contributions of this work are summarized as follows:

- A recursive VAE architecture with progressive memory compression, enabling efficient learning of hierarchical temporal patterns through section-wise latent space optimization. This design eliminates backpropagation through time while maintaining temporal continuity in latent representations.
- A dual-path attention fusion mechanism that synergizes static linear weights (enforcing temporal order) with language-enhanced dynamic attention (capturing contextual patterns). The adaptive gating module dynamically balances these components based on semantic context, achieving MSE reduction compared to Transformer baselines.
- A lightweight integration framework that enhances LightGBM's temporal awareness through memory-augmented features. Our experimental results demonstrate consistent performance improvements across varying forecast horizons (24-720 steps).

- Comprehensive empirical validation across five real-world datasets, accompanied by computational complexity analysis and ablation studies. The proposed method maintains LightGBM's native efficiency.

The remainder of this paper is organized as follows: Sect. 2 analyzes related work in temporal modeling and hybrid architectures. Section 3 details the RecLGB architecture and language-enhanced attention mechanism. Section 4 presents experimental results and comparative analysis. Section 5 concludes with future research directions.

2 Related Work

2.1 Time Series Forecasting

The development of time series forecasting methodologies has evolved through multiple paradigms, driven by diverse application requirements. Classical statistical approaches form the foundation of this field, with ARIMA [4] addressing non-stationarity through differencing techniques and Kalman filtering [24] providing state-space estimation frameworks. Modern deep learning architectures have significantly expanded these capabilities through various inductive biases. Temporal convolutional networks (TCNs) [1,29,35] employ dilated causal convolutions to model temporal causality with fixed receptive fields, while recurrent neural networks (RNNs) [18,21,46] capture dynamic temporal dependencies through sequential processing. Hybrid approaches like SutraNets [3] integrate autoregressive modeling with multi-scale decomposition to mitigate error accumulation in long-sequence forecasting.

Recent advances emphasize both efficiency and temporal dependency learning. Spiking neural networks (SNNs) [31,34] achieve energy-efficient forecasting through bioinspired spike timing mechanisms. Attention mechanisms have been particularly transformative: Temporal attention augmented RNNs [32,37] enable adaptive focus on critical time steps, while graph attention architectures [6] model multivariate dependencies. The proliferation of these techniques-spanning recurrent connections [11], attention mechanisms [19], and causal convolutions [27]-demonstrates the field's focus on sophisticated temporal relation modeling. Nevertheless, balancing computational complexity with model expressiveness remains an open challenge, particularly for resource-constrained scenarios.

While these deep learning approaches have advanced temporal dependency modeling, they exhibit inherent limitations in balancing efficiency and long-range dependency capture. Traditional RNN-based architectures, despite incorporating gating mechanisms [10,26] to mitigate gradient issues, remain constrained by their sequential processing nature and sensitivity to error accumulation in autoregressive settings [16]. TCNs leverage dilated causal convolutions to expand receptive fields [8,17], yet their fixed window sizes struggle to adaptively capture variable-range dependencies in complex time series. Although attention-augmented RNNs [25,32] enhance long-term modeling through temporal attention, the hybrid architecture often introduces computational overhead without fully resolving the inefficiencies of recurrent paradigms. These challenges have spurred the rise of pure attention mechanisms and Transformer-based models, which forgo inductive biases of recurrence or convolution to directly model global dependencies. However, such paradigm shifts come at the cost of quadratic complexity in vanilla self-attention [39], particularly problematic for resource-constrained forecasting scenarios requiring real-time inference. This tension between model expressiveness and computational efficiency motivates our subsequent analysis of attention mechanisms, ultimately informing our design of a lightweight self-attention integration within MixRecLGB framework.

2.2 Attention Models

The evolution of attention mechanisms has revolutionized sequence modeling across domains. Initially proposed for neural machine translation, additive attention [2] enabled dynamic alignment of encoder-decoder representations. Subsequent variants, such as multiplicative attention [30], improved computational efficiency through scaled dot product formulations. The paradigm shifted with self-attention in Transformer [39], which eliminated recurrence by modeling all pairwise token interactions through multi-head attention. This architecture demonstrated superior sequence alignment in language tasks [12] and later inspired time series adaptations [47]. For temporal data processing, learnable sparse attention [9] and auto-regressive masking [33] emerged to handle temporal causality constraints. Recent works further optimized attention for forecasting through frequency-aware mechanisms [41] and memory-efficient approximations [23]. Despite these advances, vanilla self-attention's quadratic complexity persists as a scalability bottleneck for long sequences, motivating our lightweight integration within residual architectures.

2.3 Models Based on LLMs

The adaptation of large language models (LLMs) for time series forecasting has emerged as a promising area of research, leveraging their robust sequence representation capabilities. Approaches utilizing LLMs can be categorized into three primary methodologies. Zero-shot adaptation methods, such as the one demonstrated by Gruver et al. [14], utilize the inherent sequence understanding of frozen LLMs to perform time series prediction without the need for task-specific training. In the realm of prompt optimization, models like Promptcast [42] enhance forecasting accuracy by reprogramming input time series to align with the sequence modeling strengths of pre-trained LLMs. Additionally, Yu et al. [43] illustrate the utility of LLMs in explainable financial time series forecasting, showcasing their adaptability to specific domains.

Furthermore, limited fine-tuning strategies have been explored to enhance performance. For instance, the generalized framework proposed [48] applies fine-tuning to selected components of LLMs for comprehensive time series analysis.

Liu et al. [28] investigate the few-shot learning capabilities of LLMs in health-related time series, while the LLM4TS model [5] implements a two-stage fine-tuning process to improve forecasting accuracy. Despite these advancements, existing methods often focus on distinct tasks rather than developing a unified representation for diverse time series data, indicating a significant area for future exploration.

3 Methodology

In the realm of time series forecasting, where the accurate prediction of future values based on historical data is of utmost importance, we introduce MixRecLGB, a groundbreaking framework. MixRecLGB aims to address the limitations of existing methods by integrating LightGBM, a highly efficient gradient - boosting algorithm, with a language - enhanced mixed attention mechanism. This integration not only improves the model's ability to capture complex temporal patterns but also enhances its understanding of contextual semantics, crucial for accurate forecasting.

3.1 Overall Framework

The overall framework of MixRecLGB, as depicted in Fig. 1, is designed to facilitate seamless integration of deep temporal modeling and efficient gradient boosting for time series forecasting.

The process begins with the input time series data. This data is first fed into the Time Series Encoder, which is based on the RecLGB architecture. RecLGB divides the long historical sequence into smaller sections. For each section, it uses a probabilistic encoder neural network to map the input observations to latent variables. These latent variables are then sampled and passed through a probabilistic decoder neural network to reconstruct the input. Through this iterative process, RecLGB compresses the time series data into hierarchical memory features, which serve as a compact representation of the long - term dependencies in the data.

Concurrently, the LLM - enhanced mixed attention mechanism processes the timestamps associated with the time series data. It starts by converting raw timestamps into meaningful textual descriptions that capture domain - relevant temporal semantics. For example, a timestamp like "2024 - 09 - 15 14:00" might be transformed into a description such as "Afternoon of a Monday in September". These descriptions are then processed by a frozen BERT - base model to extract 768 - dimensional semantic embeddings.

The semantic embeddings are used to modulate the attention weights in two ways. For the static linear attention, a learned transformation of the contextual embedding is added to the original static attention weights. This adjustment allows the model to adapt its understanding of temporal order based on semantic context while maintaining the original inductive biases. In the case of dynamic self - attention, the contextual embedding is projected into the attention space

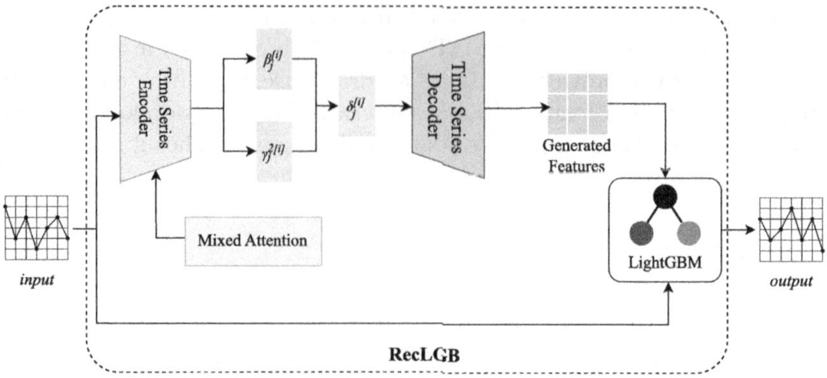

Fig. 1. Pipeline with LLM-enhanced attention.

and added as an additive bias term to the standard scaled dot - product attention scores. This enables the model to adjust its attention distribution according to the semantic context, effectively integrating numerical patterns with linguistic knowledge.

The outputs of the RecLGB encoder and the LLM - enhanced mixed attention mechanism are then combined. The resulting features are used as input for the LightGBM model. LightGBM, with its efficient gradient - boosting algorithm, processes these features to generate predictions. By leveraging the hierarchical memory features from RecLGB and the semantically - enhanced attention - weighted features, LightGBM can make more accurate forecasts, especially in long - term forecasting scenarios.

In summary, the MixRecLGB framework's overall architecture is a well - orchestrated combination of components that work in harmony. It capitalizes on the strengths of RecLGB for temporal feature extraction, the LLM - enhanced mixed attention mechanism for semantic integration, and LightGBM for efficient prediction, resulting in a powerful tool for time series forecasting.

3.2 RecLGB

The key components of MixRecLGB are the Recursive VAE (RecLGB) architecture and the LLM - enhanced mixed attention mechanism. RecLGB serves as the backbone for compressing long historical time series data. It leverages progressive latent space learning to transform extensive time series into hierarchical memory features. This process not only reduces the dimensionality of the data but also effectively captures long - range dependencies, which are often overlooked by traditional models.

Our framework introduces a progressive memory accumulation mechanism through hierarchical latent space learning. The VAE encodes input observation variables to latent variables using a probabilistic encoder neural network (NN) and then uses a probabilistic decoder NN to reconstruct the input from the latent variables. As visualized in Fig. 2, the structure of our proposed RecLGB model, in which we progressively compress a time series sequence of significant length using a VAE-like architecture.

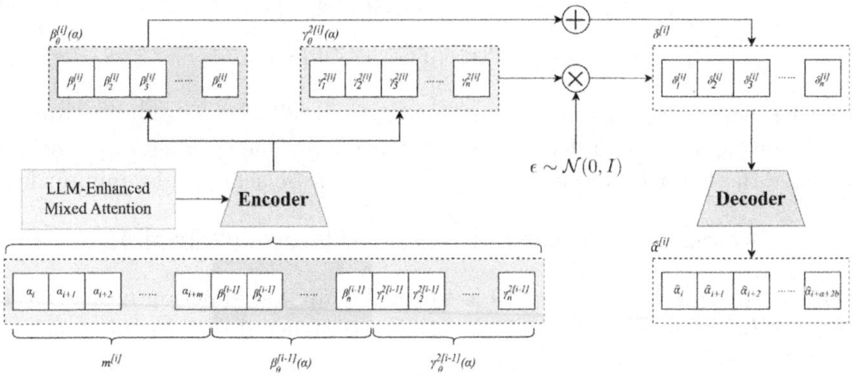

Fig. 2. Structure of Recursive VAE.

The section i contains observations of m time steps, which is a subset of the overall input observations with N time steps ($m \ll N$). Let $\alpha^{[i]} = [\alpha_i, \alpha_{i+1}, \alpha_{i+2}, \cdots, \alpha_{i+m}]$ denote Section i, and $\beta_\theta^{[i-1]}(\alpha)$ and $\gamma_\theta^{[i-1]}(x) = [\gamma_1^{[i-1]}, \gamma_2^{[i-1]}, \cdots, \gamma_n^{[i-1]}]$ denote the internal output generated from Section $i-1$. We provide the following vector to the encoder NN:

$$\alpha^{[i]} = \langle \mathbf{m}^{[i]}, \beta_\theta^{[i-1]}(\alpha), \gamma_\theta^{[i-1]}(\alpha) \rangle \in \mathbb{R}^{m+n+n},$$

where $\langle \cdot \rangle$ denotes concatenation operation.

The encoder NN parameterized by θ outputs $\beta_\theta^{[i]}(\alpha)$ and $\sigma_\theta^{[i-1]}(\alpha)$, which summarizes the input $\alpha^{[i]}$ and are used as the mean and serve as the mean and variance of different Gaussian distributions. Then latent variables $\delta^{[i]} = [\delta_1^{[i]}, \delta_2^{[i]}, \delta_3^{[i]}, \cdots, \delta_h^{[i]}]$ are then sampled from the resulting Gaussian distribution using the reparameterization trick [22]:

$$\delta^{[i]} = \beta_\theta^{[i]}(\alpha) + \gamma_\theta^{[i]}(\alpha) \odot \epsilon \sim \mathcal{N}(0, I),$$

where $\odot$ denotes the element-wise product. $\delta^{[i]}$ is then sent to decoder NN parameterized by σ to generate reconstruction $\hat{\alpha}^{[i]}$. Here we use multi-layer perceptron (MLP) as encoder NN.

For the approximation of θ and σ, consider a generative model parameterized by σ:

$$p_\sigma(\delta^{[i]}, \alpha^{[i]}) = p_\sigma(\delta^{[i]}) p_\sigma(\alpha^{[i]} | \delta^{[i]}).$$

And the log-likelihood of $\alpha^{[i]}$ is:

$$\log p_\sigma(\alpha^{[i]}) \geq \mathbb{E}_{\mathbf{z}^{[i]}\sim q_\theta(\delta^{[i]}|\alpha^{[i]})}\left[\log\frac{p_\sigma(\alpha^{[i]},\delta^{[i]})}{q_\theta(\delta^{[i]}|\alpha^{[i]})}\right]$$
$$= \mathbb{E}_{\delta^{[i]}\sim q_\theta(\delta^{[i]}|\alpha^{[i]})}\left[\log p_\sigma(\alpha^{[i]}|\delta^{[i]})\right]$$
$$-\mathrm{KL}(q_\theta(\delta^{[i]}|\alpha^{[i]})\|p(\delta^{[i]})) \triangleq \mathcal{L}^{[i]}(\sigma,\theta),$$

where KL denotes the KL divergence, and $q_\theta(\gamma^{[i]}|\alpha^{[i]})$ and $p_\sigma(\alpha^{[i]}|\gamma^{[i]})$ are modelled by encoder NN and decoder NN, respectively. The training objective is to maximize the lower bound of $\mathcal{L}^{[i]}(\sigma,\theta)$, which can be achieved by minimizing

$$\mathrm{LOSS}_{\mathrm{RecLGB}} = \mathrm{Recloss}(\hat{\alpha}^{[i]},\alpha^{[i]}) + \mathrm{KL}(q_\theta(\gamma^{[i]}|\alpha^{[i]})\|p(\gamma^{[i]})),$$

where the *Recloss*(Reconstruction loss) can be any loss function measuring the difference between the input $\alpha^{[i]}$ and the reconstructed $\hat{\alpha}^{[i]}$. In this paper, we use L2 loss, and assume $p(\gamma^{[i]})$ as $\mathcal{N}(0,I)$.

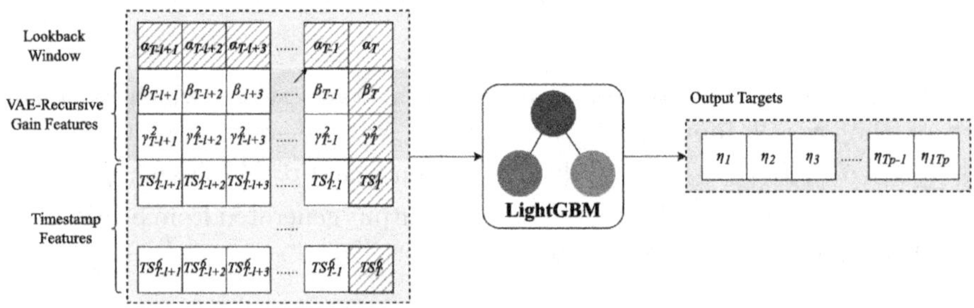

Fig. 3. Recursive Feature Generation and LightGBM Prediction Framework.

In the proposed RecLGB framework, gradient descent is applied during each summarization of $\mathbf{m}^{[i]}$, $\beta_\theta^{[i-1]}(\alpha)$, and $\gamma_\theta^{2[i-1]}(\alpha)$, thus eliminating the need for backpropagation through time in the training process. This distinguishes RecLGB from the Variational Recurrent AutoEncoder (VRAE). While deterministic approaches such as the AutoEncoder (AE) [15] are capable of reducing high-dimensional data to a lower-dimensional space, serving a similar function to the Variational AutoEncoder (VAE) in our model, RecLGB benefits from the regularization, continuity, and temporal structure intrinsic to the latent space associated with VAE. Empirical evidence suggests that combining RecLGB with AE yields superior performance compared to using AE alone. Additionally, the latent space of RecLGB is more conducive to downstream tasks, such as regression, since it facilitates the prediction of time series sequences with consistent dimensions.

Upon completion of the training process, RecLGB is capable of processing time series sequences of arbitrary length and generating compact, compressed representations. These representations serve as external memory for the subsequent Gradient Boosted Regression Trees (GBRT) model, which utilizes regression trees as weak learners to construct an additive model and applies a forward stagewise algorithm for training.

To elaborate further, for each section i, RecLGB-generated internal outputs, $\beta_{\gamma}^{[i]}(\alpha)$ (and $\sigma_{\gamma}^{[i]}(\alpha)$), are incorporated as supplementary features at each time step in section $i+1$ (including $\sigma_{\theta}^{[i]}(\alpha)$), which could potentially introduce both noise and more detailed information to the prediction phase. As such, this design choice is left to the user. In line with the methodology proposed in [13], we fit T_p instances of LightGBM for each target in the target set $\mathbf{Y}$ to improve the model's flexibility. With features generated by RecLGB, LightGBM is able to process historical time series sequences of any length. As demonstrated in Fig. 3, we employ a straightforward feature engineering approach for LightGBM, which includes six lag values of the target variable (the lookback window) along with two types of features for each time step in this window: (1) features generated by RecLGB from a sequence considerably larger than l, and (2) time-based features derived from timestamps, including the hour of the day, day of the week, day of the month, day of the year, week of the year, and month of the year. year, week of the year, and month of the year.

3.3 LLM-Enhanced Mixed Attention

The LLM-enhanced mixed attention mechanism is another crucial innovation. It injects domain - specific temporal semantics into the attention calculation. By using frozen language model embeddings, it enriches both the static linear attention and dynamic self - attention components. This allows the model to preserve the temporal order of the data while incorporating valuable contextual knowledge, bridging the gap between numerical patterns and real - world semantics.

Our language-enhanced attention mechanism introduces domain-specific temporal semantics through a carefully designed integration of LLM-derived contextual knowledge. The process consists of four main stages (in Fig. 4: context generation, semantic embedding extraction, attention weight modulation, and adaptive fusion. Each stage is explained in detail below.

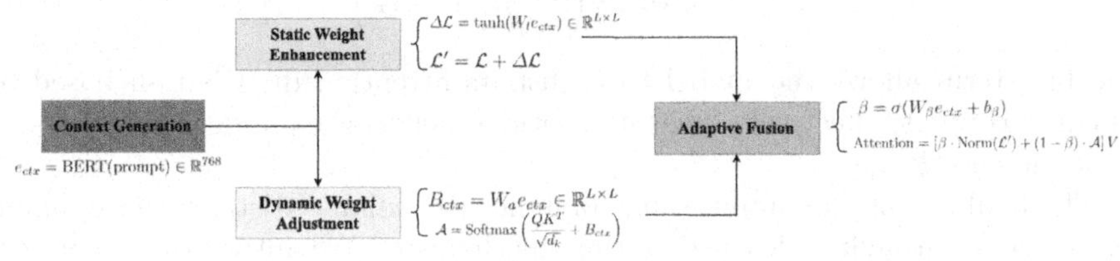

Fig. 4. Detailed process of LLM-enhanced mixed attention.

The first step converts raw timestamps into meaningful textual descriptions that capture domain-relevant temporal semantics. We employ a template-based approach to generate consistent and informative prompts. For example, given a timestamp "2024-07-04 18:00", the system generates the prompt:

```
"Time context: July Thursday 18-hour summer"
```

This structured representation ensures that key temporal attributes (month, weekday, hour, season) are explicitly encoded. The prompt is then processed through a frozen BERT-base model to extract a 768-dimensional semantic embedding:

$$e_{ctx} = \text{BERT}(\text{prompt}) \in \mathbb{R}^{768} \tag{1}$$

The use of a frozen LLM ensures computational efficiency while providing rich semantic representations. This embedding captures the contextual meaning of the timestamp in a way that complements the numerical time series data.

The original static attention weights $\mathcal{L}$ are enhanced through a learned transformation of the contextual embedding. We first project e_{ctx} into the attention space using a trainable weight matrix $W_l \in \mathbb{R}^{L\times 768}$:

$$\Delta\mathcal{L} = \tanh(W_l e_{ctx}) \in \mathbb{R}^{L\times L} \tag{2}$$

The hyperbolic tangent activation ensures that the modifications remain within a bounded range, preventing excessive distortion of the original temporal structure. The enhanced static weights become:

$$\mathcal{L}' = \mathcal{L} + \Delta\mathcal{L} \tag{3}$$

This formulation allows the model to adapt its understanding of temporal order based on semantic context while preserving the original inductive biases encoded in $\mathcal{L}$.

For the dynamic attention component, we inject contextual information through an additive bias term. The contextual embedding is first projected into the attention space using a separate weight matrix $W_a \in \mathbb{R}^{L\times 768}$:

$$B_{ctx} = W_a e_{ctx} \in \mathbb{R}^{L\times L} \tag{4}$$

This bias term is added to the standard scaled dot-product attention scores before applying the softmax function:

$$\mathcal{A} = \text{Softmax}\left(\frac{QK^T}{\sqrt{d_k}} + B_{ctx}\right) \tag{5}$$

The bias term allows the model to adjust its attention distribution based on semantic context, effectively creating a bridge between numerical patterns and linguistic knowledge.

The final attention computation combines the enhanced static and dynamic components through a learned gating mechanism. We introduce a context-dependent fusion parameter β that controls the balance between static temporal order and dynamic contextual adaptation:

$$\beta = \sigma(W_\beta e_{ctx} + b_\beta) \tag{6}$$

where $W_\beta \in \mathbb{R}^{1\times 768}$ and $b_\beta \in \mathbb{R}$ are learnable parameters, and σ denotes the sigmoid function. The final attention output is computed as:

$$\text{Attention} = [\beta \cdot \text{Norm}(\mathcal{L}') + (1-\beta) \cdot \mathcal{A}]\, V \tag{7}$$

This adaptive fusion allows the model to dynamically adjust its reliance on static temporal structure versus contextual patterns based on the semantic meaning of the current time step.

4 Experiments

4.1 Datasets

We extensively perform experiments on five datasets, comparing our approach with recent AI-driven models. The datasets contains: Traffic, ETTh1, ETTh2, Electricity, Weather. All of them are multivariate time series. We leave data descriptions in Table 1. Our results demonstrate that MixRecLGB achieves superior accuracy and efficiency, particularly in scenarios where long-range dependencies are critical.

- **Traffic** [10]: Describes road occupancy. It contains hourly highway data from July 1, 2016 to July 2, 2018 provided by the California Department of Transportation.
- **ETT** (Electricity Transformer Temperature) [11]: We use two hourly datasets (ETTh1 and ETTh2). Hourly data of oil temperature of power transformers in a county in China, each dataset contains the load characteristics of seven oil-electric transformers from July 1, 2016 to June 26, 2018.
- **Electricity**: Hourly electricity consumption of 321 customers was collected from 2012 to 2014.
- **Weather** [11]: Hourly recorded wet-bulb temperatures (in degrees Celsius) for the United States from 2010 to 2013, 4 years from the National Centers for Environmental Information. Includes 21 weather indicators, such as air temperature and humidity.

4.2 Implementation Details

Baselines. We compare the result of MixRecLGB with a wide range of advanced baselines, including:

- Autoformer [41] and Informer [47], which are two state-of-the-art Transformer-based models for time series forecasting. Autoformer leverages a decomposition block to capture both trend and seasonal components in time series data, while Informer uses a ProbSparse attention mechanism to efficiently handle long sequences and large-scale data. We adopt the original architectures suggested in their works, with input lengths tuned from 96, 168, 336, 720. For both models, we use the Adam optimizer with an initial learning rate of 0.0001 and a batch size of 32. The training process is

Table 1. Multivariate long sequence time series forecasting results on four datasets (five cases), the lower the better.

Methods		MixRecLGB		Autoformer		Informer		Transformer		DLinear		NLinear	
Metric		MSE	MAE	MSE	MAE	MSE	MAE	MSE	MAE	MSE	MAE	MSE	MAE
Traffic	24	0.159	**0.221**	0.198	0.311	**0.157**	0.223	0.482	0.469	0.240	0.256	0.239	0.253
	48	0.168	**0.228**	0.216	0.346	**0.162**	0.241	0.501	0.473	0.264	0.263	0.265	0.257
	168	0.178	**0.234**	0.252	0.365	**0.175**	0.253	0.524	0.486	0.379	0.277	0.376	0.274
	336	**0.184**	**0.243**	0.243	0.340	0.183	0.268	0.559	0.495	0.413	0.287	0.411	0.282
	720	**0.196**	**0.261**	0.266	0.352	0.204	0.293	0.594	0.514	0.455	0.295	0.451	0.296
ETTh1	24	0.145	**0.302**	**0.143**	0.305	0.577	0.549	0.486	0.462	0.188	0.327	0.182	0.321
	48	0.153	**0.314**	**0.152**	0.318	0.685	0.625	0.534	0.487	0.213	0.349	0.207	0.341
	168	0.216	**0.384**	0.231	0.402	**0.215**	0.398	0.672	0.553	0.278	0.407	0.269	0.398
	336	**0.207**	**0.323**	0.225	0.356	0.865	0.712	0.718	0.582	0.305	0.421	0.291	0.412
	720	**0.221**	**0.395**	0.254	0.417	0.912	0.754	0.803	0.635	0.347	0.453	0.333	0.441
ETTh2	24	0.102	**0.234**	**0.098**	0.241	0.720	0.665	0.512	0.451	0.127	0.261	0.121	0.255
	48	0.131	**0.251**	**0.129**	0.256	0.823	0.701	0.589	0.487	0.156	0.283	0.148	0.274
	168	0.190	**0.298**	0.214	0.323	**0.189**	0.315	0.827	0.602	0.235	0.334	0.227	0.326
	336	**0.215**	**0.337**	0.238	0.359	0.587	0.432	0.931	0.653	0.288	0.352	0.274	0.341
	720	**0.217**	**0.382**	0.254	0.403	0.642	0.467	1.125	0.732	0.327	0.387	0.315	0.379
Electricity	24	**0.141**	**0.254**	0.157	0.269	0.344	0.393	0.402	0.385	0.173	0.268	0.167	0.261
	48	**0.181**	**0.294**	0.203	0.315	0.395	0.459	0.437	0.412	0.216	0.309	0.207	0.298
	168	**0.190**	**0.320**	0.225	0.347	0.608	0.567	0.502	0.453	0.254	0.341	0.243	0.333
	336	0.233	0.338	0.241	0.358	0.702	0.620	0.576	0.487	0.240	**0.337**	**0.231**	0.329
	720	0.281	0.367	**0.275**	**0.381**	0.831	0.731	0.653	0.535	0.284	0.358	0.273	0.351
Weather	24	**0.094**	**0.213**	0.109	0.235	0.335	0.381	0.287	0.302	0.102	0.221	0.098	0.217
	48	**0.122**	**0.226**	0.135	0.248	0.395	0.459	0.327	0.331	0.131	0.239	0.127	0.233
	168	**0.156**	**0.234**	0.178	0.267	0.608	0.567	0.415	0.385	0.169	0.256	0.163	0.249
	336	0.189	0.241	0.283	0.351	0.702	0.620	0.327	0.381	0.174	0.236	**0.173**	**0.225**
	720	0.224	0.255	0.307	0.375	0.831	0.731	0.463	0.428	0.225	0.267	**0.219**	**0.249**

early stopped within 10 epochs, with patience set to 3. Time features generated from timestamps are provided to both models, as per the original implementations. These methods have shown significant improvements over various strong baselines, including Reformer, LogTrans, Prophet, LSTnet and ARIMA, and are thus the focus of our comparison.

- Transformer [39] is widely used in time series forecasting due to its ability to capture long-range dependencies. It employs multi-head self-attention and feed-forward layers to model complex temporal patterns. Transformer has been shown to perform competitively on time series tasks and is therefore included as a baseline.

– DLinear and NLinear [45], which are lightweight linear models designed specifically for time series forecasting, focusing on efficiency and simplicity. DLinear employs a decomposition strategy to separately model trend and seasonal components, while NLinear directly learns a linear mapping from input to output, avoiding redundant complexity. These models have been shown to outperform more complex architectures on various time series datasets, particularly for long-horizon forecasting tasks, making them valuable baselines for comparison.

Evaluation Mertic. Following previous studies [39,41,45,47], we use mean squared error (MSE) and mean absolute error (MAE) as the core metrics to compare the performance.

4.3 Performance Comparison

We systematically evaluate the proposed MixRecLGB method and various baseline approaches on five real-world time series datasets while progressively extending the prediction horizon, T_p. As illustrated in Table 1, the MixRecLGB method demonstrates superior performance compared to state-of-the-art baseline techniques, even without extensive feature engineering or comprehensive hyperparameter optimization tailored for each dataset. This indicates that capturing the seasonality of the data alone can yield satisfactory results in specific contexts, such as long-term forecasting of weather datasets. Moreover, utilizing historical series as a memory component can further enhance overall performance significantly.

4.4 Results and Analysis

To assess the effectiveness of our proposed MixRecLGB, we conduct analysis for two key hyperparameters, n and l. We first look at the results when the tuning range of size of features generated by MixRecLGB, n, is 0, 1 and 15. This suggests that a higher value of n is associated with a more complex representation of historical time series and a greater proportion among all features considered by MixRecLGB. Since n is a hyperparameter that is tuned before model deployment, we obtain the results on the validation set.

The results presented in Fig. 5 emphasize that our proposed approach consistently improves forecasting accuracy across all datasets for various prediction horizons. It is important to note that these results were obtained under the condition where the model receives minimal information from its lookback window (with $l = 1$), making MixRecLGB the sole mechanism for incorporating historical time series data. When compared to the case where $n = 0$, the inclusion of just one additional RecLGB-generated feature ($n = 1$) leads to an average accuracy improvement of 4.16%, 7.27%, 6.45%, 8.21%, and 6.82% for the Traffic, ETTh1, ETTh2, ECL, and Weather datasets, respectively. Moreover, increasing the value of n generally results in further enhancements in performance.

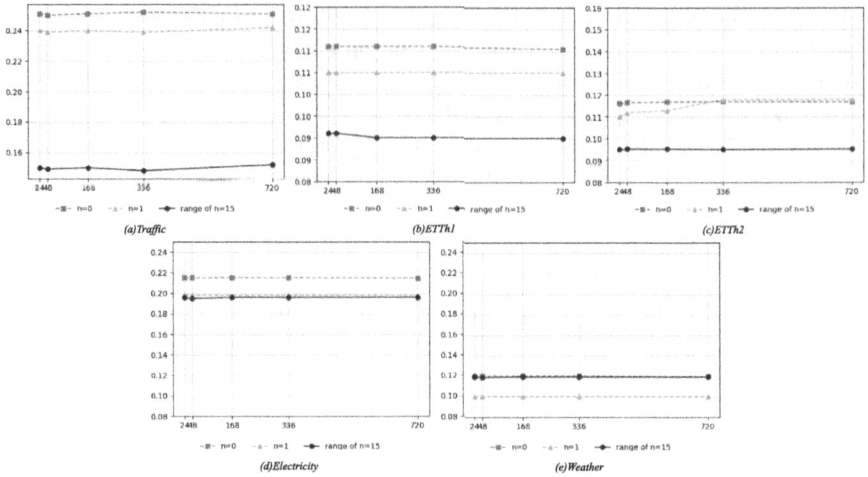

Fig. 5. MixRecLGB performance for different datasets with various tuning ranges of the size of features generated by MixRecLGB, n. The look-back window for LightGBM, n, is set to 1.

It is also important to highlight that the optimal amount of historical data to be considered varies depending on the specific characteristics of each time series. This is consistent with the common practice in deep learning, where input length is typically fine-tuned rather than using the maximum possible length. As such, the performance gain from MixRecLGB differs across datasets. Additionally, in certain cases, an extended representation of past sequences may not be necessary, meaning that larger tuning ranges do not always yield further improvements in performance.

In Fig. 6, we conduct a systematic evaluation of how features generated by RecLGB influence model performance when LightGBM is directly fed with different lookback window sizes ($l \in \{24, 96, 168, 720\}$). Our experimental results reveal four key insights:

1. Extending the lookback window generally results in higher forecasting accuracy, particularly for longer-term predictions, underscoring the advantage of incorporating extended input sequences alongside time-based features.
2. When the model is provided with insufficient historical information (e.g., $l = 24$), accuracy declines more sharply compared to models with larger lookback windows, and this performance degradation is alleviated when features generated by RecLGB are included. This demonstrates the utility of MixRecLGB in enriching the model's historical context.
3. The MixRecLGB mechanism continues to enhance performance even when as many as 720 previous time steps are directly supplied to LightGBM, highlighting the necessity of maintaining long-term memory of past sequences.

4. As l increases, the performance improvements associated with MixRecLGB become less pronounced. This could be attributed to the fact that a larger portion of the historical data is already directly input to LightGBM, thereby diminishing the relative contribution of features generated by RecLGB.

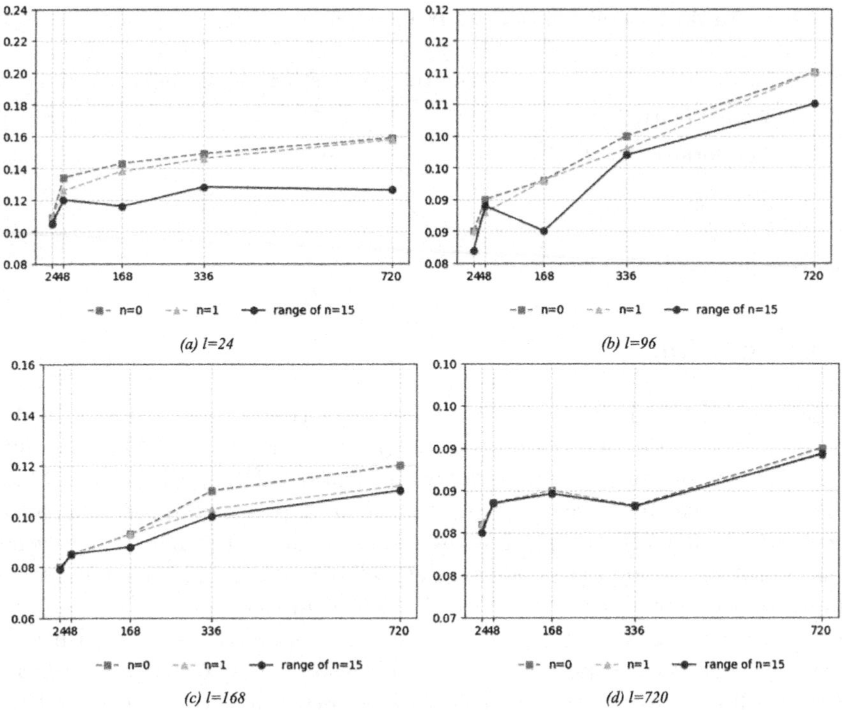

Fig. 6. MixRecLGB performance for Traffic dataset with varying lookback window sizes of LightGBM.

4.5 Computation Efficiency

To highlight the computational efficiency of our approach, we present the runtimes for both the training and testing phases on the Traffic dataset in Table 2. The results provided in Table 2 correspond to 48-step predictions, with an input length of 720 for both Informer and Autoformer. The reported runtimes for MixRecLGB, Autoformer, and Informer are based on 10 training epochs.

For MixRecLGB, the total training time comprises the time spent on MixRecLGB's training and inference, as well as the training time of LightGBM, which are 253.3, 0.9, and 100.7 s, respectively. These results demonstrate that, during the training phase, MixRecLGB exhibits a computational efficiency comparable to that of the Transformer-based baselines. In contrast, during the testing phase, our proposed method outperforms the baselines in terms of speed, benefitting from the high efficiency of LightGBM. It is worth noting that the reported runtimes for MixRecLGB, Autoformer, and Informer are all based on 10 training epochs.

Table 2. total run time for training phase and testing phase.

Methods	Training phase run time (s)	Testing phase run time (s)
MixRecLGB	354.9	2.7
Autoformer	418.2	16.4
Informer	336.7	10.8

5 Conclusion

We propose MixRecLGB, an hybrid framework that enhances LightGBM for long-term time series forecasting by integrating a recursive VAE with mixed attention. Future work will explore the integration of Large Language Models (LLMs) to further improve temporal dependency modeling and scalability. The mixed attention mechanism preserves temporal order through linear weights while capturing dynamic dependencies via self-attention, and the recursive VAE compresses extensive historical sequences into compact hierarchical features as external memory. Experiments across five datasets demonstrate MixRecLGB's superiority, achieving superior accuracy and faster inference than Transformer-based baselines. Future work will explore adaptive attention ratios and task-aligned feature learning via end-to-end joint training. This work bridges deep sequential modeling with efficient tree-based regression, offering a scalable.

Acknowledgments. This work was supported in part by the National Key Research and Development Program of China under Grant 2022YFC3302600 and in part by the Fundamental Research Funds for Central Universities of China. We would like to thank the anonymous reviewers for providing insightful suggestions and helping us to improve this paper.

References

1. Bai, S., Kolter, J. Z., Koltun, V.: An empirical evaluation of generic convolutional and recurrent networks for sequence modeling. arXiv preprint arXiv:1803.01271 (2018)
2. Bahdanau, D.: Neural machine translation by jointly learning to align and translate. arXiv preprint arXiv:1409.0473 (2014)

3. Bergsma, S., Zeyl, T., Guo, L.: SutraNets: sub-series autoregressive networks for long-sequence, probabilistic forecasting. In: Advances in Neural Information Processing Systems, vol. 36, pp. 30518–30533 (2023)
4. Box, G.E., Jenkins, G.M., Reinsel, G.C., Ljung, G.M.: Time Series Analysis: Forecasting and Control. Wiley (2015)
5. Chang, C., Peng, W.-C., Chen, T.-F.: LLM4TS: two-stage fine-tuning for time-series forecasting with pre-trained LLMs. arXiv preprint arXiv:2308.08469 (2023)
6. Liang, Z., Sun, Y.: Evolutionary neural architecture search for multivariate time series forecasting. In: Asian Conference on Machine Learning, pp. 771–786. PMLR (2024)
7. Chen, P., et al.: Pathformer: multi-scale transformers with adaptive pathways for time series forecasting. arXiv preprint arXiv:2402.05956 (2024)
8. Cheng, J., Huang, K., Zheng, Z.: Towards better forecasting by fusing near and distant future visions. In: Proceedings of the AAAI Conference on Artificial Intelligence, vol. 34, no. 4, pp. 3593–3600 (2020)
9. Child, R., Gray, S., Radford, A., Sutskever, I.: Generating long sequences with sparse transformers. arXiv preprint arXiv:1904.10509 (2019)
10. Chung, J., Gulcehre, C., Cho, K., Bengio, Y.: Gated feedback recurrent neural networks. In: International Conference on Machine Learning, pp. 2067–2075. PMLR (2015)
11. Das, A., Kong, W., Leach, A., Mathur, S., Sen, R., Yu, R.: Long-term forecasting with tide: time-series dense encoder. arXiv preprint arXiv:2304.08424 (2023)
12. Kenton, J.D.M.W.C., Toutanova, L.K.: Bert: pre-training of deep bidirectional transformers for language understanding. In: Proceedings of NAACL-HLT, vol. 1, no. 2 (2019)
13. Elsayed, S., Thyssens, D., Rashed, A., Jomaa, H.S., Schmidt-Thieme, L.: Do we really need deep learning models for time series forecasting? arXiv preprint arXiv:2101.02118 (2021)
14. Gruver, N., Finzi, M., Qiu, S., Wilson, A.G.: Large language models are zero-shot time series forecasters. arXiv preprint arXiv:2310.07820 (2023)
15. Hinton, G.E., Salakhutdinov, R.R.: Reducing the dimensionality of data with neural networks. Science **313**(5786), 504–507 (2006)
16. Hochreiter, S.: The vanishing gradient problem during learning recurrent neural nets and problem solutions. Int. J. Uncertain. Fuzziness Knowl. Based Syst. **6**(2), 107–116 (1998)
17. Huang, S., Wang, D., Wu, X., Tang, A.: Dsanet: dual self-attention network for multivariate time series forecasting. In: Proceedings of the 28th ACM International Conference on Information and Knowledge Management, pp. 2129–2132 (2019)
18. Jhin, S. Y., Kim, S., Park, N.: Addressing prediction delays in time series forecasting: a continuous GRU approach with derivative regularization. In: Proceedings of the 30th ACM SIGKDD Conference on Knowledge Discovery and Data Mining, pp. 1234–1245 (2024)
19. Kaur, K., Kaur, P.: SABDM: a self-attention based bidirectional-RNN deep model for requirements classification. J. Softw. Evol. Process **36**(2), e2430 (2024)
20. Ke, G., et al.: Lightgbm: a highly efficient gradient boosting decision tree. In: Advances in Neural Information Processing Systems, vol. 30 (2017)
21. Kim, T., Kim, J., Tae, Y., Park, C., Choi, J.H., Choo, J.: Reversible instance normalization for accurate time-series forecasting against distribution shift. In: International Conference on Learning Representations (2021)
22. Kingma, D.P., Welling, M.: Auto-encoding variational Bayes. arXiv preprint arXiv:1312.6114 (2013)

23. Kitaev, N., Kaiser, Ł., Levskaya, A.: Reformer: the efficient transformer. arXiv preprint arXiv:2001.04451 (2020)
24. Kurle, R., et al.: Deep Rao-Blackwellised particle filters for time series forecasting. In: Advances in Neural Information Processing Systems (NeurIPS), vol. 33, pp. 15371–15382 (2020)
25. Liang, Y., et al.: Geoman: multi-level attention networks for geo-sensory time series prediction. In: IJCAI, vol. 2018 (2018)
26. Liu, Q., et al.: Gated spiking neural P systems for time series forecasting. IEEE Trans. Neural Netw. Learn. Syst. **34**(9), 6227–6236 (2021)
27. Liu, M., et al.: SCINet: time series modeling and forecasting with sample convolution and interaction. In: Advances in Neural Information Processing Systems (NeurIPS), vol. 35, pp. 5816–5828 (2022)
28. Liu, X., et al.: Large language models are few-shot health learners. arXiv preprint arXiv:2305.15525 (2023)
29. Luo, D., Wang, X.: Moderntcn: a modern pure convolution structure for general time series analysis. In: The Twelfth International Conference on Learning Representations (2024)
30. Luong, M.-T.: Effective approaches to attention-based neural machine translation. arXiv preprint arXiv:1508.04025 (2015)
31. Lv, C., et al.: Efficient and Effective Time-Series Forecasting with Spiking Neural Networks. arXiv preprint arXiv:2402.01533 (2024)
32. Qin, Y., et al.: A dual - stage attention - based recurrent neural network for time series prediction. arXiv preprint arXiv:1704.02971 (2017)
33. Radford, A., et al.: Language models are unsupervised multitask learners. OpenAI Blog **1**(8), 9 (2019)
34. Salaj, D., et al.: Efficient temporal processing with spiking neural networks. In: Advances in Neural Information Processing Systems (NeurIPS) (2021)
35. Shen, L., et al.: FDNet: focal decomposed network for efficient, robust and practical time series forecasting. Knowl. Based Syst. **275**, 110666 (2023)
36. Shih, S.-Y., Sun, F.-K., Lee, H.: Temporal pattern attention for multivariate time series forecasting. Mach. Learn. 1421–1441 (2019). https://doi.org/10.1007/s10994-019-05815-0
37. Song, H., et al.: Attend and diagnose: clinical time series analysis using attention models. In: Proceedings of the AAAI Conference on Artificial Intelligence, vol. 32, no. 1 (2018)
38. Sorjamaa, A.: Methodology for long - term prediction of time series. Neurocomputing (2007)
39. Vaswani, A., et al.: Attention is all you need. In: Advances in Neural Information Processing Systems (NeurIPS) (2017)
40. Wang, H., et al.: MICN: multi-scale local and global context modeling for long-term series forecasting. In: The Eleventh International Conference on Learning Representations (2023)
41. Wu, H., Xu, J., Wang, J., et al.: Autoformer: decomposition transformers with auto-correlation for long-term series forecasting. In: Advances in Neural Information Processing Systems (NeurIPS), vol. 34, pp. 22419–22430 (2021)
42. Xue, H., Salim, F.D.: Promptcast: a new prompt-based learning paradigm for time series forecasting. IEEE Trans. Knowl. Data Eng. (2023)
43. Yu, X., Chen, Z., Ling, Y., Dong, S., Liu, Z., Lu, Y.: Temporal data meets LLM – explainable financial time series forecasting. arXiv preprint arXiv:2306.11025 (2023)

44. Yue, Z., Wang, Y., Duan, J., et al.: TS2Vec: towards universal representation of time series. In: Proceedings of AAAI Conference on Artificial Intelligence, vol. 36, no. 8, pp. 8980–8987 (2022)
45. Zeng, A., et al.: Are transformers effective for time series forecasting? In: Proceedings of the AAAI Conference on Artificial Intelligence, vol. 37, no. 9 (2023)
46. Zhang, Y., Yan, J.: Crossformer: transformer utilizing cross - dimension dependency for multivariate time series forecasting. In: Proceedings of 11th International Conference on Learning Representations (ICLR) (2023)
47. Zhou, H., et al.: Informer: beyond efficient transformer for long sequence time - series forecasting. In: Proceedings of AAAI Conference on Artificial Intelligence, vol. 35, no. 12, pp. 11106–11115 (2021)
48. Zhou, T., Niu, P., Wang, X., Sun, L., and Jin, R.: One fits all: power general time series analysis by pretrained language models. arXiv preprint arXiv:2302.11939 (2023)

Trustworthy Deep Learning

PAMUS: An Entropy-Loss-Based Poisoning Attack for Undermining Machine Unlearning

Xudong Jiang(✉), Yuhang Ma, Wei Xu, and Jiahui Wen

Key Laboratory of Aerospace Information Security and Trusted Computing, Ministry of Education, School of Cyber Science and Engineering, Wuhan University, Wuhan, China
{pixd28,yuhangm,xu_wei,jiahuiwen}@whu.edu.cn

Abstract. Deep learning has seen remarkable advancements and gained widespread adoption, while there are significant concerns about its potential misuse, including generating unsafe content, violating privacy and copyright, and perpetuating social bias. A crucial approach to mitigating these risks is machine unlearning, a technique that allows machine learning models to forget specific data and its effects. However, existing studies have found that there are risks of misuse in the unlearning process, and inappropriate or excessive unlearning can significantly corrupt the performance of models. In this paper, we conduct an in-depth analysis of the target parameter updating mechanism and potential security vulnerabilities in the unlearning process. We propose an attack strategy that combines anti-sample techniques with entropy loss optimization, proposing a data poisoning attack method named PAMUS (Poisoning Attack for Machine Unlearning Scenarios). This method reduces the model performance by increasing the impact on model parameters during unlearning. We conduct extensive experiments in both gray-box and white-box scenarios. The results demonstrate that our method reduces accuracy by 8.34%, compared to only a 4.56% reduction with traditional methods. Our approach significantly reduces the classification accuracy of the Logistic Regression model by 8.34% and the *Logistic2NN model* by 7.98%. Our insights provide new perspectives on optimizing attack methods and offer valuable references for future research focused on protecting privacy and enhancing model security.

Keywords: Machine Unlearning · Data Poisoning Attack · Entropy Loss

1 Introduction

Recently, machine learning technology has become pervasive across all sectors of society, significantly advancing the development and application of artificial intelligence. By processing and analyzing vast amounts of data, machine learning

Y. Zhou et al. (Eds.): ICECCS 2025, LNCS 15746, pp. 101–122, 2026.
https://doi.org/10.1007/978-3-032-00828-2_7

models can assist humans in making more precise predictions and decisions. This has shown substantial potential and value in areas such as medical diagnosis and intelligent recommendation systems [31]. However, as deep learning increasingly depends on private data, vulnerabilities are exposed. Attacks like membership inference and model inversion demonstrate that models can potentially leak sensitive data and exhibit specific behaviors when handling familiar datasets [22]. This can lead to privacy breaches, information cocoons, and social biases.

Consequently, the consumers have begun to request that organizations "remove personal data from the model", particularly within systems that handle sensitive information [32]. These requests coincide with a global increase in awareness regarding the protection of personal data, which has led to the implementation of the General Data Protection Regulation(GDPR) in Europe. Within this regulatory framework, the "Right to be Forgotten" has been established, allowing users to demand the deletion of all or part of their data from a system [29]. This growing demand has spurred the emergence and development of *Machine Unlearning* [5].

The primary objective of machine unlearning [6] is to entirely eliminate the influence of a specific set of data points from a trained model while minimizing any degradation in the model's overall performance. This approach serves not only as a technical solution to meet the demands for data privacy protection but also as a crucial tool to maintain the model's reliability and adaptability in complex data environments. Research in machine unlearning has concentrated on two main areas: first, developing algorithms that efficiently perform data deletion to remove the impact of specific data points without retraining the entire model; and second, studying how data deletion affects model performance and balancing data privacy with performance. Although directly removing specific data from the training set and retraining the model is ideal, the computational cost is prohibitive for modern large-scale applications. Therefore, researchers are exploring more efficient strategies. Given the diversity of model types and application scenarios, approaches to machine unlearning have diversified into several smaller directions. In application scenarios, there are several approaches: class deletion methods for face recognition applications [2], feature deletion methods [16,38] to prevent privacy leakage when similar labeled data is leaked, and data stream deletion methods [17] for forgetting online data under limited storage conditions.

However, researchers in machine learning have identified numerous security risks while optimizing existing unlearning methods or designing new approaches for emerging scenarios. One of the major security concerns is vulnerability to data poisoning [1,7,37]. The goal of a data poisoning attack is to manipulate the model's decision boundary by making strategic modifications to the training data, causing erroneous behavior during the testing phase. Since data unlearning techniques are imperfect, the decision boundaries can still be altered, making it for a gray-box model that facilitates poisoning attacks. Marchant et al. [27] pioneer benchmarking work by proposing a data poisoning attack method for the unlearning process. They suggest that the primary goal of unlearning is to completely remove the influence of specific data points from a trained model.

Fundamentally, unlearning offers a faster way to protect user privacy compared to retraining the model. Their core idea is to design added noise for data poisoning attacks to reduce the efficiency of the unlearning algorithm, preventing it from closing the time overhead gap with model retraining. Hu et al. [19] conduct excessive unlearning in a black-box environment for untargeted attacks, leading to model misclassification. While these methods have shown promising results, there remains a significant gap in research on attacks utilizing the unlearning process.

Existing methods attack by either reducing the efficiency of the unlearning algorithm or inducing excessive unlearning but do not effectively leverage model inference and decision boundaries, limiting their overall attack effectiveness. To further degrade model inference performance, we identify samples closer to the decision boundary based on model parameters and adversarial attack methods, using them for data poisoning attacks during the unlearning phase. Based on this theory, we propose PAMUS, a data poisoning attack. We extract key parameters in the unlearning process and optimize the adversarial sample generation method using the entropy loss function. By leveraging these parameters, we construct samples closer to the decision boundary and select them for unlearning, effectively reducing the classification accuracy of the *Logistic Regression model* by 8.34% and the *Logistic2NN model* by 7.98%. In summary, our contributions are:

- We identify weaknesses in the sample selection of unlearning that significantly affect model performance post-forgetting. Specifically, we propose a novel poisoning framework for machine unlearning that selects samples as close as possible to the model's decision boundary, thereby substantially influencing the model's decision-making ability during the forgetting process.
- Our PAMUS framework offers an entropy-loss-based attack that can be combined with traditional adversarial attacks to poison models. This method is specifically designed to disrupt the unlearning process, leading to a significant decline in model performance.
- We systematically validate the effectiveness, stealthiness, and robustness of PAMUS on various models and settings on the MNIST dataset. The experimentation verified that our method can successfully cause a significant drop in model accuracy (Fig. 1).

2 Related Work

2.1 Machine Unlearning

Machine unlearning aims to remove specific data from machine learning models while minimizing the impact on model performance [6]. Thudi et al. [36] propose a secondary sampling strategy, repeatedly training the model on different data subsets. This method effectively reduces the risk of membership inference attacks by mitigating the model's reliance on specific data points. To improve efficiency, Neel et al. [28] divide the training dataset into disjoint subsets and

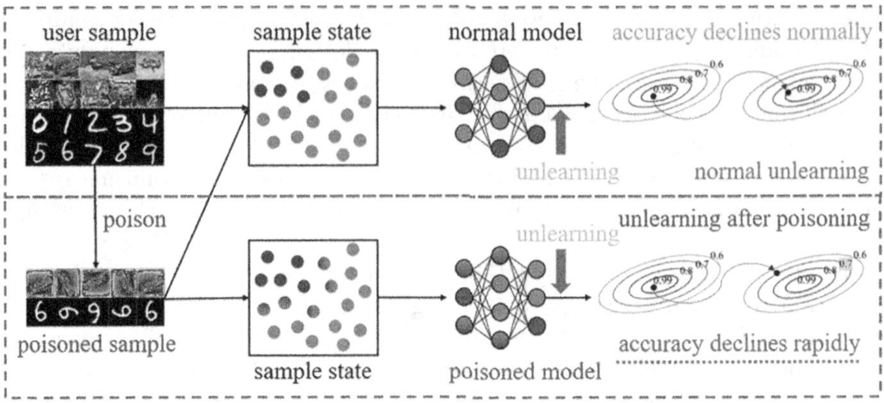

Fig. 1. An overview of our PAMUS. Different from the standard machine unlearning, we poison the user samples to be deleted and then perform unlearning on these poisoned samples, causing a rapid decline in the model's inference accuracy.

trained separate sub-models. They employ a gradient-based unlearning algorithm to remove the sub-models containing target data, achieving an effective trade-off between time overhead and performance. Meanwhile, He et al. [18] propose an unlearning algorithm for deep neural networks, which retrains only the affected sub-models. In addition, there are various unlearning methods tailored to different models and data types, such as those in [20,23,34].

In this work, we focus on the more practical approximate unlearning mechanism [13,14,30]. Approximate unlearning mitigates performance degradation by relaxing the indistinguishability requirement of the unlearning process or constraining the approximate error. Guo et al. [14] define the probabilistic concept of unlearning and propose a certified removal method for linear models, effectively removing data and enhancing privacy. To improve efficiency, Golatkar et al. [11] propose using the Fisher Information Matrix (FIM) instead of the Hessian matrix. To better respect users' personal privacy data, unlearning has been widely applied in the fields of machine learning and artificial intelligence, effectively deleting user-selected relevant data to prevent privacy leakage and other related issues.

2.2 Data Poisoning Attack

Traditional data poisoning attacks typically occur during the training phase, where the attacker manipulates the training data to degrade the model's performance during the testing phase. Indiscriminate poisoning is the most common form of data poisoning attack whose goal is to alter the model's original decision boundary by injecting malicious samples or modifying existing samples in the training dataset, leading to the misclassification of clean samples. Early label flipping methods [3] are not very effective. Later research adopts more advanced methods based on bi-level optimization [4,25], which essentially forms a max-min problem. A representative study is the attack method based on hyperparameter optimization proposed by Muñoz-González et al. [8], which utilizes reverse gradient descent to optimize poisoned samples, significantly reducing the complexity of the attack.

However, indiscriminate poisoning attacks are less feasible in real-world scenarios. Targeted poisoning mechanisms have been proposed to misclassify only the target sample without affecting others. Jagielski et al. [24] show how to generalize these attacks to subgroups within the data distribution while reducing computational costs. Guo et al. [15] extend the attack objective function, further improving the poisoning effect. Huang et al. [21] enhance the portability of such attacks. Data poisoning attacks are widely used to compromise model integrity and assess performance stability. This technique is applied in areas like spam filtering, facial recognition, and autonomous driving, where poisoned samples can mislead decision-making, posing security risks.

In this work, we focus on data poisoning attacks. We perform the poisoning attacks during the unlearning phase of models to bypass the model's defense and detection mechanisms against such attacks.

3 Background and Problem Statement

3.1 Problem Formulation

In the optimization of machine learning, it is typically necessary to find the extreme point of a function, with commonly used methods including various types of gradient descent algorithms or Newton's method. The process of unlearning is also fundamentally an optimization problem. Existing methods often involve pre-computing and caching key statistics to optimize computational resources and memory usage, while ensuring that the operational performance of the model is not significantly impacted. It has been revealed [35] that for models with approximate convex minimization and fully smoothed empirical minimization strategies, the Newton-Raphson method [33] can be used to implement the unlearning operation through pre-stored Hessian matrices efficiently.

The Hessian matrix is composed of the second-order partial derivatives of a multivariable function, revealing the curvature characteristics of the function at a local level. This matrix is commonly used in optimization problems involving the Newton-Raphson method to determine the extrema of multivariable functions. For a real-valued multivariable function $f(x_1, x_2, \ldots, x_n)$, if the second-order partial derivatives of the function f exist, then the Hessian matrix $H(f)$ of the function f is defined as:

$$H(f) = \begin{bmatrix} \frac{\partial^2 f}{\partial x_1^2} & \frac{\partial^2 f}{\partial x_1 \partial x_2} & \cdots & \frac{\partial^2 f}{\partial x_1 \partial x_n} \\ \frac{\partial^2 f}{\partial x_2 \partial x_1} & \frac{\partial^2 f}{\partial x_2^2} & \cdots & \frac{\partial^2 f}{\partial x_2 \partial x_n} \\ \vdots & \vdots & \ddots & \vdots \\ \frac{\partial^2 f}{\partial x_n \partial x_1} & \frac{\partial^2 f}{\partial x_n \partial x_2} & \cdots & \frac{\partial^2 f}{\partial x_n^2} \end{bmatrix} \tag{1}$$

In the unlearning process, for an input dataset $\mathcal{S}\{z_i\}_{i=1}^{n} \sim \mathcal{D}$ of size n, during the training process, the model parameters w are updated iteratively by $w_{t+1} = w_t - g(\hat{w}, z_i)$ until convergence. Here, $g(\cdot, z_i)$ is the stochastic gradient concerning a fixed loss function, and z_i is a randomly selected sample. After finding the converged model, the machine unlearning algorithm removes the influence of a specific sample z' from the model through a single update:

$$w' = \hat{w} + g_{\hat{w}}(z') \tag{2}$$

where $g_{\hat{w}}(z')$ represents the impact on the model parameters $\hat{w}$ caused by the removal of the specific sample $z' \in \mathcal{S}$. Therefore, the core of the unlearning process is to compute this impact, which involves the optimization problem previously mentioned in the context of the Newton-Raphson method. Due to the substantial storage and computational overhead of the Hessian matrix, it is difficult to directly implement it in the application of unlearning. As a result, many current studies are attempting to find approximate representations of $g_{\hat{w}}(z')$, such as the related works mentioned in Sect. 2. To calculate the error between the predicted result and the actual result, $f(w, z_i)$ represents the loss of the model parameters w on the data sample z_i. The $F(w) = \frac{1}{n}\sum_{i=1}^{n} f(w, z_i)$ represents the average loss across all samples, where $\hat{w} = \arg\min F(w)$ denotes the model parameters when $F(w)$ reaches its minimum value. A typical approximation method proposed in [35] expresses the impact of unlearning a target sample z' on the model as follows:

$$g(z') = \frac{1}{n-1} H'^{-1} \nabla f(\hat{w}, z') \tag{3}$$

where,

$$H' = \frac{1}{n-1}(n\nabla^2 F(\hat{w}) - \nabla^2 f(\hat{w}, z')) \tag{4}$$

However, the aforementioned algorithm entails significant computational overhead. Therefore, we opt to make improvements to this unlearning algorithm.

3.2 Local Parameter Update

The optimization scheme is illustrated in Fig. 2. In unlearning, to prevent target sample information from being leaked through membership inference attacks, noise is typically introduced during the unlearning process. Specifically, the method involves adding different noise to a single sample, performing forward propagation, and then identifying the parameters in the model's layers that are most affected by the noise. Finally, the set of parameters with the greatest impact among these samples is selected using a weighted averaging method. For further elaborating, we consider a single linear layer $l \in \mathcal{L}$ within a neural network, where $\mathcal{L}$ represents the collection of all linear layers in the network. Each linear layer l is associated with a parameter matrix $w_l \in \mathbb{R}^{a \times b}$, capable of mapping an input vector from $a - dimensional$ space to $b - dimensional$ space. For the output of the linear layer l, namely the activation value $a_l = w_l a_{l-1} \in \mathbb{R}^b$, it is obtained

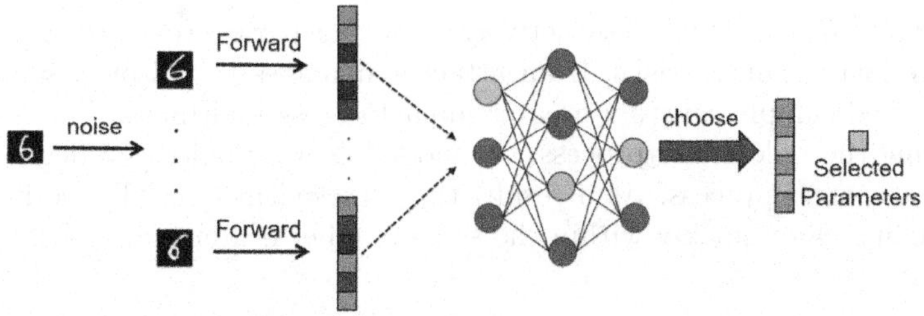

Fig. 2. Local Parameter Update Process. We add different noises to a single sample, perform forward propagation, identify the most affected parameters across layers, and select the most influential set through weighted averaging.

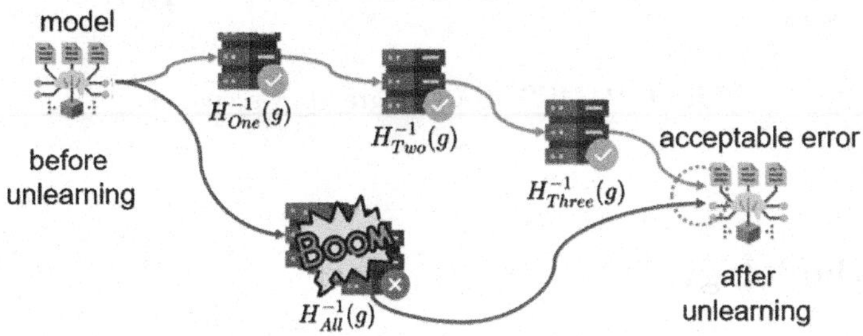

Fig. 3. Updating only the target parameters.

by multiplying the parameter matrix w_l with the output a_{l-1} of the preceding layer. Next, the network is partitioned into slices, where each slice represents a detailed view of the network parameters. By applying random perturbations to the input and collecting activation values (outputs) along all weight slices during loss computation, samples can be obtained from this collection. Specifically, for a given perturbation $\xi^j \sim N(0, \sigma^2)$:

$$x_i^j = x_i + \xi^j; \quad l^j, a_L^j = \{l(x_i^j), a_1^j, \cdots, a_{|\mathcal{L}|}^j\} \tag{5}$$

Compared to updating all the parameters of the model, this method only updates the key parameters. As shown in Fig. 3, this not only achieves an efficient unlearning effect but also significantly reduces the need to store and compute the Hessian matrix. Additionally, the noise added for privacy protection will also affect these parameters during the parameter update process, which in turn leads to a decrease in model performance. Therefore, updating fewer parameters helps to slow down the rate of model performance degradation, which is particularly important in practical applications. The specific effects of this strategy and data comparisons will be detailed in the Sect. 5. Experimental observations indicate that when running the unlearning algorithm, the speed of updating only the key parameters is significantly faster than updating all the model parameters, further validating the effectiveness and practicality of the aforementioned optimization strategy.

However, this method of selectively updating parameters in specific layers also introduces security risks. If an attacker manages to poison a sample, and this poisoned sample causes a greater impact across multiple layers of parameters during the unlearning process, the model's performance will degrade faster than in a normal process. As a result, the attacked model will lose its normal functionality more quickly within the same number of iterations.

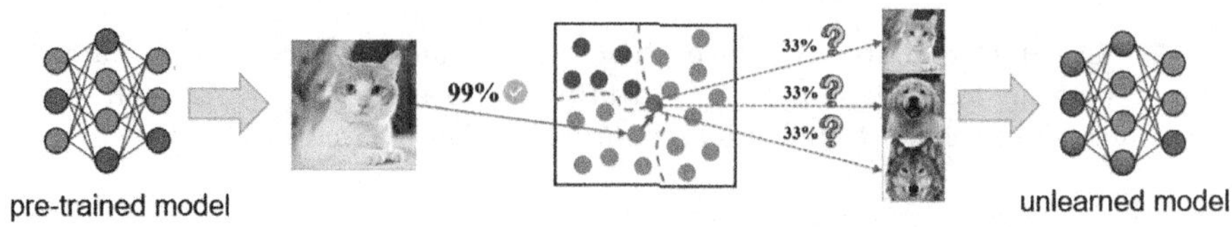

Fig. 4. PAMUS attack in gray-box scenarios.

4 Methodology

Despite advancements in data cleansing techniques and anomaly detection mechanisms, existing machine learning models have demonstrated considerable resilience against data poisoning attacks. However, the emergence of machine unlearning [6] introduces novel avenues for executing such attacks. In the work, we propose a framework for Poisoning Attacks for Machine Unlearning Scenarios(PAMUS), which is designed to exploit the unlearning process in models, enabling better poisoning attacks. PAMUS amplifies the impact of tampered samples during their removal, thereby causing significant disruptions to the model's parameter optimization and overall performance.

4.1 PAMUS

In the gray-box scenario, We adopt the adversarial sample method to perturb the target unlearning samples. The process is illustrated in Fig. 4.

Our experiment in Sect. 5.3 demonstrates that samples near the decision boundary have a greater influence on determining a model's parameters. Therefore, the goal of the adversarial sample method here is to identify samples close to the decision boundary rather than those that directly cause obvious misclassification. We implement two adversarial sample methods, FGSM [12] and PGD [26], and additionally incorporate a call to the attack process in the unlearning algorithm function, as shown in Algorithm 1.

Algorithm 1. Adversarial attack.

Require: model $\mathbf{M}$; dataset $\mathcal{S}$; Attack parameters p

Ensure: Perturbed data x'

$\mathbf{M}_{copy} \leftarrow$ deepcopy($\mathbf{M}$)

$x_i, y_i \leftarrow$ Select data and its labels from $\mathcal{S}$

$x.requires\_grad \leftarrow$ True

$res \leftarrow \mathbf{M}_{copy}(x)$

$loss \leftarrow$ Calculate the loss using the output res label y

$\mathbf{M}_{copy}.zero\_grad()$ *#Reset the gradients of the model M_{copy}*

$loss.backward()$ *#Perform loss back propagation to obtain the gradients.*

$G_x \leftarrow$ #Obtain the gradient of the data x

$x' \leftarrow$ Choose attack type based on p and generate perturbed data using G_x

Return x'

The algorithm begins by creating a copy of the original machine learning model $\mathbf{M}$, through deep copying, ensuring that the original model's state remains unaffected during the attack process. Then, sample data x_i and its corresponding target label y_i are selected from the dataset, and these data are converted into an appropriate tensor format. To meet the input requirements of the model, if the dimensions of the data images do not satisfy the input-output criteria, we employ the unsqueeze method to add a batch dimension. For instance, some datasets contain images with only three dimensions. Finally, gradient tracking is enabled for the data to facilitate gradient computation in subsequent steps. After the data is preprocessed, a forward pass through the model is conducted, and the algorithm calculates the $loss$ based on the model's predicted outputs and the actual target labels. Afterward, all gradients of the model are reset to prepare for backpropagation. After performing backpropagation, the gradients of the input data G_x are obtained. Based on the specified attack parameters p, an appropriate attack method is selected to generate the perturbed data x'.

During the attack phase, we use three structured attack methods, namely FGSM, PGD, and our optimization of the original PAMUS approach, to evaluate their impact on the model's robustness and analyze the perturbations introduced.

FGSM. By applying minor perturbations to the original input image, adversarial samples are generated that are sufficient to mislead the model while remaining imperceptible to the human eye. The algorithm computes the gradient G_x of the input image concerning the target function and extracts the sign of these gradients, $Sign_{G_x}$. These signs indicate the optimal direction for adjusting pixel values to maximize the growth of the target function. Based on these gradient signs, the pixel values of the image are modified by a preset perturbation magnitude ε, which controls the extent of the perturbation to maintain the visual coherence of the image. Finally, to ensure that the generated adversarial samples remain within a valid input range, such as pixel values between 0 and 1, a clamping operation clamp$(x', \cdot)$ is applied to restrict all pixel values within the permissible range.

PGD. Generating adversarial examples by performing multiple small-step updates on the adversarial samples, we can get a finer exploration of the input space and make adversarial examples closer to the decision boundary. As a consequence, PGD generally outperforms FGSM in terms of adversarial strength and success rate, particularly when dealing with complex models and defense strategies. Moreover, by constraining the perturbation size at each step within a predefined range (e.g., under the L-infinity norm), PGD can better control the quality of adversarial examples, enabling more covert attacks.

PAMUS. We find that regardless of whether the sample is close to the decision boundary, any sample that can confuse the model's judgment can have a greater impact on the model parameters during the unlearning process. In contrast to adversarial attacks in typical scenarios, the modified samples in unlearning scenarios need to be deleted from the model. In practical applications, users are only concerned with whether the data is deleted, rather than whether the data remains complete and valid. Therefore, PAMUS does not need to consider the quality of the samples, focusing on inducing as much confusion as possible in the model. Here, "confusion" does not mean "misclassification". For example, "misclassification" would be when the model classifies an image of a cat as "99% probability of being a dog". But "confusion" refers to situations where the model might output something like "33% probability of being a cat, 33% probability of being a dog, and 33% probability of being a wolf". Based on this approach, we replace the loss function in the PGD method with a newly designed "entropy loss function", which is capable of measuring the uncertainty in the model's output probability distribution. The attack process is detailed in Algorithm 2.

Algorithm 2. Entropy loss function

Require: output *res*

Ensure: Negative Entropy Loss $-\mathcal{H}$

1: $P \leftarrow \text{softmax}(res)$ # *The softmax probabilities of the model's output.*

2: $P_{\log} \leftarrow \text{log\_softmax}(res)$ #*Compute the log probabilities.*

3: $\mathcal{H} \leftarrow -\frac{1}{N}\sum_{i=1}^{N}\sum_j p_{ij}\log p_{ij}$ #*Compute the entropy.*

4: Return $-\mathcal{H}$

In the steps of calculating entropy, p_{ij} represents the probability that the $i-th$ sample belongs to the $j-th$ class. The outer summation $\sum_{i=1}^{N}$ iterates over all N samples, while the inner summation $\sum_j$ iterates over all classes. The final result is divided by the number of samples N to obtain the average entropy $\mathcal{H}$. The cross-entropy loss penalizes incorrect predictions while maintaining confidence, but it does not fully align with our goal. To address this, we use entropy loss, which measures the uncertainty of the model's output. Higher entropy indicates greater uncertainty, encouraging a more uniform probability distribution that better suits our needs.

4.2 White-Box Scenario

In a white-box scenario, the attacker has the capability to access internal model information, such as the gradients of the samples and detailed outputs from the softmax layer. Leveraging this information, this work designs a sample selection strategy that precisely identifies which samples have the most significant impact on the model parameters, thereby optimizing the machine unlearning process. The schematic illustration is shown in Fig. 5. Specifically, we explore the following four sample ranking methods based on different statistical metrics to identify the most critical samples for the unlearning process.

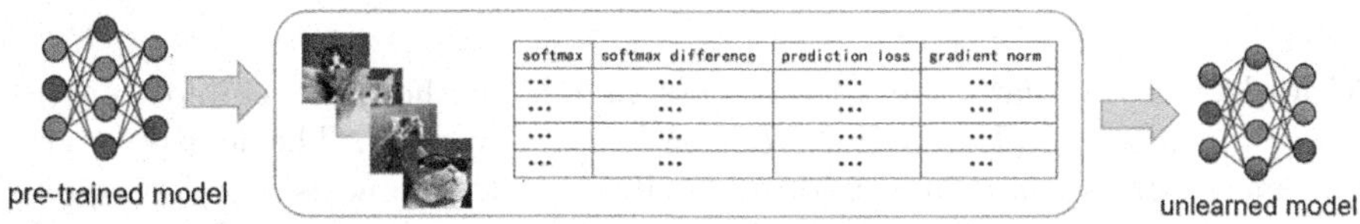

Fig. 5. PAMUS attack in white-box scenarios.

Softmax Value Ranking. This method ranks samples based on their softmax output values. High softmax values typically indicate that the model is very confident in its classification of the sample, suggesting that these samples are particularly important in defining the model's decision boundary. Unlearning such samples could significantly impact the model's overall predictive ability.

Softmax Difference Ranking. This method calculates the difference between the highest and the second-highest values in the softmax output. A larger difference usually indicates that the model is very certain about its final chosen class while being relatively less certain about other classes. Unlearning such samples may alter the model's understanding of class boundaries.

Loss Ranking. Samples are ranked based on their loss values, identifying those that have the greatest impact on model training. These samples play a critical role during training as they significantly drive the adjustment of model weights. Prioritizing the unlearning of these samples may lead to changes in the model's performance and behavior.

Gradient Norm Ranking. The gradient norm of a sample reflects its contribution to model parameter updates. By ranking samples with larger gradient norms, we can prioritize the unlearning of those that have a decisive impact on model training, potentially inducing performance changes after unlearning.

By implementing these ranking strategies, in a white-box scenario, we can effectively select the samples that have a greater impact on model performance, thus achieving an efficient and targeted unlearning process while minimizing computational resource consumption. The implementation results and specific performance impacts of these strategies will be validated and discussed in detail through experiments in Sect. 5.

5 Experiment

5.1 Experiment Settings

Datasets. In this work, we utilize the MNIST dataset [10] as the primary dataset, which is crucial for evaluating the newly proposed attack methods targeting the unlearning process. MNIST contains handwritten digit images from approximately 250 individuals, comprising 60,000 training images and 10,000 test images. Each image is a 28×28 pixel grayscale image, labeled with a digit from 0 to 9.

Models. To evaluate the effectiveness of our method, we employ *Logistic regression model* and *Logistic2NN model* as the victims. The logistic regression model [9] is commonly used in classification tasks and is a widely applied predictive analysis model, used for binary classification problems. The core idea is to use the Sigmoid function to map the linear combination of input features to the (0, 1) range, with the output representing the probability of predicting the sample to belong to a certain class. Mathematically, the prediction function of the Logistic Regression model is defined as:

$$\sigma(x) = \frac{1}{1 + e^{-x}} \tag{6}$$

Here, x represents the linear combination of input features and model parameters.

Baselines. We use the original target parameter unlearning, adversarial samples FGSM, and PGD ($\epsilon = 2.5$ and $\epsilon = 5.0$) as baselines for comparison. We implement the baselines on models trained with 200 and 500 epochs.

Metrics. To evaluate the effectiveness of our attack, we utilize accuracy (ACC) and validation accuracy in the experiments. ACC represents the proportion of correctly classified samples in the test set, while validation accuracy indicates the proportion of correctly classified samples in the validation set. They can both be defined as follows:

$$ACC = N_{correct}/N_{total} \tag{7}$$

where $N_{correct}$ represents the number of correctly classified samples, while N_{total} represents the total number of samples.

Implement Details. We train the *Logistic regression model* and *Logistic2NN* model using an SGD optimizer with a momentum of 0.9. The initial learning rate for the *Logistic Regression model* is set to 0.1, while for the *Logistic2NN* model, it is set to 0.001, with a cosine annealing method employed for learning rate adjustment. The weight decay (L2 regularization) coefficient is set to 0.0005. In this experiment, a batch size of 256 is used for training, and a total of 500 training epochs are conducted.

5.2 Effectiveness of Local Parameter Updates

We initially validate the effectiveness of the optimized unlearning method described in Sect. 3.2. In the dataset MNIST, the tests are conducted using both the *Logistic Regression model* and the *Logistic2NN model*. The results show that the classification accuracy of both models generally exhibits a downward trend. This phenomenon is primarily due to the noise introduced in Fig. 2 to ensure privacy, as well as the impact of the unlearning process itself on model performance. Therefore, the goal of this work's attack is to further reduce the accuracy based on these factors.

As is shown in Fig. 6, in the unlearning of the *Logistic Regressor model*, the validation accuracy of target parameter unlearning decreases by only 3.6% after 500 iterations, which is comparable to random parameter unlearning but significantly lower than the 15.2% drop observed in full parameter unlearning. In contrast, for the *Logistic-2NN model*, the target parameter results in only a 2.4% accuracy decline after 500 iterations, whereas the random parameter leads to a 9.4% drop, and the full parameter causes a drastic accuracy degradation with excessive computational overhead. These results demonstrate that our method effectively optimizes the unlearning process, significantly mitigating performance degradation.

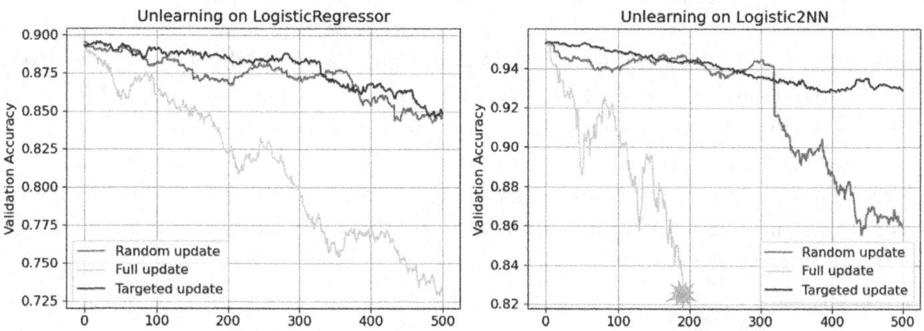

Fig. 6. Validation of local parameter update effectiveness.

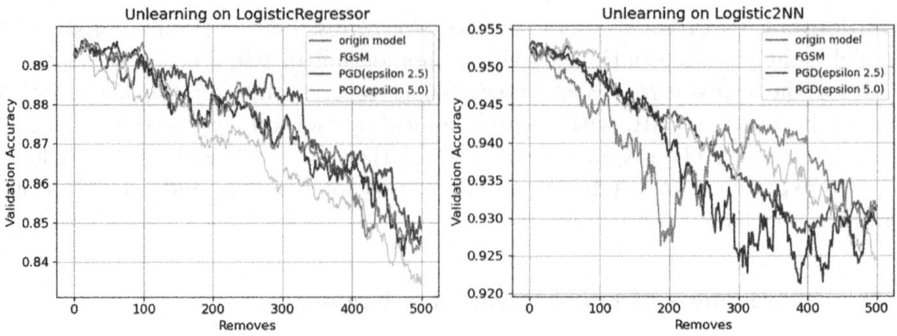

Fig. 7. Attack effectiveness of PAMUS based on adversarial attacks.

5.3 Gray-Box Scenario

We evaluated the effectiveness of adversarial example methods and entropy loss methods, conducting attribution experiments on the MNIST dataset. The detailed results can be found in Table 1. On the MNIST dataset, the initial ACC of the Logistic regression model is 89.39%, and the initial ACC of the Logistic2NN model is 95.26%.

Adversarial Example Method. The results of the adversarial example method are shown in Fig. 7. The experimental results show that, on both the Logistic regression model and the *Logistic2NN model*, the use of adversarial example methods during the unlearning phase for data poisoning attacks has demonstrated certain effectiveness. Specifically, within a limited number of experimental iterations, the adversarial attack significantly impacts the model parameters and reduces accuracy.

Comparing the two adversarial example methods, in the *Logistic regression model*, FGSM demonstrates slightly better attack performance than PGD, reaching an accuracy of 83.42% at 500 removes and 85.05% at 200 removes. Furthermore, the attack effectiveness of PGD is not significantly affected by the size of the perturbation. The accuracies for $\epsilon = 2.5$ and $\epsilon = 5.0$ are around 84.6% at 500 removes, with minimal changes. As for the *Logistic2NN model*, the FGSM attack also shows slightly better performance over 500 iterations, reaching an accuracy of 92.49% and exhibiting a smoother effect curve. In contrast, PGD shows relatively unstable behavior under different perturbation parameter settings and Its accuracy is greater than 93%.

Table 1. Gray-box experiments. We use two prefixes to abbreviate the settings of our methods: 'ϵ-' represents the perturbation parameter, and 's-' represents the perturbation step size. In addition, original unlearning is that we choose origin target parameters to unlearn, and en-loss refers to entropy loss. We report the results under 200 and 500 unlearning rounds. Our optimized entropy loss attack method achieves the best attack performance. When $\epsilon - 2.5$, $s - 25$, the accuracy of the logistic regression model drops to **81.05%**; when $\epsilon - 2.5$, $s - 10$, the accuracy of the logistic2NN model drops to **87.28%**.

removes	approach	ACC↓	
		Logistic regression	Logistic2NN
0 removes	-	89.39%	95.26%
200 removes	original unlearning	87.90%	×
	FGSM	85.05%	×
	PGD(ϵ-2.5)	85.70%	×
500 removes	original unlearning	84.83%	93.19%
	FGSM	83.42%	92.49%
	PGD(ϵ-2.5)	84.62%	93.15%
	PGD(ϵ-5.0)	84.53%	93.11%
	en-loss(ϵ-0.5 & s-25)	83.81%	89.62%
	en-loss(ϵ-2.5 & s-25)	**81.05%**	87.74%
	en-loss(ϵ-5.0 & s-25)	84.69%	91.21%
	en-loss(ϵ-2.5 & s-10)	82.85%	**87.28%**
	en-loss(ϵ-2.5 & s-50)	85.52%	89.58%

Entropy Loss Method. As described in Sect. 4.1, we optimize the loss function in the PGD attack by replacing the CrossEntropyLoss with the entropy loss function. The experimental results using this method are shown in Fig. 8. For both the Logistic regression model and the *Logistic2NN model*, data poisoning attacks based on the entropy loss method are implemented.

Specifically, we conduct multiple experiments on the Logistic regression model to explore the impact of different perturbation steps and perturbation parameters (ϵ) on the attack effectiveness. ϵ ranges from 0.5 to 5.0, while the step size varies from 10 to 50 steps. The results indicate that when the step size is set to 25 and ϵ is 2.5, the attack achieves the best performance with its accuracy dropped by 3.78% to 81.05%. Overall, the setting with $\epsilon = 2.5$ (purple line) outperforms those with $\epsilon = 0.5$ (green line) and $\epsilon = 5.0$ (light blue line).

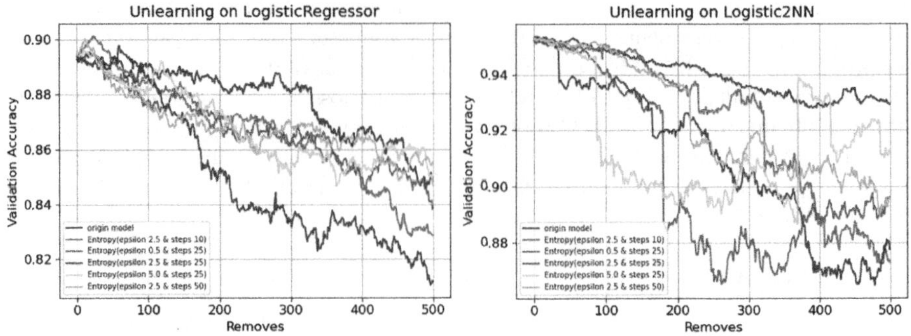

Fig. 8. Attack effectiveness of PAMUS. (Color figure online)

We find that a moderate average perturbation size is likely crucial for constructing samples that effectively influence model parameters. Neither excessively large nor excessively small average step perturbations achieve the same impact. From a practical perspective, moderate-intensity perturbations are more effective at disrupting the model's learning process in data poisoning attacks, while avoiding immediate detection and resistance by the model's defense mechanisms.

The results of the Logistic2NN model, shown in Fig. 8, demonstrate that entropy-based data poisoning attacks significantly outperform adversarial sample methods. In experiments involving 500 unlearning removes, the most effective parameter combinations are a perturbation step size of 25 with $\epsilon = 2.5$, reaching an accuracy of 87.28%.

However, compared to the experiments of the *Logistic regression model*, the *Logistic2NN model* exhibits abrupt changes in prediction accuracy under certain parameter settings. This phenomenon results from the model's sudden sensitivity to specific data during the unlearning process or uneven weight adjustments within the unlearning mechanism, leading to temporary performance fluctuations during training. But there is no doubt that an appropriate average perturbation magnitude not only ensures the effectiveness of the attack but also maintains a more stable decline in prediction accuracy throughout the unlearning process, as shown by the yellow and purple lines in Fig. 8.

Through comparative experiments, the entropy loss-based method demonstrates superior attack performance compared to the adversarial sample method on both *Logistic regression* and *Logistic2NN models*. This difference in effectiveness stems from the entropy loss method's ability to encourage the model to output a more diverse distribution of prediction probabilities, thereby increasing uncertainty and the likelihood of prediction errors. While the adversarial sample method attempts to mislead the model by introducing perturbations, its impact is often limited by the direct observability of the perturbations and the model's rapid adaptability. In contrast, the entropy loss method fundamentally increases the chances of prediction errors by altering the model's response to uncertainty.

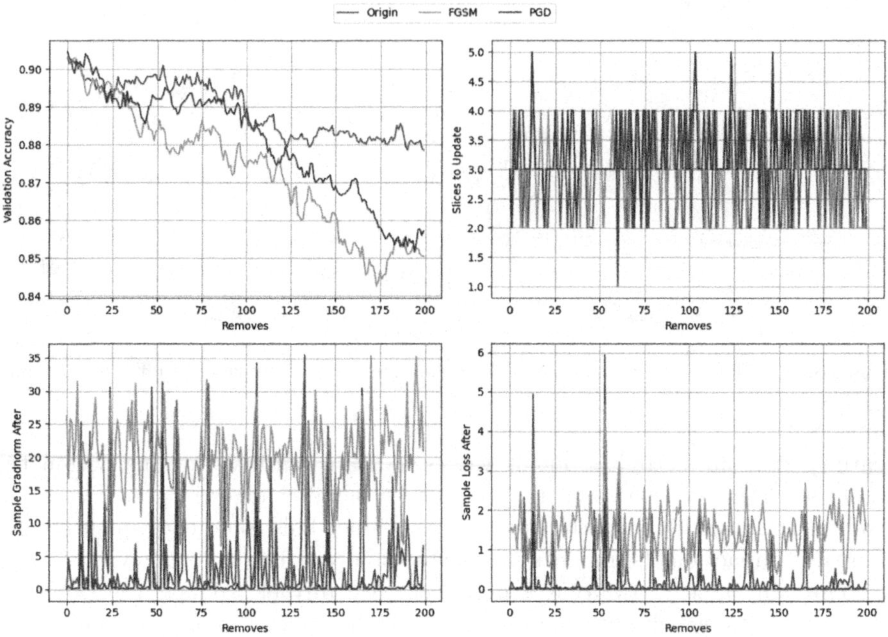

Fig. 9. Attribution experiment. (Color figure online)

5.4 Attribution Analysis

The experiments demonstrate that the perturbation magnitude in the entropy loss method significantly influences the effectiveness of data poisoning attacks. To delve deeper, we focus on the internal dynamics of the model and explore the factors affecting attack effectiveness.

To this end, we conduct a simple and rapid exploratory attribution experiment during a 200-round unlearning process. As illustrated in Fig. 9, the multi-dimensional impact of data poisoning attacks is based on adversarial examples in a gray-box scenario. The sequence of subplots, arranged from left to right and top to bottom, respectively displays the results of adversarial attack experiments. The number of layers affected by parameter changes triggered by forgotten samples, the gradients of poisoned samples, and the prediction loss of poisoned samples post-attack.

In the subplot (top-right) in Fig. 9, PGD (green line) and FGSM (orange line) appear at higher positions compared to the original model (orange line). This indicates that effective attack samples tend to impact more layers of the model's parameters. Additionally, the gradient and loss plots (bottom two subplots) demonstrate that poisoned samples exhibit higher gradient magnitudes and loss values compared to normal samples. Therefore, the disturbances introduced during the attack not only increase the uncertainty in the model's predictions but also directly enhance the influence of the samples on the model's

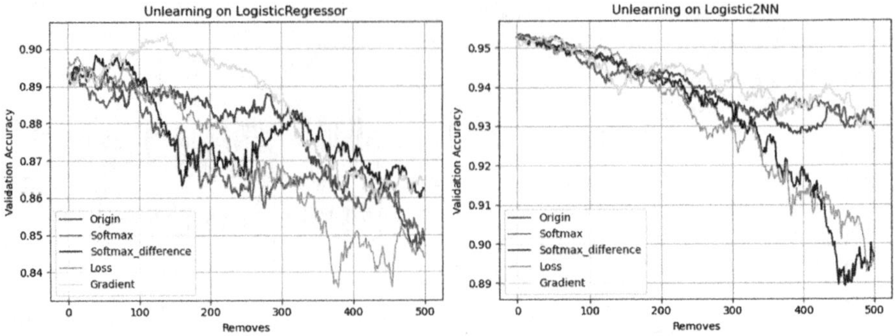

Fig. 10. Attack effectiveness of PAMUS in the white-box scenario. (Color figure online)

learning dynamics. High gradient values indicate sensitive regions within the model's parameter space, meaning that even small changes in parameters can lead to significant shifts in the loss function value. This could consequently have a greater impact on the model's parameters and prediction accuracy.

Through these attribution experiments, we further validate the potential mechanisms by which data poisoning attacks influence the model's unlearning process. Future research can leverage these findings to optimize attack strategies and develop more efficient and precise data poisoning techniques.

5.5 White-Box Scenario

In the white-box scenario, attackers have access to the information of gradients and losses of the samples. Leveraging this advantage, we conduct a series of validation experiments under white-box conditions based on the findings from the previous attribution experiments. The results, as shown in Fig. 10, aim to test the effect of prioritizing the unlearning of samples that meet specific conditions under different ranking strategies and to validate the observations from the attribution experiments.

In this experiment, the order of sample unlearning is determined based on four ranking metrics. The specific ranking strategies include: sorting samples by their softmax output values in descending order (red line), sorting by the difference between the maximum and second-highest softmax values in descending order (green line), sorting by prediction loss in descending order (purple line), and sorting by gradient norm in descending order (light blue line).

The results of each strategy are compared with the original model (blue line). In the *Logistic regression model*, across 500 unlearning iterations, all ranking strategies exhibit similar trends. Among them, the strategy based on prediction loss ranking demonstrates the most notable performance with the lowest accuracy of 83.7%, suggesting that prediction loss may be a critical factor influencing the effectiveness of model unlearning. Similarly, when testing with the *Logistic2NN model*, the difference between the prediction loss-based ranking strategy and the original becomes even more pronounced. With this strategy, the accuracy drops by 3.6% compared to the original at 500 removes, reaching 89.4%. This further supports the significance of prediction loss as a critical factor in influencing model unlearning effectiveness.

6 Discussion and Limitation

The quality of the poisoned samples generated by our PAMUS depends on the adversarial sample generation methods. These methods may produce low-quality samples that are easily distinguishable, especially when they generate out-of-distribution (OOD) samples, potentially reducing the stealthiness of our approach. However, the quality of the sets of poisoning samples can be improved by employing techniques such as manual filtering or K-means clustering with thresholds. Despite the limitation, we believe that our study provides important insights into the potential abuse of machine unlearning, especially as it relates to model performance corruption.

7 Conclusion

In this paper, we revealed that the DNNs suffer from unlearning-based data poison attacks, where the attacker could launch stealthy adversarial attacks to disrupt their performance. For the first time, we propose an attack method called PAMUS, which leverages the properties of sample deletion and parameter modification in the machine unlearning process. The core idea is to ensure that when poisoned samples are deleted, they cause more significant modifications to model parameters, leading to a faster decline in model performance compared to the normal unlearning process through multiple rounds of unlearning operations. We introduce an attack method based on entropy loss optimization, which aims to disrupt the model's functionality. This approach confuses the model's classification decisions, thereby effectively reducing its prediction accuracy. We conduct extensive experiments on the PAMUS attack method in both gray-box and white-box scenarios. The results show that the PGD attack based on the entropy loss function interferes with the model's decision-making process more effectively than traditional adversarial methods where our method reduces the accuracy by 8.34%, whereas the traditional method reduces it by only 4.77%. In experiments, our approach significantly reduces the classification accuracy of the Logistic Regression model by 8.34% and the Logistic2NN model by 7.98%. By comparing the effects of three data poisoning strategies on model performance, we highlight the potential and effectiveness of the entropy loss approach in practical applications, improving the attack effectiveness by 4.7% compared to FGSM and by 5.4% compared to the PGD attack, reaching 81.05% on the logistic regression model. This study also explores key factors affecting the attack's effectiveness through attribution experiments and white-box scenario testing, focusing on the samples sorted by prediction loss of samples, which causes the accuracy to drop by 5.69%, reaching 83.7% on the Logistic regression model, and by 5.98%, reaching 89.28% on the Logistic2NN model, significantly outperforming the original unlearning strategy. These insights offer new perspectives on optimizing attack methods and provide valuable references for future research on protecting privacy and enhancing model security.

References

1. Alfeld, S., Zhu, X., Barford, P.: Data poisoning attacks against autoregressive models. In: Proceedings of the AAAI Conference on Artificial Intelligence, vol. 30 (2016)
2. Baumhauer, T., Schöttle, P., Zeppelzauer, M.: Machine unlearning: linear filtration for logit-based classifiers. Mach. Learn. **111**(9), 3203–3226 (2022)
3. Biggio, B., Nelson, B., Laskov, P.: Support vector machines under adversarial label noise. In: Asian Conference on Machine Learning, pp. 97–112. PMLR (2011)
4. Biggio, B., Nelson, B., Laskov, P.: Poisoning attacks against support vector machines. arXiv preprint arXiv:1206.6389 (2012)
5. Bourtoule, L., et al.: Machine unlearning. In: 2021 IEEE Symposium on Security and Privacy (SP), pp. 141–159. IEEE (2021)
6. Cao, Y., Yang, J.: Towards making systems forget with machine unlearning. In: 2015 IEEE Symposium on Security and Privacy, pp. 463–480. IEEE (2015)
7. Chen, X., Liu, C., Li, B., Lu, K., Song, D.: Targeted backdoor attacks on deep learning systems using data poisoning. arXiv preprint arXiv:1712.05526 (2017)
8. Cinà, A.E., Vascon, S., Demontis, A., Biggio, B., Roli, F., Pelillo, M.: The hammer and the nut: is bilevel optimization really needed to poison linear classifiers? In: 2021 International Joint Conference on Neural Networks (IJCNN), pp. 1–8. IEEE (2021)
9. Cox, D.R.: The regression analysis of binary sequences. J. Roy. Stat. Soc.: Ser. B (Methodol.) **20**, 215–232 (1958)
10. Deng, L.: The MNIST database of handwritten digit images for machine learning research. IEEE Signal Process. Mag. **29**(6), 141–142 (2012)
11. Golatkar, A., Achille, A., Soatto, S.: Eternal sunshine of the spotless net: selective forgetting in deep networks. In: Proceedings of the IEEE/CVF Conference on Computer Vision and Pattern Recognition, pp. 9304–9312 (2020)
12. Goodfellow, I.J., Shlens, J., Szegedy, C.: Explaining and harnessing adversarial examples. arXiv preprint arXiv:1412.6572 (2014)
13. Graves, L., Nagisetty, V., Ganesh, V.: Amnesiac machine learning. In: Proceedings of the AAAI Conference on Artificial Intelligence, vol. 35, pp. 11516–11524 (2021)
14. Guo, C., Goldstein, T., Hannun, A., Van Der Maaten, L.: Certified data removal from machine learning models. arXiv preprint arXiv:1911.03030 (2019)
15. Guo, J., Liu, C.: Practical poisoning attacks on neural networks. In: Vedaldi, A., Bischof, H., Brox, T., Frahm, J.-M. (eds.) ECCV 2020. LNCS, vol. 12372, pp. 142–158. Springer, Cham (2020). https://doi.org/10.1007/978-3-030-58583-9_9
16. Guo, T., Guo, S., Zhang, J., Xu, W., Wang, J.: Efficient attribute unlearning: towards selective removal of input attributes from feature representations. arXiv preprint arXiv:2202.13295 (2022)
17. Gupta, V., Jung, C., Neel, S., Roth, A., Sharifi-Malvajerdi, S., Waites, C.: Adaptive machine unlearning. Adv. Neural. Inf. Process. Syst. **34**, 16319–16330 (2021)

18. He, Y., Meng, G., Chen, K., He, J., Hu, X.: Deepobliviate: a powerful charm for erasing data residual memory in deep neural networks. arXiv preprint arXiv:2105.06209 (2021)
19. Hu, H., et al.: A duty to forget, a right to be assured? Exposing vulnerabilities in machine unlearning services. arXiv preprint arXiv:2309.08230 (2023)
20. Huang, H., Ma, X., Erfani, S.M., Bailey, J., Wang, Y.: Unlearnable examples: making personal data unexploitable. arXiv preprint arXiv:2101.04898 (2021)
21. Huang, W.R., Geiping, J., Fowl, L., Taylor, G., Goldstein, T.: Metapoison: practical general-purpose clean-label data poisoning. Adv. Neural. Inf. Process. Syst. **33**, 12080–12091 (2020)
22. Huang, Y., et al.: Perception-guided jailbreak against text-to-image models. In: Proceedings of the AAAI Conference on Artificial Intelligence, vol. 39, pp. 26238–26247 (2025)
23. Izzo, Z., Smart, M.A., Chaudhuri, K., Zou, J.: Approximate data deletion from machine learning models. In: International Conference on Artificial Intelligence and Statistics, pp. 2008–2016. PMLR (2021)
24. Jagielski, M., Severi, G., Pousette Harger, N., Oprea, A.: Subpopulation data poisoning attacks. In: Proceedings of the 2021 ACM SIGSAC Conference on Computer and Communications Security, pp. 3104–3122 (2021)
25. Li, B., et al.: Purifying quantization-conditioned backdoors via layer-wise activation correction with distribution approximation. In: Forty-First International Conference on Machine Learning (2024)
26. Madry, A., Makelov, A., Schmidt, L., Tsipras, D., Vladu, A.: Towards deep learning models resistant to adversarial attacks. arXiv preprint arXiv:1706.06083 (2017)
27. Marchant, N.G., Rubinstein, B.I., Alfeld, S.: Hard to forget: poisoning attacks on certified machine unlearning. In: Proceedings of the AAAI Conference on Artificial Intelligence, vol. 36, pp. 7691–7700 (2022)
28. Neel, S., Roth, A., Sharifi-Malvajerdi, S.: Descent-to-delete: gradient-based methods for machine unlearning. In: Algorithmic Learning Theory, pp. 931–962. PMLR (2021)
29. Nguyen, Q.P., Low, B.K.H., Jaillet, P.: Variational bayesian unlearning. Adv. Neural. Inf. Process. Syst. **33**, 16025–16036 (2020)
30. Nguyen, T.T., Huynh, T.T., Nguyen, P.L., Liew, A.W.C., Yin, H., Nguyen, Q.V.H.: A survey of machine unlearning. arXiv preprint arXiv:2209.02299 (2022)
31. Rahal, C., Verhagen, M., Kirk, D.: The rise of machine learning in the academic social sciences. AI Soc. 1–3 (2022)
32. Ren, Z., Nguyen, T.T., Nejdl, W.: Prototype learning for interpretable respiratory sound analysis. In: ICASSP 2022-2022 IEEE International Conference on Acoustics, Speech and Signal Processing (ICASSP), pp. 9087–9091. IEEE (2022)
33. Akram, S., Ann, Q.U.: Newton raphson method. Int. J. Sci. Eng. Res. **6** (2015)
34. Schelter, S., Grafberger, S., Dunning, T.: Hedgecut: maintaining randomised trees for low-latency machine unlearning. In: Proceedings of the 2021 International Conference on Management of Data, pp. 1545–1557 (2021)
35. Sekhari, A., Acharya, J., Kamath, G., Suresh, A.T.: Remember what you want to forget: algorithms for machine unlearning. Adv. Neural. Inf. Process. Syst. **34**, 18075–18086 (2021)
36. Thudi, A., Deza, G., Chandrasekaran, V., Papernot, N.: Unrolling SGD: understanding factors influencing machine unlearning. In: 2022 IEEE 7th European Symposium on Security and Privacy (EuroS&P), pp. 303–319. IEEE (2022)

37. Tolpegin, V., Truex, S., Gursoy, M.E., Liu, L.: Data poisoning attacks against federated learning systems. In: Chen, L., Li, N., Liang, K., Schneider, S. (eds.) ESORICS 2020. LNCS, vol. 12308, pp. 480–501. Springer, Cham (2020). https://doi.org/10.1007/978-3-030-58951-6_24
38. Warnecke, A., Pirch, L., Wressnegger, C., Rieck, K.: Machine unlearning of features and labels. arXiv preprint arXiv:2108.11577 (2021)

Certified Enumeration of AI Explanations: A Focus on Monotonic Classifiers

Clément Contet(✉), Rosalie Defourné, and Aurélie Hurault

IRIT, Université de Toulouse, Toulouse, France
{clement.contet,rosalie.defourne,aurelie.hurault}@irit.fr

Abstract. The theory of minimal explanations offers a rigorous, model-based solution to the problem of producing explanations for the decisions of AI models. In some high-stakes contexts, there is a need to generate all possible explanations for a particular decision using certified programs, whose output can be trusted. We used the proof assistant Coq to certify a recently proposed algorithm for the enumeration of explanations in the case of monotonic classifiers. Our experimental results on the extracted code showcase the scalability of this approach, underscoring its potential for improving trust and reliability in AI systems.

Keywords: Formal Explainability · Explainable AI · Certification

1 Introduction

With the advancement of artificial intelligence (AI) and particularly machine learning (ML), the need to explain AI decisions has never been greater [9]. Among many different approaches (see, e.g., the recent special issue [21]), the theory of *minimal explanations* [23] offers a rigorous, model-based solution to the problem of producing explanations for the decisions of AI models. These guarantees make minimal explanations a tool particularly well suited to critical systems where rigor is paramount.

In the context of that theory, there can be several explanations for the same decision. There are several reasons why it may be desirable to compute all explanations instead of just one. Firstly, having access to all explanations makes it possible to filter quality ones and possibly select the best. Secondly, it is a straightforward way of addressing the membership problem, which asks whether a given feature can explain some decision. Thirdly, it may give useful information about the model, for example by letting us detect when a feature appears in all explanations for a given class. We provide a concrete example of this as part of the discussion following our experiments (Sect. 4.5).

Furthermore, in high-stakes contexts, explanations cannot be blindly trusted. Recent work [17,19] shows that it is important to have a rigorous formal approach

This work was supported by project ForML ANR-23-CE25-0009.

Y. Zhou et al. (Eds.): ICECCS 2025, LNCS 15746, pp. 123–142, 2026.
https://doi.org/10.1007/978-3-032-00828-2_8

to ensure the relevance of the explanation, yet few studies focus on the certification of formal explanations. However, we can mention [1], which addresses the issue of providing provably correct explanations for decision trees.

Using the proof assistant Coq[1], we prove the soundness and completeness of a recently proposed algorithm for enumerating explanations in the context of monotonic classifiers [18]. This builds on previous work that only addressed the problem of proving sound an algorithm returning one explanation [10]. This allows us to extract a certified OCaml program taking a model and instance as input, and that can be trusted to return all the possible explanations for the corresponding decision.

The paper is organized as follows. First, we provide the mathematical foundations of minimal explanations and monotonic classifiers (Sect. 2). We then describe our certified version of the enumeration algorithm, which includes proofs of soundness, completeness and termination (Sect. 3). Finally, we present our experiments demonstrating the scalability of the generated code, and illustrate the value of computing the full set of explanations with a deep dive on a concrete example supported by additional experiments on three other datasets (Sect. 4).

2 Preliminaries

2.1 Minimal Explanations

Minimal explanations are tools recently developed for explainable artificial intelligence (see, e.g., [16] for a recent survey). Given a specific instance of a classification problem, the goal is to find minimal subsets of features (in the sense that no element is superfluous) which are relevant to explain the classifier's decision.

There are two kinds of minimal explanations. *Abductive explanations*, also known as *prime implicant*, are sufficient reasons to attribute a class to an instance [8,12,23]. There are minimal sets of features such that any instance which has the same values as the original instance on those features will be associated to the same class by the classifier. Next, *contrastive explanations* are minimal sets of features such that it is possible to obtain a different prediction by changing only those features [11,20]. Both types of explanations are based on the computation of minimal conjunctions of literals representing whether the value of a feature can vary.

Formally, following the notations used by Marques-Silva [16], let $\mathcal{F}$ be a set of N features, with each ith feature taking value in domain $\mathcal{D}_i$, and let $\mathcal{K}$ be a finite set of classes. The feature space is defined by $\mathbb{F} = \mathcal{D}_1 \times \mathcal{D}_2 \times \cdots \times \mathcal{D}_N$ and a classifier is any non-constant function κ that maps the feature space $\mathbb{F}$ into the set of classes $\mathcal{K}$, i.e. $\kappa : \mathbb{F} \to \mathcal{K}$.

[1] The source code (Coq proof, extracted OCaml code, Python code to generate models, datasets, their transformation into binary classification tasks, and the corresponding models) is available at https://github.com/hurault/iceccs25.

Definition 1 (AXp and CXp). *Given $v \in \mathbb{F}$, an* abductive explanation *(*AXp*) for the classification of v by κ is any minimal subset $\mathcal{X} \subseteq \mathcal{F}$ such that*

$$\forall(x \in \mathbb{F}), \left[\left(\bigwedge_{i \in \mathcal{X}} (x_i = v_i)\right) \implies (\kappa(x) = \kappa(v))\right] \tag{1}$$

Given $v \in \mathbb{F}$, a contrastive explanation *(*CXp*) for the classification of v by κ is any minimal subset $\mathcal{Y} \subseteq \mathcal{F}$ such that*

$$\exists(x \in \mathbb{F}), \left[\left(\bigwedge_{i \in \mathcal{F} \setminus \mathcal{Y}} (x_i = v_i)\right) \wedge (\kappa(x) \neq \kappa(v))\right] \tag{2}$$

A subset of features that satisfies (1) or (2) but is not subset minimal is called a *weak* explanation. Hence, there are *weak abductive explanations* (*WAXp*) and *weak contrastive explanations* (*WCXp*). Note that being a WAXp (respectively WCXp) is a monotonic property, i.e. given a WAXp (respectively WCXp) $\mathcal{X}$ and a $\mathcal{X}' \subseteq \mathcal{F}$ such that $\mathcal{X} \subseteq \mathcal{X}'$, then $\mathcal{X}'$ is a WAXp (respectively WCXp). Intuitively this is natural since if there is enough information for the classifier to make a prediction, adding information will not change this fact. Conversely, if multiple possible outcomes exist due to the lack of information, removing extra information will not reduce the field of possibilities. This monotonicity property directly impacts explanation computation, as it means that tests for minimality can be simplified from testing all strict subsets of an AXp or CXp to testing subsets obtained by removing a single element.

2.2 Monotonic Classifiers

A classifier is said to be monotonic when increasing the value of a single feature while keeping the values of the other features unchanged can only increase the model's prediction. Monotonicity is a property naturally occurring in many real world problems. For instance, in general the cost of a house increases with the house area, the health of a patient increases with the amount of physical activity they do. In another context, a robust malware classifier has been developed, based on the principle that the probability of an application being malware increases the more it takes part in suspicious activities [7]. Monotonicity has been studied in a wide range of settings. We refer to the work of Cano *et al.* [5] for a global survey on the subject of monotonicity for classification problems. Various tools claim to support the generation of monotonic classifiers, such as COMET[2], Deep Lattice Network (DLN) [27], monoboost[3] and XGBoost[4].

To handle the case of monotonic classifiers, the feature domains $\mathcal{D}_i$ must be ordered and bounded. Before formally introducing monotonicity, we first introduce some notation. Given two points in feature space a and b, we write $a \leq b$ as a shorthand for $a_i \leq b_i$ for all features $i \in \mathcal{F}$.

[2] https://github.com/AishwaryaSivaraman/COMET.
[3] https://github.com/chriswbartley/monoboost.
[4] https://xgboost.readthedocs.io/en/latest/tutorials/monotonic.html.

Definition 2 (Monotonic and stable classifier [10]). *A classifier is (fully)* monotonic *if its associated set of classes $\mathcal{K} = \{c_1, c_2, \ldots, c_m\}$ respects a total order $\preceq$, with $c1 \preceq c2 \preceq \cdots \preceq c_m$, and its classification function κ is* monotonic *i.e. for all pairs of points $a, b \in \mathbb{F}$, $a \leq b \implies \kappa(a) \preceq \kappa(b)$.*

A classifier is stable *if its associated classification function κ is stable i.e. for all triplets of points $a, b, c \in \mathbb{F}$, $a \leq b \leq c \wedge \kappa(a) = \kappa(c) \implies \kappa(a) = \kappa(b) = \kappa(c)$.*

Stability is a weaker property than monotonicity as all monotonic classifiers are inherently stable.

Stable classifiers were introduced by Hurault and Marques-Silva [10] because it is precisely this weaker notion that is useful in the efficient computation of minimal explanations.

2.3 Computing Explanations for Monotonic Classifiers

In this section we describe the algorithms introduced by Marques-Silva *et al.* [18] to compute an AXp or a CXp for monotonic classifiers (Algorithms 1, 2, and 3), as well as to enumerate all minimal explanations (Algorithm 4). An in-depth analysis of these algorithms is not presented here, and readers are advised to refer to the original paper for further details.

First we recall why stability is useful regarding the computation of explanations. In general, computing explanations becomes tedious quickly because every possible data point needs to be checked to make sure that Eqs. 1 or 2 are satisfied. However, the stability property allows Marques-Silva *et al.* [18] to simplify the computation of explanations.

For each features $i \in \mathcal{F}$, we define $\lambda(i)$ and $\mu(i)$ as the smallest and largest values $x_i \in \mathcal{D}_i$ can take. Hence, for each $i \in \mathcal{F}$, $\lambda(i) \leq x_i \leq \mu(i)$. Let $v \in \mathbb{F}$ and $\mathcal{X} \subseteq \mathcal{F}$. The set $\mathcal{X}$ will represent features that can be relaxed in v, while its complement represents features that need to retain their values. Formally, v_L and v_U are defined such that for all features $i \in \mathcal{F}$, if $i \in \mathcal{X}$ then $v_{L_i} = \lambda(i)$ and $v_{U_i} = \mu(i)$, otherwise $v_{L_i} = v_{U_i} = v_i$. Then v_L and v_U are the lower and upper bounds allowed in the feature space restricted to the instances respecting the constraint $\mathcal{X}$. For all inputs $x \in \mathbb{F}$, if $v_i = x_i$ for all $i \in \mathcal{X}$, then $v_L \leq x \leq v_U$. Thus, if $\kappa(v_L) = \kappa(v_U)$ then $\kappa(v_L) = \kappa(x) = \kappa(v_U)$. Hence, for stable/monotonic classifiers, instead of checking each possible input, it is sufficient to compare the classes of v_L and v_U.

Now we move on to the algorithms used to compute AXps or a CXps for monotonic classifiers.

The *explainers*, i.e. the algorithms producing a single abductive or contrastive explanation for monotonic classifiers, follow the same structure since AXps and CXps are tightly connected (they are minimal hitting sets of each other [11]).

The *enumerator*, the algorithm used to enumerate all AXps and CXps for monotonic classifiers, repeatedly calls an oracle, a SAT solver, to explore the entire field of possible explanations (Algorithm 4). At each iteration, it uses Algorithm 2 and Algorithm 3 to reduce the initial seed to a minimal explanation. Finally, it updates *Map*, a boolean formula in conjunctive normal form (CNF)

Algorithm 1. Freeing/Fixing the i-th feature

function FreeAttr($i, v, v_L, v_U, \mathcal{A}, \mathcal{B}$)
  $v_L \leftarrow (v_{L_1}, \dots, \lambda(i), \dots, v_{L_N})$
  $v_U \leftarrow (v_{U_1}, \dots, \mu(i), \dots, v_{U_N})$
  $(\mathcal{A}, \mathcal{B} \leftarrow (\mathcal{A} \setminus \{i\}, \mathcal{B} \cup \{i\})$
  return $(v_L, v_U, \mathcal{A}, \mathcal{B})$

function FixAttr($i, v, v_L, v_U, \mathcal{A}, \mathcal{B}$)
  $v_L \leftarrow (v_{L_1}, \dots, v_i, \dots, v_{L_N})$
  $v_U \leftarrow (v_{U_1}, \dots, v_i, \dots, v_{U_N})$
  $(\mathcal{A}, \mathcal{B} \leftarrow (\mathcal{A} \setminus \{i\}, \mathcal{B} \cup \{i\})$
  return $(v_L, v_U, \mathcal{A}, \mathcal{B})$

Algorithm 2. Computing an AXp (Algorithm 1 in [18])

Require: $\mathcal{F} \setminus \mathcal{S}$ is a wAXp
function findAXp($\mathcal{F}, \mathcal{S}, \kappa, v$)
  $v_L \leftarrow (v_1, \dots, v_N)$
  $v_U \leftarrow (v_1, \dots, v_N)$
  $(\mathcal{C}, \mathcal{D}, \mathcal{P}) \leftarrow (\mathcal{F}, \emptyset, \emptyset)$
  for $i \in \mathcal{S}$ **do**
    $(v_L, v_U, \mathcal{C}, \mathcal{D}) \leftarrow$ FreeAttr($i, v, v_L, v_U, \mathcal{C}, \mathcal{D}$)
  for $i \in \mathcal{F} \setminus \mathcal{S}$ **do**
    $(v_L, v_U, \mathcal{C}, \mathcal{D}) \leftarrow$ FreeAttr($i, v, v_L, v_U, \mathcal{C}, \mathcal{D}$)
    if $\kappa(v_L) \neq \kappa(v_U)$ **then**
      $(v_L, v_U, \mathcal{D}, \mathcal{P}) \leftarrow$ FixAttr($i, v, v_L, v_U, \mathcal{D}, \mathcal{P}$)
  return $\mathcal{P}$

Algorithm 3. Computing a CXp (Algorithm 2 in [18])

Require: $\mathcal{F} \setminus \mathcal{S}$ is a wCXp
function findCXp($\mathcal{F}, \mathcal{S}, \kappa, v$)
  $v_L \leftarrow (\lambda(1), \dots, \lambda(N))$
  $v_U \leftarrow (\mu(1), \dots, \mu(N))$
  $(\mathcal{C}, \mathcal{D}, \mathcal{P}) \leftarrow (\mathcal{F}, \emptyset, \emptyset)$
  for $i \in \mathcal{S}$ **do**
    $(v_L, v_U, \mathcal{C}, \mathcal{D}) \leftarrow$ FixAttr($i, v, v_L, v_U, \mathcal{C}, \mathcal{D}$)
  for $i \in \mathcal{F} \setminus \mathcal{S}$ **do**
    $(v_L, v_U, \mathcal{C}, \mathcal{D}) \leftarrow$ FixAttr($i, v, v_L, v_U, \mathcal{C}, \mathcal{D}$)
    if $\kappa(v_L) = \kappa(v_U)$ **then**
      $(v_L, v_U, \mathcal{D}, \mathcal{P}) \leftarrow$ FreeAttr($i, v, v_L, v_U, \mathcal{D}, \mathcal{P}$)
  return $\mathcal{P}$

which keeps track of the explored parts of the power-set of the feature set. Although Marques-Silva *et al.* [18] present the algorithm, for a deep analysis, we strongly advice to read the work of Liffiton *et al.* [15] which inspired it. Liffiton *et al.* present an algorithm to enumerate *minimal unsatisfiable sets* (MUS) and *minimal correction sets* (MCS) that is a generalization of the enumeration of AXps and CXps (see [11]).

Algorithm 4. Enumerating all AXps and CXps (Algorithm 3 in [18])

function $\text{ENUMXP}(\mathcal{F}, \kappa, v)$
  $Map \leftarrow$ True
  while Map is satisfiable **do**
    $\mathcal{S} \leftarrow \text{SAT}(Map)$
    $\text{v}_\text{L} \leftarrow (v_{L1}, \ldots, v_{LN})$, s.t $v_{L_i} \leftarrow \text{ITE}(i, \mathcal{S}, \lambda_i, v_i)$
    $\text{v}_\text{U} \leftarrow (v_{U1}, \ldots, v_{UN})$, s.t $v_{U_i} \leftarrow \text{ITE}(i, \mathcal{S}, \mu_i, v_i)$
    if $\kappa(v_L) = \kappa(v_U)$ **then**
      $\mathcal{P} \leftarrow \text{FINDAXP}(\mathcal{F}, \mathcal{S}, \kappa, v)$
      output $AXp(\mathcal{P})$
      $Map \leftarrow Map \wedge (\bigvee_{i \in \mathcal{P}} x_i)$
    else
      $\mathcal{P} \leftarrow \text{FINDCXP}(\mathcal{F}, \mathcal{F} \setminus \mathcal{S}, \kappa, v)$
      output $CXp(\mathcal{P})$
      $Map \leftarrow Map \wedge (\bigvee_{i \in \mathcal{P}} \neg x_i)$

function $\text{ITE}(i, \mathcal{S}, v_1, v_2)$
  If $i \in \mathcal{S}$ **then return** v_1 **else return** v_2

3 Proofs and Certification of the Enumeration Algorithm

The enumeration algorithm is formally defined and proven to be sound, complete, and terminating using the Coq proof assistant. To achieve these proofs, the explainer formally verified in [10] is modified to ensure compatibility with the enumerator. This section details these modifications, discusses the challenges that came with formalizing the enumerator, and presents its soundness, termination, and completeness proofs.

3.1 Certification of the Explainer—Seeded Version

The explainers for AXps and CXps are dual to each other. For the sake of simplicity, our examples in this section will focus on the explainer producing AXps. This work is based on an existing Coq formalization that we have extended to suit our needs [10]. The algorithm has been extended to take as argument a *seed*, and the proof of soundness has been strenghtened accordingly. The seed plays a pivotal role in the interaction between explainer and enumerator, as it is used to specify constraints to the explainer and find a new explanation with each iteration.

The Coq implementation of Algorithm 2 is featured in Fig. 1. The function `findAXp` takes as input a classifier κ, an instance v, and a set of features $\mathcal{S}$ (the seed) such that the set $\mathcal{F} \setminus \mathcal{S}$ is a weak AXp. The precondition guarantees the existence of an AXp in the set $\mathcal{F} \setminus \mathcal{S}$, which is exactly what the algorithm returns.

As in the algorithm, the Coq implementation manages two vectors v_L and v_U over the feature domain and the same length as v. Features in $\mathcal{S}$ are all initially fixed in v_L and v_U, then the features in $\mathcal{F} \setminus \mathcal{S}$ are iteratively freed; if freeing one feature breaks the invariant $\kappa(v_L) = \kappa(v_U)$, then the feature is fixed back. The operations of fixing and freeing a feature are handled by the functions `fixAttr` and `freeAttr` which are not shown in the figure. Translating the algorithm from an imperative to a recursive paradigm is rather straightforward; the first loop is implemented by the function `initVectors` to initialize v_L and v_U; the main loop over $\mathcal{F} \setminus \mathcal{S}$ is now a recursive function `findAXp_aux_j` that iterates over all features but skips those in $\mathcal{S}$.

We extended the Coq proof to take into account those changes. The most important aspect of the extension is the invariant, which is presented as a set of properties R_i. The original proof featured 10 properties—we strenghtened some of them and added two. A few examples are shown in Fig. 2. Properties R_7, R_9 and R_{11} state the link between a partial result p and the vectors v_L and v_U at iteration i. Note that if the seed $\mathcal{S}$ is empty, then the condition $i \notin \mathcal{S}$ in R_7 and R_9 becomes unnecessary, and R_{11} becomes a tautology. Property R_{12} states that the partial result does not intersect with the seed. This guarantees that the final AXp is indeed a subset of $\mathcal{F} \setminus \mathcal{S}$, which is needed for proving the soundness of the enumerator next. In addition, there are four properties E_j that make up the soundness property for the function as a whole. They follow rather directly from the invariant; E_4 follows from R_{12} in the case where p is the final result.

3.2 Formalization of the Enumerator

To establish the proof of correctness of the enumerator, two key challenges had to be overcome. First, since the enumerator relies on a SAT solver, it is essential to model both the desired properties of such a solver and its corresponding calls. Second, it is necessary to find the appropriate Coq formalization to effectively unify the three proofs-soundness, termination, and completeness.

***Map* and the SAT-Solver.** *Map*, a Boolean formula in CNF, is modeled using a type `literal`, where for any $i \in \mathcal{F}$, `top`(i) represents the literal x_i and `bot`(i) represents $\neg x_i$. A clause, i.e. a disjunction of literals, is a set of literals. The type `Clause` is therefore a `MSet` of `literal`. Finally, a CNF formula, i.e. a conjunction of clauses, is a set of clauses. Type `CNF` is therefore a `MSet` of `Clause`.

Modeling a SAT-solver is an important part of this work. Indeed, while the goal is to implement a trustworthy version of ENUMXP, re-implementing a SAT-solver is not considered, due to performance reasons. This raises the question of how to represent the SAT-solver. The chosen representation is a function of `CNF` $\rightarrow$ `Option NatSet`. The codomain is of type `Option` to illustrate the fact that a SAT problem is not always satisfiable, in which case the SAT-solver returns `None`. Conversely, if the problem is satisfiable, the solver returns a `NatSet` as output, containing the indices of literals whose assignments are "true".

```
Fixpoint findAXp_aux_j
    (k : list T → Tk) (s : list nat) (j : nat)
    (v vl vu : list T) (p : list nat) {struct j} : list nat :=
match j with
| 0 ⇒ p
| S jmoins1 ⇒
  if mem_nat (nb_feature − j) s then
    findAXp_aux_j k s jmoins1 v vl vu p
  else
  let '(nvl,nvu) := freeAttr (nb_feature−j) vl vu in
    match Tk_eq_dec (k nvl) (k nvu) with
    | false ⇒ let '(nvl,nvu,np) :=
                    fixAttr (nb_feature−j) v nvl nvu p in
                findAXp_aux_j k s jmoins1 v nvl nvu np
    | true ⇒ findAXp_aux_j k s jmoins1 v nvl nvu p
    end
end.

Definition findAXp_aux
    (k : list T → Tk) (s : list nat) (i : nat)
    (v vl vu : list T) (p : list nat) : list nat :=
findAXp_aux_j k s (nb_feature−i) v vl vu p.

Fixpoint initVectors_aux
    (s : list nat) (j : nat) (vl vu : list T) :=
match j return list T * list T with
| 0 ⇒ (vl, vu)
| S j ⇒
   if mem_nat (length vl − S j) s then
      let (vl', vu') := freeAttr (length vl − S j) vl vu in
      initVectors_aux s j vl' vu'
   else
      initVectors_aux s j vl vu
end.

Definition initVectors
    (s : list nat) (v : list T) : list T * list T :=
initVectors_aux s (length v) v v.

Program Definition findAXp
    (k : list T → Tk) (s : list nat) (v: list T) : list nat :=
let (vl, vu) := initVectors s v in
findAXp_aux k s 0 v vl vu nil.
```

Fig. 1. Implementation of the Explainer in Coq

```
Definition R7 : Prop := forall (j : nat),
    j < i ∧ ¬ mem j p ∧ ¬ mem j s →
    (get j vl = lambda j) ∧ (get j vu = nu j).

Definition R9 : Prop := forall (j : nat),
    j >= i ∧ j < nb_feature ∧ i < nb_feature ∧ ¬ mem j s →
    (get j vl = get j v) ∧ (get j vu = get j v).

Definition R11 := forall (j : nat),
    j < nb_feature ∧ mem j s →
    get j vl = lambda j ∧ get j vu = nu j.

Definition R12 : Prop := forall (j : nat),
    mem j p → j < nb_feature ∧ ¬ mem j s.

Definition E4 : Prop := forall (j : nat),
    mem j (findAXp_aux k s i v vl vu p) →
    j < nb_feature ∧ ¬ mem j s.
```

Fig. 2. Some Preconditions and Postconditions for the Soundness of the Explainer

Two additional properties are expected from the SAT-solver (see Fig. 3). The first property, `sat_index_bound` ensures that if the SAT-solver receives a CNF whose literal indices are in $\mathcal{F}$ then the returned solution is a subset of $\mathcal{F}$. This property is necessary for termination. The second property, `sat_satis`, specifies the behavior of the SAT-solver. In particular, it indicates that if a solution exists, then the assignment found must satisfy all the clauses of the CNF, and that if no solution exists, it is because there is always an unsatisfied clause regardless of the assignment chosen.

On the Difficulty of Proving Soundness, Completeness, and Termination. The Coq language puts restrictions on the kind of functions that can be written, as they must be guaranteed to terminate. This makes the formalization task complicated in our case, because the termination of the enumerator is tied to its correctness. Indeed, the enumerator's termination relies on the fact that each call to the explainer returns a new valid explanation, progressively reducing the set of states to explore.

In Coq, there are several ways to define a recursive function. We choose to use a `Function`, which offers an induction mechanism crucial for proving soundness and completeness. Another approach is to use a `Program Fixpoint`, which permits the use of placeholders and generates proof obligations. This feature is particularly useful given the complexity of the termination proof. The final formalization defines the enumerator as a `Function`, making the soundness and completeness proofs more manageable. To establish termination, we leverage two key factors. To ensure the termination of the enumerator, the solution returned by the explainer must be a valid set. Therefore, the explainer is designed to

```
Definition valid_set := NatSet.For_all (gt nb_feature).

Definition valid_index (lit:literal) : Prop :=
match lit with
| bot x ⇒ gt nb_feature x
| top x ⇒ gt nb_feature x
end.

Definition valid_clause c := Clause.For_all (valid_index) c.

Definition valid_CNF c := CNF.For_all valid_clause c.

Definition sat_index_bound (sat:CNF.t → option NatSet.t) : Prop :=
    forall (p:CNF.t) (r:NatSet.t), (Some r) = (sat p) →
    (valid_CNF p) → (valid_set r).

Definition clause_satis (c:Clause.t) (s:NatSet.t) : Prop :=
    exists (e:nat), (Clause.In (top e) c ∧ NatSet.In e s)
        ∨ (Clause.In (bot e) c ∧ ¬ NatSet.In e s).

Definition sat_satis (sat:CNF.t → option NatSet.t) : Prop :=
    forall (p:CNF.t) (r:option NatSet.t), (sat p) = r →
        (exists (s0:NatSet.t), r = Some s0 ∧ (forall (c:Clause.t),
            CNF.In c p → clause_satis c s0))
        ∨ (r = None ∧ (forall (s:NatSet.t), exists (c0:Clause.t),
            CNF.In c0 p ∧ ¬ clause_satis c0 s)).

Definition sat_correct (sat:CNF.t → option NatSet.t) : Prop :=
    sat_satis sat ∧ sat_index_bound sat.
```

Fig. 3. Axioms of the SAT-solver

generate both an explanation and a proof confirming that the explanation is a valid set (Fig. 4). Then, the properties of the parameters are incorporated into the algorithm's definition (Fig. 5). Indeed, the enumeration algorithm terminates only if the SAT solver is correct and if the CNF provided to the SAT solver is valid. Therefore, these properties should be considered as parameters of the enumerator. In recursive calls, the validity of the CNF clause (lines 16 and 23) depends on the validity of the explainer's response. This validity proof is obtained in lines 14 and 21 thanks to the dependent type used to define the explainer. Note that the original explainer in Fig. 1 handles explanations as lists and only returns explanations. It has therefore been overloaded by the one in Fig. 4, which processes explanations as sets (to ensure compatibility with the enumerator) and provides a proof of the validity of the returned explanation.

```
Definition findAXp (k : list T → Tk) (v:list T) (s:NatSet.t) (ks : stable k)
(bv : length v = nb_feature ∧ is_bounded v) : {p : NatSet.t | valid_set p } := [...]
```

Fig. 4. Signature of the explainer in Coq

```
Function enumXp_aux
    (k : list T → Tk) (kstable : stable k) (knt : not_trivial k)
    (sat : CNF.t → option NatSet.t) (scorrect : sat_correct sat)
    (v: list T) (bv : length v = nb_feature ∧ is_bounded v)
    (h : CNF.t) (vcnf : valid_CNF h)
    {measure meas h} : list Xp :=
match (sat h) with
| None ⇒ nil
| Some s ⇒
    let '( vl,vu):=(build_vl_vu v s) in
    if dec (Tk_eq_dec (k vl) (k vu)) then
        let p_vp := (findAXp k v s kstable bv) in
        let p := proj1_sig p_vp in
        let vp := proj2_sig p_vp in
        (AXp p)::( enumXp_aux k kstable knt sat scorrect v bv
            (CNF.add (AXp2Clause p) h) (add_AXp_valid p h vcnf vp))
    else
        let s' := NatSet.diff featureSet s in
        let p2_vp := (findCXp k v s' kstable knt bv) in
        let p2 := proj1_sig p2_vp in
        let vp2 := proj2_sig p2_vp in
        (CXp p2)::( enumXp_aux k kstable knt sat scorrect v bv
            ( CNF.add (CXp2Clause p2) h) (add_CXp_valid p2 h vcnf vp2))
end.

Definition enumXp
    (k : list T → Tk) (kstable : stable k) (knt : not_trivial k)
    (sat : CNF.t → option NatSet.t) (scorrect : sat_correct sat)
    (v: list T) (bv : length v = nb_feature ∧ is_bounded v): list Xp :=
    enumXp_aux k kstable knt sat scorrect v bv CNF.empty valid_CNF_empty.
```

Fig. 5. Implementation of the Enumerator in Coq

3.3 Proofs of the Enumerator

The proof of ENUMXP can be broken down into three distinct parts. The *soundness* proof consists in showing that the explanations found by ENUMXP are indeed minimal explanations. The proof of *termination* consists in showing that ENUMXP, or rather in this case ENUMXP_AUX, its recursive component, does not loop indefinitely. Finally, the *completeness* proof, aims to show that ENUMXP returns all minimal explanations for the given decision. In the following, the key concepts and main structures of the proofs are presented, without delving into the details of the Coq proofs. Similar to Sect. 3.1, only the case of AXps is discussed, as the case of CXps is nearly identical.

Soundness of the Enumerator. The soundness proof of the enumerator relies on the soundness proof of the explainers. The soundness theorem in Fig. 6 is proved by induction by proving that each new explanation found by the explainers is not transformed before being added to the final list. The three cases, when *sat* returns a `None`, when the explanation found is an AXp and when the explanation is a CXp, are rather straightforward.

```
Theorem AXp_all : forall
    (k : list T → Tk) (kstable : stable k) (knt : not_trivial k)
    (sat : CNF.t → option NatSet.t) (sc : sat_correct sat)
    (v : list T) (bv : length v = nb_feature ∧ is_bounded v),
    sat_correct sat
    ∧ length v = nb_feature →
    (forall (s:NatSet.t), (List.In (AXp s) (enumXp k kstable knt sat sc v bv)) →
    (is_AXp k v s)).
```

Fig. 6. AXp Soundness Theorem

Termination of the Enumerator. Proof of termination is necessary as Coq only accepts well-founded recursive functions, i.e., those with a finite stack of recursive calls. This proof is achieved by introducing a variant that needs to have a lower bound and be strictly decreasing on the recursive calls of ENUMXP_AUX. The termination theorem is given in Fig. 7. For the enumerator, the variant is $\texttt{meas}(Map) := M - \#(Map)$ where M is an integer carefully chosen so that whatever the configuration of Map is, M is greater than the number of distinct clauses in Map. Let $M = \#\{c : \texttt{Clause} | \texttt{valid\_clause}(c)\}$ be the total number of clauses whose literals have indices less than N. On a side note, the upper bound on the number of explanations is actually smaller than 2^N; since AXps and CXps are instances of Sperner families, there is at most $2\binom{N}{\lfloor \frac{N}{2} \rfloor}$ explanations in total [26].

The proof continues by showing by induction that in all recursive calls, $\texttt{meas}(Map) \geq 0$. We prove that $Map \subseteq \{c : \texttt{Clause} | \texttt{valid\_clause}(c)\}$ using the fact that each new clause in Map satisfies `valid_clause`. This is achieved via the soundness of the explainer i.e., the explainer returns a valid AXp which is then converted into a valid clause by `AXp2Clause`. Then, we demonstrate that the new clause added to Map is not already present in Map, ensuring the strict growth of Map and consequently, that the variant is strictly decreasing. This is done using the fact that the newly found AXp was previously a solution of Map but is not a solution anymore with the extra clause.

```
Theorem AXp_term : forall (k : list T → Tk)
    (sat : CNF.t → option NatSet.t)
    (v : list T) (h : CNF.t) (s : NatSet.t),
    stable k →
    length v = nb_feature ∧
    is_bounded v →
    sat_correct sat →
    valid_CNF h →
    sat h = Some s →
    forall vl vu : list T,
    build_vl_vu v s = (vl, vu) →
    Tk_eq_dec (k vl) (k vu) = true →
    meas (CNF.add (AXp2Clause (findAXp_d k v s)) h) < meas h.
```

Fig. 7. AXp Terminaison Theorem

Completeness of the Enumerator. The completeness ensures that no explanations have been omitted during the enumeration, i.e., that every AXp for the decision is included in the list of explanations provided by ENUMXP (see Fig. 8).

```
Theorem all_AXp (k : list T → Tk) (kstable : stable k) (knt : not_trivial k)
    (sat : CNF.t → option NatSet.t) (sc : sat_correct sat)
    (v : list T) (bv : length v = nb_feature ∧ is_bounded v) :
    forall (s:NatSet.t), (is_AXp k v s) →
    List.In (AXp s) (enumXp k kstable knt sat sc v bv).
```

Fig. 8. AXp Completeness Theorem

Completeness is proven by introducing an invariant stating that any AXp which is a solution to the *Map* considered in ENUMXP_AUX will eventually be obtained (see Fig. 9). Finally, since *Map* is empty in the first call of ENUMXP_AUX, any feature subset is a solution and in particular any AXp. Hence, all AXps will eventually be obtained.

```
Lemma enumXp_aux_inv_AXp (k : list T → Tk) (kstable : stable k)
    (knt : not_trivial k) (sat : CNF.t → option NatSet.t) (sc : sat_correct sat)
    (v : list T) (bv : length v = nb_feature ∧ is_bounded v) (s : NatSet.t) :
    forall (h : CNF.t) (vcnf : valid_CNF h),
    is_AXp k v s →
    sat_sol h (diff featureSet s) →
    List.In (AXp s) (enumXp_aux k kstable knt sat sc v bv h vcnf).
```

Fig. 9. AXp Completeness Invariant

Given an AXp $\mathcal{X}$, membership is proved by induction. In the initial case, the map `h` admits no solution, hence no AXp corresponds to a solution of the SAT problem. Regarding the induction part, depending on whether ENUMXP_AUX returns an AXp or a CXp, two sub-cases appear. When ENUMXP_AUX returns a new AXp $\mathcal{Y}$ = `findAXp k v s0`, the case further divides in two sub-cases. If $\mathcal{X}$ is still a solution to the updated map `h' = (CNF.add (AXp2Clause` $\mathcal{Y}$ `h)`, ENUMXP_AUX simply needs to continue exploring the domain to find $\mathcal{X}$. If $\mathcal{X}$ is no more a solution to the updated map `h' = (CNF.add (AXp2Clause` $\mathcal{Y}$ `h)`, we have to show that $\mathcal{Y} = \mathcal{X}$. Since the new clause added to the map excludes the solution $\mathcal{X}$, $\mathcal{X} \subseteq \mathcal{Y}$. Additionally, since both $\mathcal{X}$ and $\mathcal{Y}$ are AXps, by subset minimality, $\mathcal{Y} = \mathcal{X}$. When ENUMXP_AUX returns a new CXp $\mathcal{Y}$ = `findCXp k v s0`, we must prove that $\mathcal{X}$ is still a solution to the updated map `h' = (CNF.add (CXp2Clause` $\mathcal{Y}$ `h)`. Proving that AXps are covering sets of CXps i.e. that an AXp and a CXp always share at least one element, shows that the new clause does not exclude $\mathcal{X}$ from the solutions of the updated map.

4 Experiments

This section presents a series of experiments that highlight the advantages of enumeration and demonstrate that, despite the code being unoptimized due to automatic generation, the time required to generate all explanations remains reasonable.

The strong assumption of this work is that the classifier must be stable (or monotonic). Among the multiple tools supporting the generation of such classifiers, our choice fell on XGBoost. Unfortunately, we were only able to generate monotonic models in the case of boolean features and classes. Sections 4.1 to 4.5 focus on an example of heart failure prediction and Sect. 4.6 provides additional experiments on three other datasets.

4.1 Implementation

Coq is employed to extract OCaml code that is formally verified, ensuring compliance with proven properties. This allows to offer a certified tool capable of computing correct explanations.

The extracted OCaml code remains unchanged but undergoes structural reorganization. Specifically, the *.mli* file generated by Coq is transformed into a signature module. Meanwhile, the corresponding *.ml* file is converted into a functor that adheres to this signature and is parameterized by a dataset (see `OCaml/explain.ml`). To define datasets, the axioms (N, T, Tk, Tk_eq_dec, λ, and μ) must be instantiated (see `OCaml/dataset.ml`).

The implementation of κ (see `Ocaml/bin/runAXpCXp.ml`) relies on the pyml library[5], which facilitates efficient interaction between the OCaml code extracted from Coq and the Python components responsible for generating and executing classifiers.

[5] https://github.com/thierry-martinez/pyml.

For SAT solving, the ocaml-sat-solvers library[6] is used. Note that the SAT solver plays a crucial role in the enumerator. If its implementation is not trusted, confidence in the provided explanations will be impossible. While some SAT solvers are certified (e.g., CreuSAT [25], GRAT [14], versat [22]), some others are capable of generating a replayable certificate in proof tools (e.g., kissat [4], SatAns-Cert[7]), which retrospectively guarantees the validity of their response. Since 2016, proofs have become mandatory in the main track of the international SAT solver competition [2]. Relying on such solvers allows for trust in the SAT solver calls made by the enumerator.

4.2 Dataset

We took the heart failure dataset[8] and transformed it into a binary dataset (see `XGBoost/heart_binary.py`). This transformation is necessary for XGBoost to be able to learn a monotonic classifier. The *time* feature is removed due to a lack of documentation. Features whose domains are intervals were broken into several binary features representing membership to specific subintervals. These subintervals were chosen arbitrarily for age (in 5-year sections). For features representing medical data (*creatinine_phosphokinase*, *diabetes*, *ejection_fraction*, *high_blood_pressure*, *platelets*, *serum_creatinine* and *serum_sodium*), the choice is based on what values are considered medically normal or abnormal. For example, in the case of platelets, three features were introduced corresponding to "low platelets $<$ 140 000", "extreme platelets $<$ 100 000 or $>$ 500 000", "high platelets $>$ 300 000". A patient with an extremely low level $(1,1,0)$ is ranked higher than a low level $(1,0,0)$, which is ranked higher than a normal level $(0,0,0)$. Conversely, a high level $(0,0,1)$ is ranked higher than normal, and an extremely high level $(0,1,1)$ is ranked higher than high. Note that low and high levels generate incomparable instances, which is desirable as the most beneficial situation for the patient is unknown. The original dataset has 11 features, while its transformation into a binary dataset has 32 features. Both datasets have 299 instances. The dataset is split into two parts: two-thirds for the training dataset and one-third for the testing dataset. The testing dataset is used to assess accuracy, and explanations are generated for its instances.

4.3 Models

The monotonic model is generated using XGBoost, based on research[9] [7] that also requires monotonic classifiers (for robustness, while in our work it is for explainability purposes).

To verify that precision is not lost by switching to a binary dataset and to optimally choose the number of boosting iterations, models are trained using

---

[6] https://github.com/tcsprojects/ocaml-sat-solvers.
[7] https://github.com/boulme/satans-cert.
[8] https://www.kaggle.com/datasets/andrewmvd/heart-failure-clinical-data/data.
[9] https://github.com/surrealyz/pdfclassifier.

both the binary and non-binary datasets, with boosting iterations ranging from 1 to 100. For the initial dataset, the maximum accuracy is 76.77%, while for the binary one, the maximum **accuracy is 79.80%**, which is achieved with 14 boosting iterations in the case of the binary dataset. This increase in accuracy is possibly due to the transformation of the dataset, which is designed considering the objective of obtaining a monotonic model.

4.4 Enumerating Explanations

Execution Time. The experiment are run in a HP EliteBook 840 14 in. G10 Notebook PC with 64Gio RAM and 13th Gen Intel®Core^{TM} i7-1365U × 12. The operating system is Ubuntu 24.04.2 LTS (64 bits). The execution time is computed using the Linux `time` command. To enumerate all AXps and CXps for the 99 instances in the testing dataset, the OCaml program extracted from the Coq formalization takes 1m5s, averaging **one second per instance**. The enumeration time is therefore negligible.

Number and Sizes of AXps and CXps. Table 1 summarizes the number and sizes of AXps and CXps for the 99 instances in the testing dataset. Regarding the number of explanations, note that this number can be significant. This highlights that a single explanation is not sufficient to fully justify a model's decision. Note that the model has 32 features, that the size of the AXps is approximately five times smaller, and that the size of the CXps is about ten times smaller. As a result, the explanations are much more concise than the full set of features, which means they convey essential and focused information.

Table 1. Number and sizes of explanations

	Min.	Median	Average	Max.
Number of AXp	1	12	21	161
Number of CXp	4	18	30.74	225
Size of AXp	4	6	6.54	11
Size of CXp	1	3	3.43	7

4.5 On the Importance of Computing All Explanations

AXps. When the prediction indicates no risk of heart failure, the goal is to understand how to maintain this decision, making the AXps the most relevant explanations. In all explanations across all instances, features representing age appears. Therefore, it can be concluded that age is a major factor in risk of heart failure.

A non-smoking woman between 75 and 79 years old, without anemia, with CPK > 1000, without diabetes, with normal LVEF, with high blood pressure, with high platelets, with normal creatinine and sodium level is correctly predicted as not at risk. Two different AXps are provided. The common elements, besides age, are the absence of diabetes, the normal creatinine level and the fact that she is a woman. Therefore, the patient should pay attention to these two factors. In addition to these elements, one AXp highlights the level of platelets, while the other emphasizes no anemia and no smoking. Thus, the patient can focus on whichever aspect is simplest for them to stabilize.

By analyzing the combinations of features that frequently appear in the AXps of instances identified as at risk, dangerous health combinations can be identified. For example, the combination of high creatinine and low sodium appears in 14 out of 24 heart failure risk predictions as part of explanations for the risk.

CXps. When the prediction indicates risk of heart failure, the goal is to understand how to change this decision, making the CXps the most relevant explanations.

A smoking man between 60 and 64 years old, without anemia, with CPK > 1000, without diabetes, with normal LVEF, without high blood pressure, with normal platelets, with high creatinine level, and low sodium level, is correctly predicted as at risk. The enumeration provides 5 CXp of size 1 or 2. One is about age and an other about being a man. This means that he can focus on few factors to no longer be at risk: combination of smoking and CPK, low sodium or high creatine.

4.6 Additional Datasets, Models and Experiments

In addition to the heart failure dataset, we run experiments with other datasets and models. Results are shown in Table 2. The number of boosting iterations was chosen to maximize accuracy without significantly increasing the model size. The enumeration time refers to the average time needed to compute all the explanations for a given instance over all the instances in the testing dataset.

The datasets and models used are as follows:

- **Admission Predict**[10]: This dataset is used to predict the percentage chance of admission to a university based on GRE scores, TOEFL scores, university rating, statement of purpose and letter of recommendation strength, undergraduate GPA, and research experience. In the binary version, the output indicates whether the predicted probability is greater than 0.7 or not.
- **Airline Passenger Satisfaction**[11]: This dataset is used to predict customer satisfaction after a flight. Since the dataset is very large, the explanation enumerations were performed only on the first 1,000 instances of the testing dataset.
- **Pharyngitis in Children**[12]: This dataset is used to predict RADT positivity based on signs and symptoms.

[10] https://www.kaggle.com/datasets/mohansacharya/graduate-admissions/.

[11] https://www.kaggle.com/datasets/binaryjoker/airline-passenger-satisfaction.

[12] https://www.kaggle.com/datasets/yoshifumimiya/pharyngitis.

Table 2. Experimental results on all datasets and models

Dataset	Nb instances	Nb features original	Nb features binary	Nb boosting iter.	Accuracy	Enum. time
Heart	299	11	32	14	79.80%	0.66 s
Admission	500	7	32	4	87.88%	0,35 s
Airline	129880	22	91	9	90.25%	3.62 s
Pharyngitis	676	19	34	2	72.17%	0.04 s

Dataset	Number of AXp				Number of CXp			
	Min.	Median	Average	Max.	Min.	Median	Average	Max.
Heart	1	12	21	161	4	18	30.74	225
Admission	1	7	12.19	28	3	11	13.17	28
Airline	1	15	33.06	434	3	26	45.10	364
Pharyngitis	1	1	1.15	3	1	3	2.38	3

Dataset	Size of AXp				Size of CXp			
	Min.	Median	Average	Max.	Min.	Median	Average	Max.
Heart	4	6	6.54	11	1	3	3.43	7
Admission	3	3.83	4	6	1	3.36	4	6
Airline	3	6	6.43	12	1	4	4.11	10
Pharyngitis	1	3	2.30	3	1	1	1.09	3

5 Conclusion and Perspectives

Using the proof assistant Coq, we formalized and proved correct an algorithm enumerating explanations for the decisions taken by a monotonic classifier, which is treated as a black box. We proved soundness in the context of the theory of minimal explanations—every returned set is an AXp or a CXp—and also the more challenging property of completeness—every existing AXp or CXp for the decision is eventually returned. Our evaluation of the extracted program demonstrate the scalability of this approach. We highlight the importance of being able to compute all explanations for a classifier decision, as this provides valuable information about the model that one could not infer from a single explanation and opens up the possibility of selecting particular explanations from the totality of them.

Our Coq formalization of the enumerator could be generalized in two ways. Firstly, in principle, the enumerator does not rely on the monotonicity of the AI model, it only needs functions `findAXp` and `findCXp` which take a seed as input and have been proved sound. In future work, we plan to certify an explainer for decision trees [13] and reuse the present work to enumerate explanations in this new context. Secondly, our enumerator is analogous to an existing algorithm for enumerating minimal unsatisfiable subsets (MUS) and minimal correction subsets (MCS) in the context of SAT solving [15]. This prompts the question of whether our formalization could be leveraged to extract a certified MUS enumerator.

References

1. Audemard, G., Lagniez, J., Marquis, P., Szczepanski, N.: Deriving provably correct explanations for decision trees: the impact of domain theories. In: Proceedings of the 33d International Joint Conference on Artificial Intelligence (IJCAI) (2024)
2. Balyo, T., Heule, M.J.H., Järvisalo, M.: SAT competition 2016: recent developments. In: Proceedings of the 31st Conference on Artificial Intelligence (AAAI) (2017)
3. Bartley, C., Liu, W., Reynolds, M.: A novel framework for constructing partially monotone rule ensembles. In: Proceedings of the IEEE 34th International Conference on Data Engineering (ICDE) (2018)
4. Biere, A., Faller, T., Fazekas, K., Fleury, M., Froleyks, N., Pollitt, F.: CaDiCaL, Gimsatul, IsaSAT and Kissat entering the SAT Competition 2024. In: Heule, M., Iser, M., Järvisalo, M., Suda, M. (eds.) Proceedings of the SAT Competition – Solver, Benchmark and Proof Checker Descriptions (2024)
5. Cano, J.R., Gutiérrez, P.A., Krawczyk, B., Woźniak, M., García, S.: Monotonic classification: an overview on algorithms, performance measures and data sets. Neurocomputing **341**, 168–182 (2019)
6. Chen, T., Guestrin, C.: Xgboost: a scalable tree boosting system. In: Proceedings of the 22nd ACM International Conference on Knowledge Discovery and Data Mining (SIGKDD), pp. 785–794 (2016)
7. Chen, Y., Wang, S., She, D., Jana, S.: On training robust PDF malware classifiers. In: Proceedings of the 29th USENIX Security Symposium (USENIX Security) (2020)
8. Darwiche, A., Hirth, A.: On the reasons behind decisions. In: Proceedings of the 24th European Conference on Artificial Intelligence (ECAI). IOS Press (2020)
9. Gunning, D., Aha, D.: Darpa's explainable artificial intelligence (XAI) program. AI Mag. **40**(2), 44–58 (2019)
10. Hurault, A., Marques-Silva, J.: Certified logic-based explainable AI - the case of monotonic classifiers. In: Proceedings of the 17th International Conference on Tests and Proofs (TAP) (2023)
11. Ignatiev, A., Narodytska, N., Asher, N., Marques-Silva, J.: On relating 'why?' and 'why not?' explanations. arXiv preprint arXiv:2012.11067 (2020)
12. Ignatiev, A., Narodytska, N., Marques-Silva, J.: Abduction-based explanations for machine learning models. In: Proceedings of the 33st AAAI Conference on Artificial Intelligence (AAAI) (2019)
13. Izza, Y., Ignatiev, A., Marques-Silva, J.: On explaining decision trees. CoRR abs/2010.11034 (2020)
14. Lammich, P.: The GRAT tool chain - efficient (UN)SAT certificate checking with formal correctness guarantees. In: Gaspers, S., Walsh, T. (eds.) Proceedings of 20th International Conference on Theory and Applications of Satisfiability (SAT) (2017)

15. Liffiton, M.H., Previti, A., Malik, A., Marques-Silva, J.: Fast, flexible MUS enumeration. Constraints **21**(2) (2016)
16. Marques-Silva, J.: Logic-based explainability in machine learning. In: Tutorial Lectures of the 18th International Summer School on Reasoning Web (2022)
17. Marques-Silva, J.: Disproving XAI myths with formal methods - initial results. In: Proceedings of the 27th International Conference on Engineering of Complex Computer Systems (ICECCS) (2023)
18. Marques-Silva, J., Gerspacher, T., Cooper, M.C., Ignatiev, A., Narodytska, N.: Explanations for monotonic classifiers. In: International Conference on Machine Learning, pp. 7469–7479 (2021)
19. Marques-Silva, J., Huang, X.: Explainability is not a game. Commun. ACM **67**(7), 66–75 (2024)
20. Miller, T.: Explanation in artificial intelligence: insights from the social sciences. Artif. Intell. **267**, 1–38 (2019)
21. Miller, T., Hoffman, R.R., Amir, O., Holzinger, A.: Special issue on explainable artificial intelligence (XAI). Artif. Intell. **307**, 103705 (2022)
22. Oe, D., Stump, A., Oliver, C., Clancy, K.: versat: a verified modern SAT solver. In: Proceedings of the 13th International Conference on Verification, Model Checking, and Abstract Interpretation (VMCAI) (2012)
23. Shih, A., Choi, A., Darwiche, A.: A symbolic approach to explaining Bayesian network classifiers. In: Proceedings of the 27th International Joint Conference on Artificial Intelligence (IJCAI) (2018)
24. Sivaraman, A., Farnadi, G., Millstein, T., Van den Broeck, G.: Counterexample-guided learning of monotonic neural networks. In: Advances in Neural Information Processing Systems (NeurIPS), vol. 33 (2020)
25. Skotåm, S.H.: CreuSAT, Using Rust and Creusot to create the world's fastest deductively verified SAT solver. Master's thesis, University of Oslo (2022). https://www.duo.uio.no/handle/10852/96757
26. Sperner, E.: Ein satz über untermengen einer endlichen menge. Math. Z. **27**(1), 544–548 (1928)
27. You, S., Ding, D., Canini, K.R., Pfeifer, J., Gupta, M.R.: Deep lattice networks and partial monotonic functions. In: Advances in Neural Information Processing Systems (NeurIPS), vol. 30 (2017)

Random Resampling of Training Data for Effective Verification Strategy Prediction

Bharti Chimdyalwar[1(✉)], Priyanka Darke[1], R. Venkatesh[1], and Supratik Chakraborty[2]

[1] TCS Research, Pune, India
{bharti.c,priyanka.darke,r.venky}@tcs.com
[2] Indian Institute of Technology, Bombay, Mumbai, India
supratik@cse.iitb.ac.in

Abstract. In this paper, we present a case study of two safety-critical automotive software systems. We demonstrate how applying a data balancing technique to the training dataset significantly enhanced a machine learning-based verification strategy predictor, enabling it to formally verify 55% more property specifications across the two systems. A verification strategy is a sequence of techniques ordered in the decreasing likelihood of their ability to verify a given program with respect to a property specification. Such a strategy is needed because no single technique can verify all programs, and the availability of limited resources mandates an early prediction of suitable techniques in the strategy. To the best of our knowledge, this is the first study to explore the role of data balancing in the context of verification strategy prediction.

1 Introduction

It is well known that a single verification technique cannot verify a diverse set of programs due to variations in the syntax and semantics of programs [13]. As a result, specialized techniques are required to effectively verify different classes of programs. Consequently, software verifiers use a diverse portfolio of techniques that complement each others strengths in program analysis [4,7,15,29]. The likelihood of a program being verified by a sequence of complementary techniques, called a strategy, is higher than a single technique. However, due to limited computing resources it is crucial to carefully select such a sequence of techniques for each program to improve the likelihood of a successful verification. In summary, to be able to verify a variety of programs, there has been a movement in the technology of verifiers, from implementing a single technique, to incorporating a portfolio of techniques, to using verification strategies. The latest and the most successful verifiers implement strategies [6]. As a result strategy design in verifiers is an active field of research.

Recently machine learning (ML) has been applied to train strategy predictors from source code [15,17,23,26,28]. To train machines well, training data

Y. Zhou et al. (Eds.): ICECCS 2025, LNCS 15746, pp. 143–159, 2026.
https://doi.org/10.1007/978-3-032-00828-2_9

ought to characterize the test data. Thus training data and its selection is a key influencer in the performance of strategy predictors [5]. Many strategy predictors select their training data randomly [3,12,23,24]. They label each training data point with the fastest verification technique that successfully verifies the respective program. A random sampling ensures an unbiased selection of the training data. It also improves the likelihood of the classes of programs of the training data being in proportion to the classes of programs of the input dataset. However, for large portfolios of techniques, a random selection of programs into the training data can lead to an under-representation of some techniques in the training data, as demonstrated by our findings in Sect. 3.2. This is possible when a technique needed in the portfolio is the fastest in verifying a very small percentage of programs in the training dataset compared to other techniques in the portfolio. This leads to poor training. For example, the portfolio of VeriAbs [4,11], a well known verifier, contains some techniques that verify fewer programs than others but are needed in the portfolio [4]. Further, the model in VeriAbsL [15], a best-in-class strategy prediction based verifier [1], is trained using a randomly sampled dataset of size 648. In this, data points corresponding to one technique are not sampled at all as shown under the column named 'VeriAbsL' of Table 4.

To avoid the above problem, in the past, strategy predictors with portfolios of up to 5 verification techniques [27,29] have ensured that data points corresponding to all verification techniques are sampled in the training data. But they do not study scenarios in which the training data selected this way continues to under represent some techniques. This is possible for a large portfolio in which some techniques verify a minority of programs in the training data. For example, the model trained in VeriAbsL [15] uses training data in which the data corresponding to three techniques combined, is nine data samples out of 648 data samples as shown in the second column of Table 4. Such few samples are insufficient to train the model with respect to those techniques. In general, imbalanced datasets, where some samples of interest form a minority, can adversely affect the performance of machine learning algorithms.

To overcome the problem of imbalanced class distributions in the training data, the literature proposes data balancing [21,25]. Data balancing is well-established and various methods addressing class imbalance in training data have been successfully applied across different domains [21]. In other words, data balancing ensures that the trainer is trained sufficiently for each class. However, none of the well-known verification strategy predictors [15,17,26,28] have considered balancing their training data either with respect to classes of programs or techniques. VeriAbsL [15] employs a supervised learning using multi-class classification, where each label corresponds to a technique in the portfolio. When such a kind of training data is used, then balancing the training data with respect to labels is inexpensive, and is thus explored in this paper using VeriAbsL.

In this paper, we aim to evaluate the performance of verification strategy prediction using balanced training data on practical real-life automotive applications. To this end, we use VeriAbsL, the highest scorer in the ReachSafety category at the well known competition on software verification (SV-COMP) 2025 [2]. VeriAbsL has been used previously to verify these applications with randomly sampled training data [13]. We present a case study on the impact of increasing the training data size, oversampling and balancing the training data on verification strategy prediction in VeriAbsL.

Contributions.

- We propose and present the application of a novel variation of random resampling [19], a form of oversampling, to balance training data for strategy prediction in VeriAbsL. Random resampling has been tried for the first time to predict verification strategies.
- A case study with VeriAbsL describing how training data balancing led to a rigorous verification of two automotive softwares
as compared to a random data sampling or imbalanced training data.

2 A Background on VeriAbsL

VeriAbsL [15] is a strategy prediction-based reachability verifier that utilises VeriAbs's [4] portfolio of state-of-the-art verification techniques. VeriAbsL employs a trained neural network (NN) to predict an appropriate verification strategy. Next we present VeriAbsL's NN training process and architecture in brief.

2.1 Neural Network Training

Feature Vector: VeriAbsL represents a program as a vector of Boolean features. A Boolean feature signifies the presence or absence of syntactic or semantic attributes of a program, and can hold a TRUE or a FALSE value. For example, if we use features like `has-loops` to denote the presence of loops and `has-known-bound` to indicate that a program has a known bound, then the feature vector `(has-loops, has-known-bound)` evaluating to `(1, 1)` indicates that the program has loops of known bounds. In general, features used by VeriAbsL represent the strengths and weaknesses of the techniques in its portfolio, and are computed using a light-weight static analysis [15].

Labelling: For training, every program P_i in the dataset is represented as a vector F_i of Boolean features as explained above. Each feature vector F_i is associated with an output label T_i, denoting that the verification technique T_i from VeriAbsL's portfolio is the fastest in successfully verifying program P_i. Thus, each data point L_i in the labelled data L is given by $L_i = \langle F_i, T_i \rangle$.

Neural Network: To predict a strategy, VeriAbsL employs a trained neural network as a multi-class classifier. The neural network comprises of an input layer with neurons equal to the number of features [15], two hidden layers, each with half the number of neurons than their preceding layers, and an output layer with 11 neurons for eleven different verification techniques in the portfolio. It uses categorical cross-entropy as a loss function and the output layer uses the softmax activation function. Its compact size characterises the neural network.

2.2 VeriAbsL Architecture

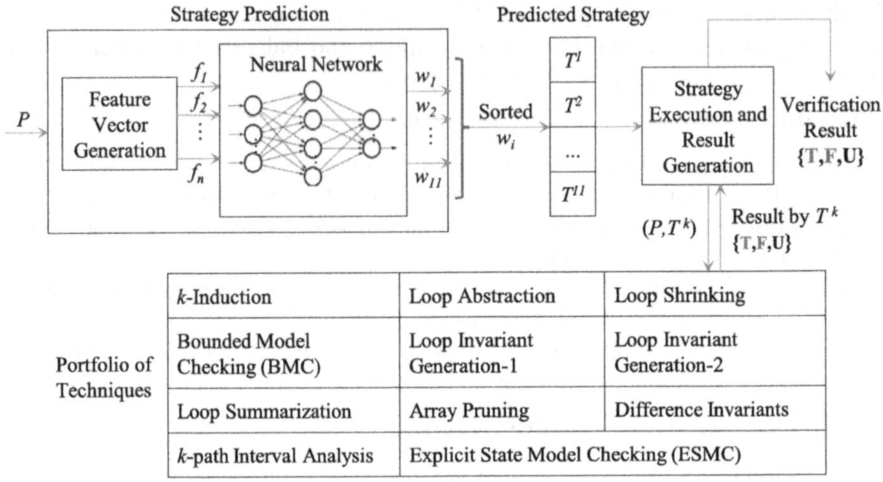

Fig. 1. Architecture of VeriAbsL.

The architecture of VeriAbsL is depicted in Fig. 1. It takes as input a program P encoded with property assertions. Then a feature vector generation module generates the Boolean features $f_1, \ldots, f_n$ indicating the presence of the respective semantic or syntactic features in P. Then it uses a trained neural network to translate these features into measures of effectiveness, referred to as weights $w_1, \ldots, w_{11}$ corresponding to verification techniques $T_1, \ldots, T_{11}$[1]. The weights $w_1, \ldots, w_{11}$ are then sorted in the decreasing order to order the corresponding techniques as, say, $T^1, \ldots, T^{11}$. Here T^1 is predicted to be the technique with the highest likelihood of verifying P successfully, and T^{11} with the smallest likelihood. This order of techniques is called a predicted strategy. The techniques are invoked in the predicted order by the 'strategy execution and result generation' module until either P is verified or some allocated resource is exhausted. VeriAbsL uses the portfolio of techniques implemented in VeriAbs.

3 A Case Study

We present a case study of two real-life industrial applications, highlighting the critical role of training data selection and data balancing in effective verification strategy prediction. The primary goal of the case study was to formally verify the input applications. In cases where full verification could not be achieved through strategy prediction, we aimed to investigate the underlying reasons. To this end, we had to perform three sets of experiments, detailed in the following

[1] VeriAbsL's portfolio contains eleven verification techniques.

sections. The study also demonstrates how a balanced training dataset enabled the successful verification of one automotive system that had remained unverified for over a decade, despite the use of state-of-the-art verification techniques.

3.1 Automotive Applications

Table 1. Automotive Applications

App.	Description	Size (KLoC)	Largest slice size (KLoC)	# Property Assertions
A1	CANopen protocol system	9	2.1	94
A2	Braking control system	34	6.3	349
Total		43	-	443

Table 1 provides a description of the two real life applications we studied. The column titled *#Property Assertions* indicates the number of property assertions in each application. They assert the absence of (1) array index out of bound, (2) division by zero and (3) arithmetic overflow or underflow. These assertions were automatically encoded into the applications based on warnings reported by a static code analyzer [14,22].

For our experiments, each application was sliced with respect to each property assertion using program slicing techniques to improve scalability [18]. This process generated a number of program slices equivalent to the number of property assertions. We then verified each program slice individually to verify the respective assertion. While slicing may not be necessary for scaling verification of small non-complex systems, it is crucial for large and/or complex systems. For example, in case of the braking control system (A2) the verification techniques and consequently the predicted strategies failed to scale without slicing. The techniques could scale and generate results by slicing A2. In Table 1 the column *largest slice size* shows the size of the largest slice analyzed for each application. The difference in sizes of the largest slice and the entire application shows the crucial role slicing plays in scaling verification.

3.2 Experimentation

To verify the given applications, we used the state of the art portfolio driven strategy prediction method implemented in VeriAbsL [15]. VeriAbsL employs a supervised multi-class classification with 11 classes where each class represents a distinct verification technique of VeriAbsL's portfolio. In general, supervised learning methods rely on labelled training data. In this case study, we attempted to improve verification by VeriAbsL by improving upon training data selection. This journey is described below. All experiments were conducted using 10 virtual processing units equipped with Ubuntu 20.04 LTS and 64 GB RAM, allowing up to 600 s per program. The results are summarised in Table 2 and discussed further in the following sections.

Table 2. Experimental Results from Automotive Applications

App.	Total Properties	#Verified properties			Time (hour)		
		Random	Labelled	Balanced	Random	Labelled	Balanced
A1	94	74	57	**86**	7.9	8.1	**6.2**
A2	349	115	128	**349**	49.6	51.3	**32.6**
Total	443	189	185	**435**	57.5	59.4	**38.8**

Experiment 1: Random Dataset (D_R). To verify the given applications using the method proposed in VeriAbsL [15] we created a training dataset called a *random dataset* (D_R). As the name suggests, the dataset D_R was formed by a random selection of data points. The data points comprised of 13% of SV-COMP 2023 ReachSafety benchmarks[2]. The number thirteen signifies the number of program categories of the ReachSafety benchmarks. A random selection of 13% programs allows for 1% per category of programs in D_R, as proposed in VeriAbsL [15]. Further, the training data we selected was from the SV-COMP 2023 ReachSafety benchmarks that the VeriAbsL team had labelled previously. Also, we did not train using the industry applications. This was due to the following two reasons: (1) In verification strategy prediction, labelling is a process in which each program in the dataset is evaluated with respect to each technique in the portfolio to label it with the fastest technique that can verify it. VeriAbsL has a large portfolio of 11 techniques. Hence labelling for VeriAbsL's portfolio is expensive. Thus we used the existing labelled data to save on resources. (2) VeriAbsL trained with similar benchmarks from SV-COMP 2022 ReachSafety[3] has been shown to perform well on these applications [13].

Findings: The results obtained by executing VeriAbsL on the industrial applications A1 and A2, using the model trained on the dataset D_R, are shown in Table 2 under the column name 'Random'. As can be seen, none of the applications were fully verified. Upon analyzing the training data, we discovered that four of the eleven techniques in the portfolio were each represented by fewer than ten data points. This is shown in the column named 'Random' of Table 4. Also, the percentage distribution of data points per technique used in the random model is shown in Table 3 under the column 'Random'. To address this issue of under-representation of techniques, we decided to explore if the performance of the model could improve by using a larger training dataset to better represent the complete portfolio and performed the next experiment.

Experiment 2: Labelled Dataset (D_L). In the second experiment, we used a large set of programs for training the model. We used the entire set of labelled benchmarks from SV-COMP 2023 ReachSafety that the VeriAbsL team had

[2] https://sv-comp.sosy-lab.org/2023/benchmarks.php.
[3] https://sv-comp.sosy-lab.org/2022/benchmarks.php.

Table 3. Technique-Wise Training Data Split of Each Model

Technique	% Data Points			
	VeriAbsL [15]	Random	Labelled	Balanced
Loop Abstraction	8.8	9.5	8.3	9.1
ESMC	26.5	16.1	17.1	9.1
Pruning	3.2	2.5	2.7	9.1
Shrinking	1.1	0.3	0.5	9.1
Difference Invariants	4	3.8	3.4	9.1
k-path Interval Analysis	0.2	1.1	1	9.1
k-Induction	16.8	12.6	13.7	9.1
BMC	36.4	28.1	29.5	9.1
Loop Summarization	0.2	0.8	0.6	9.1
Loop Invariant Gen. 1	2.5	6.1	5.5	9.1
Loop Invariant Gen. 2	0	0.4	0.4	9.1
Unverified	0.3	18.8	17.3	0
Training data size	648	800	4800	15565

labelled previously. This labelled data L contained 4,800 programs[4] from the 13 different categories of the SV-COMP 2023 ReachSafety benchmarks.

Improvements in the Training Data: As expected, the labeled data L had data points corresponding to all techniques in the portfolio in larger numbers than the randomly sampled dataset. Additionally, the techniques that verify a large number and variety of programs had a large number of points corresponding to them in the labelled data. We expected this to be useful since it would result in majority strategies containing those techniques early in their sequences of techniques. This would result in verifying more programs.

Findings: We trained another model using this training data comprising of the whole set of labelled benchmarks. We then executed VeriAbsL with this model on the industrial applications A1 and A2. The results obtained are shown in Table 2 under the column 'Labelled'. As can be seen, although there were improvements seen for A2, the verification of A1 was worse, and none of the applications were fully verified. We analyzed the training data L used for this model and found that even though more programs represented each technique, percentages corresponding to each technique were still small or non-uniform as seen in Table 3 under the column 'Labelled'. Further, a large number of programs were labelled with bounded model checking (BMC). This caused BMC to be predicted sooner in strategies even when another technique was needed. VeriAbsL ran out of time for such cases and performed worse than the random model. We thus decided to improve the model by balancing the training data and performed the next experiment.

[4] All programs that cannot be sliced by a shallow slicer [12].

Table 4. Balancing the Training Data Points

Technique	Number of Data Points			
	VeriAbsL [15]	Random	Labelled	Balanced
Loop Abstraction	57	76	399	1415
ESMC	172	129	822	1415
Pruning	21	20	131	1415
Shrinking	7	2	24	1415
Difference Invariants	26	30	165	1415
k-path interval analysis	1	9	49	1415
k-induction	109	101	656	1415
BMC	236	225	**1415**	1415
Loop Summarization	1	6	27	1415
Loop Invariant Gen. 1	16	49	262	1415
Loop Invariant Gen. 2	0	3	19	1415
Unverified	2	150	831	0
Training data size	648	800	4800	15565

Experiment 3: Balanced Dataset (D_B). We next created a balanced training dataset D_B from the labelled data L as follows. First, we removed all data points where none of the techniques in the portfolio were labelled as the best. In other words, we removed data points corresponding to programs that could not be verified by any technique in the portfolio in the given resource limits. There were 831 such data points in the labelled data L. Next, to ensure a balanced representation of all techniques, we identified the technique that was labeled as the best the most number of times and set its count as the base count b. For labelled data L, b was 1415 and corresponded to BMC. This is highlighted in Table 4 under the column 'Labelled'. Next the training data corresponding to all other techniques was oversampled up to the base count b to balance the training data. The number of data points corresponding to each technique before and after balancing the labelled data are shown in Table 4 under the columns 'Labelled' and 'Balanced'. The first two columns are for comparison only. We next explain our novel *random resampling* method for oversampling and balancing the training data.

Random Resampling Method: Let the set X represent those data points in the labelled data L for which technique T is present as a label, meaning technique T is the fastest in verifying those data points. Then if $|X| = b$, then all b data points of technique T were included in the training dataset. However, if $|X| < b$, then all $|X|$ data points of T were added n times to the training dataset such that $b > n * |X|$ and $b < (n + 1) * |X|$. Then the remaining $(b - n * |X|)$ data points were randomly sampled from X to select a total of b data points for technique T. For example, consider the loop abstraction technique shown in Table 4.

As shown the number of data points corresponding to loop abstraction in the labelled data L is 399 and for L, $b = 1415$. Thus to balance the training data, we need to have 1415 data points corresponding to loop abstraction. Hence all 399 data points of loop abstraction are added thrice to form the training data since $1415 > 3*399$ while $1415 < 4*399$. This adds $3*399 = 1197$ training data points for loop abstraction. The remaining 218 (1415 − 1197) data points for loop abstraction are added by a random sampling of the original 399 data points in L labeled with the loop abstraction technique. This process is repeated for each technique to form the balanced training dataset D_B. To summarize, this resampling method ensures that each technique is represented an equal number of times in the training data and all techniques are oversampled except the one with the maximum number of labels in the labelled data. The technique with the maximum number of labels is neither oversampled nor undersampled. Additionally, only those programs that are verified by some technique are sampled as shown in Tables 3 and 4 under the column 'Balanced'.

Findings: We trained a model using the balanced dataset D_B and executed VeriAbsL with this model on the industrial applications A1 and A2. The results obtained are shown in Table 2 under the column 'Balanced'. We found that all properties of application A2 were verified and more properties of A1 were verified. This demonstrates the advantage of using a balanced model over an unbalanced model and shows that in ML based strategy prediction, one needs to train a model comprehensively with respect to each technique to ensure that the most suitable technique is predicted early in the respective strategies. This was the *main* motivation of predicting strategies dynamically – minority techniques can be invoked early in strategies for only those programs that need those minority techniques. This may not be possible in manually predefined strategies. In the section below, we present the detailed findings of our experiments per application.

3.3 Experimental Observations

VeriAbsL was executed on a total of 43 KLoC, which included 443 property assertions. The VeriAbsL model with a balanced training dataset successfully verified 435 (98%) of these properties. This is a significant improvement of up to 135% over both the randomly selected and labelled dataset models, and atleast 128% improvement over the previous attempts to verify these software [13]. We analyzed the results of each application and made the following observations.

CANopen Protocol System (A1)

- VeriAbsL with the balanced data selection model used three techniques to verify 91% properties. On observing A1's source code, we found that it contains distinct loops with statically known or unknown bounds and linear recurrence relations. BMC, k-induction [8] and loop abstraction [16] are useful for such loops and were selected by the balanced model as required.

- The labelled and random models, on average, predicted the above three techniques late in their strategies.
  This resulted in, respectively, 29 and 12 less properties verified as compared to the balanced data model.
- Programs verified by the random model and not by the labelled model used k-induction. The labelled model predicted BMC instead.
- Of all the properties it could verify, the balanced model verified 95% programs by one of the first five techniques per strategy. The labelled model verified 75% programs and the random model verified 70% programs using the first five techniques in their strategies. This showcases the better prediction capabilities of the balanced model.

Braking Control System (A2). This control system is responsible for the operation of the braking mechanism in vehicles. This software plays a vital role in interpreting data from various sensors and executing precise commands to ensure optimal braking performance. The key functionalities include the management of braking force distribution, monitoring of system integrity, and adjustment of brake response based on real-time driving conditions. Thus, this real-time system has an outer reactive loop and all the properties to be verified are directly or indirectly present in this reactive loop. Verification of such a complex system is challenging and 69% of the properties had remained unverified despite applying state-of-the-art verification approaches [10,13].

- The balanced model could verify all 349 properties. 346 properties were verified using k-induction input with invariants from data flow analysis [8]. The remaining three were verified using a loop abstraction technique [16].
- The random and labelled models also used k-induction to verify properties. For the properties that these models could not verify, late predictions of k-induction caused the verification process to run out of resources.
- Increasing the percentages of data points for all techniques in the balanced model, even those not needed for this application A2, did not interfere with the learning and helped the learner learn when to predict the suitable technique and when *not* to predict the unsuitable techniques.

3.4 Lessons Learned

We learned the following lessons from experimental observations:

- It is essential to include representations of all techniques in the training data. A random dataset, whether small or large, does not guarantee the presence or an equal representation of all techniques. Data balancing ensures that all techniques are represented equally in the training data. This balanced representation is important for large portfolios which incorporate general techniques that verify many more programs than specialized techniques of the portfolio that verify minority programs.

- When data points corresponding to programs unsolved by any technique in the portfolio are excluded from the training data, then the learner is not misled and makes better predictions.
- A large portfolio of complementary verification techniques can be utilized better by using a strategy prediction model trained on balanced training data with respect to all techniques in the portfolio.
- Oversampling by the proposed random resampling for balancing the training data as explained above is beneficial for effective strategy prediction.
- SV-COMP benchmarks by virtue of their diversity can serve as a training set for predicting effective verification strategies for real-life applications.

3.5 Threats to Validity

We now present the limitations of our experiments in the two sections below.

Generalizability of Data Balancing. We presented the effect of balancing training data on two automotive applications. Whether the same effectiveness can be observed on other types of applications is not obvious. Yet to check this, we performed a study using VeriAbsL, the highest scoring verifier in the ReachSafety category of SV-COMP 2025 (SV25) [2]. The model used by VeriAbsL in SV25 incorporates a random sampling and ensures a representation of all verification techniques in its portfolio, but the data per technique is imbalanced. We balanced this model used in SV25 by randomly sampling data for each technique using the available labelled data L. We formed the final training data starting with the existing training data used by VeriAbsL in SV-COMP 2025 [2] and also derived the base count for oversampling using the existing training data. We then executed VeriAbsL with the original model and the new balanced model on testing data derived from SV25 benchmarks. This test data comprised of programs which were not part of either model's training data and were 10148 in number. The results of VeriAbsL with both these models are shown in Table 5.

Table 5. Results of VeriAbsL on 10148 Test Programs from SV-COMP 2025

Programs	VeriAbsL Model	
	Imbalanced [2]	Balanced
Total Verified	7184	**7287**
% Verified	70.8	**71.8**

As shown, the balanced model verified 103 more test programs. The ReachSafety category of SV-COMP is the largest category and has a diverse set of real-life and crafted benchmarks contributed by practitioners and researchers from all over the world. The performance of VeriAbsL with balanced training data on these diverse benchmarks strengthens our belief that training data balancing could generalize to software other than automotive software, and can help predict effective strategies in general.

Oversampling vs. Undersampling. In our experiments, we have performed an oversampling of the labelled data L. We did not explore undersampling, and thus have not compared the effectiveness of oversampling vs. undersampling. However, our rationale of choosing oversampling is that undersampling could remove important data points from the training data, leading to poor learning of code based features and reducing the model's ability to predict effective verification strategies. To test this hypothesis, we performed two experiments as follows.

1. Average Number of Data Points as the Balancing Pivot: In the first experiment, we calculated the average number of (no.) data points per technique in the labelled data L. This was 361 for the labelled data L. While computing the average, we did not count data points in L that were not verified by any technique and hence were not labelled by any technique. Techniques with more than the average number of labels were undersampled to match the average value of 361. There were four such techniques including loop abstraction, ESBMC, k-induction and BMC. The undersampling of programs was done by a random resampling of 361 programs from the labelled dataset with $b = 361$. Techniques with fewer than average labels were oversampled using the proposed random resampling method to balance the data. There were eleven such techniques. The data points derived this way are shown in the third column of Table 6. Here '(O)' and '(U)' indicate whether data points of the respective technique were oversampled or undersampled. It is interesting to note here that the proposed random resampling method can be used to oversample as well as undersample data points using parameter b.

Table 6. Oversampling vs. Undersampling

Technique	Number of data points		
	Labelled	Balancing Pivot	
		Average No. Data Points	No. Data Points of k-induction
Loop abstraction	399	361 (U)	656 (O)
ESMC	822	361 (U)	656 (U)
Pruning	130	361 (O)	656 (O)
Shrinking	24	361 (O)	656 (O)
Difference Inv.	165	361 (O)	656 (O)
k-path interval anal.	49	361 (O)	656 (O)
k-induction	656	361 (U)	656
BMC	1415	361 (U)	656 (U)
Loop summarization	27	361 (O)	656 (O)
Loop inv. gen. 1	262	361 (O)	656 (O)
Loop inv. gen. 2	19	361 (O)	656 (O)
Unverified	NA	0	0
Training data size	3968	3971	7216

The results of this experiment are as shown in Table 7. As can be seen, this hybrid approach led to strategies which could verify fewer properties in both applications A1 and A2 than the balanced model presented in Sect. 3.2. In particular, we observed that the prediction of k-induction was late in most strategies due to which VeriAbsL timed out for executions where k-induction was needed to verify the properties. This led to 151 fewer properties being verified than the balanced model as a result of the undersampling of k-induction.

Table 7. Data Balancing with Pivot

App.	#Properties Verified		
	Balanced	Balanced with Pivot	
		Average	k-Induction
A1	86	63	82
A2	349	222	320

2. k-Induction as the Balancing Pivot: To check if the undersampling of k-induction was responsible for verifying fewer properties, we performed a second experiment. In this experiment, we treated the k-induction technique as a pivot to decide if a technique should be oversampled or undersampled. All techniques with more data points in the labelled data L than k-induction were undersampled, and all techniques with fewer data points in L than k-induction were oversampled using the proposed random resampling method. The data points corresponding to k-induction were not over or undersampled. L contained 656 data points corresponding to k-induction as shown in the second column of Table 6. Thus the balanced model created this way contained 656 data points per technique as shown in the fourth column of Table 6. Such a sampling led to results shown in Table 7. As can be seen 116 more properties are verified using this approach than the previous hybrid model. We found that not undersampling the data points of k-induction led to the improved prediction of k-induction in the strategies. As compared to the balanced model it verified 35 fewer properties because k-induction was predicted late in strategies. Thus we can conclude that oversampling data points of k-induction helped the balanced model presented in Sect. 3.2 make predictions that could verify the most properties. This demonstrates the importance of training data balancing using oversampling rather than undersampling in the context of strategy prediction.

4 Related Work

Machine-learning techniques have been widely used in algorithm selection and strategy prediction. In some approaches, training data selection relies on random sampling, while others refine the randomly sampled data to better suit their learning mechanisms.

Random Sampling. Verifiers such as Verifolio [17], Graves-CPA [23], VeriAbsL [15] rely on randomly sampled data for training their machine learning models. Verifolio predicts the best tool from a selection of ten selected tools chosen from SV-COMP-2014. It randomly splits the verification tasks of SV-COMP from that year into a training set, $train_{\langle year \rangle}$ and a test set, $test_{\langle year \rangle}$, with a ratio of 60:40. Graves-CPA, which uses Graph Attention Networks for algorithm selection in software verification, employs five configurations from the CPAChecker framework [9]. Its model was trained on a randomly selected 20% subset of the SV-COMP benchmark set. Similarly, VeriAbsL randomly selects training data from every sub-category of well-known SV-COMP benchmarks. Our experimental results demonstrate that VeriAbsL performed better with balanced training data with respect to all verification techniques in portfolio than random selection. Both Verifolio and Graves-CPA could also benefit from balancing their training data rather than relying solely on random sampling.

Refining Randomly Sampled Data. MUX [29], PeSCo [26] and Context Syntax Trees (CST) [28] further refine randomly sampled data for better training explained as follows.

MUX predicts the best model checker for a given windows device driver annotated with a property. To avoid the under-representation of certain model checkers in the training data, MUX considers examples of drivers for which each model checker gives the least total runtime over all the properties. These drivers are then grouped according to the best-performing model checker, and each group is randomly divided into training, validation, and test sets. In this way, they aim to ensure adequate representation of the best model checkers in the training data. Our proposed data selection method is for effective verification strategy prediction across a diverse set of programs, where a particular program may be verified by multiple techniques or uniquely by a single technique in the portfolio. Just as we discard programs that are not verified by any verifier in the training data, MUX also excludes drivers that haven't been validated by any model checker. However, MUX does not currently balance the training data. Balancing the data could potentially improve MUX's prediction performance.

PeSCo ranks verifiers by representing the program in the form of graphs such as abstract syntax trees and program dependence graphs. It uses a pairwise comparison for labeling the training data [26]. The CST approach also ranks verifiers using the contextualized syntax trees of programs. The CST are input to a supervised representation learning method. This approach chose SV-COMP 2018 as their dataset, splitting it into a training and test set with ratio of 90:10 from each subcategory. On this randomly selected training set, they perform cleaning operations by deduplicating all isomorphic CSTs and removing training examples where an isomorphic counterpart exists in the test set. Additionally, they remove all programs that cannot be solved by any verifier. Their data selection process does not focus on balancing training data but on removing isomorphic entries.

Data Balancing. To address imbalanced class distributions, class balancing studies have been published previously [19,20,25] and data balancing has been successfully applied across various domains [21]. Our approach represents the first application of data balancing based on verification techniques from a portfolio of techniques to effectively utilize the portfolio and improve verification strategy prediction. Moreover, for data balancing, Nathalie Japkowicz et al. in [19,20] applies a traditional oversampling technique and calls it *random resampling*. This method randomly resamples data from minority classes whereas we propose an approach that initially resamples all elements of each minority class n times, then performs a random selection.

5 Conclusion

Machine learning based portfolio verifiers are used to predict a sequence of techniques, called a strategy, to verify a given program. The strategy predictor is trained using training data to predict the effectiveness of the techniques in the portfolio. The training data is made up of program features labelled with the fastest technique in the portfolio that can verify the given program. We presented our experience showing that a **balanced training data** created using a proposed **random resampling** method from a **large variety of programs**, helped train a model that could verify unseen automotive applications. The balanced dataset enabled the prediction model to learn effectively with respect to each technique and verify 98% properties of these practical applications. The balanced model outperformed two other models: one using the same training data before balancing, and another, a best-in-class model that involved a random sampling of the same dataset. Additionally, with two experimental studies we have shown that oversampling using the proposed random resampling performs better than undersampling. Thus we conclude that creating a balanced training data by oversampling using random resampling from a variety of programs leads to a better representation of all verification techniques in the portfolio, resulting in improved strategy prediction.

Furthermore, in the context of verification strategy prediction we presented a novel combination of two useful methods that helped verify two hard-to-verify automotive applications. The combination consisted of (1) Boolean program features labelled with a verification technique for strategy prediction, and (2) training data balancing with respect to verification techniques. Moving forward, we would like to evaluate more real-life applications from other domains for verification strategy prediction using our balanced model to showcase the generalizability of the proposed data balancing method in practice.

Finally to conclude, we present the key insights from this case study as follows:

- An equal representation of all techniques in the training data can lead to a very effective strategy prediction.
- Oversampling is useful to predict strategies from a large portfolio of varied techniques, of which some are general and some are specialised or minority.
- Random resampling, as proposed in this paper, is an effective alternative to achieve data balancing.
- A balanced training data made up of a large variety of programs, like in the SV-COMP ReachSafety benchmarks, using a small set of Boolean portfolio driven features [15], can train an effective model with respect to a variety of techniques and verify *unseen* programs.

References

1. SV-COMP 2024 Results. https://sv-comp.sosy-lab.org/2024/results/results-verified/

2. SV-COMP 2025 Results. https://sv-comp.sosy-lab.org/2025/results/results-verified/
3. Sampling Methods, chap. 4, pp. 89–121. Wiley (2021)
4. Afzal, M., et al.: Veriabs: verification by abstraction and test generation. In: 34th IEEE/ACM International Conference on Automated Software Engineering, ASE 2019, San Diego, CA, USA, 11–15 November 2019, pp. 1138–1141. IEEE (2019)
5. Albalak, A., et al.: A survey on data selection for language models. arXiv preprint arXiv:2402.16827 (2024)
6. Beyer, D.: Progress on software verification: SV-COMP 2022. In: TACAS 2022. LNCS, vol. 13244, pp. 375–402. Springer, Cham (2022). https://doi.org/10.1007/978-3-030-99527-0_20
7. Beyer, D., Dangl, M.: Strategy selection for software verification based on boolean features. In: Margaria, T., Steffen, B. (eds.) ISoLA 2018. LNCS, vol. 11245, pp. 144–159. Springer, Cham (2018). https://doi.org/10.1007/978-3-030-03421-4_11
8. Beyer, D., Dangl, M., Wendler, P.: Boosting k-induction with continuously-refined invariants. In: Kroening, D., Păsăreanu, C.S. (eds.) CAV 2015. LNCS, vol. 9206, pp. 622–640. Springer, Cham (2015). https://doi.org/10.1007/978-3-319-21690-4_42
9. Beyer, D., Keremoglu, M.E.: CPAchecker: a tool for configurable software verification. In: Gopalakrishnan, G., Qadeer, S. (eds.) CAV 2011. LNCS, vol. 6806, pp. 184–190. Springer, Heidelberg (2011). https://doi.org/10.1007/978-3-642-22110-1_16
10. Chimdyalwar, B., Darke, P., Chavda, A., Vaghani, S., Chauhan, A.: Eliminating static analysis false positives using loop abstraction and bounded model checking. In: Bjørner, N., de Boer, F. (eds.) FM 2015. LNCS, vol. 9109, pp. 573–576. Springer, Cham (2015). https://doi.org/10.1007/978-3-319-19249-9_35
11. Darke, P., Agrawal, S., Venkatesh, R.: VeriAbs: a tool for scalable verification by abstraction (competition contribution). In: TACAS 2021. LNCS, vol. 12652, pp. 458–462. Springer, Cham (2021). https://doi.org/10.1007/978-3-030-72013-1_32
12. Darke, P., Chimdyalwar, B., Agrawal, S., Kumar, S., Venkatesh, R., Chakraborty, S.: VeriAbsL: scalable verification by abstraction and strategy prediction (competition contribution). In: Sankaranarayanan, S., Sharygina, N. (eds.) TACAS 2023. LNCS, vol. 13994, pp. 588–593. Springer, Cham (2023). https://doi.org/10.1007/978-3-031-30820-8_41
13. Darke, P., Chimdyalwar, B., Alladawar, M., Sulakhe, S., Venkatesh, R., Chakraborty, S.: Learning strategies using boolean program metrics to verify industrial code. In: IEEE International Conference on Software Maintenance and Evolution, ICSME 2024, Flagstaff, AZ, USA, 6–11 October 2024, pp. 719–729 (2024)
14. Darke, P., Chimdyalwar, B., Chauhan, A., Venkatesh, R.: Efficient safety proofs for industry-scale code using abstractions and bounded model checking. In: ICST 2017, pp. 468–475 (2017)
15. Darke, P., Chimdyalwar, B., Venkatesh, R., Chakraborty, S.: The VeriAbs tool suite for code verification. In: Akshay, S., Niemetz, A., Sankaranarayanan, S. (eds.) ATVA 2024. LNCS, vol. 15054, pp. 42–64. Springer, Cham (2025). https://doi.org/10.1007/978-3-031-78709-6_3
16. Darke, P., Chimdyalwar, B., Venkatesh, R., Shrotri, U., Metta, R.: Over-approximating loops to prove properties using bounded model checking. In: DATE, pp. 1407–1412 (2015)
17. Demyanova, Y., Pani, T., Veith, H., Zuleger, F.: Empirical software metrics for benchmarking of verification tools. In: Knoop, J., Zdun, U. (eds.) Software Engineering 2016, pp. 67–68. Gesellschaft für Informatik e.V, Bonn (2016)

18. Harman, M., Hierons, R.M.: An overview of program slicing. Softw. Focus **2**(3), 85–92 (2001)
19. Japkowicz, N.: The class imbalance problem: Significance and strategies. In: Proceedings of the 2000 International Conference on Artificial Intelligence ICAI (2000)
20. Japkowicz, N., Stephen, S.: The class imbalance problem: a systematic study. Intell. Data Anal. **6**(5), 429–449 (2002)
21. Johnson, J.M., Khoshgoftaar, T.M.: Survey on deep learning with class imbalance. J. Big Data **6**(1), 1–54 (2019). https://doi.org/10.1186/s40537-019-0192-5
22. Khare, S., Saraswat, S., Kumar, S.: Static program analysis of large embedded code base: an experience. In: ISEC, pp. 99–102 (2011)
23. Leeson, W., Dwyer, M.B.: Graves-CPA: a graph-attention verifier selector (competition contribution). In: TACAS 2022. LNCS, vol. 13244, pp. 440–445. Springer, Cham (2022). https://doi.org/10.1007/978-3-030-99527-0_28
24. Leeson, W., Dwyer, M.B.: Algorithm selection for software verification using graph neural networks. ACM Trans. Softw. Eng. Methodol. (2023)
25. Mooijman, P., Catal, C., Tekinerdogan, B., Lommen, A., Blokland, M.: The effects of data balancing approaches: a case study. Appl. Soft Comput. **132**, 109853 (2023)
26. Richter, C., Hüllermeier, E., Jakobs, M.-C., Wehrheim, H.: Algorithm selection for software validation based on graph kernels. Autom. Softw. Eng. (1), 153–186 (2020). https://doi.org/10.1007/s10515-020-00270-x
27. Richter, C., Wehrheim, H.: PeSCo: predicting sequential combinations of verifiers. In: Beyer, D., Huisman, M., Kordon, F., Steffen, B. (eds.) TACAS 2019. LNCS, vol. 11429, pp. 229–233. Springer, Cham (2019). https://doi.org/10.1007/978-3-030-17502-3_19
28. Richter, C., Wehrheim, H.: Attend and represent: a novel view on algorithm selection for software verification. In: ASE, pp. 1016–1028 (2020)
29. Tulsian, V., Kanade, A., Kumar, R., Lal, A., Nori, A.V.: MUX: algorithm selection for software model checkers. In: Devanbu, P.T., Kim, S., Pinzger, M. (eds.) 11th Working Conference on Mining Software Repositories, MSR 2014, Proceedings, 31 May–1 June 2014, Hyderabad, India, pp. 132–141. ACM (2014)

DeepMR: A Learning-Based Approach for Efficient Mutation Reduction in DNN Fault Localization

Huaizhi Yin[1], Weiwei Wang[2], and Ruilian Zhao[1](✉)

[1] Beijing University of Chemical Technology, Beijing 100029, China
{2023200833,rlzhao}@mail.buct.edu.cn
[2] Beijing Institute of Petrochemical Technology, Beijing 102617, China
wangweiwei@bipt.edu.cn

Abstract. As deep neural networks (DNNs) are increasingly deployed in critical domains, ensuring their reliability and security has become a key research focus. While mutation-based fault localization (MBFL) has shown superior effectiveness in DNN testing compared to conventional methods, its practical application faces significant computational challenges due to the enormous number of mutants it generates. To tackle this challenge, we propose DeepMR, a novel learning-based approach for mutation reduction in DNN models that maintains fault localization accuracy while dramatically decreasing computational costs. The core insight behind DeepMR is that strategically targeting key neurons—those critically influencing the decision paths of test cases—with high-impact mutation operators can yield a subset of mutants that substantially improve fault localization efficacy. DeepMR dynamically distinguishes effective mutants by jointly analyzing (1) runtime neuron behaviors during training and inference and (2) mutation operator characteristics, ensuring the selection of maximally informative mutants while discarding redundant ones. To validate the effectiveness of our approach, we trained DeepMR using data from 59 DNN programs and evaluated it on 31 DNN programs. Our experimental results show that when selecting 25% of the mutants at each layer, DeepMR can identify 90.0% of the most suspicious mutants in the neural network layers, representing a 47% improvement over random sampling. In terms of fault localization precision, selecting just 15% of mutants allows DeepMR to correctly identify all 14 bugs detected by the original MBFL without mutant reduction, while reducing the overall fault localization cost reduced by 72.3%.

Keywords: Deep Neural Network · Mutation-based Fault Localization · Mutation Reduction

1 Introduction

With the rapid advancements in deep learning, deep neural networks (DNNs) have achieved remarkable success in various fields, including natural language

Y. Zhou et al. (Eds.): ICECCS 2025, LNCS 15746, pp. 160–179, 2026.
https://doi.org/10.1007/978-3-032-00828-2_10

processing, autonomous driving, and medical diagnosis. However, despite their impressive performance, DNNs still face challenges in practical applications, particularly concerning safety and reliability. The complexity and black-box nature of DNN models make them susceptible to faults, which can lead to incorrect predictions and undesired system behavior. Thus, how to effectively locate these faults has become a key issue in ensuring DNN reliability and safety.

Since the behavior of a deep neural network (DNN) is determined by its complex architecture and learned parameters, fault localization in DNNs has primarily focused on identifying faults within the model's structure. In recent years, a new research trend has emerged that integrates traditional software fault localization techniques—namely, Spectrum-Based Fault Localization (SBFL) and Mutation-Based Fault Localization (MBFL)—into the DNN context [1,2]. These approaches have demonstrated superior fault localization accuracy compared to baseline methods. Unlike traditional software, where faults are typically localized at the statement level, these DNN-oriented techniques aim to identify the most suspicious neural network layers. The DNN adaptation of SBFL relies on the coverage information of neurons with respect to test cases, whereas the DNN adaptation of MBFL captures the relationship between neural network layers and failing test inputs through mutation analysis. Specifically, MBFL for DNNs introduces small change to individual program elements of each neural network layer, such as neurons, in order to generate mutants of the model. By evaluating these mutants against test cases, a suspiciousness value is calculated for each mutant. The highest suspiciousness value is then assigned to the corresponding neural network layer, indicating its likelihood of being faulty.

However, applying MBFL to DNNs poses a significant computational challenge. Given that a single neural network layer can contain a vast number of neurons, applying all mutation operators to each neuron becomes impractical and computationally prohibitive. Previous studies and commonly used suspiciousness formulas, such as those employed in Metallaxis [3], indicate that mutants which cause failing test cases to pass are particularly informative for fault localization. These effective mutants often correspond to a subset of neurons that play a crucial role in influencing the decision paths of test cases, especially when perturbed by well-chosen mutation operators.

To address this challenge, we propose a learning-based **M**utation **R**eduction approach in fault localization of **Deep** neural network, named DeepMR. The key insight behind DeepMR is that an effective mutant—one that meaningfully contributes to fault localization—is typically created by applying a suitable mutation operator to a critical neuron. We hypothesize that a neuron's behavior, as captured by its learning trajectory during training and activation patterns during inference, offers strong cues about its importance. When this behavioral information is combined with the characteristics of different mutation operators, it can be used to estimate the likely effectiveness of each mutant.

Identifying such critical neurons and their corresponding high-impact mutation operators is non-trivial, as there are no explicit rules or heuristics to guide the selection. To overcome this, DeepMR adopts a learning-based strategy. It collects runtime data during both the training and testing phases—such as neuron weights and activation values—and applies statistical techniques to extract meaningful features. These features, along with operator-specific attributes, are used to characterize each potential mutant. A ranking model is then trained to predict the fault-localization potential of each neuron–operator pair.

DeepMR subsequently generates a ranked list of these pairs. Based on a user-defined selection ratio (e.g., top 10%), the highest-ranked combinations are selected to generate a reduced set of mutants for downstream fault localization. To the best of our knowledge, this is the first approach to reduce the computational cost of MBFL in DNNs through learned prioritization. By leveraging model-wide information, neuron-level behaviors, and operator attributes, DeepMR enables developers to focus on the most promising mutants, significantly improving the scalability and efficiency of MBFL in deep neural network.

To evaluate DeepMR, we conduct our research on 90 buggy Keras DL programs from a recent benchmark [1], covering both regression and classification models across fully connected DNNs, CNNs, and RNNs. DeepMR extracts features from 59 DNN models across three different categories and learns from over 90,000 feature vectors during training. After the pretrained model is obtained, we then evaluate DeepMR on 31 DNN models. After generating a prioritized list of mutants using DeepMR, we compare its effectiveness against random sampling, a commonly used approach for mutant reduction in traditional programs, under the same mutant selection ratio.

Our experimental results show that when selecting 25% of the mutants per layer, DeepMR can identify 90.0% of the most suspicious mutants across neural network layers, representing a 47% improvement over random sampling. When the selection ratio increases to 35%, this proportion further rises to 95.0%. Additionally, DeepMR reduces the overall fault localization cost by 72.3% when selecting 15% of mutants, significantly outperforming existing MBFL approaches in terms of efficiency. Importantly, with this reduced subset, DeepMR successfully identifies all 14 bugs detected by the original MBFL without mutant reduction. These results demonstrate that DeepMR can substantially lower the computational overhead of fault localization while preserving fault localization precision comparable to that of the original MBFL method.

In general, the contributions of this paper are as follows:

1) A learning-based mutation reduction approach for DNN fault localization, DeepMR, is proposed, which leverages training dynamics and test execution data to identify critical neurons and their corresponding effective mutation operators, resulting in a subset of efficient mutants. DeepMR significantly alleviates the high computational overhead of mutation-based fault localization.
2) A mutation-based fault localization framework incorporating DeepMR for mutation reduction has been developed, supporting three types of DNN models. The source code is publicly available[1].

[1] https://github.com/YhzDetermined/DeepMR.

3) A study on 90 DL programs was conducted to develop and evaluate DeepMR. The experimental results demonstrate that selecting only 15% of the mutants enables DeepMR to accurately identify all 14 bugs detected by the original MBFL without mutation reduction, which is significantly better than random sampling, another mutation reduction approach.

The organization of this paper is as follows: Sect. 2 provides background on mutation-based fault localization and MBFL on DNNs. Section 3 presents an working example of MBFL on DNN. Section 4 introduces our proposed method. Section 5 details the experimental evaluation, and Sect. 6 concludes the paper.

2 Background

2.1 Mutation-Based Fault Localization Approach

Mutation-based fault localization (MBFL) uses mutation analysis [4] to find bugs in software. In this section, we review a classical approach of MBFL, namely Metallaxis [3]. Metallaxis is based on the premise that mutants affecting failing test cases likely indicate that the corresponding code elements are the root cause of the test failures, while mutants affecting passing test cases suggest that the corresponding code elements are correct. In mutation analysis, test cases that exhibit different behavior on a mutant compared to the original version are said to "kill" the mutant.

Let P denote the program under test and T represent its test cases. T can be divided into two subsets: T_f (the set of failing test cases) and T_p (the set of passing test cases). Once the number of passing and failing test cases impacted by a mutant is determined, Metallaxis uses a fault localization formula to compute suspiciousness values for each program element.

The process for calculating the suspiciousness value for a program element e is as follows: Suppose $M(e)$ is the set of mutants targeting program element e. For each mutant $m \in M(e)$, m is executed against all test cases, and the results are analyzed. The test cases can then be divided into two sets: T_n, the set of test cases that do not kill (i.e., detect) the mutant, and T_k, the set of test cases that kill the mutant. Furthermore, for each mutant m, four parameters are defined: a_{np}, a_{kp}, a_{nf}, and a_{kf}, as follows:

- a_{np} represents the number of passing test cases that did not kill m,
- a_{kp} represents the number of passing test cases that killed m,
- a_{nf} represents the number of failing test cases that did not kill m,
- a_{kf} represents the number of failing test cases that killed m.

These parameters are calculated as:

$$a_{np} = |T_n \cap T_p|, \quad a_{kp} = |T_k \cap T_p|, \quad a_{nf} = |T_n \cap T_f|, \quad a_{kf} = |T_k \cap T_f|$$

Next, the suspiciousness value of mutant m, denoted as $Sus(m)$, is calculated using popular suspiciousness formulas such as SBI [5] or Ochiai [6] (as shown in

Table 1). The suspiciousness value of program element e, denoted as $Sus(e)$, is defined as the maximum suspiciousness value among the mutants in M(e) [9], as follows:

$$Sus(e) = \max(Sus(m_1), Sus(m_2), \ldots, Sus(m_l)) \tag{1}$$

where $m_1, m_2, \ldots, m_l$ are all mutants in $M(e)$. The suspiciousness value $Sus(e)$ represents the likelihood that program element e is faulty.

Finally, based on the suspiciousness values $Sus(e)$, a rank list of elements is generated, ordered in descending suspiciousness value. The elements in the list are then manually examined to identify potential faults.

Table 1. Commonly used suspiciousness formula

Name	Formula
SBI [5]	$Sus(m) = \frac{a_{kf}}{a_{kf}+a_{kp}}$
Ochiai [6]	$Sus(m) = \frac{a_{kf}}{\sqrt{(a_{kf}+a_{nf})(a_{kf}+a_{kp})}}$
Tarantula [7]	$Sus(m) = \frac{\frac{a_{kf}}{a_{kf}+a_{nf}}}{\frac{a_{kf}}{a_{kf}+a_{nf}}+\frac{a_{kp}}{a_{kp}+a_{np}}}$
Op2 [8]	$Sus(m) = a_{kf} - \frac{a_{kp}}{a_{kp}+a_{np}+1}$

2.2 Mutation Based Fault Localization of Deep Neural Network

Unlike traditional programs whose behavior is determined by their underlying code, the behavior of a Deep Neural Network (DNN) is governed by its complex model structure and parameters. Correspondingly, DNN testing primarily focuses on evaluating the model itself rather than its source code.

It is worth noting that, unlike traditional programs that often use assertions to determine whether a test case passes, in the context of DNNs, the criteria differ based on the task type. For classification tasks, a test case is considered passed if the DNN's predicted class matches the expected class. For regression tasks, a test case is deemed passed if the absolute difference between the DNN's output and the expected output is below a certain threshold (commonly set to 0.001 in prior research).

In MBFL of DNNs, program elements of the DNN—such as neurons—are modified using mutation operators to generate mutants. These modifications can include altering neuron weights, bias values, or even replacing the activation function of an entire layer. Additionally, model-specific mutation operators can be applied to modify unique structures of different types of neural networks. Once the mutants are generated, they are executed on the test cases. If a test case produces different pass/fail results on a mutant compared to the original model, it is said to kill the mutant. Based on the kill results of the mutants across the test cases, the four parameters introduced in Sect. 2.1 (a_{np}, a_{kp}, a_{nf}, a_{kf}) can be calculated. Using these parameters and the suspiciousness formulas defined in Table 1, the suspiciousness value of each mutant can be calculated. The suspiciousness of a DNN layer is then defined as the maximum suspiciousness value among all its corresponding mutants, as given by Eq. (1).

3 A Working Example of MBFL on Deep Neural Network

In this section, a simple buggy DNN program—a sequential model for a binary classification task built using the Keras API (Listing 1.1)—is used to illustrate how MBFL performs fault localization in DNN programs.

The model initializes a Sequential architecture on line 1, adds a hidden dense layer with ReLU activation on line 2, and introduces an output layer—also using ReLU as the activation function—on line 3. It is then compiled (line 4) with the `sparse_categorical_crossentropy` loss function and trained (line 5). The key issue lies in the output layer, where the activation function is incorrectly set to ReLU (line 3). ReLU is not suitable for classification tasks, as it does not normalize the output into a probability distribution. For multi-class or binary classification tasks, the output layer should typically use the *softmax* activation function to convert raw output scores into probabilities that sum to 1. Without this normalization, the model fails to produce meaningful class probabilities, leading to suboptimal training and poor predictive performance.

The network structure depicted in Fig. 1 further illustrates this issue. The input layer receives two numerical features (denoted as a and b), which are then passed to the first hidden layer, L1. This layer consists of two neurons (N1 and N2), each applying a ReLU activation function (denoted as A1). The output layer, L2, follows a similar structure with neurons (N3 and N4), again utilizing ReLU activation (denoted as A2). Weights (w_1, w_2, w_3, w_4) and biases (b_1, b_2, b_3, b_4) are applied at each connection to adjust the flow of information through the network. But the final ReLU activation in L2 renders the model incapable of producing valid classification probabilities.

```
1 model = Sequential()
2 model.add(Dense(2, input_dim=2, activation='relu'))
3 model.add(Dense(2, activation='relu'))
4 model.compile(loss='sparse_categorical_crossentropy',
5               optimizer='adam', metrics=['accuracy'])
6 model.fit(X_train, y_train, epochs=50)
```

Listing 1.1. A simple buggy DNN code

Figure 2 demonstrates how MBFL is used for fault localization in this DNN model. The first column lists the two layers of the network. For each layer, three types of mutation operators are applied: (1) halving a neuron's weight values, performed on 4 neurons, resulting in 4 mutants (M1, M3, M6, M8); (2) halving a neuron's bias values, generating 4 mutants (M2, M4, M7, M9); and (3) replacing the ReLU activation function with *Softmax*, producing 2 mutants (M5, M10).

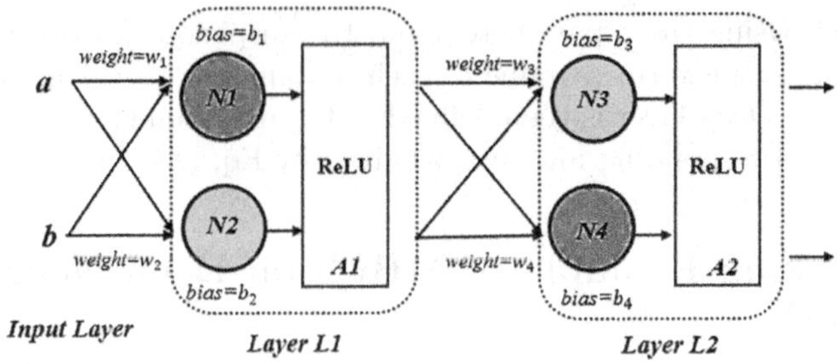

Fig. 1. Model structure built for example code in Listing 1.1.

Suppose this DNN model has 6 test cases (T1, T2, ..., T6), as shown in the table, where correctly classified cases are highlighted in green and misclassified ones in red. For each of the generated mutants (M1–M10), MBFL evaluates them by executing each test case on each mutant and comparing the results with those of the original model. If a mutant produces a different outcome from the original model, a dot (•) is placed in the corresponding cell.

Next, the suspiciousness value Sus(m) for each mutant is computed by using suspiciousness formula in Table 1, such as the Ochiai formula, with the results shown in the last column. The suspiciousness value for each layer is determined as the maximum value among its corresponding mutants (see Eq. (1)). In this example, L1 has a suspiciousness value of 0.35, whereas L2 has a higher value of 0.87, strongly suggesting that the ReLU activation in L2 is the primary fault source.

Furthermore, it can be observed that not only certain neurons but also their associated mutation operators play a critical role in generating effective mutants for fault localization. For example, using the same mutation operator, mutants derived from neurons N1 and N4 (highlighted in Fig. 1) exhibit higher suspiciousness values than those from neurons N2 and N3 within the same layer. Additionally, applying different mutation operators to the same neuron can yield mutants with varying suspiciousness values. As shown in Fig. 2, applying the halving the weights operator to neurons N3 and N4 results in suspiciousness values of 0.57 and 0.71, respectively—both of which are greater than or equal to those produced by the halving the biases operator, which yields scores of 0.35 for both neurons. Consequently, it is crucial to select the most effective neuron–operator pairs when generating mutants, as this targeted subset makes a more substantial contribution to fault localization.

Layer	Mutants		Testcase						SUS
			T1	T2	T3	T4	T5	T6	
L1	N1	M1: weight/2		•		•			0.35
		M2: bias/2		•					0
	N2	M3: weight/2		•					0
		M4: bias/2		•					0
	A1	M5: relu->softmax	•	•					0
L2	N3	M6: weight/2		•		•		•	0.57
		M7: bias/2		•		•			0.35
	N4	M8: weight/2				•		•	0.71
		M9: bias/2		•		•			0.35
	A2	M10: relu->softmax				•	•	•	0.87

Fig. 2. The fault localization process of example code in Listing 1.1. (Color figure online)

4 Approach

4.1 Overview

Based on the analytical discussion in Sect. 3, it can be concluded that applying more effective mutation operators to critical neurons can generate mutants that contribute more significantly to fault localization. This is reflected in these mutants achieving higher suspiciousness values during fault localization calculations. To identify these impactful mutants, we propose DeepMR, a learning-based mutation reduction method for DNN fault localization.

Figure 3 illustrates the overall framework of DeepMR. To capture the intrinsic characteristics of the model, the Monitor observes the model training process at regular intervals, collecting runtime data such as weights, gradients, and activation values. Additionally, Monitor tracks the inference process during testing to capture neuron activation patterns. It then performs multi-granularity statistical analyses on these large volumes of high-dimensional data (e.g., computing the mean of weights to understand overall trends), thereby extracting both model-level and neuron-level features.

To capture the characteristics of mutation operators and support the subsequent prioritization of neuron-operator pairs, the Extractor analyzes all potential combinations of neurons and their matched mutation operators. By calculating changes in neuron weights and biases before and after applying a mutation operator, it captures behavioral differences of neurons. Similar to Monitor, Extractor performs statistical analysis on the high-dimensional data to derive mutation-level features.

Next, DeepMR concatenates the model-level features, neuron-level features, and mutation-level features extracted in the previous steps to form a final feature vector, which serves as input to the Ranking Model. The Ranking Model intelligently analyzes the extracted features to assign a score to each neuron-operator pair, thereby evaluating the potential effectiveness of the corresponding mutant.

Ultimately, DeepMR produces a ranked list of neuron-mutation operator pairs. Programmers can then select a proportion of the top-ranked pairs—according to their available runtime resources—to generate mutants, which are later used for fault localization.

The following subsections provide detailed descriptions of each component in DeepMR. Section 4.2 introduces how the Monitor module tracks the model's training and inference processes, as well as its feature extraction strategy. Section 4.3 explains how the Extractor derives mutation-level features. Section 4.4 describes how the extracted features are concatenated to form the final input to the model. Finally, Sect. 4.5 presents the construction of the ranking model used to prioritize neuron–mutation operator pairs.

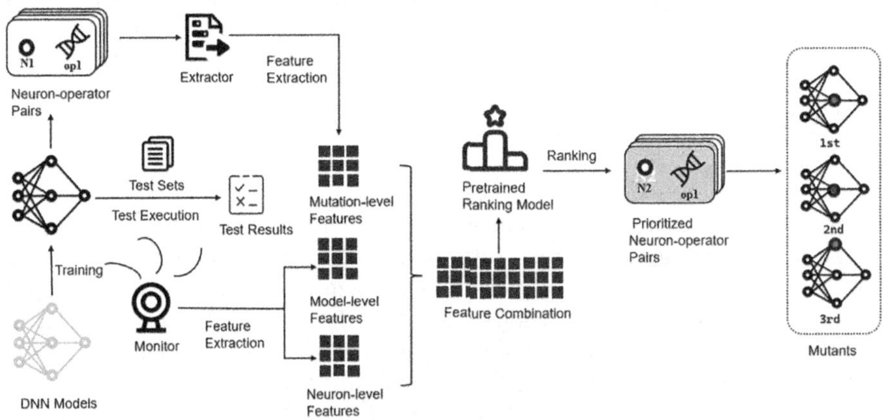

Fig. 3. The overview framework of DeepMR.

4.2 Monitor

The Monitor tracks both the model training process and the test execution, and extracts model-level and neuron-level features from the collected data.

Monitor the Model's Training Process. From our perspective, the learning trajectories of neurons provide crucial insights for identifying those neurons that significantly influence the decision paths of test cases.

During training, a DNN undergoes numerous iterations of forward and backward propagation. In each iteration, backpropagation computes gradients based on the loss from the forward pass and updates the internal weights using gradient descent to minimize the error.

As collecting detailed data at every training iteration is computationally expensive, the Monitor records neuron runtime data at fixed intervals throughout the training process. To effectively capture neuron learning dynamics, the Monitor gathers information from both the forward and backward passes at each selected iteration.

During the forward pass, the Monitor records the activation values of each neuron. Specifically, for the t-th data collection point, the activation vector of a neuron is represented as:

$$A^{(t)} = (a_1^{(t)}, a_2^{(t)}, \ldots, a_m^{(t)}),$$

where m denotes the number of training samples.

During the backward pass, the Monitor records the following information for each neuron:

(1) The weight vector and bias at the t-th collection:

$$W^{(t)} = (w_1^{(t)}, w_2^{(t)}, \ldots, w_n^{(t)}), \quad b^{(t)},$$

where n is the number of connections from the previous layer.

(2) The gradient of the weights and bias with respect to the loss at the t-th collection:

$$\nabla_w L^{(t)} = \left(\frac{\partial L^{(t)}}{\partial w_1^{(t)}}, \frac{\partial L^{(t)}}{\partial w_2^{(t)}}, \ldots, \frac{\partial L^{(t)}}{\partial w_n^{(t)}} \right), \quad \nabla_b L^{(t)}.$$

To further capture temporal learning dynamics, the Monitor also computes the change in activation values, weights, and gradients between two consecutive time points:

$$\Delta A^{(t)} = A^{(t)} - A^{(t-1)}, \quad \Delta W^{(t)} = W^{(t)} - W^{(t-1)}, \quad \Delta \nabla_w L^{(t)} = \nabla_w L^{(t)} - \nabla_w L^{(t-1)}.$$

Subsequently, DeepMR applies statistical operations (e.g., maximum, mean) listed in Table 2 to the high-dimensional vectors $A^{(t)}$, $W^{(t)}$, $\nabla_w L^{(t)}$, $\Delta A^{(t)}$, $\Delta W^{(t)}$, and $\Delta \nabla_w L^{(t)}$ to extract useful features for learning. This process results in 48 variables per iteration, representing the condensed characteristics of these vectors.

Since these variables are repeatedly collected over many training iterations, DeepMR ultimately obtains 48 data sequences after training, each representing the learning trajectory of a variable throughout the training process, DeepMR ultimately produces 48 time series, each representing the trajectory of a specific variable throughout training. It then applies the nine statistical operators listed in Table 3 to each of these data sequences, resulting in $9 \times 48 = 432$ neuron-level features.

In addition to neuron-level features, DeepMR also captures 160 model-level features that characterize the overall behavior of the model during training. The extraction methods for these features are inspired by prior work [10], where they have been successfully used for diagnosing fault types in DNNs with high accuracy. These model-level features are derived from runtime data such as training loss, accuracy, the number of times the loss increases, and other performance indicators. By incorporating these global features, DeepMR is able to more effectively model and understand the overall training dynamics of the network.

Table 2. Statistical operations for feature extraction from vectors and their formulas

Statistical Operations	Formula
max(V)	$\max\{v_1, v_2, \ldots, v_n\}$
min(V)	$\min\{v_1, v_2, \ldots, v_n\}$
mean(V)	$\frac{1}{n}\sum_{i=1}^{n} v_i$
median(V)	$\begin{cases} v_{(\frac{n+1}{2})}, & \text{if } n \text{ is odd} \\ \frac{v_{(\frac{n}{2})} + v_{(\frac{n}{2}+1)}}{2}, & \text{if } n \text{ is even} \end{cases}$
max(abs(V))	$\max\{\lvert v_1\rvert, \lvert v_2\rvert, \ldots, \lvert v_n\rvert\}$
max(mean(V))	$\frac{1}{n}\sum_{i=1}^{n} \lvert v_i\rvert$
mean square(V)	$\frac{1}{n}\sum_{i=1}^{n} v_i^2$
std(V)	$\sqrt{\frac{1}{n}\sum_{i=1}^{n}(v_i - \text{Mean}(V))^2}$
var(V)	$\frac{1}{n}\sum_{i=1}^{n}(v_i - \text{Mean}(V))^2$
zero(V)	$\frac{1}{n}\sum_{i=1}^{n} \mathbf{1}(v_i = 0)$
nan(V)	$\frac{1}{n}\sum_{i=1}^{n} \mathbf{1}(\text{isnan}(v_i))$

Monitor the Model's Test Execution Process. According to our hypothesis, neurons that influence the decision paths of test cases tend to exhibit higher sensitivity to those cases. This sensitivity is reflected in their activation patterns, which significantly affect the network's output. Therefore, DeepMR monitors the model's inference process during test execution. Specifically, it records the activation values of neurons when processing test samples, as these values provide insight into the decision paths taken by the neural network.

Table 3. Statistical Operators for Variables Aggregation

Operators	Description
max	The maximum value in a feature trace
min	The minimum value in a feature trace
mean	The mean value of a feature trace
median	The median value of a feature trace
var	The variance of a feature trace
std	The standard error of a feature trace
skew	The skewness of a feature trace
sem	The standard error of mean of a feature trace
last	The last value in a feature trace

Rather than directly using the raw activation vectors, DeepMR extracts 8 statistical neuron level features from each vector using selected statistical operations listed in Table 2. These features provide a more compact and informative representation of the neuron's behavior during inference.

In addition to neuron-level features, DeepMR also incorporates global test-level features, such as the number of passing and failing test cases, as model-level features. These values are directly utilized by specific suspiciousness formulas and are closely related to the evaluation of mutant effectiveness.

4.3 Extractor

The Extractor analyzes all neuron–mutation operator pairs to capture the characteristics exhibited by neurons after mutation operators are applied. These operators modify the neurons by altering their weights and bias values to varying degrees. Accordingly, DeepMR compares the weight vectors before and after mutation, denoted as W and W', and computes the weight difference $\Delta W = W' - W$ Similarly, it captures the bias values before and after mutation, b and b', as well as the bias change $\Delta b = b' - b$.

Since neurons in different layers of a neural network have weight vectors of varying dimensions, the raw weight vectors cannot be directly used as features for learning. Therefore, a set of statistical operations, as listed in Table 2, is applied to both W' and ΔW to extract representative features. In total, 13 mutation-level features are derived, providing a crucial basis for the selection of effective neuron–mutation operator pairs.

4.4 Feature Concatenation

Based on the aforementioned steps, DeepMR generates three types of feature vectors for each potential mutant: a model-level feature vector, a neuron-level feature vector, and a mutation-level feature vector. These vectors are then concatenated to form a comprehensive feature representation, which serves as the input to the ranking model.

4.5 Ranking Model

Once all feature vectors for neuron–mutation operator pairs are obtained, DeepMR trains a ranking model to estimate the potential contribution of each mutant to fault localization. In this section, we describe the process of constructing the ranking model and explain how it is used to prioritize neuron–mutation operator pairs based on their predicted effectiveness.

Ranking Model Building. DeepMR leverages the XGBoost ranking algorithm [11], an optimized distributed gradient boosting learning algorithm, to construct the ranking model.

XGBoost (Extreme Gradient Boosting) is a highly efficient machine learning algorithm based on the gradient boosting framework. It works by iteratively fitting decision trees to the residuals (errors) of the model's previous predictions, progressively improving the model's accuracy. In this process, a series of weak models are built to correct the mistakes made by earlier models, ultimately combining them into a robust and predictive model.

One of the main advantages of XGBoost is its high performance, especially in large datasets. DeepMR trained an XGBoost model using over 90,000 feature vectors representing mutants generated from 59 models as training data. The corresponding suspiciousness values were used as labels, obtained through fault localization. The pretrained model is generalizable and capable of prioritizing neuron–mutation operator pairs across various neural network architectures, including DNNs, CNNs, and LSTMs. By leveraging the resulting ranking, DeepMR selectively generates a subset of more effective mutants.

Neuron-Operator Pairs Prioritization via Ranking Model. It is worth noting that the ranking model used in DeepMR functions as a regression model, assigning a numerical score to each neuron–mutation operator pair to estimate the effectiveness of the corresponding mutant. These pairs are then sorted in descending order based on their scores, thereby achieving prioritized selection.

5 Evaluation

To evaluate the performance and efficiency of DeepMR, we compared it with another mutation reduction method, random sampling, in terms of fault localization efficiency and its impact on fault localization precision.

- **RQ1:** How does the accuracy of suspiciousness values across network layers in fault localization compare when mutants are reduced using DeepMR versus random sampling?

- **RQ2:** How does the time overhead of DeepMR compare to the original MBFL?
- **RQ3:** How do DeepMR and random sampling in mutation reduction impact the precision of fault localization?

5.1 Experimental Setup

Benchmark. We conducted our study on 90 buggy Keras [12] deep learning program from a recent benchmark [1], which includes regression and classification models across fully connected DNNs, CNNs, and RNNs. These programs were originally collected from StackOverflow by previous research and are implemented using Keras' Sequential API. For training, we utilized 59 of these DL programs, generating over 90,000 feature vectors. The remaining 31 programs were used to evaluate the effectiveness of mutation prioritization. We employed the Ochiai [6] formula for calculating suspiciousness value of mutants.

Environment. All experiment are implemented on a machine with Intel i9-14900HX at 2.20 GHz 32 GB RAM.

5.2 Metrics

To evaluate the effectiveness of mutation reduction, we define a new metric called **TSP** (**T**op **S**uspect **P**ercentage). TSP measures the proportion of neural network layers in which the top suspiciousness value remains unchanged when only a subset of the corresponding mutants is selected. In other words, it quantifies the likelihood of correctly identifying, per layer, the mutant with the highest suspiciousness value using a reduced mutant set. The TSP value ranges from 0 to 1, with a higher value indicating that more layers preserve the top suspiciousness value from the original MBFL, thus implying minimal degradation in fault localization accuracy. A TSP value of 1 signifies that the evaluated method successfully identifies the most suspicious mutant in every layer, achieving performance equivalent to that of the original MBFL.

We also use two additional metrics, **S-RMSE** (**S**uspect - **R**oot **M**ean **S**quare **E**rror) and **S-MAE** (**S**uspect - **M**ean **A**bsolute **E**rror), to measure the impact of missing the mutant with the highest suspiciousness value in the selected subset. Suppose the layers of the target neural network models are labeled $L_1, L_2, \ldots, L_n$. For layer L_i, let its set of corresponding mutants be M_i. Among these mutants, m_i ($m_i \in M_i$) is the mutant with the highest suspiciousness value, denoted $\text{sus}(m_i)$. According to Eq. (1), the suspiciousness value of L_i is assigned as $\text{sus}(L_i) = \text{sus}(m_i)$. Let M_i' be the subset of selected mutants for layer L_i, and let m_i' be the mutant with the highest suspiciousness value in M_i', denoted $\text{sus}(m_i')$. The metrics are calculated as follows:

$$\text{TSP} = \frac{\sum_{i=1}^{n} 1\left[\text{sus}(L_i) = \text{sus}(m_i')\right]}{n} \times 100\% \tag{2}$$

$$\text{S-RMSE} = \sqrt{\frac{1}{n}\sum_{i=1}^{n}\left(\text{sus}(L_i) - \text{sus}(m_i')\right)^2} \tag{3}$$

$$\text{S-MAE} = \frac{1}{n}\sum_{i=1}^{n}\left|\text{sus}(L_i) - \text{sus}(m_i')\right| \tag{4}$$

In these formulas, a lower S-RMSE or S-MAE indicates that the suspiciousness value calculated by the selected mutant is closer to that of the original MBFL, thus reflecting less loss in fault localization precision.

5.3 Experimental Analysis

RQ1: How does the accuracy of suspiciousness values across network layers in fault localization compare when mutants are reduced using DeepMR versus random sampling? To answer RQ1, we conducted our study on 60 dense layers from 31 deep learning programs. Some layers contain fewer than 10 neurons, or even just a single neuron, resulting in only a small number of corresponding mutants. For these layers, even without mutation reduction, the overhead of the overall process to obtain their suspiciousness value remains minimal. Therefore, these dense layers were excluded from our approach evaluation. We compared three key metrics TSP, S-RMSE, and S-MAE when applying DeepMR versus randomly sampling with different mutant ratios. Among the 60 dense layers, 29 had a suspiciousness value of 0, indicating that all corresponding mutants also had a suspiciousness value of 0. In these cases, selecting any mutant would yield the one with the highest suspiciousness value. However, faults are almost never found in layers with a suspiciousness value of 0. As such, we focus more on the selecting the corresponding mutants for the layers with none-zero suspiciousness value. Thus, we separately analyzed the impact of the two mutation reduction approaches on the remaining 31 neural network layers. To ensure the accuracy of the experimental results, we conducted 1,000 random sampling iterations for the random sampling approach and used the average values of each metric as the final results.

Figure 4 compares the performance of DeepMR and random sampling in terms of the TSP metric. As shown in Fig. 4, regardless of the mutant selection ratio, the blue line representing DeepMR consistently remains above the red line representing random sampling. As the mutant selection ratio increases, the TSP value of random sampling exhibits linear growth, while DeepMR experiences a rapid increase until reaching 90%, after which it converges and ultimately reaches 100%. The key differences between the right plot and left plot is that the right plot presents the TSP results for the two approaches after removing the 31 dense layers with a suspiciousness value of 0, providing a more refined comparison.

From the left plot, it can be observed that when selecting 25% of the mutants, DeepMR successfully identifies mutants with the highest suspiciousness value in 90.0% of dense layers, whereas random sampling achieves only 68.6%. The gap between the two approaches becomes even more pronounced after removing layers with a suspiciousness value of 0. In this case, when selecting 25% of the mutants, DeepMR identifies 80.6% of mutants with the highest suspiciousness value in dense layers, more than twice the proportion achieved by random sampling (38.9%). As the mutant selection ratio further increases to 35%, DeepMR's

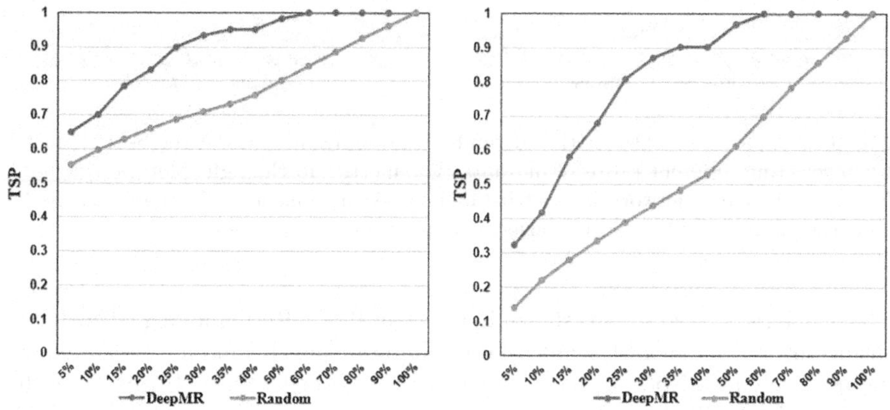

Fig. 4. Comparison of DeepMR and random sampling in terms of the TSP metric when selecting different ratios of mutants. The metrics in the right plot are calculated from the 31 neural network layers with non-zero suspiciousness. Compared to the left plot, the 29 layers with a suspiciousness value of 0 have been removed.

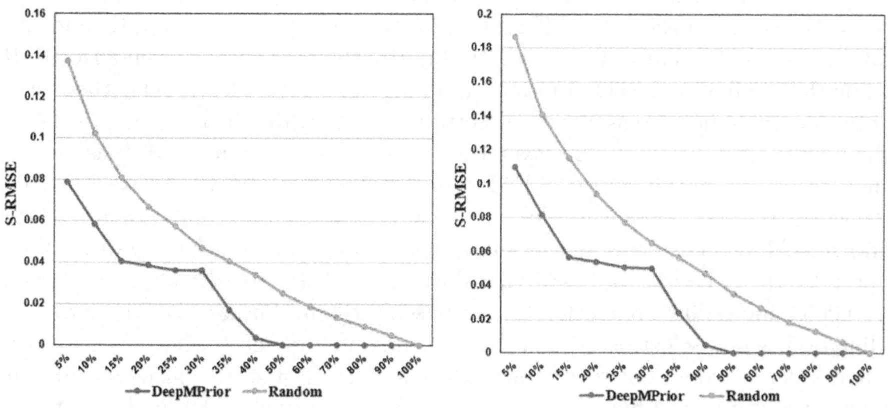

Fig. 5. Comparison of DeepMR and random sampling in terms of the S-RMSE metric when selecting different ratios of mutants. The metrics in the right plot are calculated from the 31 neural network layers with non-zero suspiciousness. Compared to the left plot, the 29 layers with a suspiciousness value of 0 have been removed.

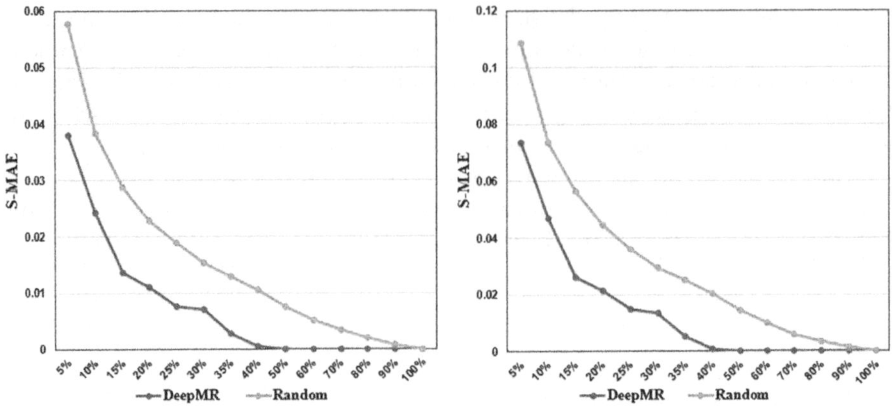

Fig. 6. Comparison of DeepMR and random sampling in terms of the S-MAE metric when selecting different ratios of mutants. The metrics in the right plot are calculated from the 31 neural network layers with non-zero suspiciousness. Compared to the left plot, the 29 layers with a suspiciousness value of 0 have been removed.

TSP value rises to 90.3% (as shown in the right plot, after removing layers with a suspiciousness value of 0), while random sampling lags behind at 48.4%, remaining relatively low. Notably, when selecting 60% of the mutants, DeepMR reaches a TSP value of 100%, meaning it successfully identifies the mutants with the highest suspiciousness value in all layers. In contrast, even when selecting 90% of the mutants, random sampling only achieves a TSP value of 92.8%, failing to guarantee the identification of the mutant with the highest suspiciousness value in each layer.

Figure 5 and Fig. 6 present the evaluation results of S-RMSE and S-MAE, respectively, when selecting different ratios of mutants using DeepMR and random sampling. Similar to Fig. 4, in both figures, the blue line represents DeepMR, while the red line represents random sampling. The left plot evaluates the results of both approaches across 60 neural network layers, while the right plot evaluates the results after removing 29 layer with suspiciousness value of 0. It is evident that, regardless of the metric (S-RMSE or S-MAE), the blue line consistently lies below the red line, indicating that DeepMR consistently achieves lower S-RMSE and S-MAE values compared to random sampling. When selecting 40% of the mutants, the S-RMSE and S-MAE values of DeepMR are already very close to 0 (0.0034 and 0.0005, respectively), surpassing the performance of random sampling even when selecting 90% of the mutants. This suggests that, even in cases where DeepMR does not select the mutant with highest suspiciousness value, the selected mutants still have a suspiciousness value very close to the highest.

Overall, when selecting 15% of the mutants (DeepMR-15%), our approach already achieves performance close to the original MBFL, with a 78.3% probability of selecting the highest-suspiciousness mutant. At this selection ratio, the S-RMSE is 0.0407 and the S-MAE is 0.0135, indicating that the suspiciousness values computed by DeepMR-15% are highly similar to the actual suspiciousness values of the neural network layers. Furthermore, when selecting 35% of the mutants (DeepMR-35%), DeepMR achieves performance nearly equivalent to the original MBFL, with a 95% probability of selecting mutant with the highest suspiciousness value. At this selection ratio, the S-RMSE is 0.0170 and the S-MAE is 0.0027, both of which are less than half of the corresponding values obtained using random sampling.

RQ2: How does the time cost of applying DeepMR compare to that of the original MBFL? To answer RQ2, we measured the average time overhead of DeepMR with different configurations, as well as the original MBFL, across 31 faulty neural network models. Specifically, the configurations of DeepMR include selecting 15% (DeepMR-15%), 20% (DeepMR-20%), 25% (DeepMR-25%), 30% (DeepMR-30%), and 35% (DeepMR-35%) of the mutants.

We recorded the average time overhead for each configuration at different stages of fault localization, including the model training phase, mutant generation phase, and mutant execution phase, across all 31 neural network models. The detailed time overhead statistics are presented in Table 4.

As shown in Table 4, adopting DeepMR slightly increases the training time, as it monitors model variables during each iteration and computes feature values using statistical operators. This results in an average increase of 27.3 s in the training phase. However, this additional time is negligible compared to the time required for mutation generation and execution. More importantly, DeepMR significantly reduces both mutation generation and execution time, greatly lowering the overall cost of fault localization. Table 4 illustrate that DeepMR-15% reduces the overall time cost by 72.3% compared to the original MBFL, while DeepMR-35% achieves a 56.0% reduction. This demonstrates that DeepMR provides a substantial improvement in efficiency while maintaining accuracy in mutation prioritization.

Table 4. The time cost of applying DeepMR with different implements compare to original MBFL

Time (s)	origin	15%	20%	25%	30%	35%
Training	113.29	140.32	140.32	140.32	140.32	140.32
Mutation Generation	1345.37	229.79	292.43	352.97	418.48	488.86
Mutation Execution	2558.28	753.86	845.27	935.66	1027.02	1154.13
Total	4051.88	1123.97	1278.02	1428.95	1585.82	1783.31

RQ3: How do DeepMR and random sampling in mutation reduction impact the precision of fault localization? To address RQ3, we compared the fault localization accuracy of DeepMR and random sampling across 31 neural

network models. The original MBFL approach successfully localized 14 faults, as shown in Table 5. Notably, DeepMR-15% achieved the same accuracy as the original MBFL, correctly identifying all 14 faults.

In contrast, Random-15% failed to localize two faults, demonstrating a loss in precision. Even when the random sampling ratio increased to 25%, one fault remained incorrectly localized. This indicates that DeepMR incurs less precision loss in fault localization compared to random sampling, making it a more effective approach for prioritizing mutants.

Table 5. Comparison of Fault Localization Accuracy Between DeepMR and random sampling

selected mutants	Random	DeepMR
15%	12	14
25%	13	14

6 Conclusion

To address the excessive time cost of the original MBFL, we proposed DeepMR, a mutation reduction method. DeepMR monitors the training and testing execution processes, extracting model-level, neuron-level, and mutation-level features. By leveraging a learning-based approach, it constructs a model capable of prioritizing mutants. Our results demonstrate that DeepMR significantly reduces time costs while maintaining fault localization accuracy, making it an effective and efficient alternative to traditional MBFL methods.

Acknowledgments. The work described in this paper is supported by the National Natural Science Foundation of China (Grant nos. 61902015).

References

1. Ghanbari, A., Thomas, D.-G., Arshad, M.A., Rajan, H.: Mutation-based fault localization of deep neural networks. In: 2023 38th IEEE/ACM International Conference on Automated Software Engineering (ASE), Luxembourg, Luxembourg, pp. 1301–1313. IEEE (2023). https://doi.org/10.1109/ASE56229.2023.00171
2. Xu, W., Li, Y., Ma, M., Chen, L., Zhou, Y.: Weighted suspiciousness and balanced aggregation to boost spectrum-based fault localization of deep learning models. ACM Trans. Softw. Eng. Methodol. 3716849 (2025). https://doi.org/10.1145/3716849
3. Papadakis, M., Traon, Y.: Metallaxis-FL: mutation-based fault localization. Softw. Test. Verif. Reliab. **25**, 605–628 (2015). https://doi.org/10.1002/stvr.1509
4. DeMillo, R.A., Lipton, R.J., Sayward, F.G.: Hints on test data selection: help for the practicing programmer. Computer **11**, 34–41 (1978). https://doi.org/10.1109/C-M.1978.218136

5. Liblit, B., Naik, M., Zheng, A.X., Aiken, A., Jordan, M.I.: Scalable statistical bug isolation. SIGPLAN Not. **40**, 15–26 (2005). https://doi.org/10.1145/1064978.1065014
6. Abreu, R., Zoeteweij, P., Van Gemund, A.J.: An evaluation of similarity coefficients for software fault localization. In: 2006 12th Pacific Rim International Symposium on Dependable Computing (PRDC 2006), pp. 39–46 (2006). https://doi.org/10.1109/PRDC.2006.18
7. Jones, J.A., Harrold, M.J.: Empirical evaluation of the tarantula automatic fault-localization technique. In: Proceedings of the 20th IEEE/ACM International Conference on Automated Software Engineering, Long Beach, CA, USA. ACM (2005). https://doi.org/10.1145/1101908.1101949
8. Naish, L., Lee, H.J., Ramamohanarao, K.: A model for spectra-based software diagnosis. ACM Trans. Softw. Eng. Methodol. **20**, 1–32 (2011). https://doi.org/10.1145/2000791.2000795
9. Gong, P., Zhao, R., Li, Z.: Faster mutation-based fault localization with a novel mutation execution strategy. In: 2015 IEEE Eighth International Conference on Software Testing, Verification and Validation Workshops (ICSTW), pp. 1–10 (2015). https://doi.org/10.1109/ICSTW.2015.7107448
10. Cao, J., et al.: DeepFD: automated fault diagnosis and localization for deep learning programs. In: Proceedings of the 44th International Conference on Software Engineering, Pittsburgh, Pennsylvania, pp. 573–585. ACM (2022). https://doi.org/10.1145/3510003.3510099
11. Chen, T., Guestrin, C.: XGBoost: a scalable tree boosting system. In: 22nd ACM SIGKDD International Conference on Knowledge Discovery and Data Mining (KDD), pp. 785–794. ACM (2016)
12. Chollet, F., et al.: Keras (2015). https://keras.io
13. Wardat, M., Le, W., Rajan, H.: DeepLocalize: fault localization for deep neural networks. In: 2021 IEEE/ACM 43rd International Conference on Software Engineering (ICSE), pp. 251–262 (2021). https://doi.org/10.1109/ICSE43902.2021.00034
14. Shen, J., Li, Z., Pan, M., Li, X.: Prioritizing test inputs for DNNs using training dynamics. In: Proceedings of the 39th IEEE/ACM International Conference on Automated Software Engineering, Sacramento, CA, USA, pp. 1219–1231. ACM (2024). https://doi.org/10.1145/3691620.3695498
15. Liu, Y., Li, Z., Wang, L., Hu, Z., Zhao, R.: Statement-oriented mutant reduction strategy for mutation based fault localization. In: 2017 IEEE International Conference on Software Quality, Reliability and Security (QRS), pp. 126–137 (2017). https://doi.org/10.1109/QRS.2017.23
16. Dang, X., Li, Y., Papadakis, M., Klein, J., Bissyandé, T.F., Traon, Y.L.: Test input prioritization for machine learning classifiers. IEEE Trans. Software Eng. **50**, 413–442 (2024). https://doi.org/10.1109/TSE.2024.3350019
17. Papadakis, M., Le Traon, Y.: Using mutants to locate "unknown" faults. In: Verification and Validation 2012 IEEE Fifth International Conference on Software Testing, pp. 691–700 (2012). https://doi.org/10.1109/ICST.2012.159

Investigating the OOV Problem and Its Impacts on Neural Program Repair

Weijun Guo, Xuedan Zheng, and Mingyue Jiang(✉)

School of Computer Science and Technology, Zhejiang Sci-Tech University, Hangzhou, Zhejiang, China
{202230603060,202230603145}@mails.zstu.edu.cn, mjiang@zstu.edu.cn

Abstract. Neural Program Repair (NPR) has emerged as a promising approach to automatically fix bugs in software programs. By leveraging large datasets of buggy and patched code, NPR models learn patterns and transformations to generate patches. Nevertheless, one fundamental challenge in NPR is the Out-of-Vocabulary (OOV) problem, which occurs when the model encounters tokens that were not seen during training. Due to the diversity and variability of code, the OOV problem is particularly prevalent in the context of NPR, and it may affect the model's ability to generalize and repair unseen or uncommon code. To comprehensively understand the characteristics of OOV problem and its impacts on NPR, this study conduct an empirical study on three NPR models and two datasets. Our results reveal that the OOV rate decreases with the increasing of the vocabulary of the NPR model, and that the most common types of OOV words in NPR are variable name and parameter name. The results also confirm the negative impact of OOV words on the repair effectiveness of NPR models. Our findings highlight the importance of addressing the OOV problem to enhance the effectiveness and real-world utility of NPR models.

Keywords: Neural program repair · OOV problem · Repair effectiveness · Vocabulary size

1 Introduction

Neural program repair (NPR) [1], which leverages deep learning models to automatically generate patches for fixing buggy programs, is an emerging technique in the field of software engineering. Unlike traditional program repair methods, which are often heuristic-based, constraint-based or pattern-based [2], NPR utilizes large-scale data-driven models to learn patterns in code, as well as to learn potential relationships between buggy programs and their corresponding patches. NPR has shown promising repair effectiveness and offers the potential for scalable and automated bug fixing that can help developers improve software quality while reducing the time and effort spent on manual debugging [3].

Y. Zhou et al. (Eds.): ICECCS 2025, LNCS 15746, pp. 180–197, 2026.
https://doi.org/10.1007/978-3-032-00828-2_11

Generally, NPR treats the task of program repair as a neural machine translation (NMT) task. NPR models, which are typically built upon the *encoder-decoder* architecture, are trained on large datasets of code snippets and bug-fix pairs, with the goal of generating patches for a wide range of buggy programs. More specifically, the encoder processes the input sequence (e.g., a buggy program) and converts it into a latent representation, while the decoder generates an output sequence (e.g., a patch) based on this representation. It is worth noting that vocabulary plays a critical role in these models, since it defines the set of tokens the model can understand and generate.

However, NPR models are commonly equipped with a fixed-sized vocabulary that contains a set of words or tokens from the training dataset. That is, during the model training phrase, the vocabulary is constructed based on the most frequent words in the training dataset, while less frequent words are excluded with the consideration of reducing computational complexity and memory usage [3]. This, thus, leads to the issue of out-of-vocabulary (OOV) words or tokens during the inference phrase. The reason for this is that the model may encounter words that are not in the vocabulary when repairing a given buggy program. Since OOV words are unknown to the model, they cannot be processed effectively, often resulting in ignoring the OOV words, or misinterpreting the meaning or semantics of OOV words. This OOV problem is particularly significant in tasks that require rare or domain-specific vocabulary, where OOV words can contain critical information [4]. For a NPR model, it aims to fix bugs in code, and thus it heavily relies on accurately understanding and generating identifiers, keywords, and domain-specific tokens. As a consequence, when the OOV problem occurs, it could prevent the model from suggesting valid repairs, especially for unique or project-specific variable names or function calls, potentially limiting its real-world applicability. In other words, the inability of NPR model to handle OOV words may decrease its repair effectiveness, failing to generate a patch or leading to incorrect patches.

Compared to natural language texts, programs tend to generate a much larger vocabulary and contain more rare words due to the unique nature of programming languages. On one hand, programs include numerous identifiers such as variable names, function names, class names, and custom keywords, which are often developer-specific and context-dependent. These identifiers are rarely reused across different programs, leading to a significant increase in the vocabulary size and a higher prevalence of rare or unique tokens. Additionally, programs often combine symbols, numbers, and text in unconventional ways, further expanding the vocabulary. These characteristics pose much more challenges for models processing code, as handling such a diverse and sparse words may face more severe OOV problem.

Currently, the OOV problem has been well-documented in many software engineering tasks, such as code completion and code summarization, where unseen or rare tokens like unique variable names or domain-specific functions often lead to reduced model performance. For example, in code summarization, missing critical identifiers due to the OOV problem can result in vague or incomplete summaries [5]. In addition, it is found that OOV tokens hinder models from accessing deeper semantic information in the code comment generation task [6]. However, in the specific context of NPR, little is known about its OOV problem and how the OOV problem affects repair effectiveness. This gap in understanding highlights the need for further investigation into the characteristics of OOV words in NPR as well as the way the OOV problem affects the effectiveness of NPR.

To fill this gap, we conduct comprehensive empirical investigations of various NPR models with respect to OOV words and their impacts. Specifically, we adopt three NPR models, Tufano [7], SequenceR [8] and CoCoNut [9], and use two widely recognized datasets, Defects4J [10] and Bugs.jar [11]. By training these models with varying vocabulary sizes (which is one of the configurations that influence the occurrence of OOV word), we analyze the characteristics of OOV issues in NPR, and also evaluate how OOV words affect the repair effectiveness of NPR models.

Our findings confirm a clear correlation between the model's vocabulary size and the frequency of OOV words (namely, the OOV rate). Notably, variable names and parameter names are the most common types of OOV words encountered in these models. Furthermore, our results reveal that OOV words have a detrimental effect on the repair performance of NPR models-lower OOV rates generally lead to higher repair effectiveness. However, we also observe that different OOV rates can result in the models repairing distinct sets of bugs, highlighting the nuanced role of OOV handling in program repair tasks.

The rest of the paper is structured as follows. Section 2 presents the background and related work. Section 3 details our methodology, including the objectives of our study and the experimental design. Section 4 provides our experimental results and analysis, followed by a conclusion in Sect. 5.

2 Background and Related Work

2.1 OOV Problem in Neural Program Repair

Neural program repair (NPR) is an emerging paradigm that leverages machine learning, particularly neural networks, to automatically fix bugs in software code [1]. The NPR model, often built on sequence-to-sequence architectures like encoder-decoder models, processes the input code to identify and understand bugs in the code, and aims to generate a patch for fixing code [7]. The paradigm relies on training models using large datasets of buggy and fixed code pairs, enabling the model to learn patterns of common programming errors and their fixes. During inference, the model generates potential fixes for the input code, which are then validated, often through automated testing, to ensure correctness [12].

The out-of-vocabulary (OOV) problem in NPR refers to the challenge of handling tokens in source code that are not present in the training vocabulary [3]. While the vocabulary is built based on the training dataset, for a given buggy program, program identifiers [13] such as variable names, function names, and custom class names are often highly specific to a particular program or developer, leading to a vast number of rare or unique tokens. When a NPR model encounters OOV tokens, it may struggle to generate valid fixes, as these tokens often carry essential semantic information for understanding and repairing the code [14].

Figure 1 illustrates an example of a bug that was not successfully fixed by SequenceR on the Defects4J dataset. According to the ground truth, the bug should have correctly replaced **script.getName()** with **script**. However, because the pre-defined vocabulary in SequenceR does not include **guessCJS-ModuleName**, this OOV word was replaced with the special token <UNK> during code tokenization. Since <UNK> does not carry any meaningful semantic information, the model failed to correctly understand the intent of the source code. As a result, the model generated an incorrect patch that mistakenly replaced **guessCJSModuleName** with **getName**.

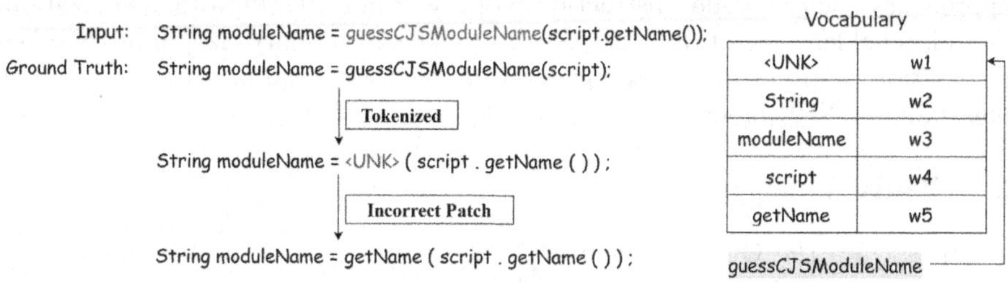

Fig. 1. An illustration showing that the NPR model cannot correctly fix the bug since the OOV token.

2.2 Progress in Handling NPR's OOV Problem

Tufano et al. [7] proposed the first code abstraction method in NPR, which generates abstract source code by replacing rare tokens with specific identifiers while preserving frequently occurring tokens. This method significantly reduces the vocabulary size while retaining the semantic information of important tokens. Chen et al. [8] introduced a copy mechanism to alleviate the OOV problem, and experiments showed that this mechanism helps the model fix more defects. Li et al. [15] proposed a novel abstraction strategy called α-renaming, which retains the type of a variable during renaming. This approach not only reduces the occurrence of rare tokens but also helps the model learn repair relationships between methods that use different variable names in similar scenarios. Lutellier et al. [9] proposed a word-level enhanced tokenization method based on programming language characteristics, which significantly reduces the vocabulary size and lowers the frequency of infrequent tokens.

Jiang et al. [4] observed that many composite identifiers are not recognized by word-level enhanced tokenization, so they employed Byte-Pair Encoding (BPE) to address the OOV problem. Using BPE, they reduced the vocabulary size from 139,423 to 50,057, helping the model generate more correct patches, thus demonstrating the effectiveness of subword tokenization. Yuan et al. [16] utilized a subword tokenization method to address the OOV problem. However, instead of building a new token vocabulary, they use the original tokenization vocabulary from T5, allowing them to fully exploit the pre-trained knowledge. Zhu et al. [17] adopted a novel edit-based patch generation method and proposed Recoder. It first abstracts infrequent identifiers with placeholders, then replaces these placeholders with identifiers from the buggy code if they meet the syntactic and semantic requirements for the placeholder's position. Jiang et al. [18] combined the code abstraction method with placeholder generation for tokenization. This not only alleviates the computational pressure on the encoder but also allows their newly designed three-stage tree decoder to generate more correct patches.

Recent advancements in handling the OOV problem in NPR include approaches such as code abstraction, copy mechanism, subword tokenization, and placeholder generation. They aim to reduce vocabulary size, improve token recognition, and enhance patch generation accuracy, leading to more effective bug fixing in NPR models.

3 Study Design

To investigate the OOV problem in NPR and its impact on NPR's effectiveness, we trained NPR models with different vocabulary sizes, and evaluated NPR models based on test datasets. This section presents the methodologies and configurations used for the experiments, including the NPR models selected for evaluation, the datasets utilized, the vocabulary size configurations, and the evaluation metrics adopted.

3.1 Research Questions

In order to study the characteristics of the OOV problem and its impacts on NPR, this study mainly focuses on the following research questions.

- **RQ1**. *How does the vocabulary size of an NPR model affect the OOV rates?* Vocabulary size is one of the configuration of NPR models, which is regarded to be important for the OOV problem. This RQ seeks to analyze the OOV rate for different vocabulary configurations to determine how the vocabulary size influences the occurrence of OOV tokens. This will help us understand the trade-off between a large vocabulary size and its impact on OOV reduction.
- **RQ2**. *What are the typical types of OOV words in the context of program repair?* Existing studies have shown that identifiers dominate the OOV words for models of source code. However, there are various categories of identifier in a program. For example, Frantzeskou et al. [13] classified Java identifiers into four categories: method names, variable names, parameter names, and class names. RQ2 analyzes the distribution of OOV tokens with respect to different categories of identifiers, aiming to provide a clearer understanding about the characteristics of OOV words in NPR.

- **RQ3**. *How do NPR techniques perform under varying OOV rates?* RQ3 will evaluate the repair effectiveness of NPR models for different OOV rates and then analyze the similarities and differences in the repair results of different models.

3.2 NPR Models

Different NPR techniques have varying potential for fixing different types of bugs. In order to investigate different NPR techniques, this study mainly focuses on their ability in fixing single-line bugs, which is one type of bugs that are targeted by most of NPR techniques. We thus follow a recent empirical study [19] on NPR techniques to include Tufano [7], SequenceR [8] and CoCoNut [9] as study subjects.

Tufano [7]. The model employs an RNN-based encoder-decoder structure with attention mechanisms, enabling it to capture the syntactic and semantic structure of code effectively. Tufano is trained on large datasets of buggy and fixed code pairs, allowing it to learn patterns of common bug fixes. It classifies common tokens as idioms and maps rare tokens to specific IDs during abstraction, which is able to narrow down the search space and thus improves the performance of the model. Additionally, it emphasizes lightweight pre-processing and tokenization tailored to programming languages, ensuring scalability and efficiency for real-world software development tasks.

SequenceR [8]. It employs a sequence-to-sequence learning model for generating one-line patches. During data pre-processing, it uses the tokens (<START_BUG> and <END_BUG>) to mark buggy lines and incorporate the abstract buggy context to support program repair. In the patch generation phase, the use of copy mechanism enables the model to replace OOV tokens by selecting tokens directly from the input tokens, thereby improving the model's accuracy.

CoCoNut [9]. The model utilizes ensemble learning and leverages a context-aware neural machine translation architecture. Unlike traditional sequence-to-sequence models, CoCoNut employs dual encoders: one encoder focuses on the buggy code snippet, while the other captures the broader program context. This design allows CoCoNut to account for dependencies and semantic nuances in the surrounding code, enhancing its repair accuracy. Additionally, its contextual copy mechanism ensures that the model can directly reuse tokens from the input, preserving the syntactic and semantic integrity of the repaired code.

To thoroughly investigate the impact of the OOV problem on NPR repair performance, we disable the strategies employed by all three NPR methods that were designed to mitigate OOV issues. This ensures that the models rely solely on their vocabulary, without fallback mechanisms like the copy mechanism or abstraction techniques, allowing us to observe the direct effects of OOV tokens on repair accuracy and performance.

3.3 Vocabulary Size Configuration

Vocabulary is important for NPR models to learn bug-fixing transformation patterns [7]. A large vocabulary can lower the frequency of OOV tokens by covering rare tokens, but it may also introduce noise that negatively affects the repair performance of the NPR model. On the other hand, a smaller vocabulary can result in numerous OOV tokens in buggy code, hindering the model's ability to capture sufficient semantic information. There seems to be a trade-off relationship between vocabulary size and OOV tokens. Therefore, to investigate the OOV problem, we control the frequency of OOV tokens by adjusting the vocabulary size and then study its impact on the repair efficiency of NPR models.

3.4 Datasets

To ensure a fair comparison and comprehensively reveal the impact of the OOV problem on NPR, we follow previous work [19] and use their publicly available dataset. To maintain consistency and fairness in our evaluation, the same dataset is used for both training and testing the NPR models.

Training. Zhong et al. [19] published a method-level bug-fix pairs dataset containing only single-line modifications, comprising a total of 144,641 samples, which we used as the training dataset for models.

Testing. **Defects4J** [10] is the most widely used real-world Java dataset in the field of automated program repair (APR) for evaluating repair capabilities, while **Bugs.jar** [11] is a large and diverse dataset of real-world Java defects. Zhong et al. [19] split and purify these benchmarks, so we focus on all single-line bugs (bugs that can be fixed with a single-line modification) from them, which include 400 bugs and 1013 bugs respectively.

3.5 OOV Tokens Collection

During the inference phase, for each vocabulary size configuration, for both datasets (Defects4J and Bugs.jar), and for each NPR model, we tokenize the buggy code snippets into tokens. We collect the OOV tokens, which are replaced by <UNK> in the tokenization results.

3.6 Evaluation Metrics

We measure the occurence of OOV words via *OOV rate*, which is the percentage of OOV words among all tokens of the given buggy program.

To measure the repair effectiveness of NPR, we follow previous work [20–22] to adopt the following two metrics.

- *Exact match.* The exact match metric measures the number of buggy programs that an approach can successfully repair. In other words, it reflects the number of correct patches generated by an approach. Specifically, it considers a patch to be correct if and only if it perfectly matches the human-written fix.

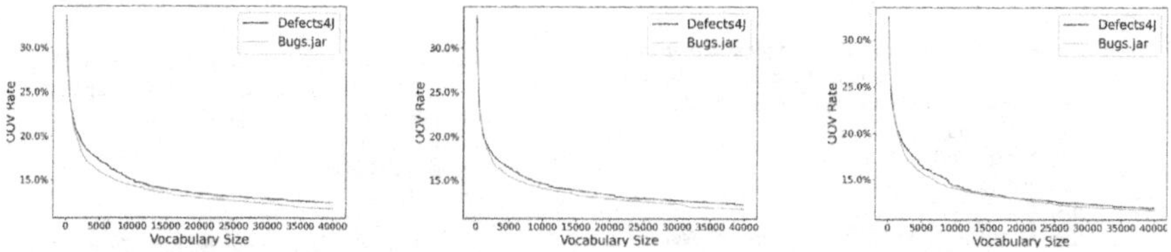

(a) Tufano (b) SequenceR (c) CoCoNut

Fig. 2. Variation of OOV rates with the increase of vocabulary size.

- *CodeBLEU.* Apart from the number of correct patches, another important aspect of NPR refers to the quality of all generated patches. In this study, we use CodeBLEU [23] to assess the similarity between patches generated by NPR approach and manually written ones so as to measure the quality of generated patches. CodeBLEU is a weighted combination of n-gram match (BLEU), weighted n-gram match (BLEU-weighted), AST match and data-flow match scores, incorporating semantic and syntactic information to more accurately assess the similarity between codes.

4 Results and Analysis

To answer our research questions, we carry out a series of experiments by training each of the NPR models with varying vocabulary sizes, and perform extensive analysis of OOV words and their impacts on the repair effectiveness of NPR models. Next, we present the results with respect to our three research questions.

4.1 RQ1: Correlation Between Vocabulary Size and OOV Rate

Configuring a NPR model with different vocabulary sizes may lead to different OOV rates. To clearly reveal the relationship between the size of NPR model's vocabulary and its OOV rate, we trained each of the three NPR models with a set of different vocabulary sizes. Specifically, we predefined a set of vocabulary sizes {100, 1000, 5000, 10,000, 15,000, 20,000, 25,000, 30,000, 35,000, 40,000}, and trained a model with each of the vocabulary size, respectively. In total, 3×10 trained models are obtained. We further applied each trained model to the two datasets (Defects4J and Bugs.jar), and collected the OOV words during repairing each of the subject programs. Based on this, we calculated the OOV rates under individual configurations of the vocabulary.

Figure 2 reports the results, where the horizontal axis represents a NPR model configured with different vocabulary sizes and the vertical axis shows different OOV rates. It can be observed that the OOV rates of all models exhibit similar trends on both datasets. The OOV rate initially drops sharply as the vocabulary size increases, and then it gradually become stable. This follows a

```java
@Override
public int parseArguments ( Parameters setParams)
                                throws CmdLineException {
    String param = setParams.getParameter(0);
    if (param == null) {
      setter.addValue(true);
      return 0;
    } else {
      String lowerParam = param.toLowerCase();
    }
```

(a) Vocabulary Size = 100

```java
@Override
public int parseArguments ( Parameters setParams)
                                throws CmdLineException {
    String param = setParams.getParameter(0);
    if (param == null) {
      setter.addValue(true);
      return 0;
    } else {
      String lowerParam = param.toLowerCase();
    }
```

(b) Vocabulary Size = 1000

```java
@Override
public int parseArguments ( Parameters setParams)
                                throws CmdLineException {
    String param = setParams.getParameter(0);
    if (param == null) {
      setter.addValue(true);
      return 0;
    } else {
      String lowerParam = param.toLowerCase();
    }
```

(c) Vocabulary Size = 10000

```java
@Override
public int parseArguments ( Parameters setParams)
                                throws CmdLineException {
    String param = setParams.getParameter(0);
    if (param == null) {
      setter.addValue(true);
      return 0;
    } else {
      String lowerParam = param.toLowerCase();
    }
```

(d) Vocabulary Size = 20000

Fig. 3. OOV tokens of SequenceR for repairing a buggy program from Defects4J dataset. ▒ represents the OOV tokens under the corresponding vocabulary size.

typical power-law distribution with a long tail, evident across all three NPR models. Specifically, as the vocabulary size increases from 100 to 10,000, the OOV rate significantly decreases from over 30% to below 15%. Beyond this point, further increases in vocabulary size result in a more gradual reduction, eventually stabilizing.

Figure 3 presents an illustrative example, where OOV tokens of SequenceR for repairing a buggy program from Defects4J dataset are displayed. It is obvious that the number of OOV tokens keeps decreasing when the vocabulary size of SequenceR is increased. When the vocabulary size is 100, only a few programming language-specific keywords are not OOV tokens. As the vocabulary increases, common class and method names are further included in the vocabulary.

Answer to RQ1: For NPR models, the vocabulary size directly impacts the OOV rate, indicating that increasing the vocabulary size can effectively reduce the OOV rate. However, once the vocabulary size reaches a certain threshold, its effect on the OOV rate becomes trivial. This finding consolidates observations reported by existing studies, emphasizing that an appropriate vocabulary size is crucial for NPR methods, while an extremely large vocabulary may not necessarily benefits a lot for the OOV problem.

4.2 RQ2: Distributions of OOV Words

Since OOV words are prevalent in the context of NPR, it is important to know the distributions of different types of OOV words. Identifiers, as assigned by

```
@Override
public int parseArguments ( Parameters setParams)
                    throws CmdLineException {
   String param = setParams.getParameter(0);
   if (param == null) {
      setter.addValue(true);
      return 0;
   } else {
      String lowerParam = param.toLowerCase();
   }
```

Fig. 4. A buggy code snippet from Defects4J [10]. Different colors represent distinct types of OOV words: parseArguments is a method name, setParams is a parameter name, lowerParam is a variable name, and CmdLineException is a class name.

developers, often carry rich semantic meaning in code [24], though they can also be arbitrarily created and infrequent. Given their significance, we focused primarily on program identifiers. By following previous work [13], we classified identifiers into four categories: *method names*, *parameter names*, *variable names*, and *class names*. An example illustrating these four types of OOV words is shown in Fig. 4.

To analyze different types of OOV words, we selected each subject model with four different OOV rates-15%, 20%, 25%, and 30% (by using corresponding vocabulary sizes for each rate). We also applied JavaParser [25], which discerns the role of each identifier, to identify the types of OOV words. We further collected different types of OOV words with respect to individual NPR models and datasets.

The results are shown in Fig. 5, where each subfig reports the percentages of different types of OOV words encountered by an NPR model with varying OOV rates. Firstly, it can be observed that even for the same NPR model, the percentage of one type of OOV words may be different with different OOV rates. For example, consider the application of Tufano on the Defects4J dataset, the model with an OOV rate of 15% encounters 28.6% OOV words that are *method names*, while the model with an OOV rate of 30% only encounters 16.9% *method names* among all OOV words (as shonw in Fig. 5(a)). Similar trend can also be observed on the other NPR models. Secondly, among the four types of OOV words under investigation, *method names* and *parameter names* are relatively have higher proportions. It can be found from Fig. 5 that for all the NPR models, the proportion of *method names* is between 40% and 50%, while the proportion of *parameter names* is between 25% and 30%. While for the *class names*, it rarely occurs as an OOV words, since its proportions are always lower than 5%. Thus, it can be concluded that *variable names* and *parameter names* are the most common types of OOV words in the context of NPR, regardless of the overall OOV rate of the NPR model.

Answer to RQ2: Among the four types of identifiers under investigation, *variable names* and *parameter names* are the most common types of OOV words

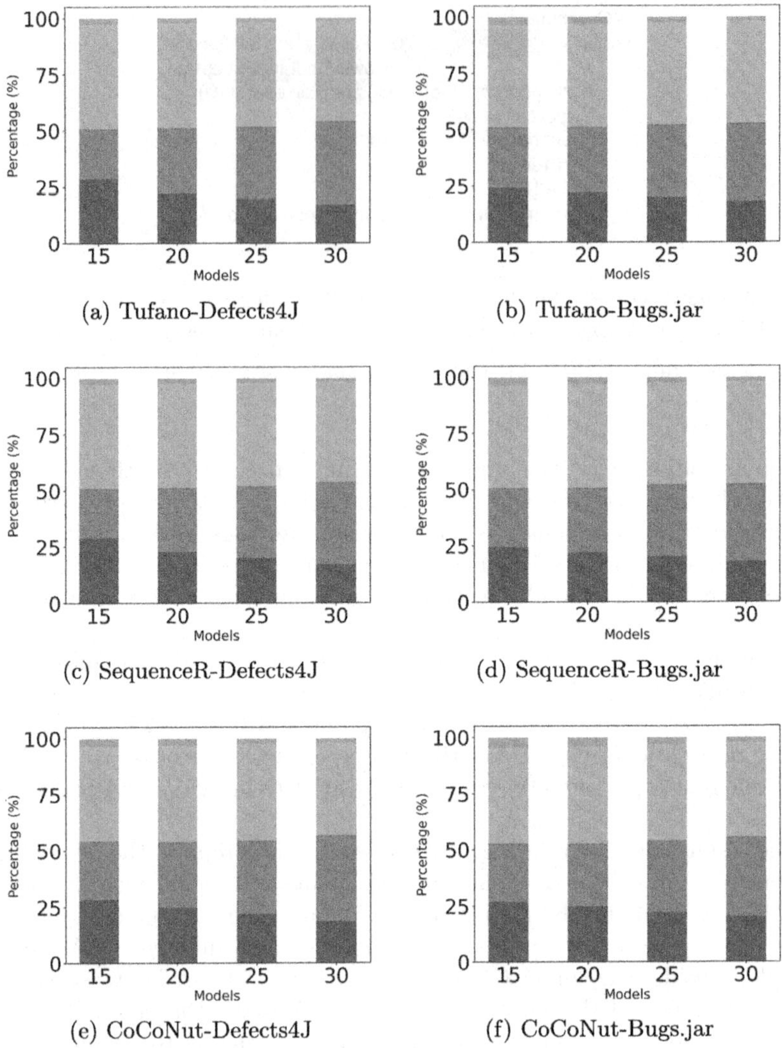

Fig. 5. The distribution of OOV words types. ■ represents method names, ■ represents parameter names, ■ represents variable names, ■ represents class names.

for the task of NPR. This further indicates that researchers should devote more attention and effort to handle these two types of OOV words.

4.3 RQ3: The Impact of OOV on NPR's Repair Effectiveness

To study the impact of OOV problem on the repair effectiveness of NPR models, we selected four models (with 15%, 20%, 25%, and 30% OOV rates) with respect to each subject NPR model, and then evaluated them on two test datasets

Table 1. Number of correct patches.

Models	OOV Rate	Defects4J	Bugs.jar
		400 bugs	1013 bugs
Tufano	15%	28	82
	20%	22	60
	25%	20	50
	30%	13	1
SequenceR	15%	42	72
	20%	45	79
	25%	42	68
	30%	38	56
CoCoNut	15%	14	60
	20%	12	43
	25%	8	32
	30%	6	17

(Defects4J and Bugs.jar). We collected the generated patches, and also measures the number of correct patches (via the Exact match metric) and the repair quality of patches (via the CodeBLEU metric).

Number of Bug Repaired. Table 1 reports the number of buggy programs that have been successfully repaired by individual NPR models. That is, the number of correct patches generated by the NPR model. A larger number of correct patches indicates that the NPR model has a higher repair effectiveness in terms of correctly repairing more buggy programs. It is found that for each subject model, a lower OOV rate leads to a larger number of correct patches. Consider, Tufano, as an example, it successfully fixes 28 buggy program of the Defect4J dataset when its OOV rate is 15%, while it only generates 13 correct patches on the same dataset when it has an OOV rate of 30%. More significant discrepancies can be observed on the Bugs.jar dataset. For instance, CoCoNut fixed 60 programs with an OOV rate of 15%, while it only fixes 17 programs when its OOV rate is 30%. All of these results suggest that decreasing the OOV rate will help the NPR model to generate more correct patches. This finding is reasonable since the NPR model can better understand and manipulate the buggy program with few OOV words.

However, previous research [7] suggests that an excessive number of tokens may introduce noise for real defects, hindering the model's ability to fix them correctly. Furthermore, upon reviewing our results, we observe that the model "spontaneously" fails to fix a bug at a certain OOV rate v, even though it correctly fixes the bug at other OOV rates. To gain deeper insights, we follow the approach in [20] and categorize the bugs correctly fixed at some OOV rates into four groups:

Table 2. Different groups of bugs repaired by NPR models

Model	Benchmark	Group1	Group2	Group3	Group4
Tufano	Defects4J	38.7%	48.4%	3.2%	9.7%
	Bugs.jar	1.1%	85.4%	0%	13.5%
SequenceR	Defects4J	38.3%	18.3%	13.3%	30%
	Bugs.jar	31.5%	26.1%	10.8%	31.5%
CoCoNut	Defects4J	37.5%	50%	0%	12.5%
	Bugs.jar	27.0%	66.7%	0%	6.3%

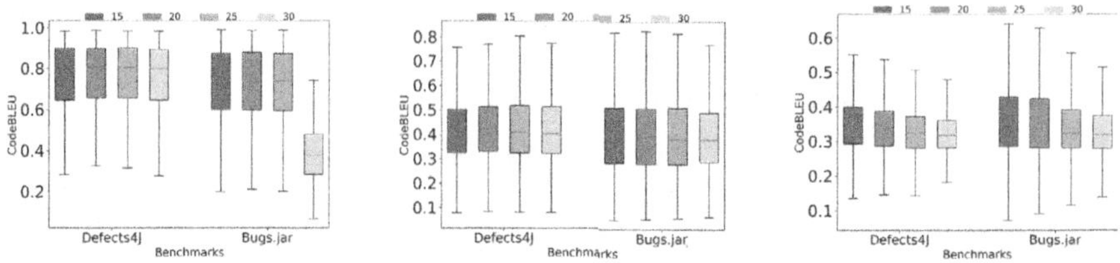

(a) Tufano (b) SequenceR (c) CoCoNut

Fig. 6. CodeBLEU values of Candidate Patches generated under different OOV rates.

1. *Group1*: Bugs fixed at all OOV rates;
2. *Group2*: Bugs that fixed with decreasing OOV rates (they are not fixed at a certain OOV rate v, but are fixed for all OOV rates lower than v);
3. *Group3*: Bugs that only get fixed above a certain OOV rate v (and are not fixed at OOV rates lower than v);
4. *Group4*: Erratic bugs with more complex patterns (e.g., the bug might be fixed at OOV rates of 15% and 25%, but not at 20%, with no clear reason for the failure).

Through the analysis of Table 2, we find that approximately one-third of the bugs can be fixed at all OOV rates (e.g., Group 1). Tufano and CoCoNut exhibit the highest percentage of defect repairs in Group 2, strongly supporting the importance of reducing the OOV rate. Additionally, their low percentage of defects in Group 3 demonstrates that the benefits of increasing the vocabulary size far outweigh the drawbacks. However, we observe that SequenceR has a Group 4 repair rate as high as 30%, indicating a lack of robustness in the model.

Quality of Patches. For bugs that are not correctly fixed (i.e., where the NPR fails to generate the correct patch), we further analyze the impact of OOV rates on the quality of all generated patches. The similarity between the candidate patches and human-written patches is measured using the CodeBLEU metric, with the results presented in Fig. 6.

1. **Tufano**. Although our experiments focus only on single-line bugs, Tufano generates the entire fixed method. This results in candidate patches that

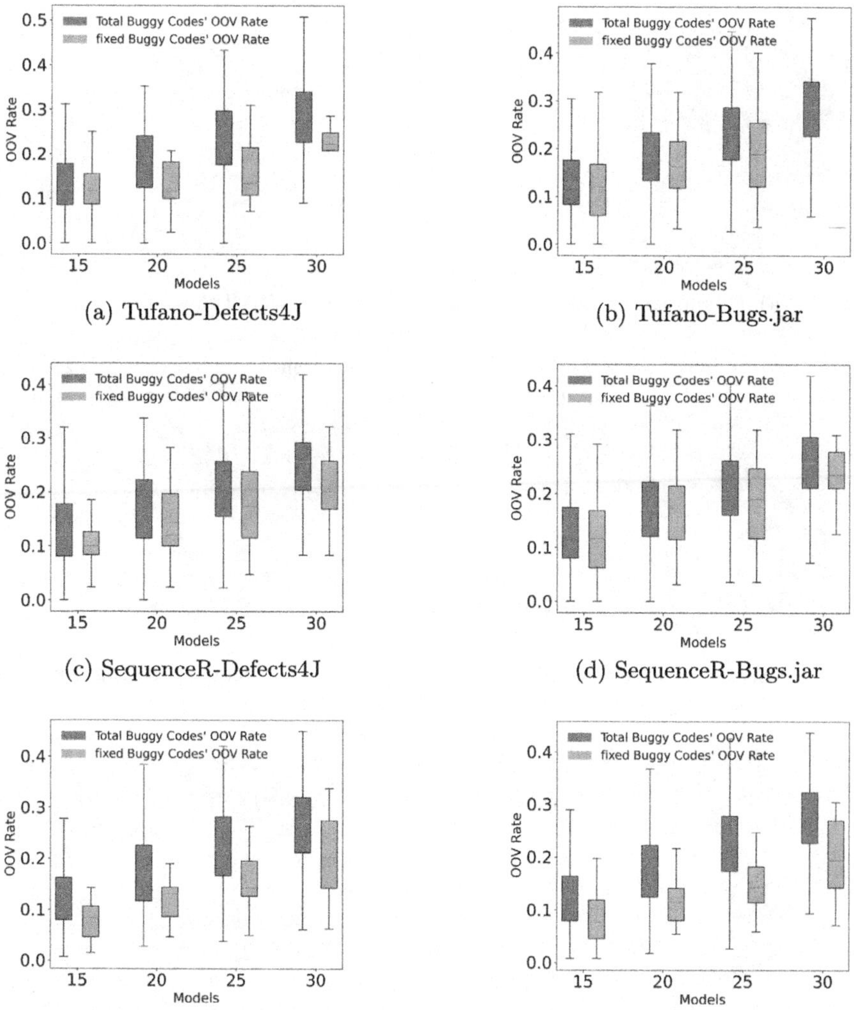

(a) Tufano-Defects4J

(b) Tufano-Bugs.jar

(c) SequenceR-Defects4J

(d) SequenceR-Bugs.jar

(e) CoCoNut-Defects4J

(f) CoCoNut-Bugs.jar

Fig. 7. Distribution of OOV rates for buggy programs. ▒ represents all buggy programs and ▒ represents buggy programs that have been successfully repaired by NPR models.

share many tokens with the correct code, contributing to its higher overall CodeBLEU score.

2. **SequenceR**. For SequenceR, although the CodeBLEU scores do not drop significantly, a noticeable declining trend is evident as the OOV rate increases.
3. **CoCoNut**. For CoCoNut, we observe that as the OOV rate increases, the CodeBLEU score decreases significantly, and the distribution narrows, indicating a reduced number of high scores.

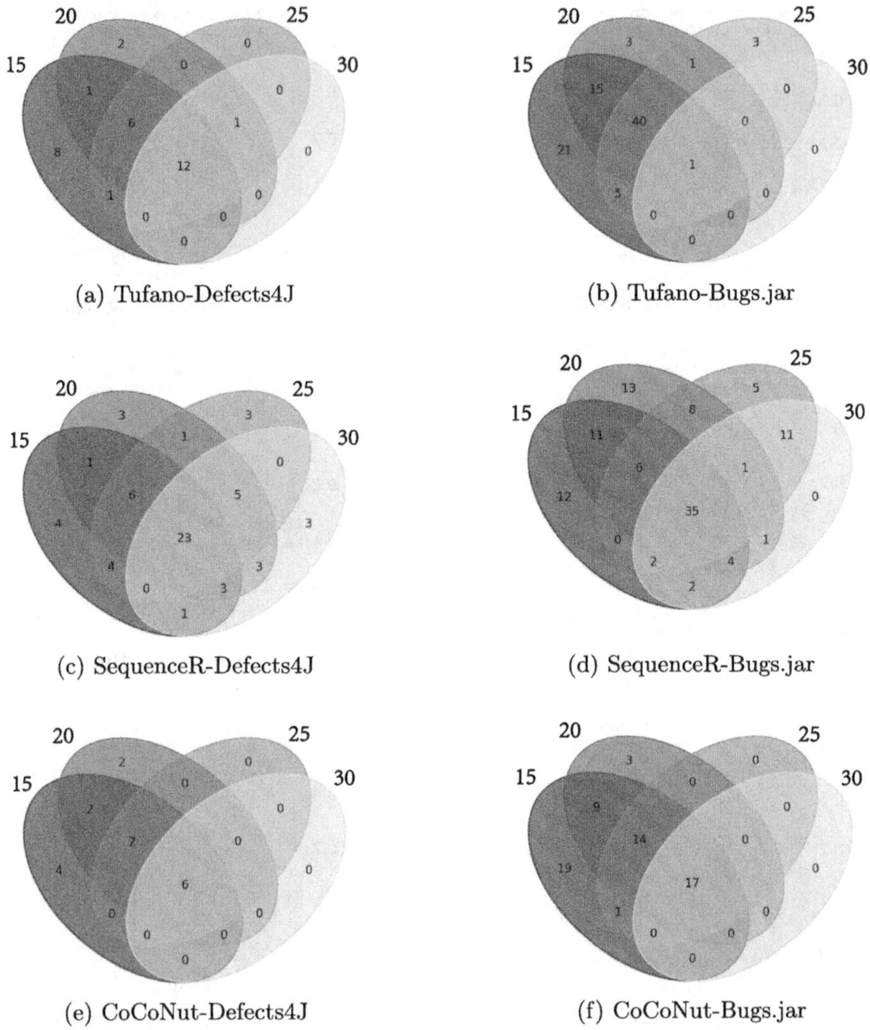

Fig. 8. The repair results for NPR models under different OOV rates.

Tendency. We hypothesize that the fewer OOV tokens a piece of buggy code contains, the more effectively the model can capture the underlying semantic information of the code. This is because OOV tokens, which are absent from the model's vocabulary, introduce uncertainty and hinder the model's ability to understand the context of the code. As a result, we believe that models are more likely to successfully fix bugs with lower OOV rates in the dataset, as these bugs provide fewer challenges in terms of token comprehension and representation. Specifically, we gathered the OOV rate distributions for the buggy programs correctly fixed by each model and compared them with the overall OOV rate distribution of all buggy programs in the dataset.

Figure 7 presents the distribution analysis of OOV rates across different buggy programs. The results show a clear trend: models tend to perform better on bugs with relatively low OOV rates in the test datasets. Specifically, when applying Tufano to the Defects4J dataset, the model with an OOV rate of 15% demonstrates a narrower and lower distribution of repaired buggy programs compared to the distribution of all buggy programs, and the model with an OOV rate of 30% exhibits a more pronounced narrowing of the repaired test case distribution. This suggests that the model is more efficient at repairing bugs with fewer OOV tokens, leading to a higher concentration of successful fixes.

The findings from this analysis provide strong support for our hypothesis, indicating that test models tend to focus on and perform better at fixing bugs with relatively low OOV rates in the test datasets.

Complementarity. A natural question arises as to whether the model is capable of fixing distinct sets of bugs at different OOV rates, or in other words, whether different OOV rates exhibit complementary effects in bug repair. To address this, we conducted an analysis on four models (with 15%, 20%, 25%, and 30% OOV rates), examining the extent to which the bugs fixed at each OOV rate are unique to that particular rate or common across multiple OOV rates. Specifically, we analyze how many bugs are exclusively fixed by one OOV rate, and how many are repaired across different OOV rate settings.

The results of this analysis are illustrated in the Venn diagrams shown in Fig. 8. As the diagrams reveal, between 62% and 78% of the bugs can be successfully fixed by at least two or more models, indicating a significant overlap in the bug repair capabilities across different OOV rates. Notably, when combining the predictions from the four models, each trained on a different OOV rate, we observe a considerable performance improvement. The enhancement ranges from 5% (for CoCoNut on the Bugs.jar dataset) to 40% (for SequenceR on the Bugs.jar dataset), demonstrating that combining models trained at varying OOV rates can lead to substantial gains in bug repair accuracy.

This complementary nature of different OOV rates highlights the importance of leveraging diverse OOV rate settings to enhance the robustness and overall performance of neural program repair models. The ability to fix a broader range of bugs across different OOV settings underscores the potential for combining multiple models as a strategy for improving the effectiveness of automatic program repair systems.

Answer to RQ3: Overall, the OOV problem significantly affects NPR's effectiveness. Lower OOV rates help models fix more bugs accurately, with a preference for bugs at lower rates. Increasing vocabulary size offers more benefits than drawbacks, though some bugs are inconsistently fixed across OOV settings. Additionally, different OOV rates enable the model to fix different bugs, and this complementarity can be leveraged by combining models trained at various OOV rates into an ensemble.

5 Conclusion

In this work we studied the effect of OOV problem in NPR from multiple perspectives. Using two test datasets (Defects4J and Bugs.jar), we first found that increasing the vocabulary size effectively reduces the OOV rate by approximately 15%, with *variable names* and *parameter names* being the most common types of OOV words in NPR. Furthermore, OOV words negatively affect the repair effectiveness of NPR models, including both the number of correct patches and the overall quality of the generated repairs. Our analysis of repair complementarity shows that ensembling models trained at different OOV rates leads to a relative improvement of 5–40%.

Our results have several implications. First, there remains significant potential for improvement, as the OOV problem can be addressed more effectively. On the other hand, increasing the vocabulary introduces challenges, particularly regarding robustness to small variations in vocabulary. We believe that future researchers can draw valuable insights from our work when designing NPR models, particularly in terms of addressing the OOV problem.

References

1. Zhong, W., Li, C., Ge, J., Luo, B.: Neural program repair: systems, challenges and solutions. In: Proceedings of the 13th Asia-Pacific Symposium on Internetware, pp. 96–106 (2022)
2. Huang, K., et al.: A survey on automated program repair techniques. arXiv preprint arXiv:2303.18184 (2023)
3. Zhang, Q., Fang, C., Ma, Y., Sun, W., Chen, Z.: A survey of learning-based automated program repair. ACM Trans. Softw. Eng. Methodol. **33**(2), 1–69 (2023)
4. Jiang, N., Lutellier, T., Tan, L.: Cure: code-aware neural machine translation for automatic program repair. In: 2021 IEEE/ACM 43rd International Conference on Software Engineering (ICSE), pp. 1161–1173. IEEE (2021)
5. Karampatsis, R.-M., Babii, H., Robbes, R., Sutton, C., Janes, A.: Big code!= big vocabulary: open-vocabulary models for source code. In: Proceedings of the ACM/IEEE 42nd International Conference on Software Engineering, pp. 1073–1085 (2020)
6. Hu, X., Li, G., Xia, X., Lo, D., Jin, Z.: Deep code comment generation with hybrid lexical and syntactical information. Empir. Softw. Eng. **25**, 2179–2217 (2020)
7. Tufano, M., Watson, C., Bavota, G., Di Penta, M., White, M., Poshyvanyk, D.: An empirical investigation into learning bug-fixing patches in the wild via neural machine translation. In: Proceedings of the 33rd ACM/IEEE International Conference on Automated Software Engineering, pp. 832–837 (2018)
8. Chen, Z., Kommrusch, S., Tufano, M., Pouchet, L.-N., Poshyvanyk, D., Monperrus, M.: Sequencer: sequence-to-sequence learning for end-to-end program repair. IEEE Trans. Softw. Eng. **47**(9), 1943–1959 (2019)
9. Lutellier, T., Pham, H.V., Pang, L., Li, Y., Wei, M., Tan, L.: Coconut: combining context-aware neural translation models using ensemble for program repair. In: Proceedings of the 29th ACM SIGSOFT International Symposium on Software Testing and Analysis, pp. 101–114 (2020)

10. Just, R., Jalali, D., Ernst, M.D.: Defects4j: a database of existing faults to enable controlled testing studies for Java programs. In: Proceedings of the 2014 International Symposium on Software Testing and Analysis, pp. 437–440 (2014)
11. Saha, R.K., Lyu, Y., Lam, W., Yoshida, H., Prasad, M.R.: Bugs.jar: a large-scale, diverse dataset of real-world Java bugs. In: Proceedings of the 15th International Conference on Mining Software Repositories, pp. 10–13 (2018)
12. Ouyang, Y., Yang, J., Zhang, L.: Benchmarking automated program repair: an extensive study on both real-world and artificial bugs. In: Proceedings of the 33rd ACM SIGSOFT International Symposium on Software Testing and Analysis, pp. 440–452 (2024)
13. Frantzeskou, G., MacDonell, S.G., Stamatatos, E., Georgiou, S., Gritzalis, S.: The significance of user-defined identifiers in Java source code authorship identification. arXiv preprint arXiv:2101.12384 (2021)
14. Moon, S., Okazaki, N.: Effects and mitigation of out-of-vocabulary in universal language models. J. Inf. Process. **29**, 490–503 (2021)
15. Li, Y., Wang, S., Nguyen, T.N.: Dlfix: context-based code transformation learning for automated program repair. In: Proceedings of the ACM/IEEE 42nd International Conference on Software Engineering, pp. 602–614 (2020)
16. Yuan, W., et al.: Circle: continual repair across programming languages. In: Proceedings of the 31st ACM SIGSOFT International Symposium on Software Testing and Analysis, pp. 678–690 (2022)
17. Zhu, Q., et al.: A syntax-guided edit decoder for neural program repair. In: Proceedings of the 29th ACM Joint Meeting on European Software Engineering Conference and Symposium on the Foundations of Software Engineering, pp. 341–353 (2021)
18. Jiang, N., Lutellier, T., Lou, Y., Tan, L., Goldwasser, D., Zhang, X.: Knod: domain knowledge distilled tree decoder for automated program repair. In: 2023 IEEE/ACM 45th International Conference on Software Engineering (ICSE), pp. 1251–1263. IEEE (2023)
19. Zhong, W., et al.: Standup4npr: standardizing setup for empirically comparing neural program repair systems. In: Proceedings of the 37th IEEE/ACM International Conference on Automated Software Engineering, pp. 1–13 (2022)
20. Prenner, J.A., Robbes, R.: Out of context: how important is local context in neural program repair? In: Proceedings of the IEEE/ACM 46th International Conference on Software Engineering, pp. 1–13 (2024)
21. Ding, Y., Ray, B., Devanbu, P., Hellendoorn, V.J.: Patching as translation: the data and the metaphor. In: Proceedings of the 35th IEEE/ACM International Conference on Automated Software Engineering, pp. 275–286 (2020)
22. Zhang, Y., Li, G., Jin, Z., Xing, Y.: Neural program repair with program dependence analysis and effective filter mechanism. arXiv preprint arXiv:2305.09315 (2023)
23. Ren, S., et al.: Codebleu: a method for automatic evaluation of code synthesis. arXiv preprint arXiv:2009.10297 (2020)
24. Wang, Y., Wang, W., Joty, S., Hoi, S.C.: Codet5: identifier-aware unified pre-trained encoder-decoder models for code understanding and generation. arXiv preprint arXiv:2109.00859 (2021)
25. Tomassetti, F., Smith, N., Maximilien, C., Kirsch, S.: Javaparser (2021)

Edge Computing Systems

Auction-Based Caching Decision Algorithm for IoT Traffic with Popular and Fresh Content

Hao Xu[1], Alvin Valera[1], Wuyungerile Li[2(✉)], and Winston K. G. Seah[1]

[1] School of Engineering and Computer Science, Victoria University of Wellington, Wellington, New Zealand
{hao.xu,alvin.valera,winston.seah}@ecs.vuw.ac.nz

[2] School of Computer Science, Inner Mongolia University, Hohhot, China
gerile@imu.edu.cn

Abstract. The proliferation of Internet of Things (IoT) devices presents challenges for data transmission efficiency, including network congestion and data retrieval latency. Named Data Networking (NDN), a key architecture within Information-Centric Networking (ICN), has proven to be a promising solution to these issues through in-network caching. Unlike traditional ICN, IoT data traffic exhibits distinct characteristics in terms of content popularity dynamics and freshness requirements due to the diversity of IoT application scenarios. Efficient caching of IoT data becomes challenging due to the need to balance both the popularity and freshness of content, as popular items may quickly become outdated, and fresh content is often only relevant for a limited period. In this paper, we propose Auction-Based Caching Decision (ABCD) Algorithm, a caching strategy for IoT data traffic which simultaneously considers content popularity and freshness to prioritize caching of high-demand and timely content. ABCD utilizes an auction mechanism whereby content bids to be cached based on a combined recency-frequency and freshness-aware criteria. Simulation results using NDNsim demonstrate significant improvements in cache hit ratio, data retrieval latency, and content freshness in comparison with LCE, LCD, ProbCache and CFPC.

Keywords: Internet of Things (IoT) · Named Data Networking (NDN) · In-Network Caching

1 Introduction

The Internet of Things (IoT) aims to connect various physical devices, sensors, machines, and everyday objects through the internet, creating an intelligent networked ecosystem. These devices can communicate and exchange data autonomously without human intervention. It is estimated that by 2030, up to 500 billion IoT devices will be connected to the internet [1]. Due to the widespread deployment, real-time nature, and diversity of IoT devices, massive

Y. Zhou et al. (Eds.): ICECCS 2025, LNCS 15746, pp. 201–220, 2026.
https://doi.org/10.1007/978-3-032-00828-2_12

amounts of data will be generated. Consequently, IoT communications encounter substantial challenges, most notably increased network overhead, data retrieval delays, and network congestion.

While Information-Centric Networking (ICN) was not originally developed to address IoT-specific challenges, its principles offer potential solutions for some of the key issues in IoT [2]. ICN shifts from the traditional IP address-based, end-to-end communication model of the internet to a content-centric model, focusing on data retrieval by content identifiers rather than device addresses. Named Data Networking (NDN), a key ICN architecture, is particularly beneficial for IoT environments due to its *name-based content retrieval* and *in-network caching* capabilities [2].

In-network caching has gained considerable attention due to its potential to reduce latency, bandwidth usage, and overall network traffic. Various caching strategies have been proposed, focusing on content placement, cache eviction, and optimization strategies that consider factors such as device energy, and node types [2]. In traditional ICN, caching strategies primarily focus on improving content distribution efficiency, *i.e.*, reducing network traffic, and minimizing content retrieval latency [3].

However, IoT data traffic exhibits distinct characteristics, particularly in terms of content popularity and freshness dynamics. Unlike traditional ICN, IoT data is typically generated by numerous distributed, resource-constrained devices, with varying access patterns and freshness requirements across different scenarios. *Freshness* refers to how recently the data was generated, which is critical in IoT environments where data can quickly become outdated. While popularity has been extensively studied in prior research, freshness has received relatively limited attention in the literature [8]. Moreover, AI-based or overly complex algorithms cannot operate on IoT devices with limited energy and computational resources, highlighting the need for simpler and more efficient caching strategies [13].

In this paper, we study the problem of caching IoT data within NDN by considering both content popularity and freshness to prioritize the caching of high-demand and timely content. We propose the ABCD scheme, a simple and efficient caching solution tailored to the NDN architecture for IoT scenarios. Unlike the major related works [8,9,11], which focus primarily on edge caching scenarios, ABCD naturally extends to hybrid network environments and allows the algorithm to operate independently on each caching node without requiring additional network management. By doing so, ABCD effectively and naturally caches popular content on nodes where caching utility is high.

The main contributions of this paper are as follows:

- We introduce Auction-Based Caching Decision (ABCD), a novel auction-based caching strategy that is suitable for IoT data traffic. ABCD enables nodes to autonomously perform caching decisions based on the content's combined recency-frequency and freshness-aware metric value. This distributed approach reduces communication overhead, enhances scalability, and is applicable to various IoT scenarios.

- We propose an innovative integration of the auction mechanism into the caching algorithm, optimizing content placement by simulating an auction process that dynamically prioritizes higher-value nodes for caching. This approach not only reduces the computational complexity at individual cache nodes but also facilitates collaborative optimization across nodes during the propagation of content requests. By enhancing the efficiency of network caching and the effectiveness of content distribution, this design significantly improves the applicability and performance of caching strategies in IoT scenarios.
- We conducted an extensive evaluation of the proposed algorithm in multiple IoT scenarios using the NDNsim simulator. Compared against several benchmark caching strategies, our ABCD strategy demonstrates significant performance improvements in content freshness, hit ratio and delay.

The remainder of this paper is organized as follows. Section 2 discusses in-network caching in ICN and related work. Section 3 describes our proposed caching strategy. Section 4 presents and analyzes the simulation results, followed by the conclusion in Sect. 5.

2 Related Work

In NDN, caching occurs at intermediate nodes to store frequently accessed content, reducing retrieval latency and increasing cache hit rates. Traditional caching strategies, such as Leave Cache Everywhere (LCE) and Leave Cache Down (LCD), have been widely adopted. The LCE strategy caches content at every node along the path, while LCD caches content only at nodes close to the content requester [14,15].

To address the limitations of finite cache space and diverse content demands, more advanced caching strategies have been proposed. For instance, Kim et al. [4] introduced a cache-aware content placement strategy that optimizes content distribution by balancing cache capacity and content popularity within local networks. Asmat et al. proposed the Edge-Linked Caching (ELC) mechanism, which focuses on maintaining the freshness of cached IoT content while minimizing energy consumption. The strategy ensures that outdated content is updated only when requested, thus avoiding unnecessary overhead. This approach simplifies the caching and eviction process, improving the overall efficiency of content dissemination in IoT environments [25]. Similarly, Amadeo et al. [7] proposed a freshness-driven caching strategy tailored for vehicular networks, ensuring that cached content remains fresh and relevant at the time of user requests. These strategies highlight the importance of content freshness, aligning with our goal to optimize caching performance by considering both content popularity and freshness in IoT environments.

Auction mechanisms which are widely applied in resource allocation, have found increasing use in network caching optimization. Auction-based caching strategies dynamically allocate cache resources through bidding, ensuring that the most valuable content is stored within limited cache space [2]. For example, BidCache optimizes caching in ICN through an auction mechanism between nodes, preventing redundant caching caused by independent node decisions. BidCache enables nodes along the data request path to participate in an auction for the right to cache content, improving cache utilization and reducing latency [21]. In addition, several other auction-based caching strategies have been proposed for diverse network environments. Cao et al. developed an optimal auction mechanism for mobile edge caching, where service providers allocate cache space based on user bids to maximize revenue while ensuring truthfulness and user participation [26]. Jedari and Di Francesco introduced DOCAT, a double auction-based trading system for scalable video content in multi-provider networks. DOCAT balances economic properties such as rationality and budget balance while maximizing social welfare [27]. Similarly, DeepAuC combines deep learning with auction mechanisms to optimize caching in NDN. By predicting future network traffic, this method not only prevents congestion but also allows paid content to be acquired at optimal prices through auctions, enabling Internet Service Providers (ISPs) to resell cached content. These auction-based caching management methods help ISPs acquire high-demand content while reducing network congestion and latency, as well as providing ISPs the ability to monetize cached paid content [23].

3 Auction-Based Caching Decision Algorithm (ABCD)

In this section, we introduce the ABCD algorithm, designed to maximize the caching of fresh and frequently accessed content. The algorithm uses an auction mechanism, where nodes dynamically adjust their caching strategy based on content popularity and freshness. IoT data has the characteristic of a limited lifespan, and if its time in the cache exceeds its lifespan, it is considered *expired* [2]. Since content can expire, the algorithm aims to cache as much fresh content as possible.

3.1 NDN Data Structures

In NDN, communication is initiated by the receiver or consumer through the exchange of *interest* and *data* packets. Consumers send interest packets to request named content, and the data packet (which encapsulates the requested content) is returned by either the source node (also known as producer or origin) or a cache node. Each node maintains three key data structures: the *Content Store* (CS) for caching data packets, the *Pending Interest Table* (PIT) for recording unanswered interest packets, and the *Forwarding Information Base* (FIB) for determining forwarding paths of interest packets. When a node receives an interest packet, if matching content is found in the CS, it is immediately returned; otherwise, the packet is processed using the FIB. Data packets follow the chain of PIT entries back to the requesters, **and each node along the path decides whether to cache the data**.

3.2 IoT Data Packet Fields

The NDN data packet format is designed to be flexible and extensible, allowing the inclusion of custom fields in addition to the predefined name, content, and signature fields. To support freshness calculation and the auction process, we added the following three fields to the data packet: (*i*) *GeneratedTime* which represents the packet's creation time; (*ii*) *FreshnessPeriod* which indicates its validity period; and (*iii*) *BidThreshold* which is used to decide whether an auction should be conducted in order to cache this data packet. It is initialized to 0 by the node (which can satisfy the interest) when it sends the corresponding data packet.

IoT producers periodically generate new content which is encapsulated in a data packet and includes the above-mentioned fields. Now, when a consumer requests for a **fresh** data, the corresponding data packet reply must be valid, i.e., it has not yet exceeded its *FreshnessPeriod*. Data packets that have exceeded their *FreshnessPeriod* cannot be used to satisfy such requests, and this may require the retrieval of content from other nodes or even the original producer.

3.3 Bidding Function Design

In this auction-based caching mechanism, nodes act as **auctioneers** while content objects act as **participants**. When a new content arrives and the cache is full, the node (acting as the auctioneer) initiates an auction to determine whether the new content should replace an existing item. This mechanism adopts characteristics of a multi-unit English auction [24], where in each round, all participating content (including new content and cached content) submit their **bids** based on their popularity and freshness. As mentioned, the *BidThreshold* field of the new content is used to trigger the auction which reduces the number of auctions.

The bidding function is the core of the auction mechanism, used to evaluate the utility of caching content at a specific node. It considers two key factors: **content popularity** and **freshness**. The combination of these factors ensures that frequently requested and highly relevant (fresh) content is prioritized for caching.

Popularity Calculation. Content popularity is calculated using a method similar to the Least Recently Frequently Used (LRFU) algorithm, where each cached item is associated with a Combined Recency and Frequency (CRF) value [16]. This value decays over time but increases with each new access, balancing both frequency and recency of request. The CRF of content x at time t is calculated as follows:

$$CRF(x,t) = CRF(x,\tau) \times \left(\frac{1}{2}\right)^{\epsilon \Delta t} \tag{1}$$

where τ is the previous time that the CRF of content x was last calculated, ϵ is the decay factor that controls the rate at which the historical value diminishes, and Δ t denotes the time elapsed since the last access.

Freshness Calculation. In an IoT environment, content freshness is a critical factor that should influence cache decisions because it ensures that cached data remains relevant and useful for timely responses to requests. For a content x at time t, we introduce a freshness factor as follows:

$$FreshnessFactor(x,t) = \max\left(0, 1 - \frac{t - \text{GeneratedTime}(x)}{\text{FreshnessPeriod}(x)}\right). \tag{2}$$

where GeneratedTime(x) and FreshnessPeriod(x) denote the corresponding data packet fields discussed in Sect. 3.2. This normalization allows packets with different freshness periods to be directly comparable.

Finally, we can now define the adjusted bidding function incorporating freshness of content x at time t as:

$$Bid(x,t) = CRF(x,t) \cdot FreshnessFactor(x,t). \tag{3}$$

Essentially, a higher freshness factor increases the bid value which increases likelihood of caching more timely content.

3.4 Content Table

To enable the computation of CRF and *FreshnessFactor*, and ultimately the bid of a content, each cache node maintains a **Content Table** that tracks the following information:

- **Content Name**: A unique identifier for each content item.
- **Last Access Time**: Timestamp of last request.
- **CRF**: Content's CRF at last access.

When a new content request arrives, the node updates the relevant entry in the content table. If any content has expired or surpassed its valid lifetime, the corresponding entry is deleted from the Content Table.

3.5 Algorithm

The ABCD algorithm is listed in Algorithm 1 and consists of four main steps:

Data Packet Arrival. When a data packet arrives at a cache node, the node first checks whether there is available space in the cache. If the cache is not full, the data packet is immediately cached. Otherwise, the node proceeds to evaluate whether the data packet should be cached.

Bidding Function Calculation. The node performs a valuation of the content using Eq. (3), which reflects the content's popularity and freshness at the current node.

Auction Trigger Conditions. The node reads the *BidThreshold* field from the data packet and compares *BidThreshold* with its valuation:

- **If the node's valuation exceeds *BidThreshold***, the auction is triggered. The node evaluates all cached content and compares their bids. If the new content's bid is higher than the lowest bid among the cached items, the data packet is considered to have won the auction and is therefore cached in the node. Otherwise, the data packet is not cached and is only forwarded to the next node if a corresponding record exists in the PIT. This mechanism ensures that only content with sufficiently high value (in terms of popularity and freshness) participates in the auction process, significantly reducing unnecessary computational overhead. By doing so, the node avoids evaluating all cached content for every incoming data packet, making the system more efficient, especially in resource-constrained IoT scenarios.
- **If the node's valuation does not exceed the *BidThreshold***, the auction is skipped, and the content is not cached. This threshold-driven design also prevents low-value content from occupying valuable cache space or triggering frequent auctions, further optimizing network caching efficiency. The data packet is forwarded to the next node only if a corresponding record exists in the PIT.

Algorithm 1: ABCD Algorithm

```
Input: Content object P, Content store C, Current time t
Output: Cache decision
if C is full then
    bid ← Bid(P, t);
    if bid > BidThreshold of P then
        minBid ← ∞;
        for every content i in C do
            b ← Bid(i, t);
            if b < minBid then
                minBid ← b;
        if bid > minBid then
            Cache P in C;
            BidThreshold of P ← bid;
        else
            Do not cache P;
    else
        Do not cache P;
else
    Cache P in C;
Forward P to the next node;
```

Update of *BidThreshold*. If the auction is triggered and the new content wins, the node updates the *BidThreshold* of the packet to reflect its updated valuation across the network. This updated BidThreshold effectively communicates the caching decision to downstream nodes, enabling them to dynamically adjust their caching strategies based on the current value of the content. By propagating this updated threshold, the system achieves a form of "collaboration" among nodes, ensuring that the most valuable content is cached at the most suitable nodes, maximizing cache utility. Otherwise, the *BidThreshold* remains unchanged.

Since ABCD is a caching decision strategy, it can be used alongside any existing cache replacement strategy. Once ABCD decides to cache a new content, the replacement strategy is first invoked to evict existing content from the cache before storing the new content.

4 Performance Evaluation

In this section, we evaluate the performance of the proposed caching algorithm in a variety of network settings through simulations. We compare it against several existing caching strategies using key performance metrics. The simulations were conducted using realistic network topologies and diverse IoT scenarios to ensure thorough evaluation and comparison of the algorithm under different conditions.

4.1 Simulation Scenarios and Settings

Using the ns-3 simulator with NDN extensions (NDNsim) [19], we designed a hybrid network scenario where the backbone network connects multiple IoT edge domains. The core network is modeled using the CERNET [18] (36 nodes), GEANT [20] (40 nodes), and UNINETT [30] (69 nodes) topologies, with 10 nodes randomly selected from the core network as access routers for the edge domains. Each edge domain used a two-level NDN content router topology, forming a binary tree structure with 6 nodes (2 aggregation and 4 content routers).

Each edge domain contains 40 leaf nodes, serving as access points for IoT producer devices. Each leaf node is connected to 250 IoT devices, generating a total of 100,000 unique content items, which are small enough to fit into a single data packet [28]. Additionally, each content item is associated with a freshness period, uniformly distributed between 2 and 20 s to reflect varying IoT application freshness requirements.

The content request rate follows a Poisson distribution with parameter λ set to 100 requests per second [22]. Requests are generated by consumer nodes and randomly assigned to consumers connected to the leaf nodes, with the number of consumers set to 20. The requests are forwarded through NDN routers to the IoT producer devices for retrieval and response. To simulate content popularity, we employed both Zipf and uniform random distributions. We evaluated the performance of the algorithm under different request patterns using these two distribution models, with the Zipf distribution having a skewness parameter $\alpha = 1$. We varied the cache capacity of the nodes from 100 to 1000 [28], treating it as one of the independent variables in the experiments. To ensure reliable results, we conducted a 10-minute warm-up phase where all content items were requested at least once, followed by a 10-minute evaluation phase to assess the performance metrics accurately. Additionally, the simulation was repeated 10 times, and a 95% confidence interval was calculated for the experimental results. Table 1 provides a summary of the simulation setup and the parameters used.

4.2 Benchmarks and Metrics

We studied the performance of ABCD, comparing it with four existing caching strategies. These strategies include LCE (Leave Cache Everywhere) [29], LCD (Leave Cache Down) [15], ProbCache (probabilistic cache with a caching probability of $p = 0.5$) [2], and CFPC (Caching Popular and Fresh Content). The latter is a recent algorithm that focuses on caching popular content with longer residual lifetimes [8]. For ABCD, we tuned $\epsilon = 0.5$ as it provided optimal cache hit rate performance. LRU (Least Recently Used) was employed as the cache replacement policy.

To evaluate and compare the performance of the proposed caching placement algorithm and benchmarks, we employ three key metrics:

Content Freshness Ratio. This metric evaluates the freshness of content received by a consumer relative to its total lifetime. For each content item x_i received at time t, CFR is defined as:

$$CFR(x_i, t) = 1 - \frac{t - \text{GeneratedTime}(x_i)}{\text{FreshnessPeriod}(x_i)} \tag{4}$$

where $\{x_i, i = 1, \ldots, N\}$ represents the set of content items received, and FreshnessPeriod(x_i) is the total valid duration of x_i. To compute the overall performance, the **Average Content Freshness Ratio (ACFR)** is calculated as the average of all CFR values over the simulation period:

$$ACFR = \frac{1}{M} \sum_{i=1}^{M} CFR(x_i, t) \tag{5}$$

where M is the total number of content items received. ACFR indicates the freshness of content at the time of reception, with values closer to 1 representing fresher content.

Cache Hit Ratio. This metric measures the percentage of requests satisfied by the local cache, defined as the ratio of cache hits (successful local cache responses) to the total number of requests.

Packet Delay. This metric represents the time taken from the consumer sending an interest packet to receiving the corresponding IoT data packet.

Table 1. Simulation Parameters.

Parameter	Value
Core network topology	CERNET, GEANT and UNINETT
Access routers	10 randomly selected nodes
Edge domain topology	2-level binary tree
Total catalog size	100,000 content items
Freshness period	Uniformly distributed [2–20] s
Request rate	Poisson, $\lambda = 100$ requests/sec
Network bandwidth	Core: 10 Gbps; Edge: 100 Mbps
Network latency	Core: 5 ms; Edge: 50 ms

4.3 Results

The simulation results are presented in Figs. 1, 2, 3, 4, 5 and 6, each representing a combination of distributions and performance metrics. Each figure consists of three subfigures corresponding to the CERNET, GEANT, and UNINETT topologies. The first two figures illustrate the cache hit ratio, the middle two figures focus on latency performance, and the last two figures show the results for the Average Content Freshness Ratio (ACFR). To facilitate comparison, the results of the three subfigures in each figure are plotted on the same coordinate scale.

Under the uniform distribution, the cache hit ratio of all algorithms increases as cache capacity grows, as shown in Fig. 1. This trend is particularly pronounced in the simpler CERNET topology, where the growth is nearly linear. However, in more complex topologies such as GEANT (Fig. 1b) and UNINETT (Fig. 1c), the growth rate slows. Log analysis reveals that as cache capacity increases, the number of cached items grows, leading to longer retention times. Consequently, some content expires before being requested, reducing the benefits of increasing cache capacity. Among the algorithms, **ABCD** achieves the best performance under the uniform distribution, despite the lack of concentrated content requests. By prioritizing fresher content for caching, ABCD significantly improves the cache hit ratio, highlighting the importance of content freshness under uniform distribution. **CFPC** and **ProbCache** also perform relatively well, while **LCD** performs similarly to **LCE** but slightly worse in most cases due to limitations in its caching strategy. In contrast, ProbCache outperforms LCE by reducing cache redundancy, while LCE's frequent content updates improve freshness but provide limited benefits to hit ratio. Overall, ABCD improves the cache hit ratio by approximately 50% compared to LCE and 15% compared to CFPC. The generally low cache hit ratio under uniform distribution further emphasizes the significant impact of content freshness.

Under the Zipf distribution, as shown in Fig. 2, all algorithms show substantial improvements in cache hit ratio, with performance approximately doubling in the CERNET topology. Unlike the uniform distribution, the growth in cache

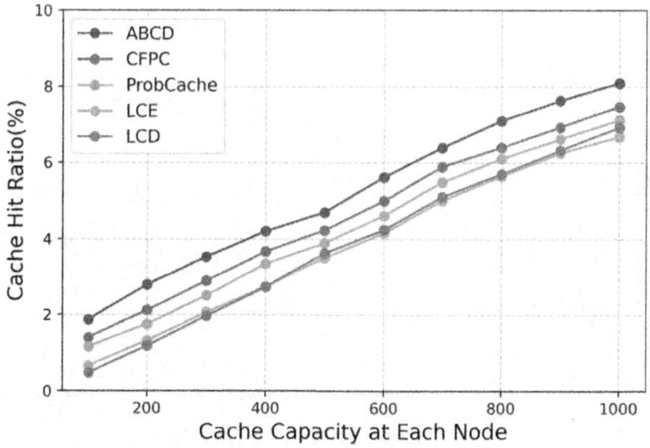

(a) CERNET

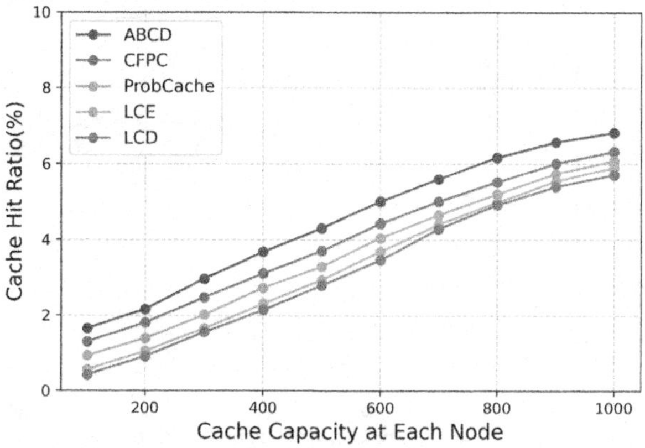

(b) GEANT

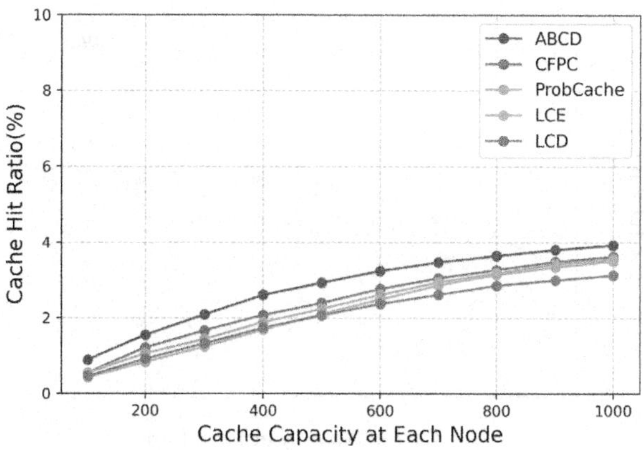

(c) UNINETT

Fig. 1. Hit rate performance under uniform distribution.

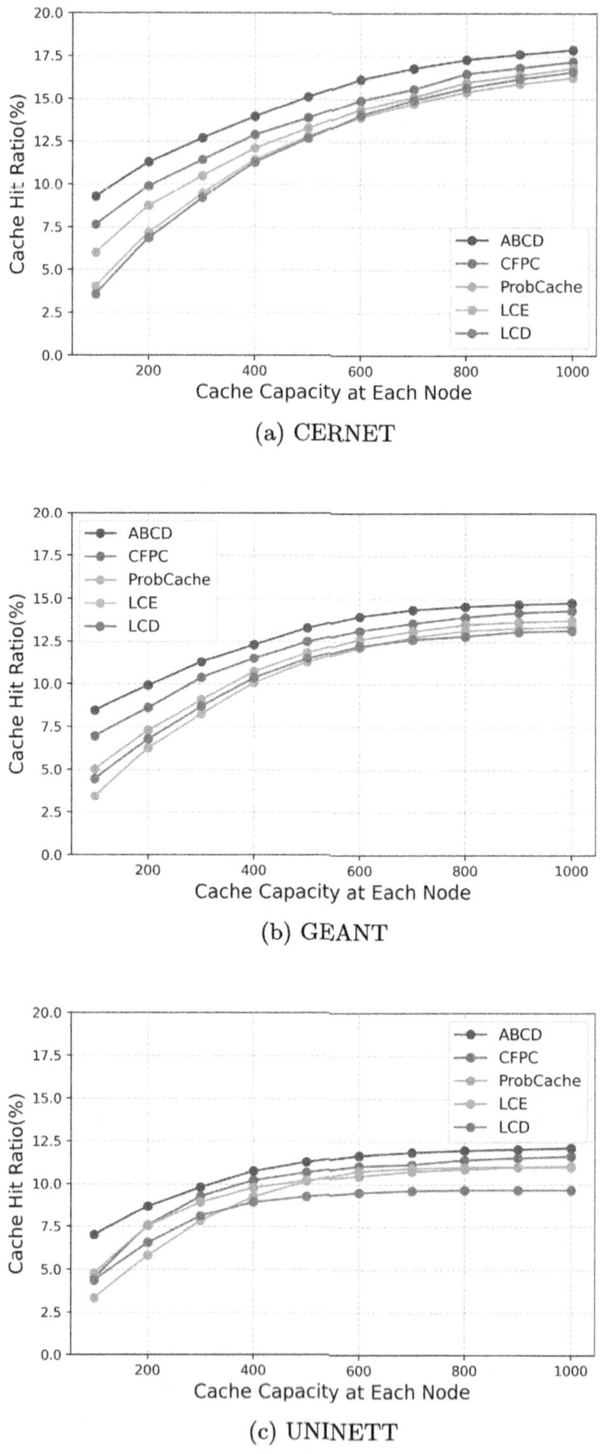

Fig. 2. Hit rate performance under zipf distribution.

hit ratio under the Zipf distribution exhibits diminishing returns, particularly in complex topologies such as GEANT and UNINETT. The performance gap between LCD and LCE widens in complex topologies, where LCD lags behind due to its caching mechanism. At low cache capacities, LCD outperforms LCE because LCE's frequent updates may replace popular content. However, as cache capacity grows, LCE gradually surpasses LCD by retaining fresher content. **ABCD** demonstrates greater advantages under the Zipf distribution, especially at low cache capacities, where its ability to identify and cache popular, fresh content significantly enhances performance. Overall, ABCD improves the cache hit ratio by approximately 20% compared to LCE and 10% compared to CFPC, consistently outperforming all other algorithms across all topologies.

Figure 3 shows the latency performance of the algorithms under the uniform distribution. The trends in latency closely align with the cache hit ratio results, with latency decreasing nearly linearly as cache capacity increases. **ABCD** achieves the lowest latency and exhibits significant advantages over other algorithms, while **LCD** has the highest latency. This outcome aligns with its low cache hit ratio. Log analysis indicates that LCD's content delivery mechanism introduces delays, causing more content to expire before being served. Additionally, LCD does not significantly shorten request paths, whereas **LCE** and **ProbCache** can occasionally locate cached content through shorter paths, effectively reducing latency. As cache capacity increases, the latency gap between LCD and other algorithms widens due to the higher proportion of expired content in complex topologies. **CFPC** demonstrates lower latency compared to LCE and LCD but performs similarly to ProbCache, suggesting that while CFPC caches fresher content more effectively, its retention capability remains limited. Under the uniform distribution, ABCD reduces latency by approximately 10% compared to LCE.

Figure 4 illustrates the latency performance under the Zipf distribution. Compared to the uniform distribution, latency is significantly lower across all cache capacities, and the performance gap between algorithms becomes more pronounced. The latency difference between CFPC and other algorithms is more evident under the Zipf distribution. ABCD maintains the best latency performance, reducing latency by approximately 15% compared to LCE and 5% compared to CFPC. At low cache capacities, ABCD exhibits the most significant advantage, further demonstrating its ability to identify popular and fresh content. LCD continues its trend from the uniform distribution, with the latency gap between LCD and other algorithms increasing as cache capacity grows. Additionally, LCD reaches latency saturation more quickly, highlighting the critical impact of content freshness on caching efficiency.

Figure 5 presents the ACFR performance of the algorithms under the uniform distribution. Higher ACFR values indicate that most of the content received by nodes is relatively fresh. The ACFR performance closely mirrors the cache hit ratio trends, showing a linear growth pattern as cache capacity increases. Due to their consideration of content freshness, **ABCD** and **CFPC** significantly outperform other traditional algorithms, with ABCD improving ACFR by approx-

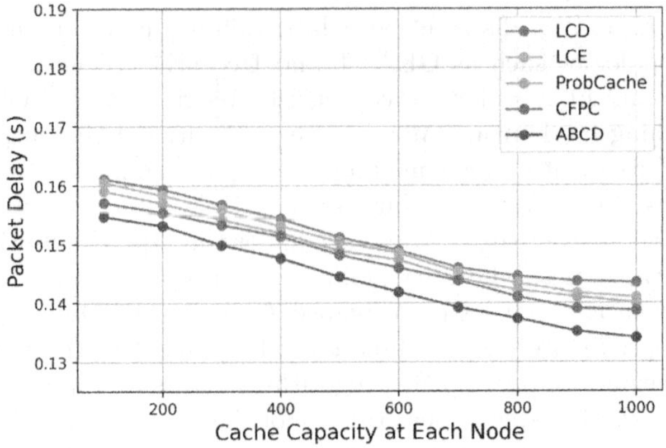

(a) CERNET

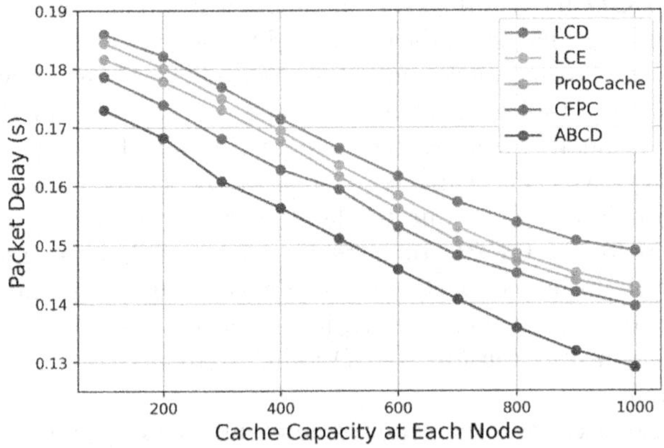

(b) GEANT

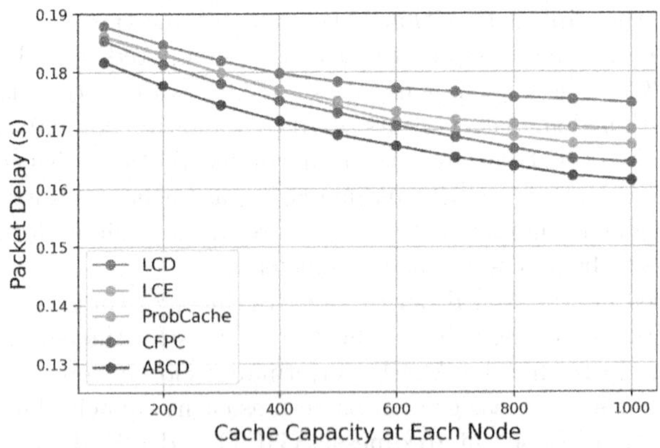

(c) UNINETT

Fig. 3. Packet Delay under uniform distribution.

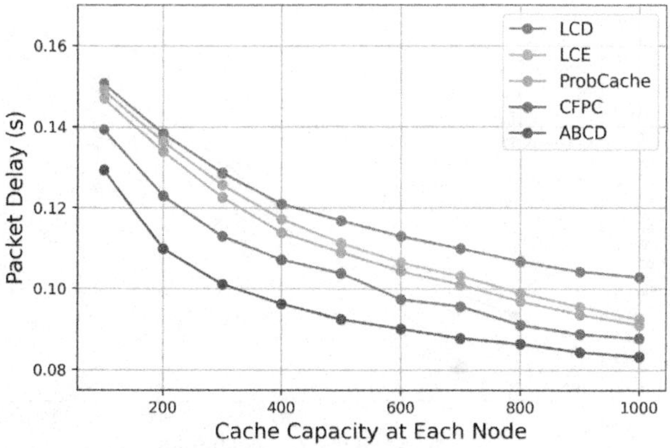

(a) CERNET

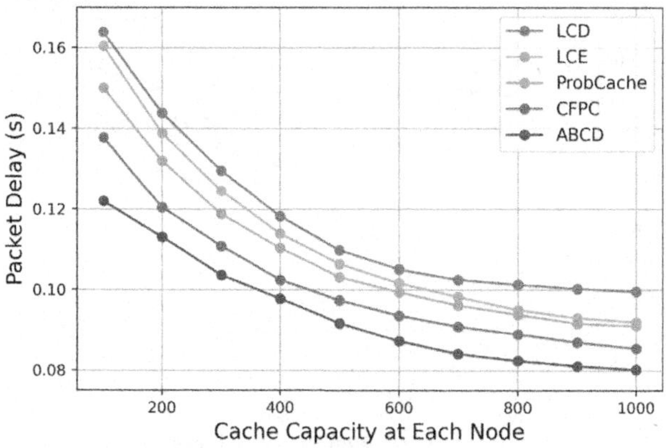

(b) GEANT

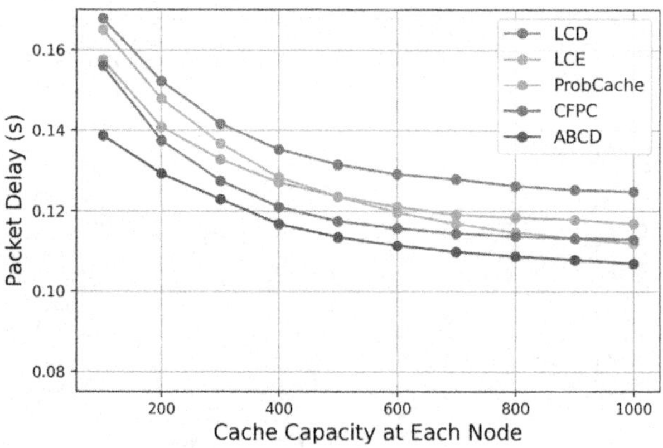

(c) UNINETT

Fig. 4. Packet Delay under zipf distribution.

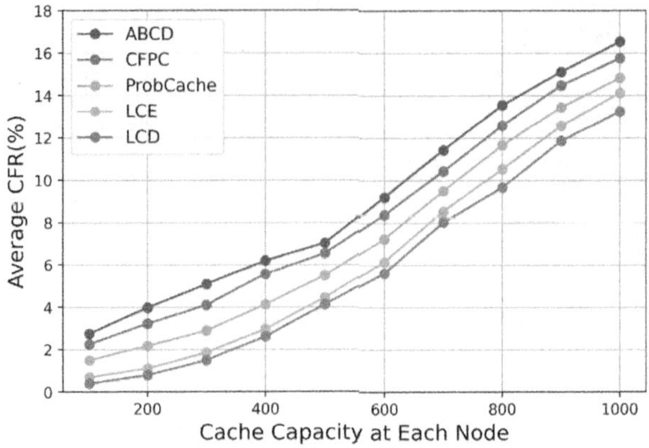

(a) CERNET

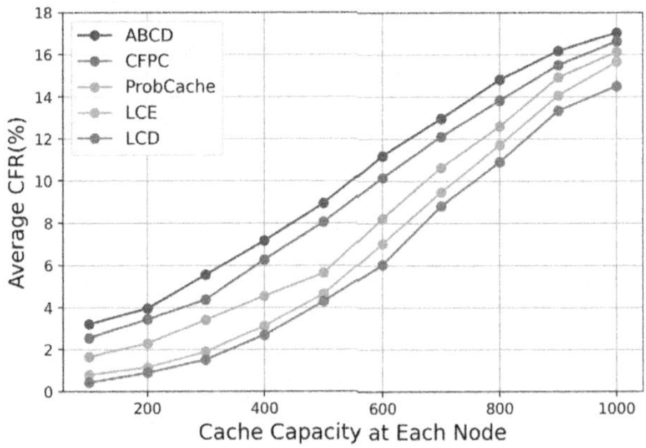

(b) GEANT

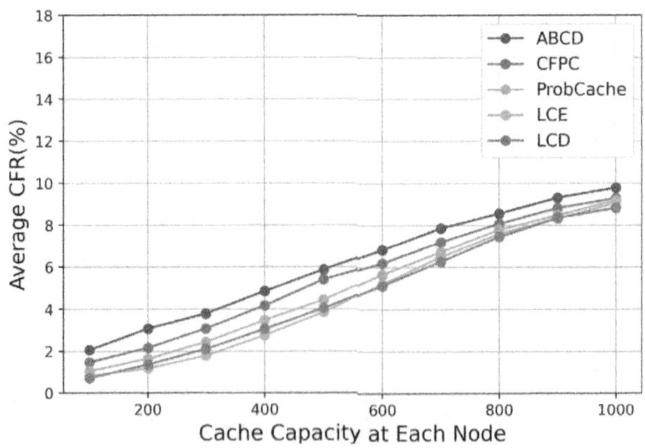

(c) UNINETT

Fig. 5. ACFR under uniform distribution.

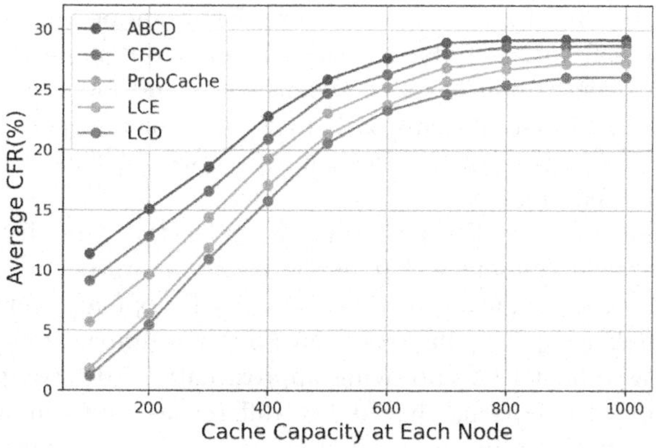

(a) CERNET

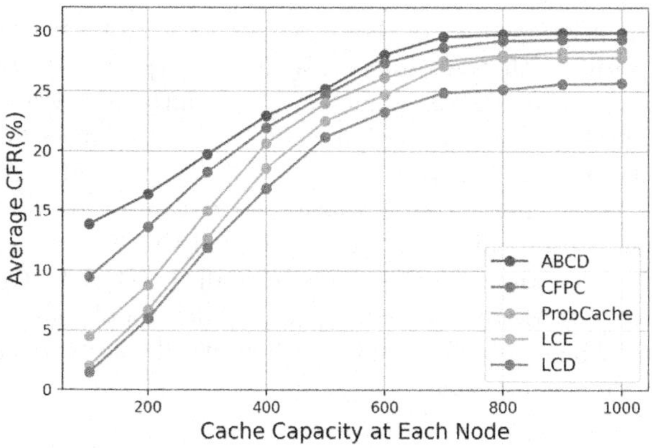

(b) GEANT

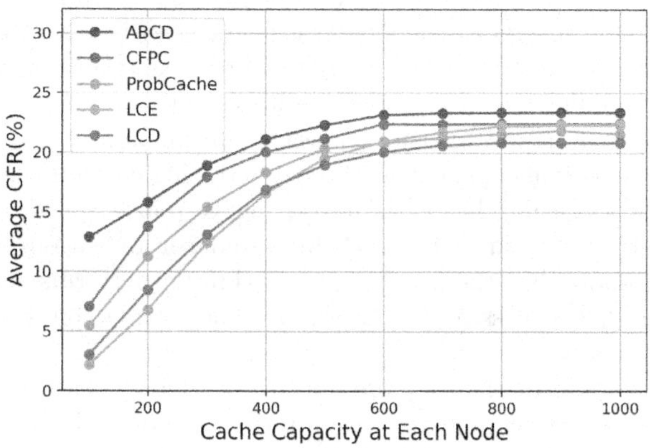

(c) UNINETT

Fig. 6. ACFR under zipf distribution.

imately 20% compared to LCE. Furthermore, **ProbCache** outperforms LCE in ACFR, as LCE's frequent updates result in more content being fetched from server nodes, leading to longer transmission paths and lower ACFR. Although LCD performs the worst, its gap with LCE is smaller in complex topologies such as UNINETT, where LCD's mechanism reduces inefficient cache updates, mitigating cache redundancy.

Figure 6 shows the ACFR performance under the Zipf distribution. The ACFR growth trend resembles that of the cache hit ratio but saturates more quickly. When cache capacity reaches 500, most popular content is already cached, and further capacity increases have minimal impact on ACFR. ABCD achieves the highest ACFR, improving approximately 10% compared to LCE. Under the Zipf distribution, the ACFR differences between algorithms are smaller than under the uniform distribution, as all algorithms prioritize caching popular content. However, at low cache capacities, ABCD retains a significant advantage, demonstrating its effectiveness in improving content freshness across caching nodes.

The comprehensive analysis of the three metrics—**cache hit ratio**, **latency**, and **ACFR**—confirms that **ABCD** consistently outperforms other algorithms across various scenarios. ABCD achieves significantly higher cache hit ratios, particularly under the Zipf distribution, and effectively reduces latency by leveraging higher hit ratios and shorter request paths. Additionally, ABCD substantially enhances ACFR, highlighting its superior capability to identify and cache both popular and fresh content. While CFPC and ProbCache perform competitively in certain scenarios, they fall short overall. LCD and LCE demonstrate relatively weaker performance, especially in complex topologies and with higher cache capacities. These results emphasize the critical role of incorporating content freshness into caching strategies to improve performance.

5 Conclusion

IoT data are typically transient, and producers frequently update the data, which imposes high requirements on caching placement strategies and data freshness. We propose an auction-based caching algorithm that simultaneously considers both content popularity and freshness, suitable for IoT data traffic. Through this distributed caching mechanism, nodes can autonomously make caching decisions based on real-time evaluations, thereby reducing communication overhead, enhancing network scalability, and improving response speed. We conducted extensive experiments using the NDNsim simulator in various IoT scenarios, and the results show that the proposed algorithm outperforms existing schemes in terms of cache freshness and network efficiency while significantly reducing data retrieval latency.

Future work could further explore optimizing this algorithm for IoT devices by focusing on reducing energy consumption. Since IoT devices are often resource-constrained, it is crucial to design caching placement strategies that also consider energy efficiency. Furthermore, considering the mobility of IoT devices, future research should investigate the impact of consumer and producer mobility on caching strategies to ensure the validity and availability of cached content in dynamic network environments.

References

1. Qadir, Z., et al.: Towards 6G Internet of Things: recent advances, use cases, and open challenges. ICT Express **9**(3), 296–312 (2023)
2. Zhang, Z., et al.: In-network caching for ICN-based IoT (ICN-IoT): a comprehensive survey. IEEE Internet Things J. **10**(16), 14595–14620 (2023)
3. Mishra, G.P., Dave, M.: A review on content centric networking and caching strategies. In: Proceedings of the International Conference on Communication Systems and Network Technologies, pp. 925–929
4. Kim, D., et al.: Cache capacity-aware content centric networking under flash crowds. J. Netw. Comput. Appl. **50**, 101–113 (2015)
5. Amadeo, M., et al.: Information-centric networking for the internet of things: challenges and opportunities. IEEE Netw. **30**(2), 92–100 (2016)
6. Serhane, O., et al.: Energy-aware cache placement scheme for IoT-based ICN networks. In: Proceedings of the IEEE International Conference on Communications (ICC), pp. 1–6 (2021)
7. Amadeo, M., et al.: Caching transient contents in vehicular named data networking: a performance analysis. Sensors **20**(7), 1–17 (2020)
8. Amadeo, M., et al.: Caching popular and fresh IoT contents at the edge via named data networking. In: IEEE INFOCOM Workshops, pp. 610–615 (2020)
9. Meddeb, M., et al.: Least fresh first cache replacement policy for NDN-based IoT networks. Pervasive Mob. Comput. **52**, 60–70 (2019)
10. Zhang, Z., et al.: IoT data lifetime-based cooperative caching scheme for ICN-IoT networks. In: Proceedings of the IEEE International Conference on Communications (ICC), pp. 1–7 (2018)
11. Meddeb, M., et al.: Cache freshness in named data networking for the Internet of Things. Comput. J. **61**(10), 1496–1511 (2018)
12. He, X., et al.: EABC: energy-aware centrality-based caching for named data networking in the IoT. In: Proceedings of the IEEE WoWMoM, pp. 1–6 (2024)
13. Sheraz, M., et al.: Artificial intelligence for wireless caching: schemes, performance, and challenges. IEEE Commun. Surv. Tutor. 631–661 (2020)
14. Jacobson, V., et al.: Networking named content. In: Proceedings of the 5th International Conference on Emerging Networking Experiments and Technologies (CoNEXT), Rome, Italy, pp. 1–12 (2009)
15. Laoutaris, N., et al.: The LCD interconnection of LRU caches and its analysis. Perform. Eval. **63**(7), 609–634 (2006)
16. Lee, D., et al.: LRFU: a spectrum of policies that subsumes the least recently used and least frequently used policies. IEEE Trans. Comput. **50**(12), 1352–1361 (2001)
17. Xu, X., et al.: Proactive edge caching in content-centric networks with massive dynamic content requests. IEEE Access **8**, 59906–59921 (2020)
18. Tong, T.-C., et al.: Mitigation strategy for the cascading failure of complex networks based on node capacity control function. IEEE Access **7**, 184743–184758 (2019)
19. Mastorakis, S., et al.: ndnSIM 2.0: a new version of the NDN simulator for NS-3. NDN, Technical Report NDN-0028 (2015)

20. Saino, L., et al.: Icarus: a caching simulator for information centric networking (ICN). In: Proceedings of the 7th International Conference on Simulation Tools and Techniques (SIMUTools), Portugal, pp. 66–75 (2014)
21. Gill, A.S., et al.: BidCache: auction-based in-network caching in ICN. In: Proceedings of the IEEE Globecom Workshops, Washington, DC, USA, pp. 1–6 (2016)
22. Herouala, A.T., et al.: CaDaCa: a new caching strategy in NDN using data categorization. Multimedia Syst. **29**, 2935–2950 (2023)
23. Ndikumana, A., et al.: DeepAuC: joint deep learning and auction for congestion-aware caching in named data networking. PLoS ONE **14**(8), e0220813 (2019)
24. Hubbard, T.P., Paarsch, H.J.: Auctions. MIT Press, Cambridge (2016)
25. Asmat, H., Din, I.U., Ullah, F., Talha, M., Khan, M., Guizani, M.: ELC: edge linked caching for content updating in information-centric Internet of Things. Comput. Commun. **156**, 174–182 (2020)
26. Cao, X., Zhang, J., Poor, H.V.: An optimal auction mechanism for mobile edge caching. In: Proceedings of the IEEE 38th International Conference on Distributed Computing Systems (ICDCS), pp. 388–399 (2018)
27. Jedari, B., Francesco, M.D.: Auction-based cache trading for scalable videos in multi-provider heterogeneous networks. In: Proceedings of the IEEE INFOCOM, pp. 1864–1872 (2019)
28. Araldo, A., et al.: Cost-aware caching: caching more (costly items) for less (ISPs operational expenditures). IEEE Trans. Parallel Distrib. Syst. **27**(5), 1316–1330 (2016)
29. Zhang, L., et al.: Named data networking. SIGCOMM Comput. Commun. Rev. **44**(3), 66–73 (2014)
30. Gonzalez, A.J., Helvik, B.E.: Characterisation of router and link failure processes in UNINETT's IP backbone network. Int. J. Space-Based Situated Comput. 7 **2**(1), 3–11 (2012)

Maximizing Long-Term Task Completion Ratio of 3D-UAV-Enabled Wirelessly Powered MEC System

Tixin Chen, Guanqun Shen, Xinnan Zhu, Shaojun Zhu, Bincheng Zhu(✉), and Kaikai Chi

Zhejiang University of Technology, Hangzhou, China
{chentx,1121812003,zxn,sjzhu,bczhu,kkchi}@zjut.edu.cn

Abstract. In recent years, Mobile Edge Computing (MEC) and Wireless Power Transfer (WPT) technologies have been widely applied to wireless devices (WDs). However, in remote areas or during disaster events, data and energy transmission cannot be accomplished through conventional ways. To address this challenge, this paper explores a WPT-MEC system using Unmanned Aerial Vehicle (UAV) with 3D flying and obstacle avoidance. Our goal is to maximize the long-term task completion ratio while considering the constraints of UAV coverage, time resources, energy, and task validity duration. We first model this problem into multiple equal-sized time slots, with each time slot involving two main actions. The first action is the UAV selecting its flight direction based on the tasks of the on-site WDs. The second action is after UAV's flying, the WDs which are in the UAV's coverage offload their tasks to UAV. For each action decision, we design a Deep Reinforcement Learning (DRL) algorithm. By training two models to accomplish this task, our algorithm significantly improves the long-term task completion ratio, with performance improvements reaching up to 40% in certain scenarios compared to baseline methods.

Keywords: Unmanned aerial vehicle · Edge computing · Deep reinforcement learning

1 Introduction

Recent advancements in Internet of Things (IoT) and wireless communication have expanded their applications across various fields. However, IoT devices face limitations in computational power and battery life due to cost constraints, necessitating external resources to meet their requirements. Mobile Edge Computing (MEC), powered by edge servers, addresses these challenges effectively.

This paper explores Unmanned Aerial Vehicle(UAV)-based MEC (UAV-MEC), which is ideal for some scenarios like disaster relief scene where the devices for computation task offloading and energy supply are unavailable. UAV which work as edge servers are highly mobile, offering rapid deployment in remote

Y. Zhou et al. (Eds.): ICECCS 2025, LNCS 15746, pp. 221–240, 2026.
https://doi.org/10.1007/978-3-032-00828-2_13

areas to provide computation service and solve the computational power issues at IoT nodes.

For energy supply, Wireless Power Transfer (WPT) technology provides a promising solution [1,10]. UAV can conduct WPT to wireless nodes during computation task completion, ensuring energy provision even when conventional facilities are damaged.

In recent studies, [6,7] respectively studied how to maximize the total computational capacity of edge computing systems in the context of Sparse Code Multiple Access (SCMA) and Non-Orthogonal Multiple Access (NOMA), with [6] collaborating UAV and Reconfigurable Intelligent Surfaces (RIS). [2,12] aimed to address the information security issues in UAV-MEC systems during communication between UAV and wireless nodes, employing a Block Coordinate Descent (BCD)-based approach. [8] divided the IoT devices into two groups, the active devices and the idle devices, investigating the assistance of the UAV and the idle devices in task offloading for active devices. [3,5] used traditional mathematical models to solve the problems, with [5] utilizing Mixed-Integer Nonlinear Programming (MINLP) and Penalty Successive Convex Approximation (PSCA), and [3] adopting a Dinkelbach iterative algorithm-based approach. [11] used traditional mathematical models to plan the UAV's 3D spatial flight. [4] utilized a deep reinforcement learning (DRL)-based multi-step adversarial DDQN approach to address the UAV's 3D spatial flight, taking into account the height of buildings in the environment. [9] considered the scenario where tasks are indivisible and employed a shortest job first approach for task offloading. It should be noted that, in many practical MEC scenarios, the computation tasks have limited lifetime. However, in [2–9,11,12], the lifetime issue of computation tasks is not considered. Additionally, except [3], very few works have been done on the MEC networks using UAV for WPT. Moreover, except [4], most of these studies do not account for no-fly zones or restricted areas in the UAV's flight environment.

In this work, we aim to maximize the long-term task completion ratio of a WPT-enabled 3D-UAV-MEC system with independent task and no-fly areas. In this setup, the UAV flies in a 3D space, and each task generated by WDs has an effective lifetime. Each task can only be offloaded and computed individually. The WPT-enabled UAV-MEC system must optimize the energy supply time and task offloading time in each time slot. Given the presence of many obstacles and no-fly zones in the real environment, this paper introduces no-fly zones into the model, requiring the UAV to avoid these areas while flying.

The main contributions of this paper are as follows:

- We investigate more realistic 3D-UAV-MEC system where UAV flies in 3D space with no-fly zones, UAV conducts both WPT and task offloading, and each computation task has its lifetime.
- The long-term task computation ratio maximization problem of the WPT-enabled UAV-MEC system is formulated as a nonlinear and non-convex optimization problem. To solve it efficiently, we decompose it into two subproblems: one is the top-level problem of determining the UAV flight tra-

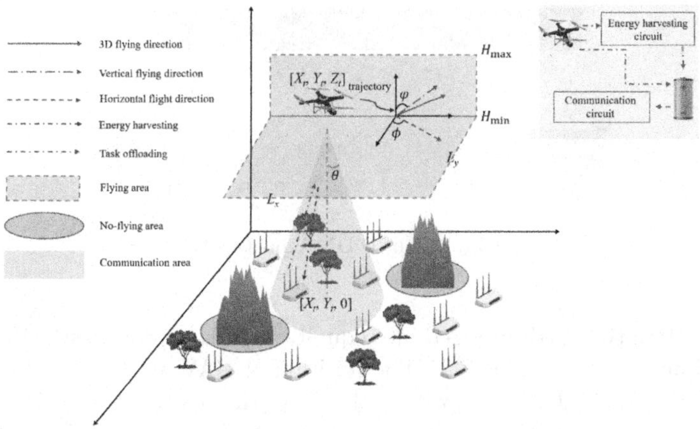

Fig. 1. The considered 3D-UAV-enabled wireless powered MEC.

jectory, and the other is the sub-problem of optimizing WPT time and task offloading time allocation for each WD given the UAV trajectory decision.
- For the two sub-problems, a deep reinforcement learning network algorithm based on Deep Deterministic Policy Gradient(DDPG) is designed to train two independent models, called UAV-DDPG and time-division multiple access(TDMA) -DDPG, that output the UAV's flight trajectory and the WPT time and task offloading time for edge nodes, respectively. In this algorithm, some random exploration methods are employed to enhance the stability and generalization ability of the trained models.
- Through extensive simulation results, we demonstrate that the proposed dual-model algorithm based on DRL achieves higher long-term task completion ratio and better network generalization ability compared to other benchmark algorithms and single-model algorithm.

The structure of this paper is as follows. Section 2 provides the system model. Section 3 formulates the problem and introduces the DRL-based algorithm. Simulation results are presented in Sect. 4. Finally, Sect. 5 concludes the paper.

2 System Model

2.1 Environment Model

The considered wireless powered 3D-UAV-enabled MEC system is shown in Fig. 1. The UAV is equipped with a radio frequency (RF) energy transmitter and an MEC server. UAV can wirelessly transmit RF energy to N wireless devices (WDs) for wireless power supply and provide MEC service to these WDs. UAV can fly within a limited height and range, completing task offloading while avoiding regions such as impassable mountains or no-fly zones. The set of WDs is denoted as $\mathcal{N} = \{1, 2, ..., N\}$.

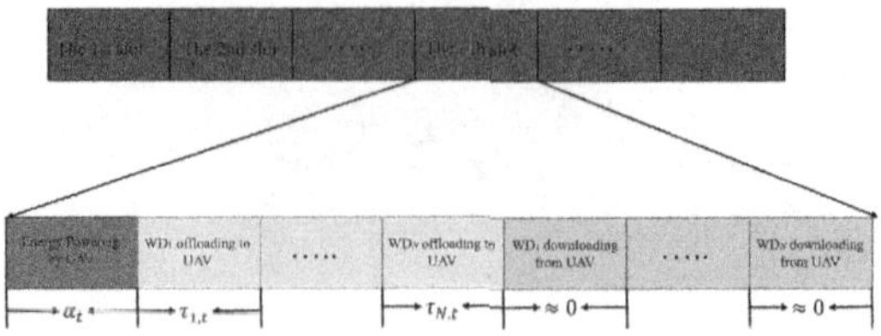

Fig. 2. The TDMA protocol.

The system time is discretized into equally sized time slots, with the duration of each time slot denoted as ΔT. The position of UAV at time slot t is denoted as $\mathbf{q}_t^U = [x_t^u, y_t^u, z_t^u]$. UAV flies within the network area with the WDs for better communication and safety reasons, i.e., $0 \le x_t^u \le L_x$, $0 \le y_t^u \le L_y$ and $H_{min} \le z_t^u \le H_{max}$. At each slots, the UAV maintains a constant flight speed denoted by v, and has two angels (denoted by ϕ_t and φ_t) to describe its direction. ϕ_t is the horizontal angle of fly action and φ_t is the vertical angle of fly action. $\phi_t \in [-\pi, \pi]$ and $\varphi_t \in [0, \pi]$. So the UAV's next state is $[X_{t-1} + v_{xy} * cos(\phi_t), Y_{t-1} + v_{xy} * sin(\phi_t), Z_{t-1} + v * cos(\varphi_t)]$, and $v_{xy} = v * sin(\varphi_t)$.

Each WD can store the collected energy and offload tasks to the UAV. WDs are randomly located on the ground, which is denoted by q_i, where $q_i = [x_i, y_i, 0]$. x_i and y_i are the horizontal plane coordinates of the WD_i.

Due to cost and size constraints, WDs have no local computing capabilities. They are primarily used for collecting environmental data, such as climate temperature, soil moisture, and other environmental information. At the beginning of each time slot, each WD randomly generates some tasks.

The UAV and WDs operate on the same frequency band for both WPT and task offloading. A TDMA protocol is applied, as shown in Fig. 2.

The important symbols are listed in Table 1.

2.2 Task Generation and Dropping Model

The tasks of the WDs are generated in a random arrival manner, like Poisson arrival process. The task size and maximum tolerable delay are random values. The tasks are represented as $\{w_i^s, w_i^t\}$, where w_i^s and w_i^t denote the task's transmission size and current tolerable delay, respectively. For WD_i, its tasks are stored in its buffered task queue $B_i(t)$.

After the offloading operation in each time slot, the current tolerable delay w_i^t is decreased by 1 before the end of each time slot. According to the system's computation delay requirements, any task with a current tolerable delay w_i^t equal to 0 must be discarded.

For example, suppose that the buffered task $B_i(t)$ of WD_i is $[\{w_i^s,w_i^t = 2\}, \{w_i^s,w_i^t = 1\},\{w_i^s,w_i^t = 6\}]$ at the begin of t-th slot. Then at the end of the t-slot,the $B_i(t)$ is change to $[\{w_i^s,w_i^t = 1\},\{w_i^s,w_i^t = 0\},\{w_i^s,w_i^t = 5\}]$. So the second task should be remove out of the $B_i(t)$ and discarded.

Table 1. Table 1 Notations used throughout the paper.

Notation	Description
L_x, L_y	The length and width of the flight area
ΔT	Time duration for each slot
$i, N, \mathcal{N}$	Index,number,set of WDs
$\mathcal{M}$	set of no-fly-area
H_{max}, H_{min}	The maximum and minimum flight height for UAV
v	The speed of UAV
θ	The communication angle of UAV
$\mathcal{R}$	The maximum communication number of WDs at one slot
P	The energy transmit power of UAV
t	Index of time slot
ϕ_t, φ_t	The horizontal and vertical fly angle of UAV
$\mathbf{q}_i, \mathbf{q}_t^U, \mathbf{q}_t^N$	Position vector of the WD_i, UAV, no-fly-area
$[x_t^u, y_t^u, z_t^u]$	Position of the UAV
$[x_i, y_i, 0]$	Position of the WD
$[x_i^n, y_i^n, 0, r_i^n]$	Position and radius of the no-fly-area
$[w_i^s, w_i^t]$	Task's transmission size and current tolerable delay
$d_{i,t}$	Distance between the WD_i and UAV
$h_{i,t}$	Channel gain between the WD_i and UAV
$E_{i,t}$	The amount of energy captured by WD_i
α_t	WPT time
$\tau_{i,t}$	The offloading time allocated for WD_i
$B_i(t)$	The total amount of buffered tasks of WD_i of the t-th slot
$b_{task}(i,j)$	one task of WD_i
$Z_{in}(t)$	The indexes from all WDs within the UAV communication range of the t-th slot
$Z_{can}(t)$	The indexes from can offload WDs within the UAV communication range of the t-th slot
Z_t	Number of WDs
$B_i^{max}(t)$	The max completed data of WD_i of the t-th slot
$B_i^{waste}(t)$	The waste of computational resources allocated to WD_i
ψ	The long-term task completion ratio
$s(t), a(t), r(t)$	State, action and reward of the t-th slot
$\pi(\cdot), Q(\cdot)$	Policy function and Q function
ω	Parameters of the Neural Network
$\delta(t)$	The temporal difference (TD)-error
γ	The discount ratio of the value with future state
e	The random exploration of action

2.3 Channel Model

All WDs are located on the ground, remaining stationary. To calculate the distance between UAV and WDs, a three-dimensional (3D) Euclidean coordinate system is established. The relative distance between the UAV and WDs depends solely on their coordinates. The wireless channel between the UAV and each WD is primarily a Line-of-Sight. Therefore, the channel gain $h_{i,t}$ between the UAV and WD_i at the t-th slot can be expressed as:

$$h_{i,t} = \beta_0 d_{i,t}^{-2} = \frac{\beta_0}{\left\|\mathbf{q}_t^U - \mathbf{q}_i\right\|^2} \tag{1}$$

where β_0 is the channel power gain at a reference distance $d_0 = 1m$, and $d_{i,t}$ is the distance between the UAV and WD$_i$ at the t-th slot.

2.4 Energy Harvesting Model

Referring to the TDMA protocol outlined in Fig. 2, it can be observed that each time slot is divided into two parts: WPT phase and the task offloading phase.

In the WPT phase, the UAV hovers above the WDs and transmits RF energy. The offloading phase includes task offloading, UAV computation, and downloading the computation results. During the WPT phase, the amount of energy captured by WD$_i$ at the t-th slot can be expressed as:

$$E_{i,t} = \mu P h_{i,t} \alpha_t \tag{2}$$

where μ denotes the energy conservation efficiency, $0 < \mu < 1$, α_t represents the WPT duration at the t-th time slot, and P is the transmit power of the UAV.

The UAV maintains a constant power output during energy transmission because it is equipped with a powerful battery capable of supporting prolonged wireless device charging. When the UAV's energy is depleted after extended flight, it will return for recharging. At this point, a fully charged UAV will immediately replace the energy-depleted UAV, ensuring that the task offloading continues uninterrupted.

2.5 Task Computing Model

For each WD, tasks arrive randomly with different sizes, and each task can only be offloaded independently. While passing over the WDs, the UAV provides energy to the WDs within its coverage range, enabling them to offload tasks.

Let $R_{\max}$ represent the coverage radius of UAV at the current time slot. $R_{\max}$ is related to the current height of the UAV and satisfies the following:

$$R_{max} = z_t^u * tan(\theta) \tag{3}$$

where θ is the max communication angle of UAV.

At time slot t, if WD$_i$ satisfies the following communication distance condition, it is able to collect RF energy and offload tasks to the UAV:

$$\sqrt{(x_t^u - x_i)^2 + (y_t^u - y_i)^2} \leq R_{max}. \tag{4}$$

The set of all WDs within the communication range is denoted as $Z_{in}(t)$, that is

$$Z_{in}(t) = \{i | \sqrt{(x_t^u - x_i)^2 + (y_t^u - y_i)^2} \leq R_{max}, \forall i \in \mathcal{N}\}. \tag{5}$$

This means that not all WDs can communicate with the UAV at the current time slot. To facilitate the input of the model, we set that only $\mathcal{R}$ WDs can communicate at a time. Let Z_t be the number of wireless devices in the communicable set Z_t, that is, $Z_t = |Z_{in}(t)|$.

When the number of communicative WDs Z_t is greater than $\mathcal{R}$, we need a selection method to choose communication WDs. For such cases, we select the top $\mathcal{R}$ WDs with the strongest channel gains $h_{i,t}$ for WPT and task offloading. The set of all WDs we select is denoted as $Z_{can}(t)$

During the offloading phase, tasks are offloaded to the UAV. These tasks are then processed by the server mounted on the UAV. The computational capability of the UAV server is sufficient to efficiently process these tasks. Therefore, the time spent on computation is negligible. Additionally, since the amount of data for the computational results is very small, the download time can also be ignored. Thus, the time allocation for WPT and task offloading must satisfy the following constraints:

$$\alpha_t + \sum_{i \in Z_{can}(t)} \tau_{i,t} \leq \Delta T \tag{6}$$

where $\tau_{i,t}$ is the offloading time of WD_i in the t-th time slot.

During the task offloading process, the task transmission power of WD_i is $\frac{E_{i,t}}{\tau_{i,t}}$. If the remaining battery threshold of the WDs is taken into account, the available energy for WD_i at time slot t is $E_{i,t}$ minus the remaining battery threshold, which does not bring any other changes to the considered problem. Then, according to Shannon's formula, the maximum task offloading amount that WD_i can achieve at time slot t is expressed as:

$$B_i^{max}(t) = \tau_{i,t} W log_2(1 + \frac{\mu P h_{i,t}^2 \alpha_t}{\tau_{i,t}\sigma^2}) \tag{7}$$

where W is the communication bandwidth and σ^2 denotes the noise power.

In the task offloading process, each WD has a task queue $B_i(t)$. After the model outputs the corresponding α_t and $\tau_{i,t}$, the maximum data that each WD can offload is calculated. The tasks in $B_i(t)$ are sorted based on the current tolerance time, with tasks having smaller tolerance times given higher priority. Offloading is performed according to this order, until no one more task can be fully offloaded.

2.6 No-Fly-Area Model

In practical applications, there are areas such as no-fly zones set by the government, terrains that are difficult for UAV to traverse, and regions with poor signal quality. We model the no-fly zone as a circle. Note that our algorithm is applicable to flight restriction zones of any shape. In the cylindrical space with this circle as its base, flying is prohibited.

The no-fly-area is described as $q_i^N = [x_i^n, y_i^n, 0, r_i]$. x_i^n and y_i^n is the horizontal plane and r_i is the radius.

2.7 Task Completion Ratio

In the t-th slot, the number of tasks offloaded to UAV for each WD is $N_{i,t}^{off}$, and the number of tasks which are discarded is $N_{i,t}^{dis}$. Until to the t_0-th slot, the task completion ratio for each WD is:

$$r_i(t_0) = \frac{\sum_{t=1}^{t=t_0} N_{i,t}^{off}}{\sum_{t=1}^{t=t_0} N_{i,t}^{off} + \sum_{t=1}^{t=t_0} N_{i,t}^{dis}} \tag{8}$$

Therefore, the long-term task completion ratio for the entire system is:

$$\psi = \lim_{T \to \infty} \frac{1}{N} \sum_{i=1}^{N} r_i(T) \tag{9}$$

3 Problem Formulation and Efficient Algorithm

In this section, we formulate a mathematical model for the problem of maximizing the long-term task completion ratio. In this model, the task is divided into two independent components: determining 3D-fly UAV's terajectory and allocating time in TDMA. To address this, we introduce a deep reinforcement learning algorithm based on DDPG, training two models, UAV-DDPG and TDMA-DDPG, to solve these two problems, respectively.

3.1 Problem Formulation

The objective of this paper is to maximize the long-term task completion ratio. This task is defined as P1.

$$P1 : \psi = \lim_{T \to \infty} \frac{1}{N} \sum_{i=1}^{N} r_i(T). \tag{10}$$

The problem is constrained by the following conditions.

$$0 \le x_t^u \le L_x, \quad 0 \le y_t^u \le L_y, \quad H_{min} \le z_t^u \le H_{max}, \forall t \in T \tag{11}$$

$$-\pi \le \phi_t \le \pi, \quad 0 \le \varphi_t \le \pi, \forall t \in T \tag{12}$$

$$0 \le \alpha_t + \sum_{i \in Z_{can}(t)} \tau_{i,t} \le \Delta T, \forall i \in Z_{can}(t), \forall t \in T \tag{13}$$

$$\sqrt{(x_t^u - x_i^n)^2 + (y_t^u - y_i^n)^2} \ge r_i, \forall i \in \mathcal{M}, \forall t \in T \tag{14}$$

Constraint 11 indicates that the UAV can only fly within the specified range. Constraint 12 defines the range of the vertical and horizontal angles of the UAV's flight. Constraint 13 represents the allocation of WPT time and task offloading time in the TDMA protocol. Constraint 14 represents the UAV can not fly in the no-fly area.

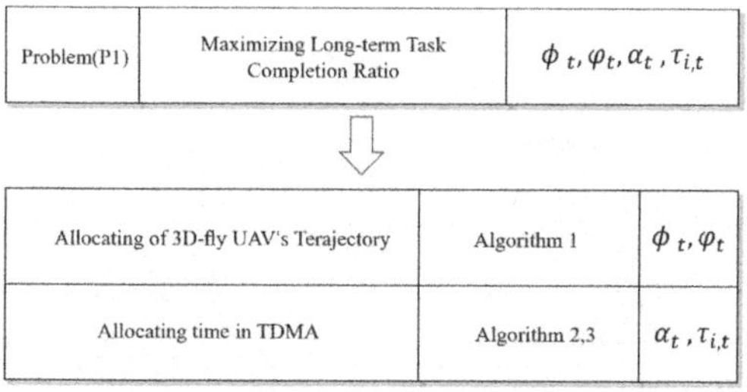

Fig. 3. The structure of the algorithm.

Clearly, problem (P1) is non-convex and highly challenging. If we attempt to use a Deep Reinforcement Learning (DRL) model to directly output the values of all optimization parameters, the high dimensionality of both inputs and outputs results in an overly complex network mapping between them. This complexity makes it difficult for the model to converge and learn effective actions, leading to potentially infeasible solutions.

To address this issue effectively, we propose a novel approach. We implement these two parts using separate models, UAV-DDPG and TDMA-DDPG, to decouple this complex problem.

To tackle the issue of fixed model input size and the uncertainty in the number of communicable WDs, the second model adopts a fixed number of WDs as input, with any excess WDs being excluded from communication. The workflow of our proposed scheme is illustrated in Fig. 3.

3.2 The DDPG Algorithm

In this subsection, we present a reinforcement learning framework based on the DDPG algorithm. This framework is used to train UAV-DDPG and TDMA-DDPG. Notably, The actions output by both models are continuous actions. And the DDPG algorithm is particularly well-suited for such problems due to its inherent capability to handle continuous variables.

The DDPG algorithm employs a dual-network architecture, comprising an actor network and a critic network. The actor network is responsible for generating deterministic actions based on the current state, while the critic network evaluates the quality of these actions by estimating the corresponding state-action value function (Q-value). Specifically, the actor network maps states to actions within the continuous action space, thereby facilitating exploration and policy optimization. Concurrently, the critic network provides a feedback mechanism by assessing the long term value of the selected actions, guiding the actor network toward more optimal policies. This synergistic interaction between the actor and critic networks enables the DDPG algorithm to effectively navigate high-dimensional, continuous state and action spaces, making it a powerful tool for solving complex decision-making problems in UAV trajectory planning and

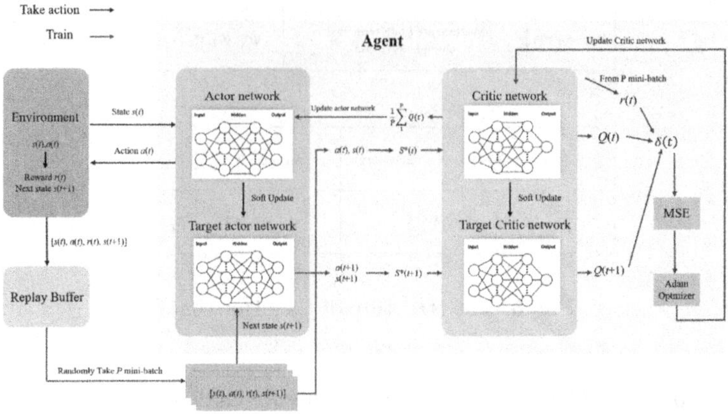

Fig. 4. The detailed structure and training process of the DDPG network.

resource allocation. The detailed structure and training process of the DDPG network are shown in Fig. 4.

We applied the reinforcement learning DDPG algorithm, with its outputs serving as the actions of algorithms, denoted as $a(t)$. The algorithm utilizes an actor network model, referred to as the Actor, to train the action policy function $\pi(s(t)|\omega^{\pi})$, given the state $s(t)$, where ω^{π} represents the parameters of the actor network model. After obtaining the system state and its corresponding action, the critic network model, referred to as the Critic, is trained to evaluate the potential value of the action. This evaluation process generates a value function $Q(s(t), a(t)|\omega^{Q})$, where ω^{Q} represents the parameters of the critic network.

To enhance the stability of model training and prevent oscillations during the training process, two target networks are established based on the DDPG algorithm, denoted as $\pi'(\cdot)$ and $Q'(\cdot)$, with parameters $\omega^{\pi'}$ and $\omega^{Q'}$, respectively. These target networks adjust their network parameters through a soft update mechanism, as specified below.

$$\omega^{\pi'} = 0.995 * \omega^{\pi'} + 0.005 * \omega^{\pi} \tag{15}$$

$$\omega^{Q'} = 0.995 * \omega^{Q'} + 0.005 * \omega^{Q} \tag{16}$$

During parameter updates, we adopt the experience replay mechanism. By storing and randomly sampling historical experience data, the temporal correlation of training samples is effectively disrupted. This approach enhances model generalization and prevents issues caused by locality, thereby addressing the problems of data autocorrelation and sample utilization. In each training epoch, a mini-batch containing $\mathcal{P}$ samples is randomly sampled from the experience replay buffer. The temporal difference (TD) error for each sample, denoted as $\delta(i)$, is calculated to measure the discrepancy between the critic network and its target network based on the temporal difference algorithm. These tasks can be treated as regression tasks, where the mean squared error is used as the loss function, denoted as $\delta_{\mathcal{P}}$. This loss function is then backpropagated to update the critic network parameters.

$$\delta_{\mathcal{P}} = \sum_{i=1}^{\mathcal{P}} \frac{\delta(i)^2}{2} \tag{17}$$

$$a(i) = \pi(s(i)|\omega^{\pi}) \tag{18}$$

$$a'(i+1) = \pi'(s(i+1)|\omega^{\pi'}) \tag{19}$$

$$\delta(i) = z(i) + \gamma Q'[s(i+1), a'(i+1)|\omega^{Q'}] - Q[s(i), a(i)|\omega^{Q}] \tag{20}$$

where $a'(i+1)$ is the action obtained from $\pi'(\cdot)$ based on $s(i+1)$.

The actor network is updated according to the policy gradient:

$$\begin{aligned}\nabla_{\omega^{\pi}} J &\approx \frac{1}{K}\sum_{k=1}^{K} \nabla_a Q(s, a \mid \omega^Q)\Big|_{s=s(k), a=\pi(s(k)|\omega^{\pi})} \\ &= \frac{1}{K}\sum_{k=1}^{K}\left[\nabla_a Q(s, a \mid \omega^Q)\Big|_{s=s(k), a=\pi(s(k))} \cdot \nabla_{\omega^{\pi}} \pi(s \mid \omega^{\pi})\Big|_{s=s(k)}\right]\end{aligned} \tag{21}$$

In the following two sections, we will introduce the state, action, reward and next_state in DDPG for the two subproblems.

3.3 The DDPG Algorithm for Allocating of 3D-Fly Terajectory

The following are the state, action, reward and next_state in UAV-DDPG.

- **State**: $s_{UAV}(t)$ represents the set comprising the UAV's position and the task quantities of N WDs in the t-th time slot.

$$s_{UAV}(t) = [x_t^u, y_t^u, z_t^u, B_1(t), B_2(t), ..., B_N(t)] \tag{22}$$

- **Action**: $a_{UAV}(t) = [\phi_t, \varphi_t]$, where ϕ_t is the horizontal flight angle of the UAV, and φ_t is the vertical flight angle of the UAV. Based on this action, the UAV moves according to the angle outputs from this network.
  During the training process, the exploration of the action space has a significant impact on both the convergence speed of the training and its inference performance. A typical exploration mechanism involves adding noise with a fixed variance to the original output actions. In this paper, noise is added to both angles, with the noise decreasing as the training epochs progress. This approach allows for sufficient space exploration in the early to middle stages of training, thus enhancing the model's generalization capability. The following is the noise addition formula:

$$a_{UAV}(t) = a_{UAV}(t) + e \tag{23}$$

  where e is a 1×2 matrix, consisting of two random variables sampled from normal distributions with a mean of 0 and a variance of $0.1 \times cos(\frac{i \times \pi}{2 \times m})$.

i represents the current training epoch, while m denotes the total number of training epochs we will conduct for the models. As i increases, i.e., as training progresses, the variance of e gradually decreases from 0.1 to 0. More specifically, during the early stages of training, random exploration is significantly more extensive, allowing the model to explore a wider range of possibilities. As training continues, random exploration gradually decreases, and after reaching the set epoch, it is entirely eliminated, ultimately reducing its impact on actions and stabilizing the model.

- **reward**: The purpose of setting the flight reward is to ensure that the UAV can cover as many tasks as possible and offload them in the second algorithm. $N_{UAV}(t)$ represents the total amount of tasks from all WDs within the UAV's communication range at time slot t, and it can be used to evaluate the quality of the action output by the actor in time slot t. However, since the cumulative amount of tasks within the UAV's communication range varies from one time slot to another, $N_{UAV}(t)$ does not accurately reflect the quality of the action. For example, at time slot t_1, the number of tasks in environment is 120 and the number of tasks in UAV's communication range $N_{UAV}(t_1)$ is 60. At time slot t_2, the number of tasks in environment is 700 and $N_{UAV}(t_2)$ is 70. Therefore, although $N_{UAV}(t_1) < N_{UAV}(t_2)$, $a_{UAV}(t_2)$ is not good than $a_{UAV}(t_1)$. Hence, we define the reward as the ratio of the UAV-covered task amount to the total task amount at the beginning of the time slot, that is,

$$r_{UAV}(t) = \frac{\sum_{i \in Z_{in}(t)} B_i(t)}{\sum_{j=0}^{N} B_j(t)}. \tag{24}$$

When the UAV's position results in it going outside the network area due to the current action, a penalty parameter $\eta = 0.9$ is applied to discount the reward.

$$r_{UAV}(t) = \eta \times r_{UAV}(t). \tag{25}$$

When the UAV is in a no-fly zone, since the normal offloading task reward range is between 0 and 1, a corresponding penalty is applied to the reward:

$$r_{UAV}(t) = -0.1. \tag{26}$$

- **Next_state**:$s_{UAV}(t+1)$ represents the environmental state after executing the flight action at time slot t and completing Algorithm 2 (WPT and offloading task). This state includes the UAV's position and the remaining tasks of each WD,

$$s_{UAV}(t+1) = [x^u_{t+1}, y^u_{t+1}, z^u_{t+1}, B_1(t+1), B_2(t+1), ..., B_N(t+1)]. \tag{27}$$

Once a new sample $(s_{UAV}(t), a_{UAV}(t), r_{UAV}(t), s_{UAV}(t+1))$ is obtained, it is stored in the experience replay buffer, and the oldest sample is discarded if the buffer is full. Subsequently, mini-batches are periodically sampled from this buffer.

Algorithm 1. The DDPG algorithm for Allocating of 3D-fly UAV-Terajectory.

Initialize the Actor network $\pi(s(t)|\omega^{\pi})$ with parameters ω^{π} and the Critic network $Q(s(t), a(t)|\omega^{Q})$ with parameters ω^{Q}. Set the target networks $\pi'(\cdot) = \pi(\cdot)$ and $Q'(\cdot) = Q(\cdot)$.
Initialize the training's epoch times M., minibatch size $\mathcal{P}$.
for epoch $= 1, 2, \ldots, M$ **do**
    $t \leftarrow 0$
    Initialize the environment and clear all task in WDs
    Set the UAV's takeoff point to $[0, 0, 10]$, and set action noise e based on (23).
    while $t < T$ **do**
        Gain $s_{UAV}(t)$ from the environment.
        Input $s_{UAV}(t)$ to UAV-actor network and obtain the UAV action $a_{UAV}(t)$,
        Use $a_{UAV}(t)$ to update the environment and obtain the state of TDMA $s_{TDMA}(t)$, $Z_{can}(t)$ and $r_{UAV}(t)$;
        Input $s_{TDMA}(t)$ to TDMA-actor network and obtain the TDMA action $a_{TDMA}(t)$,
        Use $a_{TDMA}(t)$ and $Z_{can}(t)$ to update the environment by Algorithm 2 and obtain the next-state of UAV $s_{UAV}(t+1)$;
        Store $(s_{UAV}(t), a_{UAV}(t), r_{UAV}(t), s_{UAV}(t+1))$ into the experience replay buffer and drop the oldest sample if the buffer is full;
        if the length of replay buffer $\geq$ min_train_size **then**
            Take $\mathcal{P}$ sample from the replay buffer, Samples $=$
            $(s_{UAV}(p_t), a_{UAV}(p_t), r_{UAV}(p_t), s_{UAV}(p_{t+1})), p = 1, 2, ..., \mathcal{P}$
            Use samples calculate $\delta_{\mathcal{P}}$ based on (17), (18), (19), (20)
            Backward and update the Critic's parameters with $\delta_{\mathcal{P}}$;
            Input $(s_{UAV}(t), a_{UAV}(t))$ to the Critic and calculate by (21), then backward and update the Actor
            Perform a soft update of two target networks' parameters according to (15) and (16);
        end if
        $t \leftarrow t + 1$
    end while
end for

In summary, this is the network setup for the UAV 3D flight algorithm. The detailed process of the algorithm is shown in Algorithm 1. First, initialize the parameters of the networks in DDPG. Based on the parameters, the environment is initialized, and the environment state is obtained. The model then outputs an action based on the environment and its reward. After executing the flight action, task offloading is performed using Algorithm 2, resulting in the updated state. These are stored as a training data set in the buffer pool. Algorithm 2 uses a model that has already been pre-trained offline, and the training process of the model in Algorithm 2 will be introduced later.

Algorithm 2. The algorithm for WPT and offloading task.

Input: $a_{TDMA}(t)$, $Z_{can}(t)$
Get α_t from $a_{TDMA}(t)$
for each i in $Z_{can}(t)$ **do**
  Get $\tau_{i,t}$ from $a_{TDMA}(t)$
  Calculate $B_i^{max}(t)$ with α_t and $\tau_{i,t}$ by (1), (2), (7)
  Sort $B_i(t)$ from small to large by the current tolerance time.
  $B_i^{waste}(t) \leftarrow B_i^{max}(t)$
  for each j in $B_i(t)$ **do**
    if $b_{task}(i,j) \leq B_i^{waste}(t)$ **then**
      Remove $b_{task}(i,j)$ from $B_i(t)$
      $B_i^{waste}(t) \leftarrow B_i^{waste}(t) - b_{task}(i,j)$
    end if
  end for
end for
Calculate $r_{TDMA}(t)$ by $\sum_i B_i^{waste}(t), \sum_i B_i^{max}(t)$, with (31)
Output: $r_{TDMA}(t)$

3.4 The DDPG Algorithm for Allocating of Time Slots in TDMA

The following are the state, action, reward and next_state in DDPG for the TDMA time allocation.

- **State:** $s_{TDMA}(t)$ represents the state input of the TDMA time allocation model. To prevent the input dimension of $s_{TDMA}(t)$ from becoming too large and to avoid conflicts between the varying number of communicable WDs and the fixed input requirement of the model, we set the model's input to a fixed value. The model communicates with a fixed number $\mathcal{R}$ of WDs. Each WD inputs $\mathcal{Y}$ task sizes. If the number of tasks exceeds $\mathcal{Y}$, the tasks are sorted based on the current tolerable time; if fewer, zeros are padded as input. Similarly, if the number of WDs is fewer than $\mathcal{R}$, zeros are padded as input. If the number of WDs exceeds $\mathcal{R}$, the WDs are selected based on channel gain ranking.

$$\begin{aligned} s_{WD}(i,t) &= [h_{i,t}, b_{task}(1), b_{task}(2), ..., b_{task}(\mathcal{Y})] \\ s_{TDMA}(t) &= [s_{WD}(1,t), s_{WD}(2,t), ..., s_{WD}(\mathcal{R},t)] \end{aligned} \tag{28}$$

- **Action:** $a_{TDMA}(t)$ is the action output of the network, consisting of $\mathcal{R}+1$ floating-point numbers, which represent the time allocated to WPT and $\mathcal{R}$ WDs for task offloading. These $\mathcal{R}+1$ floating-point numbers must sum up to ΔT, ensuring that the entire TDMA time slot is used.

$$a_{TDMA}(t) = [\alpha_t, \tau_{1,t}, \tau_{2,t}, ...\tau_{\mathcal{R},t}] \tag{29}$$

To enforce this constraint, the output layer of the TDMA time allocation model adds a softmax layer on top of the original outputs, ensuring that all outputs sum to 1, and then multiplies the result by ΔT, to guarantee the constraint is satisfied.

Algorithm 3. The DDPG algorithm for TDMA time allocation.

Initialize the Actor network $\pi(s(t)|\omega^{\pi})$ with parameters ω^{π} and the Critic network $Q(s(t), a(t)|\omega^{Q})$ with parameters ω^{Q}. Set the target networks $\pi'(\cdot) = \pi(\cdot)$ and $Q'(\cdot) = Q(\cdot)$.
Initialize the training's epoch times M., minibatch size $\mathcal{P}$.
for epoch $= 1, 2, \ldots, M$ **do**
    $t \leftarrow 0$
    Initialize the environment and clear all task in WDs
    Set the UAV's takeoff point to $[50, 50, 10]$, and set action noise e based on (23).
    Generate some WD randomly within the area where UAV can communicate.
    while $t < T$ **do**
        Set UAV's z_t^u randomly in the range of $[H_{min}, H_{max}]$
        Gain $s_{TDMA}(t)$ and $Z_{can}(t)$ from the environment.
        Input $s_{TDMA}(t)$ to TDMA-actor network and obtain the TDMA action $a_{TDMA}(t)$,
        Use $a_{TDMA}(t)$ and $Z_{can}(t)$ to update the environment by Algorithm 2 and obtain the next-state of TDMA $s_{TDMA}(t+1)$ and the reward of the action $r_{TDMA}(t)$;
        Store $(s_{TDMA}(t), a_{TDMA}(t), r_{TDMA}(t), s_{TDMA}(t+1))$ into the experience replay buffer and drop the oldest sample if the buffer is full;
        if the length of replay buffer $\geq$ min_train_size **then**
            Take $\mathcal{P}$ sample from the replay buffer, Samples =
            $(s_{TDMA}(p_t), a_{TDMA}(p_t), r_{TDMA}(p_t), s_{TDMA}(p_{t+1})), p = 1, 2, ..., \mathcal{P}$
            Use samples calculate $\delta_{\mathcal{P}}$ based on (17), (18), (19), (20)
            Backward and update the Critic's parameters with $\delta_{\mathcal{P}}$;
            Input $(s_{TDMA}(t), a_{TDMA}(t))$ to the Critic and calculate by (21), then backward and update the Actor
            Perform a soft update of two target networks' parameters according to (15) and (16);
        end if
        $t \leftarrow t + 1$
    end while
end for

To enhance the model's generalization ability, similar to the UAV flight model, we introduce noise to promote exploration, thus improving the model's generalization capability. Noise e, drawn from a normal distribution with a mean of 0 and a standard deviation of $0.1 \times \Delta T \times cos(\frac{i \times \pi}{2 \times m})$, is added to the model's output, which is a $1 \times (\mathcal{R}+1)$ matrix and then a softmax layer is applied to ensure that the action output meets the requirements.

$$a_{TDMA}(t) = a_{TDMA}(t) + e \tag{30}$$

- **reward**: In this model, the reward $r_{TDMA}(t)$ is designed to encourage the model to offload as many tasks (in bits) as possible from the selected R offloading WDs. The reward range designed in this study is between -1 and 0. More specifically, first, notice that the tasks of offloading WDs are offloaded one by one, i.e., they are offloaded in the unit of task rather than bit. This means that for each offloading WD, some of its allocated offloading time will be redundant which is not enough for offloading one more task, or there is some redundent time as the WD has quite few buffered tasks. To prevent an excessive number of tasks that cannot be offloaded within time ΔT, we record two metrics for each WD$_i$: the total number of bits B_i^{max} that can be offloaded and the remaining bits B_i^{waste} that are not offloaded under the given action $a_{TDMA}(t)$. The reward is defined as:

$$B_{waste} = \sum_{i \in Z_{can}(t)} B_i^{waste}, \quad B_{max} = \sum_{i \in Z_{can}(t)} B_i^{max} \\ r_{TDMA}(t) = -\frac{B_{waste}}{B_{max}} \tag{31}$$

Clearly, if all tasks of offloading WDs are completely offloaded, $r_{TDMA}(t) = 0$. Additionally, if the total redundent offloading time of WDs is insufficient to offload any another task of any offloading WD, we define $r_{TDMA}(t) = 0$ because this action is good enough, although $r_{TDMA}(t)$ calculated based on the above formula is not zero.

A potential issue arises in cases where the WPT time is too short, leading to insufficient total offloading capacity but the reward is $r_{TDMA}(t) = 0$. For example, when the WPT time is 0.05, $B_{max} = 10$, and after offloading a 9.8-bit task, 0.2 bits of offloading capacity remain, which is insufficient to offload any other tasks. So the $r_{TDMA}(t) = 0$, but this action is suboptimal due to the low WPT time.

In order to deal with this cases, based on the parameter calculations for the environment in this paper, we selected a reasonable WPT time allocation range, $0.1 < \alpha_t < 0.5$. For WPT times outside this range, $r_{TDMA}(t) = -1$, ensuring the rationality of WPT time allocation.

- **Next_state**: $s_{TDMA}(t+1)$ represents the environmental state after completing Algorithm 2, based on the model output during the t-th time slot. This state includes the channel gain and tasks of each WD after the task offloading process,

$$s_{TDMA}(t+1) = [s_{WD}(1, t+1), s_{WD}(2, t+1), ..., s_{WD}(\mathcal{R}, t+1)] \tag{32}$$

Once a new sample $(s_{TDMA}(t), a_{TDMA}(t), r_{TDMA}(t), s_{TDMA}(t+1))$ is obtained, it is stored in the experience replay buffer. If the buffer is full, the oldest sample is discarded. Subsequently, mini-batches are periodically sampled from this buffer.

In summary, this is the network setup for the TDMA time allocation algorithm. The model and training process are described in Algorithm 3. First, the parameters of all networks in DDPG are initialized. Based on these parameters, the environment is initialized, and the environmental state is obtained. The model outputs an action based on the environment and provides a reward for the action. After executing the offloading action, task offloading is performed according to Algorithm 2, resulting in an updated state. These data are stored as a training set in the buffer pool. The trained model is then integrated into Algorithm 1 to train the UAV-3D flight model.

4 Numerical Results

This section evaluates our proposed algorithm with the simulations implemented on NVIDIA GeForce RTX 3060, Python 3.9.18, and Torch 1.12.0. In the DDPG network of this paper, three fully connected hidden layers are used, with Adam as the optimizer and tanh as the activation function. The output of the TDMA is additionally connected to a softmax layer. The learning rates for the actor and critic of the 3D-fly UAV-Terajectory network are 0.00001 and 0.0005, respectively. And the learning rates for the actor and critic of the TDMA time allocation network are 0.0001 and 0.001, respectively.

The UAV operating area is a square region with side length 100 m, and the flight height is limited to the range $[H_{\min}, H_{\max}]$, where $H_{\min} = 10\,m$ and $H_{\max} = 15\,m$. There are two no-fly zones, each in the shape of a circle with a radius of 6.5 m. The environment contains 20 randomly distributed WDs (unless otherwise specified), and the WDs are not located within the no-fly zones. At the beginning of each time slot, every WD generates a task with a probability $\mathbf{p} = 0.2$ (unless otherwise specified). The size of the newly generated task falls within the range $(0, B_{\max}]$, where $B_{\max} = 100$ bits, and the task's tolerance time randomly falls within the range $[T_{\min}, T_{\max}]$, where $T_{\min} = 15\Delta T$ and $T_{\max} = 20\Delta T$. Other parameters are set as follows (unless otherwise specified): power $P = 0.1$ W, energy conversion efficiency $\mu = 0.2$, channel bandwidth $W = 1$ MHz, noise power $\sigma^2 = 10^{-5}$ W, UAV speed $v = 10$ m/s, maximum communication angle $= 50°$, training epochs $= 30000$, and time slot length $\Delta T = 1$ s.

4.1 Model Convergence Performance Evaluation

We evaluate the convergence performance of our DDPG model (UAV-DDPG + TDMA-DDPG) and compare it with the traditional Acotr-Critic algorithm (UAV-AC + TDMA-DDPG) and the DDPG model that combines UAV flight and TDMA time allocation into a single model (ONE-DDPG).

Figure 5 plots the long-term task completion ratio curves for the three models, where the y-axis represents the long-term task completion ratio per training epoch, and the x-axis represents the number of training iterations. In the figure, we can find that the long-term task completion ratio of UAV-DDPG + TDMA-DDPG improves before 10,000 epochs. After 25,000 epoch, having explored sufficient scenarios, ratio stabilizes at around 75%. Due to the complexity of the tasks in this study, the other two models fail to converge.

Figure 6 shows the convergence curve of the reward function during the training epochs of TDMA-DDPG. In the figure, the TDMA-DDPG model get low rewards before 500 epochs due to insufficient exposure. However, after 1000 epochs, having explored sufficient scenarios, the model gradually converges and is able to effectively handle most task offloading scenarios.

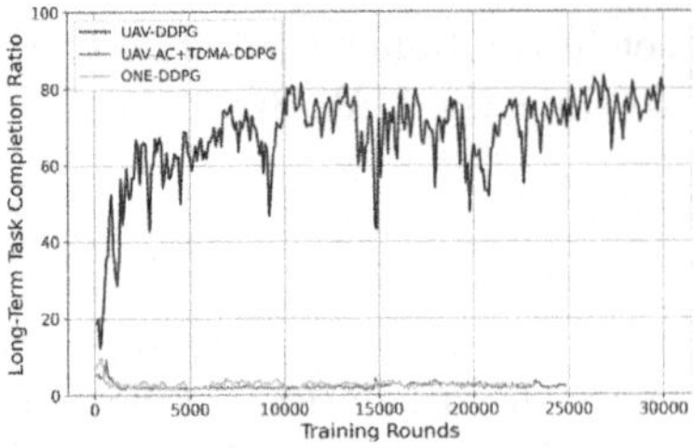

Fig. 5. The reward of the three models.

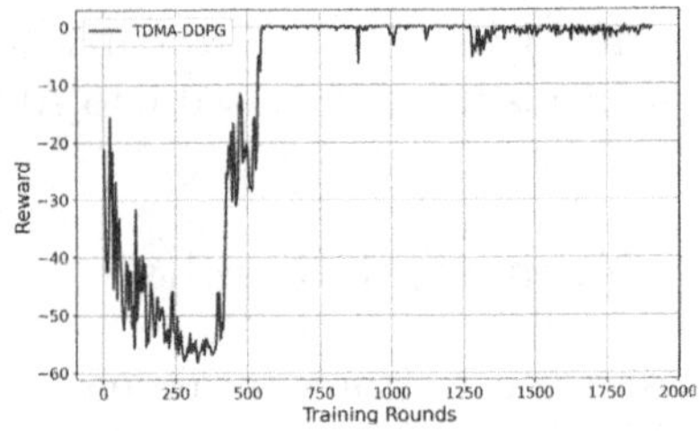

Fig. 6. The reward of TDMA-DDPG.

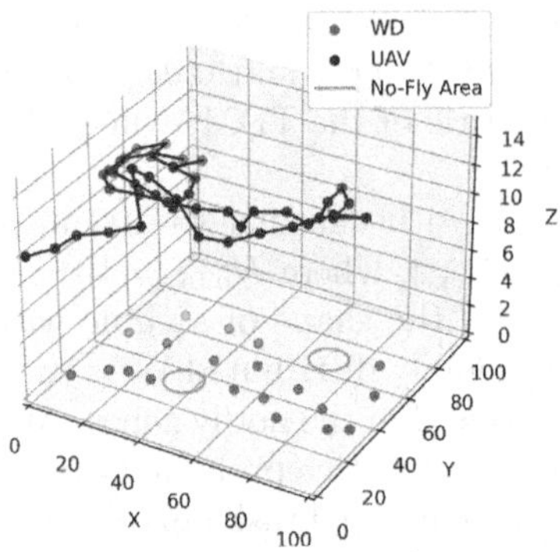

Fig. 7. The UAV 3D-flight trajectory.

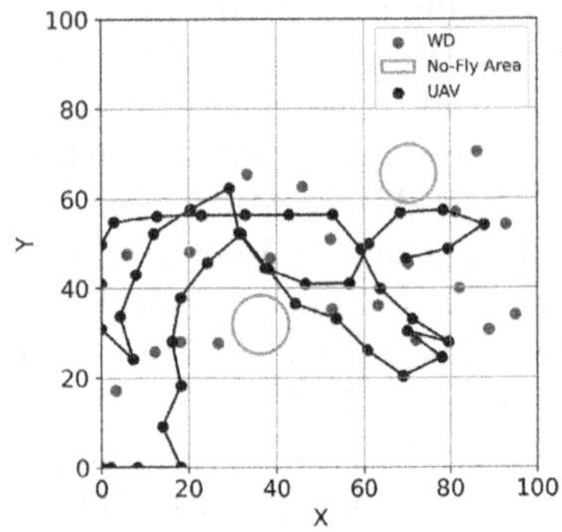

Fig. 8. The vertical view of UAV.

Finally, Fig. 7 and Fig. 8 presents the UAV flight trajectory generated by our model in different perspectives. It can be seen that the UAV successfully avoids the no-fly zones and plans a reasonable trajectory.

4.2 Long-Term Task Completion Ratio

We evaluate the generalization ability of the DDPG algorithm trained model under different scenarios, comparing our approach with two other baseline schemes. For these baseline schemes, after making the flight direction decision, the TDMA time allocation model trained by our method is used for task offloading.

The details of the two baseline schemes are as follows:

1. **Random Trajectory (RT) Scheme:** During UAV flight, two flight angles are randomly generated.
2. **Predetermined Trajectory (ST) Scheme:** The UAV flight trajectory is a pre-designed, relatively reasonable trajectory.

To ensure the validity of the evaluation data, we run 1000 time slots per round and perform the test 10 times to average the long-term task completion ratio of each scheme. However, considering that the random flight strategy of the RT scheme easily leads the UAV out of bounds, causing the long-term data completion ratio to approach zero, we impose an additional constraint on the RT scheme to prevent the UAV from flying out of the task flight area.

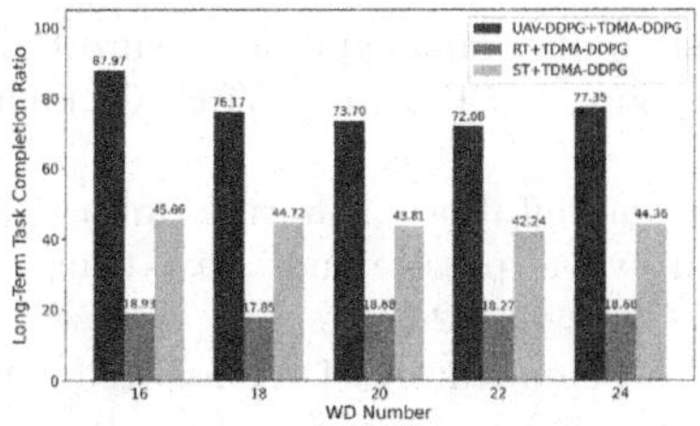

Fig. 9. The average computation ratio under varying numbers of WD

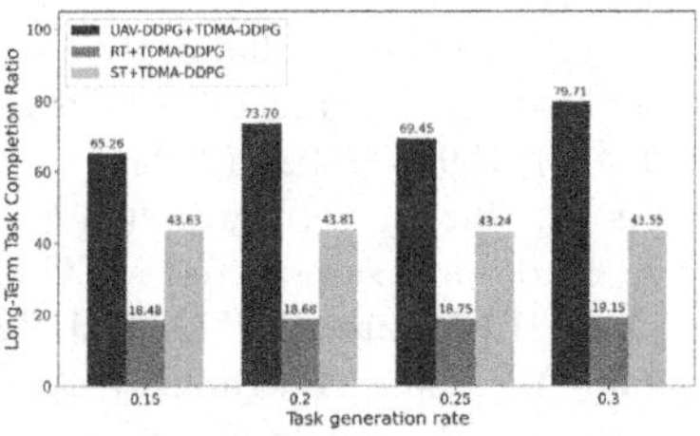

Fig. 10. The average computation ratio under varying task generation

Figure 9 compares the long-term task completion ratio of the three trajectory scheduling schemes in scenarios with different numbers of WDs, using various trajectory scheduling schemes. As the number of WDs increases, because the number of WDs that the UAV can handle is limited, the long-term task completion ratio decreases. However, it still shows an improvement of around 40% compared to the baseline solutions.

Figure 10 compares the long-term task completion ratio of the three trajectory scheduling schemes in scenarios with different task generation probability **p**, using various trajectory scheduling schemes. When the task generation rate increases, because the UAV still has remaining task offloading capacity under the current environment, the long-term task completion ratio gradually improves, with the comparative solution ultimately achieving an improvement of nearly 50%.

5 Conclusion

This paper focuses on a wireless-powered UAV-supported edge computing system, where the UAV performs 3D flight and needs to avoid no-fly zones. Each task is independent and generated randomly, with the ultimate goal of maximizing the long-term task completion ratio while minimizing the number of abandoned tasks. In order to effectively integrate reinforcement learning algorithms into the system and decouple the model complexity, this paper decomposes the problem into two subproblems and solves them using two submodels. Subsequent comparative results show that our model achieves a high long-term task completion ratio.

Acknowledgments. This work was supported in part by the National Natural Science Foundation of China under Grant No. 62272414 and the Zhejiang Provincial Natural Science Foundation of China under Grant No. LR20F020003.

References

1. Chen, W., et al.: Computation time minimized offloading in NOMA-enabled wireless powered mobile edge computing. IEEE Trans. Commun. **72**(11), 7182–7197 (2024)
2. Ding, Y., et al.: Collaborative communication and computation for secure UAV-enabled MEC against active aerial eavesdropping. IEEE Trans. Wirel. Commun. **23**(11), 15915–15929 (2024)
3. Fu, Z., Shi, L., Ye, Y., Zhang, Y., Zheng, G.: Computation EE fairness for a UAV-enabled wireless powered MEC network with hybrid passive and active transmissions. IEEE Internet Things J. **11**(11), 20152–20164 (2024)
4. Gao, Y., Yuan, X., Yang, D., Hu, Y., Cao, Y., Schmeink, A.: UAV-assisted MEC system with mobile ground terminals: DRL-based joint terminal scheduling and UAV 3D trajectory design. IEEE Trans. Veh. Technol. **73**(7), 10164–10180 (2024)
5. He, H., Yang, X., Huang, F., Shen, H., Tian, H.: Enhancing QOE in large-scale U-MEC networks via joint optimization of task offloading and UAV trajectories. IEEE Internet Things J. **11**(21), 35710–35723 (2024)
6. Hu, H., Sheng, Z., Nasir, A.A., Yu, H., Fang, Y.: Computation capacity maximization for UAV and RIS cooperative MEC system with NOMA. IEEE Commun. Lett. **28**(3), 592–596 (2024)
7. Liu, P., An, K., Lei, J., Sun, Y., Liu, W., Chatzinotas, S.: Computation rate maximization for SCMA-aided edge computing in IoT networks: a multi-agent reinforcement learning approach. IEEE Trans. Wirel. Commun. **23**(8), 10414–10429 (2024)
8. Liu, W., et al.: Joint trajectory design and resource allocation in UAV-enabled heterogeneous MEC systems. IEEE Internet Things J. **11**(19), 30817–30832 (2024)
9. Tang, Q., Li, B., Yang, H.H., Li, Y., He, S., Yang, K.: Delay and load fairness optimization with queuing model in multi-UAV assisted MEC: a deep reinforcement learning approach. IEEE Trans. Netw. Serv. Manage. (2024). https://doi.org/10.1109/TNSM.2024.3520632
10. Wang, X., et al.: Wireless powered mobile edge computing networks: a survey. ACM Comput. Surv. **55**(13s), 1–37 (2023)
11. Xu, Y., Zhang, T., Liu, Y., Yang, D., Xiao, L., Tao, M.: 3D multi-UAV computing networks: Computation capacity and energy consumption tradeoff. IEEE Trans. Veh. Technol. **73**(7), 10627–10641 (2024)
12. Zhang, Y., Kuang, Z., Feng, Y., Hou, F.: Task offloading and trajectory optimization for secure communications in dynamic user multi-UAV MEC systems. IEEE Trans. Mob. Comput. **23**(12), 14427–14440 (2024)

Towards Efficient and Secure Multimodal Misinformation Detection

Jianhao Wei[1], Yixiao Li[2], Xiaolong Li[2(✉)], Ming Zhao[3], Jin Zhang[4(✉)], Limei Liu[1], and Junfeng Yang[1]

[1] School of Frontier and Interdisciplinary Studies, Hunan University of Technology and Business, Changsha, China
{jianhao,seagullm}@hutb.edu.cn, b12100031@hnu.edu.cn

[2] School of Computer Science, Hunan University of Technology and Business, Changsha, China
lxl@hutb.edu.cn

[3] School of Computer Science and Engineering, Central South University, Changsha, China
meanzhao@csu.edu.cn

[4] School of Computer and Communication Engineering, Changsha University of Science and Technology, Changsha, China
mail_zhangjin@163.com

Abstract. The rapid development of AI-generated content (AIGC) has heightened the threat of multimodal misinformation, posing significant security concerns. Existing misinformation detection methods have not addressed privacy concerns or have only considered the privacy of single-modal data, overlooking the semantic correlation privacy among multimodal data. In this paper, we propose a cloud-edge-end collaboration-based privacy-preserving multimodal misinformation detection (CPMD) scheme, safeguarding the correlation privacy of multimodal data while efficiently detecting misinformation. To achieve this, we introduce a local differential privacy-based multimodal Fourier dynamic protection (MFDP) scheme, thereby achieving efficient multimodal fusion and semantic correlation protection. We also design a multi-head spatiotemporal correlation attention-based large model pre-training protection (MSLP) method and DP-based Gradient Correlation Protection (DPGC) method, which ensure high-utility gradient correlation protection. Furthermore, we utilize a multimodal misinformation detection transformer (MMDT) to perform high accuracy recognition. Extensive experiments demonstrate that, compared to the HAMMER method, our CPMD method improves the accuracy of multimodal misinformation detection by 5.08%.

Keywords: Multimodal misinformation detection · Semantic correlation protection · Cloud-edge-end collaboration · Spatiotemporal correlation

Y. Zhou et al. (Eds.): ICECCS 2025, LNCS 15746, pp. 241–260, 2026.
https://doi.org/10.1007/978-3-032-00828-2_14

1 Introduction

With the rise of AI-generated content (AIGC) models, social network data is no longer confined to single-document data, but rather encompasses large-scale multimodal data (e.g., documents and images). The generated multimodal data may contain some misinformation, significantly influencing the development of individuals and society [1–3]. For example, despite OpenAI's correctness checks on ChatGPT outputs, issues like "over-generation" and "under-generation" still occur [4,5]. The multimodal misinformation detection task aims to identify and localize false content in multimodal media (e.g., image-text pairs), with its core challenge lying in simultaneously detecting forgery traces in both images and text while precisely localizing false regions (such as forged facial bounding boxes in images or false terms in text). To efficiently detect misinformation, as shown in Fig. 1, cloud-edge-end collaboration frameworks are gaining popularity. End devices submit multimodal data (e.g., text ads, news images) to edge nodes, which collaborate with cloud servers to train models for performing efficient and accurate multimodal misinformation detection.

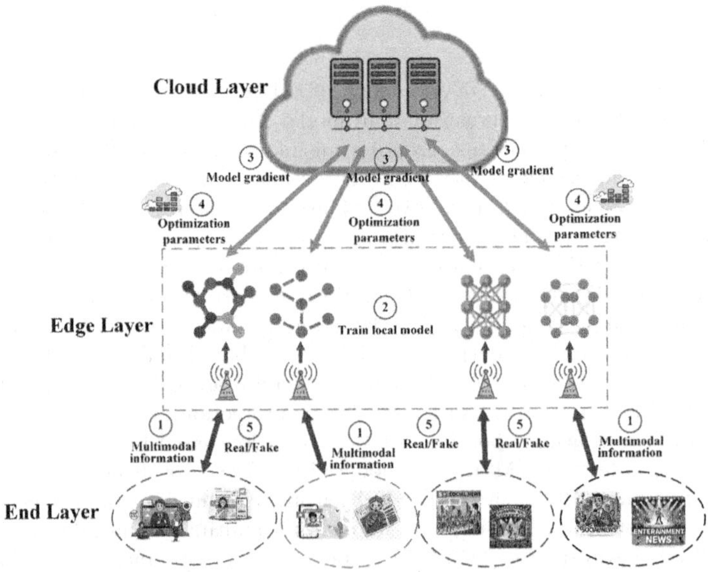

Fig. 1. Multimodal misinformation detection.

However, multimodal misinformation detection within the cloud-edge-end framework faces significant security challenges. The multimodal data collected by end devices contain a large amount of sensitive user information, such as personal historical browsing records, important documents, and health status. On one hand, when end devices upload multimodal data to edge nodes, they are vulnerable to attacks [6]. For example, untrusted edge nodes can exploit link attacks to analyze the semantic correlations of multimodal data, thereby inferring users' private information, including interests and hobbies [7]. Additionally, during model collaborative training between edge nodes and cloud servers, untrusted cloud servers can infer the internal structure and data privacy of pre-trained models by analyzing gradient correlations, which severely compromises user interests [8,9].

Currently, most misinformation detection methods, such as DartBlur [10] and FedForgery [11], primarily target single-modal data, such as image data. However, these methods fail to address multimodal misinformation detection [12]. In recent years, some multimodal misinformation detection methods, such as HAMMER [12], IMQ [13], and Sniffer [14], have achieved good detection accuracy. Nevertheless, these methods do not focus on the privacy protection issues in multimodal misinformation detection. To protect data privacy within the cloud-edge-end framework, researchers have introduced federated learning, anonymization, and differential privacy (DP) mechanisms [10,11,15]. For example, DartBlur uses anonymization to obscure facial features in pre-trained models, but it cannot defend against re-identification attacks. Some studies [11,15] utilize DP-based federated learning methods to protect training data privacy but overlook the correlation privacy of model gradients. Furthermore, these methods primarily focus on unimodal data privacy at edge nodes, neglecting the privacy of multimodal data released by end devices.

A few multimodal privacy protection methods, such as the SecMdp method, protect multimodal data privacy within the cloud-edge-end framework. However, they overlook the highly correlated privacy between multimodal data and training model gradients, which may lead to potential privacy leakage [6]. Additionally, simultaneous privacy protection for both multimodal data and model gradients can result in reduced accuracy in misinformation detection. Therefore, the key issue addressed in this paper is how to simultaneously protect the privacy of multimodal data and model gradients within the cloud-edge-end framework, while achieving efficient misinformation detection.

To achieve both privacy protection for multimodal data and high-accuracy misinformation detection, we face three key challenges: 1) Traditional multimodal deep learning fusion methods suffer from inefficient hyperparameter tuning, and existing unimodal privacy-preserving techniques disrupt the semantic correlation of multimodal data. Therefore, the first challenge is how to efficiently fuse multimodal misinformation data while preserving its semantic consistency. 2) Multimodal data collected at the edge nodes exhibit strong spatiotemporal correlations, which traditional misinformation detection methods (such as contrastive loss and binary classification) fail to capture effectively. Additionally, current privacy-preserving techniques for pretrained models only add noise to model gradients, neglecting their spatiotemporal correlation during multiple rounds of training, leading to potential privacy leakage. Thus, the second challenge is how to mine the spatiotemporal correlation of pretrained multimodal data while preserving the privacy of model gradient correlations. 3) Since both multimodal data and pretrained model parameters are protected by noise, the complexity of misinformation detection is further added, significantly impacts the accuracy of multimodal misinformation detection. Therefore, the critical challenge addressed in this paper is how to balance privacy protection of multimodal data with the usability of misinformation detection.

To address these issues, to the best of our knowledge, we are the first to propose a cloud-edge-end collaboration-based privacy-preserving multimodal misinformation detection (CPMD) scheme. Specifically, to tackle the first challenge, we introduce a local DP-based multimodal Fourier dynamic protection (MFDP) scheme at the end layer. This approach employs a dynamic gradient signal-to-noise ratio and a multimodal semantic fusion layer to efficiently integrate multimodal data. We design a dynamic Fourier filtering ratio to add noise protection to the semantic correlation of the multimodal embeddings, thereby mitigating the impact of extreme noise. To address the second challenge, we propose a multi-head spatiotemporal correlation attention-based large model pre-training protection (MSLP) method, which efficiently extracts spatiotemporal correlations using multimodal contrastive learning, thereby improving the accuracy of model pretraining. Additionally, we design a DP-based Gradient Correlation Protection (DPGC) method to safeguard the correlation privacy of model gradients. To address the final challenge, we propose a multimodal misinformation detection Transformer (MMDF) method, which utilizes fully connected layers and a Sigmoid activation function to minimize the total loss function, achieving high-quality multimodal misinformation detection. Through security analysis, we demonstrate that our CPMD scheme satisfies a high level of DP protection. Our main contributions are as follows:

- We propose, for the first time, a CPMD scheme that simultaneously protects the semantic correlations of multimodal data and the correlations of pretrained model gradients, enabling highly available multimodal misinformation detection.
- We introduce the MFDP method, which provides effective privacy protection for multimodal semantic correlations. We design the DPGC method to protect the correlations of model gradients, thereby ensuring the security of pretrained models. The MSCL method is leveraged to mine the spatiotemporal correlations for achieving efficient multimodal misinformation detection.
- Security analysis proves that our CPMD scheme satisfies (ϵ, δ)-DP, and extensive experimental results show that, compared with the existing state-of-the-art method HAMMER, our method achieves better performance in multimodal misinformation detection through the multi-head spatiotemporal correlation attention mechanism.

2 Methodology

2.1 System Model

As shown in Fig. 2, our CPMD scheme contains three layers: end, edge, and cloud, with a federated learning framework implemented between the edge and cloud

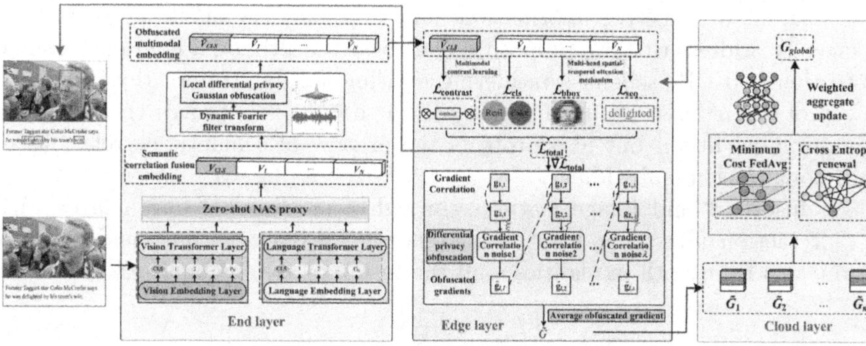

Fig. 2. The process of our CPMD framework.

layers. In the end layer, for multimodal text and image data, users encode them separately with language and vision Transformer models. Text features are $P = (CLS, p_1, \dots, p_{N-1})$ and image features are $C = (CLS, c_1, \dots, c_{N-1})$, where CLS is the global feature and $N+1$ is the number of encoded features. Then, a Zero-shot NAS Transformer fuses these features into a multimodal embedding $V = (v_{CLS}, v_1, \dots, v_{N-1})$, with v_{CLS} being the global fused embedding. To protect its semantic integrity, V is transformed into the frequency domain F by Fourier transform. Noise $N(0, \sigma^2 S^2)$ is added to obfuscate F, and a dynamic filtering mechanism removes extreme noise. Finally, the obfuscated embedding $\widetilde{V}$ is obtained by inverse Fourier transform and uploaded to the edge layer.

In the edge layer, edge nodes gather the obfuscated multimodal fused embeddings $\widetilde{V}$ from all users and pre-train local models using a multi-head spatiotemporal correlation attention mechanism. The training uses multimodal contrastive loss $L_{contrast}$, bounding box loss L_{bbox}, and sequence labeling loss L_{seq}. Based on these losses, local model gradients are computed. To protect the privacy of model gradient correlation, adaptive Gaussian noise is added between each layer's gradients according to their correlation, safeguarding gradient relationship privacy and improving local model training accuracy.

In the cloud layer, the cloud server aggregates the obfuscated local model gradients to train the global model and get optimized global parameters. These parameters are distributed to edge nodes, allowing local edge models to be updated for high-quality misinformation detection.

2.2 Multimodal Fusion and Semantic Correlation Protection

In the end layer, there are inefficiencies in fusion due to hyperparameter tuning in the traditional fusion network layer [16]. Recent work uses gradient signal-to-noise ratio (ξ-GSNR) [17] as a zero-shot proxy and optimizes fusion accuracy via optimal neural architecture search (NAS), reducing computational overhead. However, static ξ parameters may fail to maintain prediction consistency [18,19]. Moreover, the multimodal fusion embeddings obtained through fusion contain a large amount of sensitive information, and thus face the challenge of privacy leakage. To address this, we propose a LDP-based Multimodal Fourier Dynamic Protection (MFDP) scheme considering multimodal data interactions and privacy protection for text and images. MFDP not only improves the efficiency of multimodal fusion but also protects the privacy of semantic correlations in multimodal fusion embeddings.

We fuse text and image features through a multimodal fusion layer with an "interaction phase" and a "fusion phase". The interaction phase extracts information from both modalities, and the fusion phase combines it:

$$GSNR = \sum_{j=1}^{H} \log \left(\sum_{\omega \in \theta_j} \frac{(\mathbb{E}_{(x,y)\sim Z}[g(x,y,\omega)])^2}{\text{Var}_{(x,y)\sim Z}[g(x,y,\omega)] + \xi} \right)$$
$$\xi = \frac{\xi_0}{1 + Var(g)} + \frac{\xi_0}{1 + L_{val}} \tag{1}$$

Here, H is the number of network parameters, $\mathbb{E}_{(x,y)\sim Z}[g(x,y,\omega)]$ is the gradient expectation of parameter ω, Var is the variance, ξ_0 is the initial value and L_{val} is the validation loss.

Finally, the process of multimodal fusion can be expressed as:

$$V = \text{Fusion}_{GSNR}^{h}\left(V^h; \theta\right) = (v_{cls}, \ldots, v_{N-1}) \tag{2}$$

where V represents the multimodal fused embedding, Fusion^h denotes the fusion network at the h-th layer, V^h is the fusion result at the h-th layer, and θ represents the learned parameters.

To protect the semantic correlation privacy of the multimodal fused embedding, we obfuscate the user's multimodal fused embedding. We first apply a Fourier transform to convert the multimodal fused embedding V into a frequency domain representation:

$$f_i = \frac{1}{\sqrt{N}} \sum_{n=0}^{N-1} v_n \cdot e^{\frac{j2\pi}{N} in} \tag{3}$$

where f_i represents the Fourier-transformed element, v_n denotes the elements of the multimodal fused embedding V, N is the embedding length, and j is the imaginary unit.

Based on the obtained Fourier transform representation $F = (f_0, \ldots, f_{N-1})$, we add Gaussian noise with a mean of 0 and variance equal to the maximum sensitivity of F:

$$\Delta F = \max \|f_i - f_j\|_2$$
$$\widetilde{F} = F + \gamma \tag{4}$$

where ΔF represents the maximum sensitivity in the frequency domain, $\|\cdot\|_2$ denotes the L_2-norm, $\widetilde{F}$ is the obfuscated frequency domain vector, and γ is the noise vector drawn from a distribution with a mean of 0 and variance $\sigma^2 \Delta F^2$.

Due to the presence of extreme noise values in the frequency domain after noise addition, the data's usability may be compromised. Therefore, frequency domain filtering is a key mechanism to mitigate the impact of extreme noise. However, traditional fixed blurring filtering ratios may either filter out critical information or retain excessive noise [20]. To address this, considering that the frequency energy distribution and energy variations can reflect the scale of key information and noise [21], we design a dynamic filtering ratio as follows:

$$\begin{aligned} C_f[k] &= \frac{\sum_{i=0}^{k} E_f[i]cos\left(\frac{(2i-1)\pi}{2(N)}\right)}{\sum_{j=0}^{N} E_f[j]cos\left(\frac{(2j-1)\pi}{2(N)}\right)} \\ M_f &= \sum_{i=0}^{N-1} |E_f[i+1] - E_f[i]|_2^2 \\ \rho &= 1/(1+\exp\left(-(\alpha \cdot \frac{C_f[k]}{\parallel C_f \parallel_2} + (1-\alpha) \cdot \frac{M_f}{\parallel M_f \parallel_2}\right)) \end{aligned} \tag{5}$$

Here, $C_f[k]$ represents the energy ratio of the first k frequency domain elements, E_f denotes the frequency domain energy distribution, and M_f represents the frequency domain energy variation. ρ is the dynamic filtering ratio, and α is a tuning parameter.

Finally, by dynamically filtering the obfuscated multimodal frequency domain representation, we apply the inverse Fourier transform to the filtered obfuscated multimodal frequency domain representation, obtaining the obfuscated multimodal fused embedding $\widetilde{V}$, expressed as:

$$\begin{aligned} P_K(\widetilde{F}) &= \begin{cases} f_i & \text{if } i < K \\ 0 & \text{if } i \geq K \end{cases} \\ K &= N - \rho N \\ \widetilde{V} &= \text{IF}(P_K(\widetilde{F})) \end{aligned} \tag{6}$$

where $P_K(\widetilde{F})$ represents the dynamic filtering mechanism, K is the retention coefficient, $\text{IF}(\cdot)$ denotes the inverse Fourier transform, and $\widetilde{V}$ is the obfuscated multimodal fused embedding. The user fuses multimodal data and obfuscates it at the end layer, then uploads the obfuscated multimodal fused embedding to the edge node.

2.3 Local Multi-head Spatiotemporal Correlation Pretraining

The edge node collects the obfuscated multimodal embeddings uploaded by users for pre-training detection. Traditional detection methods use contrastive and binary classification losses for misinformation pre-training detection [12]. However, the spatiotemporal correlation between multimodal data contains a significant amount of information, and traditional methods that do not account for these correlations may result in lower detection accuracy. To address this, we propose a multi-head spatiotemporal correlation attention-based large model pre-training protection (MSLP) method. First, based on traditional contrastive learning loss, we calculate the contrastive learning loss between the obfuscated multimodal fused embeddings from different users:

$$\mathcal{L}_{\widetilde{V}_i,\ \widetilde{V}_j} = \frac{1}{B}\sum_{i=1}^{B} \log \frac{exp(d_m^2(\widetilde{V}_i,\ \widetilde{V}_j)/\tau)}{\sum_{j=1}^{u} exp(d_m^2(\widetilde{V}_i,\ \widetilde{V}_j)/\tau)} \tag{7}$$

where $L_{\widetilde{V}_i,\widetilde{V}_j}$ represents the contrastive learning loss of $\widetilde{V}_i$ with respect to $\widetilde{V}_j$, and d_m denotes the Mahalanobis distance. We also consider the directional differences in the loss between $\widetilde{V}_i$ and $\widetilde{V}_j$. Therefore, the user multimodal contrastive learning loss is represented as:

$$\mathcal{L}_{contrast} = \mathcal{L}_{\widetilde{V}_i,\widetilde{V}_j} + \mathcal{L}_{\widetilde{V}_j,\widetilde{V}_i} \tag{8}$$

where $L_{contrast}$ is the multimodal contrastive learning loss.

Similarly, based on the sample size B and v_{cls}, we calculate the binary classification detection loss for the obfuscated multimodal fused embedding as follows:

$$\mathcal{L}_{cls} = \frac{1}{B}\sum_{i=1}^{B}[y_{cls}\log(\hat{y}_{cls}) + (1-y_{cls})\log(1-\hat{y}_{cls})] \tag{9}$$

Here, L_{cls} is the binary classification detection loss, $\hat{y}_{cls}$ is the predicted binary classification probability, and y_{cls} is the ground truth probability.

In addition to the traditional contrastive learning loss and binary classification detection loss, we also design a multi-head spatiotemporal correlation attention mechanism to detect misinformation regions.

We use the mean pooling method along the spatial embeddings to obtain the spatial feature S, and use the word-level pooling method to obtain word feature W. Then we apply cross attention between S and W, choosing top-k_1 related features to get spatial representation V_S. Similarly, after the time feature T is extracted along the token pool of the time dimension, we calculate the top-k_2 related features to obtain time representation V_T. Finally, we design a multi-head self-attention mechanism to calculate the spatiotemporal correlation V_{ST}.

$$V_{ST} = \text{MultiHead}\left(\left[\phi_S\left(V_S\right), \phi_T\left(V_T\right), \phi_W\left(W\right)\right]\right) \tag{10}$$

Next, based on V_{ST}, we use a linear layer ϕ to predict the mapped image bounding boxes $\hat{p}_{img}$ and text labels $\hat{t}_{txt}$ for achieving detection grounding. Thus, we compute the bounding box loss $\mathcal{L}_{bbox}$ and the sequence labeling loss $\mathcal{L}_{seq}$ as follows:

$$\begin{gathered} \hat{p}_{img} = \phi(\omega_{img}V_{ST} + b_{img}) \quad \hat{t}_{txt} = \phi(\omega_{txt}V_{ST} + b_{txt}) \\ \mathcal{L}_{bbox} = \frac{1}{B}\sum_{i=1}^{B} \parallel p_{img} - \hat{p}_{img} \parallel_1 \\ \mathcal{L}_{seq} = \frac{1}{B}\sum_{j=1}^{B}\sum_{k=1}^{K} t_{txt}log(\hat{t}_{txt}) \end{gathered} \tag{11}$$

Here, $\mathcal{L}_{bbox}$ represents the image bounding box L_1 regression loss, $\mathcal{L}_{seq}$ denotes the text sequence labeling cross-entropy loss, p_{img} is the ground truth false region bounding box mapping, $\hat{p}_{img}$ is the predicted bounding box mapping, K is the length of the text sequence, t_{txt} represents the ground truth text label mapping, and $\hat{t}_{txt}$ represents the predicted label mapping. ω_{img} and b_{img} represent the weight and bias for predicting image bounding boxes, ω_{txt} and b_{txt} denote the weight and bias for predicting text tokens.

Based on all the loss values from the edge server, we compute the total loss for the entire local misinformation detection model, expressed as:

$$\mathcal{L}_{total} = \mathcal{L}_{contrast} + \mathcal{L}_{cls} + \mathcal{L}_{bbox} + \mathcal{L}_{seq} \tag{12}$$

Among them, L_{total} represents the total model loss, $L_{contrast}$ represents the multimodal contrastive learning loss, L_{cls} is the binary classification detection loss, L_{bbox} is the image bounding box L1 regression loss, and L_{seq} is the text sequence labeling cross-entropy loss.

2.4 Local Model Gradient Correlation Obfuscation

In cloud-edge collaboration, multiple interactions of data and gradients risk privacy attacks like gradient inversion. Even if the noise-added data is uploaded to the model pre-training, the correlation of training parameters can still reveal internal model privacy [23]. Existing work mainly focuses on protecting the privacy of the model gradients themselves while overlooking the privacy of gradient correlations. Attackers can infer sensitive gradient information from the correlations between gradients of different layers [22], which leads to severe privacy issues. To address this, we propose a Differential Privacy-based Gradient Correlation Protection (DPGC) method, which safeguards the privacy of layer-wise gradients during model pretraining by considering their inter-layer correlations.

Specifically, during the model's backpropagation update, the gradient for each layer, $g = \nabla L_{\text{total}}$, is computed from the total loss L_{total}. We then obfuscate the gradients of each layer based on the correlations between gradients. First, for the gradient g_l at layer l, due to potential issues such as vanishing or exploding gradients, we apply gradient clipping based on gradient sensitivity:

$$\begin{aligned} \bar{g}_l &= \frac{g_l}{max\left(1, \frac{||g_l||_2}{S}\right)} \\ S &= max||g_l^i - g_l^j||_2 \end{aligned} \tag{13}$$

where $\bar{g}_l$ is the clipped gradient for layer l, S represents the sensitivity, $\|\cdot\|_2$ is the L_2 norm, and g_l^i is the i-th element of the gradient g_l at layer l.

Next, we add Gaussian noise with a mean of 0 and variance $\zeta = \sigma_l^2 S^2$ to the current gradient, based on the information entropy of the current gradient and the correlation with the previous layer's gradient. Specifically, we dynamically adjust the noise size by calculating the information entropy of each layer's gradient and the correlation between the current gradient and the previous layer's gradient. The gradient information entropy and correlation are computed as follows:

$$H(\bar{g}_l) = \sum_{i=1}^{L} \left(\frac{|\bar{g}_l^i|}{\sum_{j=1}^{L} |\bar{g}_l^j|} \right) \log \left(\frac{|\bar{g}_l^i|}{\sum_{j=1}^{L} |\bar{g}_l^j|} \right)$$
$$c(\bar{g}_l, \bar{g}_{l-1}) = \sqrt{(\bar{g}_l - \bar{g}_{l-1})^T X^{-1} (\bar{g}_l - \bar{g}_{l-1})} \tag{14}$$

where $H(\bar{g}_l)$ is the information entropy of the gradient at layer l, L is the gradient length, $c(\bar{g}_l, \bar{g}_{l-1})$ is the correlation between the gradients of two layers, and X is the covariance matrix.

Considering that privacy is inversely proportional to gradient correlation [24], we design an adaptive noise scaling method for gradient correlation privacy protection, which integrates all the above conditions. Specifically, it is expressed as follows:

$$\sigma_l = \frac{\sigma_0}{e^{H(\bar{g}_l)}} \left(cos \left(\frac{\pi}{2} \cdot \frac{correlation\,(\bar{g}_l, \bar{g}_{l-1})}{d_{max}} \right) + 1 \right)$$
$$\widetilde{G} = \frac{1}{\lambda} \sum_{k=1}^{\lambda} (\bar{g}_{l,k} + \mathcal{N}(0, \sigma_l^2 S^2)) \tag{15}$$

where σ_l is the noise scale, σ_0 is initial noise scale, $H(\bar{g}_l)$ is the gradient entropy, $\bar{g}_l$ is clipped gradient, and d_{max} is the maximum Mahalanobis distance. $\bar{g}_{l,k}$ represents the gradient of the l-th layer in the k-th round, E is the model pre-training batch.

Each edge node pretrains the model based on the user-disturbed multimodal fusion embeddings, then uploads the disturbed model gradients to the cloud service for global model aggregation. The cloud server then distributes the aggregated global model parameters back to each edge node for local model updates.

2.5 Efficient Multimodal Misinformation Detection Transformer

The cloud server feedback the global parameters to the edge nodes for updating local models. We propose a multimodal misinformation detection transformer (MMDF) method. Misinformation detection is carried out for $\widetilde{v}_{cls}$ of each user through two fully connected layers and the sigmoid activation function. Leveraging contrastive learning to capture global and local semantic inconsistencies in fake information, which determine the authenticity of multimodal data and pinpoint forged regions through bounding boxes and text tokens. Classification detection is:

$$\mathcal{X} = sigmoid(\omega_3 \mathcal{O}_2 + b_3)$$
$$\mathcal{O}_2 = \xi(\omega_2 \mathcal{O}_1 + b_2) \tag{16}$$
$$\mathcal{O}_1 = \xi(\omega_1 v_{cls} + b_1)$$

Here, $\mathcal{X}$ is the detection classification probability and $\mathcal{O}$ the output of the fully connected layer, ξ denote the activation function, ω represent the weight of the network layer, and b stand for the bias.

3 Security Analysis

Our CPMD scheme contains four algorithms: MFDP, MSLP, DPGC, and MMDT. Due to MSLP and MMDT do not add any noise. Thus, these two methods satisfy 0-DP according to the nature of DP. MFDP and DPGC algorithms add DP noise to protect multimodal fusion embeddings and model gradient privacy. To ensure user privacy, we analyze the MFDP algorithm satisfies (ϵ_1, δ)-DP and prove that the DPGC algorithm satisfies (ϵ_2, δ)-DP. Subsequently, we prove that our CPMD scheme achieves (ϵ, δ)-DP.

Theorem 1. *Let each noise γ_i is drawn from $N(0, \sigma^2 \Delta F^2)$. Consider $\widetilde{V} = IF(P_K(\widetilde{F}))$, then we need to prove that $\widetilde{V}$ follows a normal distribution $N(0, \frac{K}{N}\sigma^2 \Delta F^2)$.*

Proof. Let $\gamma_i^K = P_K(\gamma_i)$. The resulting $\widetilde{V} = \text{IF}(\gamma_i^K)$. It can be formulated as:

$$\begin{aligned}
\widetilde{V} &= \frac{1}{\sqrt{N}} \sum_{i=0}^{N} \gamma_i^K e^{\frac{j2\pi}{N} in} \\
&= \frac{1}{\sqrt{N}} \sum_{i=0}^{K} \gamma_i e^{\frac{j2\pi}{N} in} \\
&= \frac{1}{\sqrt{N}} \sum_{i=0}^{K-1} \{\gamma_i\} \cos\left(\frac{2\pi}{N} in\right) + j\frac{1}{\sqrt{N}} \sum_{i=0}^{K-1} \{\gamma_i\} \sin\left(\frac{2\pi}{N} in\right)
\end{aligned}$$

Define $c_{n,i} = \frac{1}{\sqrt{N}}\{\gamma_i\}\cos(\frac{2\pi}{N}in)$, then we have $\frac{1}{\sqrt{N}}\sum_{i=0}^{K-1}\{V_i\}\cos(\frac{2\pi}{N}in) = \sum_{i=0}^{K-1} c_{n,i}$. Following the property of the normal distribution, we have $\sum_{i=0}^{K-1} c_{n,i} \sim \mathcal{N}(0, \sum_{i=0}^{K-1} \frac{1}{N}\cos^2(\frac{2\pi}{N}in)\sigma^2\Delta F^2)$. Simplifying the variance of the distribution, we have $\sum_{i=0}^{K-1} c_{n,i} \sim \mathcal{N}(\frac{K}{N}\frac{\sigma^2\Delta F^2}{2})$.

Similarly, we have $\frac{1}{\sqrt{N}}\sum_{i=0}^{K}\{\gamma_i\} \cdot \sin(\frac{2\pi}{N}in) \sim \mathcal{N}(\frac{K}{N}\frac{\sigma^2\Delta F^2}{2})$. This indicates that $v_n \sim \mathbb{CN}(\frac{K}{N}\sigma^2\Delta F^2)$ has the same scale of $N(\frac{K}{N}\sigma^2\Delta F^2)$.

Theorem 2. *For a training sample of size B, add the Gaussian distribution noise function $\frac{1}{\xi}e^{-\lambda||\tau||}$ to the gradient $\nabla L_{total}(x, \omega_l)$, it is guaranteed that when $\lambda = \frac{B\epsilon_l}{2S}$, the DPGC satisfies (ϵ_2, δ)-DP. $S > ||\nabla L_{total}(x, \omega_l)||_2$ is the sensitivity at the lth epoch.*

Proof. Given two continuous differentiable functions $O(x, \omega)$ and $o(x, \omega)$, when we sampl τ from a Gaussian distribution, the density at a specific τ_0 is directly proportional to $e^{-\lambda||\tau_0||}$. Thus, given x_1 and x_2, any ω is distinct values in two separate batches within an instance:

$$\frac{O(x_1, w)}{O(x_2, w)} = \frac{\frac{1}{\xi}e^{-\lambda||\tau_1||}}{\frac{1}{\xi}e^{-\lambda||\tau_2||}} = e^{-\rho(||\tau_1||-||\tau_2||)} \tag{17}$$

Let ω_1 and ω_2 be the solutions of x_1 and x_2 respectively under the training function. According to the triangle inequality, we get:

$$||\tau_1|| - ||\tau_2|| \leq ||\tau_1 - \tau_2|| = ||\omega_1 - \omega_2|| \tag{18}$$

When $O(\omega)$ and $o(\omega)$ are α-convex functions. We believe that all functions f_1, f_2 and $\beta \in (0,1)$ satisfy $\chi(\beta f_1 + (1-\beta)f_2) \leq \beta\chi(f_1) + (1-\beta)G(f_2) - \frac{1}{2}\alpha\beta(1-\beta)||f_1 - f_2||_2^2$ [25]. Assign $O(\omega)$ to $L(x_1, \omega_l)$, and $o(\omega)$ to $L(x_2, \omega_l) - L(x_1, \omega_l)$, ω_1 is assigned to $argmin_\omega L(x_1, \omega_l)$, and ω_2 is assigned to $argmin_\omega L(x_2, \omega_l)$. Then, we can get the following formula:

$$\nabla O(\omega_1) = \nabla O(\omega_2) + \nabla o(\omega_2) = 0$$

Due to the α-convex function property:

$$(\nabla O(\omega_1) - \nabla O(\omega_1))^\top(\omega_1 - \omega_2) \geq \alpha||(\omega_1 - \omega_2)||^2$$

Combine the above two equations, we can get:

$$\begin{aligned} ||\omega_1 - \omega_2|| \times ||\nabla o(\omega_2)|| &\geq (\omega_1 - \omega_2)^\top \nabla o(\omega_2)) \\ &= (\nabla O(\omega_1) - \nabla O(\omega_1))^\top(\omega_1 - \omega_2) \geq \alpha||(\omega_1 - \omega_2)||^2 \end{aligned}$$

When α=1, we can get:

$$\begin{aligned} ||\omega_1 - \omega_2|| &\leq \max_\omega ||\nabla o(\omega)|| \\ \nabla o(\omega) &= \frac{1}{B}(x_1 \nabla L(x_1, \omega_l) - x_2 \nabla L(x_2, \omega_2)) \leq \frac{2S}{B} \end{aligned}$$

According to Eq. (17) and Eq. (18), we can have:

$$\frac{O(x_1, w)}{O(x_2, w)} = e^{-\lambda(||\tau_1|| - ||\tau_2||)} \leq e^{-\lambda(||\omega_1 - \omega_2||)} \leq e^{-\lambda\frac{2S}{B}}$$

According to the concept of DP, when $\lambda = \frac{B\epsilon_l}{2S}$ is, our $\frac{O(x_1,w)}{O(x_2,w)} < \epsilon_l$. Therefore, we prove that the DPGC algorithm satisfies (ϵ_2, δ)-DP.

Theorem 3. *The CPMD scheme follows (ϵ, δ)-DP.*

Proof. In Theorem 1 and 2, we prove that the MFDP algorithm satisfies (ϵ_1, δ)-DP, and the DPGC algorithm satisfies (ϵ_2, δ)-DP. MSLP and MMDT algorithms satisfy 0-DP. According to the sequential composition theorem of DP, we can conclude that the CPMD scheme satisfies (ϵ, δ)-DP, where $\epsilon = \epsilon_1 + \epsilon_2$.

4 Experiment

4.1 Datasets and Evaluation

We use the Detecting and Grounding Multi-Modal Media Manipulation (DGM^4) dataset, which focuses on large-scale machine-generated multimodal manipulations [12]. Root mean square error (RMSE) is employed to evaluate the accuracy of obfuscated data. For the fake detection performance, we use the Area Under the Receiver Operating Characteristic Curve (AUC), Equal Error Rate (EER), and Accuracy (ACC) to evaluate the binary classification task. For multi-label classification, we adopt the mean Average Precision (mAP), average per-class F1 score (CF1), and average overall F1 score (OF1) to assess the detection of fine-grained manipulation types. Regarding image bounding box localization, we calculate the mean Intersection over Union (IoUmean) between the ground truth coordinates and the predicted coordinates of all test samples to examine the performance of the predicted manipulated bounding boxes. Meanwhile, two IoU thresholds of 0.5 and 0.75 are set to calculate the average accuracy. For text token localization, we use Precision, Recall, and F1 score as evaluation metrics to evaluate the manipulated text token localization task more fairly and reasonably [12]. Although the Sniffer [14] method demonstrates excellent detection performance, it is limited by the size and diversity of the training dataset, particularly when the proportion of the training set is small, which can affect the model's detection capability. Therefore, we compare our approach with three state-of-the-art multimodal detection models CLIP [26], ViLT [27], and HAMMER [12].

4.2 Parameter Settings

During the multimodal fusion phase, we set the initial ξ_0 for ξ-GSNR to 1e-4. In the obfuscated embedding phase, we configure the weight factor $\alpha \in [0.1, 1]$ for the dynamic filtering ratio and set the privacy budget $\epsilon_1 \in [1, 3]$. For the edge pretraining, we use a batch size of 32, validation batch size of 64, learning rate of 1e-5, weight decay of 0.02 and a τ value of 0.07. For the gradient obfuscation, we set the initial noise scale $\sigma_0 \in \{10, 15, 20\}$ and privacy budget $\epsilon_2 \in [0.1, 1]$. For detection, the binary classifier, multi-head self-attention mechanism, image bounding box detector, and text token detector all employ a two-layer MLP, with output dimensions of 2 (true/false classification), 4 (four types of forgery), 4 (bounding box coordinates), and 2 (text token authenticity). We have demonstrated through Theorem 1 and Theorem 2 that our scheme achieves a high level of differential

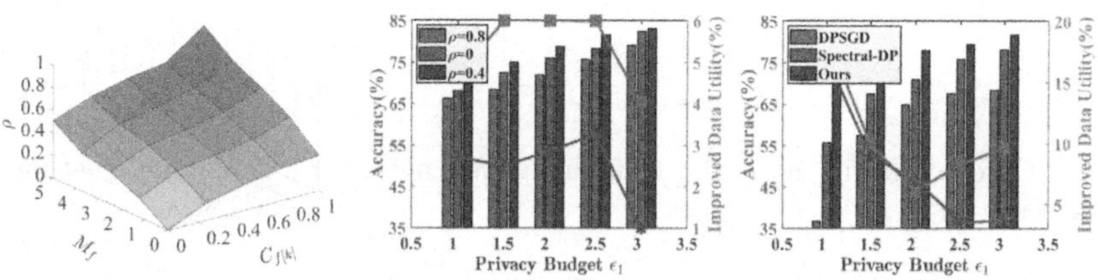

(a) ρ under different $C_{f[k]}$ and M_f. (b) Different ρ comparison. (c) Different method comparison.

Fig. 3. Performance evaluation of our MFDP method. The red line indicates the accuracy difference between $\rho = 0.4$ and $\rho = 0.8$, blue line indicates the accuracy difference between $\rho = 0.4$ and $\rho = 0$. (Color figure online) privacy protection. Thus, in the experiments, we will evaluate the performance of each algorithm in terms of aspects such as usability and detection accuracy.

4.3 Performance Analysis

Privacy Utility Comparison. Figure 3(a) shows the influence of the energy proportion $C_{f[k]}$ and energy change M_f on the filtration ratio ρ. It can be observed that ρ is jointly affected by both $C_{f[k]}$ and M_f. As shown in Fig. 3(b), increasing the MFDP filtering ratio removes more information from the multi-modal embeddings, reducing accuracy. When $\rho = 0.4$, the data usability reaches its maximum value of 83.24%. Figure 3(c) shows that, compared to a fixed filtering ratio, the MFDP method can dynamically adjust the filtering ratio, achieving an average accuracy improvement of 9.4%, thereby providing higher data utility. Figure 4(a) indicates that our DPGC's initial noise scale affects data utility. When the initial noise scale $\sigma_0 = 10$, the DPGC method exhibits the best performance, reaching 91.2%. Figure 4(b) shows that our method is capable of adding relatively large noise at the early stage of training and gradually reducing the noise as the training progresses, which benefits from the combination of dynamic sensitivity and dynamic noise scale. In contrast, the baseline maintains a constant noise variance during the training process due to the use of fixed parameters. Although Fed-αCDP [22] employs dynamic sensitivity, its noise scale is fixed, and thus the variation of its noise variance is not as favorable as that of our DPGC method. In Fig. 4(c), the DPGC method takes gradient correlation into account and achieves an accuracy of 90%., outperforming the existing federated learning DP methods, Fed-CDP [32] and the Fed-αCDP [22], which uses dynamic noise scaling, in terms of data utility. Although Fed-αCDP iteratively reduces noise, it poses a risk of cumulative privacy loss. Our DPGC method adjusts noise scale based on intrinsic features, providing privacy protection.

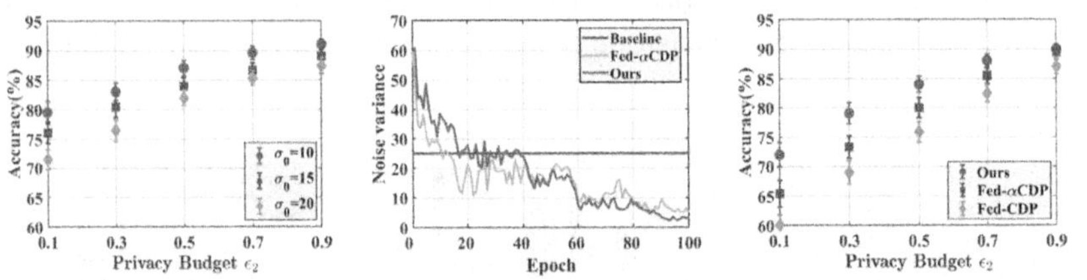

(a) Different initial noise scales. (b) Different initial noise scales. (c) Different methods comparison.

Fig. 4. Performance evaluation of our DPGC method. The horizontal line above and below is the accuracy error range.

Detection Performance Comparison. In Table 1, we compare the detection performance of our CPMD method with that of HAMMER, TS [28], and

Table 1. Different image grounding methods comparison.

Categories	Binary Cls			Image Grounding		
Methods	AUC	EER	ACC	IoUmean	IoU50	IoU75
TS	91.80	17.11	82.89	72.85	79.12	74.06
MST	91.31	17.65	82.36	72.88	78.98	74.70
HAMMER	94.40	13.18	86.80	75.69	82.93	75.65
Ours	**94.77**	**13.10**	**87.03**	**76.11**	82.67	**76.40**

Table 2. Different text grounding methods comparison.

Categories	Binary Cls			Text Grounding		
Methods	AUC	EER	ACC	Precision	Recall	F1
BERT	80.82	28.02	68.98	41.39	63.85	50.23
LUKE	81.39	27.88	76.18	50.52	37.93	43.33
HAMMER	93.44	13.83	87.39	70.90	73.30	72.08
Ours	**94.57**	**12.63**	**88.55**	**72.48**	**73.9**	70.84

MST [29] in image grounding. When the learning rate is 1e-4, the weight decay is 0.02, and the batch size is 64, our binary classification detection accuracy reaches an optimal value of 94.77%, and the optimal value of the image grounding accuracy is 76.40%. Table 2 compares HAMMER, BERT [30], and LUKE [31] in text grounding. Our method achieves the best performance of 94.57% in binary classification detection and 74.58% in text grounding. In Table 3, we compare the performance in misinformation detection between our method and ViLT, CLIP, and HAMMER. Our method demonstrates excellent performance. In some cases, although our method does not achieve the best performance, such as IoU50 in Table 1 and F1 in Table 2, our method has better privacy protection effect because it considers the multi-modal semantic association and gradient correlation privacy of data. This shows the strong competitiveness of our spatialtemporal correlation mechanism in misinformation detection.

Table 3. Comparison of different misinformation detection methods.

Methods	Binary Cls			Multi-Label Cls			Image Grounding			Text Grounding		
	AUC	EER	ACC	mAP	CF1	OF1	IoUmean	IoU50	IoU75	Precision	Recall	F1
CLIP	83.22	24.61	76.40	66.00	59.52	62.31	49.51	50.03	38.79	58.12	22.11	32.03
ViLT	85.16	22.88	78.38	72.37	66.14	66.00	59.32	65.18	48.10	66.48	49.88	57.00
HAMMER	93.19	14.10	86.39	86.22	79.37	80.37	76.45	83.75	76.06	75.01	68.02	71.35
Ours	**94.21**	**11.04**	**89.42**	**88.94**	**83.98**	**85.45**	**77.55**	82.01	**77.37**	72.46	**72.13**	**73.85**

Ablation Study of Losses. The losses taken into account in each situation along with the corresponding outcomes are presented in Table 4. It is quite clear that the removal of the contrastive learning loss, i.e. $\mathcal{L}_{contrast}$, gives rise to performance deterioration in nearly all respects. This indicates that the multimodal contrastive learning loss is indispensable for our method. Upon the elimination of any one of the other specific losses, namely $\mathcal{L}_{bbox}$ or $\mathcal{L}_{seq}$, not only does the performance of the relevant task drop significantly, but also the overall binary classification performance may be reduced. In contrast to the baseline approach [12], our complete loss function model attains the optimal performance, which manifests the efficacy and complementarity of all losses.

Fig. 5. Visual comparison of multimodal misinformation detection.

Table 4. Ablation study of losses in the our method.

Methods	AUC	mAP	IoUmean	F1	Avg
Baseline	93.19	86.22	76.45	71.35	81.8
Ours exc. $\mathcal{L}_{contrast}$	89.85	58.66	74.63	73.58	74.11
Ours exc. $\mathcal{L}_{bbox}$	91.94	86.13	59.43	73.51	77.7
Ours exc. $\mathcal{L}_{seq}$	91.05	85.32	75.14	60.39	77.9
Ours	94.21	88.94	77.55	73.85	83.63

Time Cost Analysis. As shown in Table 5, we observe that CPMD achieves a shorter runtime compared to ZiCo [33] and AZ-NAS [34]. Specifically, ZiCo

Table 5. Search cost of different methods.

Method	Sample size	Search cost
ZiCo	1005M	0.46
AZ-NAS	1022M	0.71
Our CPMD	1048M	0.4

inherently favors networks with a large number of #Params, resulting in a limited synergy effect between these computational searches and #Params and making it difficult to improve the NAS performance. Although the AZ-NAS method devises several zero-cost proxies, in the context of some special network architectures, calculating the relevant indicators of the trainability proxy may augment the computational load.

Visualization. Figure 5 shows the visual comparison of detection. In the top three images, we observe that HAMMER [12] may encounter competition between two modalities, leading to bias in marker detection. In the subsequent three images, our method successfully detects multimodal misinformation and accurately recognizes fake regions.

5 Related Work

Multimodal Misinformation Detection. In the field of multimodal misinformation detection, a series of influential methods have emerged in recent years [12–14]. Among them, the HAMMER method conducts misinformation detection and grounding through unimodal contrastive learning and multimodal aggregation cross-learning [12]. IMQ employs the dual-branch cross-attention mechanism (DCA) and decoupled fine-grained classifiers (DFC) to fuse modal features, and discovers forged details via implicit manipulation query (IMQ) [13]. Sniffer designs two stages for misinformation detection. The first stage aligns multimodal information, and the second stage utilizes out-of-context (OOC)-specific instruction data to fine-tune the recognition ability of the model [14]. However, in practical applications, multimodal data often contains rich personal information and sensitive content. Although these methods have made progress in detection accuracy, none of them can address the privacy issues in multimodal data.

Misinformation Detection Privacy Protection. In the field of privacy protection for misinformation detection, numerous research efforts are dedicated to addressing the challenges of data privacy [6,10,11,15]. For example, the DartBlur method employs anonymization techniques to blur facial features, thereby achieving privacy protection [10]. FedForgery utilizes a DP-based federated learning approach to safeguard the privacy of training data on clients [11]. FIND is a sparse update perturbation method that further enhances system security [15]. However, they overlook the privacy of multimodal data and the correlation privacy of gradients. Additionally, the SecMdp method has contributed to the privacy protection of multimodal data in the cloud-edge architecture [6]. Nevertheless, it neglects the privacy concerning the correlation of multimodal data.

6 Conclusion

In this paper, we propose the CPMD scheme to address the challenges of multimodal misinformation detection and privacy protection in the cloud-edge-end framework. Our CPMD scheme integrates the MFDP, MSLP, DPGC, and MMDT methods. In the end layer, the MFDP efficiently fuses multimodal data and protects semantic correlation privacy using dynamic mechanisms. In the edge layer, the MSLP extracts spatiotemporal correlations, enhancing pre-training accuracy, and the DPGC safeguards gradient correlation privacy. Finally, the MMDT method enables accurate misinformation detection. Security analysis proves that CPMD satisfies (ϵ, δ)-DP. Extensive experiments on a large-scale misinformation dataset, compared with advanced models like HAMMER, ViLT, and CLIP, demonstrated the superiority of our methods in privacy-utility trade-off and detection performance.

Acknowledgments. We appreciate the anonymous reviewers for their insightful and constructive suggestions. This work was supported in part by the Major Project of Xiangjiang Laboratory (No. 23XJ01002, No. 22XJ01001), National Natural Science Foundation of China (No. 62402177, No. 62376092, No. 62273140), Humanity and Social Science Youth foundation of Ministry of Education (No. 23YJCZH233), Hunan Provincial Natural Science Foundation of China (No. 2023JJ40237), Scientific Research Fund of Hunan Provincial Education Department (No. 22B0648, No. 22A0460), Teaching Reform Research Project of Ordinary Higher Education Institutions in Hunan Province (No. HNJG-20230772), and Postgraduate Scientific Research Innovation Project of Hunan Province (No. CX20231128).

References

1. Wan, L., Yan, C., Meng, M.H., Wang, K., Wang, H.: Analyzing excessive permission requests in Google workspace add-ons. In: Bai, G., Ishikawa, F., Ait-Ameur, Y., Papadopoulos, G.A. (eds.) ICECCS 2024. LNCS, vol. 14784, pp. 323–345. Springer, Cham (2025)
2. Sharevski, F., Vander Loop, J.: Children, parents, and misinformation on social media. In: IEEE Symposium on Security and Privacy (SP), pp. 1536–1553 (2024)
3. Hans, W., Hanley, A., Kumar, D., Durumeric, Z.: Specious sites: tracking the spread and sway of spurious news stories at scale. In: IEEE Symposium on Security and Privacy (SP), pp. 1609–1627 (2024)
4. Gao, C., Xu, Q., Qiao, P., Xu, K., Qian, X., Dou, Y.: Adapter-based incremental learning for face forgery detection. In: IEEE International Conference on Acoustics, Speech and Signal Processing (ICASSP), pp. 4690–4694 (2024)
5. Saha Roy, S., Thota, P., Naragam, K., Nilizadeh, S.: From chatbots to phishbots?: phishing scam generation in commercial large language models. In: IEEE Symposium on Security and Privacy (SP), pp. 36–54 (2024)

6. Bai, Z., Wang, M., Guo, F., Guo, Y., Cai, C., Bie, R.: SecMdp: towards privacy-preserving multimodal deep learning in end-edge-cloud. In: IEEE International Conference on Data Engineering (ICDE), pp. 1659–1670 (2024)
7. Bourdellès, M., El-Hachem, J., Sadou, S.: Confidentiality management in complex systems design. In: Bai, G., Ishikawa, F., Ait-Ameur, Y., Papadopoulos, G.A. (eds.) ICECCS 2024. LNCS, vol. 14784, pp. 303–322. Springer, Cham (2025). https://doi.org/10.1007/978-3-031-66456-4_17
8. Wang, X., Wang, Y., Yang, M., Li, F., Wu, X., Fan, L.: FedSiam-DA: dual-aggregated federated learning via Siamese network for non-IID data. IEEE Trans. Mob. Comput. **24**(2), 985–998 (2025)
9. Ma, J., Zhou, Y., Cui, L., Guo, S.: An optimized sparse response mechanism for differentially private federated learning. IEEE Trans. Dependable Secure Comput. **21**(4), 2285–2295 (2024)
10. Jiang, B., Bai, B., Lin, H., Wang, Y., Guo, Y., Fang, L.: DartBlur: privacy preservation with detection artifact suppression. In: IEEE/CVF Conference on Computer Vision and Pattern Recognition (CVPR), pp. 16479–16488 (2023)
11. Liu, D., et al.: FedForgery: generalized face forgery detection with residual federated learning. IEEE Trans. Inf. Forensics Secur. **18**, 4272–4284 (2023)
12. Shao, R., Wu, T., Wu, J., Nie, L., Liu, Z.: Detecting and grounding multi-modal media manipulation and beyond. IEEE Trans. Pattern Anal. Mach. Intell. **46**(8), 5556–5574 (2024)
13. Wang, J., et al.: Exploiting modality-specific features for multi-modal manipulation detection and grounding. In: IEEE International Conference on Acoustics, Speech and Signal Processing (ICASSP), pp. 4935–4939 (2024)
14. Qi, P., Yan, Z., Hsu, W., Lee, L.: Sniffer: multimodal large language model for explainable out-of-context misinformation detection. In: IEEE/CVF Conference on Computer Vision and Pattern Recognition (CVPR), pp. 13052–13062 (2024)
15. Lian, Z., Zhang, C., Su, C., Dharejo, A., Almutiq, M., Memon, H.: FIND: privacy-enhanced federated learning for intelligent fake news detection. IEEE Trans. Comput. Soc. Syst. **11**(4), 5005–5014 (2024)
16. Li, Y., Quan, R., Zhu, L., Yang, Y.: Efficient multi-modal fusion via interactive prompting. In: IEEE/CVF Conference on Computer Vision and Pattern Recognition (CVPR), pp. 2604–2613 (2023)
17. Sun, Z., et al.: Unleashing the power of gradient signal-to-noise ratio for zero-shot NAS. In: IEEE/CVF International Conference on Computer Vision (ICCV), pp. 5740–5750 (2023)
18. Michalkiewicz, M., Faraki, M., Yu, X., Chandraker, M., Baktashmotlagh, M.: Domain generalization guided by gradient signal to noise ratio of parameters. In: IEEE/CVF International Conference on Computer Vision (ICCV), pp. 6154–6165 (2023)
19. Zhang, Z., Zhang, Z., Wang, X., Qin, Y., Qin, Z., Zhu, W.: Dynamic heterogeneous graph attention neural architecture search. In: AAAI Conference on Artificial Intelligence (AAAI), pp. 1269–1277 (2023)
20. Feng, C., Xu, N., Wen, W., Venkitasubramaniam, P., Ding, C.: Spectral-DP: differentially private deep learning through spectral perturbation and filtering. In: IEEE Symposium on Security and Privacy (SP), pp. 1944–1960 (2023)
21. Liu, C., Wang, X., Li, S., Wang, Y., Qian, X.: FSI: frequency and spatial interactive learning for image restoration in under-display cameras. In: IEEE/CVF International Conference on Computer Vision (ICCV), pp. 12503–12512 (2023)

22. Wei, W., Liu, L., Zhou, J., Chow, K., Wu, Y.: Securing distributed SGD against gradient leakage threats. IEEE Trans. Parallel Distrib. Syst. **34**(7), 2040–2054 (2023)
23. Ye, Z., Luo, W., Zhou, Q., Tang, Y., Zhu, Z., Shi, Y.: Gradient inversion of text-modal data in distributed learning. IEEE Trans. Inf. Forensics Secur. **20**, 928–943 (2025)
24. Sun, P., Liao, G., Chen, X., Huang, J.: A socially optimal data marketplace with differentially private federated learning. IEEE/ACM Trans. Netw. **32**(3), 2221–2236 (2024)
25. Zhu, Y., Yu, W., Wen, G., Chen, G.: Projected primal-dual dynamics for distributed constrained nonsmooth convex optimization. IEEE Trans. Cybern. **50**(4), 1776–1782 (2020)
26. Alec, R., et al.: Learning transferable visual models from natural language supervision. In: International Conference on Machine Learning (ICML), pp. 8748–8763 (2021)
27. Kim, W., Son, B., Kim, I.: ViLT: vision-and-language transformer without convolution or region supervision. In: International Conference on Machine Learning (ICML), pp. 5583–5594 (2021)
28. Luo, Y., Zhang, Y., Yan, J., Liu, W.: Generalizing face forgery detection with high-frequency features. In: IEEE/CVF Conference on Computer Vision and Pattern Recognition (CVPR), pp. 16312–16321 (2021)
29. Zhao, H., Wei, T., Zhou, W., Zhang, W., Chen, D., Yu, N.: Multi-attentional deepfake detection. In: IEEE/CVF Conference on Computer Vision and Pattern Recognition (CVPR), pp. 2185–2194 (2021)
30. Devlin, J., Chang, M., Lee, K., Toutanova, K.: BERT: pre-training of deep bidirectional transformers for language understanding. In: Conference of the North American Chapter of the Association for Computational Linguistics: Human Language Technologies, pp. 4171–4186 (2019)
31. Yamada, I., Asai, A., Shindo, H., Takeda, H., Matsumoto, Y.: LUKE: deep contextualized entity representations with entity-aware self-attention. In: Conference on Empirical Methods in Natural Language Processing (EMNLP), pp. 6442–6454 (2020)
32. Wei, W., Liu, L., Wu, Y., Su, G., Iyengar, A.: Gradient-leakage resilient federated learning. In: IEEE International Conference on Distributed Computing Systems (ICDCS), pp. 797–807 (2021)
33. Li, G., Yang, Y., Bhardwaj, K., Marculescu, R.: ZiCo: zero-shot NAS via inverse coefficient of variation on gradients. In: the Eleventh International Conference on Learning Representations (ICLR) (2023)
34. Lee, J., Ham, B.: AZ-NAS: assembling zero-cost proxies for network architecture search. In: IEEE/CVF Conference on Computer Vision and Pattern Recognition (CVPR), pp. 5893–5903 (2024)

Large Language Models Empowered Software Engineering

Leveraging Large Language Models for Feature Envy Detection: A Context-Aware and Reasoning-Driven Approach

Jiamin Guo[1], Yangyang Zhao[1(✉)], Zhifei Chen[2], and Liming Nie[3]

[1] Zhejiang Sci-Tech University, Hangzhou, China
yangyangzhao@zstu.edu.cn
[2] Nanjing University of Science and Technology, Nanjing, China
chenzhifei@njust.edu.cn
[3] Shenzhen Technology University, Shenzhen, China
nieliming@sztu.edu.cn

Abstract. Feature Envy, a common code smell characterized by excessive reliance on external classes, undermines software maintainability by violating principles of cohesion and coupling. Traditional detection methods, which rely on heuristic thresholds and machine learning approaches, face limitations in generalizability and semantic understanding. In contrast, large language models (LLMs) offer promising capabilities for code analysis through deep semantic modeling. This study explores the performance of LLMs in Feature Envy detection, proposing a context-aware and reasoning-driven detection framework. The framework extracts relevant information from the target method and its containing class, incorporating reasoning-structured prompt designs to enhance detection accuracy. We examine three research questions: (1) the impact of prompt design on detection performance, particularly reasoning-based prompts (e.g., Chain-of-Thought and Tree-of-Thought), (2) the comparative effectiveness of state-of-the-art LLMs, and (3) model adaptability across four severity levels of Feature Envy. Experimental results reveal that reasoning-based prompts outperform non-reasoning prompts in 75% of scenarios, with significant improvements in F1-score, MCC, and Recall. Among evaluated models, DeepSeek-V3 achieves the highest overall performance, while GPT-4 excels in precision-critical tasks. Severity-level analysis shows DeepSeek-V3 and CodeLlama-7b excel in detecting high-severity instances, whereas GPT-4 demonstrates proficiency in identifying non-smell cases. These findings underscore the potential of LLMs in code smell detection and provide valuable insights for LLM-driven tools in technical debt management.

Keywords: Feature Envy Detection · Large Language Model · Prompt Engineering · Code Smell

Y. Zhou et al. (Eds.): ICECCS 2025, LNCS 15746, pp. 263–282, 2026.
https://doi.org/10.1007/978-3-032-00828-2_15

1 Introduction

During software development, code smells often indicate underlying design flaws [1]. If not addressed promptly, they can reduce code maintainability and readability [2,3], and escalate debugging and refactoring costs, thereby exacerbating technical debt. Feature Envy is one of the most well-known and extensively studied code smells [4]. It occurs when a method excessively depends on the attributes or methods of other classes rather than utilizing the resources of its own class [5,6]. This phenomenon typically signals an issue with functional decomposition, leading to reduced cohesion and increased coupling within the system. Such a code smell violates the Single Responsibility Principle, posing significant challenges for future maintenance and expansion [7]. Therefore, detecting Feature Envy is crucial for ensuring software quality.

Traditional Feature Envy detection methods typically rely on heuristic rules, determining the presence of code smells by setting specific threshold values [8]. However, the effectiveness of these methods is highly dependent on the choice of rules and thresholds, and identifying the optimal thresholds for different scenarios is a complex and time-consuming task [9]. To overcome the limitations of traditional approaches, researchers have introduced machine learning (ML) [10,11] and deep learning (DL) [12] techniques, which automatically learn the characteristics of code smells from labeled data and optimize the classification thresholds using algorithms. However, these approaches heavily rely on large amounts of labeled data and are significantly affected by changes in application scenarios. Additionally, they primarily focus on shallow features, making it difficult to capture deep semantic relationships and contextual dependencies within the code. These limitations affect the accuracy of code smell detection and presents significant challenges in real-world applications [13,14].

In recent years, the emergence of large language models (LLMs) has brought unprecedented breakthroughs to natural language processing (NLP) tasks [15–17]. Trained on large-scale corpora through self-supervised learning, these models can effectively capture complex semantic relationships and demonstrate exceptional text comprehension and generation capabilities. In the field of software engineering, the application of LLMs has been expanding, covering various tasks such as code generation and vulnerability detection [18–21]. LLMs can accurately capture structural and logical features of code, providing robust technical support for solving complex software engineering problems. Although LLMs have achieved remarkable progress in many code-related tasks, their effectiveness in code smell detection—particularly in detecting Feature Envy—remains to be further validated. Given the significant impact of Feature Envy on code quality, exploring the potential of LLMs in this domain not only enhances the accuracy of Feature Envy detection but also lays a theoretical foundation for the development of more effective detection tools.

This study focuses on evaluating the performance of LLMs in the Feature Envy detection and proposes a detection framework based on contextual information and prompt engineering. The framework extracts relevant information from the target method and its containing class, incorporating reasoning-structured prompt designs to support more accurate detection decisions. To investigate the impact of prompt design on LLM performance, we compare reasoning-structured prompts (e.g., Chain-of-Thought [22] and Tree-of-Thought [23]) with non-reasoning prompts (RQ1), aiming to reveal how prompting strategies guide models in analyzing code features and contextual information. Additionally, we evaluate the performance of various state-of-the-art LLMs with different scales and characteristics in Feature Envy detection (RQ2) and compare their applicability and limitations in detection. On the other hand, the severity of code smells is a critical factor that developers must prioritize in code quality management and refactoring [24–27]. While previous studies have discussed the concept of code smell severity [24], there is still a lack of comprehensive evaluation of LLM performance across different severity levels of code smells. To bridge this research gap, this study further analyzes LLM performance in detecting Feature Envy smells across four severity levels (RQ3), shedding light on the adaptability of LLMs in handling complex scenarios.

The main contributions of this work are as follows:

1) A context-aware and reasoning-driven framework is proposed that leverages LLMs, integrating contextual information and prompt engineering to enhance Feature Envy detection.
2) This study is the first to systematically evaluate the capability of LLMs in Feature Envy detection, addressing a research gap in this field. It demonstrates the impact of prompt engineering, evaluates the effectiveness of different models, and assesses LLM performance in detecting Feature Envy smells of varying severities.
3) This study offers new insights into automated code smell detection. The findings indicate that DeepSeek-V3 achieves the best overall performance, providing valuable theoretical guidance for optimizing LLM applications in code smell detection.

The rest of this paper is structured as follows: Sect. 2 reviews related work, while Sect. 3 presents our approach. Section 4 details the experimental design, and Sect. 5 analyzes the results. Section 6 discusses key findings and limitations, with threats to validity outlined in Sect. 7. Finally, Sect. 8 concludes the paper.

2 Related Work

The detection of Feature Envy smells is crucial for software quality maintenance. However, manual identification is both time-consuming and costly, prompting researchers to explore more efficient automated detection methods. Currently, mainstream Feature Envy detection approaches can be categorized into three types: heuristic-based, machine learning-based, and deep learning-based methods.

Heuristic-Based Approaches: Heuristic-based detection methods typically rely on predefined rules to identify suspicious code fragments. For instance,

Tsantalis and Chatzigeorgiou [28] proposed a distance-based analysis method to identify refactoring opportunities for movable methods, integrating it into the JDeodorant tool [29]. Additionally, textual information has been leveraged for Feature Envy detection. Bavota et al. [30] employed a Relational Topic Model to extract textual and structural information for identifying Feature Envy smells. Palomba et al. [31,32] discovered that methods affected by Feature Envy are more likely to co-change with the "envied class" rather than their actual containing class. Based on this insight, they proposed a history-based detection method. However, these heuristic approaches often rely on manually defined rules and thresholds, making it challenging to determine effective detection thresholds.

Machine Learning-Based Approaches: To overcome the limitations of heuristic methods, researchers have introduced machine learning techniques. Fontana et al. [24,33] conducted an empirical study comparing 16 machine learning techniques in code smell detection, evaluating their performance on four types of code smells across 74 software systems. Guo et al. [34] further validated the effectiveness of machine learning in Feature Envy detection and proposed a data-balancing strategy to enhance detection performance.

Deep Learning-Based Approaches: In recent years, deep learning techniques have been increasingly applied to Feature Envy detection. Liu et al. [12] employed deep neural networks to automatically extract and select features from source code, mapping them to detection labels. Barbez et al. [35] utilized a Multi-Layer Perceptron model for Feature Envy detection. Sharma et al. [36] compared the performance of Convolutional Neural Networks, Recurrent Neural Networks, and Autoencoders in code smell detection. More recently, Wu et al. [37] trained a Mixture of Experts (MoE) model, leveraging specialized sub-model integration techniques to improve detection performance.

With the growing potential of LLMs in code understanding and software engineering tasks [38,39], their effectiveness in Feature Envy detection has also attracted significant attention. However, a systematic evaluation of LLMs in this task remains lacking. To address this gap, we conduct a comprehensive assessment of LLMs' potential in Feature Envy detection.

3 Approach

To evaluate the performance of LLMs in detecting Feature Envy, we propose a systematic three-phase framework, as illustrated in Fig. 1. This framework consists of three key stages: Context Collection, Prompt Construction, and Feature Envy Detection. The process begins with extracting and preparing contextual data, followed by designing prompts, and finally leveraging LLMs to analyze code snippets and generate predictions. The details of each stage are as follows:

1) **Context Collection:** We used SciTools Understand to extract the target methods and their corresponding class code and contextual information from Java repositories. The extracted code was then preprocessed by removing

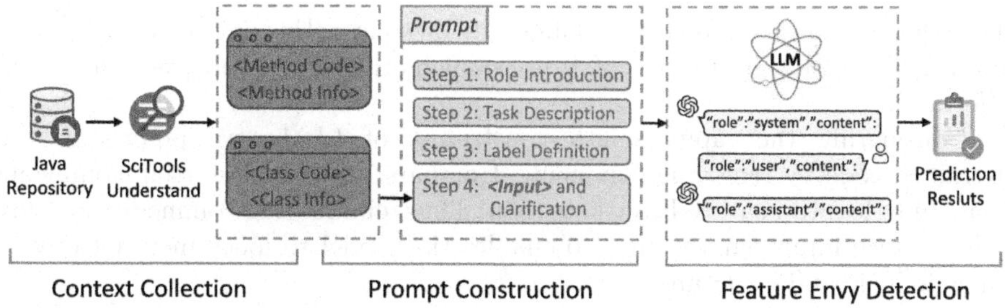

Fig. 1. Framework of the approach.

comments and optimizing inputs. For excessively long code, we employed method information sets and class information sets as alternatives to preserve the interaction between methods and classes as much as possible, ensuring the reliability of Feature Envy detection.

2) **Prompt Construction:** The design of prompts is crucial for optimizing LLMs inference. We introduce a structured four-step prompt framework comprising role introduction, task description, label definition, and input clarification. This structured approach ensures that the model receives clear task instructions, enhancing its reasoning efficiency.
3) **Feature Envy Detection:** In this phase, we input the contextual information along with prompts into multiple LLMs. These models analyze the code and predict whether a given method exhibits Feature Envy. Through extensive experimentation, we systematically evaluate the performance of different LLMs in this task, offering deeper insights into their understanding and reasoning capabilities.

The framework aims to assess whether LLMs can leverage their strong reasoning capabilities to improve Feature Envy detection, particularly when integrating contextual information and reasoning-structured prompts. In the following sections, we provide a detailed discussion of the implementation process and strategies for each stage.

3.1 Context Collection

Context collection is a crucial prerequisite for prompt construction and Feature Envy detection. This study employs the SciTools Understand static analysis tool to extract Java code and relevant information, enabling code structure analysis and capturing attributes and dependencies of code fragments. This approach ensures comprehensive contextual support for LLMs.

Code Extraction and Preprocessing: To accurately reflect the core logic of each target method, we extract its complete code. Additionally, to enhance contextual information, we retrieve the full code of the enclosing class, allowing for a more comprehensive analysis of method-class interactions. Since the primary criterion for Feature Envy detection is whether a method exhibits stronger dependencies on external classes than on its own class, this data collection strategy addresses the limitations of traditional methods in leveraging contextual information.

Considering the input length constraints of LLMs, we preprocess the extracted code by removing comments. Compared to the code itself, comments contribute less to Feature Envy detection. Thus, eliminating comments not only helps reduce input length but also enables the model to focus more effectively on code logic and structure.

Optimized Input Strategy: Despite preprocessing, some LLMs may still be unable to process the full code due to input length limitations. Traditional approaches often truncate excessively long code, which can result in the loss of crucial contextual information, thereby compromising the model's ability to perform a comprehensive analysis. To address this issue, we propose an optimized input strategy that prioritizes retaining as much contextual information as possible to fully capture method-class dependencies. When providing the complete code is infeasible, we adopt a structured representation that extracts key features, ensuring that LLMs can still accurately recognize code characteristics and dependencies. Specifically, we define two structured representations: Method Information Set and Class Information Set, which encapsulate the core characteristics of the code:

$$\begin{aligned} Method\ Information = \{&Class\ Name, Invoked\ Methods, Accessed\ Fields, \\ &Instantiated\ Objects, Method\ Parameter\ Types, \\ &Return\ Type\} \qquad (1) \\ Class\ Information = \{&Class\ Name, Fields, Methods, Constructors, \\ &Interfaces, Superclass\} \qquad (2) \end{aligned}$$

In cases where input constraints apply, we use these structured representations as substitutes, effectively reducing input length while preserving critical interaction relationships. Although the information is condensed, its core semantics remain intact, ensuring that LLMs can accurately identify both method dependencies on external classes and relationships within its enclosing class, thereby supporting Feature Envy detection. Detailed application rules can be found in Sect. 3.2.

3.2 Prompt Construction

To efficiently guide LLMs in code smell detection tasks, we designed two prompt construction strategies: Chain-of-Thought (CoT) prompts (referred to as $\text{prompt}_{\text{CoT}}$) and Tree-of-Thought (ToT) prompts (referred to as $\text{prompt}_{\text{ToT}}$). These two strategies are based on different reasoning approaches and aim to harness the LLM's ability to understand and analyze code context.

$\text{Prompt}_{\text{CoT}}$ employs a linear reasoning approach, guiding the LLM to analyze code step by step (Fig. 2). First (Step 1), the model is defined as an intelligent assistant specializing in Feature Envy detection. Next (Step 2), it is instructed to analyze the interaction between the target method, its enclosing class, and

Chain-of-Thought Prompt

Step1: Role Introduction

"role": "system", "content": "You are a highly skilled code analysis assistant specialized in detecting code smells, such as Feature Envy."

Step2: Task Description

"role": "user", "content": "Your task is to determine whether the following method exhibits Feature Envy. Please analyze the given method's code step by step: Start by analyzing the method's interactions with its own class and other classes. **Respond strictly with 'yes' or 'no,' without any additional text or explanation.**"

Step3: Label Definition

"role": "assistant", "content": "Got it. Can you provide more details about Feature Envy?"
"role": "user", "content": "Here is the definition of Feature Envy: *[label definition]*"

Step4: Input Clarification

"role": "user", "content": "Here is the *[method-related content]* and *[class-related content]*"

Fig. 2. The definition of the proposed $\text{prompt}_{\text{CoT}}$.

external classes, ultimately providing a binary "Yes" or "No" judgment. Then (Step 3), the definition of Feature Envy is explicitly provided to ensure consistency in evaluation standards. Finally (Step 4), the target method's code and its contextual information are inputted to furnish a comprehensive basis for analysis.

$\text{Prompt}_{\text{ToT}}$, in contrast, adopts a multi-perspective reasoning approach (Fig. 3, simulating an expert discussion process. It guides the model to independently analyze the code along different logical paths and then integrates conclusions from multiple perspectives to reach a final decision. While its overall workflow is similar to $\text{prompt}_{\text{CoT}}$, a key distinction lies in the task description stage (Step 3), where $\text{prompt}_{\text{ToT}}$ creates multiple virtual "experts". Each expert represents an independent reasoning path and analyzes the code from a distinct perspective. By leveraging multi-path reasoning, the model can develop a more comprehensive understanding of code characteristics in complex environments.

To address the context length limitations of LLMs, we adopt a hierarchical prioritization strategy. The method code and class code are prioritized as a complete unit to provide the richest semantic information. If the input length exceeds the limit, a stepwise compression strategy is applied. Specifically, the method code is retained first, while the class code is replaced with a condensed version extracted in Sect. 3.1. The priority given to method code is due to its direct representation of the target method's logical structure and dependencies, which are critical for Feature Envy detection. In contrast, class code mainly provides auxiliary context and can be appropriately condensed under resource constraints. If the input still exceeds the limit, the method code is further replaced with a simplified version. This strategy ensures that input compression preserves

Tree-of-Thought Prompt
Step1: Role Introduction
"role": "system", "content": "You are a highly skilled code analysis assistant specialized in detecting code smells, such as Feature Envy."
Step2: Task Description
"role": "user", "content": **"Imagine there are three experts analyzing and discussing whether the given code exhibits Feature Envy. They will approach the analysis from different perspectives and, in the end, arrive at a unified conclusion: **'yes' or 'no', without additional explanation or text.**"**
Step3: Label Definition
"role": "assistant", "content": "I see. Could you explain Feature Envy in more detail?" **"role": "user", "content":** "The definition of Feature Envy is as follows: ***[label definition]***"
Step4: Input Clarification
"role": "user", "content": "Here is the ***[method-related content]*** and ***[class-related content]***"

Fig. 3. The definition of the $\text{prompt}_{\text{ToT}}$.

the core semantic relationships between methods and classes while minimizing the risk of information loss caused by direct truncation.

3.3 Feature Envy Detection

After constructing the prompts, we input them into the LLMs to perform Feature Envy detection. The LLMs analyze the interaction between the target method and its class based on the input, determining whether Feature Envy exists. By explicitly providing the definition of Feature Envy in the prompt, the detection task can be focused on its core characteristics, thereby improving the detection accuracy. The detection follows a binary classification approach, where the LLM analyzes the code and its context and outputs either "yes" or "no" to present the detection result in a straightforward manner, facilitating subsequent analysis and validation.

4 Experimental Design

4.1 Research Questions

This study investigates the capability of LLMs in detecting Feature Envy smells and proposes three core research questions. These questions explore the performance variations of the proposed framework when equipped with different prompt strategies and large language models, as well as the effectiveness in identifying code smells of varying severity.

- **RQ1: Does the design of prompts affect the performance of LLMs in detecting Feature Envy?** Traditional prompts often rely on direct

Prompt$_{TI}$

only the task and input description, without the label definition

prompt = "Your task is to determine if the following method exhibits Feature Envy. **Respond strictly with 'yes' or 'no', without additional explanation or text.** Here is the *[method-related content]* and *[class-related content]*"

Fig. 4. The definition of the prompt$_{\mathrm{TI}}$.

Prompt$_{TDI}$

includes task, label, and input introduction, without CoT structure.

prompt = "Your task is to determine whether the following method demonstrates Feature Envy. **Respond only with 'yes' or 'no', without providing any further explanation or text.** Below is the definition of Feature Envy: *[feature envy definition]* The following includes the *[method-related content]* and *[class-related content]*."

Fig. 5. The definition of the prompt$_{\mathrm{TDI}}$.

question-answering, which may not fully stimulate the model's reasoning abilities. Research indicates that prompts with reasoning structures (such as CoT and ToT) can guide the model to gain a deeper understanding of the task context, thereby enhancing reasoning performance. Given the complexity of code smell detection, prompt design may be a key factor affecting model performance. Therefore, this study explores whether the design of prompts influences the performance of LLMs in Feature Envy detection. In particular, does a reasoning-structured prompt demonstrate a significant advantage over a simple prompt?

- **RQ2: How do different LLMs perform in Feature Envy detection?** The scale and training data of LLMs influence their performance across various tasks, and systematically evaluating their performance in Feature Envy detection is crucial. This not only reveals the strengths and weaknesses of current models but also provides theoretical support for future optimization. Therefore, this study compares the detection capabilities of different LLMs and analyzes their differences in this task.
- **RQ3: How do LLMs perform in detecting Feature Envy with different levels of severity?** The severity of code smells significantly impacts software quality, and varying levels of severity may present different challenges to the LLM's detection abilities. This study analyzes the performance of LLMs in detecting Feature Envy with different levels of severity, aiming to explore whether models can maintain stable and reliable detection performance across varying complexities and impacts, thereby supporting developers in prioritizing critical issues.

For RQ1, we designed and compared four prompt strategies. The prompt$_{\mathrm{CoT}}$ strategy, based on chain-of-thought (CoT) reasoning, and prompt$_{\mathrm{ToT}}$, based on tree-of-thought (ToT) reasoning, guide the model to use step-by-step reasoning and multi-perspective analysis to uncover the complex relationships between methods and classes. Additionally, we designed two baseline prompts: $\text{prompt}_{\text{TI}}$ (Fig. 4), which includes only the task and input descriptions, and $\text{prompt}_{\text{TDI}}$ (Fig. 5), which extends $\text{prompt}_{\text{TI}}$ by incorporating the definition of "Feature Envy" to enhance task contextual information. For RQ2, we selected five advanced LLMs, including DeepSeek-V3, GPT-3.5-Turbo, GPT-4, CodeLlama-7b and Llama-3-8b-Instruct, to analyze their performance in the Feature Envy detection task. Regarding RQ3, we evaluated the accuracy of different models in detecting Feature Envy across four severity levels to investigate their adaptability to varying complexity scenarios.

4.2 Dataset Construction

This study employs the code smell dataset proposed by Fontana et al. [33], which contains labeled instances from 74 software systems and covers various common types of code smells. Fontana et al. initially detected code smells using five detection tools and subsequently validated the results manually with the assistance of three graduate students to ensure the accuracy and reliability of the labels.

This study focuses on 420 instances related to Feature Envy, of which 33% are labeled as smelly code and 67% as non-smelly code. This dataset has been widely used in code smell detection research and is considered one of the standard datasets for evaluating detection methods [40–42].

To obtain complete code information for each instance to support subsequent analysis, we performed necessary preprocessing on the dataset. Instances that could not meet the experimental requirements due to unavailable code repositories or other factors were reasonably excluded. This adjustment affected only a small portion of the data, while the retained instances remained representative, providing a high-quality and reliable data foundation for the study.

Additionally, each instance is also assigned a code smell severity label, categorized into four levels: (1) No Smell, indicating no impact from code smells; (2) Non-Severe Smell, signifying that the method is partially affected by code smells; (3) Smell, meaning that the method fully exhibits the characteristics of a code smell; and (4) Severe Smell, which denotes that the method not only fully possesses the characteristics of a code smell but also exhibits exceptionally high size, complexity, or coupling. These severity classifications provide a more granular basis for analyzing the detection capability of LLMs across different levels of code smells.

4.3 Large Language Model

This study selects five large language models (LLMs) to evaluate their performance in the Feature Envy detection task, primarily based on their capabilities in code analysis, feature extraction, and pattern recognition, while also considering the representativeness of both open-source and closed-source models. To ensure the selected models are suitable for Feature Envy detection and provide a reference for future research, we prioritize models that excel in programming-related tasks and instruction-tuned models that demonstrate strong generalization ability in classification tasks. The introduction of these LLMs is as follows:

- DeepSeek-V3 [17]: Optimized for programming and reasoning tasks, with strong capabilities in long-text processing, code generation, and mathematical reasoning.
- GPT-3.5-Turbo [43]: An optimized version of GPT-3.5, offering higher computational efficiency and lower cost, suitable for various tasks.
- GPT-4 [44]: An upgraded version in the GPT series with enhanced reasoning, code comprehension, and contextual analysis abilities, making it highly competitive in code analysis tasks.
- CodeLlama-7b [45]: A code-specific model optimized based on the Llama architecture, trained explicitly for programming tasks, demonstrating strong adaptability in code generation and understanding.
- Llama-3-8b-Instruct [46]: An instruction-tuned model developed by Meta, designed for various NLP tasks, with reasoning capabilities for code analysis.

4.4 Performance Measures

To evaluate the performance of the Feature Envy prediction models, we employed four commonly used metrics: Accuracy, Precision, Recall, F1-score, and Matthews Correlation Co-efficient (MCC). These metrics have been widely applied in previous research to assess the performance of prediction models. In the context of Feature Envy detection tasks, smelly instances are labeled as positive, while non-smelly instances are labeled as negative.

5 Result Analysis

5.1 RQ1: Impact of Prompt Design on Feature Envy Detection

The experimental results are shown in Table 1. In terms of the Accuracy metric, $\text{prompt}_{\text{CoT}}$ and $\text{prompt}_{\text{ToT}}$ generally outperform PromptTI and PromptTDI. Notably, $\text{prompt}_{\text{CoT}}$ achieved the best accuracy on DeepSeek-V3, GPT-4, and Llama-3-8b-Instruct, reaching 0.8540, 0.7950, and 0.6925, respectively. However, on GPT-3.5-Turbo and CodeLlama-7b, $\text{prompt}_{\text{CoT}}$ and $\text{prompt}_{\text{ToT}}$ performed slightly worse than other prompts.

In terms of the Precision metric, $\text{prompt}_{\text{CoT}}$ and $\text{prompt}_{\text{ToT}}$ also showed significant advantages. In particular, $\text{prompt}_{\text{CoT}}$ ranked first on DeepSeek-V3, GPT-4, and Llama-3-8b-Instruct, with precision scores of 0.7522, 0.8276, and 0.5258, respectively. However, $\text{prompt}_{\text{ToT}}$ exhibited slightly lower precision in certain scenarios, such as on DeepSeek-V3 (0.6159) and CodeLlama-7b (0.3278), which may be attributed to its design prioritizing Recall.

Table 1. Performance evaluation of prompts across models and metrics.

Model	Prompt	Accuracy	Precision	Recall	F1-score	MCC
DeepSeek-V3	$\text{prompt}_{\text{TI}}$	0.8106	0.7416	0.6346	0.6839	0.5532
	$\text{prompt}_{\text{TDI}}$	0.8509	0.7456	0.8173	0.7798	0.6691
	$\text{prompt}_{\text{CoT}}$	**0.8540**	**0.7522**	0.8173	**0.7834**	**0.6749**
	$\text{prompt}_{\text{ToT}}$	0.7950	0.6159	**0.9712**	0.7537	0.6381
GPT-3.5-Turbo	$\text{prompt}_{\text{TI}}$	0.6646	0.4231	0.1058	0.1692	0.0634
	$\text{prompt}_{\text{TDI}}$	**0.7019**	**0.6111**	0.2115	0.3143	0.2186
	$\text{prompt}_{\text{CoT}}$	0.6801	0.5051	0.4808	0.4926	**0.2594**
	$\text{prompt}_{\text{ToT}}$	0.5559	0.3889	**0.6796**	**0.4947**	0.1666
GPT-4	$\text{prompt}_{\text{TI}}$	0.7453	0.8056	0.2788	0.4143	0.3661
	$\text{prompt}_{\text{TDI}}$	0.7795	0.7391	**0.4904**	0.5896	0.4648
	$\text{prompt}_{\text{CoT}}$	**0.7950**	**0.8276**	0.4615	0.5926	**0.5058**
	$\text{prompt}_{\text{ToT}}$	**0.7950**	0.8065	0.4808	**0.6024**	0.5049
CodeLlama-7b	$\text{prompt}_{\text{TI}}$	**0.5901**	**0.3986**	0.5288	0.4545	**0.1400**
	$\text{prompt}_{\text{TDI}}$	0.5528	0.3780	0.5962	0.4627	0.1200
	$\text{prompt}_{\text{CoT}}$	0.3416	0.3213	0.9515	0.4804	0.0130
	$\text{prompt}_{\text{ToT}}$	0.3602	0.3278	**0.9706**	**0.4901**	0.0923
Llama-3-8b-Instruct	$\text{prompt}_{\text{TI}}$	0.5813	0.3491	0.3627	0.3558	0.0458
	$\text{prompt}_{\text{TDI}}$	0.6104	0.3684	0.2800	0.3182	0.0535
	$\text{prompt}_{\text{CoT}}$	**0.6925**	**0.5258**	0.4904	0.5075	0.2847
	$\text{prompt}_{\text{ToT}}$	0.6025	0.4362	**0.7885**	**0.5616**	**0.2867**
TI:TDI:CoT:ToT Scores		1:1:3:1	1:1:3:0	0:1:0:4	0:0:1:4	1:0:3:1

Regarding the Recall metric, $\text{prompt}_{\text{ToT}}$ demonstrated a remarkable advantage. For instance, on DeepSeek-V3 and CodeLlama-7b, $\text{prompt}_{\text{ToT}}$ achieved recall rates of 0.9712 and 0.9706, significantly surpassing other prompts. Furthermore, $\text{prompt}_{\text{ToT}}$ also maintained a leading recall rate on GPT-3.5-Turbo and Llama-3-8b-Instruct. These results suggest that prompts with tree-structured reasoning are more effective in comprehensively identifying potential instances of Feature Envy in code.

In terms of the F1-score metric, $\text{prompt}_{\text{CoT}}$ and $\text{prompt}_{\text{ToT}}$ generally outperform prompts without reasoning structures. Among these, $\text{prompt}_{\text{CoT}}$ achieved the highest F1-score on DeepSeek-V3 (0.7834), while $\text{prompt}_{\text{ToT}}$ delivered the best performance on GPT-4, Llama-3-8b-Instruct, GPT-3.5-Turbo, and CodeLlama-7b, with scores of 0.6024, 0.5616, 0.4947, and 0.4804, respectively. These results suggest that prompts with reasoning structures perform better in balancing Precision and Recall, effectively combining detection accuracy with comprehensiveness.

Regarding the MCC metric, $\text{prompt}_{\text{CoT}}$ performed particularly well on DeepSeek-V3 and GPT-4, achieving scores of 0.6749 and 0.5058, respectively.

This indicates that prompts with reasoning structures not only exhibit more stable performance but also handle the detection of complex code features more effectively.

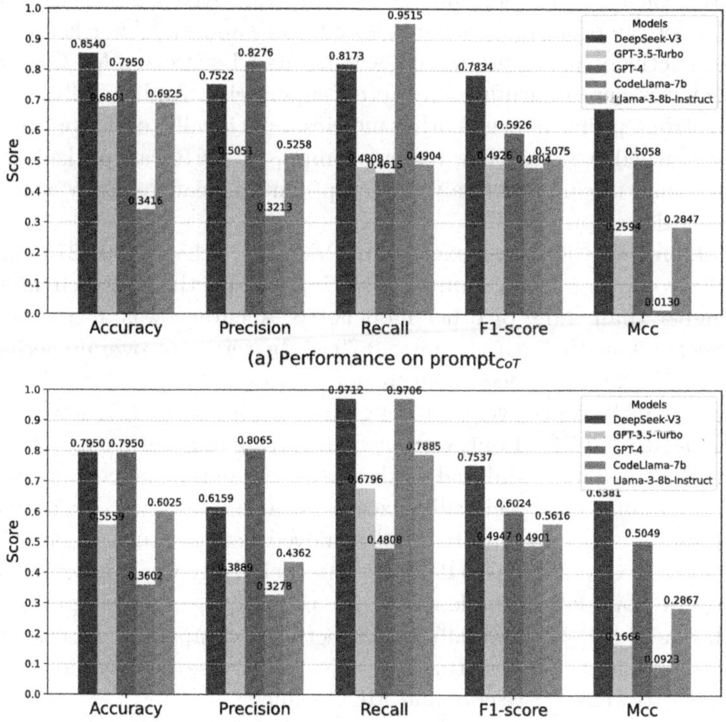

(a) Performance on prompt_{CoT}

(b) Performance on prompt_{ToT}

Fig. 6. Results comparison of different large language models.

Answer to RQ1: The design of prompts has a significant impact on the performance of LLMs in the Feature Envy detection task. Experimental results indicate that prompts with reasoning structures ($\text{prompt}_{\text{CoT}}$ and $\text{prompt}_{\text{ToT}}$) outperform non-reasoning prompts in key metrics such as F1-score, MCC, and Recall, achieving the best performance in over 75% of scenarios. This demonstrates that reasoning-structured prompts can more effectively activate the model's reasoning capabilities, enabling it to capture complex task features more comprehensively and thereby significantly improving detection accuracy and completeness.

5.2 RQ2: Performance of Different LLMs in Feature Envy Detection

Based on the conclusions of RQ1, we further compared the performance of five different LLMs in the Feature Envy detection task under the prompt settings of reasoning structures. As shown in Fig. 6, there are significant differences in the performance of different models across both overall and individual evaluation metrics.

DeepSeek-V3 demonstrated the most balanced performance in comprehensive metrics such as F1-score and MCC, indicating strong generalization capabilities. Under the $prompt_{CoT}$ setting, its F1-score and MCC reached 0.7834 and 0.6749, respectively. In the $prompt_{ToT}$ setting, its F1-score and MCC were 0.7537 and 0.6381, further confirming its overall superiority. Additionally, this model exhibited strong performance in other metrics. Specifically, under $prompt_{CoT}$, its Accuracy reached 0.8540, while under $prompt_{ToT}$, its Recall peaked at 0.9712, suggesting that it can effectively detect potential Feature Envy smells while maintaining detection stability.

GPT-4, on the other hand, excelled in Precision, achieving 0.8276 and 0.8065 under the $prompt_{CoT}$ and $prompt_{ToT}$ settings, respectively, which were significantly higher than those of other models. Its Accuracy was also close to that of DeepSeek-V3, with both reaching 0.7950. In terms of overall performance, GPT-4's MCC values exceeded 0.5 in both prompt settings, with F1-scores of 0.5926 and 0.6024, respectively. Although its Recall was slightly lower than that of GPT-3.5-Turbo, GPT-4 outperformed the latter in all other metrics.

Llama-3-8b-Instruct exhibited moderate overall performance but still outperformed CodeLlama-7b. Specifically, except for a slightly lower Recall compared to CodeLlama-7b, Llama-3-8b-Instruct achieved better results in all other metrics. In contrast, CodeLlama-7b demonstrated relatively weaker performance but stood out in Recall. For example, under the $prompt_{CoT}$ and $prompt_{ToT}$ settings, its Recall reached 0.9515 and 0.9706, respectively, comparable to DeepSeek-V3. However, CodeLlama-7b performed significantly worse in Precision and Accuracy, leading to weaker F1-score and MCC values.

Answer to RQ2: DeepSeek-V3 demonstrates the best overall performance, particularly excelling in F1-score and MCC, showcasing good balance and stability. GPT-4 consistently leads in the Precision metric, and although its composite metrics are slightly lower than DeepSeek-V3, it outperforms GPT-3.5-Turbo overall. Llama-3-8b-Instruct exhibits moderate performance, with all metrics surpassing CodeLlama-7b, except for Recall, which is slightly lower. In contrast, CodeLlama-7b, despite its strong Recall performance, suffers from low Accuracy and Precision, leading to weaker overall performance. These results suggest that model size and training characteristics significantly influence performance in the Feature Envy detection task.

5.3 RQ3: LLM Performance in Detection at Varying Severity Levels

Figure 7 illustrates the detection accuracy (represented by the probability of correct detection on the vertical axis) of various models under two reasoning-structured prompt settings across different Severity levels. Severity 1 indicates instances with no code smells, while Severities 2 to 4 represent instances with code smells, with increasing severity.

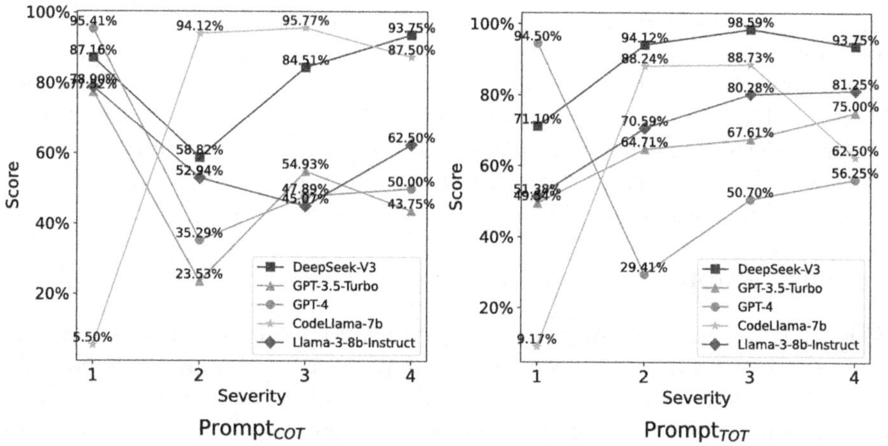

Fig. 7. Accuracy comparison of large language models across different severity levels.

For non-smelly instances (Severity 1), GPT-4 achieves the highest accuracy, with 95.41% under the prompt$_{\text{CoT}}$ setting and 94.50% under the prompt$_{\text{ToT}}$ setting. DeepSeek-V3 follows, with accuracy rates of 87.16% (prompt$_{\text{CoT}}$) and 71.10% (prompt$_{\text{ToT}}$). In contrast, CodeLLaMA-7b performs poorly in this task, with accuracy below 10%. These results indicate that GPT-4 and DeepSeek-V3 are more effective in identifying non-smelly code, whereas CodeLLaMA-7b has significant limitations in this regard. For low-severity instances (Severity = 2), CodeLLaMA-7b's performance improves substantially, achieving accuracy rates of 94.12% (prompt$_{\text{CoT}}$) and 88.24% (prompt$_{\text{ToT}}$). DeepSeek-V3 also performs well, particularly under the prompt$_{\text{ToT}}$ setting, where it reaches 94.12% accuracy. In contrast, GPT-4 and GPT-3.5-Turbo exhibit relatively lower detection accuracy, suggesting that the GPT series models may have limitations in detecting low-severity code smells.

For medium-severity instances (Severity 3), DeepSeek-V3 demonstrates the strongest detection capability, achieving accuracy rates of 84.51% (prompt$_{\text{CoT}}$) and 98.58% (prompt$_{\text{ToT}}$). CodeLLaMA-7b also maintains stable performance, with accuracy rates of 95.77% and 88.73%, respectively. Additionally, Llama-3-8b-Instruct performs well under the prompt$_{\text{ToT}}$ setting, with an accuracy of 80.28%. This trend suggests that as severity increases, DeepSeek-V3 and CodeLLaMA-7b are more consistently effective in detecting medium-severity Feature Envy smells.

For high-severity instances (Severity 4), DeepSeek-V3 performs best, achieving 93.75% accuracy under both prompt settings. CodeLLaMA-7b also achieves high accuracy under the prompt$_{\text{CoT}}$ setting (87.50%), while Llama-3-8b-Instruct and GPT-3.5-Turbo achieve accuracy rates of 81.25% and 75.00%, respectively, under the prompt$_{\text{ToT}}$ setting.

Answer to RQ3: Different models exhibit varying performance in detecting the severity of Feature Envy smells. DeepSeek-V3 demonstrates exceptional stability and accuracy in high-severity instances, making it suitable for prioritizing critical code issues. GPT-4 performs best in detecting non-smelly instances, but its ability to detect low-severity code smells is relatively weaker. Although CodeLLaMA-7b shows weaker detection capability for non-smelly instances, it performs better in identifying smelly instances. The study highlights that different models have varying adaptability to changes in severity, offering valuable insights for developers to optimize issue prioritization.

6 Discussion

This study proposes a framework based on contextual information and prompt engineering, leveraging the contextual information of the method's enclosing class and structured reasoning prompts to guide LLMs in deeper code analysis. Experimental results demonstrate that this framework effectively enhances the performance of LLMs in Feature Envy smells detection.

Impact of Prompt Design on LLM Detection Performance: Compared to conventional prompts, structured reasoning prompts significantly improve the model's understanding of code structure and dependencies. PromptCoT enhances the model's ability to identify Feature Envy smells through step-by-step reasoning, while PromptToT encourages the model to analyze the problem from multiple perspectives, optimizing the reasoning process and reducing misclassifications. These findings indicate that prompts not only serve as an input mechanism but also profoundly influence the reasoning strategy and detection performance of LLMs.

Performance Differences Among LLMs: Further experiments reveal performance differences among various LLMs in Feature Envy detection. DeepSeek-V3 demonstrates the best performance in key metrics such as F1-score and MCC, showcasing exceptional generalization ability. GPT-4 excels in precision, making it more suitable for high-accuracy tasks. Although CodeLlama-7b achieves higher recall, its lower precision leads to a higher false positive rate. The balanced performance of DeepSeek-V3 makes it a more promising choice for large-scale code scanning tasks, where it can more effectively identify potential Feature Envy smells.

Detection Performance Across Different Severity Levels: Additionally, this study further analyzes the performance of LLMs under different severity levels of Feature Envy smells. Results show that DeepSeek-V3 and CodeLlama-7b perform well in detecting high-severity smells (Severity 3 and 4), making them suitable for prioritizing critical code segments. GPT-4, in contrast, excels at identifying non-smelly instances (Severity 1) but performs relatively weaker on low-severity smells (Severity 2). Notably, DeepSeek-V3 maintains high stability across all severity levels, further validating its strong adaptability in Feature Envy smells detection.

Future research can further optimize the performance of LLMs in code smell detection from the following aspects: First, refining prompt strategies by exploring more efficient reasoning prompts to enhance detection accuracy. Second, leveraging the strengths of multiple LLMs by investigating model fusion and ensemble learning methods to improve overall detection performance. Additionally, given DeepSeek-V3's strong adaptability in the Feature Envy detection task, further optimization of its detection capabilities can enable it to play a more significant role in code analysis tasks. These research directions will provide new insights for developing more efficient and reliable code quality management tools, facilitating automated code detection and optimization in software engineering practice.

7 Threats to Validity

Internal Validity: The choice of prompts has a significant impact on the detection performance of LLMs. Although this study employs reasoning-structured prompts such as PromptCoT and PromptToT, variations in prompting strategies may still lead to differences in results. To mitigate this effect, we evaluated multiple prompt configurations and selected the optimal approach. Additionally, to ensure the comparability of experimental results, we maintained prompt consistency across different models and task scenarios.

External Validity: This study is based on the dataset proposed by Fontana et al. While this dataset has been widely used, its coverage may be insufficient to represent all code structures and styles, potentially limiting the generalizability of the findings. Future research could expand the dataset to encompass a broader range of code types and domains, thereby improving external validity. Moreover, as this study primarily focuses on Java code, the applicability of LLMs to different programming languages remains an open question that requires further investigation.

Construct Validity: The construct validity of this study may be influenced by the choice of evaluation metrics. We adopt commonly used metrics such as Accuracy, Precision, Recall, F1-score, and MCC to assess the accuracy of Feature Envy detection, all of which have been widely recognized in related research. However, alternative metrics may offer different analytical perspectives. Future studies could incorporate additional evaluation methods to enhance the comprehensiveness and reliability of the research findings.

8 Conclusion

This study systematically evaluates the performance of LLMs in Feature Envy detection and proposes a detection framework that integrates contextual information and prompt engineering. It focuses on analyzing the impact of prompt design, model characteristics, and smell severity on detection effectiveness. Experimental results show that reasoning-structured prompts significantly enhance detection performance, outperforming conventional prompts in key metrics. Significant performance differences are observed among the selected

LLMs: DeepSeek-V3 demonstrates the most balanced overall performance, GPT-4 excels in precision, making it suitable for high-accuracy detection tasks, while CodeLlama-7b stands out in recall, making it preferable for high-recall scenarios. Additionally, they exhibit varying detection capabilities across different severity levels of code smells: DeepSeek-V3 and CodeLlama-7b perform exceptionally well in detecting high-severity code smells, whereas GPT-4 is more effective in identifying non-smelly code. These findings not only highlight the potential of LLMs in Feature Envy detection but also offer valuable insights for developing more effective intelligent tools for code quality analysis.

References

1. Yamashita, A., Counsell, S.: Code smells as system-level indicators of maintainability: an empirical study. J. Syst. Softw. **86**(10), 2639–2653 (2013)
2. Palomba, F., Bavota, G., Di Penta, M., Fasano, F., Oliveto, R., De Lucia, A.: On the diffuseness and the impact on maintainability of code smells: a large scale empirical investigation. In: Proceedings of the 40th International Conference on Software Engineering, pp. 482–482 (2018)
3. Abbes, M., Khomh, F., Gueheneuc, Y.-G., Antoniol, G.: An empirical study of the impact of two antipatterns, blob and spaghetti code, on program comprehension. In: 2011 15Th European Conference on Software Maintenance and Reengineering, pp. 181–190. IEEE (2011)
4. Mumtaz, H., Alshayeb, M., Mahmood, S., Niazi, M.: An empirical study to improve software security through the application of code refactoring. Inf. Softw. Technol. **96**, 112–125 (2018)
5. Fowler, M.: Refactoring: Improving the Design of Existing Code. Addison-Wesley Professional (2018)
6. D'Ambros, M., Bacchelli, A., Lanza, M.: On the impact of design flaws on software defects. In: 2010 10th International Conference on Quality Software, pp. 23–31. IEEE (2010)
7. Sjøberg, D.I.K., Anda, B., Mockus, A.: Questioning software maintenance metrics: a comparative case study. In: Proceedings of the ACM-IEEE International Symposium on Empirical Software Engineering and Measurement, pp. 107–110 (2012)
8. Azeem, M.I., Palomba, F., Shi, L., Wang, Q.: Machine learning techniques for code smell detection: a systematic literature review and meta-analysis. Inf. Softw. Technol. **108**, 115–138 (2019)
9. Ghannem, A., Boussaidi, G., Kessentini, M.: On the use of design defect examples to detect model refactoring opportunities. Softw. Qual. J. **24**, 947–965 (2016)
10. Di Nucci, D., Palomba, F., Tamburri, D.A., Serebrenik, A., De Lucia, A.: Detecting code smells using machine learning techniques: are we there yet? In: 2018 IEEE 25th International Conference on Software Analysis, Evolution and Reengineering (SANER), pp. 612–621. IEEE (2018)
11. Pecorelli, F., Palomba, F., Di Nucci, D., De Lucia, A.: Comparing heuristic and machine learning approaches for metric-based code smell detection. In: 2019 IEEE/ACM 27th International Conference on Program Comprehension (ICPC), pp. 93–104. IEEE (2019)
12. Liu, H., Jin, J., Zhifeng, X., Zou, Y., Yifan, B., Zhang, L.: Deep learning based code smell detection. IEEE Trans. Softw. Eng. **47**(9), 1811–1837 (2019)

13. dos Reis, J.P., Brito e Abreu, F., de Figueiredo Carneiro, G., Anslow, C.: Code smells detection and visualization: a systematic literature review. Arch. Comput. Methods Eng. **29**(1), 47–94 (2022)
14. Alazba, A., Aljamaan, H., Alshayeb, M.: Deep learning approaches for bad smell detection: a systematic literature review. Empir. Softw. Eng. **28**(3), 77 (2023)
15. Dubey, A., et al.: The llama 3 herd of models. arXiv preprint arXiv:2407.21783 (2024)
16. Achiam, J., et al.: GPT-4 technical report. arXiv preprint arXiv:2303.08774 (2023)
17. Liu, A., et al.: Deepseek-v3 technical report. arXiv preprint arXiv:2412.19437 (2024)
18. Dilhara, M., Bellur, A., Bryksin, T., Dig, D.: Unprecedented code change automation: the fusion of LLMs and transformation by example. Proc. ACM Softw. Eng. **1**(FSE), 631–653 (2024)
19. Feng, S., Chen, C.: Prompting is all you need: automated android bug replay with large language models. In: Proceedings of the 46th IEEE/ACM International Conference on Software Engineering, pp. 1–13 (2024)
20. Lin, F., Kim, D.J., Chen, T.H.: Soen-101: code generation by emulating software process models using large language model agents. arXiv preprint arXiv:2403.15852 (2024)
21. Wang, H., Xu, Z., Tan, S.H.: Testing refactoring engine via historical bug report driven LLM. arXiv e-prints, p. arXiv–2501 (2025)
22. Wei, J., et al.: Chain-of-thought prompting elicits reasoning in large language models. In: Advances in Neural Information Processing Systems, vol. 35, pp. 24824–24837 (2022)
23. Yao, S., et al.: Tree of thoughts: deliberate problem solving with large language models. In: Advances in Neural Information Processing Systems, vol. 36 (2024)
24. Fontana, F.A., Zanoni, M.: Code smell severity classification using machine learning techniques. Knowl.-Based Syst. **128**, 43–58 (2017)
25. Abdou, A., Darwish, N.: Severity classification of software code smells using machine learning techniques: a comparative study. J. Softw. Evol. Process **36**(1), e2454 (2024)
26. Tiwari, O., Joshi, R.K.: Functionality based code smell detection and severity classification. In: Proceedings of the 13th Innovations in Software Engineering Conference (Formerly Known as India Software Engineering Conference), pp. 1–5 (2020)
27. Dewangan, S., Rao, R.S., Chowdhuri, S.R., Gupta, M.: Severity classification of code smells using machine-learning methods. SN Comput. Sci. **4**(5), 564 (2023)
28. Tsantalis, N., Chatzigeorgiou, A.: Identification of move method refactoring opportunities. IEEE Trans. Softw. Eng. **35**(3), 347–367 (2009)
29. Fokaefs, M., Tsantalis, N., Chatzigeorgiou, A.: Jdeodorant: identification and removal of feature envy bad smells. In: 2007 IEEE International Conference on Software Maintenance, pp. 519–520. IEEE (2007)
30. Bavota, G., Oliveto, R., Gethers, M., Poshyvanyk, D., Lucia, A.: Methodbook: recommending move method refactorings via relational topic models. IEEE Trans. Softw. Eng. **40**(7), 671–694 (2013)
31. Palomba, F., Bavota, G., Di Penta, M., Oliveto, R., De Lucia, A., Poshyvanyk, D.: Detecting bad smells in source code using change history information. In: 2013 28th IEEE/ACM International Conference on Automated Software Engineering (ASE), pp. 268–278. IEEE (2013)
32. Palomba, F., Bavota, G., Penta, M., Oliveto, R., Poshyvanyk, D., Lucia, A.: Mining version histories for detecting code smells. IEEE Trans. Softw. Eng. **41**(5), 462–489 (2014)

33. Fontana, F.A., Mäntylä, M.V., Zanoni, M., Marino, A.: Comparing and experimenting machine learning techniques for code smell detection. Empirical Softw. Eng. **21**, 1143–1191 (2016)
34. Guo, J., Zhao, Y., Zheng, T., Chen, Z., Jiang, M., Ding, Z.: Alleviating class imbalance in feature envy prediction: an oversampling technique based on code entity attributes. Inf. Softw. Technol. 107673 (2025)
35. Barbez, A., Khomh, F., Guéhéneuc, Y.-G.: A machine-learning based ensemble method for anti-patterns detection. J. Syst. Softw. **161**, 110486 (2020)
36. Sharma, T., Efstathiou, V., Louridas, P., Spinellis, D.: Code smell detection by deep direct-learning and transfer-learning. J. Syst. Softw. **176**, 110936 (2021)
37. Wu, D., et al.: ismell: assembling LLMs with expert toolsets for code smell detection and refactoring. In: Proceedings of the 39th IEEE/ACM International Conference on Automated Software Engineering, pp. 1345–1357 (2024)
38. Zhang, Y., et al.: Patch: empowering large language model with programmer-intent guidance and collaborative-behavior simulation for automatic bug fixing. ACM Trans. Softw. Eng. Methodol. (2025)
39. Du, X., et al.: Vul-rag: enhancing LLM-based vulnerability detection via knowledge-level rag. arXiv preprint arXiv:2406.11147 (2024)
40. Alazba, A., Aljamaan, H.: Code smell detection using feature selection and stacking ensemble: an empirical investigation. Inf. Softw. Technol. **138**, 106648 (2021)
41. Jain, S., Saha, A.: Improving performance with hybrid feature selection and ensemble machine learning techniques for code smell detection. Sci. Comput. Program. **212**, 102713 (2021)
42. Khleel, N.A.A., Nehéz, K.: Deep convolutional neural network model for bad code smells detection based on oversampling method. Indones. J. Electr. Eng. Comput. Sci **26**(3), 1725–1735 (2022)
43. OpenAI. GPT-3.5-turbo (2023). Accessed June 2024
44. OpenAI. GPT-4 (2023). Accessed June 2024
45. Roziere, B., et al.: Code llama: open foundation models for code. arXiv preprint arXiv:2308.12950 (2023)
46. AI Meta. Introducing meta llama 3: The most capable openly available LLM to date. Meta AI (2024)

RustMap: Towards Project-Scale C-to-Rust Migration via Program Analysis and LLM

Xuemeng Cai[1(✉)], Jiakun Liu[1(✉)], Xiping Huang[1], Yijun Yu[2(✉)], Haitao Wu[3(✉)], Chunmiao Li[4(✉)], Bo Wang[5(✉)], Imam Nur Bani Yusuf[1(✉)], and Lingxiao Jiang[1(✉)]

[1] Singapore Management University, Singapore, Singapore
{xuemengcai,jkliu,xphuang,imamy.2020,lxjiang}@smu.edu.sg
[2] The Open University, Milton Keynes, UK
y.yu@open.ac.uk
[3] Beijing, China
wain303009@hotmail.com
[4] Beijing Academy of Blockchain and Edge Computing, Beijing, China
chunmiaoli1993@gmail.com
[5] Beijing Jiaotong University, Beijing, China
wangbo_cs@bjtu.edu.cn

Abstract. Migrating existing C programs into Rust is increasingly desired, as Rust offers superior memory safety while maintaining C's high performance. Existing automated translation tools, such as C2Rust, may rely too much on syntactic, template-based translation and generate unsafe Rust code that is hard for human developers to read, maintain, or even compile. More semantic-aware translation that produces safer, idiomatic, and runnable Rust code is much needed. This paper introduces a novel dependency-guided and large language model (LLM)-based C-to-Rust translation approach, RustMap, based on three key ideas: (1) Utilize LLM's capabilities to produce idiomatic Rust code from given *small* pieces of C code, (2) Mitigate LLM's incapability in handling large codebases by breaking project-scale C programs into smaller units for translation according to their usage dependencies, and (3) Enhance the correctness of the translated Rust program by utilizing available test cases to check input/output equivalence between C and Rust code, and iteratively utilizing the feedback from compilation and testing errors for LLM to refine translated Rust code. We have empirically evaluated RustMap on 126 sample real-world programs, including 125 programs from Rosetta Code and a complex bzip2 program containing more than 7000 lines of code, using GPT-4o as the LLM. RustMap shows promising results in guiding GPT-4o to translate most of the C code into more idiomatic, readable, and functional Rust code with significantly less unsafe code than other translation tools, presenting non-trivial translation patterns that may be reusable for future research.

H. Wu—Independent Researcher.

Y. Zhou et al. (Eds.): ICECCS 2025, LNCS 15746, pp. 283–302, 2026.
https://doi.org/10.1007/978-3-032-00828-2_16

Keywords: Program translation · C2Rust · Dependency analysis · LLM

1 Introduction

Rust is increasingly popular as it not only offers better safety guarantees but also has performance on par with that of C [2,32]. In industry, there is a growing trend to rewrite existing C projects in Rust [3,19,36], including the Linux kernel [41,42]. To help developers to translate C code into Rust, several tools have been proposed. For example, C2Rust [26] aims to automatically convert C code to Rust with mostly syntax-based rules. However, such tools often produce too much unsafe code that is not idiomatic in Rust and hard to read or maintain since C and Rust languages have very different features, e.g., object ownership and lifetime rules. To tackle the drawbacks, more tools, such as CRustS [23], Crown [49], and Laertes [9,10], have been proposed on top of C2Rust to analyze specific C & Rust language features and enhance transformation between them. However, due to the lack of one-to-one syntactic mapping between C and Rust language features (e.g., incompatible data types, macros, vastly different usages of pointers and references, language-specific programming idioms, and Rust-specific ownership and lifetime rules), these tools are still very limited in translating diverse code patterns, and the translated Rust code still contain lots of unsafe code blocks that are hard to read, maintain, or even compile—Challenge ①. In addition, these tools often fail to translate project-scale C programs to produce executable Rust programs, due to inadequate management of various kinds of dependencies among code, such as language-specific libraries, linker files, global data types and variables defined in many header files scattered across different locations in the project but dependent on by a piece of code to be translated. When a C project is translated to Rust, the resultant Rust project structure should accommodate all the dependent code from C to ensure their compilation and execution—Challenge ②. Also, the translated Rust code should naturally be functionally equivalent to the original C code—Challenge ③.[1]

To address these challenges, we propose a novel LLM-prompting-based translation approach guided by program dependency analyses, named **RustMap**. We utilize the capabilities of a LLM (specifically ChatGPT [14,39]) for code translation [45]. To deal with LLM's limits in handling large input data and avoiding bugs [24,30], RustMap utilizes program dependency analyses and functional testing, combined with customized prompts, to extend LLM's translation capabilities to project-scale programs.

Specifically, RustMap first breaks down a C program into relatively smaller and standalone translation units, which can be a global variable definition, a datatype `struct` definition, a macro, a preprocessor directive, a function, or a set of inter-dependent functions, by utilizing both static and dynamic analyses of the C source code and a given set of functional test cases. Then RustMap determines the translation order of these units according to their dependencies,

[1] except for the cases when the C code contains bugs.

and constructs a Rust project that contains sufficient Rust files or modules to hold all the code translated from the translation units for the whole-program translation. This dependency-guided break-down of C programs and construction of Rust project structures, which we call *project scaffolding* tackles the Challenges ① and ②: (1) Suitable prompts for each translation unit are formulated and fed to ChatGPT for translation, utilizing ChatGPT's capabilities in producing functionally the same, but syntactically different code, so that the translated Rust code can be safer and more idiomatic. (2) With the broken-down smaller and relatively standalone translation units, RustMap makes it possible to apply LLMs to large programs. For Challenge ③, RustMap also utilizes the functional tests together with ChatGPT to enhance the correctness of translated Rust code: Whenever there are compilation or testing errors in the translated Rust, the error information, either compilation error messages or code execution states, is extracted and formulated as suitable prompts for ChatGPT to locate and adjust faulty translated code until the code passes the provided functional tests or time out. Thus, RustMap provides an operational roadmap for translating project-scale C programs into Rust through a LLM-prompting-based, dependency-guided translation process to enhance the correctness, readability, safety, executability of translated Rust programs.

We have evaluated RustMap on 126 real-world C programs ranging from tens of lines to more than 7000 lines of code, including sample Rosetta Code [28], and a file compression program `bzip2` [34]. Our results show that RustMap can translate most of the C programs into idiomatic Rust programs without the need of defining specific transformation rules. Most programs translated by RustMap are compilable and runnable, passing a set of functional tests. RustMap also significantly reduces unsafe code and improves readability in the translated programs compared with other tools.

In short, the main contribution of our paper is RustMap, a novel dependency-guided, LLM-prompting-based approach for project-scale C to Rust translation. It leverages functional testing and dependency analyses to guide the project-scale translation process, utilizes LLMs to perform actual translation, produces more idiomatic and safer code than other tools, and enhance the correctness of translated code. Although not without limitations, our approach and the translated Rust code for typical difficult cases faced by other tools provide meaningful and reusable solutions for future research and tools. Our code and translation results are publicly available at https://github.com/Cxm211/RustMap.

Paper Organization: Section 2 provides an overview of RustMap. Section 3 introduces the project-level organization of translated code. Section 4 describes more details about translating C code into Rust using LLM. Section 5 evaluates our approach and discusses its limitations and threats to validity. Section 6 reviews related work. Section 7 concludes with future work.

2 RustMap Overview

Figure 1 illustrates an overview of RustMap. We focus on migrating a C project to Rust by translating C functions and their dependencies one by one. Given a C

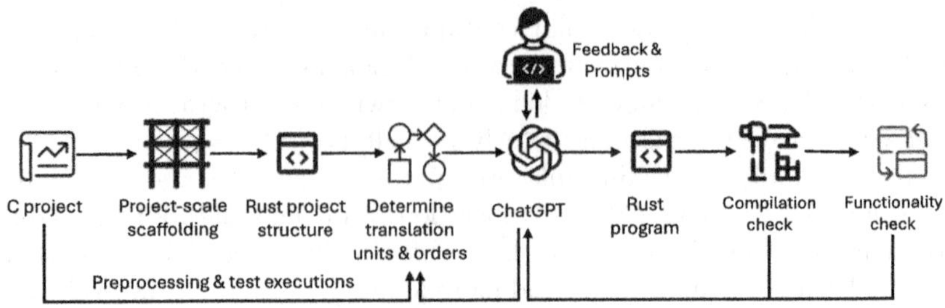

Fig. 1. Overview of RustMap

project, RustMap first generates a Rust project scaffolding where each C header file and each C function is mapped to a Rust file; the Rust files are initially empty, but when more C functions or header file contents are translated, the translated code will gradually be merged into the files. RustMap also preprocesses the C files, compiles the whole program, and run its available tests, which provides static and dynamic call graphs to identify the dependencies of each function (e.g., other functions, data types, global variables, and macros used by it). Sections 3.1 and 3.2 have more details.

Then, RustMap determines the units for translation and their translation order based on dependencies among code elements. Each translation unit may have one or many code elements, such as `struct` definitions, global variables, macros, a function definition, a statement, etc. The translation units and order can be adjusted according to LLM's outputs (e.g., when ChatGPT identifies more dependent code elements to be translated). Section 3.3 has more details.

A translation unit (e.g., a function and its dependencies) along with custom prompts is fed to LLM for translation (see Sect. 4.1). If LLM fails to produce translated Rust code, we try again with another translation unit or adjust the translation unit (e.g., splitting a large unit into smaller ones) according to its outputs. When the LLM produces Rust code for the unit, RustMap applies the Rust compiler to check its syntactic correctness. If there were any compilation errors, RustMap will try to fix them by using the error messages as additional prompts to LLM and instructing ChatGPT to retranslate the code and fix the given error (see Sect. 4.3).

When all the units needed to run a given test have been translated, RustMap will try to compile them together to produce an executable Rust program. Similar to the above, if there were any compilation errors in the translated code, RustMap will try to fix them by using the error messages as additional prompts to LLM. RustMap will execute the compiled Rust program with the given test input and compare its execution states with those of the original C program executed with the same test input to identify any semantic differences. If there was any difference, RustMap will try to locate the error and fix it by using the execution state context as additional prompts to LLM and instructing ChatGPT to retranslate the code so that the execution states in the translated Rust code can match their C counterparts (see Sect. 4.4).

As a result, RustMap will generate a project-scale Rust program with sufficient C functions and their dependencies translated so that it can run the same given tests to produce the same outputs, while maintaining close mapping between the original C functions and the translated Rust code.

3 Project-Scale Scaffolding

A project can contain a large amount of code, and it is impractical to translate the code all at once. When translating a C project to a Rust project, we temporarily organize the C project in a way that allows each C function and/or its relevant dependencies to be translated separately. For this purpose, we need to identify the boundaries of *translation units* where each unit is a set of C code and/or their dependencies to be translated together, and determine the order in which they can be translated. We also construct a Rust project containing temporary files corresponding to the translation units, to save intermediate translation results, track dependencies, and prepare for integrated compilation and execution of the whole translated Rust program. We refer to such preparations as *scaffolding*. The following subsections detail the preparations.

3.1 Initial Rust Project Structure

Our overarching idea is to use a function and/or its dependencies as a translation unit and translate one or multiple units at a time as long as the LLM can handle them. We use functions as translation units mainly because C programs start executions from their `main` functions and functions are often natural modular units of code and have well-defined interfaces and dependencies.[2]

We use the `cargo new` command to initialize a Rust project. The command generates a `Cargo.toml` file, which contains the metadata about the project and its dependencies. The metadata will be updated when new Rust files are generated during the translation and is used to compile and run the project. For each `.c` file in the given C project, we automatically map the C file to a set of Rust `.rs` files. Each Rust file corresponds to either a function from the C file, or a set of global variables, data types, or preprocessor directives and macros defined in the C file, and is put in a directory of the same name (without the `.c` suffix) as the C file. For each `.h` header file in the C project, a corresponding `.rs` file is also generated and placed in the *headers* folder to be shared across the project. If a `.h` file also happens to include function definitions (in addition to function declarations), those functions are processed in the same way as `.c` files.

Figure 2 is a sample generated Rust project scaffolding for the bzip2 program used in our evaluation, where various scaffolding folders and files are created for storing code according to either globals, functions, or headers that will be handled as translation units. The scaffolding files can be merged or split during translation, depending on how well LLM handles the translation units.

[2] For functions longer than the input length limit of LLM, we divide function bodies and their dependencies into smaller statements for translation.

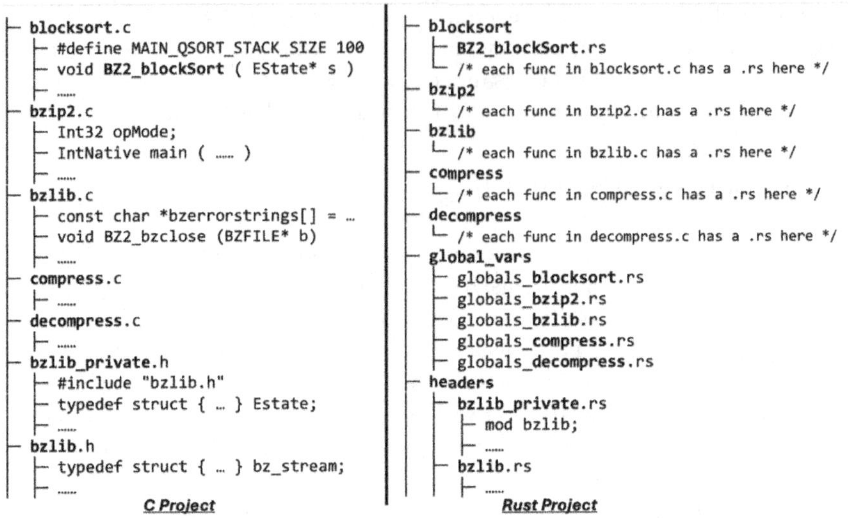

Fig. 2. An example of project scaffolding structure

3.2 Handling C Preprocessor Directives

A C file can include many kinds of preprocessor directives, e.g., `#include` for file inclusions, `#define` for macro definition, `#if` for conditional compilation, `#pragma` for specific compilation features, etc., which may bring many challenges when being translated into Rust. To the best of our knowledge, all prior C-to-Rust translation tools use C's preprocessor to turn a `.c` file into a `.i` file so that all directives are preprocessed and removed so that they do not actually translate directives. However, preprocessed directives, especially macro expansions, can lead to much bloated code from the included libraries and much repetitive code that is less readable. It would be beneficial for users if the directives and macros can be translated to corresponding Rust code elements as much as possible to retain code readability and maintainability.

Thus, for each `.c` file, we treat all the preprocessor directives as a translation unit, together with other code elements from the file that may directly depend on them according to a simple def-use static analysis, and feed them into LLM. The unit may be split according to the def-use dependency order[3] if it is too large to fit in the length limit of LLM.

Handling File Inclusions. When the directives include commonly used libraries, such as `#include <stdlib.h>`, we observe that ChatGPT can recognize the functions and macros defined in the libraries and used in the C code to be translated, and replace those C functions and macros with appropriate

[3] Intuitively, we handle the declarations or definitions of directives first before handling other code elements that *use* the definitions.

Rust library functions and macros. Thus, we can leave out such directives from further processing.

For directives that include project-specific header files, e.g., `#include"bzlib.h"`, we will translate each header file and replace the directive with a `mod` declaration (translated as `mod bzlib;`) in the corresponding scaffolding file and later add a `use` statement if an element from the header file is used somewhere (see Sect. 4.2), to indicate the dependencies.

Handling C Macros. The existing tool C2Rust [18] preprocesses C programs before translating C files to Rust. Thus, C2Rust expands all macro uses into concrete C code, including primitive-type numerical macros, complex macros [8], and others, leading to duplicate and less readable code. For better code readability and alignment with the original C code, we propose to retain the macro definitions as much as possible based on LLM's capabilities in translating some of C macros to Rust macros and simple rule-based refactoring.

Replacing Numerical Macros with Const Global Variables. For primitive-type numerical macros, we use LLM to infer the data type of each numerical value and use rule-based automation to rewrite them into const global variables in Rust. A detailed example of this transformation can be found in the corresponding section[4] in our Github repository.

Replacing Complex Macros with Functions. There can be complex macros, such as "`#define GET_MTF_VAL(label1,label2,lval) ...`", that accept arguments and implement complex logic and are reused many times in C code. For better code readability and alignment with the original C code again, we rewrite the complex macros as the functions that have the same names as the macros by using LLM before applying our translation to the code using such macros. Note that the arguments in complex macros are not typed and will be merely determined by the values passed to the macro when used. Therefore, when we prompt[5] ChatGPT to rewrite the macro as a function, we also provide the code of the functions that use the macro, and instruct ChatGPT to replace the macro use with a function call if possible. Taking the functions that use the macro as the context, ChatGPT is able to infer the data types of the macro arguments. Finally, the complex macros are replaced with the new functions, and the code using the macro is updated with the function call. The corresponding sectionm (see footnote 4) in our repo provides a detailed example of complex macro handling.

Note that there are also macros that would correspond to syntactically invalid C code by itself, which are allowed by C but not allowed by Rust, and cannot be easily rewritten as simple variables or functions. It would be challenging to still retain such macros during translation, and we opted to apply the usual C preprocessor to expand such macros like other unhandled directives below.

---

[4] https://github.com/Cxm211/RustMap/blob/main/README_example.md.

[5] https://github.com/Cxm211/RustMap/blob/main/prompt-templates/prompt_for_LLM_to_generate_code.txt.

Unhandled Conditional Compilations and Other Directives. Although many preprocessor directives can be translated by LLM, there are still many other directives (e.g., `#if`, `#pragma`, `#line`, etc.) that may depend on system environment settings and require specialized handling and more advanced Rust macro features if to be retained and translated to Rust. One example of unhandled directives is provided in the examples section (see footnote 4) in our repo.

To ensure the generation of compilable and executable Rust programs when LLM fails to translate such diverse directives, we use the same approach of other C-to-Rust translation tools, by preprocessing the directives using the GCC preprocessor to remove them or expand them into usual C code so that they can be translated with other code. As a result, for each C file (`.c` or `.h`), we will have a preprocessed C file (`.i`) that contains only usual C code and the directives that can be translated. Such `.i` files will be analyzed by RustMap further to identify dependencies and translation units.

3.3 Function Dependencies and Translation Order

Project-scale C programs can contain numerous functions to be translated, necessitating a strategic prioritization of their translations. Intuitively, the functions that are called by other functions should be translated before their callers; and data types used by a function should be translated before the function. If there are circular dependencies (e.g., recursive functions and data types), they can be put into one translation unit to be translated together, as long as their combined size is within the length limit of LLM. In addition, to help check functionality based on a given test case, functions that are executed should be prioritized before others that are not.

To achieve this goal, we utilize both dynamic and static call graphs of the C program preprocessed (see Sect. 3.2) by our approach to determine the translation order of functions and their dependencies. A dynamic call graph represents the function call relations in a program, by recording the actual calling sequence when running the program in debug mode with one or more test cases. A static call graph represents conservatively all possible call relations.[6] While dynamic call graphs are more precise than static ones so that we can prioritize the translation of the executed functions with respect to given test cases as the Rust program can still compile and run if other non-executed code is cut off, static ones capture more call relations so that our translation for the program can be more complete in case more test cases will be used.[7]

We also note that there can be functions that call each other directly or indirectly, similarly for recursive data type definitions. For such cases, translating either function alone without referring to others may lead to translation errors. This motivates us to put inter-dependent functions and/or data types together

[6] We used gprof [13] to get dynamic call graphs, and cflow [31] to get function call graphs and data type dependencies.

[7] Due to this translation strategy, RustMap cannot ensure the functional correctness of non-executed functions yet.

for translation. To do so, we use the Tarjan algorithm [37] to identify Strongly Connected Components (SCCs) in a call graph and their dependencies, and treat all the code belonging to one SCC as a translation unit.[8]

Thus, to determine the translation units and their translation order, we start from the `main` entry of a call graph of the project, we perform a post-order depth-first search, recursively visiting all nodes and translating all the children of a node before translating the node itself, ensuring that each function is translated after all its callees and dependencies have been translated.

During this process, we have observed and utilized an important capability and flexibility of LLM in dealing with unknown function or data type: we can instruct LLM to ignore an unknown dependency when the C code for translation contains references to functions or data types *not* defined in the code itself, or to replace the unknown with a generic no-op placeholder, or to ask human users to provide additional definitions of those dependencies. This is also a reason why we can just translate the functions that appear in dynamic call graphs to produce compilable and executable Rust program without the need to translate all functions in static call graphs.[9]

4 Translating C Functions to Rust Using LLM

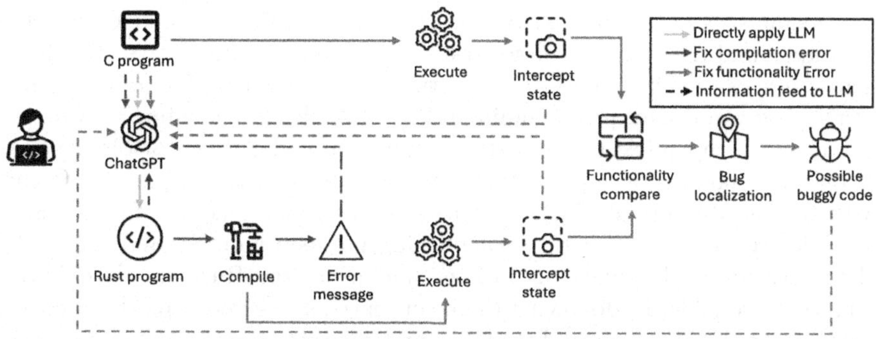

Fig. 3. Workflow of translating a C program via LLM

Translating C programs to Rust programs needs to ensure that the Rust programs (1) can be compiled successfully, and (2) should behave consistently with

[8] If the number of lines of code of an SCC is beyond the length limit of LLM, we still break down it into smaller units for translation.

[9] This capability and flexibility of LLM is also applicable to any reasonable code chunk, not limited to a complete function. Thus, when the number of lines of code of just one function is beyond the length limit of LLM, we can break down the function into shorter code chunks at various syntactically valid places, e.g., the call sites to other functions, the boundaries of a `while` statement, a `case` in a `switch` statement, etc., and treat each smaller code chunk as a translation unit and merge them back to a function after they are translated into Rust.

the C programs. We leverage ChatGPT 4o [20,29] with human prompts and test cases for these purposes. Each program is broken down into translation units as described in the previous section; each unit is fed to LLM for translation, and their translation results are merged together to form the Rust program.

Figure 3 shows an overview of our uses of LLM. Specifically, given a C program and its translation units, we first prompt ChatGPT to translate the program (if the whole program can fit within the LLM input length limit) or one of its translation units (Sect. 4.1). If the Rust compiler fails to compile the Rust code translated by ChatGPT, we will include the compiler error messages in the prompt to ChatGPT for the next round of trial (Sect. 4.3). If the program and all its translation units can be translated and compiled, we continue to execute the translated program in the debug mode and check their execution states. If there is a functional inconsistency between the Rust program and the C program when they execute, we perform bug localization to locate possible buggy code in the translated Rust code and its corresponding C code, and then prompt ChatGPT to re-translate the code to fix the bug (Sect. 4.4). All prompt templates we use are provided in our repo.[10]

4.1 Leveraging ChatGPT for Translation

Rust and C are two distinct languages with different syntax and semantics. This requires extensive pre-existing knowledge of both Rust and C, which is demanding and the main reason for translation errors by other tools. To address such issues, we utilize ChatGPT for translation, as ChatGPT is pre-trained with a large amount of programming-related knowledge, including C and Rust programs, which equips it with a strong ability to understand both languages.

Figure 4 shows a prompt template we used to translate a piece of C code to Rust. The prompt considers various Rust programming conventions useful for idiomatic Rust code, e.g., distinguishing between mutable and immutable references, adding lifetime annotations, and using the Rust standard library as much as possible. By following these conventions, the generated Rust code is more likely to be idiomatic and readable, and adhere to Rust's safety guarantees.

4.2 Adding Dependencies Into Translated Files

As our approach can divide a C file into multiple Rust files (cf. Sect. 3.1) during translation, we need to spell out the dependencies between the files so that the entire translated Rust project can be compiled successfully. We identify the dependencies based on the original C code and add reference relations into the files. Specifically, given a Rust file containing a translated function, we first identify all its callee functions using call graphs. Then, we locate the corresponding Rust files for the callees and identify their module name. Finally, we add Rust `use` statements to import those modules at the beginning of the initial Rust file. For example, `BZ2_decompress` function calls `BZ2_hbCreateDecodeTables` function,

[10] https://github.com/Cxm211/RustMap/tree/main/prompt-templates.

Please take on the role of an expert developer familiar with the Rust and C and C++ programming languages.

Convert the given code to idiomatic Rust, keeping its functionality. Use minimal unsafe traits and follow the requirements below. Don't translate unknown variables or functions, and avoid assumptions. If the C code references other vital functions or structures, *ask me first* and wait for my provided input.

1. If a variable inside the function is modified, add the `mut` specifier.
2. Distinguish between mutable and immutable references by storing intermediate values.
3. If necessary, add lifetime annotations.
4. Add clear comments for all numeric types and pay attention to type conversions, especially between `usize` and others.
5. Be cautious of potential out-of-bound errors in the C code.
6. Use the Rust standard library as much as possible.
7. When performing arithmetic operations, be mindful of potential overflow or underflow.

(...Here is C Code to be translated...)

Fig. 4. Prompt for directly applying ChatGPT to translate

which is defined in `huffman.c`. We use the file path from the scaffolding step as the module name (i.e., `huffman::BZ2_hbCreateDecodeTables`), and import the module using `use` statement at the beginning of the file containing the `BZ2_decompress` function. When some dependent functions are put into the same translation unit and their translation results are merged into one Rust file, the relevant `use` statements would be removed. This restructuring maintains the original dependencies between functions, enhancing the maintainability and readability of the translated Rust codebase.

4.3 Fixing Compilation Errors

We adapt a prior study [7] that uses LLMs to produce fixes for compilation errors in Rust programs. When a function and its necessary dependencies are translated, we use the `rustc` compiler to check whether they can be compiled successfully. If compilation fails, we will locate the Rust function or code construct that cause the failure, and take the compilation error messages, along with the buggy Rust code and its corresponding original C code, as the input prompt for ChatGPT to fix the errors in the Rust code. We will conduct this process three times until the generated Rust code can be compiled without an error.

4.4 Locating and Fixing Functionality Errors

When the `main` entry function and its necessary dependencies are translated and the whole Rust program is compiled, we run the compiled Rust program with the test inputs available from the original C project. To ensure they produce the same outputs for the same test inputs, we instrument the Rust program and intercept its runtime execution states, and then compare the states with those from the C program.[11] If there is any inconsistency, we follow the steps below to **locate** and **fix** the possible faulty code fragments or functions.

To effectively **locate** bug locations causing runtime state inconsistencies in programs, we adopt a binary-search-based method on the C and Rust programs at the same time. First, we consider all the statements in the buggy Rust program as bug candidate statements. Then, a breakpoint in the Rust program is set around the halfway point of the sequential execution of all bug candidate statements; the breakpoint in the C program is set at the corresponding C statement semantically equivalent to the Rust breakpoint statement. Then, we check the state of the Rust program and the state of the C program at the breakpoints. If they are consistent, the bug candidate statements should be narrowed to its second half; otherwise, we narrow the bug candidate statements into its first half only (although the second half may still contain more bugs). This process will be executed repeatedly until the number of bug candidate statements is small (fewer than 10 within a function) and the statements are relatively simple without complex control-flow changes (e.g., simple code blocks with less than 5 Cyclomatic Complexity [6,40]). As a result, we locate a code fragment in Rust with bug candidate statements (also called faulty code fragment), as well as a corresponding code fragment in the original C program that is supposed to be functionally equivalent to the Rust code fragment.

To **fix** a possible faulty code fragment, we instantiate the prompt template shown in Fig. 5 and ask ChatGPT to fix. We take (1) the corresponding code fragment from the C program with the states before and after executing the C code, and (2) the faulty Rust code fragment with the state before executing the faulty code, as the input prompt for ChatGPT to correct the Rust code so that it produces the same output state as the C code. This fix process for each located buggy code fragment will be iterated three times. If ChatGPT fails to fix the Rust code to produce states consistent with the C code, we leave it as a translation failure case. The whole locate-and-fix process will also be repeated many times until time out or the whole Rust program can run the given test cases to produce outputs consistent with the C program.

[11] In our implementation, we inserted various `print` statements at needed locations in both C and Rust programs to print out *relevant inputs and outputs* and compared the printed values. Relevant inputs of a function are the function parameters; Relevant outputs of a function are the variables or expressions returned by the function. Relevant inputs of any code fragment are selected by LLM with a simple use-def static analysis of data that is used in the code fragment; Relevant outputs of any code fragment are selected by LLM with a simple use-def static analysis of data that is modified in the code fragment.

```
// C code fragment with its before- and after-states:
{
    (before-state of C)
    (...Here is the C code to be translated to Rust...)
    (after-state of C)
}

// Rust code generation:
{
    (before-state in Rust)
    (...Here is the possibily faulty Rust code...)
    /** please fix the Rust code fragment here to have
        consistent states as the C code above
      */
}
```

Fig. 5. Prompt template for ChatGPT to resolve functionality errors. The instantiated prompt will include the same requirements as shown in the prompt in Fig. 4.

5 Empirical Evaluation

To evaluate the effectiveness of RustMap in translating C code to Rust, we perform studies on real-world C programs, including a set of RosettaCode programs and a file compression program `bzip2`, ranging from tens of lines to tens of thousands of lines of code. Section 5.1 shows the overall performance of RustMap in various functionality, safety, readability metrics. Sample translation results (e.g., involving thread-safe global variables, interdependent data structures, and pointer aliasing, control-flow goto) are provided in our repo[12] for potential reuses by future research. Sect. 5.2 discusses our limitations.

5.1 Effectiveness

Functionality Evaluation. After applying RustMap, we successfully converted 125 RosettaCode programs and a file compression program `bzip2` from C to Rust. Unlike prior studies that only output Rust code snippets, we generated compilable Rust codebases that can execute and produce the same outputs as the original C programs for their given test cases. For example, the converted `bzip2` program can successfully compress and decompress given test files, while none of the existing tools can achieve this level of functionality.[13]

On the other hand, there can be some C code that is not translated by our approach, as the C code can contain some functions, macros, or branches that are not executed by the given test cases. To gauge the likely deficit, Table 1 shows the proportion of C functions and lines that are translated into Rust *with respect to* the C functions and lines that are executed/covered by the test cases.

[12] https://github.com/Cxm211/RustMap/tree/main/case_study.

[13] The translated Rust code for bzip2 is at: https://github.com/Cxm211/RustMap/tree/main/rust-code/bzip2_rs_gpt.
The translated Rust code for RosettaCode programs is at: https://github.com/Cxm211/RustMap/tree/main/rust-code/rosetta_code_gpt/125-rosetta-code-gpt.

Table 1. Proportion of C functions and lines that are translated into Rust *with respect to* the C functions and lines that are executed in the given test cases.

C File	Function Coverage	Line Coverage
`bzip2`		
blocksort.c	66.7%	71.7%
bzip2.c	100.0%	100.0%
bzlib.c	100.0%	93.3%
compress.c	100.0%	100.0%
decompress.c	100.0%	93.2%
huffman.c	100.0%	98.8%
Average	**94.4%**	**92.8%**
Rosetta Code		
125 .c files	**95.3%**	**93.2%**

We observe that the differences between the amount of C code that is translated and the amount of C code that is executed are small, indicating that the translated Rust projects have close functionality as the original C projects.

> RustMap can produce runnable Rust projects that pass the same test cases as the original C projects.

Unsafety Evaluation. We compare the number of unsafe code blocks in the Rust projects translated by RustMap with those translated by other tools. Laertes [10] implemented a tool to categorize unsafe code, and we used it for measuring unsafe code in Rust projects. Table 2 shows the numbers of unsafe code blocks in the Rust projects translated by RustMap, C2Rust, CRustS, and Laertes. We measure the unsafe code declared in Rust's official document [22]: Read From Union (reading from a field of a C-style untagged union), MutGlobal Access (reading, writing, or referencing to mutable global(static)/external vars), RawPtr Deref (dereferencing a raw pointer), Alloc (direct external function calls to malloc and free), Extern Call (calling an external function other than 'Alloc').

> RustMap is much more effective in reducing unsafe code when translating C to functionally equivalent Rust.

Readability Assessment. To measure RustMap's capability in terms of code readability, we compare the *Cognitive Complexity* (CC) scores of the Rust projects generated by different tools. Cognitive Complexity quantifies code readability and maintainability, assessing the cognitive load on developers. To do so, we apply the complexity crate [6] to the functions in the generated Rust projects. Figure 6 shows the comparison between RustMap and C2Rust in terms

Table 2. Numbers of unsafe code blocks

Tool	Read From Union	Mut Global Access	Raw Ptr Deref	Alloc	Extern Call	Unsafe Cast
`bzip2`						
C2Rust	0	386	3424	14	1	0
CRustS	0	386	3424	14	1	0
Laertes	0	386	3359	14	1	0
RustMap*	0	126	122	5	0	0
Rosetta Code						
C2Rust	0	339	572	68	593	19
CRustS	0	339	572	68	593	19
Laertes	0	339	572	68	593	19
RustMap*	0	3	0	0	0	0

of CC scores. We observe that the complexity of the Rust projects translated by RustMap is significant lower than the ones generated by C2Rust (p-value $<$ 0.05).

> Rust code translated by RustMap is easier to read than the code translated by C2Rust.

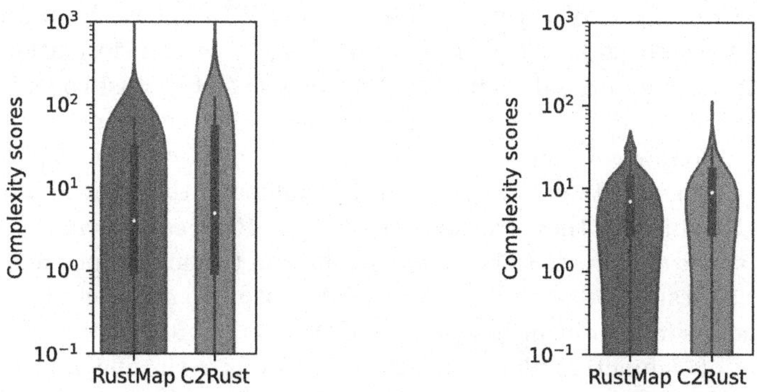

(a) BZip2 (b) RosettaCode

Fig. 6. Cognitive Complexity of Rust code translated by RustMap and C2Rust. Note that the y-axes are in **log scale**.

5.2 Discussion and Threats to Validity

C includes various coding features that pose challenges during translation to Rust. Common practices such as pointer punning [43] and aliasing, where multiple array pointers reference the same memory, conflict with Rust's safety guarantees, which prohibit multiple mutable references to avoid memory errors. RustMap addresses this by converting such pointers to `Vec<>` and relying on value copying for data access, though this is less efficient than in C. Future work may investigate the semantics of shared memory access (e.g., there may be at most one writer to the shared memory at any time) to support more efficient and idiomatic Rust translations.

Concurrent C programs often rely on shared memory, employing coding patterns that differ significantly from Rust's concurrency model. Our current evaluation does not cover multi-threaded C code; future work will explore leveraging Rust's safe concurrency mechanisms to ensure idiomatic and correct translation of parallel programs.

RustMap relies on customized prompts to handle diverse code patterns and translation issues, requiring substantial manual effort to design and select suitable prompt templates. Future work could aim to automate and standardize this process using LLM-based agents, particularly for scaling to larger codebases.

6 Related Work

Unsafe Rust code has been used extensively [1] by developers, as it is difficult to write safe code that implements complex and efficient operations under the restrictions of the Rust type system. Efforts to reduce the amount of unsafe code in Rust, in the context of Rust translated using C2Rust, have been diverse and significant. CRustS [23] utilizes TXL source-to-source transformation rules to minimize the extent of unsafe expressions in the translated Rust code. Laertes [9, 10] concentrates on diminishing unsafe code by addressing import and lifetime errors related to raw pointers, a common issue in translations from C. Meanwhile, Crown [49] offers a suite of analyses aimed at inferring the ownership models of C pointers, facilitating their translation into safe Rust equivalents. Hong et al. [15] used a static analysis based on abstract interpretation, complemented by the concept of abstract read/write sets, to replace output parameters (i.e., pointer-type parameters for producing outputs) in C programs with 'Option/Result' (the return type of a function that represents functions returning multiple values and may fail) in the translated Rust code. Hong et al. [16] further developed static analysis to identify tag fields and values, using must-points-to analysis and heuristics, to replace unions with tagged unions during C-to-Rust translation. Further, Hong et al. [17] proposed tools to port entire C programs to Rust by translating each C function to a Rust function with a signature containing proper Rust types through type migration with the help of LLM, but they have not been able to resolve all type errors to produce executable Rust programs.

LLMs have also been applied in different ways to help translate programs to Rust. Zhang et al. [48] utilize type compatibility and feature mapping between source and target languages to facilitate translation and have achieved meaningful results when translating Go code to Rust. Eniser et al. [11] evaluate various LLM models on translating a few Go and C programs to Rust; they use differential fuzzing to check if a Rust translation is I/O equivalent to the original source program and use feedback mechanisms to repair faulty translation. They achieved a translation success rate of about 47% and provided insights for improvements. Although we share a similar high-level idea of using LLMs for translation, our approach uses different code break-down strategy and different mechanisms to check code correctness and provide feedback for LLMs. It would be valuable future work to explore and compare different strategies in using LLMs and agent workflows to improve the translation results further.

In the realm of Rust synthesis, there have been innovative attempts to enhance safety and correctness. Synthetic Ownership Logic (SOL) [12] aims to provide correct-by-construction programs in safe Rust. Furthermore, the program synthesis for Rust library API testing [35] explores the synthesis of safe Rust code while dealing with unsafe code.

Regarding the verification of Unsafe Rust, notable advancements have been made. RustBelt [21] offers the first formal (and machine-checked) safety proof for Rust. Building on this, RustHornBelt [25] extends these proofs to ensure the soundness of Rust APIs implemented with unsafe Rust code. Recently, [33] has studied on how to implement a novel embedding of Rust code into fixed-sized vectors to categorize and find Rust common fix patterns.

Recent research covers a range of topics: [4] explores the impact of unstable features on package compilation, [50] presents a technique for automatic fuzz target synthesis in Rust libraries, [27] studies safety requirements in unsafe Rust code, [47] examines differences between paid and volunteer developers in the Rust community, [38] introduces a tool for fixing ownership-rule violations, [5] analyzes the effectiveness of Clippy lints, [44] investigates security vulnerabilities in Rust packages, and [46] demonstrates the use of KLEE for detecting unrecoverable errors. These papers provide significant insights and tools that contribute to the security, reliability, and development practices of the Rust ecosystem, while targeting different problems from our C-to-Rust code translation problem.

7 Conclusion and Future Work

Unlike previous translation tools such as C2Rust, which focused primarily on syntactic conversions without considering functional integrity, our approach, RustMap, with large language models (LLM) and program analysis, shows much potential in performing more semantic-aware, project-scale code translation. We have successfully translated 125 RosettaCode programs and the bzip2 file compression program into Rust, enhancing the functional usability of the translated Rust code with better code safety and readability.

Looking ahead, we plan to expand our project scope to include more comprehensive translations from C to Rust, to further explore the capabilities of LLMs in aiding code conversion of diverse features and to conduct more performance evaluations. Our long-term aim is to ensure not only the functionality, readability, safety, but also performance of translated code and their compatibility with untranslated code.

Acknowledgments. We thank the anonymous reviewers for their valuable feedback, suggesting many meaningful improvements. A version of this paper with more details is publicly available at https://doi.org/10.48550/arXiv.2503.17741.

References

1. Astrauskas, V., Matheja, C., Poli, F., Müller, P., Summers, A.J.: How do programmers use unsafe rust? Proc. ACM Program. Lang. **4**(OOPSLA) (2020). https://doi.org/10.1145/3428204
2. Bang, I., Kayondo, M., Moon, H., Paek, Y.: TRUST: a compilation framework for in-process isolation to protect safe rust against untrusted code. In: 32nd USENIX Security Symposium (USENIX Security), Baltimore, MD, USA (2023)
3. casey: Awesome rewrite it in rust (2024). https://github.com/casey/awesome-rewrite-it-in-rust. A curated list of replacements for existing software written in Rust
4. Li, C., Wu, Y.: Demystifying compiler unstable feature usage and impacts in the rust ecosystem. In: Proceedings of the International Conference on Software Engineering (ICSE) (2024)
5. Li, C., Yu, Y.: Unleashing the power of clippy in real-world rust projects. In: Proceedings of the International Conference on Software Engineering (ICSE) (2024)
6. Crates.io: Complexity—calculate cognitive complexity of rust code (2024). https://crates.io/crates/complexity
7. Deligiannis, P., Lal, A., Mehrotra, N., Rastogi, A.: Fixing rust compilation errors using LLMs. arXiv preprint arXiv:2308.05177 (2023)
8. developer.arm.com: Complex macros in C (2024). https://developer.arm.com/documentation/101655/latest/Cx51-User-s-Guide/Preprocessor/Macros/Complex-Macros
9. Emre, M., Boyland, P., Parekh, A., Schroeder, R., Dewey, K., Hardekopf, B.: Aliasing limits on translating C to safe rust. Proc. ACM Program. Lang. **7**(OOPSLA1), 551–579 (2023)
10. Emre, M., Schroeder, R., Dewey, K., Hardekopf, B.: Translating C to safer rust. Proc. ACM Program. Lang. **5**(OOPSLA), 1–29 (2021)
11. Eniser, H.F., et al.: Towards translating real-world code with LLMs: a study of translating to rust. arXiv preprint arXiv:2405.11514 (2024)
12. Fiala, J., Itzhaky, S., Müller, P., Polikarpova, N., Sergey, I.: Leveraging rust types for program synthesis. Proc. ACM Program. Lang. **7**(PLDI), 1414–1437 (2023)
13. u Graham, S.L., Kessler, P.B., McKusick, M.K.: Gprof: a call graph execution profiler. ACM Sigplan Not. **17**(6), 120–126 (1982). https://sourceware.org/binutils/docs/gprof/
14. Guo, Q., et al.: Exploring the potential of ChatGPT in automated code refinement: an empirical study. CoRR abs/2309.08221 (2023). https://doi.org/10.48550/ARXIV.2309.08221
15. Hong, J., Ryu, S.: Don't write, but return: replacing output parameters with algebraic data types in C-to-Rust translation. Proc. ACM Program. Lang. **8**(PLDI), 716–740 (2024)

16. Hong, J., Ryu, S.: To tag, or not to tag: Translating C's unions to Rust's tagged unions. In: Proceedings of the 39th IEEE/ACM International Conference on Automated Software Engineering, pp. 40–52 (2024)
17. Hong, J., Ryu, S.: Type-migrating C-to-Rust translation using a large language model. Empir. Softw. Eng. **30**(1), 3 (2025)
18. Immunant, I.: c2rust - c to rust translation and more (2024). https://github.com/immunant/c2rust#faq. Accessed 03 June 2024
19. InfoQ: Rust reviewed: the current trends and pitfalls of the ecosystem (2023). https://www.infoq.com/articles/rust-ecosystem-review-2023/. A review of the current trends and pitfalls in the Rust ecosystem
20. Islam, R., Moushi, O.M.: GPT-4o: The cutting-edge advancement in multimodal LLM. Authorea Preprints (2024)
21. Jung, R., Jourdan, J.H., Krebbers, R., Dreyer, D.: RustBelt: securing the foundations of the rust programming language. Proc. ACM Program. Lang. **2**(POPL), 1–34 (2017)
22. rust lang.org: Unsafe rust (2023). https://doc.rust-lang.org/book/ch19-01-unsafe-rust.html. Accessed 18 Nov 2023
23. Ling, M., Yu, Y., Wu, H., Wang, Y., Cordy, J.R., Hassan, A.E.: In rust we trust: a transpiler from unsafe c to safer rust. In: Proceedings of the ACM/IEEE 44th International Conference on Software Engineering: Companion Proceedings, pp. 354–355 (2022)
24. Liu, J., Xia, C.S., Wang, Y., Zhang, L.: Is your code generated by chatGPT really correct? Rigorous evaluation of large language models for code generation. Adv. Neural Inf. Process. Syst. **36** (2024)
25. Matsushita, Y., Denis, X., Jourdan, J.H., Dreyer, D.: RustHornBelt: a semantic foundation for functional verification of rust programs with unsafe code. In: Proceedings of the 43rd ACM SIGPLAN International Conference on Programming Language Design and Implementation, pp. 841–856 (2022)
26. Mertens, E., Langley, T.: C2Rust: migrating C to safe rust (2018). https://galois.com/blog/2018/08/c2rust/. Accessed 24 May 2024
27. Cui, M., Sun, S.: Is unsafe an Achilles' heel? A comprehensive study of safety requirements in unsafe rust programming. In: Proceedings of the International Conference on Software Engineering (ICSE) (2024)
28. Mol, M.: Rosetta code. https://rosettacode.org. Accessed 29 May 2024
29. OpenAI: GPT-4 technical report. Technical report, OpenAI (2024)
30. Pan, R., et al.: Lost in translation: a study of bugs introduced by large language models while translating code. In: Proceedings of the IEEE/ACM 46th International Conference on Software Engineering, pp. 1–13 (2024)
31. Poznyakoff, S.: GNU cflow (2005). https://www.gnu.org/software/cflow/
32. Qin, B., Chen, Y., Yu, Z., Song, L., Zhang, Y.: Understanding memory and thread safety practices and issues in real-world rust programs. In: Proceedings of the 41st ACM SIGPLAN Conference on Programming Language Design and Implementation, PLDI 2020, pp. 763–779. Association for Computing Machinery, New York (2020). https://doi.org/10.1145/3385412.3386036
33. Robati Shirzad, M., Lam, P.: A study of common bug fix patterns in rust. Empir. Softw. Eng. **29**(2), 44 (2024)
34. Seward, J.: bzip2 (2023). https://sourceware.org/bzip2/. Accessed 04 June 2024
35. Takashima, Y., Martins, R., Jia, L., Păsăreanu, C.S.: SyRust: automatic testing of rust libraries with semantic-aware program synthesis. In: Proceedings of the 42nd ACM SIGPLAN International Conference on Programming Language Design and

Implementation, PLDI 2021, pp. 899–913. Association for Computing Machinery, New York (2021). https://doi.org/10.1145/3453483.3454084
36. TaKO8Ki: Awesome alternatives in rust (2024). https://github.com/TaKO8Ki/awesome-alternatives-in-rust. A curated list of replacements for existing software written in Rust
37. Tarjan, R.: Depth-first search and linear graph algorithms. SIAM J. Comput. **1**(2), 146–160 (1972)
38. Wenzhang Yang, L.S.: Rust-lancet: automated ownership-rule-violation fixing with behavior preservation. In: Proceedings of the International Conference on Software Engineering (ICSE) (2024)
39. White, J., Other, A.: ChatGPT prompt patterns for improving code quality, refactoring, requirements elicitation, and software design. arXiv preprint arXiv:2303.07839 (2023)
40. Wikipedia: Cyclomatic complexity (2024). https://en.wikipedia.org/wiki/Cyclomatic_complexity
41. Wikipedia: Redox (operating system) (2024). https://en.wikipedia.org/wiki/Redox_(operating_system)
42. Wikipedia: Rust for Linux (2024). https://en.wikipedia.org/wiki/Rust_for_Linux
43. Wikipedia: Type punning (2024). https://en.wikipedia.org/wiki/Type_punning#C_and_C++
44. Zheng, X., Wan, Z.: A closer look at the security risks in the rust ecosystem. ACM Trans. Softw. Eng. Methodol. (TOSEM) (2024)
45. Yang, Z., et al.: Exploring and unleashing the power of large language models in automated code translation. arXiv preprint arXiv:2404.14646 (2024)
46. Ying Zhang, P.L.: Broadly enabling Klee to effortlessly find unrecoverable errors in rust. In: Proceedings of the International Conference on Software Engineering (ICSE) (2024)
47. Yuxia Zhang, M.Q.: How are paid and volunteer open source developers different? A study of the rust project. In: Proceedings of the International Conference on Software Engineering (ICSE) (2024)
48. Zhang, H., David, C., Wang, M., Paulsen, B., Kroening, D.: Scalable, validated code translation of entire projects using large language models. arXiv preprint arXiv:2412.08035 (2024)
49. Zhang, H., David, C., Yu, Y., Wang, M.: Ownership guided C to Rust translation. arXiv preprint arXiv:2303.10515 (2023)
50. Xu, Z., Wu, B.: RPG: rust library fuzzing with pool-based fuzz target generation and generic support. In: Proceedings of the International Conference on Software Engineering (ICSE) (2024)

Formal Methods

LTL Model Checking of Concurrent Self Modifying Code

Tayssir Touili and Olzhas Zhangeldinov(✉)

IRIF, CNRS, and University Paris Cité, Paris, France
{touili,zhangeldinov}@irif.fr

Abstract. We consider the LTL model-checking problem of concurrent self modifying code, i.e., concurrent code that has the ability to modify its own instructions during execution time. This style of code is frequently utilized by malware developers to make their malicious code hard to detect. To model such programs, we consider Self-Modifying Dynamic Pushdown Networks (SM-DPN). A SM-DPN is a network of Self-Modifying Pushdown processes, where each process has the ability to modify its current set of rules and to spawn new processes during execution time. We consider model checking SM-DPNs against single indexed LTL formulas, i.e., conjunctions of separate LTL formulas on each single process. This problem is non trivial since the number of spawned processes in a given run can be infinite. Our approach is based on computing finite automata representing the set of configurations from which the SM-DPN has a run that satisfies the single-indexed LTL formula. We implemented our techniques in a tool and obtained promising results. In particular, our tool was able to detect concurrent, self-modifying malware.

1 Introduction

Most programs implement concurrent routines for efficiency. However, analysis of concurrent programs is a notoriously hard challenge. Therefore, significant efforts were made in the direction of automatic verification of concurrent programs [8,13,17,19–21,25].

On the other hand, self-modifying code is a code that modifies its own instructions during the execution time. This technique is widely used by packers to decrease the size of a program and by malware developers to confuse anti-virus software and make their malware hard to detect. The problem of analysing self-modifying code was approached by more recent studies [7,9,19,26].

This paper focuses on analysing programs that are both *concurrent* and *self-modifying*. Indeed, modern malware employs concurrency for parallel execution of different tasks and contains self-modifying code to stay undetected for as long as possible.

This work was partially funded by the French ANR grant Defmal "ANR-22-PECY-0007".

Y. Zhou et al. (Eds.): ICECCS 2025, LNCS 15746, pp. 305–325, 2026.
https://doi.org/10.1007/978-3-032-00828-2_17

```
# Address   Bytecode            Assembly
  0x10       0x31c0              xor    eax, eax
  0x14       0xb001              mov    al, 1
  0x18       0xbb80cd02b0        mov    ebx, 0xb002cd80
  0x1d       0x891d04000000      mov    [0x04], ebx
  0x23       0xebe7              jmp    0x04
```

Listing 1.1. Binary code with a self-modifying instruction.

```
# Address   Assembly
  0x04       xor  eax, eax   #-  executing  --> mov al, 0x2
                             #  mov [0x04], ebx
  0x06       mov  al, 1      #-  executing  --> int 0x80
                             #  mov [0x04], ebx
  0x08       mov  ebx, 0xb002cd80
  0x0d       mov  [0x04], ebx
  0x13       jmp  0x04
```

Listing 1.2. Binary code after executing a self-modifying instruction.

Self-modifying behaviour of a program is achieved by writing to the executable region of the binary, which is a memory segment from where a computer can read instructions to execute. Self-modification can be implemented using different techniques. For example, let us consider a self-modifying concurrent binary code of a Linux program running on a CPU with x86 architecture. Programs for this architecture mostly use `mov` instructions to write data into memory, including the memory of executable instructions. A portion of the program's assembly is demonstrated in Listing 1.1. The first column denotes relative addresses of instructions. The second column contains bytes stored at that address, and the third column is the corresponding assembly code for the binary code. `eax` and `ebx` are CPU registers, and `al` points to the lowest byte of `eax`.

Let us explain why this code is self-modifying and concurrent. First, a process starts executing the program at the address `0x04` and reads bytes `0x31c0` stored at this location. Bytecode `0x31c0` corresponds to the instruction `xor eax, eax`, which means the process sets `eax` to 0. This instruction is two bytes long, so the process reads the next instruction from the address `0x06`. This address contains bytes `0xb001`, which is the bytecode of the instruction `mov al, 0x1`, which sets the lowest byte of `eax` to `0x1`. Then, the process executes the instruction `mov ebx, 0xb002cd80`, which corresponds to the bytecode `0xbb80cd02b0` stored at the address `0x08`. This sets `ebx` to `0xb002cd80`. Next, the process executes the instruction stored at the address `0x0d`. This instruction is `mov [0x04], ebx` and it stores the value of `ebx` (previously set to `0xb002cd80`) to the address `0x04`. This changes the instructions stored at address `0x04`. Since `0xb002cd80` is the binary code for instructions `mov al, 0x2` and `int, 0x80`, the instructions at the addresses `0x04` and `0x06` will be replaced by these two instructions. Therefore, `mov [0x04], ebx` is a self-modifying instruction. The code of the program after self-modification occurs is presented in Listing 1.2. The next instruction the process reads will be `jmp 0x04` (corresponding to the bytecode `0xebe7` contained at the location `0x13`), which will make the process jump to the address `0x04`. As explained, this address now contains a modified instruction with the bytecode `0xcd80`. The new assembly is `mov al, 0x2`, which sets `eax` to 2 (remember that we set higher bytes of `eax` to 0 with `xor eax, eax`). Then, the process will execute the modified instruction at the address `0x06` with the new bytecode `0xcd80`, which corresponds to the assembly `int, 0x80`. This instruction tells Linux kernel to execute a system function with the function code stored in `eax`. The function code `0x2` corresponds to the kernel's *fork* function, which spawns a copy of the current process. Since the previous instruction sets `eax` to `0x2`, Linux kernel executes the *fork* function, making this program also concurrent.

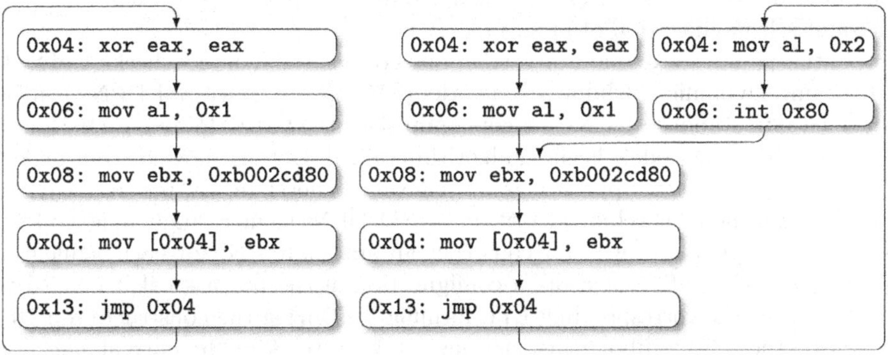

(a) Naive CFG (b) Accurate CFG

Fig. 1. Naive and accurate CFGs of code from Listing 1.1.

You can see that if we analyse this program blindly, using the instructions of Listing 1.1, without taking into account the self-modifying nature of the instruction `mov [0x04], ebx`, then we will obtain the Control Flow Graph (CFG) shown in Fig. 1(a). However in reality, the program will spawn parallel processes indefinitely. This is clear if we look at the more accurate CFG in Fig. 1(b). This is one of the tecnhiques malware developers use to obscure the real behaviour of the malware from antivirus software. Therefore, it is necessary to take into account the self-modifying nature of the code for an accurate analysis.

The aim of this paper is to provide an efficient algorithm for model checking such self-modifying and concurrent code. To analyse such kind of programs, we need an abstract model suitable for both self-modifications and concurrency. Pushdown System (PDS) was shown to be a natural abstraction for sequential programs [14]. To deal with concurrency, Dynamic Pushdown Networks (DPNs) were proposed to model how a program can spawn parallel processes [8]. A DPN is a network of pushdown systems where each PDS is able to spawn new processes controlled by other PDSs. On the other hand, to model programs with self-modifying instructions, Touili and Ye [26] proposed Self-Modifying Pushdown Systems (SM-PDS). Intuitively, SM-PDS is a PDS with the ability to modify its set of rules during runtime. To model both concurrent and self-modifying programs, a previous work [19] introduced Self-Modifying Dynamic Pushdown Networks (SM-DPNs) as a network of self-modifying pushdown systems. [19] proposed an efficient algorithm for reachability analysis of SM-DPNs. In this work, we go one step further and propose an efficient LTL model checking algorithm for SM-DPNs.

Model checking concurrent programs imposes additional challenges. In fact, model checking LTL formulas that reason about two concurrent processes is undecidable [16], even in the absence of thread creation. To overcome this problem, we consider single-indexed LTL formulas of the form $f = \bigwedge_i f_i$, such that f_i is an LTL formula over process i. This problem of single-indexed LTL model checking of DPNs was tackled by [25], however, this work does not take into account self-modification of programs.

In this paper, we go one step further and consider LTL model checking of Self-Modifying Dynamic Pushdown Networks (SM-DPNs). Since SM-DPNs can be encoded into standard DPNs, we could translate the SM-DPN into a DPN, and then use the LTL model checking algorithm of [25]. But, as shown by our experiments in Sect. 4, this approach is not efficient. Therefore, we propose a *direct* and *efficient* model checking algorithm for SM-DPNs against single-indexed LTL formulas. To this aim, we first construct an automaton $\mathcal{A}_i$ for each sequential process i, such that $\mathcal{A}_i$ accepts a configuration of the process i if it has a run that satisfies the corresponding LTL formula f_i. During the construction of $\mathcal{A}_i$, to tackle the self-modifying instructions, we keep track of the current *phase* of the process i (the current set of the transitions of the process). $\mathcal{A}_i$ also keeps track of the spawned processes during the execution because we need to check that every spawned process j satisfies the formula f_j as well. Then, we use all of the obtained automata to compute the largest set of processes $\mathcal{D}_{fp}$, such that every process i in $\mathcal{D}_{fp}$ satisfies the LTL formula f_i, and does not spawn a process j that violates the formula f_j $(j \geq 0)$. Then, we check that every initial process satisfies the LTL formula and spawns only processes from $\mathcal{D}_{fp}$. Our experiments show that our direct approach is much more efficient than model checking an equivalent DPN using the approach in [25]. Moreover, we show the applicability of our approach for malware detection.

Related Works. Model checking of sequential binaries has been extensively studied in [4,5,16,24]. However, these studies do not consider either concurrency of programs, or self-modifying instructions.

To solve the problem of model checking concurrent programs, different models were proposed. Some studies use Dynamic Pushdown Network (DPN) model [8,20,25] and its extensions [13,19]. Other studies [17,21,22] performed model checking on networks of pushdown systems. However, these works do not consider self-modifying code.

To analyse self-modifying programs, several dynamic analysis approaches were proposed [11,27], which imply executing the binary in a debugger and observing the behaviour of the program. However, these techniques do not allow to analyse every possible behaviour of the program. Static analysis of self-modifying code was proposed in, for example, [7,9,12]. However, [9] needs extra invariant annotations, [12] can deal with only packing and unpacking of binaries. As for [7], it proposes an abstract representation without a specific approach to automated analysis. Another model to represent self-modifying code is State-Enhanced Control Flow Graph (SE-CFG) [3]. Reachability analysis of binaries with self-modifying instructions was also proposed by [6]. However, both of these studies [3,6] do not take into account the stack of the program, and thus, do not provide an accurate enough model of execution. Self-modifying pushdown systems (SM-PDS) were successfully used for model checking self-modifying programs [26]. However, this work does not support concurrency.

As far as we know, the only work that considers both concurrent and self-modifying programs is [19], where the SM-DPN model was proposed. But, [19] considers only reachability analysis. In this paper, we go one step further and propose an efficient LTL model checking of SM-DPNs. Moreover, we extend the SM-DPN model to allow modelling programs when an instruction can modify *several* instructions (not only one as in [19]).

Outline. Section 2 introduces our SM-DPN model. Section 3 describes the proposed algorithm for efficient model checking SM-DPNs. Section 4 provides results of practical experiments conducted using the proposed LTL model checking.

2 Preliminaries

In this section, we introduce Self-Modifying Pushdown Networks (SM-DPNs).

2.1 Self-Modifying Pushdown Network

A *Self-Modifying Dynamic Pushdown Network* (SM-DPN) is an extension of standard Pushdown Systems (PDS) that models programs that can spawn parallel processes and can change their instruction set in real-time. SM-DPN consists of several *Self-Modifying Dynamic Pushdown Systems* (SM-DPDS) each modelling a single sequential process. Formally:

Definition 1. *A Self-Modifying Dynamic Pushdown Network (SM-DPN) is a tuple $\mathcal{M} = (\mathcal{P}_1, \mathcal{P}_2, \ldots, \mathcal{P}_n)$, s.t. for every i, $1 \leq i \leq n$, $\mathcal{P}_i = (P_i, \Gamma_i, \Delta_i, \Delta_i^c)$ is a Self-Modifying Dynamic Pushdown System (SM-DPDS), where P_i is a finite set of control locations (for every $j \neq k$, $P_j \cap P_k = \emptyset$), Γ_i is the stack alphabet, Δ_i is a finite set of rules of the forms: (a) $p\gamma \hookrightarrow p_1\omega_1$ and (b) $p\gamma \hookrightarrow p_1\omega_1 \triangleright p_2\omega_2\theta_2$, such that $p, p_1 \in P_i$, $\gamma \in \Gamma_i$, $\omega_1 \in \Gamma_i^*$, $p_2 \in P_j$, $\omega_2 \in \Gamma_j^*$, $\theta_2 \subseteq \Delta_j \cup \Delta_j^c$ for some j, $1 \leq j \leq n$, and Δ_i^c is a finite set of self-modifying rules of the form $p \xhookrightarrow{(\rho_1,\rho_2)} p_1$, such that $\rho_1, \rho_2 \subseteq \Delta_i \cup \Delta_i^c$. A Dynamic Pushdown System (DPDS) is an SM-DPDS, such that $\Delta_i^c = \emptyset$. A Dynamic Pushdown Network (DPN) is an SM-DPN, such that for every $1 \leq i \leq n$, $\mathcal{P}_i$ is a DPDS.*

Consider an SM-DPN $\mathcal{M} = (\mathcal{P}_1, \mathcal{P}_2, \ldots, \mathcal{P}_n)$. An SM-DPDS $\mathcal{P}_i = (P_i, \Gamma_i, \Delta_i, \Delta_i^c)$ can be seen as a Pushdown System with the ability (1) to spawn a new process and (2) to change its current set of rules during its execution.

Because a process modelled by an SM-DPDS can change its set of rules at runtime, we introduce the notion of a *phase*. A phase $\theta \subseteq \Delta_i \cup \Delta_i^c$ is the current set of rules that can be applied. θ changes when a self-modifying rule of type $p \xrightarrow{(\rho_1,\rho_2)} p_1 \in \theta$ is applied. Such rule denotes that if the process is at the control location p, it can transition to the control location p_1 while removing rules in ρ_1 from θ and adding rules from ρ_2 to θ. Note that unlike the definition of SM-DPN in [19], we allow ρ_1 and ρ_2 to have different numbers of rules. The rules of type $p\gamma \hookrightarrow p_1\omega_1 \in \theta$ define that if the process is at the control location p and has γ on the top of its stack, then it can pop γ from the stack, push ω_1 onto it, and go to the control location p_1. Similarly, the rules of type $p\gamma \hookrightarrow p_1\omega_1 \triangleright p_2\omega_2\theta_2 \in \theta$ describe the same behaviour as $p\gamma \hookrightarrow p_1\omega_1$ but additionally, the rule spawns another process at the control location p_2, with ω_2 as content of the stack, and phase θ_2. This new process will be executed by its corresponding SM-DPDS $\mathcal{P}_j = (P_j, \Gamma_j, \Delta_j, \Delta_j^c) \in \mathcal{M}$, such that $p_2 \in P_j$.

2.2 Configurations and DCLICs

A *local configuration* of an SM-DPDS $\mathcal{P}_i$ is a tuple $(\langle p_i, \omega_i\rangle, \theta_i)$, where $p_i \in P_i$ is the current state of the process, $\omega_i \in \Gamma_i^*$ is the current stack content, and $\theta_i \subseteq \Delta_i \cup \Delta_i^c$ is the current phase. The set of all local configurations of a process of $\mathcal{P}_i$ is denoted as $Conf_i$. A *global configuration* of an SM-DPN is a multi-set over $\bigcup_{i=1}^n Conf_i$.

When a process can spawn a new process starting at the local configuration $(\langle p_j, \omega_j\rangle, \theta_j)$, we say that $p_j\omega_j\theta_j$ is a *Dynamically Created Local Initial Configuration* (DCLIC). The finite set of all DCLICs created by a process of $\mathcal{P}_i$ is denoted as $\mathcal{D}_i$ and is equal to $\{p_2\omega_2\theta_2 \in P_j \times \Gamma_j^* \times 2^{\Delta_j \cup \Delta_j^c} \mid \exists p, p' \in P_i, \gamma \in \Gamma_i, \omega' \in \Gamma_i^*, p\gamma \hookrightarrow p'\omega' \triangleright p_2\omega_2\theta_2 \in \Delta_i\}$.

For an SM-DPDS $\mathcal{P}_i$ and a set of DCLICs $D \subseteq \mathcal{D}_i$, we define the *successor operator* $\xRightarrow{D}_i$ on a pair of local configurations of $\mathcal{P}_i$ as follows: $(\langle p, \omega\rangle, \theta) \xRightarrow{D}_i (\langle p', \omega'\rangle, \theta')$ means that a process at the configuration $(\langle p, \omega\rangle, \theta)$ can transition into the configuration $(\langle p', \omega'\rangle, \theta')$ by applying one of the rules in the current phase θ and the rule applied spawns processes with DCLICs D. Formally, $(\langle p, \omega\rangle, \theta) \xRightarrow{D}_i (\langle p', \omega'\rangle, \theta')$ iff one of these conditions holds:

1. $\exists \gamma \in \Gamma_i, u, v \in \Gamma_i^*$, s.t. $\omega = \gamma u$, $\omega' = vu$, $\theta = \theta'$, $D = \emptyset$, and $p\gamma \hookrightarrow p'v \in \theta$, or
2. $\omega = \gamma u$, $\omega' = vu$, $\theta = \theta'$, $D = \{p_2\omega_2\theta_2\}$, and $p\gamma \hookrightarrow p'v \triangleright p_2\omega_2\theta_2 \in \theta$, or
3. $\omega = \omega'$, $D = \emptyset$, $p \xrightarrow{(\rho_1,\rho_2)} p' \in \theta$, $\rho_1 \subseteq \theta$, $\theta' = (\theta \backslash \rho_1) \cup \rho_2$.

Intuitively, condition 1 specifies that if the process is at the local configuration $(\langle p, \gamma u\rangle, \theta)$, such that the rule $p\gamma \hookrightarrow p'v$ is in the current phase θ, then the process can pop γ from the stack, push v onto it, and transition to the state p' without spawning any new process, getting $(\langle p', vu\rangle, \theta)$. Condition 2 means that if the process is at the local configuration $(\langle p, \gamma u\rangle, \theta)$, such that the current phase θ contains a rule $p\gamma \hookrightarrow p'v \triangleright p_2\omega_2\theta_2$, then it can pop γ from the top of the stack, push v, go to p', getting $(\langle p', vu\rangle, \theta)$, and also spawn a new process with the DCLIC $p_2\omega_2\theta_2$, i.e. starting at local configuration $((\langle p_2, \omega_2\rangle, \theta_2)$. Condition 3 defines that if the process is at the local configuration $((\langle p, \omega\rangle, \theta)$, such that the rule $p \xhookrightarrow{(\rho_1,\rho_2)} p'$ is in the current phase θ, the process can remove all rules $r_1 \in \rho_1$ from the phase θ and add all rules $r_2 \in \rho_2$ to θ, changing the current state to p', getting $((\langle p', \omega\rangle, \theta')$, such that $\theta' = (\theta \backslash \rho_1) \cup \rho_2$.

For local configurations $c, c' \in Conf_i$ and set of DCLICs $D \subseteq \mathcal{D}_i$, we define a reflexive-transitive closure $c \xRightarrow{D}_i^* c'$ as follows, where $c'' \in Conf_i$ and $D', D'' \subseteq \mathcal{D}_i$: (1) $c \xRightarrow{\emptyset}_i^* c$ and (2) if $c \xRightarrow{D'}_i c'$ and $c' \xRightarrow{D''}_i^* c''$, then $c \xRightarrow{D}_i^* c''$, where $D = D' \cup D''$. We also define the non-reflexive transitive closure $c \xRightarrow{D}_i^+ c'$ as follows: $c \xRightarrow{D}_i^+ c'$ iff $\exists D', D'' \subseteq \mathcal{D}_i$, such that $D = D' \cup D''$, $c \xRightarrow{D'}_i c''$ and $c'' \xRightarrow{D''}_i^* c'$.

Consider an arbitrary set of pairs of local configurations and sets of DCLICs $W \subseteq Conf_i \times 2^{\mathcal{D}_i}$. Let $pre : 2^{Conf_i \times 2^{\mathcal{D}_i}} \rightarrow 2^{Conf_i \times 2^{\mathcal{D}_i}}$ be such that $pre(W) = \{(c, D \cup D'), c \in Conf_i \mid \exists D \subseteq \mathcal{D}_i, (c', D') \in W : c \xRightarrow{D}_i c'\}$. Let pre^+ and pre^* be the transitive and reflexive-transitive closures of pre, respectively. In other words, pre takes a pair of a local configuration and a set of DCLICs, and returns a set of predecessors of the given configurations paired with a superset of the given DCLICs that will be generated by the predecessors.

A *local run* of $\mathcal{P}_i$ is a possibly infinite sequence of local configurations $c_0c_1\ldots$, s.t. $\forall j \geq 0 : \exists D \subseteq \mathcal{D}_i : c_j \xRightarrow{D}_i c_{j+1}$. A *global run* σ starting from a global configuration $g_0 = c_0^0c_0^1c_0^2 \ldots c_0^m$, $m \geq 0$, is a (potentially infinite) set of local runs. Initially, σ contains local runs for m given processes, with each starting from initial local configuration c_0^i for $0 \leq i \leq m$. Whenever an SM-DPDS responsible for a local run spawns a new process with the DCLIC $p_2\omega_2\theta_2$, a local run starting from $((\langle p_2, \omega_2\rangle, \theta_2)$ is added to σ. From now on, we will omit the index i for $\xRightarrow{D}_i$ when it is understood from the context.

2.3 From SM-DPN to DPN

We show in this section that every SM-DPN model is equivalent to a non self-modifying DPN. Since the number of phases is finite, we can show that encoding every phase into the state set gives an equivalent DPN. Our translation follows the logic of the translation given in [19].

Let $\mathcal{M} = (\mathcal{P}_1, \mathcal{P}_2, \ldots, \mathcal{P}_n)$ be an SM-DPN for $n \in \mathbb{N}$, such that for $i \leq n$, $\mathcal{P}_i = (P_i, \Gamma_i, \Delta_i, \Delta_i^c)$ is an SM-DPDS. We can construct an equivalent DPN $\mathcal{M}' = (\mathcal{P}_1', \mathcal{P}_2', \ldots, \mathcal{P}_n')$, where for $i \leq n$, $\mathcal{P}_i' = (P_i', \Gamma_i, \Delta_i')$ is a DPDS equivalent to $\mathcal{P}_i$, such that $P_i' = P_i \times 2^{\Delta_i \cup \Delta_i^c}$ and Δ_i' is computed as follows. Initially, Δ_i' is empty. For every $r \in \Delta_i \cup \Delta_i^c$ and for every phase $\theta \in 2^{\Delta_i \cup \Delta_i^c}$, such that $r \in \theta$:

1. if $r = p\gamma \hookrightarrow p_1\omega_1$, then add $(p, \theta)\gamma \hookrightarrow (p_1, \theta)\omega_1 \in \Delta_i'$;
2. if $r = p\gamma \hookrightarrow p_1\omega_1 \triangleright p_2\omega_2\theta_2$, then add $(p, \theta)\gamma \hookrightarrow (p_1, \theta)\omega_1 \triangleright (p_2, \theta_2)\omega_2 \in \Delta_i'$;
3. if $r = p \xhookrightarrow{(\rho_1,\rho_2)} p_1$ and $\rho_1 \subseteq \theta$, then for every $\gamma \in \Gamma$, add $(p, \theta)\gamma \hookrightarrow (p_1, (\theta \backslash \rho_1) \cup \rho_2)\gamma \in \Delta_i'$.

This algorithm terminates because we have a finite number of rules and hence, a finite number of phases. We can show that:

Proposition 1. *Let* $(\langle p, \omega\rangle, \theta)$ *and* $(\langle p_1, \omega_1\rangle, \theta_1)$ *be configurations of* $\mathcal{P}_i$*, and* $D \subseteq \mathcal{D}_i$*.* $(\langle p, \omega\rangle, \theta) \xRightarrow{D}_{\mathcal{M}} (\langle p_1, \omega_1\rangle, \theta_1)$ *iff* $\langle (p, \theta), \omega\rangle \xRightarrow{D'}_{\mathcal{M}'} \langle (p_1, \theta_1), \omega_1\rangle$*, such that* $D' = \{(p_2, \theta_2)\omega_2 \mid p_2\omega_2\theta_2 \in D\}$*.*

Thus, we get:

Theorem 1. *Let* $\mathcal{M} = (\mathcal{P}_1, \mathcal{P}_2, \dots, \mathcal{P}_n)$ *be an SM-DPN for* $n \in \mathbb{N}$*, such that for* $i \leq n$*,* $\mathcal{P}_i = (P_i, \Gamma_i, \Delta_i, \Delta_i^c)$ *is an SM-DPDS. We can construct an equivalent DPN* $\mathcal{M}' = (\mathcal{P}_1', \mathcal{P}_2', \dots, \mathcal{P}_n')$*, where for* $i \leq n$*,* $\mathcal{P}_i' = (P_i', \Gamma_i, \Delta_i')$ *such that* $O(|P_i'|) = |P_i| \cdot 2^{O(|\Delta_i| + |\Delta_i^c|)}$ *and* $O(|\Delta_i'|) = (|\Delta_i| + |\Delta_i^c||\Gamma|) \cdot 2^{O(|\Delta_i| + |\Delta_i^c|)}$*.*

2.4 Modelling Self-modifying Concurrent Code with SM-DPN

We give in this section a general process of converting a binary executable containing self-modifying code and concurrency into an SM-DPN. We suppose that we have an oracle that translates a binary program into a Control Flow Graph (CFG), such that each CFG transition corresponds to one instruction. One can obtain such an oracle using existing tools like Jakstab [18], IDA Pro [15], Radare2 [2], or ANGR [23].

We use the translation of [24] that models non self-modifying *sequential* instructions of the program by a standard PDS. We concentrate here on the translation of self-modifying and spawning instructions. For more details on the translation for sequential instructions, we refer the reader to [24].

If a CFG transition spawns a new thread, we add a rule $p\gamma \hookrightarrow p'\omega \rhd p_2\omega_2\theta_2$, where $(\langle p_2, \omega_2\rangle, \theta)$ is the initial configuration of the newly created process.

A self-modifying CFG transition that writes a binary value $\mathtt{v}$ to an address $\mathtt{d}$, where $\mathtt{d}$ is the destination address for an executable region and $\mathtt{v}$ is a new value, is translated as follows: let ρ_1 be the set of SM-DPN rules obtained by our translation from instructions at $\mathtt{d}$ before self-modification and let ρ_2 be the set of SM-DPN rules obtained by our translation at $\mathtt{d}$ after the memory is modified. Suppose the CFG transition starts at control location p and leads to a control location p'. In this case, we add a rule $p \xhookrightarrow{(\rho_1, \rho_2)} p'$ to the SM-DPN model.

2.5 LTL and Büchi Automata

In this section, we consider standard LTL formulas and Büchi Automata. Let AP be a set of atomic propositions.

Definition 2. *An LTL formula* ψ *is defined as follows (where* $a \in AP$*):*

$$\psi ::= \top \mid \bot \mid a \mid \neg\psi \mid \psi \wedge \psi \mid \boldsymbol{X}\psi \mid \psi \boldsymbol{U} \psi$$

Let $w = \alpha_0\alpha_1\alpha_2\ldots$ be an ω-word over 2^{AP} and ψ be an LTL formula. Let $w^i = \alpha_i\alpha_{i+1}\ldots$ be the subsequence of w starting from the i-th symbol, where $i \geq 0$. The satisfaction $w \models \psi$ is defined as follows: $w \models \top$; $w \not\models \bot$; $w \models a$ iff $a \in \alpha_0$; $w \models \neg\psi$ iff $w \not\models \psi$; $w \models \psi_1 \wedge \psi_2$ iff $w \models \psi_1$ and $w \models \psi_2$; $w \models \mathbf{X}\psi$ iff $w^1 \models \psi$; $w \models \psi_1\mathbf{U}\psi_2$ iff there exists $k \geq 0$ such that for $j < k$, $w^j \models \psi_1$, and $w^k \models \psi_2$. We define the *eventually* operator as follows: $\mathbf{F}\psi = \top\mathbf{U}\psi$, which means that ψ will hold at some point of the run. The *globally* operator $\mathbf{G}\psi = \neg\mathbf{F}\neg\psi$ means that ψ holds universally along the run.

Definition 3. *A Büchi Automaton (BA) is a tuple $\mathcal{B} = (G, \Sigma, T, g_0, F)$, where G is a finite set of states, $T \subseteq G \times \Sigma \times G$ is the set of transitions, $g_0 \in G$ is the initial state, and $F \subseteq G$ is the set of accepting states.*

For an ω-word $w = \alpha_0\alpha_1\alpha_2\ldots$, such that $\alpha_i \in \Sigma, i \geq 0$, a *run* on a BA $\mathcal{B}$ is an infinite sequence $r = g_0g_1g_2\ldots$, such that $(g_{i-1}, \alpha_{i-1}, g_i) \in T$ for $i \geq 1$. A run r is *accepting* if it visits some accepting states in F infinitely often. $\mathcal{B}$ accepts an infinite word iff there is an accepting run on $\mathcal{B}$. It is well known that given an LTL formula ψ, we can construct a Büchi Automaton (BA) $\mathcal{B}_\psi$ on words over $\Sigma = 2^{AP}$ that accepts all ω-words that satisfy ψ [28].

2.6 Single-Indexed LTL for SM-DPNs

Let $AP = AP_1 \cup AP_2 \cup \cdots \cup AP_n$ be a set of atomic propositions, such that AP_i is the set of atomic propositions for process $\mathcal{P}_i$, $1 \leq i \leq n$ (for $i \neq j$, $AP_i \cap AP_j = \emptyset$).

Definition 4. *A single-indexed LTL formula is a formula of the form $f = \bigwedge_{i=1}^{n} f_i$, where f_i is a standard LTL formula over AP_i.*

Let us consider an SM-DPN $\mathcal{M} = (\mathcal{P}_1, \mathcal{P}_2, \ldots, \mathcal{P}_n)$, where $\mathcal{P}_i = (P_i, \Gamma_i, \Delta_i, \Delta_i^c)$, $1 \leq i \leq n$, and a single-indexed LTL formula $f = \bigwedge_{i=1}^{n} f_i$ over AP, where f_i is an LTL formula over AP_i for $\mathcal{P}_i$, and let λ_i be a labelling function $\lambda_i : P_i \to 2^{AP_i}$. For each control location $p \in \bigcup_{i=1}^{n} P_i$, let $\pi(p)$ be a function that maps p to the index i of its corresponding SM-DPDS, i.e. $\pi(p) = i$ if $p \in P_i$. For a local run $\sigma = (\langle p_0, \omega_0\rangle, \theta_0)(\langle p_1, \omega_1\rangle, \theta_1)\ldots$, let $\pi(\sigma) = \pi(p_0)$. Let $\tau = \sigma_0\sigma_1\ldots$ be a global run on $\mathcal{M}$, where for $j \geq 0$, σ_j is a local run in τ. We define the satisfaction condition for a global run $\tau = \sigma_0\sigma_1\ldots$ on SM-DPN $\mathcal{M}$ and a single-indexed LTL formula f as follows:

Definition 5. *For a local run of $\mathcal{P}_i$ $\sigma = (\langle p_0, \omega_0\rangle, \theta_0)(\langle p_1, \omega_1\rangle, \theta_1)\ldots$ and a set of DCLICs $D \subseteq \mathcal{D}_i$, we say that $\sigma \models_D f_i$ if the ω-word $w = \lambda_i(p_0)\lambda_i(p_1)\ldots$ satisfies f_i and σ spawns D. For a local configuration c, $c \models_D f_i$ if $\mathcal{P}_i$ has a local run $\sigma_c = cc_2c_3\ldots$, such that $\sigma_c \models_D f_i$.*
For a global run $\tau = \sigma_0\sigma_1\ldots$, we say that $\tau \models f$ if for every local run $\sigma_j \in \tau$, where $j \geq 0$:

1. *there exists $D_j = \{p_j^0\omega_j^0\theta_j^0, p_j^1\omega_j^1\theta_j^1, \ldots, p_j^m\omega_j^m\theta_j^m\}$, such that $\sigma_j \models_{D_j} f_{\pi(\sigma_j)}$,*

2. *for every* $0 \leq k \leq m$ *there exists a local run* σ_j^k *starting from* $(\langle p_j^k, \omega_j^k \rangle, \theta_j^k)$, *such that* $\sigma_j^k \models f$.

In other words, a global run $\tau = \sigma_0 \sigma_1 \ldots$ satisfies a single-indexed LTL formula f if every local run σ in τ satisfies $f_{\pi(\sigma)}$ and if for every local run σ_j^k spawned during σ, σ_j^k satisfies f.

3 LTL Model-Checking for SM-DPNs

From now on, we fix an SM-DPN $\mathcal{M} = (\mathcal{P}_1, \mathcal{P}_2, \ldots, \mathcal{P}_n)$, where for $1 \leq i \leq n$, $\mathcal{P}_i = (P_i, \Gamma_i, \Delta_i, \Delta_i^c)$ is an SM-DPDS, and a single-indexed LTL formula $f = \bigwedge_{i=1}^{n} f_i$, such that f_i is an LTL formula over atomic propositions AP_i corresponding to $\mathcal{P}_i$. Let $\mathcal{B}_i = (G_i, 2^{AP_i}, T_i, g_i^0, F_i)$ be a Büchi automaton for the corresponding LTL formula f_i. Model checking a global configuration $\mathcal{G}$ of $\mathcal{M}$ over f is not trivial for two reasons. First, it is not enough to check every local run starting from local configurations in $\mathcal{G}$, because we also need to check spawned processes. Second, model checking every possibly spawned process is too restrictive, because not all processes are required to be spawned during an accepting run, so even if they violate their LTL formulas, a global run would still be accepting if it does not spawn such processes. Therefore, when model checking $\mathcal{P}_i$ over f_i, it is important to remember which processes were spawned during the accepting run. We divide the problem of checking whether a global run starting from $\mathcal{G}$ satisfies f into the following steps:

1. We compute a Self-Modifying Büchi Dynamic Pushdown System $\mathcal{BP}_i$ for each pair of $\mathcal{P}_i$ and $\mathcal{B}_i$, $1 \leq i \leq n$, which corresponds to a kind of synchronization between the SM-DPDS $\mathcal{P}_i$ and the LTL formula f_i.
2. For each $\mathcal{BP}_i$, we compute the set of pairs of local configurations and DCLICs of the form (c, D), such that $c \models_D f_i$. For this, we need to be able to finitely represent potentially infinite sets of such pairs. To this aim, we use a kind of finite automata. Then, we perform a kind of reachability analysis on $\mathcal{BP}_i$ and construct a finite automaton $\mathcal{A}_i$, that accepts all pairs (c, D) for a configuration c and set of DCLICs D spawned during the run of $\mathcal{P}_i$ from c satisfying f_i, i.e. $c \models_D f_i$.
3. Using the automata $\mathcal{A}_i$, we compute the maximal set of DCLICs $\mathcal{D}_{fp}$, such that it contains only DCLICs for local configurations that satisfy their LTL formulas, and that the accepting runs on that configurations spawn only DCLICs in $\mathcal{D}_{fp}$.
4. For every local configuration $(\langle p, \omega \rangle, \theta) \in \mathcal{G}$, we use the automaton $\mathcal{A}_{\pi(p)}$ to check that there exists $D' \subseteq \mathcal{D}_{fp}$, such that $(\langle p, \omega \rangle, \theta) \models_{D'} f_{\pi(p)}$.

These different steps are detailed in the following sections.

3.1 Self-Modifying Büchi Dynamic Pushdown Systems

We compute a Self-Modifying Büchi Dynamic Pushdown System (SM-BDPDS) as a product of an SM-DPDS and a BA:

Definition 6. *A Self-Modifying Büchi Dynamic Pushdown System is an SM-DPDS $\mathcal{BP} = (P, \Gamma, \Delta, \Delta^c, I, F)$ with extra elements $I \subseteq P$, which is a set of initial states, and $F \subseteq P$, which is a set of accepting states.*

Let $\mathcal{BP} = (P, \Gamma, \Delta, \Delta^c, I, F)$ be an SM-BDPDS, $c_0 = (\langle p_0, \omega_0\rangle, \theta_0)$ be a local configuration and D be a set of DCLICs. (c_0, D) is accepted by $\mathcal{BP}$ iff $p_0 \in I$ and there is a local run $\sigma = c_0c_1c_2\ldots$ in $\mathcal{BP}$, such that $\mathcal{BP}$ spawns new processes with DCLICs D during σ and there is an infinite subsequence of configurations $c_{k_0}c_{k_1}\ldots$, where $c_{k_j} = (\langle p_{k_j}, \omega_{k_j}\rangle, \theta_{k_j})$ for $j \geq 0$ and $p_{k_j} \in F$. We denote by $\mathcal{L}(\mathcal{BP})$ the pairs of all configurations and DCLICs in the form (c, D) accepted by $\mathcal{BP}$, where c is a configuration and D is a set of DCLICs.

For an SM-DPDS $\mathcal{P}_i = (P_i, \Gamma_i, \Delta_i, \Delta_i^c)$, a BA $\mathcal{B}_i = (G, 2^{AP_i}, T, g_0, F)$ that corresponds to an LTL formula f_i, and a labelling function λ_i, we can compute an SM-BDPDS $\mathcal{BP}_i = (P_i', \Gamma_i, \Delta_i', \Delta_i^{c'}, I_i', F_i')$, where $P_i' = P_i \times G$, $I_i' = P_i \times \{g_0\}$, and $F_i' = P_i \times F$. Let $p, p_1, \in P_i$, $g_1, g_2 \in G_i$, $\gamma \in \Gamma$, $\omega_1 \in \Gamma^*$, $\rho_1, \rho_2 \subseteq \Delta_i \cup \Delta_i^c$, $p_2 \in P_j$, $\omega_2 \in \Gamma_j^*$, $\theta_2 \in 2^{\Delta_j \cup \Delta_j^c}$. Let $prod_{\mathcal{B}_i}(\delta)$ be a set of rules of $\mathcal{BP}_i$ obtained by applying the following procedure, where $\delta \subseteq \Delta_i \cup \Delta_i^c$:

1. $[p, g_1]\gamma \hookrightarrow [p_1, g_2]\omega_1 \in prod_{\mathcal{B}_i}(\delta)$ iff $p\gamma \hookrightarrow p_1\omega_1 \in \delta$ and $(g_1, \lambda_i(p), g_2) \in T_i$,
2. $[p, g_1]\gamma \hookrightarrow [p_1, g_2]\omega_1 \rhd p_2\omega_2\theta_2 \in prod_{\mathcal{B}_i}(\delta)$ iff $p\gamma \hookrightarrow p_1\omega_1 \rhd p_2\omega_2\theta_2 \in \delta$ and $(g_1, \lambda_i(p), g_2) \in T_i$,
3. $[p, g_1] \xhookrightarrow{(\sigma_1,\sigma_2)} [p_1, g_2] \in prod_{\mathcal{B}_i}(\delta)$ iff $p \xhookrightarrow{(\rho_1,\rho_2)} p_1 \in \delta$, $(g_1, \lambda_i(p), g_2) \in T_i$, $\sigma_1 = prod_{\mathcal{B}_i}(\rho_1)$, and $\sigma_2 = prod_{\mathcal{B}_i}(\rho_2)$.

We construct rules for $\mathcal{BP}_i$ as follows: $\Delta_i' = prod_{\mathcal{B}_i}(\Delta_i)$ and $\Delta_i^{c'} = prod_{\mathcal{B}_i}(\Delta_i^c)$. Intuitively, $\mathcal{BP}_i$ is a product of $\mathcal{P}_i$ and the BA $\mathcal{B}_i$. The behavior of the constructed SM-BDPDS $\mathcal{BP}_i$ is the same as of $\mathcal{P}_i$ synchronized with $\mathcal{B}_i$ for the LTL formula f_i. The intuition behind this construction is that if there is a run on the SM-BDPDS $\sigma = (\langle [p_0, g_0], \omega_0\rangle, \theta_0)(\langle [p_1, g_1], \omega_1\rangle, \theta_1)\ldots$, then there should be a valid run $\sigma^{\mathcal{P}_i} = (\langle p_0, \omega_0\rangle, \theta_0)(\langle p_1, \omega_1\rangle, \theta_1)\ldots$ on $\mathcal{P}_i$ and a valid run $\sigma^{\mathcal{B}_i} = g_0g_1\ldots$ on $\mathcal{B}_i$. Assume the run $\sigma^{\mathcal{P}_i}$ spawns DCLICs D, then, $\sigma^{\mathcal{P}_i} \models_D f_i$ iff $(((\langle [p_0, g_0], \omega_0\rangle, \theta_0), D) \in \mathcal{L}(\mathcal{BP}_i)$.

3.2 Characterizing $\mathcal{L}(\mathcal{BP}_i)$ Using Reachability

We show in this sections how $\mathcal{L}(\mathcal{BP}_i)$ can be computed by performing a kind of reachability analysis.

Theorem 2. *For an SM-BDPDS $\mathcal{BP}_i = (P_i', \Gamma_i, \Delta_i', \Delta_i^{c'}, I_i, F_i)$, a local configuration $(\langle p, \omega\rangle, \theta)$ and a set of DCLICs D, $(((\langle p, \omega\rangle, \theta), D) \in \mathcal{L}(\mathcal{BP}_i)$ iff $p \in I_i$ and $\exists D_1, D_2, D_3 \subseteq \mathcal{D}_i$, s.t. $D = D_1 \cup D_2 \cup D_3$ and the following conditions hold:*

α_1 *$(\langle p, \omega\rangle, \theta) \xRightarrow{D_1}{}^* (\langle p', \gamma\omega'\rangle, \theta')$ for some $p' \in P_i'$, $\theta, \theta' \subseteq (\Delta_i' \cup \Delta_i^{c'})$, $\gamma \in \Gamma_i$, $\omega' \in \Gamma^*$, and*

α_2 *$(\langle p', \gamma\rangle, \theta') \xRightarrow{D_2}{}^+ (\langle g, u\rangle, \theta'')$ and $(\langle g, u\rangle, \theta'') \xRightarrow{D_3}{}^* (\langle p', \gamma v\rangle, \theta')$ for some $g \in F_i$, $\theta'' \subseteq (\Delta_i' \cup \Delta_i^{c'})$, $u, v \in \Gamma^*$.*

Let us explain the intuition behind the theorem. Since $\big(((\langle p,\omega\rangle,\theta),D\big) \in \mathcal{L}(\mathcal{BP}_i)$, there must be an infinite sequence of local configurations with an accepting state g. This sequence is produced by an infinite cycle starting from some $(\langle p',\gamma\rangle,\theta')$, visiting $(\langle g,u\rangle,\theta'')$, and then going to $(\langle p',\gamma v\rangle,\theta')$. Since rules of $\mathcal{BP}_i$ only look at the top symbol of the stack content, $\mathcal{BP}_i$ can apply the same rules on $(\langle p',\gamma v\rangle,\theta')$ and end up at $(\langle p',\gamma vv\rangle,\theta')$ and so on. During this cycle, $\mathcal{BP}_i$ spawns processes with DCLICs $D_2 \cup D_3$ (D_2 to reach $(\langle g,u\rangle,\theta'')$ and D_3 to go back). This is ensured by the condition α_1. Moreover, the starting state $(\langle p,\omega\rangle,\theta)$ must be backwards reachable from $(\langle p',\gamma\rangle,\theta')$, which is ensured by the condition α_1. Assume that $\mathcal{BP}_i$ spawns processes with DCLICs D_1 along the path from $(\langle p,\omega\rangle,\theta)$ to $(\langle p',\gamma\rangle,\theta')$. Therefore, $\mathcal{BP}_i$ spawns $D_1 \cup D_2 \cup D_3$ during the accepting run and hence, $\big((\langle p,\omega\rangle,\theta),D\big)$ is accepted by $\mathcal{BP}_i$.

Corollary 1. *For an SM-BDPDS $\mathcal{BP}_i = (P_i', \Gamma_i, \Delta_i', \Delta_i^{c'}, I_i, F_i)$, a local configuration $(\langle p,\omega\rangle,\theta)$ and a set of DCLICs D, $\big((\langle p,\omega\rangle,\theta),D\big) \in \mathcal{L}(\mathcal{BP}_i)$ iff $p \in I_i$ and $\exists D_1, D_2' \subseteq \mathcal{D}_i$, $\exists \theta' \subseteq \Delta_i' \cup \Delta_i^{c'}$, s.t. $D = D_1 \cup D_2'$ and the following conditions hold:*

β_1 $\big((\langle p,\omega\rangle,\theta),D_1\big) \in pre^*(\{p'\} \times \gamma\Gamma_i^* \times \{\theta'\} \times \{\emptyset\})$, *and*

β_2 $\big((\langle p',\gamma\rangle,\theta'),D_2'\big) \in pre^+((F_i \times \Gamma_i^* \times 2^{\Delta_i' \cup \Delta_i^{c'}} \times 2^{\mathcal{D}_i}) \cap pre^*(\{p'\} \times \gamma\Gamma_i^* \times \{\theta'\} \times \{\emptyset\}))$.

The corollary is a rewording of Theorem 2 using *pre* notation instead of successor relationship, and where D_2' equals to $D_2 \cup D_3$. Intuitively, for the condition β_1, if $(\langle p,\omega\rangle,\theta) \xRightarrow{D_1}{}^* (\langle p',\gamma\omega'\rangle,\theta')$, then $\big((\langle p,\omega\rangle,\theta),D_1\big) \in pre^*(\{p'\} \times \gamma\Gamma_i^* \times \{\theta'\} \times \{\emptyset\})$. And for condition β_2, if $(\langle g,u\rangle,\theta'') \xRightarrow{D_3}{}^* (\langle p',\gamma v\rangle,\theta')$, then $\big((\langle g,u\rangle,\theta''),D_3\big) \in (F_i \times \Gamma_i^* \times 2^{\Delta_i' \cup \Delta_i^{c'}} \times 2^{\mathcal{D}_i}) \cap pre^*(\{p'\} \times \gamma\Gamma_i^* \times \{\theta'\} \times \{\emptyset\})$. And since $(\langle p',\gamma\rangle,\theta') \xRightarrow{D_2}{}^+ (\langle g,u\rangle,\theta'')$, then $\big((\langle p',\gamma\rangle,\theta'),D_2'\big)$ is in pre^+ of all such $\big((\langle g,u\rangle,\theta''),D_3\big)$, where $D_2' = D_2 \cup D_3$.

Thus, computing $\mathcal{L}(\mathcal{BP}_i)$ boils down to finding pre^* of regular sets of pairs of local configurations and DCLICs of an SM-DPDS.

3.3 Multi Automata

As explained previously, we need to compute pre^* of regular sets of local configurations and DCLICs. For this, we need to be able to finitely represent potentially infinite sets of such pairs. Following [25], we use *Multi Automata* (MA) to represent sets of local configurations and DCLICs of SM-DPDS. Note that our definition of MA extends the standard one introduced in [14] by encoding the current *phase* into the state set, and labelling each transition with DCLICs to track which processes were spawned.

Definition 7. *A Multi-Automaton is a tuple $\mathcal{A}_i = (Q_i, \Gamma_i, \delta_i, I_i, Acc_i)$, where Q_i is a finite set of states, Γ_i is the alphabet of $\mathcal{P}_i$, $\delta_i \subseteq Q_i \times (\Gamma_i \cup \{\varepsilon\}) \times 2^{\mathcal{D}_i} \times Q_i$ is a set of transitions, $I_i = P_i \times 2^{\Delta_i \cup \Delta_i^c} \subseteq Q_i$ is a set of initial states representing* *the control point and the phase of the configuration, and* $Acc_i \subseteq Q_i$ *is a set of accepting states. Transition* $(q, \gamma, D, q') \in \delta_i$ *can be denoted as* $q \xrightarrow{\gamma/D}_i q'$.

The reflexive-transitive closure $q \xrightarrow{\omega/D}{}^*_i q'$ for transitions is defined as: (1) $q \xrightarrow{\varepsilon/\emptyset}{}^*_i q$, (2) if $q \xrightarrow{\gamma/D}_i q''$ and $q'' \xrightarrow{\omega/D'}{}^*_i q'$, then $q \xrightarrow{\gamma\omega/D\cup D'}{}^*_i q'$, where $\omega \in \Gamma_i^*$, $D' \subseteq \mathcal{D}_i$.

For a local configuration $(\langle p, \omega\rangle, \theta)$ and a set of DCLICs D, the MA accepts tuples $\big((\langle p, \omega\rangle, \theta), D\big)$ iff there is a path $(p, \theta) \xrightarrow{\omega/D}{}^*_i q_f$ for some $q_f \in Acc_i$. From now on, we will omit the index i for $\rightarrow_i$ when it is understood from the context.

Let $\mathcal{L}(\mathcal{A}_i)$ be the set of configurations and DCLICs accepted by the MA $\mathcal{A}_i$. We say that a set of configurations and DCLICs W is *regular* iff there exists a MA $\mathcal{A}_i$, such that $W = \mathcal{L}(\mathcal{A}_i)$.

3.4 Algorithm for *pre** Computation

We prove in this section that given an SM-DPDS $\mathcal{P}_i$ and a regular set of pairs of configurations and DCLICs W accepted by a MA $\mathcal{A}_i$, we can compute a new MA $\mathcal{A}_i^{pre^*}$ that accepts $pre^*(W)$ using the following saturation procedure. Let $\mathcal{A}_i = (Q_i, \Gamma_i \cup \{\varepsilon\}, \delta_i, I_i, Acc_i)$ be the original MA that accepts configurations of an SM-DPDS $\mathcal{P}_i = (P_i, \Gamma_i, \Delta_i, \Delta_i^c)$.

Without loss of generality, we assume that the SM-DPDS has no rules that remove themselves. I.e., there are no rules of type $r = p \xhookrightarrow{(\rho_1,\rho_2)} p' \in \Delta_i^c$, such that $r \in \rho_1$. This is not a restriction since we can substitute such rules with two rules: $r = p \xhookrightarrow{(\emptyset,\emptyset)} p^r$ and $r' = p^r \xhookrightarrow{(\rho_1,\rho_2)} p'$, where r' is a new rule and p^r is a new state. Moreover, we assume w.l.o.g. that δ_i has no transitions into initial states, i.e. there exists no transitions of the form $q \xrightarrow{\gamma/D} (p, \theta)$ in δ_i, for any $q \in Q_i$, $\gamma \in \Gamma_i$, $D \subseteq \mathcal{D}_i$, $(p, \theta) \in I_i$.

Now, we can construct $\mathcal{A}_i^{pre^*} = (Q_i, \Gamma_i, \delta_i', I_i, Acc_i)$. Initially, $\delta_i' = \delta_i$. Then, we apply the following saturation rules:

μ_1 If $r = p\gamma \hookrightarrow p'\omega \in \Delta_i$, then for every $\theta \in 2^{\Delta_i \cup \Delta_i^c}$, s.t. $r \in \theta$ and $(p', \theta) \xrightarrow{\omega/D}{}^* q \in \delta_i'$, add transition $(p, \theta) \xrightarrow{\gamma/D} q$ to δ_i';

μ_2 if $r = p\gamma \hookrightarrow p'\omega \rhd p''\omega''\theta'' \in \Delta_i$, then for every $\theta \in 2^{\Delta_i \cup \Delta_i^c}$, s.t. $r \in \theta$ and $(p', \theta) \xrightarrow{\omega/D}{}^* q \in \delta_i'$, add transition $(p, \theta) \xrightarrow{\gamma/D\cup\{p''\omega''\theta''\}} q$ to δ_i';

μ_3 If $r = p \xhookrightarrow{(\rho_1,\rho_2)} p' \in \Delta_i^c$, then for every $\theta' \in 2^{\Delta_i \cup \Delta_i^c}$ and $\gamma \in \Gamma_i$, s.t. $r \in \theta'$, $\rho_2 \subseteq \theta'$ and $(p', \theta') \xrightarrow{\gamma/D} q$, then add $(p, \theta) \xrightarrow{\gamma/D} q$ to δ_i', such that $\theta' = (\theta \backslash \rho_1) \cup \rho_2$.

This procedure terminates because there is a finite number of transitions we can add, which is $|(P_i \times 2^{\Delta_i \cup \Delta_i^c}) \cup Q_i|^2 |\Gamma \cup \{\varepsilon\}||2^{\mathcal{D}_i}|$.

Let us explain the intuition behind the saturation rules. Rule μ_1 adds predecessors obtained from standard pushdown rules. Consider a rule $r = p\gamma \hookrightarrow p'\omega \in$

Δ_i and let us consider a path of $\mathcal{A}_i^{pre^*}$ of the form $(p', \theta) \xrightarrow{\omega/D}{}^* q \xrightarrow{\omega'/D'}{}^* q_f$ such that $q_f \in Acc_i$ and $r \in \theta$, which means $\big(((p', \omega\omega'), \theta), D \cup D'\big) \in \mathcal{L}(\mathcal{A}_i^{pre^*})$. Since the phase θ contains r, then $(\langle p, \gamma\omega'\rangle, \theta)$ is a direct predecessor of $(\langle p', \omega\omega'\rangle, \theta)$. Since r does not spawn new processes, there is no need to update the DCLICs D. Therefore, we add the new transition $(p, \theta) \xrightarrow{\gamma/D} q$ to $\mathcal{A}_i^{pre^*}$, so that $\big((\langle p, \gamma\omega'\rangle, \theta), D \cup D'\big)$ will be accepted by the path $(p, \theta) \xrightarrow{\gamma/D} q \xrightarrow{\omega'/D'}{}^* q_f$ in $\mathcal{A}_i^{pre^*}$.

Similarly, rule μ_2 adds predecessors that require a process to be spawned. In this case, consider a rule $r = p\gamma \hookrightarrow p'\omega \triangleright p''\omega''\theta'' \in \Delta_i$ and let there be a path of the form $(p', \theta) \xrightarrow{\omega/D}{}^* q \xrightarrow{\omega'/D'}{}^* q_f$ such that $q_f \in Acc_i$ and $r \in \theta$. Therefore, $\big((\langle p', \omega\omega'\rangle, \theta), D \cup D'\big) \in \mathcal{L}(\mathcal{A}_i^{pre^*})$. Since the phase θ contains r, then $(\langle p, \gamma\omega'\rangle, \theta)$ is a direct predecessor of $(\langle p', \omega\omega'\rangle, \theta)$. Since r spawns a new process with the DCLIC $p''\omega''\theta''$, we add $p''\omega''\theta''$ to the DCLICs D. Therefore, we add the new transition $(p, \theta) \xrightarrow{\gamma/D \cup \{p''\omega''\theta''\}} q$, so that $\big((\langle p, \gamma\omega'\rangle, \theta), D \cup D' \cup \{p''\omega''\theta''\}\big)$ will be accepted by the path $(p, \theta) \xrightarrow{\gamma/D \cup \{p''\omega''\theta''\}} q \xrightarrow{\omega'/D'}{}^* q_f$.

The saturation rule μ_3 adds the predecessors that are obtained by self-modifying rules. Consider a rule $r = p \xhookrightarrow{(\rho_1, \rho_2)} p' \in \Delta_i^c$ and a path in $\mathcal{A}_i^{pre^*}$ of the form $(p', \theta') \xrightarrow{\gamma/D} q \xrightarrow{\omega/D'}{}^* q_f$, such that $q_f \in Acc_i$, $r \in \theta'$, $\rho_2 \subseteq \theta'$. Therefore, $\big((\langle p', \gamma\omega\rangle, \theta'), D \cup D'\big) \in \mathcal{L}(\mathcal{A}_i^{pre^*})$. Since the phase θ' contains r and all rules in ρ_2, then $(\langle p, \gamma\omega\rangle, \theta)$ is a direct predecessor of $(\langle p', \gamma\omega\rangle, \theta')$, where $\theta = (\theta' \backslash \rho_2) \cup \rho_1$. Since this transition does not spawn any new processes, there is no need to update DCLICs D. Therefore, we add the new transition $(p, \theta) \xrightarrow{\gamma/D} q$ to $\mathcal{A}_i^{pre^*}$, so that $\big((\langle p, \gamma\omega\rangle, \theta), D \cup D'\big)$ will be accepted by the path $(p, \theta) \xrightarrow{\gamma/D} q \xrightarrow{\omega/D'}{}^* q_f$ in $\mathcal{A}_i^{pre^*}$.

We can show that the saturation algorithm described above computes MA $\mathcal{A}_i^{pre^*}$ that accepts $pre^*(\mathcal{L}(\mathcal{A}_i))$.

Lemma 1. *Given a regular set of configurations and DCLICs W recognized by MA a $\mathcal{A}_i = (Q_i, \Gamma_i, \delta_i, I_i, Acc_i)$, we can effectively compute the Multi-Automaton $\mathcal{A}_i^{pre^*} = (Q_i, \Gamma_i, \delta'_i, I_i, Acc_i)$, such that $\mathcal{L}(\mathcal{A}_i^{pre^*}) = pre^*(W)$.*

Thus, we get:

Theorem 3. *For a regular set of local configurations and DCLICs $W \subseteq P_i \times \Gamma_i^* \times 2^{\Delta_i \cup \Delta_i^c} \times 2^{\mathcal{D}_i}$, the set $pre^*(W)$ is also regular and can be effectively computed.*

3.5 Effective Algorithm for Model Checking SM-DPNs

Now, we are ready to tackle the main problem of this paper - effective LTL model checking of SM-DPNs. Using Corollary 1 and our saturation procedure, we can compute $\mathcal{L}(\mathcal{BP}_i)$ for every i, $1 \leq i \leq n$, by constructing a MA $\mathcal{A}_i$, such that $\mathcal{L}(\mathcal{A}_i) = \mathcal{L}(\mathcal{BP}_i)$. To construct $\mathcal{A}_i$, we iterate over possible $p' \in P'_i, \gamma' \in$

Γ_i, and $\theta' \subseteq \Delta'_i \cup \Delta_i^{c'}$. For every such triple, we construct the MA $\mathcal{A}_i^1$, s.t. $\mathcal{L}(\mathcal{A}_i^1) = pre^*(\{p'\} \times \{\theta'\} \times \gamma'\Gamma_i^* \times \{\emptyset\})$. Then, we compute the MA $\mathcal{A}_i^2$, s.t. $\mathcal{L}(\mathcal{A}_i^2) = (F_i \times 2^{\Delta'_i \cup \Delta_i^{c'}} \times \Gamma_i^* \times 2^{\mathcal{D}_i})$. We compute then the product $\mathcal{A}_i^3$, s.t. $\mathcal{L}(\mathcal{A}_i^3) = \mathcal{L}(\mathcal{A}_i^1) \cap \mathcal{L}(\mathcal{A}_i^2)$. After that, we construct the pre^+ of the intersection: $\mathcal{L}(\mathcal{A}_i^4) = pre^+(\mathcal{L}(\mathcal{A}_i^3)$, and test whether $(((\langle p', \gamma' \rangle, \theta'), D'_2) \in \mathcal{L}(\mathcal{A}_i^4)$ for a set of DCLICs D'_2. If the $\mathcal{A}_i^4$ automaton accepts $(((\langle p', \gamma' \rangle, \theta'), D'_2)$, then we add the transition $(p', \theta') \xrightarrow{\gamma'/D'_2} q_f$ to a MA $\mathcal{A}'_i$, where q_f is a final state. Next, we compute pre^* of $\mathcal{A}'_i$ to get the final automaton $\mathcal{A}_i$, s.t. $\mathcal{L}(\mathcal{A}_i) = pre^*(\mathcal{L}(\mathcal{A}'_i))$. From Corollary 1, this $\mathcal{A}_i$ is such that if $(c, D) \in \mathcal{L}(\mathcal{A}_i)$, then $c \models_D f_i$.

Now, we can use the constructed MAs $\mathcal{A}_i$ to model check $\mathcal{M}$. First, we need to compute the largest set of DCLICs that have an accepting run and spawn DCLICs that also have an accepting run. We call this set $\mathcal{D}_{fp}$. This set contains DCLICs that satisfy f. Let $D_I = \bigcup_{k=1}^{n} \mathcal{D}_k$ be the set of all DCLICs spawned in $\mathcal{M}$. Let $F : 2^{D_I} \to 2^{D_I}$ be defined as $F(D) = \{p\omega\theta \in D_I \mid \exists D' \subseteq D : (((\langle [p, g^0_{\pi(p)}], \omega \rangle, \theta), D') \in \mathcal{L}(\mathcal{A}_{\pi(i)})\}$. Let $D^0 D^1 D^2 \ldots$ be a sequence generated by the recursive application of F, such that $D^0 = D_I$, and $D^j = F(D^{j-1})$ for $j \geq 1$. We can show that $\mathcal{D}_{fp} = \bigcap_j D^j$ and can be effectively computed by finding the greatest fixpoint on F:

Theorem 4. *We can effectively compute* $\mathcal{D}_{fp}$*, s.t. for every DCLIC* $p\omega\theta \in \bigcup_{k=1}^{n} \mathcal{D}_k$*,* $(\langle p, \omega \rangle, \theta) \models f$ *iff* $p\omega\theta \in \mathcal{D}_{fp}$*.*

Intuitively, the function F takes a set of DCLICs D that *hypothetically* satisfy their corresponding LTL formulas. The function returns a smaller set of DCLICs D', where for every DCLIC $p'\omega'\theta' \in D'$, there exists another set of DCLICs $D'' \subseteq D$, such that $(\langle p', \omega' \rangle, \theta') \models_{D''} f_{\pi(p')}$. Initially, D^0 is the set of all DCLICs D_I. At the first step, we exclude DCLICs that cannot satisfy f regardless of what DCLICs they generate. Then, every next iteration excludes such DCLICs that spawn unsatisfiable DCLICs during their accepting runs. At the end, the function should converge at a constant set of DCLICs that satisfy f. In other words, we can compute the greatest fixpoint $\mathcal{D}_{fp}$ on the recursion starting from D_I because this function reduces a countable set of DCLICs for each step. Therefore, we can use Theorem 4 to find the set of valid DCLICs for a single-indexed LTL formula.

Now, for a global configuration $\mathcal{G} = c_0 c_1 c_2 \ldots c_m$ and a single indexed formula $f = \bigwedge_{i=1}^{n} f_i$, we can determine whether $\mathcal{G}$ satisfies f as follows: we check for each local configuration $c_j = (\langle p_j, \omega_j \rangle, \theta_j)$, if there exists $D \subseteq \mathcal{D}_{fp}$, such that $c_j \models_D f_{\pi(p_j)}$. $\mathcal{G} \models f$ iff all configurations $c_j \in \mathcal{G}$ satisfy their corresponding $f_{\pi(p_j)}$ and spawn DCLICs $D \subseteq \mathcal{D}_{fp}$.

4 Experiments

4.1 Comparison with Model Checking DPNs

Since SM-DPNs are equivalent to normal DPNs, we compared our *direct* model checking approach with the approach that consists of translating SM-DPN to

Table 1. Performance comparison of proposed algorithm to the algorithm of [25] on an equivalent DPN.

			Our approach		SM-DPN to DPN	
$\|\mathcal{M}\|$	$\|f_i\|$	$\|\Delta_i\| + \|\Delta_i^c\|$	**T**, sec	**mem**, KiB	**T**, sec	**mem**, KiB
1	5	10 + 3	0.01	63.57	0.4	1 153.93
1	6	10 + 3	3.98	236.29	2 927.27	2 017.56
1	7	10 + 3	2.87	325.34	815.80	1 232.78
1	8	10 + 3	5.29	674.29	8 894.93	2 420.37
1	5	10 + 1	0.30	63.57	7.23	134.47
1	6	10 + 1	0.10	63.57	3.11	116.18
1	**7**	**10 + 1**	**2.12**	**642.30**	**389.87**	**1 045.70**
2	1	12 + 2	1.24	71.24	21.76	561.31
2	1	22 + 2	1.53	78.41	39.49	706.41
2	**1**	**32 + 2**	**10.04**	**179.01**	**1 473.41**	**1 542.21**
2	12	32 + 2	114.78	1 433.08	timeout	timeout
3	4	31 + 3	29.19	483.58	3 586.07	10 920.32
3	5	32 + 5	0.02	72.42	4.21	41 818.15
3	5	42 + 5	1401.31	3 661.34	timeout	timeout
2	7	32 + 4	253.80	1 347.30	timeout	timeout
3	8	50 + 4	607.18	1 717.22	timeout	timeout
2	9	34 + 5	904.25	2 924.89	timeout	timeout
2	13	40 + 3	0.02	72.50	1.09	5 212.05
4	**1**	**22 + 2**	**31.92**	**476.02**	**4 644.77**	**2 492.78**
3	14	37 + 2	32.93	585.57	1 824.50	8 695.83
3	41	43 + 2	275.18	5 206.40	timeout	timeout
4	1	52 + 2	47.35	919.43	timeout	timeout
4	1	62 + 2	60.15	920.29	timeout	timeout
5	1	12 + 2	5.03	167.78	232.47	1 341.30
5	1	22 + 2	13.99	291.78	1 804.86	2 088.73
5	**2**	**102 + 2**	**151.66**	**587.85**	**10 392.94**	**3 288.55**
2	2	28 + 3	18.21	246.90	866.46	7 962.37
3	**1**	**33 + 5**	**54.72**	**400.27**	**14 310.20**	**23 819.53**
2	1	48 + 4	251.91	560.40	timeout	timeout
4	1	38 + 7	7 548.30	12 901.00	OOM	OOM
1	2	81 + 8	56 501.63	11 606.98	OOM	OOM
2	2	134 + 4	2 878.35	2 131.24	timeout	timeout
4	2	42 + 9	26 804.35	19 890.16	OOM	OOM
1	3	59 + 4	184.98	545.51	timeout	timeout
1	3	66 + 1	77.44	1 325.73	1 442.53	10 312.03
2	3	149 + 4	7 467.28	3 901.95	timeout	timeout
3	**1**	**129 + 2**	**769.27**	**3 005.60**	**151 403.08**	**52 682.78**
3	3	63 + 3	105.41	621.27	81 637.13	41 098.79
3	3	197 + 1	1 115.17	6 529.34	26 151.43	55 853.34
3	3	127 + 4	8 154.62	8 112.27	timeout	timeout
4	3	134 + 3	4 002.69	9 294.60	timeout	timeout
3	10	161 + 2	981.33	4 854.11	timeout	timeout
4	6	90 + 7	14 090.17	5 948.56	OOM	OOM

the equivalent DPN and applying the algorithm proposed by [25]. We implemented both algorithms using Python and tested them on random SM-DPNs. We summarized our results in Table 1. The column $|\mathcal{M}|$ specifies the number of SM-DPDSs in a SM-DPN, $|f_i|$ is the number of transitions in a BA corresponding to the i-th LTL formula, $|\Delta_i|$ is the number of non self-modifying rules in each SM-DPDS, $|\Delta_i^c|$ is the number of self-modifying rules in each SM-DPDS, **T** is the time taken for the algorithm and **mem** is the amount of memory used during the computation. We put *timeout* for executions longer than 10 h, and *OOM* (out-of-memory) if the computer ran out of memory resource for the computations. The experiments were conducted on a laptop with a CPU AMD Ryzen 7 8845HS and 10 GB of available memory (8 GB RAM and 2 GB swap pages).

From Table 1, we can see that our algorithm performs consistently better in terms of time and memory than translating SM-DPNs into standard DPNs and applying the LTL algorithm for standard DPNs from [25]. We highlighted some cases where our algorithm performed significantly better. For example, when an SM-DPN contains 3 processes, 129 standard rules and 2 self-modifying rules, our direct LTL model checking took 769.27 s (~13 min), while the naive approach took almost 2 days. The DPN approach timed out and required too much memory in a lot of cases, taking more than 10 h to complete. Whereas our approach could finish model checking in a few minutes for most cases.

4.2 Specifying Malicious Behaviour as Single-Indexed LTL Formulas

We evaluated the applicability of our approach for malware detection. We have collected reported malware from malware databases, such as Virus Share [10] and Malware Bazaar [1]. We consider a variant of Mirai malware and a variant of Gozi malware that are both *concurrent* and *self-modifying*. We also considered a self-modifying version of a concurrent generic backdoor.

In what follows, we describe the malicious behaviour of the mentioned malware as single-indexed LTL formulas of the form $f = \bigwedge_i f_i$. For readability, we write $[f_i]_i$ to denote that f_i describes the malicious behavior related to process i.

Mirai malware is a botnet virus that targets IoT devices running on Linux. It has two parallel processes. One process communicates with a Command and Control (C2) server. The other process evades detection and maintains persistence on the host machine. The single-indexed LTL formula for Mirai can be described as:

$$f_{Mirai} = \Big[\mathbf{F}\big(accept \wedge \mathbf{F} fork\big)\Big]_1 \wedge \Big[\mathbf{F}\big(setsid \wedge \mathbf{F} kill\big)\Big]_2$$

Intuitively, the first process waits for a command from the C2 server using the *accept* syscall and then creates a parallel process to perform malicious activity using the $fork$ syscall. The second process disguises itself as a legitimate software. First, it calls *setsid* to move itself to a new group of processes and kills the parent process by calling *kill* to avoid detection.

Gozi malware is a Windows virus that targets the banking field and steals credentials of critical systems such as banking software. The first thread tries to hide the presence of the malware by manipulating the filesystem. The second avoids automatic detection by antivirus software and connects to the C2 server or executes an external program. The third thread steals credentials from browsers. Here is the single-indexed formula for such behaviour:

$$f_{Gozi} = \Big[\mathbf{F}\big(FindFirstFileW \wedge \mathbf{F}(DeleteFileW \vee SetFileAttributesW)\big)\Big]_1 \wedge \Big[\mathbf{F}\big(Sleep \wedge \mathbf{F}(CreateProcessW \vee connect)\big)\Big]_2 \wedge \Big[\mathbf{G}\big(GetWindowTextW \implies \mathbf{F}CreateFileW\big)\Big]_3$$

The first thread finds the file of itself using *FindFirstFileW* and hides it by either deleting it with *DeleteFileW*, or modifying it visibility with the *SetFileAttributesW* syscall. The second thread waits until antivirus software marks the program as safe by calling *Sleep* and then, establishes connection with C2 using *connect* or calls another malicious process using *CreateProcessW*. The third thread performs credential stealing by calling *GetWindowTextW* on a browser, and saving the credentials into a new file created by the syscall *CreateFileW*.

Generic Backdoor is a group of different malware that obtains a full access to the infected machine. Its first thread modifies the system registry to execute the malware at the startup of the system. The second thread establishes connection with a C2 server. The third thread sends data to the C2. And the fourth thread waits for commands from the C2. The behaviour is described using the following formula:

$$f_{Backdoor} = \Big[\mathbf{F}(GetModuleFileNameA \wedge \mathbf{F}RegSetValueExA)\big)\Big]_1 \wedge \Big[\mathbf{F}(gethostbyname \wedge \mathbf{F}recv)\Big]_2 \wedge \Big[\mathbf{F}send\Big]_3 \wedge \Big[\mathbf{GF}(accept \wedge \mathbf{F}CreateThread)\Big]_4$$

The first thread gets its own filename using *GetModuleFileNameA*, and puts it into the registry for automatic execution on system startup using the system call *RegSetValueExA*. The second formula finds the C2 server using *gethostbyname* and configures a socket to receive incoming messages with *recv*. The third thread sends data using *send* syscall. And the fourth thread waits for incoming messages using *accept* and, on receiving the message, spawns a new thread using *CreateThread* to perform malicious activities.

4.3 Applying Our Approach for Malware Detection

We applied our tool to detect malicious behaviour of the malware mentioned above. We translated the binary code of the malware into SM-DPNs using the method described in Sect. 2.4. We obtained the CFGs of malware using the ANGR analyzer [23]. We made use of its symbolic execution to resolve system calls as control points, identify self-modifying instructions, and compute states of spawned processes. Then, we model checked the obtained SM-DPNs against single-indexed LTL formulas f_{Mirai}, f_{Gozi}, and $f_{Backdoor}$ describing the malicious behaviors. We used system calls as atomic propositions AP. Our labelling function λ is that if there is a system call x at a control point p, then $\lambda(p) = \{x\}$ and otherwise, $\lambda(p) = \emptyset$.

Our tool successfully detected the malicious behaviours specified by the above single-indexed LTL formulas, by checking that the corresponding SM-DPN of each program satisfies the corresponding malicious single-indexed LTL formula. Thus, our tool was able to check that these programs are malicious in a few minutes (e.g., the analysis of the backdoor malware took only 2 min).

5 Conclusion

In this work, we tackle the problem of LTL model checking of concurrent self-modifying code. We propose a *direct* and *efficient* algorithm for model checking of SM-DPNs over single-indexed LTL formulas. First, we show an algorithm for reducing model checking SM-DPDS to the reachability analysis of Self-Modifying Büchi Dynamic Pushdown Systems using Multi-Automata. Then, we give an algorithm for single-indexed LTL model checking by computing fixpoint of DCLICs. During the experiments, we compared our algorithm with an approach of translating SM-DPN into standard DPN and performing LTL model checking on DPN, and the results show the efficiency of our approach. Finally, we show how our model checking approach can be applied for detecting self-modifying and concurrent malware.

References

1. abuse.ch: Malwarebazaar. https://bazaar.abuse.ch/about/. Accessed 30 Jan 2025
2. Àlvarez, S.: The official radare2 book. https://book.rada.re/credits/credits.html. Accessed 15 Jan 2025
3. Anckaert, B., Madou, M., Bosschere, K.: A model for self-modifying code. In: Camenisch, J.L., Collberg, C.S., Johnson, N.F., Sallee, P. (eds.) IH 2006. LNCS, vol. 4437, pp. 232–248. Springer, Heidelberg (2007). https://doi.org/10.1007/978-3-540-74124-4_16
4. Balakrishnan, G., et al.: Model checking x86 executables with CodeSurfer/x86 and WPDS++. In: Etessami, K., Rajamani, S.K. (eds.) CAV 2005. LNCS, vol. 3576, pp. 158–163. Springer, Heidelberg (2005). https://doi.org/10.1007/11513988_17
5. Bergeron, J., et al.: Static detection of malicious code in executable programs. Int. J. Req. Eng. **2001**(184–189), 79 (2001)
6. Blazy, S., Laporte, V., Pichardie, D.: Verified abstract interpretation techniques for disassembling low-level self-modifying code. J. Autom. Reason. **56**, 283–308 (2016)
7. Bonfante, G., Marion, J.Y., Reynaud-Plantey, D.: A computability perspective on self-modifying programs. In: SEFM 2009, pp. 231–239. IEEE (2009)

8. Bouajjani, A., Müller-Olm, M., Touili, T.: Regular symbolic analysis of dynamic networks of pushdown systems. In: Abadi, M., de Alfaro, L. (eds.) CONCUR 2005. LNCS, vol. 3653, pp. 473–487. Springer, Heidelberg (2005). https://doi.org/10.1007/11539452_36
9. Cai, H., Shao, Z., Vaynberg, A.: Certified self-modifying code. In: ACM SIGPLAN PLDI 2007, pp. 66–77 (2007)
10. Corvus Forensics: Virusshare. https://virusshare.com/. Accessed 30 Jan 2025
11. Dawei, S., Delong, L., Zhibin, Y.: Dynamic self-modifying code detection based on backward analysis. In: Proceedings of the 2018 10th International Conference on Computer and Automation Engineering, pp. 199–204 (2018)
12. Debray, S.K., Coogan, K.P., Townsend, G.M.: On the semantics of self-unpacking malware code. Technical report, Citeseer (2008)
13. Diaz, M., Touili, T.: Model checking dynamic pushdown networks with locks and priorities. In: Podelski, A., Taïani, F. (eds.) NETYS 2018. LNCS, vol. 11028, pp. 240–251. Springer, Cham (2019). https://doi.org/10.1007/978-3-030-05529-5_16
14. Esparza, J., Kučera, A., Schwoon, S.: Model checking LTL with regular valuations for pushdown systems. Inf. Comput. **186**(2), 355–376 (2003)
15. Hex-Rays: Ida pro. https://hex-rays.com/ida-pro. Accessed 15 Jan 2025
16. Kahlon, V., Gupta, A.: An automata-theoretic approach for model checking threads for LTL properties. In: LICS 2006, pp. 101–110. IEEE (2006)
17. Kidd, N., Lammich, P., Touili, T., Reps, T.: A decision procedure for detecting atomicity violations for communicating processes with locks. Int. J. Softw. Tools Technol. Transf. **13**(1), 37–60 (2011)
18. Kinder, J., Veith, H.: Jakstab: a static analysis platform for binaries. In: Gupta, A., Malik, S. (eds.) CAV 2008. LNCS, vol. 5123, pp. 423–427. Springer, Heidelberg (2008). https://doi.org/10.1007/978-3-540-70545-1_40
19. Messahel, W., Touili, T.: Reachability analysis of concurrent self-modifying code. In: Bai, G., Ishikawa, F., Ait-Ameur, Y., Papadopoulos, G.A. (eds.) ICECCS 2024. LNCS, vol. 14784, pp. 257–271. Springer, Cham (2024). https://doi.org/10.1007/978-3-031-66456-4_14
20. Nguyen, H.-V., Touili, T.: CARET analysis of multithreaded programs. In: Fioravanti, F., Gallagher, J.P. (eds.) LOPSTR 2017. LNCS, vol. 10855, pp. 73–90. Springer, Cham (2018). https://doi.org/10.1007/978-3-319-94460-9_5
21. Pommellet, A., Touili, T.: LTL model checking for communicating concurrent programs. Innov. Syst. Softw. Eng. **16**(2), 161–179 (2020). https://doi.org/10.1007/s11334-020-00363-6
22. Qadeer, S., Rehof, J.: Context-bounded model checking of concurrent software. In: Halbwachs, N., Zuck, L.D. (eds.) TACAS 2005. LNCS, vol. 3440, pp. 93–107. Springer, Heidelberg (2005). https://doi.org/10.1007/978-3-540-31980-1_7
23. Shoshitaishvili, Y., et al.: SoK: (state of) the art of war: offensive techniques in binary analysis. In: 2016 IEEE Symposium on Security and Privacy (SP), pp. 138–157. IEEE (2016)
24. Song, F., Touili, T.: Efficient malware detection using model-checking. In: Giannakopoulou, D., Méry, D. (eds.) FM 2012. LNCS, vol. 7436, pp. 418–433. Springer, Heidelberg (2012). https://doi.org/10.1007/978-3-642-32759-9_34
25. Song, F., Touili, T.: Model checking dynamic pushdown networks. Formal Aspects Comput. **27**(2), 397–421 (2015). https://doi.org/10.1007/s00165-014-0330-y
26. Touili, T., Ye, X.: LTL model checking of self modifying code. Formal Methods Syst. Design **60**(2), 195–227 (2022)

27. Ugarte-Pedrero, X., Balzarotti, D., Santos, I., Bringas, P.G.: SoK: deep packer inspection: a longitudinal study of the complexity of run-time packers. In: 2015 IEEE Symposium on Security and Privacy, pp. 659–673. IEEE (2015)
28. Vardi, M.Y., Wolper, P.: Automata theoretic techniques for modal logics of programs. In: ACM STOC 1984, pp. 446–456 (1984)

Checking Linearizability of Multi-core Task Management and Scheduling System

Qiaowen Jia[1], Liangjie Lv[2], Yuting Yang[2], Bohua Zhan[3], Peng Wu[4,5], Jifeng Hao[6], Hong Ye[6], Chao Wang[2(✉)], and Yi Lv[4,5(✉)]

[1] China Electronics Corporation, Shenzhen, China
[2] Centre for Research and Innovation in Software Engineering, College of Computer and Information Science, Southwest University, Chongqing, China
wangch1@swu.edu.cn
[3] Huawei Technologies Co. Ltd., Beijing, China
[4] Key Laboratory of System Software, Institute of Software, Chinese Academy of Sciences, Beijing, China
lvyi@ios.ac.cn
[5] University of Chinese Academy of Sciences, Beijing, China
[6] Aeronautics Computing Technique Research Institute, Xi'an, China

Abstract. Checking the correctness of complex concurrent programs is inherently challenging due to the large amount of code and complex structures. Three key issues are required to addressed: choosing a proper correctness condition as a goal of checking, proposing an effective approach for checking the correctness condition, and adapting the architectural details of complex concurrent programs. In this paper we propose an efficient methodology to address these issues by considering complex concurrent programs as concurrent objects. To solve the first issue, linearizability, a *de facto* correctness criterion for concurrent objects, is chosen as the correctness condition for complex concurrent programs. To solve the second issue, we propose an effective approach to reduce the potential exponential explosion in linearizability checking. Sequential executions are referred to as sequential specifications with their correctness guaranteed via a combination of a replay mechanism and the insertion of assertions. The third issue requires to solve architecture-relevant problems that hinder linearizability checking. We propose a notion called "macro operations" to assemble "fragments" of operations. This is quite suitable for dealing with inter-core interrupt mechanisms. To demonstrate the effectiveness of our methodology, we verify a task management and scheduling system, which is a critical component of a multi-core embedded operating system kernel, supporting the preemptive multi-core task scheduling and inter-core interrupts. During this process, we found and fixed numerous errors in the original system design, which were confirmed by the system developer.

1 Introduction

Concurrent objects are designed to conform to sequential specifications, and linearizability [1] is a *de facto* correctness condition for concurrent objects. Intu-

Y. Zhou et al. (Eds.): ICECCS 2025, LNCS 15746, pp. 326–337, 2026.
https://doi.org/10.1007/978-3-032-00828-2_18

itively, linearizability requires that each operation appears to take effect instantaneously at some time point between its invocation and return.

Complex and critical components of fundamental software have begun to adopt the acceleration techniques of multi-core architectures, which inevitably complicates the design, testing and verification of fundamental software. One such example occurs in a proprietary multi-core embedded operating system kernel, of which the task management and scheduling system is optimized via fine-grained locks. This system manages the life cycle and scheduling of a task. Its implementation is rather complex with a hierarchy of storage for each process, resulting in more than 3,000 lines of C code. Ensuring the correctness of the task management and scheduling system is crucial. In our opinion, it will aid programmers for rapid development if there is a tool that can check the correctness of complex concurrent programs, respond in reasonable time, and does not require theoretical knowledge about the verification. However, this field has not yet been thoroughly investigated and leaves the following issues to address.

First, testing for typical concurrency vulnerabilities, such as data races, atomicity violations and order violations, are insufficient for checking the correctness of complex concurrent programs. These vulnerabilities lack mechanisms of sequential specifications and thus cannot precisely describe abstract behaviors. Moreover, the absence of these vulnerabilities does not necessarily imply the correctness of the whole system. To solve this issue, we model complex concurrent programs as concurrent objects, and adopt linearizability as the correctness condition for checking complex concurrent programs. Linearizability uses sequential specifications to precisely describe the desired abstract behaviors.

Second, there lacks an efficient approach to check linearizability of concurrent executions with sufficiently many operations. It is known that checking the linearizability of a single execution is NP-complete [2]. Existing tools of linearizability checking, such as VeriTrace [3], TFL [4] and lincheck [5], have limited efficiency and can only handle executions with a small number of operations. Due to the large scale and complex logic of a concurrent program, one may have to check concurrent executions with sufficiently many operations to explore potential violations in the program. It is also difficult to obtain *a priori* the sequential specifications for complex concurrent programs. To solve this issue, we propose an effective approach to check the linearizability of long executions with sufficiently many operations. There are two key points in our approach. The first point is to adjust the shape of an execution such that most interleavings comprise operations of a small number of threads. The second point is the generation and validation of sequential specifications. We treat sequential executions of complex concurrent programs as their sequential specifications, and perform testing for sequential executions by inserting assertions based on the experiences of checking complex concurrent programs. A replay mechanism is required herein to enable precise identifications of error contexts when assertions fail.

Third, fundamental software are performance critical and require dealing with details of underlying software and even hardware. For example, the aforementioned task management and scheduling system has to deal with inter-core interrupts, where an operation executes on a thread may initiate an interrupt request to a specified target thread, and the target thread is then required to handle the interrupt request and continue to execute that operation. Inter-core interrupts break the convention of linearizability, where each operation happens on one thread. To solve the third issue, we provide abstractions for underlying software and hardware details. We abstract such phenomena as macro operations, which combine fragments of an operation cross multiple threads into a single operation.

To demonstrate the effectiveness of our methodology, we check the linearizability of the aforementioned task management and scheduling system with an extended version of our linearizability checking tool VeriLin [6]. To manipulate the shape of executions, VeriLin provides a mechanism that can insert and adjust delay times both inside and outside operations. VeriLin provides object file specifications, where sequential executions of object files under test are treated as sequential specifications. To check the correctness of these sequential executions, we extend VeriLin via inserting assertions into the sequential executions. To deal with inter-core interrupts, we extend VeriLin via introducing macro operations. With our methodology we successfully conduct the linearizability checking of the task management and scheduling system, and identify and fix several new bugs of the system. The experimental results demonstrate that our methodology can effectively manage executions with 40,000 concurrent operations. To the best of our knowledge, this is the first time that linearizability checking has been successfully applied to complex concurrent programs at an industrial scale.

Related Work: Linearizability has been thoroughly investigated from various aspects, including monitoring [7], testing [3–5,8,9], theorem proving [10,11] and model checking [12]. The monitoring approach intends to separate verification of linearizability for certain sequential specifications into verifications of several simple properties. However, it seems infeasible to separate sequential specifications of complex concurrent programs into simple properties.

Researchers have proposed several approach for checking linearizability for concurrent objects. Wing et al. [8] propose a backtracking algorithm to check linearizability, which traverses all possible sequential sequences of operations. Lowe et al. [4] propose the Just-In-Time algorithm to optimize the algorithm of [8]. Horn et al. [9] propose P-compositionality, which generalizes the notion of locality principle [1] to operations on the same concurrent objects. Currently the typical linearizable checking tools include VeriTrace [3], TFL [4] and lincheck [5]. However, these tools suffers from limited efficiency, and they requires hours to deal with executions with hundreds of operations, which makes them infeasible to check complex concurrent objects.

Theorem proving is one of mainstream verification methods for operating system kernels. Klein et al. [13] prove the correctness of the seL4 microkernel with theorem proving tool Isabelle. Gu et al. [14] propose the concurrent operating system kernel verification framework CertiKOS with the theorem proving tool Coq. Xu et al. [15] propose a concurrent refinement program logic based on observational refinement and completed the correctness proof of the key functional modules of the μC/OS-II kernel. Zou et al. [16] use concurrent relational logic to verify the correctness of an embedded concurrent file system.

Model checking is another one of mainstream verification methods for operating system kernels. Cui et al. [17] use the temporal logic with time extension (TMSVL) tool to model check μC/OS-III. Choi et al. [18] use the Spin tool to perform model checking on the safety properties of the vehicle operating system.

2 Linearizability

A typical concurrent object may access shared memory and provides methods to programmers. The behavior of an object is typically represented by histories of interactions between the object and the thread that accesses the object. A history is a sequence of call and return actions. In a history, a return action matches a call action, if the return action is after the call action, they happen on a same thread and are of a same method. A history is sequential if it starts with a call action and each call (respectively, return) action is immediately followed by a matching return (respectively, a call) action unless it is the last action. A call action of a history is pending if there is no matching return action of this call action in the history. A thread subhistory $h|_i$ is a history consisting of all and only the actions of thread i of h. Two histories h and h' are equivalent, if for each thread i, $h|_i = h'|_i$. Given a history h, $complete(h)$ is the maximal subsequence of h consisting of all the matching call and return actions. In a history, an operation *op* consists of a pair of a call action, denoted $inv(o)$, and the follow-up matching return action, denoted $res(o)$. A history h induces a happen-before relation $<_h$ over operations, denoted $o_1 <_h o_2$, if $res(o_1)$ occurs before $inv(o_2)$ in h. A sequential specification is a prefix closed set of sequential histories. The notion of linearizability is defined as follows.

Definition 1 (linearizability [1]). *A history h is linearizable with respect to a sequential specification Spec, if h can be extended (by appending zero or more return actions) to a history h', and there exists a sequential history $s \in Spec$, such that*

- *$complete(h')$ is equivalent to s.*
- *For each pair of operations o_1, o_2 of h, if $o_1 <_h o_2$, then $o_1 <_s o_2$.*

A concurrent object $\mathcal{O}$ is linearizable with respect to *Spec*, if for each execution e of $\mathcal{O}$, the projection of e into call and return actions is linearizable with respect to *Spec*.

3 Task Management and Scheduling System

The multi-core task management and scheduling system presented in this paper originates from a multi-core embedded operating system kernel, which supports

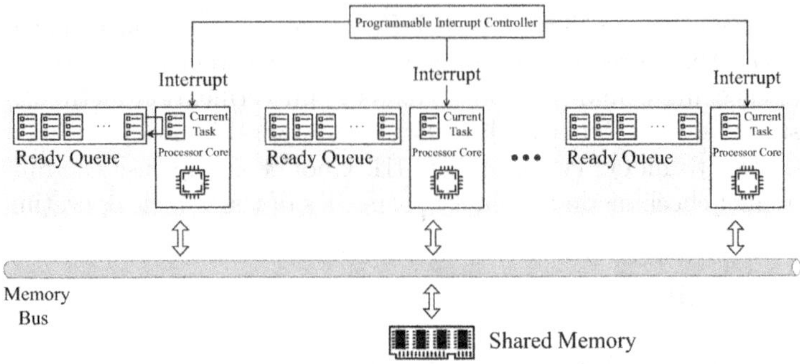

Fig. 1. Structure of multi-core task management and scheduling system

scalable architecture, multi-core techniques, real-time processing and 64-bit compatibility. The multi-core task management and scheduling system serves as the central component of the operating system kernel. It is intricate in both functionality and structure. The system's architecture is depicted in Fig. 1.

A task operates on a processor core and communicates with tasks on other cores through an inter-core interrupt mechanism. Each task is assigned a (modifiable) priority level. Each processor core maintains its own priority bitmap and a set of ready task queues for tasks at each priority level. Furthermore, there is a global priority bitmap and a global ready task queue that serve the entire system. Since tasks access various resources, the system includes multiple resource queues that allow tasks to share resources among themselves.

Task management is responsible for a variety of operations on tasks, including life cycle management and resource management. A task can be in one of several states: dormant, ready, and suspended. The task management system is also responsible for recording task state and transition of task states.

Task scheduling system supports a priority-based preemptive scheduling algorithm. The task scheduling system provides two schedule modes: the global schedule mode and the local schedule mode. In the local schedule mode, during each scheduling cycle of a processor core, the scheduling system only seeks out the highest priority task from the core's own ready task queue.

4 Methodology for Checking Complex Concurrent Programs

In this section we state our methodology for checking complex concurrent programs that can solve these issues stated in the introduction.

Complex Concurrent Programs as Concurrent Objects. To solve the first issue, we model complex concurrent programs as concurrent objects, and choose linearizability as correctness conditions for complex concurrent programs.

The task management and scheduling system is implemented with C language, complemented by a minimal amount of assembly language. As a contrast, VeriLin is initially designed for checking Java multi-threaded programs.

We decide to rewrite the system in Java. The rewritten Java model will then serve as concurrent objects to be checked as well as sequential specification in linearizability checking with VeriLin. Our rewriting generates a Java implementation that contains over 4,500 lines of Java code with a sophisticated structure, encompassing more than 20 member variables. This system is implemented with hierarchy of methods, and to check linearizability we focus on the following top-level methods, such as taskCreate, taskStart, taskSuspend, taskResume, taskSet-priority, taskStop, taskDelete, acqResource and relResource.

Effective Approach for Checking Linearizability. We intend to propose a heuristic approach that can effectively solve linearizability checking. Our idea is to decrease the size of segments. A segment h_1 of a history h is a sub-trace of h, such that one of the following cases holds: (1) h_1 consists of a call action and its matching return action, or (2) h_1 contains multiple call and return actions, all call actions (resp., return actions) of operations of h_1 are contained in h_1, and at any time of h_1 there are at least two operations o_1 and o_2 such that $o_1 \not<_{h_1} o_2 \wedge o_2 \not<_{h_1} o_1$. Our approach for effectively checking linearizability focus on the executions where most segments are of small number of operations.

VeriLin permits to add delay time both inside and outside operations, and thus fine-tune the delay of operations. An internal delay involves adding a fixed time delay immediately after the call action of each operation, while an external delay adds a fixed time delay between two operations on the same thread. With this mechanism we can make operations not gather too closely, and thus decrease the number of operations in segment and decrease the number of threads running concurrently with high probability.

Generation and Testing of Sequential Specifications. We consider the sequential executions of complex concurrent programs as their sequential specifications, as stated in [19]. There may exist errors in the sequential executions of complex concurrent programs, as we find in the example of the task management and scheduling system. VeriLin makes up for this deficiency and proposes a method to check the sequential executions via checking assertion and replaying the sequential executions. However, this holds in VeriLin only for user-provided specifications, where specifications are provided by users. We extend VeriLin and add assertion for object file specifications, where sequential executions of object files under test are treated as sequential specifications. These assertions are generated according to experience. We then validate the correctness of the sequential executions against these assertions. When an assertion fails, we proceed to replay it sequentially (possibly on multiple threads) and employ debug mode to scrutinize the task and system status and pinpoint the error.

It is not always suitable to use sequential executions of one thread of complex concurrent programs as sequential specifications. One such example is the task management and scheduling system, where each processor core maintains its own priority bitmap and a set of ready task queues for tasks at each priority level. To expose the error from communication between storage of different threads, it requires to use multiple threads. Thus, to generate sequential specifications, we execute the system on multiple threads, and force operations to run sequentially.

Macro Operation Abstraction for Inter-core Interrupts. The inter-core interrupts of the multi-core operating system kernel break the requirement of linearizability. Inter-core interrupts permits an interrupt generated by one processor core be recognized and handled by a different processor core. Upon the occurrence of an inter-core interrupt, a thread utilizes the cpcinvoke() function to dispatch the interrupt message to the intended message queue. The ISR_HANDLE() serves as the the interface to response to inter-core interrupt. When interrupts are enabled on the destination processor core, ISR_HANDLE() invokes the corresponding interrupt service routines based on the type of interrupt message. The messages in the message queue are dealt with in a FIFO manner.

To simulate the inter-core interrupt mechanism within our Java version of the task management and scheduling system, we generate an ISR class which records the permitted level of interrupts, and logs the list of interrupt messages received with a queue. We scatter ISR_HANDLE() at each step within the non-atomic execution methods of our model to ensure a thread to be able to continuously monitor content of interrupt message queue of its core and be ready to process interrupt message. This simulates the interrupt mechanism at statement-level granularity, and ensures that our Java version of the system accurately reflects the complex behavior of inter-core interrupt handling in the original system.

To effectively handle inter-core interrupts, we propose the concept of macro operations. A macro operation contains several sequences of actions on different threads, where essentially these sequences belongs to one operation. It encapsulates several sequences on different thread as a entire operation, and provides a comprehensive perspective for analyzing and verifying the system's behavior under inter-core interrupts. To use macro operations in VeriLin, it is crucial to ensure that the initiation and conclusion of a same macro operation are placed within a same segment. To achieve this, it requires to continuously monitor the existence of macro operation, and merge the segment of initiation of macro operation and the segment of conclusion of macro operation into a larger segment.

5 Linearizability Checking Framework

Based on our methodology we build a linearizability checking framework via extending VeriLin according to discussion of previous section. The framework is organized into three main modules shown in Fig. 2: preprocessing, history generation, and linearizability checking.

1. **Preprocessing.** The preprocessing module takes the implementation file of the test object as input and produces an instrumented test object as output. The framework supports instrumentation at any point within the implementation, and print information about certain execution details of operations in a well-designated format. This paper focuses on instrumenting the internal functions ISR_HANDLE() within the multi-core system. Another significant task in the preprocessing module is designing an appropriate output format for task information.

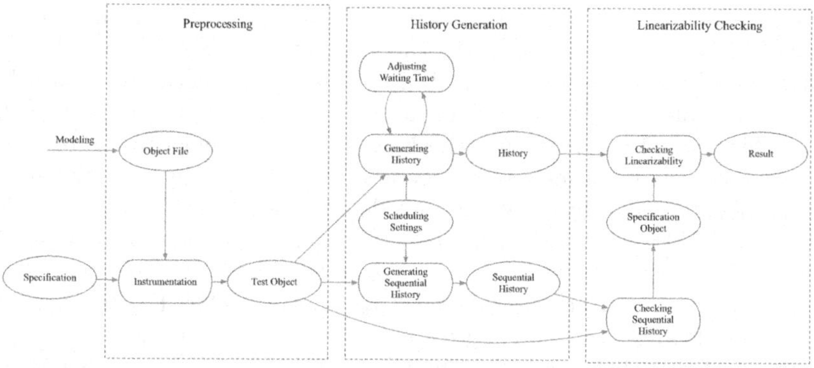

Fig. 2. Linearizability Checking Framework

2. **History Generation.** The history generation module takes the instrumented test file and the scheduling scheme of tasks within the multi-core system as input, producing a series of sequential and concurrent histories as output. It comprises two main components: sequential history generation and concurrent history generation. To generate concurrent histories with sufficient many operations, we adjust the delay of the operations to manage segment size. This requires manually fine-tune delay time. The native history generation module of VeriLin generates a vast number of trivial histories for the task management and scheduling system. To mitigate this, we design an adapter module that filters out such trivial histories optionally by selecting appropriate next task actions based on the system's current state.
3. **Linearizability Checking.** The input of this module are concurrent histories that are to be checked, and their sequential specifications in the form of sequential histories. This module outputs whether these concurrent histories are linearizable. This module is responsible for checking sequential histories and checking concurrent histories. For sequential history checking, assertions are inserted into the test object based on experience to catch exceptions during sequential execution. Violation of assertion will trigger a replay mechanism to debug the sequential sequence, identify abnormal return values, and determine the error environment. The module checks linearizability with VeriLin and the aforementioned optimization strategies. It identifies erroneous histories, and report the shortest prefix of erroneous executions.

6 Experimental Results and Analysis

Experimental Environment: The checking were executed on an Azure VM with an Intel(R) Xeon(R) CPU E5-2673 v4 @ 2.30 GHz, running Ubuntu 20.04, and equipped with 512 GB of memory.

Fine-Tune Delays: We adjust the segment size via adding delay time. Delays are divided into internal delays and external delays. During the experiment, we found that external delays plays greater impact on the segment size, while internal delays can assist in adjusting the segment size when external delays are already used. Therefore, we designed an experiment to perform linearizability checking on different external delays at scales to observe the impact of delay on the efficiency of linearizability checking. Here scale refers to the product of thread number and the number of operations performed by each thread. The case when external delays and internal delays are both 0 ms are considered as baseline. Table 1 shows the experimental results of several delay schemes at different scales. For each case we test 100 concurrent executions and use the local schedule mode. Here latency refers to external delay. For the case when the external delay is 0 ms (resp., greater than 0 ms), the internal delay is set to 0 ms (resp., 1 ms). The average maximum segment size refers to the arithmetic mean of the maximum segment length among all segments of 100 histories. The number of passes refers to the number of executions for which our methodology is not timeout (the time limit is set to 30 min). The checking time is the average checking time of the passed executions.

Table 1. Comparison of results of various sizes of history at different delays

Size	Latency (ms)	Segments	Size	Passes	Time (ms)
$4 * 100$	0	96	17	93/100	167
	1	63	8	100/100	143
	10	135	3	100/100	124
$4 * 1{,}000$	0	620	84	56/100	857
	1	580	12	98/100	514
	10	1,376	3	100/100	658
$4 * 5{,}000$	0	3,114	100	48/100	5,111
	1	2,421	15	96/100	4,534
	10	6,313	4	100/100	6,114
$4 * 10{,}000$	0	5,469	97	54/100	17,217
	1	5,262	16	93/100	16,883
	10	12,580	4	100/100	21,655

Error Reporting and Analysis: We find some errors when checking the sequential histories and concurrent executions. We check them and ensure that they recur in the original C version of the task management and scheduling system.

The first error involves resource management and is found in sequential histories. The resource waiting queue is shared among processor cores to store the tasks waiting to obtain resources. A task tsk_1 of processor core 1 applies for a resource. Since the resource is already occupied by a task on processor core 2,

tsk_1 is thus placed into the resource waiting queue. Then the system use taskSetpriority() to reset the priority of tsk_1. Although the priority of tsk_1 is modified and tsk_1 is then inserted into the ready queue, the task management and scheduling system forget to remove tsk_1 from the resource waiting queue. This makes tsk_1 be in both the ready queue and the resource waiting queue, which violates the design guidelines. To make it worse, tsk_1 may still occupy resource even if tsk_1 is stopped via calling taskStop(), which is ridiculous and violates intuition of resource management.

The second error involves inter-core interrupts and is found in concurrent histories. A global task tsk_2 is created and starts to execute on processor core 1, and its state is the ready state. Then tsk_2 performs a taskSuspend() operation on processor core 1, but the scheduler require this taskSuspend() operation to execute on processor core 2. Then, tsk_2 begins to perform a taskStop() operation on processor core 1, while the scheduler requires this taskStop() operation to execute on processor core 2. Processor core 2 executes the taskSuspend() operation from processor core 1 and modify the state of tsk_2 to state suspended. Then, processor core 2 continues to execute the taskStop() operation from processor core 1 and prepares to set the state of tsk_2 to state dormant. However, in experience we find that the state of tsk_2 is modified into a superimposed state of the dormant state and the suspended state. This is because that in the ISR_HANDLE() of taskStop() the state suspended is not cleared before modify the state into dormant state.

7 Conclusion

Due to the inherent intractability in linearizability checking problems, linearizability checking has not traditionally been applied to checking large-scale complex concurrent programs. In this paper, we have undertaken the task of checking an industrial level multi-core task management and scheduling system. We have identified the principal issues that must be addressed, and propose our methodology to solve these issues. We consider complex concurrent programs as concurrent objects and choose linearizability as correctness condition to check. We implement our methodology via extending the linearizability checking tool VeriLin. To deal with inter-core interrupts, we propose the notion of macro operations and implement it in our framework. This work contributes to the advancement of linearizability checking techniques, making them more applicable to complex systems encountered in real-world industrial scenarios.

We have successfully completed the linearizability checking of the task management and scheduling system, and identified several bugs in the systems. This is the first time that linearizability checking has been applied to complex concurrent programs at an industrial scale. Our linearizability detection framework can serve as an effective verification platform for complex concurrent programs.

As the first time of checking linearizability for complex concurrent programs, there leaves several future works. The linearizability checking acceleration of VeriLin lacks elaborate manipulation of shape of histories. It will be worthwhile to investigate which executions are more suitable to expose error, and how to manipulate the executions more elaborately. The linearizability violations we find often contain a large number of operations, and it is necessary to investigate how to effectively locate the error and explain the error.

Acknowledgments. This work is partially supported by the National Natural Science Foundation of China under Grants No. 62002298, No. 62372439, No. 62032019, No. 62372386, Beijing Natural Science Foundation (Grant Nos. F251021 and 4232038), the Fundamental Research Funds for the Central Universities (SWU019036), and the Capacity Development Grant of Southwest University (SWU116007).

References

1. Herlihy, M.P., Wing, J.M.: Linearizability: a correctness condition for concurrent objects. TOPLAS **12**, 463–492 (1990)
2. Gibbons, P.B., Korach, E.: Testing shared memories. SIAM J. Comput. **26**, 1208–1244 (1997)
3. Long, Z., Zhang, Y.: Checking linearizability with fine-grained traces. In: SAC 2016, pp. 1394–1400. ACM (2016)
4. Lowe, G.: Testing for linearizability. Concurr. Comput.: Pract. Exp. **29**, e3928 (2017)
5. Koval, N., Fedorov, A., Sokolova, M., Tsitelov, D., Alistarh, D.: Lincheck: a practical framework for testing concurrent data structures on JVM. In: Enea, C., Lal, A. (eds.) CAV 2023. LNCS, vol. 13964, pp. 156–169. Springer, Cham (2023). https://doi.org/10.1007/978-3-031-37706-8_8
6. Jia, Q., et al.: VeriLin: A linearizability checker for large-scale concurrent objects. In: David, C., Sun, M. (eds.) TASE 2023. LNCS, vol. 13931, pp. 202–220. Springer, Cham (2023). https://doi.org/10.1007/978-3-031-35257-7_12
7. Emmi, M., Enea, C.: Sound, complete, and tractable linearizability monitoring for concurrent collections. Proc. ACM Program. Lang. **2**, 25:1–25:27 (2018)
8. Wing, J.M., Gong, C.: Testing and verifying concurrent objects. J. Parallel Distrib. Comput. 164–182 (1993)
9. Horn, A., Kroening, D.: Faster linearizability checking via P-compositionality. In: Graf, S., Viswanathan, M. (eds.) FORTE 2015. LNCS, vol. 9039, pp. 50–65. Springer, Cham (2015). https://doi.org/10.1007/978-3-319-19195-9_4
10. Liang, H., Feng, X.: Modular verification of linearizability with non-fixed linearization points. In: POPL 2013, pp. 459–470 (2013)
11. Vafeiadis, V.: Modular fine-grained concurrency verification. Technical report, University of Cambridge, Computer Laboratory (2008)
12. Alur, R., McMillan, K., Peled, D.: Model-checking of correctness conditions for concurrent objects. Inf. Comput. **160**, 167–188 (2000)
13. Klein, G., et al.: seL4: formal verification of an OS kernel. In: SOSP 2009, pp. 207–220 (2009)
14. Gu, R., et al.: CertiKOS: an extensible architecture for building certified concurrent OS kernels. In: OSDI 2016, pp. 653–669. ACM (2016)
15. Xu, F., Fu, M., Feng, X., Zhang, X., Zhang, H., Li, Z.: A practical verification framework for preemptive OS kernels. In: Chaudhuri, S., Farzan, A. (eds.) CAV 2016. LNCS, vol. 9780, pp. 59–79. Springer, Cham (2016). https://doi.org/10.1007/978-3-319-41540-6_4

16. Zou, M., Ding, H., Du, D., Fu, M., Gu, R., Chen, H.: Using concurrent relational logic with helpers for verifying the AtomFS file system. In: SOSP 2019, pp. 259–274. ACM (2019)
17. Cui, J., Duan, Z., Tian, C., Zhang, N., Zhou, C.: Model checking μC/OS-III multi-task system with TMSVL. In: Butler, M., Conchon, S., Zaïdi, F. (eds.) ICFEM 2015. LNCS, vol. 9407, pp. 187–200. Springer, Cham (2015). https://doi.org/10.1007/978-3-319-25423-4_12
18. Choi, Y.: Model checking trampoline OS: a case study on safety analysis for automotive software. Softw. Test. Verif. Reliab. **24**, 38–60 (2014)
19. Herlihy, M., Shavit, N., Luchangco, V., Spear, M.: The Art of Multiprocessor Programming. Newnes, New York (2020)

Contract-Based Verification of Digital Twins

Muhammad Naeem(✉) and Cristina Seceleanu(✉)

School of Innovation, Design, and Engineering, Mälardalen University, Västerås, Sweden
{muhammad.naeem,cristina.seceleanu}@mdu.se

Abstract. Digital twins are becoming powerful tools in industrial applications, offering virtual representations of cyber-physical systems. However, verification of these models remains a significant challenge due to the potentially large datasets used by the digital twin. This paper introduces an innovative methodology for verifying neural network-based digital twin models, in a black-box fashion, by integrating model checking into the process. The latter relies on defining and applying system-level contracts that capture the system's requirements, to verify the behavior of digital twin models, implemented in Simulink. We develop an automated solution that simulates the digital twin model for certain inputs, and feeds the predicted outputs together with the inputs to the contract model described as a network of timed automata in the UPPAAL model checker. The latter verifies whether the predicted outputs fulfill the specified contracts. This approach allows us to identify scenarios where the digital twin's behavior fails to meet the contracts, without requiring the digital twin's design technicalities. We apply our method to a boiler system case study for which we identify prediction errors via contract verification. Our work demonstrates the effectiveness of integrating model checking with digital twin models for continuous improvement.

Keywords: Digital Twin · Model Checking · UPPAAL · Neural Networks · Simulink

1 Introduction

The emergence of Industry 4.0 has propelled Digital Twins (DT) to the forefront of industrial digitalization, offering virtual representations of cyber-physical systems that facilitate precise simulations, analysis, and control [19]. As industrial systems grow in complexity, ensuring the reliability and correctness of these DT becomes crucial.

This work is a part of the Dynamic and Robust Distributed Systems (D-RODS) project [1] aiming to develop an adaptable and dependable framework for

[1] https://www.es.mdu.se/projects/615-D_RODS.

Y. Zhou et al. (Eds.): ICECCS 2025, LNCS 15746, pp. 338–357, 2026.
https://doi.org/10.1007/978-3-032-00828-2_19

the implementation and operation of DT, tackling issues in industrial digitalization including system integration, performance enhancement, and compatibility with legacy systems [8,17]. In the current study, we focus on the Verification and Validation (V&V) of Neural Network-based Digital Twins (NNDT) models using model-checking techniques. NNDT have the potential to predict system behavior, conduct real-time tests, and identify optimization opportunities. However, their effectiveness depends on their ability to represent and accurately respond to real-world conditions [7].

Recent advancements in model-driven engineering, such as the CoCoSim framework, have demonstrated the value of integrating formal verification techniques with model-based design, especially for multi-periodic discrete systems [3].

Our research applies a similar concept to the domain of DT, proposing a novel approach that employs model checking to verify monotonicity, functional, and infrastructure contracts specified for black-box NNDT. Since our DT is in fact an NNDT, the correctness of its output is not guaranteed. We propose a methodology for systematically verifying the behavior of DT models implemented in `Simulink` by defining system contracts, as networks of UPPAAL timed automata [1]. We present an automated solution that connects a simulation environment with model checking, allowing for the continuous validation and improvement of NNDT models. Our approach detects situations where the NNDT generates incorrect outcomes.

Due to their dynamic nature and complex interactions with cyber-physical systems, verifying DT models is challenging. Dahmen et al. emphasize the importance of systematic methods to verify and validate DT models [5], and propose an approach that breaks down the verification problem into smaller, more manageable components. This research aligns with our methodology of using (sub-) system contracts to verify specific aspects of DT behavior.

Given the importance of ensuring the correctness of DT behavior, our research aims to address the following research question: **RQ:** How can we design an automated solution to model check a black-box NNDT model?

To answer it, this paper presents a contract-based approach for verifying black-box NNDT models in UPPAAL. The solution simulates the `Simulink` NNDT model for certain inputs, and feeds the predicted outputs together with the inputs to the contract model described as a network of timed automata in the UPPAAL model checker. The latter verifies if the predicted outputs fulfill the specified contracts. In brief, our contributions are as follows:

- *Model-Checking-based Methodology:* We propose a methodology that uses contracts modeled as UPPAAL timed automata, and employs model checking to verify the correctness of black-box NNDT.
- *System Contract Implementation:* We define a systematic approach for modeling system contracts that specify expected behaviors, enabling precise verification of model outputs against system requirements.
- *Practical Validation:* Our approach is illustrated through a burner-boiler system case study, showcasing its effectiveness on an industrial application.

Our approach facilitates the identification of scenarios where the DT's behavior fails to meet the contracts, without requiring knowledge of the model's internal structural and functional details.

The remainder of this paper is organized as follows. Section 2 provides the necessary background information. Section 3 details our methodology for verifying NNDT models using contract-based model checking. Section 4 describes our case study of a burner-boiler system, including the DT model implemented in `Simulink`, as well as the system's contracts. Section 5 presents the implementation of contracts in UPPAAL, for model checking, and Sect. 6 discusses the verification results. Finally, Sect. 7 presents and compares to relevant related work, before Sect. 8 concludes the paper, summarizing our contributions and discussing potential lines of future work.

2 Preliminaries

This section presents the background information necessary to understand the concepts and methodologies employed in our study.

2.1 UPPAAL Timed Automata

Model checking is a formal verification technique that systematically and exhaustively verifies whether a system model meets specified requirements. UPPAAL [1] is a state-of-the-art model checker designed for modeling, verification, and simulation of distributed systems. Its modeling framework is based on Timed Automata (TA), which extends traditional finite-state machines by incorporating real-valued clocks. These clocks allow for the precise timing of events, enabling the modeling of systems where timing is critical.

In UPPAAL, the concept of TA is further enhanced through the use of UPPAAL Timed Automata (UTA). UTA introduces discrete data variables, such as integers and Boolean values, which can act as guards or expressions to control transitions between states. Additionally, UTA supports specifications in the C programming language, facilitating the observation and control of the model's discrete states.

A UTA can be formally defined as a tuple: $\langle L, l_0, C_h, V, E, I\rangle$, where: L is a finite set of locations in the automata model, l_o represents the initial location, $C_h = C_h! \cup C_h?$ denotes a set of channels for communication, with $C_h!$ and $C_h?$ representing sending and receiving channels, respectively [14]. V includes a set of data variables and clocks, E consists of edges connecting locations, I specifies invariants that must hold true for certain expressions.

UPPAAL's ability to model and verify real-time systems makes it particularly valuable in safety-critical domains. The tool offers a user-friendly graphical interface for designing models and simulating their behavior, along with a command-line interface for efficient verification processes [15].

Figure 1(a) shows a *network of UTA* modeling a simple lamp and its user [16]. The lamp has three locations: off, low, and bright. If the user presses a button,

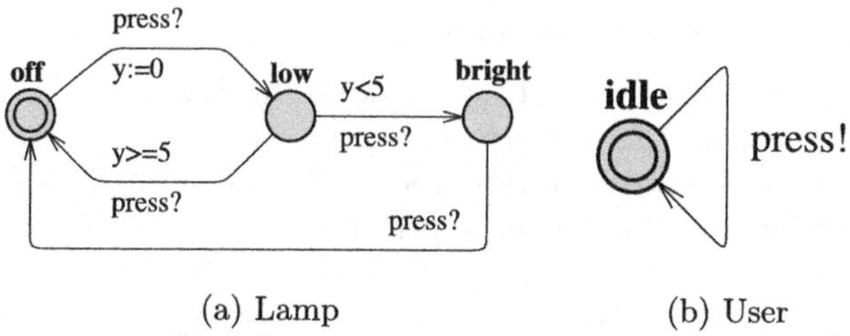

Fig. 1. The simple lamp example.

i.e., synchronizes with the press? then the lamp is turned on. If the user presses the button again, the lamp is turned off. However, if the user is fast and rapidly presses the button twice, the lamp is turned on and becomes bright. The user model is shown in Fig. 1(b). The user can press the button randomly at any time or even not press the button at all. The clock y of the lamp is used to detect if the user is fast ($y < 5$) or slow ($y >= 5$).

The contracts (queries in UPPAAL) to be verified by model checking on the resulting network are specified in a decidable subset of (Timed) Computation Tree Logic ((T)CTL). In this paper, we verify (T)CTL queries of the following kinds (p is a state property): (i) Reachability: $E \lozenge p$ - the query evaluates to true if there exists a path where p eventually holds, and (ii) Invariance: $A \square p$ - the query evaluates to true if (and only if) every reachable state satisfies p, in other words, for all paths p always holds.

3 Proposed Methodology

In this section, we describe our methodology for verifying NNDT models in a black-box fashion, by integrating model checking into the process.

3.1 Digital Twin Model as a Neural Network

The starting point of our methodology is a black box NNDT model, implemented in `Simulink` (in this paper). However, the approach can be applied to other modeling frameworks, straightforwardly. The NNDT serves as a virtual representation of the cyber-physical system, continuously updated with real-time data to mirror its current state and behavior.

The black-box nature of this neural network-based model allows us to capture complex, non-linear relationships within the system without requiring detailed knowledge of its internal structure. This approach provides flexibility and accuracy in representing the system's behavior across various operating conditions. The inputs and outputs form the basis for our subsequent contract verification process, allowing us to assess the NNDT's performance against predefined system contracts.

3.2 Contract Model Development

We develop a comprehensive contract model using UTA, and provide contract verification in UPPAAL. These contracts capture the system's requirements and serve as a formal specification of the expected behavior of the NNDT. We categorize the contracts into three main types (Fig. 2):

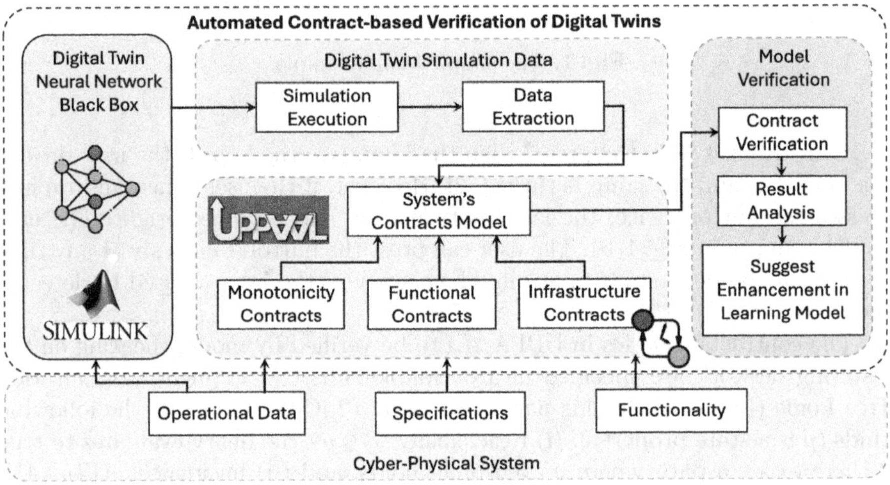

Fig. 2. Methodology

- *Monotonicity Contracts:* These contracts are designed to verify that the output of the NNDT behaves monotonically with respect to certain inputs. This means that if an input's value increases, the NNDT's output value should also increase, and vice versa. This property is crucial in many industrial applications where a predictable relationship between inputs and outputs is expected.
- *Functional Contracts:* These contracts specify the expected functional behavior of the digital twin, defining relationships between inputs and outputs that must be maintained throughout the operation of the model. These contracts ensure that the digital twin follows the intended operational specifications.
- *Infrastructure Contracts:* These contracts focus on the operational aspects of the digital twin, such as response times, resource usage, and system stability. These contracts ensure that the digital twin operates within acceptable performance limits.

Contracts for Neural Networks-based Digital Twins (NNDT). In the following, we define our notion of *NNDT contract*, as used in this paper.

Definition 1 (NNDT Contract). *Let $\mathcal{N} : \mathbb{R}^n \to \mathbb{R}^m$ be a digital twin represented by a neural network, mapping an input vector $x \in \mathbb{R}^n$ to an output vector $y \in \mathbb{R}^m$. We define the* assume-guarantee *contract for the digital twin, as the pair (A, G), as follows:*

- Assumption (A): *We assume that the input and output of the digital twin at time t, denoted as $x(t)$, and $y(t)$, respectively, are represented by a moving average over the last m time steps (m is a constant that depends on the application), to mitigate the effects of inaccurate sensing, and predictions, respectively:*

$$\hat{x}(t) = \frac{1}{m} \sum_{i=1}^{m} x(t-i), \tag{1}$$

where $\hat{x}(t)$ is the stabilized input, and:

$$\hat{y}(t) = \frac{1}{m} \sum_{i=1}^{m} y(t-i), \tag{2}$$

where $\hat{y}(t)$ is the stabilized output. To these cross-cutting assumptions (they hold for all contracts), we add predicate p that captures the requirements on inputs $x(t)$.
- Guarantee (G): *A predicate q that captures the NNDT's expected output behavior. As an example,* a monotonicity contract *that states that, if the input $\hat{x}$ increases component-wise, then the output of the neural network, $\mathcal{N}(\hat{x})$, should also increase component-wise, can be expressed formally as follows (similarly, for the decreasing case):*

$$((\forall \hat{x}, \hat{x}' \in \mathbb{R}^n \,.\, \hat{x} \preceq \hat{x}'), (\mathcal{N}(\hat{x}) \preceq \mathcal{N}(\hat{x}')) \tag{3}$$

Here, $\preceq$ denotes component-wise inequality (that is, inequality that is applied individually to each entry, which can be the average value over m previous ones, as explained above). This ensures that the neural network maintains monotonicity and avoids erratic behavior in response to changes in input.

The semantics of the (A, G) contract of Definition 1 is given in terms of UPPAAL*timed automata* (UTA), as follows.

Definition 2 (Semantics of NNDT Contracts). *A contract for a neural-network-based digital twin is a pair (A, G), where $A = ||_i UTA_{A_i}$ represents the network of $i \neq 0$* ***assumption UTA****, and $G = ||_j UTA_{G_j}$ is the network of $j \neq 0$* ***guarantee UTA****. The semantic contract is then defined by the parallel composition $A||G$.*

3.3 Role of Contracts in Verification

The contracts mentioned above play a critical role in the verification process because they set clear expectations for how the digital twin should behave. During the model-checking phase, we compare the outputs predicted by the NNDT model to these contracts. If the outputs do not meet any of the contracts, it shows that there might be a problem with how the model is working.

By using these contracts in a structured way, we can ensure that the digital twin meets its required functions and follows the necessary rules for operation. This helps to improve the reliability and safety of the system that it represents.

Verifying Satisfaction of NNDT Contracts. In our approach, the verification of NNDT contracts reduces to model checking the UTA parallel composition $A||G$ of Definition 2, against *invariance* properties of the form $A\Box\, q$, where q is the predicate that models the guarantee, per component. As sometimes it proves faster, we can also check *reachability* properties of the form $E <> \neg q$, where a witness trace returned by UPPAAL identifies a breach of contract.

3.4 Automated Verification Process

To verify the behavior of neural network-based digital twins (NNDTs) in a systematic and scalable manner, we developed an automated workflow managed by a shell script. This script coordinates each stage of the process, including simulation, contract verification, and result analysis. It ensures consistent execution across multiple test scenarios.

The automated process consists of the following components:

- *Digital Twin Simulation (`DT.slx`):* We begin with a trained NNDT model implemented in `Simulink`, derived from datasets and modeling work in the D-RODS [2]project. The shell script triggers simulations of this model for various predefined input scenarios.
- *Prediction Generation:* Each simulation produces time-series output traces (e.g., in our case study presented later int he paper, burner and boiler temperatures, wood and water mass), which are saved as text files. These represent the model's predicted behavior under the given inputs.
- *Data Preprocessing (`DataProcessForUPPAAL.m`):* A `MATLAB` script processes the simulation outputs to generate structured input files suitable for contract verification in UPPAAL.
- *Contract Verification in* UPPAAL: The shell script initiates UPPAAL model checking using predefined queries and contract models. For each simulation, the processed inputs and predictions are fed into the UPPAAL automata, and verification is performed using reachability queries ($E\langle\rangle \neg p$).
- *Diagnostic Output and Visualization:* If a contract is violated, UPPAAL generates a diagnostic trace that is saved automatically. The trace can be visualized to highlight when and how the violation occurred. The script also logs verification outcomes for each scenario.

This automated workflow enables scalable and repeatable contract-based verification of NNDT models with minimal manual intervention (Fig. 3).

3.5 Results Analysis

We analyze the verification results, identifying any violations of the contracts, where the NNDT's behavior fails to meet the contracts. This process involves:

[2] https://www.es.mdu.se/projects/615-D_RODS.

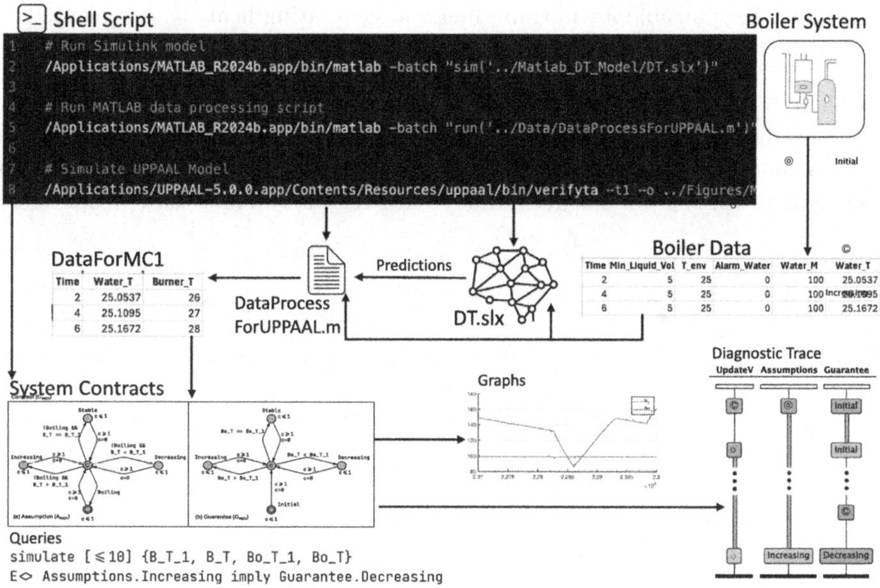

Fig. 3. Workflow of the contract-based verification process for boiler usecase

- Pinpointing the exact input conditions that lead to contract violations.
- Categorizing errors based on the type of contract breached (monotonicity, functional, or infrastructure).

4 Case Study: Burner-Boiler System

To illustrate our approach, we apply it on a case study focused on heating different liquids until they evaporate (Fig. 4). This model includes several parts that work together to achieve the goal.

At the center of the system, there is a *wood provider*, which supplies fuel to a *warehouse*. From there, a *burner system* takes the fuel to heat up a *boiler*. The boiler heats containers made of various materials, each holding different types of liquids. The system's complexity comes from several randomly assigned rates. These include how efficiently the wood burns, how well heat transfers in the containers, and how quickly each liquid heats up. Key parameters, such as the starting amounts of wood and liquid, sizes of wood deliveries, and the evaporation temperatures of the liquids, are also randomly set. This randomness allows for generating a variety of scenarios in our study.

Figure 4 shows a simple diagram of this setup, highlighting the main parts, as well as how information flows through the system. The model is built around the *System of Interest (SoI)*, which includes three main subsystems:

- *Warehouse:* The central place for storing and distributing fuel.

- *Burner:* Responsible for burning fuel and generating heat.
- *Boiler:* The part where liquids are heated.

There is also an external *Wood Delivery System* that interacts with the SoI but operates separately. While this system is important for supplying wood, it is not included in our DT modeling. We can change its delivery conditions—like when and how much wood is delivered—but it remains outside our current focus.

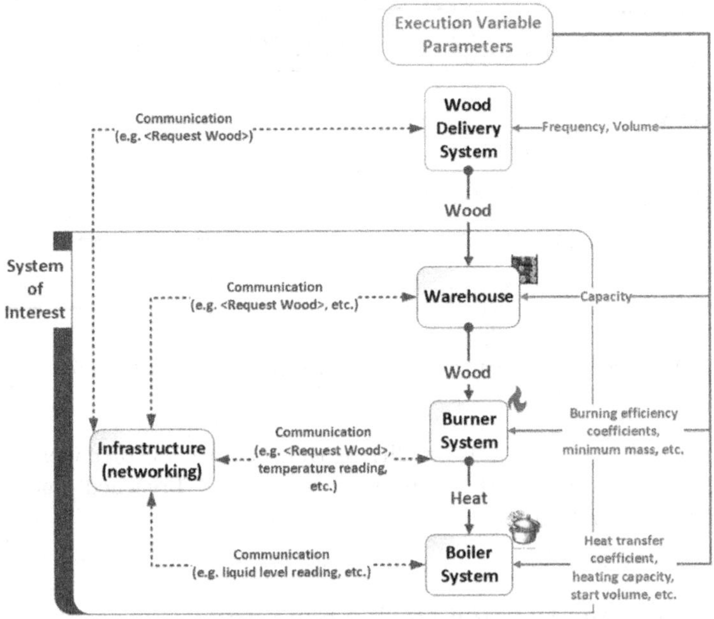

Fig. 4. The heating system.

Our main goal is to create efficient and accurate DT models. In this paper, we focus on the verification of a black-box NNDT model developed in our previous work. This model represents the complex interactions within the burner-boiler system, and our current efforts aim to ensure its correctness and reliability using *contract-based verification* in the UPPAAL tool.

4.1 Digital Twin Model

The Fig. 5 illustrates the DT model in `Simulink`. The NNDT model for the burner-boiler system is implemented in `Simulink` and serves as a virtual representation of the physical boiler. This model integrates real-time data to accurately reflect the current state and behavior of the boiler.

We use the following notation to describe the DT model for this use case:

B_T: Burner Temperature
Bo_T: Boiler Temperature
W_T: Water Temperature
W_M: Water Mass
Wo_M: Wood Mass
T_{env}: Environmental Temperature
t: Current time step
$T_{\mathbf{Boil}}$: Boiling Temperature
W_A: Water Alarm
Wo_D: Wood Delivered
Wo_A: Wood Alarm
Wo_R: Wood Request
A: Assumption
G: Guarantee

The model takes several input parameters, including temperatures, burner characteristics (Alpha, Beta, Delta), wood and water mass and alarms. These inputs allow the DT to adapt to changing conditions and predict the boiler's operations effectively.

Key outputs from the model include predictions for B_T, Bo_T, W_M, Wo_M, W_A, Wo_A, Wo_R and Wo_D. The DT uses a neural network to process these inputs and generate accurate predictions about future states of the system.

While the model has been trained on specific datasets and validated with known data, there remains a potential for errors due to limitations in the available data. This aspect is critical as it highlights the scope of our work in this paper. We focus on model-checking the NNDT black-box model using the contract-based approach described in Sect. 3.

Through the use of its neural network architecture, this DT captures complex relationships within the boiler system. Our contract-based verification method enables us to capture specific behavioral requirements for the NNDT, allowing us to assess its contract compliance. This approach ultimately aims to improve the reliability and accuracy of real-world applications NNDT.

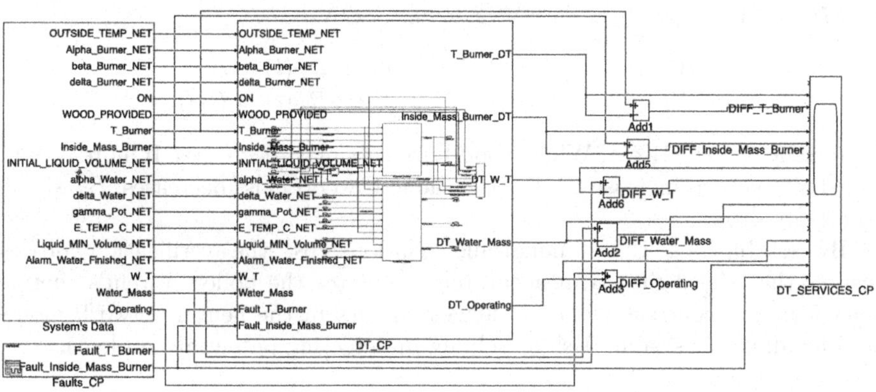

Fig. 5. DT Model

4.2 System Contracts

We define three categories of contracts for our DT model: *Monotonicity Contracts (MC)*, *Functionality Contracts (FC)*, and *Infrastructure Contracts (IC)*. Each contract is formulated as a pair, (A, G), using the notation described in Sect. 3.2. In cases where multiple assumptions exist, we have: $A = \wedge_i A_i$, and similar for multiple guarantees: $G = \wedge_i G_i$.

Monotonicity Contracts (MC). These contracts are designed to verify that the output of the NNDT behaves monotonically with respect to certain inputs, which is a crucial property of NN.

MC1 (B_T vs Bo_T): $A1: \; \forall t, \quad B_T(t) < T_{\text{Boil}}$

$$\begin{aligned} A2: \; \hat{B_T}(t) > \hat{B_T}(t-1) \;&,\; G1: \; \hat{Bo_T}(t) \geq \hat{Bo_T}(t-1) \\ A3: \; \hat{B_T}(t) < \hat{B_T}(t-1) \;&,\; G2: \; \hat{Bo_T}(t) \leq \hat{Bo_T}(t-1) \end{aligned}$$

When the burner temperature $\hat{B_T}$ is below the boiling point T_{Boil}, it may increase or decrease smoothly over time. The boiler temperature $\hat{Bo_T}$ must follow the trend of the burner temperature, either increasing or decreasing, accordingly.

MC2 (W_M vs Bo_T):

$$\begin{aligned} A1: \; \hat{Bo_T}(t) > T_{\text{Boil}} \;&,\; G1: \; \hat{W_M}(t) \leq \hat{W_M}(t-1) \\ A2: \; \hat{Bo_T}(t) \leq T_{\text{Boil}} \;&,\; G2: \; \hat{W_M}(t) \approx \hat{W_M}(t-1) \end{aligned}$$

When $\hat{Bo_T}$ exceeds T_{Boil}, evaporation occurs, causing W_M to decrease over time. However, if the $\hat{Bo_T}$ drops to or below T_{Boil}, the evaporation should slow down or stop, stabilizing the $\hat{W_M}$. This ensures that the system correctly models the evaporation dynamics, maintaining a realistic relationship between Bo_T and W_M.

MC3 (Wo_M vs B_T): $A1: \; \forall t, Burner = ON$

$$\begin{aligned} A2: \; \hat{Wo_M}(t) > \hat{Wo_M}(t-1) \;&,\; G1: \; \hat{B_T}(t) \geq \hat{B_T}(t-1) \\ A3: \; \hat{Wo_M}(t) < \hat{Wo_M}(t-1) \;&,\; G2: \; \hat{B_T}(t) \leq \hat{B_T}(t-1) \end{aligned}$$

$\hat{B_T}$ depends on the $\hat{Wo_M}$. When wood burns, its mass decreases. If more wood is added, $\hat{B_T}$ should increase or stay the same. If wood mass decreases, $\hat{B_T}$ should eventually drop.

By establishing these monotonic relationships, the verification process ensures that the digital twin accurately simulates the boiler system's thermal behavior. Any contract violation suggests issues in the neural network model, data handling, or system design, helping in detecting potential problems.

Functionality Contracts (FC). The functionality contracts define the expected operational behavior of the system, by specifying how different components should respond to certain conditions.

1- Burner System FC:

The *burner system* ensures safe and efficient operation by managing wood supply, monitoring temperature, and responding to boiler signals.

FC1: $A: \hat{Wo_M}(t) < Wo_{M_{min}}$, $G:$ RequestWood()
The burner must request wood when the $\hat{Wo_M}$ falls below a certain threshold.

FC2: $A1: (Wo_R(t) \wedge \neg Wo_D(t + \Delta t)$ where $\Delta t = 60s)$, $A2: (\hat{Wo_M} < Wo_{M_{min}})$, $G: W_A$
The W_A should be triggered if no wood is received within 1 minute after the wood request, or when $\hat{Wo_M}$ falls below the minimum level.

FC3: $A: \hat{Wo_M}(t) > Wo_{min}$, $G1: \neg Wo_R(t)$, $G2: \neg Wo_D(t)$
This states that there should be no wood request or delivery when the $\hat{Wo_M}$ is above Wo_{min}.

FC4: $A1:$ $ReachedIdealRange(t) =$ True , $A2: \hat{B_T}(t) < 130°C \vee \hat{B_T}(t) > 160°C)$, $G:$ CriticalTemperatureAlarm(t)
The system must enable the *CriticalTemperatureAlarm*, if $\hat{B_T}$ leaves the ideal operational range after reaching once.

FC5: $A: TurnOffSignal(t) =$ True , $G:$ Burner = Off
The burner must shut down immediately when it receives a *TurnOffSignal* from the boiler.

FC6: $A: \hat{W_M}(t) > W_{min}$, $G: \hat{Wo_M}(t) > 0$
The $\hat{Wo_M}$ must always remain above zero if the $\hat{W_M}$ is above the minimum level, to keep the burner functional.

2- Boiler System FC:

The *boiler system* ensures stable operation by maintaining boiling conditions, monitoring water levels, and responding appropriately to critical conditions.

FC7: $A1:$ *ReachedBoilingState(t)* , $A2: \hat{W_M}(t) > W_{M_{min}}$, $G: \hat{Bo_T}(t) \approx T_{\text{Boil}}$
If the boiler system has reached the boiling state and the $\hat{W_M}$ is above the minimum level, the $\hat{Bo_T}$ should remain around T_{Boil}.

FC8: $A: \hat{W_M}(t) < W_{M_{min}}$, $G1: W_A(t)$, $G2: TurnOffSignal(t)$
If the $\hat{W_M}$ falls below the minimum level, the system must generate W_A and send a *TurnOffSignal* to the burner to prevent unsafe operation.

FC9: $A: \hat{W_M}(t) > W_{M_{min}}$, $G1: \neg W_A(t)$, $G2: \neg TurnOffSignal(t)$
When the $\hat{W_M}$ is above the minimum level, W_A should not be triggered, and no *TurnOffSignal* should be sent to the burner.

FC10: $A1: \forall t, Burner = off$, $G1: \hat{B_T}(t) \geq T_{env}(t),$, $G2: \hat{Bo_T}(t) \geq T_{env}(t)$
The B_T and Bo_T should always stay above or equal to the T_{env}, even if the burner is off. They may gradually decrease but should never drop below the ambient temperature, unless an external cooling source is applied.

4.3 Infrastructure Contracts (IC)

IC1: A : $\exists t, t_0$ such that (CriticalAlarm(t_0) = True) $\wedge$ ($\forall t' \in [t_0, t_0 + 5]$, CriticalAlarm($t'$) = True) , G : ShutDownBurner() If a critical alarm remains active for more than $5minutes$, the burner must shut down to prevent system damage and ensure safety.

5 Contract Modeling in UPPAAL

The UTA models presented in this section demonstrate how contract-based verification can check the correctness of a digital twin model, systematically. By mapping component and system contracts onto UPPAAL timed automata, we ensure that key constraints are validated. UPPAAL allows for efficient verification, as it explores all possible states and detects contract violations.

5.1 Contract Model for MC1

The Monotonicity Contract (MC1) ensures that the Bo_T follows the changes in the B_T. This contract guarantees a realistic and predictable behavior of the heating system. The UPPAAL model designed for MC1 is implemented as a timed automaton (Fig. 6), effectively capturing the dynamic relationship between the temperatures. To model this contract in UPPAAL, we used three templates: *UpdateV* (Variable Update), A_{MC1}, and G_{MC1}. The *UpdateV* template updates B_T and Bo_T values periodically. The A_{MC1} template represents the expected behavior of the B_T, while the G_{MC1} template ensures that the Bo_Tv follows the B_T's trend.

The *UpdateV* template maintains the system's temperature changes using global variables: B_T (current burner temperature), B_{T_1} (previous burner temperature), Bo_T (current boiler temperature), and Bo_{T_1} (previous boiler temperature). The function *UpdateVar()* updates these values using a moving average. A clock variable `(c)` ensures that updates occur at regular time steps.

A_{MC1} template defines three possible states for the burner temperature: `Increasing` ($B_T > B_{T_1}$), `Decreasing` ($B_T < B_{T_1}$), and `Stable` ($B_T == B_{T_1}$). The system transitions between these states based on the changes in B_T. If the burner reaches the boiling point, the system enters a special state (Boiling).

The G_{MC1} template enforces the expected reaction of the boiler temperature. It includes three states: `Increasing` ($Bo_T > Bo_{T_1}$), `Decreasing` ($Bo_T < Bo_{T_1}$), and `Stable` ($Bo_T == Bo_{T_1}$). The transitions ensure that the boiler temperature behaves consistently with the burner temperature.

Verification in UPPAAL. UPPAAL provides a query language to verify system properties [1]. The verification is done using queries, which check whether certain properties hold in all possible executions of the system. To verify the correctness of the model, we define the following queries:

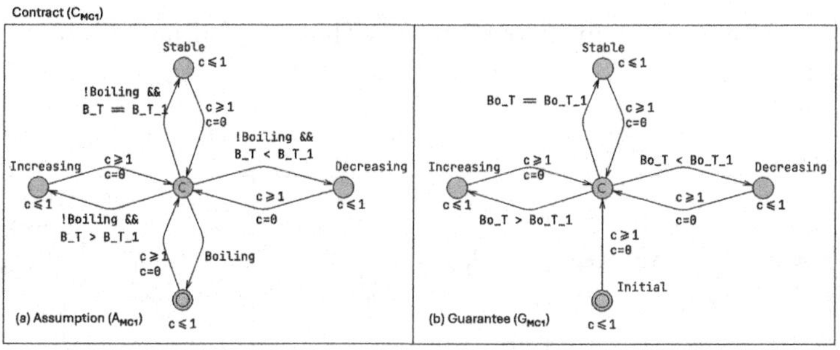

Fig. 6. Monotonicity Contract UTA Model for MC1

Safety Property Check: This ensures that the system always satisfies the monotonicity requirement:

```
A[] Assumption.Increasing imply Guarantee.Increasing
```

If this query fails, it indicates that there are case(s) where the boiler temperature does not always follow the burner temperature correctly. Additionally, UPPAAL provides diagnostic traces, which help locate errors by showing a counterexample when a property does not hold.

5.2 Contract Model for FC9

The Functional Contract (FC9) ensures that when W_M is above a defined minimum threshold, the alarm should not be triggered, and no turn-off signal should be sent to the burner. This contract prevents unnecessary interruptions in the heating system and ensures efficient operation.

In Fig. 7, the UPPAAL model represents a contract (FC9) for a boiler system. To model this contract in UPPAAL, we define three key templates: A_{FC9} (Water Level Monitoring), $G1_{FC9}$ (Alarm Condition), and $G2_{FC9}$ (TurnOffSignal). Additionally, a UpdateV (Variable Update) template periodically updates the monitored water level, similarly as that described in MC1 Model.

The A_{FC9} template maintains the state of the water level, defining two primary locations: `AboveW_min`, and `BelowW_min`, where. A clock variable (c) ensures regular updates, and the system transitions between these states based on the water level condition.

The $G1_{FC9}$ template models the alarm behavior by defining two states: `NotAlarm`, and `Alarm`. The transition to the Alarm state occurs only if the water level falls below the threshold. If the water level is above the threshold, the system remains in the NotAlarm state, ensuring that the contract requirement is met.

The $G2_{FC9}$ template models the burner control system by ensuring that the burner remains on as long as the water level is above the minimum threshold. The states in this template include `B_off_false`, and `B_off_true`. The transition to

`B_off_true` is allowed only if one ensures that the burner is not turned off unnecessarily.

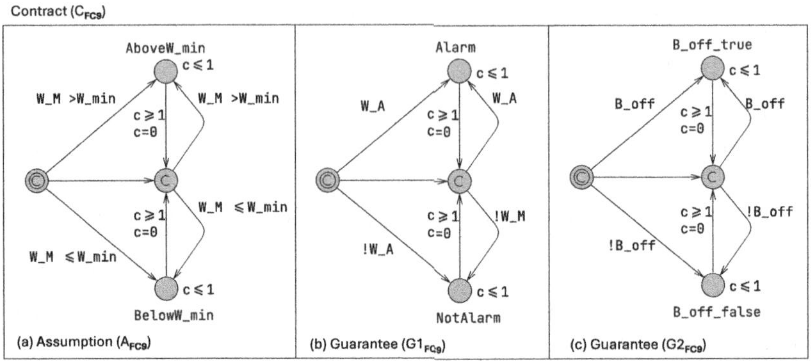

Fig. 7. Functionality Contract UTA Model for FC9

Verification in UPPAAL. To verify the accuracy of the model, we define the following queries. The *invariance property check* ensures that, when the water level is above the threshold, neither the water alarm is triggered, nor the burner is turned off. This is expressed as:

```
A[] A_FC9.AboveW_min imply (not (G1_FC9.Alarm || G2_FC9.B_off_true))
```

If this property fails, it indicates that W_A or *turn-off* signal is incorrectly triggered despite sufficient water level. The reachability check verifies whether a violation of the contract is possible:

```
E<> A_FC9.AboveW_min imply (G1_FC9.Alarm || G2_FC9.B_off_true)
```

6 Verification Results

Our contract-based verification approach using UPPAAL revealed some scenarios in which the predictions of the NNDT model deviated from the specified contracts. These findings highlight areas for improvement in the model and potential safety concerns regarding the boiler system's operation.

6.1 MC1: Relation Between the Burner and the Boiler Temperatures

We simulate the contract automaton model described in Sect. 5.1 to verify the relation between the burner and the boiler temperatures. The results illustrate a

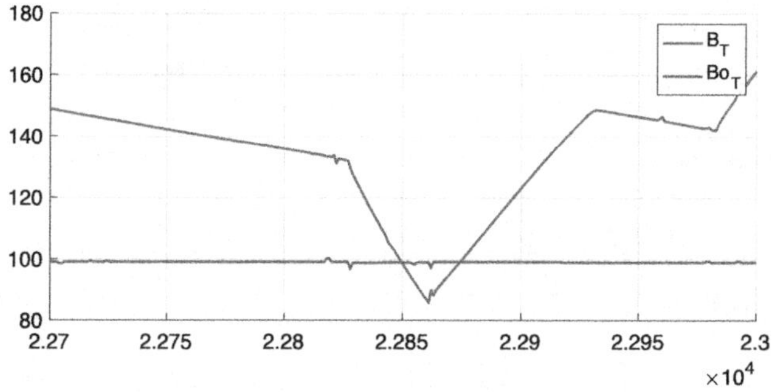

Fig. 8. Contract violation in MC1

violation of the expected relationship between burner and boiler temperatures. According to MC1, the boiler temperature should correlate with the burner temperature, allowing for an acceptable delay δ, particularly when the burner temperature is below the boiling threshold.

In Fig. 8, the graph shows that the burner temperature gradually decreases with time, even dropping below the boiling temperature at certain points. Despite this, the boiler temperature remains unchanged and does not follow the expected correlation. This discrepancy suggests that the heat transfer dynamics between the burner and the boiler are not accurately trained in the digital twin model.

The impact of this contract breach is significant. It may result in erroneous system behavior, such as the boiler maintaining a high temperature despite a decrease in burner temperature, which could lead to incorrect operational conditions. This conclusion emphasizes the need for model refinement to ensure that the digital twin accurately represents temperature dependencies and state transitions, enhancing its fidelity and reliability as a predictive tool.

6.2 FC3: Erroneous Wood Request

The results indicate a contract violation in the wood request mechanism, leading to an unnecessary wood supply. According to FC3, a wood request should only be triggered when the wood mass falls below the minimum threshold. However, as shown in Fig. 9, noise in the wood request signal causes the system to falsely detect a low wood level, even when there is enough wood available.

As a result, the model requests unnecessarily additional wood, leading to an excessive amount of wood in the burner. This misbehavior can affect system efficiency and fuel management, potentially causing overheating or inefficient combustion.

Improvements in the wood request signal processing are required to avoid such errors. Possible solutions include noise-filtering techniques or threshold adjustments to avoid false triggers and ensure accurate wood requests.

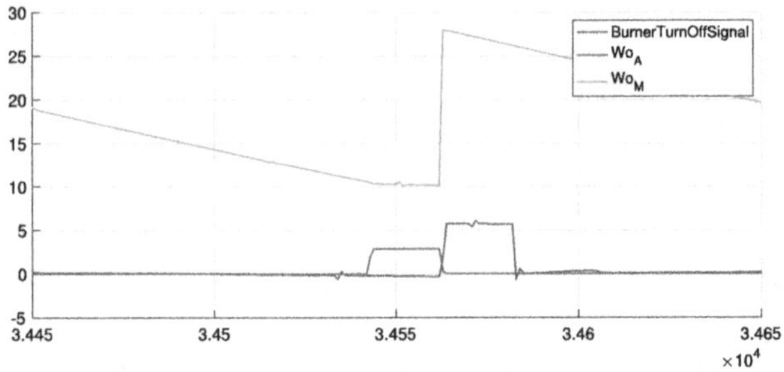

Fig. 9. Contract violation in FC3

These verification results highlight the importance of refining the DT model, particularly in areas of wood mass management, temperature control, and system state consistency. They also demonstrate the effectiveness of contract-based verification in identifying potential safety and operational issues that might not be apparent through traditional testing methods.

6.3 FC9: Alarm Water Finished False Trigger

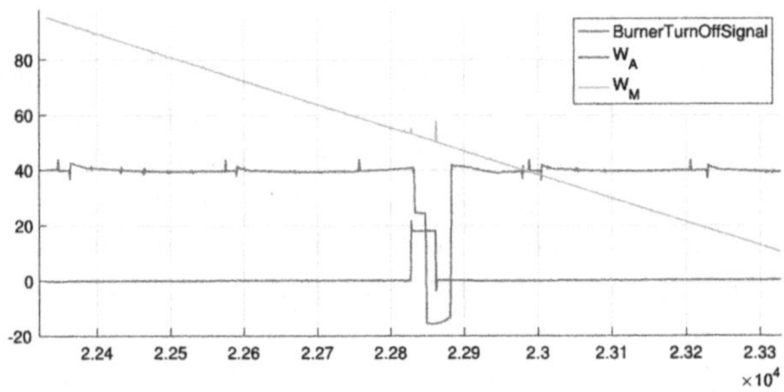

Fig. 10. Contract violation in FC9

The findings highlight a contract violation in the Water_Finished_Alarm, which led to an incorrect shutdown of the burner. According to FC9, the alarm should activate only when the water mass falls below the minimum threshold. However, as illustrated in Fig. 10, interference in the alarm signal leads to a false burner shutdown, even when the water mass remains above the minimum level.

Improvements in alarm signal processing are necessary to address this issue. Possible solutions include implementing signal filtering techniques, adjusting threshold conditions, or introducing hysteresis mechanisms to prevent minor fluctuations from causing false shutdowns.

7 Related Work

The verification of DT is a growing area of research due to its increasing use in critical applications.

Cimatti et al. provide the OCRA tool [4] that enables a *design-by-contract* methodology for reactive systems. In OCRA, the system's DT is its contract, which consists of an assumption on the system inputs, and a guarantee of the system outputs under the given assumptions, both described in Linear Temporal Logic. In comparison, our approach distinguishes between the DT, which is a neural network, and its contracts, and specifies the latter as timed automata that are fed with the DT's inputs and predicted outputs, to verify the black-box behavior of the DT by model checking.

Perhaps the closest research to ours is the approach used in CoCoSim [3], which is a toolbox that can be called directly from the Matlab Simulink environment, and can be used for code generation (e.g. Lustre) or property verification via contracts. The contracts are specified directly in Simulink, as model components, and the verification is carried out on the generated code, by using modular SMT-based verification engines (such as Zustre) that also generate assume-guarantee style formal contracts. However, the difference from our approach comes from the fact that the verification is not a black-box one, it instead uses the functional details of Simulink's model blocks that are transformed into code. The fact that our approach uses contracts modeled as simple timed automata that encode the properties to be model checked makes the verification very fast and scalable.

Notable work for *verifying neural networks*, which in our case describes the DT, has been carried out for a while now. Katz et al. introduce the "Reluplex" method [10], designed to verify deep neural networks by solving satisfiability problems, particularly in networks utilizing ReLU activation functions. In comparison, our method is agnostic of the NNDT's activation function, being based only on inputs, predicted outputs and their check of whether they satisfy the timed automata contracts.

Another strand of research focuses on *reachability analysis*, where methods such as *symbolic interval propagation* [11] and *abstract interpretation* [6,12,13,18,20] are used to estimate possible outputs of neural networks within a bounded input space. This is crucial for safety-critical systems to ensure that neural networks do not produce unexpected or unsafe outputs. For instance, the Neural Network Verification tool (NNV) [20] supports over-approximate analysis by combining the star set analysis used for feed-forward neural network controllers with zonotope-based analysis for nonlinear plant dynamics. In general, neural network verification approaches based on abstract interpretation are supported by tools that represent the inputs as a set, called abstract domain, which is then passed along the neural network, yielding a set that over-approximates the output that is used to evaluate the property under verification. The verification accuracy depends heavily on the abstract domain chosen [12]. If the abstraction is too rough, the tool might not be able to decide if the property is verified or falsified, therefore other methods need to be employed. By using contracts that encode the actual NNDT properties that need to be verified, we avoid such problems, providing a fast and scalable solution that can potentially be employed at run-time too, due to its insignificant overhead.

Additionally, researchers explore *probabilistic verification* [2] to handle the inherent uncertainty in data-driven models like neural networks. Techniques based on Bayesian methods and Monte Carlo simulations have been proposed to evaluate the performance and robustness of neural networks DT in dynamic environments. Kapteyn et al. [9] explore the mathematical foundations of digital twins, focusing on probabilistic graphical models, including dynamic Bayesian networks, to model complex systems and inform decision-making processes.

8 Conclusions and Future Work

This paper presents a novel methodology for verifying black-box neural network-based digital twin models using contract-based model checking. Our approach, which uses UPPAAL timed automata to define system contracts, allows for black-box verification without requiring knowledge of the digital twin's internal details. This makes it particularly valuable for complex industrial applications. We validated our methodology using an existing neural network-based digital twin model of a boiler system developed in Simulink. By modeling contracts as UPPAAL timed automata, we demonstrated how our approach can be applied to real-world industrial processes, ensuring digital twin predictions align with physical constraints and expected behaviors.

Our contract models show fast simulation times, making them suitable for runtime verification. This efficiency enables real-time monitoring of the digital twin's behavior during system operation without significantly impacting overall performance.

Future work will focus on analyzing the digital twin's performance under various input conditions and exploring ways to improve predictions for more complex systems. We aim to enhance the reliability and utility of digital twins in industrial applications, leading to improved efficiency and safety in operations.

Acknowledgments. The research was supported by vinnova's advanced digitalization program in the project D-RODS (ID: 2023-00244).

References

1. Behrmann, G., David, A., Larsen, K.G.: A Tutorial on Uppaal 4.0. Dept. Comput. Sci., Aalborg Univ. **1**(1), 1–48 (2006)
2. Boetius, D., Leue, S., Sutter, T.: Probabilistic verification of neural networks using branch and bound (2024). arXiv:2405.17556
3. Bourbouh, H., Garoche, P.L., Loquen, T., Noulard, É., Pagetti, C.: CoCoSim, a code generation framework for control/command applications: an overview of CoCoSim for multi-periodic discrete simulink models. In: Embedded Real Time Systems (ERTS) 2020 (ARC-E-DAA-TN74591) (2020)

4. Cimatti, A., Dorigatti, M., Tonetta, S.: OCRA: a tool for checking the refinement of temporal contracts. In: 2013 28th IEEE/ACM International Conference on Automated Software Engineering (ASE), pp. 702–705 (2013)
5. Dahmen, U., Osterloh, T., Roßmann, J.: Verification and validation of digital twins and virtual testbeds. Int. J. Adv. Appl. Sci. **11**(1), 47–64 (2022)
6. Gehr, T., Mirman, M., Drachsler-Cohen, D., Tsankov, P., Chaudhuri, S., Vechev, M.: Ai2: safety and robustness certification of neural networks with abstract interpretation. In: 2018 IEEE Symposium on Security and Privacy (SP), pp. 3–18. IEEE (2018)
7. Grieves, M., Vickers, J.: Digital twin: mitigating unpredictable, undesirable emergent behavior in complex systems. Transdisc. Perspect. Complex Syst.: New Find. Approaches, 85–113 (2017)
8. Gu, R., Seceleanu, T., Xiong, N., Naeem, M.: A service-oriented digital twin framework for dynamic and robust distributed systems. In: 2024 IEEE International Conference on Software Services Engineering (SSE), pp. 66–73. IEEE (2024)
9. Kapteyn, M., Pretorius, J., Willcox, K.: A probabilistic graphical model foundation for enabling predictive digital twins at scale. Nat. Comput. Sci. **1**(5), 337–347 (2021)
10. Katz, G., Barrett, C., Dill, D.L., Julian, K., Kochenderfer, M.J.: Reluplex: an efficient SMT solver for verifying deep neural networks. In: Majumdar, R., Kunčak, V. (eds.) CAV 2017. LNCS, vol. 10426, pp. 97–117. Springer, Cham (2017). https://doi.org/10.1007/978-3-319-63387-9_5
11. Kern, P., Büning, M.K., Sinz, C.: Optimized symbolic interval propagation for neural network verification (2022). arXiv:2212.08567
12. Lemesle, A., Lehmann, J., Gall, T.L.: Neural network verification with PyRAT (2024). arXiv:2410.23903
13. Mazzucato, D., Urban, C.: Reduced products of abstract domains for fairness certification of neural networks. In: Drăgoi, C., Mukherjee, S., Namjoshi, K. (eds.) SAS 2021. LNCS, vol. 12913, pp. 308–322. Springer, Cham (2021). https://doi.org/10.1007/978-3-030-88806-0_15
14. Naeem, M.: Energy-efficient cyber-physical systems: a model-based approach (2024)
15. Naeem, M., Albano, M., Larsen, K.G., Nielsen, B., Høedholt, A., Laursen, C.Ø.: Battery aware analysis of sensor networks in UPPAAL SMC. In: 2021 10th Mediterranean Conference on Embedded Computing (MECO), pp. 1–6. IEEE (2021)
16. Naeem, M., Albano, M., Larsen, K.G., Nielsen, B., Høedholt, A., Laursen, C.Ø.: Modelling and analysis of a sigfox-based IoT network using UPPAALSMC. IEEE Sens. J. **23**(10), 10577–10587 (2023)
17. Seceleanu, T., Xiong, N., Enoiu, E.P., Seceleanu, C.: Building a digital twin framework for dynamic and robust distributed systems. In: International Conference on Engineering of Computer-Based Systems, pp. 254–258. Springer (2023)
18. Singh, G., Gehr, T., Püschel, M., Vechev, M.T.: An abstract domain for certifying neural networks. Proc. ACM Program. Lang. **3**(POPL), 1–30 (2019)
19. Tao, F., Zhang, H., Liu, A., Nee, A.Y.: Digital twin in industry: state-of-the-art. IEEE Trans. Industr. Inf. **15**(4), 2405–2415 (2018)
20. Tran, H.D., et al.: NNV: the neural network verification tool for deep neural networks and learning-enabled cyber-physical systems. In: Proc. of the 32nd International Conference on Computer-Aided Verification (CAV) (2020)

Verifying Neural Network Controlled Systems by Combining Taylor Models and Linear Abstract Domains

Minghao Li[1], Liqian Chen[1,2(✉)], Xinyu Wang[1], Shifu Yang[1], Yuan Zhou[3], and Ji Wang[1,2]

[1] College of Computer Science and Technology, National University of Defense Technology, Changsha 410073, China
{liminghao,lqchen,wangxinyu23,yangshifu_,wj}@nudt.edu.cn
[2] State Key Laboratory of Complex and Critical Software Environment, National University of Defense Technology, Changsha 410073, China
[3] Intelligent Game and Decision Lab (IGDL), Beijing, China

Abstract. Verifying the safety properties of neural network controlled systems (NNCSs) is essential before their deployment in safety-critical scenarios. NNCSs face significant verification challenges due to the complex nonlinear interactions between neural network controllers and dynamic systems. While Taylor models (TMs) excel in capturing nonlinear dynamics of the system and linear abstract domains efficiently verify neural networks, their isolated use faces two limitations: TMs struggle with neural network scalability, while linear abstract domains cannot precisely represent nonlinear system states. To overcome these limitations, we present a verification approach that synergistically integrates TMs with linear abstract domains. Since naive interval-based approximations often destroy variable dependencies between TMs and linear abstract domains, we further propose a parity-characteristic-driven linearization method to construct interval linear abstraction of TMs, preserving variable dependencies by extracting relationships in nonlinear terms and incorporating them into linear terms. Based on the interval linear abstraction of TMs, our approach enables bidirectional conversion between TMs and different linear abstract domains while reducing precision loss during abstraction conversion. We implemented a prototype named TTLA. Experimental results show that TTLA outperforms the tools in terms of both efficiency and tightness of the reachable set overapproximation. In addition, TTLA enables scalable verification, with neural network analysis time under 0.7 s even for large networks.

Keywords: Neural Network Controlled Systems · Verification · Abstract Domains · Taylor Models · Reachability Analysis

1 Introduction

Neural networks (NNs) are increasingly used as decision-makers in autonomous systems, such as autonomous vehicles [1,2], air traffic collision avoidance sys-

Y. Zhou et al. (Eds.): ICECCS 2025, LNCS 15746, pp. 358–378, 2026.
https://doi.org/10.1007/978-3-032-00828-2_20

tems [3] and other cyber-physical systems (CPS) [4,5], due to their strong representation learning capabilities. At the same time, NNs are known to be highly susceptible to input perturbations [6], such as adversarial attacks [7], and often lack formal robustness guarantees. This poses a significant challenge for their deployment in safety-critical systems, where even small errors can lead to catastrophic consequences. Therefore, formal verification of safety properties and reliability is essential before deploying NN-based controlled systems in real-world applications, particularly in safety-critical scenarios.

In this paper, we consider neural network controlled systems (NNCSs) which integrate neural networks as the controller with dynamic systems. The plant model is typically described by nonlinear ordinary differential equations (ODEs), while the NN controller computes control inputs based on the system's state variables at discrete time steps [8]. This hybrid structure introduces significant complexity, as the NN's nonlinearity interacts with the plant's dynamics. Reachability analysis is an effective and sound method for verifying the safety of NNCSs. It computes the reachable set, encompassing all possible system trajectories from an initial state set over a finite time horizon. If the reachable set avoids the unsafe region and reaches the goal set, the system is considered safe.

Reachability analysis for NNCSs is challenging due to the nonlinearity of both the NN controller and the plant dynamics. These nonlinear interactions make it infeasible to compute exact reachable sets, necessitating the use of overapproximations, which can introduce conservatism and reduce verification precision. Moreover, the closed-loop interaction between the NN controller and the plant over multiple control steps significantly increases system complexity. As a result, current verification approaches [9,10] for standalone NNs or dynamic systems cannot be applied directly to NNCSs. Existing approaches for NNCS verification can be categorized into three categories. Firstly, NNV [11] leverages abstract domains to unify representations across the plant and NNs. However, the lack of consideration of the interactions leads to overapproximation errors that quickly accumulate after a few control steps, also known as the wrapping effect [12]. JuliaReach [13] tames the approximation error when converting between two set representations of different reachability analysis tools, but the improvement is limited. Secondly, Verisig [14] employs hybrid automaton conversion for NNs. Thirdly, some tools such as Sherlock [15], ReachNN [16], and ReachNN* [17] utilize function overapproximation of NNs based on sampling, while Verisig2.0 [18] propagating Taylor models layer-by-layer in networks, yet both face scalability bottlenecks.

To alleviate the above weakness, we propose a generic verification approach for NNCSs by combining TMs and linear abstract domains. Taylor models are particularly effective in computing rigorous bounds on the complex trajectories of nonlinear differential equations, making them powerful for verifying the properties of nonlinear continuous systems. The use of different abstract domains [19,20] allows for the computation of the reachable set for larger neural networks with various activation functions while TMs can only handle differentiable activation functions.

To reduce the errors introduced by the conversion of higher-order Taylor models into different linear abstract domains, we propose a method to construct the interval linear abstraction of TMs. This approach extracts dependencies from higher-order terms of TMs based on their even and odd characteristics, integrating them into linear terms. As a result, the conversion between the Taylor models and various linear abstract domains is both more accurate and computationally efficient. Based on this, we improve the general verification framework by combining Taylor models for dynamic systems and linear abstract domains for NNs. In each iteration, an interval linear abstraction of TMs is constructed and converted into various linear abstract domains, enabling seamless integration of NN verification tools based on different abstract domains.

In summary, the contribution of this paper can be concluded as follows:

1. We propose a method to construct the interval linear abstraction of TMs, enabling more accurate and efficient conversions between Taylor models and various linear abstract domains.
2. We improve the generic verification framework for NNCSs by using the interval linear abstraction of TMs and linear abstract domains to achieve high precision and scalability.
3. We perform extensive experiments on diverse benchmarks, including systems of varying types, scales, and activation functions, demonstrating the superior accuracy and efficiency of our approach compared to state-of-the-art tools.

2 Preliminaries

2.1 Neural Network Controlled Systems

NNCSs consist of two main components: the plant which represents the system being controlled, and the neural network controller as shown in Fig. 1. Unlike traditional controllers, the neural network controller is typically trained using advanced techniques like reinforcement learning [1,21]. It takes the current system state as input and generates the corresponding control signal as output.

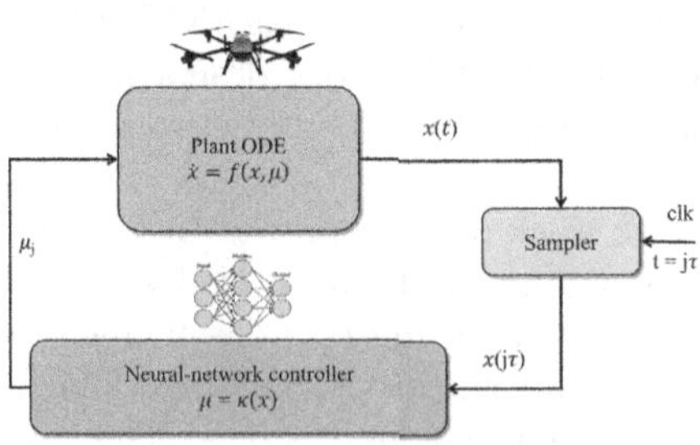

Fig. 1. Overview of neural network controlled systems

Formally, the NNCSs can be defined by a tuple $(\mathcal{X}, f, \mu, \kappa, \tau, X_0)$,where:

- $\mathcal{X}$ is the state space, with its dimension equal to the number of state variables;
- f describes the continuous dynamics of the plant;
- μ represents the control input set, with its dimension equal to the number of control variables;
- κ defines the input-output mapping of the neural network controller;
- τ is the control period;
- X_0 is the initial state space of the NNCS.

This formulation captures the essential components of the NNCS and provides a foundation for their formal analysis and verification.

2.2 Reachability Analysis

Bounded-time reachability analysis for NNCSs aims to compute an over-approximation of the reachable set, which contains all possible system trajectories starting from an initial set of states. Given the NNCS S and an initial state set $x_0 \in X_0$, the reachable set R_t at time t can be defined as:

$$R_t = \{x \in \mathcal{X} |\ \forall x_0 \in X_0,\ S(x_0, t) = x\} \tag{1}$$

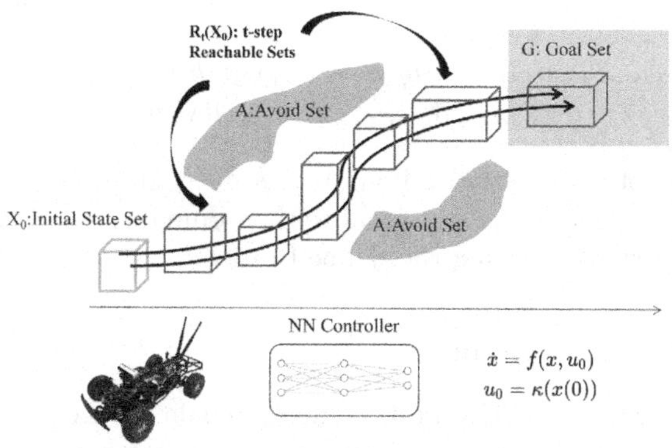

Fig. 2. Reachability analysis for NNCSs

As illustrated in Fig. 2, safety verification based on reachability analysis involves checking whether the reachable set R_t over a finite time horizon $[0, T]$ satisfies two conditions:

1. R_T is entirely contained within the goal set G;
2. $R_{[0:T]}$ has no intersection with the avoidance set A.

If both conditions are met, the NNCS is deemed safe. This approach provides a rigorous framework for ensuring the reliability of NNCSs in safety-critical applications.

2.3 Taylor Models

Taylor Models (TMs) [22] provide a powerful framework for approximating functions using higher-order Taylor polynomials combined with an interval remainder to capture approximation errors [23]. A TM is represented as a pair (p, I), where p is a polynomial of degree at most k, defined over a finite set of variables $x_1, \ldots, x_n$ within an interval domain $D \subset \mathbb{R}^n$, and I is a remainder interval. The pair (p, I) serves as a k-order overapproximation of a function f, satisfying the condition:

$$\forall x \in D, f(x) \in p(x) + I, \text{ i.e., } f(x) \in \{p(x) + y \mid y \in I\} \tag{2}$$

The range of a TM is the Minkowski sum of the range of its polynomial and the remainder interval [24]. TM arithmetic [25] supports fundamental operations such as addition, scaling, and multiplication, all of which are closed over the same domain. Interval multiplication and addition are defined as follows:

$$\begin{aligned} [\ell_1, u_1] \otimes [\ell_2, u_2] &:= \left[\min_{c_i \in \{\ell_i, u_i\}} (c_1 c_2), \max_{c_i \in \{\ell_i, u_i\}} (c_1 c_2)\right] \\ [\ell_1, u_1] \oplus [\ell_2, u_2] &:= [\ell_1 + \ell_2, u_1 + u_2] \end{aligned} \tag{3}$$

Consider two Taylor models $TM_1 = (p_1, I_1)$ and $TM_2 = (p_2, I_2)$ defined over the same domain D. For any given scalars a and b, the addition and multiplication of these Taylor models are defined as:

$$\begin{aligned} a(p_1, I_1) + b(p_2, I_2) &:= (ap_1 + bp_2, (a \otimes I_1) \oplus (b \otimes I_2)) \\ (p_1, I_1) \cdot (p_2, I_2) &:= (p_1 \cdot p_2, (\mathrm{Itv}(p_2) \otimes I_1) \oplus (\mathrm{Itv}(p_1) \otimes I_2) \oplus (I_1 \otimes I_2)) \end{aligned} \tag{4}$$

where $\mathrm{Itv}(p)$ denotes an interval bound of p over the domain D. A common practice with Taylor models is to normalize their domains to $[-1, 1]^n$ using Taylor model arithmetic while keeping the defined range unchanged.

2.4 Linear Abstract Domains

Given the complexity of NNCSs and the need to balance accuracy and efficiency, linear abstract domains provide a promising choice for neural network verification. These domains have been widely adopted in numerous neural network verification tools and provide a precision-scalability trade-off. Common examples include Box [26], Zonotope [19], Starset [27], and Polyhedra [20].

In this paper, we focus on Box and Zonotope due to their efficiency in handling affine transformations, which are fundamental to neural network operations. However, the interval linear abstraction of TMs construction and conversion algorithms we describe are also applicable to other linear abstract domains. A Box denotes the union of a finite number of intervals and a Zonotope $\mathcal{Z} \subset \mathbb{R}^n$ is defined as follows:

$$\mathcal{Z} := \left\{ c + \sum_{i=1}^{p} \beta_i g^{(i)} \mid \beta_i \in [-1, 1] \right\} \tag{5}$$

where $c \in \mathbb{R}^n$ represents the center and $g^{(i)} \in \mathbb{R}^n$ are the generators. These generators are typically arranged as columns in a matrix $G_{\mathcal{Z}} = [g_1, g_2, \cdots, g_p]$. The order of a Zonotope is given by the ratio p/n of generators per dimension.

A Zonotope can be viewed as the Minkowski sum of line segments [25]. The zonotope is particularly efficient for manipulation under affine transformations in each layer of the neural network (including multiplication with weights and addition of biases). This domain was already shown to be a suitable basis for analyzing neural networks by Gehr et al. [26].

3 Conversion Between Taylor Models and Linear Abstract Domains

The computation of the reachable set using TMs requires different orders of Taylor expansion, depending on the dynamic system's complexity.

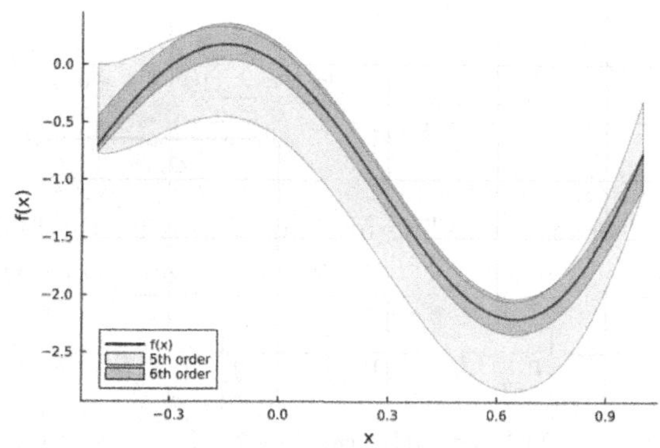

Fig. 3. 5th-order and 6th-order Taylor expansions of $f(x)$

Figure 3 illustrates an example where fifth-order and sixth-order Taylor expansions are used to overapproximate the function $f(x)$ over the interval $[-0.5, 1.5]$. With respect to $f(x) = x \cdot (x - 1.1) \cdot (x + 2) \cdot (x + 2.2) \cdot \sin(1.7x + 0.5)$, the error of the sixth-order expansion is considerably reduced compared to the fifth-order expansion. Indeed, in the analysis of more complex dynamic systems, higher-order expansions are shown to be necessary for capturing nonlinear dynamics beyond affine approximations.

However, two fundamental limitations hinder the direct application of Taylor models (TMs) in neural network verification:

- Taylor models are limited by Taylor arithmetic and can only handle differentiable activation functions [18].
- The interval remainder error accumulates rapidly during propagation through the network, after degenerating TMs into interval analysis.

Therefore, we propose to use different linear abstract domains for reachable set computation in the neural network instead of TMs. It is evident that the conversion from high-order Taylor models to linear abstract domains inevitably introduces precision loss, moreover, during the closed-loop process, the over-approximation error accumulates continuously, ultimately preventing successfully verifying safety properties. To resolve this challenge, we adopt a method of constructing the interval linear abstraction of TMs to reduce the error introduced during the conversion of abstract representations.

3.1 Interval Linear Abstraction of TMs

Before introducing our method of constructing the interval linear abstraction of TMs, we first describe a direct way to construct the linear abstraction of TMs using the remainder to bound errors caused by the linearization of higher-order polynomials. Firstly, split the polynomial into linear terms $P_1(x)$ and nonlinear terms $Q_n(x)$ where $n \geq 2$ like (6),

$$P_n(x) = \underbrace{a_0 + a_1(x - x_0)}_{P_1(x)} + \underbrace{\sum_{k=2}^{n} a_k(x - x_0)^k}_{Q_n(x)} \tag{6}$$

then we compute the corresponding interval bounds for the higher-order terms using interval arithmetic and accumulate these bounds into the remainder I, getting

$$I_1 = \left[\min_{x \in D} Q_n(x),\ \max_{x \in D} Q_n(x)\right], I = I_0 \oplus I_1 \tag{7}$$

Finally we get the TM-linear Abstraction $\mathcal{T}(x) = P_1(x) + I$.

However, this approach has two critical limitations:

- approximating higher-order terms with intervals completely destroys the variable dependencies encoded in these terms.
- the lack of consideration for constraints on the variables introduces additional approximation errors into the computed remainder term.

To effectively capture dependency relationships encoded in higher-order terms while reducing approximation-induced remainder errors, we propose a parity-characteristic-driven method to construct interval linear abstractions of Taylor models.

Consider the nonlinear polynomial in its most general form:

$$P(x_1, x_2, \ldots, x_n) = \sum_{i_1=0}^{d_1} \sum_{i_2=0}^{d_2} \cdots \sum_{i_n=0}^{d_n} a_{i_1 i_2 \cdots i_n} x_1^{i_1} x_2^{i_2} \cdots x_n^{i_n} \tag{8}$$

First, we decouple the linear and nonlinear terms, where the linear terms serve as the foundation for the interval linear abstraction like (6). To address the equality constraints among variables, we employ parity-based dynamic partitioning and order reduction for the higher-order terms. Subsequently, interval arithmetic operations are performed between the processed terms and the linear components to construct an intermediate representation—the interval-linear expression, in the form of

$$p(x) = b + [l_1, u_1]x_1 + [l_2, u_2]x_2 + \cdots + [l_n, u_n]x_n \tag{9}$$

where $[l_i, u_i] \subseteq \mathbb{R}$ $(1 \leq i \leq n)$ denotes interval values.

The specific procedure is as follows: we apply dynamic parity-based partitioning to decompose the polynomial into linear-absorbable terms ($\mathcal{A}_{\text{lin}}$) and remainder-absorbable terms ($\mathcal{A}_{\text{res}}$).

$$Q_n(x) = \sum_{\alpha \in \mathcal{A}_{\text{lin}}} a_\alpha \mathbf{x}^\alpha + \sum_{\beta \in \mathcal{A}_{\text{res}}} a_\beta \mathbf{x}^\beta, \tag{10}$$

$\alpha, \beta = (i_1, i_2, \ldots, i_n)$ is the index vector, $\mathcal{A}_{\text{lin}}$ is the set of terms selected by the dynamic parity partition strategy, and $\mathbf{x}^\alpha, \mathbf{x}^\beta = x_1^{i_1} x_2^{i_2} \cdots x_n^{i_n}$, $\mathcal{A}_{\text{res}} = \{\beta \mid \beta \notin \mathcal{A}_{\text{lin}}\}$.

For linear-absorbable terms containing single-variable monomials such as $a_k x^k$ where $k > 2$ and $k\%2 \neq 0$, we split them into the form:

$$a_k x^k = a_k \cdot \underbrace{x^{k-1}}_{I_{x^{k-1}}} \cdot x, \quad I_{x^{k-1}} = \left[\min_{x \in D} x^{k-1}, \max_{x \in D} x^{k-1}\right] \tag{11}$$

For other multivariate monomials like $T_n = a_k x_1^{\alpha_1} \cdots x_p^{\alpha_p}$ $(\alpha_1 + \ldots + \alpha_p = n)$, we convert the even-powered components to intervals while preserving the linear univariate terms, extend the original constant coefficients to interval forms.

$$T_n = \underbrace{\left(\prod_{\substack{j-1 \\ i_j \text{ even}}}^{m} x_j^{i_j}\right)}_{I_a} \cdot \left(\prod_{\substack{k=1 \\ i_k \text{ odd}}}^{n-m} x_k\right), I_\alpha = \left[\min_{\mathbf{x} \in D}\left(\prod_{j:i_j \text{ even}} x_j^{i_j}\right), \max_{\mathbf{x} \in D}\left(\prod_{j:i_j \text{ even}} x_j^{i_j}\right)\right] \tag{12}$$

Then, interval arithmetic is applied to merge terms of the same variable, resulting in the interval-linear expression:

$$P_{\text{linear}}(\mathbf{x}) = \left(a_0 + \sum_{i=1}^{n} \left[\underline{c_i}, \overline{c_i}\right] x_i\right), \quad c_i = \sum_{\alpha \in \mathcal{A}_{\text{lin}}} a_\alpha \otimes \prod [\underline{I_{x_j}}, \overline{I_{x_j}}] \tag{13}$$

The detailed process for constructing the interval linear abstraction of TMs is outlined in Algorithm 1. We extract information from higher-order terms based on their parity characteristics and integrate it into linear terms or the remainder using the methods described earlier.

Algorithm 1. Constructing the interval linear abstraction of TMs

Input: Origin Taylor models vTM_0;
Output: the interval linear abstraction of TMs vTM_l ;

```
for each polynomial p in vTM_0 do
    pol, dom, r ← polynomial(p), domain(p), reminder(p)
    n, order ← dim(pol), highest_term(pol)
    pol ← normalize_taylor(pol, dom, true)            ▷ Normalize Taylor models
    if order > 1 then
        coeffs[1...n][l, u] ← linear_pol(pol)         ▷ Get linear term coefficients
        for each term t in pol do
            if t.order%2 == 0 then
                r ← r ⊕ evaluate(t, dom)              ▷ Calculate the interval value of t
            else
                pos, interval ← linearization(t, dom) ▷ Get linearized coefficients
                coeffs[pos] ← coeffs[pos] ⊕ interval
            end if
        end for
    end if
    vTM_l ← vTM_l ∪ {(pol, r)}
end for
return vTM_l
```

Here, we provide an example to demonstrate in detail how to construct the interval linear abstraction of TMs.

Example 1. Consider the normalized Taylor Models $\mathcal{T} = (p, I) = (p, [-0.5, 0.5]^2)$ where

$$p_1(x) = 1.0x_1^3 + 0.3x_2^3 + 0.2x_1x_2^2 - 0.6x_1 - 0.1x_2 + 1$$
$$p_2(x) = 0.5x_1^3 + 0.4x_1^2 - 0.3x_1 + 0.4x_2 + 1$$

Firstly, we decompose the polynomial into linear-absorbable terms and remainder-absorbable terms, then the corresponding parts of the linear-absorbable terms and the remainder-absorbable terms are transformed into intervals, and finally, the interval linear abstraction of TMs is obtained by interval arithmetic.

$$\begin{aligned} p_1(x) &= \underbrace{1.0x_1^2 \times x_1 + 0.3x_2^2 \times x_2 + 0.2x_2^2 \times x1 - 0.6x_1 - 0.1x_2}_{linear-absorbable} + 1, I_1 = [-0.5, 0.5] \\ &\subset [0, 1.0]x_1 + [0, 0.3]x_2 + [0, 0.2]x_1 - 0.6x_1 - 0.1x_2 + 1, I_1 = [-0.5, 0.5] \\ &\subset [-0.6, 0.6]x_1 + [-0.1, 0.2]x_2 + 1, I_1 = [-0.5, 0.5] \end{aligned}$$

$$\begin{aligned} p_2(x) &= \underbrace{0.5x_1^2 \times x_1 - 0.3x_1 + 0.4x_2}_{linear-absorbable} + 1 + \underbrace{0.4x_1^2}_{remainder-absorbable}, I_2 = [-0.5, 0.5] \\ &\subset [0, 0.5]x_1 - 0.3x_1 + 0.4x_2 + 1 + [0, 0.4], I_2 = [-0.5, 0.5] \\ &\subset [-0.3, 0.2]x_1 + 0.4x_2 + 1.2, I_2 = [-0.7, 0.7] \end{aligned}$$

By constructing the interval-linear expression, two key accuracy improvements are achieved.

- For precision in linear term absorption, tighter bounds are achieved via **equality constraints** (e.g., variable self-identity like $x_1 = x_1$) and by merging interval-linear terms of the same variables.
- By integrating most polynomial terms into linear components while retaining only even-order terms to be absorbed into the remainder, we significantly reduce the over-approximation error in the remainder after linearization.

3.2 Conversion Between Interval Linear Abstraction of TMs and Linear Abstract Domains

In abstract interpretation, while some abstract domains (e.g., interval polyhedra) natively support interval linear form, commonly used abstract domains in neural network verification—such as zonotope and starset—lack direct support for such representations. This section focuses on transforming interval linear abstractions of TMs into these linear abstract domains.

Firstly, to derive a linear expression from the interval-linear expression, we replace interval-valued coefficients with constant ones. Since the polynomial of TMs is normalized, we select the bound with the larger absolute magnitude within each coefficient interval as the constant coefficient for each linear term. This approach reduces over-approximation errors as much as possible while ensuring computational soundness. For example, $[-0.6, 0.6]x_1 + [-0.1, 0.2]x_2 + 1$ can be overapproximate as $0.6x_1 + 0.2x_2 + 1$ in example 1 since $D_{x_1} = [-1, 1]$.

Conversion from the linear abstraction of TMs to the box merely requires computing the interval bounds for each variable. A conversion example involving two variables is provided below:

$$B = \left\{ P(x,y) = \sum_{i=0}^{n}\sum_{j=0}^{n} c_{i,j} x^i y^j \,|\, x \in [\underline{x}, \overline{x}], y \in [\underline{y}, \overline{y}] \right\} \subseteq \sum_{i=0}^{n}\sum_{j=0}^{n} c_{i,j} [\underline{x}, \overline{x}]^i [\underline{y}, \overline{y}]^j \tag{14}$$

The reverse conversion is also straightforward. For a given single-variable interval a, we derive the corresponding linear TMs using the following formula:

$$T = P(x) + I = (0.5(\overline{a} + \underline{a}) + 0.5(\overline{a} - \underline{a})x) + [0, 0], \text{ where } x \in [-1, 1]. \tag{15}$$

Converting between the linear abstraction of TM and the zonotope is more complex than the box. Zonotope conversion requires encoding the polynomial coefficient as a generator matrix of the zonotope and bounding the remainder within the zonotope's noise terms. Let the linear abstraction of TMs be:

$$p_i(\mathbf{x}) = \mathbf{a}_i \mathbf{x} + b_i, r_i \in [-e_i, e_i] \tag{16}$$

where $\mathbf{x} \in [-1, 1]^n$, $1 \leq i \leq m$, $\mathbf{x} = (x_1, x_2, \ldots, x_n)^T$ is an n-dimensional vector representing variable, $\mathbf{a}_i = (a_{i1}, a_{i2}, \ldots, a_{in})^T$ is the coefficient vector of the i-th polynomial. The center of the zonotope is composed of the constant terms from all polynomials. The generator matrix G consists of two components: the linear term generator matrix which corresponds to the polynomial coefficient vectors and the remainder term generator matrix which is derived from a diagonal matrix converted from the remainder interval.

It is imperative to introduce new variables for the zonotope during the propagation of the neural network in order to represent the error caused by the approximate activation function. It is required to perform order reduction on the zonotope, convert it into the representation given by (17), and subsequently derive the corresponding Taylor models.

$$\begin{aligned} \mathbf{c} = \mathbf{b} &= \begin{bmatrix} b_1 \; b_2 \cdots b_m \end{bmatrix} \\ G_{\text{linear}} &= \begin{bmatrix} \mathbf{a}_1 \; \mathbf{a}_2 \cdots \mathbf{a}_m \end{bmatrix}, \quad G_{\text{residual}} = \text{diag}(e_1, e_2, \ldots, e_m) \\ G &= \begin{bmatrix} G_{\text{linear}} \; G_{\text{residual}} \end{bmatrix} \end{aligned} \tag{17}$$

By applying the linear abstraction of TMs, we ensure that the overapproximation remains tight while reducing the loss of linear dependencies within the abstract domain as demonstrated in the following example.

Example 2. Following our approach described above, we get the linear abstractions of TMs like $p_1(x) = 0.6x_1 + 0.2x_2 + 1, r_1 = [-0.5, 0.5]$, $p_2(x) = 0.3x_1 + 0.4x_2 + 1.2, r_2 = [-0.7, 0.7]$ from example 1. For box domain, we get the Box $\mathcal{B}_1 = \begin{bmatrix} -1.7 \; 3.7 \\ -0.7, \; 3.1 \end{bmatrix}$ from direct conversion, the Box $\mathcal{B}_2 = \begin{bmatrix} -0.3 \; 2.3 \\ -0.0 \; 2.6 \end{bmatrix}$ from our method, as shown in Fig. 4(a). For Zonotope, we get the $C_{\mathcal{Z}_1} = C_{\mathcal{Z}_2} = [1.0, 1.2]$, $\text{generator}_{\mathcal{Z}_1} = \begin{bmatrix} 0.0 & -0.1 & 2.2 & 0.0 \\ -0.3 & 0.4 & 0.0 & 1.2 \end{bmatrix}$, $\text{generator}_{\mathcal{Z}_2} = \begin{bmatrix} 0.6 \; 0.2 \; 0.5 \; 0.0 \\ 0.3 \; 0.4 \; 0.0 \; 0.7 \end{bmatrix}$ from our method, as shown in Fig. 4(b).

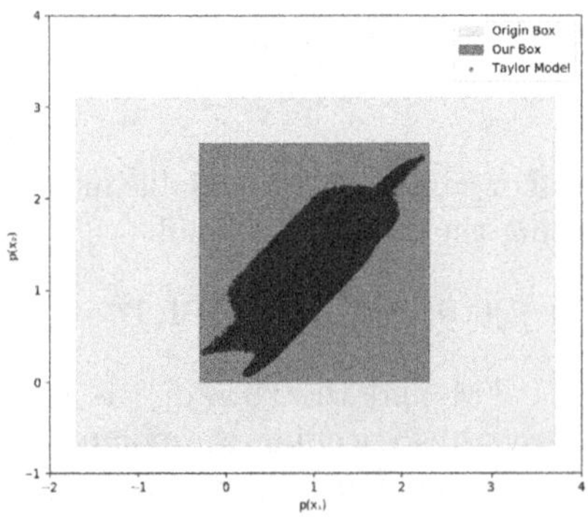

(a) Comparison of Box $\mathcal{B}_1$ and $\mathcal{B}_2$

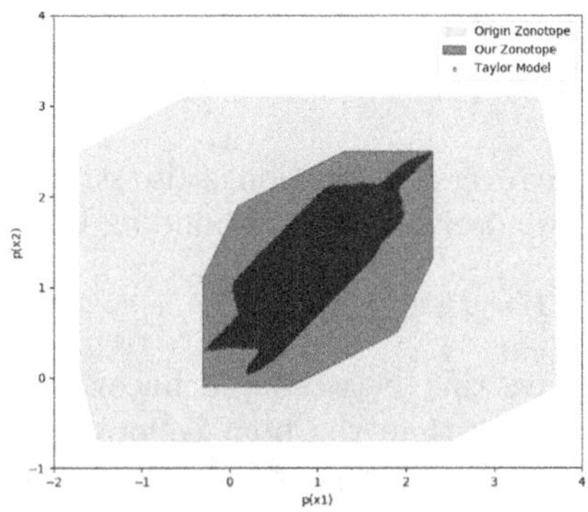

(b) Comparison of Zonotope $\mathcal{Z}_1$ and $\mathcal{Z}_2$

Fig. 4. Box example and Zonotope example. The yellow area is obtained by the direct conversion, the blue area is obtained by our method, and the 300000 red points are the simulation of the Taylor models (Color figure online)

4 The Overall Workflow

In this section, we present our workflow for reachable set computation in NNCSs based on TMs and linear abstract domains (Fig. 5).

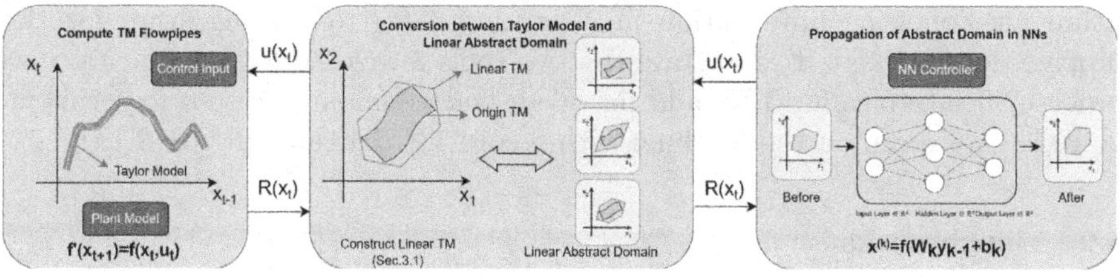

Fig. 5. The overall workflow

The verification process follows an iterative procedure:

Compute TM Flowpipes: Based on the state set $X_{(t-1)}$ at time step $t-1$ and the current control input $u_{(t-1)}$, the Taylor flowpipe computation method generates a Taylor model approximation $R(x_t)$ of the state $x_{(t)}$ at time step t.

Conversion Between TM and Linear Abstract Domains: Apply the interval linear abstraction of TMs method proposed in Sects. 3.1 and 3.2 to decompose the original Taylor model into an interval linear form and convert it to the corresponding linear abstract domain.

Propagation of Abstract Domains in NNs: Using the linear abstract domain of $R(x_t)$ as input constraints, perform forward propagation of the NN, and output the feasible control input $u(x_t)$. Then $u(x_t)$ is converted to the linear abstraction of TMs and propagated to the next time step for computation.

The Algorithm 2 outlines the workflow of our reachability algorithm.

Algorithm 2. Reachability Algorithm combining Taylor models and linear abstract domains

Input: Initial states X_0; time horizon $T = K\tau$; abstract domain type *ad_type*;
Output: Reachable set R; verification results V

$TM_x \leftarrow \text{constructTM}(X_0)$
for $k \leftarrow 0$ **to** $K-1$ **do**
  $TM_{linear} \leftarrow \text{linear\_TM}(TM_x)$ ▷ Construct the linear abstraction of TMs
  $AD_k^{'} \leftarrow \text{convertT2A}(TM_{linear}, ad\_type)$
  $AD_k \leftarrow P_\kappa(AD_k^{'})$ ▷ Compute NN reachable set
  $TM_{ad} \leftarrow \text{convertA2T}(AD_k, ad\_type)$ ▷ Convert to Taylor models
  $TM^{'} \leftarrow \text{merge}(TM_x, TM_{ad})$ ▷ Merge Taylor models
  $R_k, TM_x \leftarrow P_f(f, TM^{'}, \tau)$ ▷ Compute plant reachable set
end for
$R \leftarrow \bigcup_{i=0}^{K-1} R_i$
return R

5 Experimental Evaluation

5.1 Implementation

We implemented a prototype called TTLA in conjunction with the TaylorModel.jl implemented TM Flowpipe calculation [28] and DeepZ [19] (an algorithm for Zonotope propagation in NNs) and AI^2 [26](an algorithm for Box propagation in NNs). To integrate the two tools for closed-loop verification, we provide an interface for TMs and linear abstract domains. All our experiments of TTLA were run on the machine with 8-core 3.2 GHz and 16 GB RAM.

5.2 Benchmarks

We used 8 benchmarks to evaluate our approach. These benchmarks are from the competition on NNCSs at ARCH-COMP 2023 [3] and 2024 [29] covering a wide range of dynamic systems and NN controllers with various activation functions. All of the benchmarks are shown in Table 1.

Table 1. List of benchmarks from ARCH-COMP 2023 and 2024. V denotes the dimension of the state variable

Name	V	Initial set	Specifications
ACC	5	$x_{\text{lead}}(0) \in [90, 110], v_{\text{lead}}(0) \in [32, 32.2], a_{\text{lead}}(0) = a_{\text{ego}}(0) = 0, v_{\text{ego}}(0) \in [30, 30.2], x_{\text{ego}} \in [10, 11]$	$D_{\text{rel}} \geq D_{\text{safe}}, D_{\text{safe}} = D_{\text{default}} + T_{\text{gap}} \cdot v_{\text{ego}}$
SP	2	$x_1 \in [1.0, 1.175], x_2 \in [0.0, 0.2]$	$x_1 \in [0, 1]$
DP	4	$x \in [1.0, 1.3]^4$	$x \in [-1.5, 1.5]^4$
Airplane	12	$x = y = z = r = p = q = 0, [v_x, v_y, v_z, \phi, \theta, \psi] \in [0.0, 1.0]^6$	$s_y \in [-1.0, 1.0], [\phi, \theta, \psi] \in [-1.0, 1.0]^3$
Unicycle	4	$x_1 \in [9.5, 9.55], x_2 \in [-4.5, -4.45], x_3 \in [2.1, 2.11], x_4 \in [1.5, 1.51]$	$x_1 \in [-0.6, 0.6], x_2 \in [-0.2, 0.2], x_3 \in [-0.06, 0.06], x_4 \in [-0.3, 0.3]$
TORA	4	$x_1 \in [-0.77, -0.75], x_2 \in [-0.45, -0.43], x_3 \in [0.51, 0.54], x_4 \in [-0.3, -0.28]$	$x_1 \in [-0.1, 0.2], x_2 \in [-0.9, -0.6]$
AC	6	$\omega_1 \in [-0.45, -0.44], \omega_2 \in [-0.55, -0.54], \omega_3 \in [0.65, 0.66], \psi_1 \in [-0.75, -0.74], \psi_2 \in [0.85, 0.86], \psi_3 \in [-0.65, -0.64]$	$\omega_1 \in [-0.2, 0], \omega_2 \in [-0.5, -0.4], \omega_3 \in [0, 0.2], \psi_1 \in [-0.7, -0.6], \psi_2 \in [0.7, 0.8], \psi_3 \in [-0.4, -0.2]$
QUAD	12	$[x_1, x_2, x_3, x_4, x_5, x_6] \in [-0.0045, 0.0045], [x_7, x_8, x_9, x_{10}, x_{11}, x_{12}] = 0$	$x_3 \in [0.94, 1.06]$

5.3 Result

Comparison with Prior Work. We conduct a comprehensive evaluation of TTLA against state-of-the-art NNCS verification tools of different categories:

- **NNV2.0** [30]**:** A hybrid approach combining star sets (for neural networks) and zonotopes (for dynamic systems)
- **JuliaReach** [13]**:** Taylor model-based plant analysis with zonotopic neural network abstraction
- **Verisig2.0** [18]**:** Taylor models propagation through neural networks using Flow* for verification
- **Sherlock** [15]**:** Sampling-based functional over-approximation of NNs using Flow* for verification

The evaluation covers 8 benchmarks from ARCH-COMP 2023–2024 [3,29], spanning autonomous vehicles (ACC, Unicycle), flight systems (Quadrotor), mechanical and classical control systems(TORA). Since the box cannot effectively track variable dependencies [8,11], we present the results using the zonotope.

Table 2. Result over ARCH-COMP 23 and 24 Benchmark. V: number of state variables; σ: activation functions; M: number of hidden layers; n: number of neurons in each hidden layer; 'time(s)': runtime in seconds; 'unknown': the property could not be verified; '': the approach cannot be applied to support σ

Benchmark	V	NN Controller			time(s)				
		σ	M	n	TTLA	JuliaReach	NNV2.0	Verisig2.0	Sherlock
ACC	5	ReLU	5	20	**0.33**	0.36	9.5	529[1]	1.4
SP	2	ReLU	2	25	1.3	1.8	1.9	–	**0.3**
DPm	4	ReLU	2	25	**0.56**	0.57	20.1	–	unknown
DPl	4	ReLU	2	25	**1.27**	1.77	19.4	–	unknown
Airplane	12	ReLU	3	100	**6.7**	7.7	20.0	–	unknown
Unicycle	4	ReLU	1	500	**40.32**	40.86	unknown	-	167.6
TORA	4	ReLU-Tanh	3	20	**1.5**	1.9	1684.7	43[2]	–
	4	Sigmoid	3	20	**4.1**	4.5	4363.3	50	–
AC	6	Sigmoid	3	64	**1.0**	1.5	unknown	–	–
QUAD[3]	12	Sigmoid	3	64	**7.2**	unknown	unknown	–	–

[1] ACC's NN structure is adopted to 3×20 with Sigmoid for using Verisig2.0.
[2] TORA's activation function is adopted to Tanh for using Verisig2.0.
[3] The initial set of QUAD is $[-0.0045, 0.0045]^6 \times \{0\}^6$.

According to Table 2, our tool TTLA outperforms NNV2.0, Verisig2.0, and Sherlock in terms of both accuracy and efficiency. Key metrics include verification success rate and computational efficiency.

1) **Verification Success Rate:** The verification success rate reflects the comprehensive capability of a tool, primarily determined by the types of activation functions supported and the overapproximated precision of reachable sets. Only TTLA successfully verifies all benchmarks. By employing diverse abstract domains for neural network analysis, TTLA, JuliaReach, and NNV2.0 are capable of handling all types of activation functions. But Sherlock can only handle ReLU and Verisig2.0 can only handle differential activation functions. The unknown verification results indicate that the overapproximation of the reachable set is too large to verify the safe property.

2) **Computational Efficiency:** TTLA achieves 9/10 fastest verification times with an average runtime of 6.3 s. By calculating the average computation time, TTLA achieves speedup factors of **1.08**×**, 8.94**×**, 32.86**×**, and 140.66**× over JuliaReach, Sherlock, Verisig 2.0, and NNV2.0, respectively.

Initial State Set Ranges. In the verification of the SP system, it is necessary to check for intersections with unsafe regions and verify property by identifying counterexamples. For counterexample simulation in small-scale initial state sets, Sherlock demonstrates faster verification speeds compared to our tool. However, in other benchmarks, as the initial state set ranges expand, Sherlock either requires significantly more computation time or fails to verify the target properties due to insufficient precision.

Partitioning Strategy. In the verification of TORA, our tool demonstrates remarkable speedup ratios compared to NNV2.0. NNV2.0's limited verification precision necessitates partitioning the initial state sets to compute tighter reachable sets from smaller initial subsets. We adopted the same strategy in the Unicycle. However, unlike NNV2.0, TTLA maintains efficient verification times due to its low time consumption of single verification and parallelization.

Abstract Representation Conversion. JuliaReach provides a method for directly converting in Eq. (6) and (7). Our acceleration compared to JuliaReach originates from two algorithmic innovations:

- For benchmarks using linear Taylor expansion, we directly convert them into the corresponding abstract domains without going through operations such as extracting linear polynomials.
- As for higher-order Taylor models, our method of constructing interval linear abstractions is comparable to the time consumption of computing the intervals directly but is faster in the conversion.

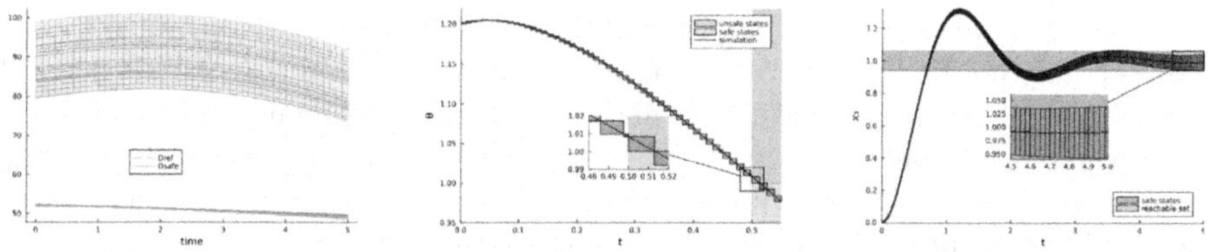

(a) ACC (b) SP (c) QUAD

Fig. 6. Verification results of different specifications from TTLA. We additionally plot simulations from the extreme points of X_0. (Color figure online)

The visualization results of TTLA across various benchmarks with different specifications are presented in Fig. 6. Case (a) shows the verification results of ACC, the safety specification of the system can be expressed $D_{rel}(\text{orange}) \geq D_{safe}(\text{blue})$; Case (b) shows a violation of safety by constructing a counterexample; while Case (c) demonstrates compliance with the reachability specification.

Precision Comparison. This section presents a further discussion of the improvement of the TTLA, with a particular focus on the exploration of the linear abstraction of TMs. We focus on the reachable set reduction for the properties that need to be verified, which directly reflects the difference in accuracy.

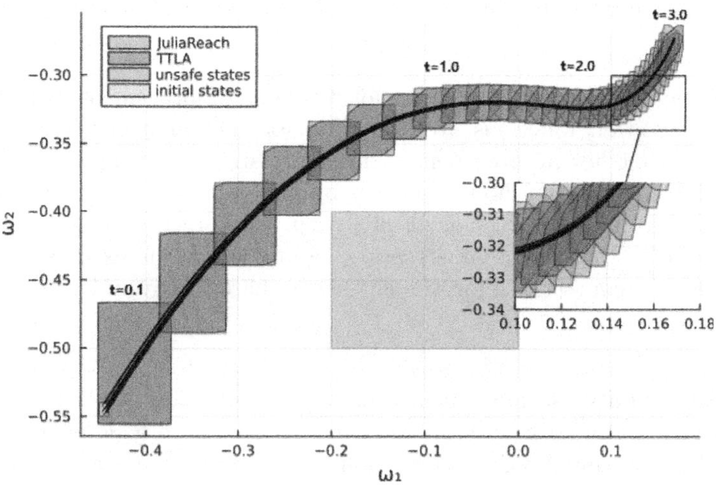

Fig. 7. Comparison of reachable sets in AC

As illustrated in Fig. 7, a comparison is made between the reachable sets computed by the interval linear abstraction of TMs and the original reachable sets by JuliaReach. It is evident that during the initial phase ranging from 0.1 s to

1.0 s, the improvement in the precision of the reachable sets, as determined by our method, may not be immediately apparent. Since the linear terms of TMs derived from Taylor expansion contain the majority of the dependency information in the initial phase. Consequently, the upper approximation error introduced by the linearization of the higher terms is significantly reduced. However, as the closed-loop verification process is iterated, the improvement in accuracy becomes more apparent from 2.0 s to 3.0 s. More importantly, the abstractions generated by our method are better at tracking the relationships among system variables, which is visually reflected in the plots as the blue regions more closely align with the black simulation trajectories.

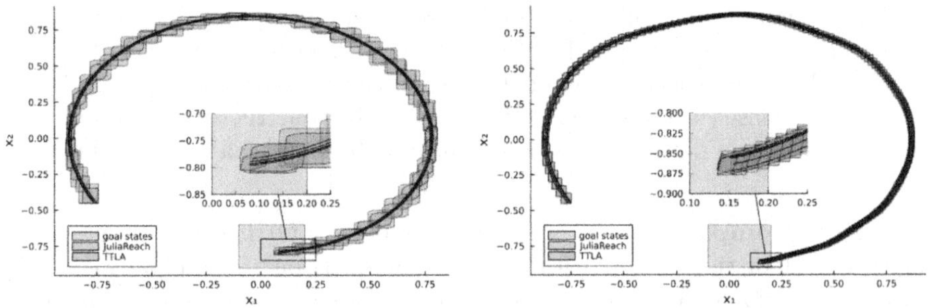

(a) TORA with ReLU-Tanh (b) TORA with Sigmoid

Fig. 8. Comparison of reachable sets in TORA with different activation functions

the linear abstraction of TMs demonstrates an improvement in Fig. 8 when different activation functions are employed for the same benchmark TORA. We observe that our improvement yields more significant improvements when the direct conversion method described by Eq. (6) and (7) is not sufficiently tight as shown in Fig. 8(a). Conversely, when the direct conversion method is already close to the optimal abstraction—approaching the expressive limits of the abstract domain—the improvement benefits are relatively limited as shown in Fig. 8(b).

Scalability Analysis. Since neural network verification tools such as DeepZ exhibit significantly stronger scalability in handling large-scale neural networks compared to existing NNCSs verification tools, this section focuses on demonstrating how our approach leverages and enhances the scalability of NNCS verification by integrating these advanced neural network verification capabilities.

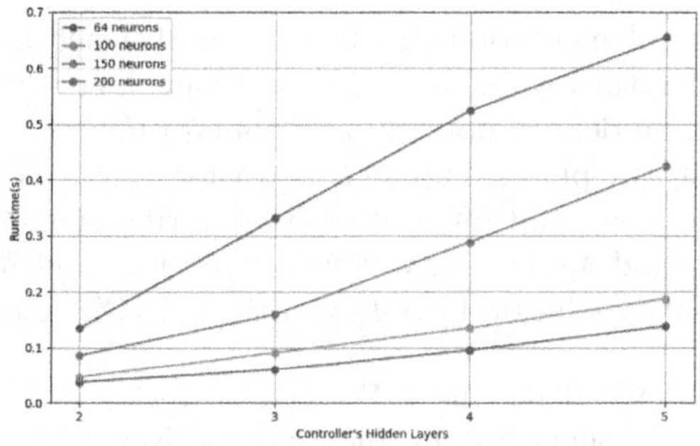

Fig. 9. Runtimes of the neural network component with different configurations

Using QUAD as a benchmark, we conduct scalability experiments by replacing the original neural network controller with architectures of varying depths and widths. Then we compare the verification time required for the neural network component with networks of different sizes, as shown in Fig. 9. While the verification time grows with network complexity, our approach maintains sub-second execution times (under 0.7 s) for abstract domain propagation through large-scale networks (up to 5 hidden layers) across multiple closed-loop verification cycles.

6 Conclusion

This paper presents a verification approach for NNCSs by combining Taylor models (TMs) with linear abstract domains. Our key contribution lies in a method for constructing the interval linear abstraction of TMs, which effectively extracts dependency information from higher-order terms and reduces overapproximation errors introduced during linearization. By leveraging the even and odd characteristics of TMs, our method enables precise and scalable conversions between TMs and various linear abstract domains.

The proposed approach achieves two critical advantages:

1) **Preservation of Variable Dependencies:** Our interval linear abstraction method retains variable dependencies in control inputs, which is essential for tracking input-output mappings of neural networks across multiple control steps. This capability is particularly vital for closed-loop verification, where relational abstract domains (e.g., Zonotopes) outperform non-relational domains like Box, which discard dependency information and fail to verify most safety properties.

2) **Accuracy, Efficiency, and Scalability:** Experimental results demonstrate that our method outperforms existing tools on most benchmarks in both accuracy and efficiency. Our tool demonstrates excellent scalability. Even when the neural network is scaled to a 5 × 200 configuration, it maintains the computation time for the neural network component within 0.7 s.

Currently, our implementation only uses linear abstract domains such as Box and Zonotope. For future work, we will investigate how structural features of TMs (e.g., polynomial degree, domain partitioning) influence linear abstraction quality. Additionally, we plan to extend support for advanced relational domains (e.g., Polytopes, Starset) and integrate hybrid verification tools like Flow* to enhance scalability and applicability. These extensions will further solidify our approach as a versatile solution for safety-critical NNCS verification.

Acknowledgement. We thank the ICECCS 2025 reviewers for their constructive feedback. This work is supported by the National Key R&D Program of China (No. 2022YFA1005101) and the National Natural Science Foundation of China (Nos. 62032024).

References

1. Mnih, V., et al.: Human-level control through deep reinforcement learning. Nature **518**(7540), 529–533 (2015)
2. Hu, Y., et al.: Planning-oriented autonomous driving. In: Proceedings of the IEEE/CVF Conference on Computer Vision and Pattern Recognition, pp. 17853–17862 (2023)
3. Manzanas Lopez, D., Althoff, M., Forets, M., Johnson, T.T., Ladner, T., Schilling, C.: ARCH-COMP23 category report: artificial intelligence and neural network control systems (AINNCS) for continuous and hybrid systems plants. In: EPiC Series in Computing (2023)
4. Kumpati, S.N., Kannan, P., et al.: Identification and control of dynamical systems using neural networks. IEEE Trans. Neural Netw. **1**(1), 4–27 (1990)
5. Chen, P.Y., Sharma, Y., Zhang, H., Yi, J., Hsieh, C.J.: EAD: elastic-net attacks to deep neural networks via adversarial examples. In: Proceedings of the AAAI Conference on Artificial Intelligence, vol. 32 (2018)
6. Szegedy, C., et al.: Intriguing properties of neural networks. arXiv preprint arXiv:1312.6199 (2013)
7. Kurakin, A., Goodfellow, I.J., Bengio, S.: Adversarial examples in the physical world. In: Artificial Intelligence Safety and Security, pp. 99–112. Chapman and Hall/CRC (2018)
8. Huang, C., Fan, J., Chen, X., Li, W., Zhu, Q.: POLAR: a polynomial arithmetic framework for verifying neural-network controlled systems. In: Bouajjani, A., Holík, L., Wu, Z. (eds.) ATVA 2022. LNCS, vol. 13505, pp. 414–430. Springer, Cham (2022). https://doi.org/10.1007/978-3-031-19992-9_27
9. Chen, X., Abraham, E., Sankaranarayanan, S.: Taylor model flowpipe construction for non-linear hybrid systems. In: 2012 IEEE 33rd Real-Time Systems Symposium, pp. 183–192. IEEE (2012)
10. Singh, G., Gehr, T., Püschel, M., Vechev, M.: Boosting robustness certification of neural networks. In: International Conference on Learning Representations (2019)
11. Tran, H.-D., et al.: NNV: the neural network verification tool for deep neural networks and learning-enabled cyber-physical systems. In: Lahiri, S.K., Wang, C. (eds.) CAV 2020. LNCS, vol. 12224, pp. 3–17. Springer, Cham (2020). https://doi.org/10.1007/978-3-030-53288-8_1

12. Neumaier, A.: The wrapping effect, ellipsoid arithmetic, stability and confidence regions. In: Albrecht, R., Alefeld, G., Stetter, H.J. (eds.) Validation Numerics. Computing Supplementum, vol. 9, pp. 175–190. Springer, Vienna (1993). https://doi.org/10.1007/978-3-7091-6918-6_14
13. Schilling, C., Forets, M., Guadalupe, S.: Verification of neural-network control systems by integrating Taylor models and zonotopes. In: Proceedings of the AAAI Conference on Artificial Intelligence, vol. 36, pp. 8169–8177 (2022)
14. Ivanov, R., Weimer, J., Alur, R., Pappas, G.J., Lee, I.: Verisig: verifying safety properties of hybrid systems with neural network controllers. In: Proceedings of the 22nd ACM International Conference on Hybrid Systems: Computation and Control, pp. 169–178 (2019)
15. Dutta, S., Chen, X., Sankaranarayanan, S.: Reachability analysis for neural feedback systems using regressive polynomial rule inference. In: Proceedings of the 22nd ACM International Conference on Hybrid Systems: Computation and Control, pp. 157–168 (2019)
16. Huang, C., Fan, J., Li, W., Chen, X., Zhu, Q.: ReachNN: reachability analysis of neural-network controlled systems. ACM Trans. Embed. Comput. Syst. (TECS) **18**(5s), 1–22 (2019)
17. Fan, J., Huang, C., Chen, X., Li, W., Zhu, Q.: ReachNN*: a tool for reachability analysis of neural-network controlled systems. In: Hung, D.V., Sokolsky, O. (eds.) ATVA 2020. LNCS, vol. 12302, pp. 537–542. Springer, Cham (2020). https://doi.org/10.1007/978-3-030-59152-6_30
18. Ivanov, R., Carpenter, T., Weimer, J., Alur, R., Pappas, G., Lee, I.: Verisig 2.0: verification of neural network controllers using Taylor model preconditioning. In: Silva, A., Leino, K.R.M. (eds.) CAV 2021. LNCS, vol. 12759, pp. 249–262. Springer, Cham (2021). https://doi.org/10.1007/978-3-030-81685-8_11
19. Singh, G., Gehr, T., Mirman, M., Püschel, M., Vechev, M.: Fast and effective robustness certification. In: Advances in Neural Information Processing Systems, vol. 31 (2018)
20. Singh, G., Gehr, T., Püschel, M., Vechev, M.: An abstract domain for certifying neural networks. Proc. ACM Program. Lang. **3**(POPL), 1–30 (2019)
21. Van Hasselt, H., Guez, A., Silver, D.: Deep reinforcement learning with double Q-learning. In: Proceedings of the AAAI Conference on Artificial Intelligence, vol. 30 (2016)
22. Hawkes, P.W.: Modern Map Methods in Particle Beam Physics. Academic Press (1999)
23. Chen, X., Ábrahám, E., Sankaranarayanan, S.: Flow*: an analyzer for non-linear hybrid systems. In: Sharygina, N., Veith, H. (eds.) CAV 2013. LNCS, vol. 8044, pp. 258–263. Springer, Heidelberg (2013). https://doi.org/10.1007/978-3-642-39799-8_18
24. Berz, M., Makino, K.: Verified integration of odes and flows using differential algebraic methods on high-order Taylor models. Reliable Comput. **4**(4), 361–369 (1998)
25. Neher, M., Jackson, K.R., Nedialkov, N.S.: On Taylor model based integration of odes. SIAM J. Numer. Anal. **45**(1), 236–262 (2007)
26. Gehr, T., Mirman, M., Drachsler-Cohen, D., Tsankov, P., Chaudhuri, S., Vechev, M.: AI2: safety and robustness certification of neural networks with abstract interpretation. In: 2018 IEEE Symposium on Security and Privacy (SP), pp. 3–18. IEEE (2018)
27. Tran, H.-D., et al.: Verification of piecewise deep neural networks: a star set approach with zonotope pre-filter. Formal Aspects Comput. **33**, 519–545 (2021). https://doi.org/10.1007/s00165-021-00553-4

28. Bogomolov, S., Forets, M., Frehse, G., Potomkin, K., Schilling, C.: JuliaReach: a toolbox for set-based reachability. In: Proceedings of the 22nd ACM International Conference on Hybrid Systems: Computation and Control, pp. 39–44 (2019)
29. Manzanas Lopez, D., et al.: ARCH-COMP24 category report: artificial intelligence and neural network control systems (AINNCS) for continuous and hybrid systems plants. In: EPiC Series in Computing (2024)
30. Lopez, D.M., Choi, S.W., Tran, H.D., Johnson, T.T.: NNV 2.0: the neural network verification tool. In: Enea, C., Lal, A. (eds.) CAV 2023. LNCS, vol. 13965, pp. 397–412. Springer, Cham (2023). https://doi.org/10.1007/978-3-031-37703-7_19

Model Checking Nondeterministic Behaviours in the Tendermint Byzantine Fault Tolerant Blockchain Consensus Protocol

Yisong Yu[1,2](✉), Zhe Hou[3], Naipeng Dong[4](✉), and Jin Song Dong[2]

[1] Ningbo University, Ningbo 315211, Zhejiang, China
[2] National University of Singapore, 21 Lower Kent Ridge Road, 119077 Singapore, Singapore
e0792458@u.nus.edu, dcsdjs@nus.edu.sg
[3] Griffith University, 170 Kessels Rd, Nathan, Brisbane, QLD 4111, Australia
z.hou@griffith.edu.au
[4] The University of Queensland, St. Lucia, Brisbane, QLD 4072, Australia
n.dong@uq.edu.au

Abstract. We investigated the Tendermint protocol, a core Byzantine Fault Tolerance (BFT) consensus engine for the Cosmos Blockchain. When modelling this protocol, we faced significant challenges in the computational performance of verification. To mitigate the state-space explosion issue, we improve the model with optimisation techniques, such as partial-order reduction and role-based symmetry reduction. Through verification, we discovered vulnerabilities in the design of Tendermint, and we proposed fixes that regained both the safety and liveness properties. This paper describes our modelling techniques and optimisations, analyses the vulnerabilities and fixes, and discusses how the optimisations impact verification runtime and results.

Keywords: Model Checking · Formal Verification · Blockchain · Consensus Protocol · Byzantine Fault Tolerance

1 Introduction

Blockchain is gaining widespread adoption, serving as the backbone of decentralized systems, such as cryptocurrencies, decentralized finance, and supply chain management. It fundamentally shifts how data is stored, verified, and processed to eliminate single points of failure, making it resilient to fraud, tampering, or unauthorized operations. These qualities heavily depend on the underlying consensus mechanism, which plays a critical role in validating data changes and maintaining the security and consistency of the applications built on top. The robustness and efficiency of consensus mechanisms directly impact the reliability, scalability, and overall performance of blockchain-based decentralized systems.

Despite their widespread use, rigorous proof of Blockchain consensus mechanisms is scarce. This is largely due to the complexity of achieving consensus, which

Y. Zhou et al. (Eds.): ICECCS 2025, LNCS 15746, pp. 379–400, 2026.
https://doi.org/10.1007/978-3-032-00828-2_21

requires cooperative execution of geographically distributed nodes exchanging information asynchronously. Challenges arise from issues such as partial connectivity of the network, unreliable communication channels and malicious nodes (with Byzantine behaviour). The concurrent and nondeterministic nature of node interactions introduces significant challenges for formal verification.

We aim to investigate the capability of formal verification, particularly automatic verification technology, for consensus mechanisms, taking the Tendermint consensus protocol as a case study. We focus on model checking technique, which is widely used in existing consensus verification efforts. Tendermint was chosen due to its practical significance—it powers numerous real-world blockchain platforms like Cosmos. Also, unlike Bitcoin's probabilistic protocols, Tendermint's non-probabilistic nature makes it more feasible for automatic proof.

Previous research on verifying Tendermint consensus protocol has primarily focused on verifying safety (maintaining data integrity) because liveness (ensuring continuing operation) verification poses significant challenges due to the extensive state space when naively translating the pseudocode into formal specifications. Our goal is to verify both safety and liveness in the presence of Byzantine nodes. To overcome the challenges, we apply state space reduction techniques such as partial order reduction and role-based symmetry reduction, which are crucial for efficient verification of both safety and liveness properties.

We have successfully verified the correctness of this algorithm using the PAT model checker [8,23] in the CSP# formal language, and we believe that we are the first to have verified both the safety and liveness properties of Tendermint. The verification is non-trivial due to the state-space explosion challenges, and the optimisation techniques in this work have the potential to be adopted in verifying other consensus protocols. As a highlight, during our investigation, we identified a critical vulnerability hidden within the Tendermint design that could be exploited to orchestrate a denial-of-service attack, potentially jeopardizing the entire system. This finding emphasizes the importance of rigorous validation of blockchain security. Moreover, we discussed the generalization of our reduction techniques beyond this case study.

In summary, this work makes the following contributions:

- We modelled the Tendermint protocol and proposed optimisations to make verification efficient. We proved that our optimisations preserve the correct semantics of the model, and they are also applicable to similar BFT protocols.
- We identified a vulnerability of Tendermint, and we give an attack demonstration as well as a fix.
- With the help of model optimisations, we verified the Tendermint protocol's safety and liveness after the vulnerability was patched.

2 The Tendermint Consensus Protocol

The Tendermint consensus protocol [10] is implemented in the Tendermint Core of the Cosmos SDK, and is a *state machine replication* algorithm [20] that is inspired by the Practical Byzantine Fault Tolerance (PBFT) algorithm [11] and the DLS algorithm [18].

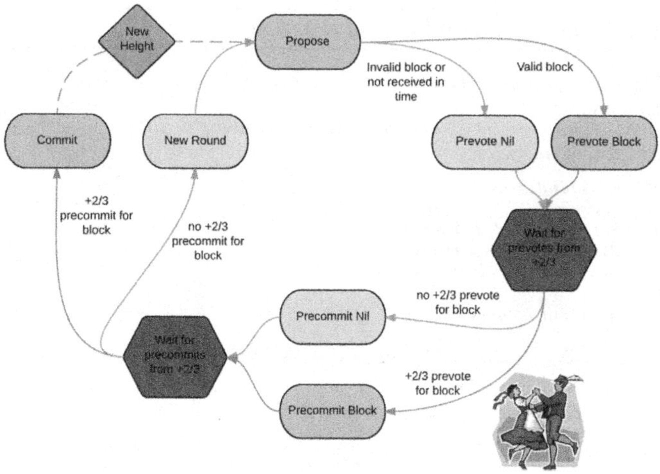

Fig. 1. Overview of Tendermint consensus protocol [24].

Protocol Overview. The protocol proceeds in rounds, and the communication pattern of each round follows a simple state machine as depicted in Fig. 1, resembling the normal case in PBFT [11]. Each round features a proposer selected through a weighted round-robin function based on voting power. Participants are usually referred to as validators which verify the proposed blocks of transactions to be sequentially committed in a chain, each at a new height. Although the state machine diagram seems simple with only ten states, it reflects a limited, single-node perspective, omitting concurrent actions by other nodes. The entire network operation is much more complex, making manual analysis challenging and error-prone.

Protocol Specification. The protocol is detailed in the Tendermint consensus algorithm from the literature [10], shown in Algorithm 1. It uses atomically executed "upon rules", triggered when a local message log accumulates enough messages to satisfy conditions based on validators' voting power. Messages exchanged among nodes include PROPOSAL, PREVOTE, and PRECOMMIT to trigger an upon rules. In addition, the protocol ensures timeliness and reliability through timeout mechanisms (e.g., $timeoutPropose$, $timeoutPrevote$, $timeoutPrecommit$) which are incrementally adjusted for each new round to prevent indefinite delays.

Processes exchange three types of messages to agree on a proposed block of transactions: the proposer sends a PROPOSAL, and nodes respond with PREVOTE and PRECOMMIT messages. PREVOTE and PRECOMMIT carry a small identifier (e.g., a hash of the proposed block) to confirm agreement. To reach a decision, nodes require a PROPOSAL and enough PRECOMMIT messages (i.e., from validators representing at least two-thirds of the voting power). Processes maintain internal variables like $lockedValue$, $lockedRound$, $validValue$, and $validRound$ to track their decision progress and ensure termination and agreement. A correct process updates $validValue$ and $validRound$ when it receives a valid proposal backed by sufficient votes. This guarantees that if a process locks on a value, all correct processes will eventually converge on that decision.

Algorithm 1: The Tendermint Algorithm [10]

```
Initialization:
    h_p, round_p := 0; step_p ∈ {propose, prevote, precommit};
    validRound_p := −1;
    decision_p[], lockedValue_p, lockedRound_p, validValue_p := nil;
upon start do StartRound(0)
Function StartRound(round):
    round_p ← round; step_p ← step;
    if proposer(h_p, round_p) = p then
        if validValue_p ≠ nil then
            proposal ← validValue_p;
        else
            proposal ← getValue();
        broadcast ⟨PROPOSAL, h_p, round_p, proposal, validRound_p⟩;
    else
        schedule OnTimeoutPropose(h_p, round_p) to be executed after
          timeoutPropose(round_p);
upon ⟨PROPOSAL, h_p, round_p, v, −1⟩ from proposer(h_p, round_p) while
  step_p = propose do
    if valid(v) ∧ (lockedRound_p = −1 ∨ lockedValue_p = v) then
        broadcast ⟨PREVOTE, h_p, round_p, id(v)⟩;
    else
        broadcast ⟨PREVOTE, h_p, round_p, nil⟩;
    step_p ← prevote;
upon ⟨PROPOSAL, h_p, round_p, v, vr⟩ from proposer(h_p, round_p) AND
  2f + 1 ⟨PREVOTE, h_p, vr, id(v)⟩ while step_p = propose ∧ (vr ≥ 0 ∧ vr < round_p) do
    if valid(v) ∧ (lockedRound_p ≤ vr ∨ lockedValue_p = v) then
        broadcast ⟨PREVOTE, h_p, round_p, id(v)⟩;
    else
        broadcast ⟨PREVOTE, h_p, round_p, nil⟩;
    step_p ← prevote;
upon 2f + 1 ⟨PREVOTE, h_p, round_p, ∗⟩ while step_p = prevote first time do
    schedule OnTimeoutPrevote(h_p, round_p) to be executed after
      timeoutPrevote(round_p);
```

The gossip communication property ensures messages are propagated across all nodes, enabling processes to synchronize their decisions. The termination mechanism ensures that, even in prolonged rounds, the protocol will eventually finalize a decision. This is achieved without extra messages, making Tendermint efficient and reliable for consensus in distributed systems.

Correctness Criteria. We adopt the correctness criteria from distributed systems [11] in the Tendermint setting as follows:

Safety requires that correct validators all decide on the same value, or formally $\forall p, q \in validators : honest(p) \wedge honest(q) \Rightarrow decision[h_p] = decision[h_q]$.

Liveness requires that all correct validators must eventually decide on a value, or formally $\forall p \in validators : \exists v \in values : honest(p) \Rightarrow decision[h_p] = v$.

3 Our Modelling of Tendermint

Modelling and verifying the Tendermint protocol presented tremendous challenges, especially in verification time. Faithfully modelling the protocol leads to non-termination within a few days. Realising that modelling is an art, we went through 13 versions of modelling; each one included some optimisations to improve runtime to finally achieve a realistic model that is efficient in verification. This section begins with an overview of the overall modelling approach, followed by a detailed analysis of a vulnerability identified during the model checking of our initial, unoptimized model. Finally, we present a walkthrough of the key optimizations that brought the most significant improvements to our verification process, addressing the inherent state-space explosion issue that persists even in the patched model.

Algorithm 1: The Tendermint Algorithm (Continued) [10]

```
upon ⟨PROPOSAL, h_p, round_p, v, ∗⟩ from proposer(h_p, round_p) AND
  2f + 1 ⟨PREVOTE, h_p, round_p, id(v)⟩ while valid(v) ∧ step_p ≥ prevote for the first
  time do
    if step_p = prevote then
        lockedValue_p ← v; lockedRound_p ← round_p;
        broadcast ⟨PRECOMMIT, h_p, round_p, id(v)⟩;
        step_p ← precommit;
    validValue_p ← v; validRound_p ← round_p;

upon 2f + 1 ⟨PREVOTE, h_p, round_p, nil⟩ while step_p = prevote do
    broadcast ⟨PRECOMMIT, h_p, round_p, nil⟩;
    step_p ← precommit;

upon 2f + 1 ⟨PRECOMMIT, h_p, round_p, ∗⟩ for the first time do
    schedule OnTimeoutPrecommit(h_p, round_p) to be executed after
      timeoutPrecommit(round_p);

upon ⟨PROPOSAL, h_p, r, v, ∗⟩ from proposer(h_p, r) AND
  2f + 1 ⟨PRECOMMIT, h_p, r, id(v)⟩ while decision_p[h_p] = nil do
    if valid(v) then
        decision_p[h_p] = v; h_p ← h_p + 1;
        reset lockedRound_p, lockedValue_p, validRound_p, validValue_p to initial values
          and empty message log;
        StartRound(0);

upon f + 1 ⟨∗, h_p, round, ∗, ∗⟩ with round > round_p do
    StartRound(0);

Function OnTimeoutPropose(height, round):
    if height = h_p ∧ round = round_p ∧ step_p = propose then
        broadcast ⟨PREVOTE, h_p, round_p, nil⟩;
        step_p ← prevote;

Function OnTimeoutPrevote(height, round):
    if height = h_p ∧ round = round_p ∧ step_p = prevote then
        broadcast ⟨PRECOMMIT, h_p, round_p, nil⟩;
        step_p ← precommit;

Function OnTimeoutPrecommit(height, round):
    if height = h_p ∧ round = round_p then StartRound(round_p + 1);
```

3.1 Protocol Assumptions

Processor: The protocol considers a system of spatially separated ***asynchronous*** processors that communicate with each other by exchanging messages because they do not belong to the same administrative domain and are therefore not directly connected. Each process has some voting power, usually proportional to the amount of stakes (e.g., cryptocurrencies) it commits to participate in the consensus as a validator.

Network: The protocol assumes a *reliably authenticated* ***partially synchronous*** network on which processors communicate with each other. Here, "reliable" implies that messages cannot be lost, duplicated, altered, or corrupted during their transmission through the communication channels, although they may be delivered out of order, "authenticated" means the recipient can verify the identity of the sender, and "partially synchronous" means messages will be eventually delivered within an upper bound of delay.

Communication: The protocol assumes the following auxiliary *communication property* that captures *gossip-based* nature of communication, where GST is Global Stabilization Time and Δ is the upper bound of delay: If a correct node sends some message m at time t, all correct nodes will receive m before $max\{t, GST\} + \Delta$. If a correct node receives some message m at time t, all correct nodes will receive m before $max\{t, GST\} + \Delta$.

Failure Model: Two types of participants are considered in the design of a consensus algorithm [9]: *honest/non-faulty* nodes always engage in benign behaviours by strictly following the pre-defined protocol, and *corrupted/faulty* nodes may randomly crash, or have malicious (Byzantine) intent, e.g., withholding messages, sending invalid messages, and violating expected timing assumptions.

Computation Model: The protocol assumes an atomic execution of each logical entity in the form of an *upon rule* is truly atomic. In addition, a simple ***send*** and its aggregated counterpart ***broadcast*** both operate similarly atomically.

3.2 Introduction to CSP# and PAT

The input language of PAT is CSP#, whose syntax is shown in Definition 1. We chose PAT due to its support for state variables, common programming constructs, and moreover external libraries and functions.

Definition 1 (Syntax of Processes in CSP#).

$$P,\ Q ::= Stop \mid Skip \mid e \rightarrow P \mid e\{prog\} \rightarrow P \mid c!exp \rightarrow P \mid c?x \rightarrow P \mid P[]Q \mid \\ if(b)\{P\}\ else\ \{Q\} \mid ifa(b)\{P\}\ else\ \{Q\} \mid P;Q \mid P||Q \mid P|||Q$$

```
StartRound(p, round) =
 reset_all_flags_in_effective_rounds_for_process.p{effective_rounds[p]=0;} ->
 update_round_and_step_for_process_in_round.p.round{rounds[p]=round; steps[p]=
     PROPOSE;} ->
 ifa (round%N==p) {
  ifa (valid_values[p]!=NIL) {
   update_proposal_for_process_in_round.p.round{proposals[p]=valid_values[p];} ->
    Skip}
   else {
    update_proposal_for_process_in_round.p.round{
     if (honest_processes[p]==true) {proposals[p]=DECISION_T;}
     else {proposals[p]=DECISION_F;}} -> Skip};
   BroadcastProposalMessage(p, rounds[p], proposals[p], valid_rounds[p])
  } else {ScheduleOnTimeoutPropose(p, rounds[p])};
```

Fig. 2. Process StartRound.

```
BroadcastProposalMessage(p, round, proposal, valid_round) =
 broadcast_proposal_message_to_all_processes_from_process.p{message_log.AddProposal(
     new ProposalMessage(p, round, proposal, valid_round));} -> Skip;
```

Fig. 3. Process BroadcastProposalMessage.

Stop and *Skip* are processes denoting inaction and termination, respectively. Process $e \rightarrow P$ engages in an atomic event e first and then behaves as process P. The event is allowed to attach an atomically executed program, denoted as $e\{prog\} \rightarrow P$. Channel communication is supported: $c!exp \rightarrow P$ denotes sending exp over channel c, while $c?x \rightarrow P$ denotes reading from channel c and referring to the message as x. Two types of choices are supported: $P[]Q$ denotes unconditional choice, and $if(b)\{P\}\ else\ \{Q\}$ is conditional branching, where b is a boolean expression. $ifa(b)\{P\}\ else\ \{Q\}$ is a variation of conditional branching that performs the condition checking and first operation of P/Q together. There are three types of process relations: Process $P;Q$ behaves as P until P terminates and then behaves as Q. The parallel composition of two processes is written as $P||Q$, where P and Q may communicate via multi-party event synchronisation. If P and Q only communicate through variables, then it is written as $P|||Q$.

3.3 Overall Modelling

The process *StartRound* in Fig. 2 models the function **StartRound** from line 7 to line 17 of the protocol. It resets $effective\_rounds[p]$, updates $rounds[p]$ and $steps[p]$, and either updates $proposals[p]$ (to $valid\_values[p]$, $DECISION\_T$, or $DECISION\_F$) or schedules *OnTimeoutPropose*, depending on whether p is the proposer. It prevents reverting to a previous round if $round < rounds[p]$.

The process *BroadcastProposalMessage*, shown in Fig. 3, models the behaviour of broadcasting the *PROPOSAL* message by a proposer (line 15 of the protocol). It wraps the proposal data into a *ProposalMessage* instance from the C# library, then adds it to the message log by calling the *AddProposal* method on the $message\_log$ variable, completing the broadcast. The other messages, such as *PREVOTE* and *PRECOMMIT* are modelled similarly.

```
ScheduleOnTimeoutPropose(p, round) =
[BOUND_DELTA>INIT_TIMEOUT_PROPOSE+round*TIMEOUT_DELTA
|| honest_processes[round%N]!=honest_processes[p]]OnTimeoutPropose(p, round) []
[honest_processes[round%N]==honest_processes[p]]Skip;
OnTimeoutPropose(p, round) =
 ifa (round==rounds[p]&&steps[p]==PROPOSE) {
  BroadcastPrevoteMessage(p, round, NIL);
  update_step_for_process_in_round.p.round{steps[p]=PREVOTE;} -> Skip};
```

Fig. 4. Process (Schedule)OnTimeoutPropose.

Then each upon rule from line 18 to line 52 of the protocol is modelled following their corresponding algorithms. To illustrate, we take one upon rule (line 32–39 of the protocol) as an example, and show our non-trivial modelling techniques in Fig. 8 (detailed in Sect. 3.5). We omit the details of other upon rules due to limited space (for details, see the online code).

The process *ScheduleOnTimeoutPropose*, shown in Fig. 4, models how a process p in round *round* schedules the handler *OnTimeoutPropose* (line 53-56 of the protocol). This allows p to simulate both the expiration and non-expiration of the timer, controlled by conditional expressions composed with a choice operator.

If the timeout for the *round* ($INIT\_TIMEOUT\_PROPOSE + round * TIMEOUT\_DELTA$) meets or exceeds a predefined bound $BOUND\_DELTA$ for message delivery in a partially synchronous network, and if p's honesty matches the proposer's in that round, p cannot choose to timeout. In this case, the timer will not expire before p receives a valid $PROPOSAL$ message. This prevents p from prematurely sending a $PREVOTE$ message for *nil* before the proper rule is invoked.

However, if these conditions are not met, p may opt to timeout, even if the $PROPOSAL$ message is cached in the message log. This model's possible behaviours simulate scenarios where p pretends not to have received the message on time, thus covering all potential timeout behaviours.

The other two functions *onTimeoutPrevote* (line 57–60 of the protocol) and *onTimeoutPrecommit* (line 61–62) are modelled in the same manner.

The entire process of Tendermint is shown in Fig. 7, where the left side shows a straightforward modelling that leads to state exploration and right hand side shows our final modelling with partial-order reduction.

3.4 Identified Vulnerability and Fix

This vulnerability was revealed when model checking our early model without any optimization strategies. A counterexample trace was generated, showing that the execution of $StartRound(p)$ may be delayed after a given process p has advanced into a later round.

This vulnerability could occur if a node is reverted from a later round ($round \neq 0$) back to $round = 0$ by delaying the initial $StartRound(0)$ execution. This flaw could deadlock the entire system as the protocol does not explicitly

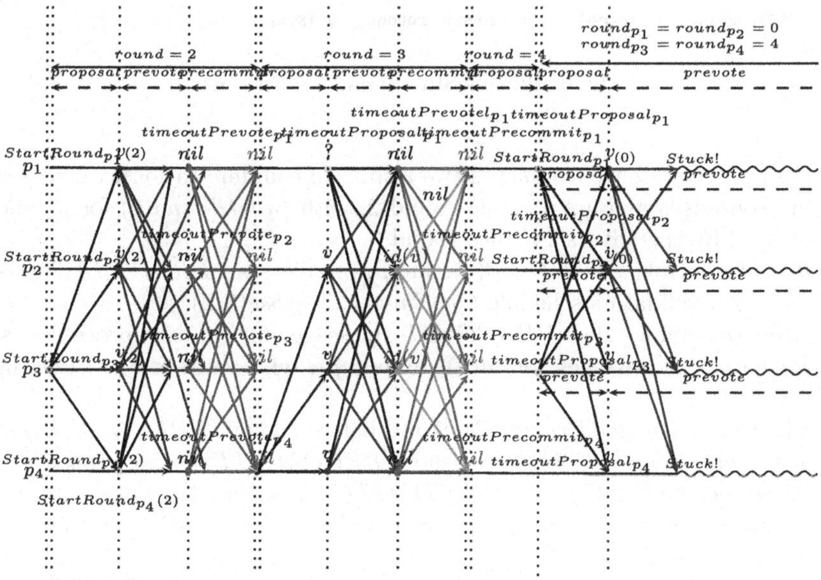

Fig. 5. An attack example demonstrating the identified vulnerability. (Color figure online)

require the function to be completed before other rules are executed, making it vulnerable.

The space-time diagram in Fig. 5 illustrates how a denial-of-service (DoS) attack could exploit the vulnerability. The horizontal axis represents time, segmented into rounds and steps, while the vertical axis represents processes. Events (message send/receive) are marked with dots, and coloured arrows depict message transmission between processes. Each color indicates a specific message type: orange for *PROPOSAL* messages, brown for *PREVOTE* messages for $id(v)$, yellow for *PREVOTE* messages for nil, purple for *PRECOMMIT* messages for $id(v)$, and blue for *PRECOMMIT* messages for nil. The grey text above each event shows which function or rule is activated, leading to the corresponding event below. In this diagram, synchronized message arrivals are shown, although in reality, communication delays are often unstable.

The DoS attack occurs by exploiting the system's vulnerability, where a delayed $StartRound(0)$ invocation can revert nodes back to $round = 0$, disrupting the consensus and eventually deadlocking the system. This example highlights how the absence of a strict requirement for completing certain protocol functions before others enable the attack, making it a significant vulnerability.

In this scenario, all nodes in green are honest, except for p_4 in red, which is Byzantine and behaves arbitrarily. p_4 can delay functions or message transmissions, selectively withhold messages, or send conflicting ones, disrupting the consensus process without completely halting the system. More specifically:

```
StartRoundFixed(p, round) = ifa (round>=rounds[p]) {StartRound(p, round)};
```

Fig. 6. Process StartRound (Fixed ver.).

1. Four processes have completed two rounds of communication without reaching consensus and are starting round 2, with *StartRound*(0) for p_1 and p_2 delayed by the adversary since round 0.
2. p_3 and p_4 invoke *StartRound*(2), and p_3 broadcasts a *PROPOSAL* message for v. All validators schedule $OnTimeoutPropose(0, 2)$.
3. After receiving the *PROPOSAL* message for v, all processes send *PREVOTE* messages for $id(v)$, except p_4, who votes for nil, creating a split vote.
4. The timers $timeoutPrevote(2)$ expire before enough *PREVOTE* messages are received, and all processes send *PRECOMMIT* messages for nil.
5. After receiving sufficient *PRECOMMIT* messages for nil, all processes advance to round 3, with p_4 as proposer, broadcasting $PROPOSAL(v)$ to all except p_1.
6. p_2, p_3, and p_4 send $PREVOTE(id(v))$, while p_4 sends $PREVOTE(nil)$ to p_1, who then votes nil upon timeout.
7. p_2 and p_3 send $PRECOMMIT(id(v))$, while p_1 and p_4 send $PRECOMMIT$ (nil), resulting in another split vote.
8. Upon $timeoutPrecommit(3)$ expiry, all processes start round 4, with p_4 withholding *PROPOSAL* messages.
9. The adversary relinquishes control over p_1 and p_2, reverting them to round 0, causing p_1 to broadcast a *PROPOSAL* for v.
10. p_1 and p_2 send obsolete $PREVOTE(id(v))$ messages for round 0, which are discarded by others.
11. The system reaches deadlock with p_1 and p_2 stuck in round 0, and p_3 and p_4 in round 4, resulting in a denial-of-service attack.

To fix this vulnerability and prevent a malicious entity from exploiting it, we need to wrap the entire body of the function *StartRound* into an if statement that checks if the round *round* to be entered is not smaller than the round the process p is currently in, i.e., if $round >= rounds[p]$, as shown in Fig. 6.

3.5 Reduction Techniques

With the vulnerability identified above addressed, it remains crucial to verify the patched protocol to ensure that the fix does not introduce new bugs and that the protocol continues to satisfy both safety and liveness properties. However, model-checking the corrected version still presents a significant challenge due to the state-space explosion problem, as the number of states grows combinatorially with all possible interleavings of rules across processes, often causing the verification engine to exceed memory limits and abort.

Among those well-known strategies for state space minimization, we applied two key optimizations that are considered most effective in our model, partial-order reduction and symmetry reduction, designed to address the intractability of model checking highly concurrent distributed protocols like Tendermint; we ensure that the optimizations reduce state space without omitting any potential counterexamples from the full model in tools like PAT.

Partial-Order Reduction (POR). POR reduces state space by representing multiple interleaving executions with a single partial order execution, leveraging the connection between interleaving semantics, which treats executions differing only in independent transition order as equivalent, and partial order semantics, which orders events causally. This mitigates the *state space explosion* problem in concurrent systems by generating a compact state space that ensures counterexamples, if present, are preserved in the reduced state space.

We present an example of applying POR in Fig. 7, where our model's separation into two distinct processes, *TendermintBootstrap* and *Tendermint*, shown on the bottom, is preferred over the more intuitive but naive approach of interleaving all participating validators into a single process, shown on the top. In our optimized model, each validator is represented by its own process, *Validator*, consisting of a general choice of those processes denoting upon rules, which is then general-choiced with processes denoting other validators in *Tendermint*, which is then sequentially composed with the process *StartRound* of all validators to enforce a total ordering on the execution sequence of the function *StartRound* at the beginning of model checking, given that this approach significantly reduces the state space—by an order of magnitude—by mitigating the complexity introduced by the interleaving operator, which otherwise generates all possible execution orders, thereby successfully addressing the timeout and out-of-memory issues encountered in earlier models that naively modelled *concurrency*. The decision to impose a predefined order in *TendermintBootstrap* and replace interleaving with general choice operators in *Tendermint* is driven by the observation that nearly all transitions (*i.e.*, operations at each step) are

```
Tendermint() = ||| p: {0..N-1} @ (
  StartRound(p,0) ||| DaemonThread(p) ||| Mutex(p) |||
  UponProposalNewValue(p) ||| UponProposalOldValue(p) |||
  UponSufficientPrevoteAny(p, 0) ||| UponSufficientPrevoteValue(p, 0) |||
  UponSufficientPrevoteNil(p) ||| UponSufficientPrecommitAny(p, 0) |||
  UponSufficientPrecommitValue(p) ||| UponSufficientMessageAny(p, 0));
```

```
Validator(p) = UponProposalValue(p) []
  UponSufficientPrevoteAny(p) [] UponSufficientPrevoteValue(p) []
  UponSufficientPrevoteNil(p) [] UponSufficientPrecommitAny(p) []
  UponSufficientPrecommitValue(p) [] UponSufficientMessageAny(p);
TendermintBootstrap() = StartRound(0, 0); StartRound(1, 0);
  StartRound(2, 0); StartRound(3, 0); Tendermint();
Tendermint() = Validator(0) [] Validator(1) [] Validator(2) [] Validator(3) []
               OnTimeoutPrevoteManual() [] OnTimeoutPrecommitManual();
```

Fig. 7. A comparison of example code without (top) & with (bottom) POR.

local/internal. Excluding pure events that do not introduce side effects to the global states, these transitions only mutate local variables, neither interfering with other processes nor disabling each other (*i.e.*, satisfying *enabledness*), and can be commutated with each other while leading to the same final state (*i.e.*, satisfying *commutativity*), indicating their *independence.*

Correctness of our POR. Next, we discuss the correctness of our partial-order reduction. We adopt the definitions from Clarke et al.'s partial-order reduction technique [13,14]. This technique operates within a model checking algorithm applied to a transition system modelled as a Kripke structure $\mathcal{K} = \langle S, I, R, L, AP \rangle$ over a set of atomic propositions AP where S is a set of states, $I \subseteq S$ is a set of initial states, $R \subseteq S \times S$ is a transition relation between states, and $L : S \to 2^{AP}$ is a labelling function that maps each state to a subset of atomic propositions. A transition α is considered *enabled* in state s if there is another state s' where $(s, s') \in R$. If only one transition is enabled from s, α is a *deterministic transition*, expressible as $s' = \alpha(s)$. Additionally, execution paths are assumed infinite, even if deadlocks occur, by introducing self-transitions. This framework supports reasoning about transition *reordering* in model checking algorithms.

Definition 2 (Independence Relation). *The* independence relation $IR \subseteq R \times R$ *is a symmetric and anti-reflexive relation on transitions. A pair of* independent *transitions* $(\alpha, \beta) \in IR$ *satisfies the following for each state* $s \in S$*:*

- Enabledness*: If* $\alpha, \beta \in enabled(s)$*, then* α *and* β *remain enabled in each other's resulting state.*
- Commutativity*: If* $\alpha, \beta \in enabled(s)$*, then executing* α *followed by* β *gives the same result as executing* β *followed by* α*.*

We introduce the concept of *invisible* transitions to address the variability in verification outcomes caused by reordered execution sequences with independent transitions. These transitions help clarify how specifications differentiate between states, despite the states appearing equivalent based on their transition orders.

Definition 3 (Invisible Transitions). *A transition* $\alpha \in R$ *is termed* invisible *concerning a subset* AP' *of atomic propositions* AP *if its execution between any two states does not alter their labellings. This means for states* s *and* s' *where* $s' = \alpha(s)$*, it holds that* $L(s) \cap AP' = L(s') \cap AP'$*.*

Definition 4 (Stuttering Equivalence of Paths). *Two infinite paths* $\sigma = s_0, s_1, s_2, ...$ *and* $\rho = r_0, r_1, r_2, ...$ *are* stuttering equivalent, *denoted* $\sigma \equiv_{st} \rho$*, if there exist sequences of indices* $0 = i_0 < i_1 < ...$ *and* $0 = j_0 < j_1 < ...$ *such that for all* $k \geq 0$*,* $L(s_{i_k}) = L(s_{i_{k+1}}) = L(r_{j_k}) = L(r_{j_{k+1}})$*, indicating matching labelled subsequences in both paths.*

Definition 5 (Stuttering Invariance of LTL Formulas). *An* LTL_{-X} *formula* ψ *(without "next") is* invariant under stuttering *if for any two* stuttering equivalent *paths* σ *and* σ' *(i.e.,* $\sigma \equiv_{st} \sigma'$*), it holds that* $\sigma \models \psi$ *iff* $\sigma' \models \psi$*.*

Definition 6 (Stuttering Equivalence of State Transition Systems). *Two state transition systems M and M' are considered* stuttering equivalent *if:*

- *For every path σ starting from an initial state of M, there exists a path σ' from an initial state of M' such that $\sigma \equiv_{st} \sigma'$.*
- *For every path σ' starting from an initial state of M', there exists a path σ from an initial state of M such that $\sigma' \equiv_{st} \sigma$.*

Based on the definitions of *stuttering equivalence* of state transition systems in Definition 6 and *stuttering invariance* of LTL_{-X} formulas in Definition 5, we conclude that if two state transition systems M and M' are *stuttering equivalent*, then $M \models \psi$ iff $M' \models \psi$ for any LTL_{-X} formula ψ. This justifies the validity of using the partial order reduction technique to create a structure that is *stuttering equivalent* to the original system.

Lemma 1 (Correctness of Partial-Order Reduction). *Given a transition system represented as a Kripke structure $\mathcal{K} = \langle S, I, R, L, AP\rangle$ and the reduced structure $\mathcal{K}_p = \langle S_p, I_p, R_p, L_p, AP\rangle$ via the above partial-order reduction, $\mathcal{K}$ and $\mathcal{K}_P$ are stuttering equivalent.*

Theorem 1 (Correctness of POR Tendermint Model). *Given the Tendermint consensus protocol modelled as $\mathcal{K} = \langle S, I, R, L, AP\rangle$ and the reduced model $\mathcal{K}_p = \langle S_p, I_p, R_p, L_p, AP\rangle$ via partial-order reduction, if a counterexample exists in the state space of $\mathcal{K}$ then it also exists in the state space of $\mathcal{K}_p$.*

Role-Based Symmetry Reduction (SR). Structural symmetries, such as replicated components in concurrent systems, often go unnoticed but can help reduce the *state space explosion* problem. Symmetry reduction treats states that differ only in the arrangement of identical processes as equivalent. This technique collapses these symmetric states, called *orbits*, into a single representative during model checking. Unlike partial order reduction, which minimizes independent transition interleavings, symmetry reduction focuses on collapsing equivalent states. It ensures that any counterexample in the full state space is still found in the reduced space, improving efficiency without sacrificing verification accuracy.

We show an example code snippet modified for symmetry reduction in Fig. 8 where in addition to the original conditions for the upon rule two extra constraints added to the guarded expression of our corresponding process *UponSufficientPrevoteValue*(p) with respect to two orthogonal dimensions in data values, namely *round* and *step* serve as the key to a significant reduction of the state space by an order of magnitude, via imposing a strict total ordering on the executions of upon rules by different processes at different steps within the same round (*i.e.*, $p == 0 || (rounds[p-1] == rounds[p] \&\& steps[p-1] >= PRECOMMIT)$), as well as those executions of this upon rule similarly by different processes at potentially same or different steps across different rounds (*i.e.*, $p == 0 || rounds[p-1] > rounds[p]$), so that unnecessary exploration of symmetric executions may be avoided to enable a faster termination of the model

```
UponSufficientPrevoteValue(p) =
[decisions[p]==NIL && steps[p]>=PREVOTE && (effective_rounds[p]/2)%2==0 &&
    message_log.ContainsProposalAndSufficientPrevotesForPrecommitting(all_messages,
     rounds[p]) &&
 ((honest_processes[p]==true && message_log.GetProposalValue(all_messages, rounds[p]
    )==DECISION_T) ||
 (honest_processes[p]==false && message_log.GetProposalValue(all_messages, rounds[p]
    )==DECISION_F))]
enable_second_flag_in_effective_round_for_process.p{effective_rounds[p]=
    effective_rounds[p]+2;} -> UponSufficientPrevoteValueAuxiliary(p, rounds[p]);
UponSufficientPrevoteValueAuxiliary(p, round) =
ifa (steps[p]==PREVOTE) {
 update_locked_value_and_locked_round_for_process_in_round.p.round{locked_values[p]=
    message_log.GetProposalValue(all_messages, round); locked_rounds[p]=round;} ->
 BroadcastPrecommitMessage(p, round, message_log.GetProposalValue(all_messages,
    round));
 update_step_for_process_in_round.p.round{steps[p]=PRECOMMIT;} -> Skip};
 update_valid_value_round_for.p.round{valid_values[p]=message_log.GetProposalValue(
    all_messages, round); valid_rounds[p]=round;} -> Tendermint();
```

```
UponSufficientPrevoteValue(p) =
[(p==0 || (rounds[p-1]==rounds[p] && steps[p-1]>=PRECOMMIT) || rounds[p-1]>rounds[p]
    ) && decisions[p]==NIL &&
 (effective_rounds[p]/2)%2==0 && steps[p]>=PREVOTE && message_log.
    ContainsProposalAndSufficientPrevotesForPrecommitting(all_messages, rounds[p])
    &&
 ((honest_processes[p]==true && message_log.GetProposalValue(all_messages, rounds[p]
    )==DECISION_T) ||
  (honest_processes[p]==false && message_log.GetProposalValue(all_messages, rounds[p
    ])==DECISION_F))]
enable_second_flag_in_effective_round_for_process.p{effective_rounds[p]=
    effective_rounds[p]+2;} ->
ifa (steps[p]==PREVOTE) {
 update_locked_value_and_locked_round_for_process_in_round.p.rounds[p]{locked_values
    [p]=message_log.GetProposalValue(all_messages, rounds[p]); locked_rounds[p]=
    rounds[p];} ->
 BroadcastPrecommitMessage(p, rounds[p], message_log.GetProposalValue(all_messages,
    rounds[p]));
 update_step_for_process_in_round.p.rounds[p]{steps[p]=PRECOMMIT;} -> Skip};
 update_valid_value_and_valid_round_for_process_in_round.p.rounds[p]{valid_values[p]
    =message_log.GetProposalValue(all_messages, rounds[p]); valid_rounds[p]=rounds[
    p];} -> Tendermint();
```

Fig. 8. A comparison of example code without (top) & with (bottom) SR.

checking process. Note that other upon rules (omitted here for brevity) also apply the same modifications to their guarded conditions to enforce a total ordering on their executions as well.

Correctness of our SR. We now show, on a high level, the correctness of our symmetry reduction. We again use a Kripke structure $\mathcal{K} = \langle S, I, R, L, AP \rangle$, and its associated behaviours (enabled transitions, deterministic paths, and infinite execution paths). We adopt definitions from prior work [12,15,19] to reason about the correctness of symmetry reduction applied at the model level for distributed protocols modelled into a state transition system.

To formalize the definitions of *symmetric* states and paths, which help in selecting one representative from each equivalence class for analysis, we begin with the concept of a *permutation*. From this, we define the *symmetry group* and *orbit* within a transition system.

Definition 7 (Permutation). *A permutation* $\sigma : S \rightarrow S$ *on a set* S *is a* bijection *of* S *onto itself, meaning* $(\forall s \in S : \exists_{=1}\sigma(s) \in S) \wedge (\forall \sigma(s) \in S : \exists_{=1} s \in S)$, *where* $\exists_{=1}$ *means exists only one.*

Definition 8 (Symmetry Group). *In a Kripke structure* $\mathcal{K} = \langle S, I, R, L, AP\rangle$, *a subgroup* G *of all permutations of* S *(denoted* $Perm(S)$*) is a* symmetry group *if every permutation* $\sigma \in G$ *preserves the transition relation* R, *meaning* $(s_1, s_2) \in R$ *iff* $(\sigma(s_1), \sigma(s_2)) \in R$. *Each* $\sigma \in G$ *is called an* automorphism *of* $\mathcal{K}$.

Definition 9 (Equivalence Relation & Orbit). *A symmetry group* G *acting on a Kripke structure* $\mathcal{K}$ *defines an* equivalence relation $\equiv$ *on* S, *where* $s_1 \equiv s_2$ *if* $\exists \sigma \in G$ *such that* $s_2 = \sigma(s_1)$. *The* equivalence class $[s] = \{t \mid \exists \sigma \in G : \sigma(s) = t\}$ *is called the* orbit *of* s *under* G, *with* $rep([s])$ *as the representative.*

Definition 10 (Quotient Structure). *Given a Kripke structure* $\mathcal{K} = \langle S, I, R, L, AP\rangle$ *and a symmetry group* G *acting on* $\mathcal{K}$, *the quotient structure for* $\mathcal{K}$ *modulo* G *is a Kripke structure* $\mathcal{K}_G = \langle S_G, I_G, R_G, L_G, AP\rangle$, *where* $S_G = \{[s] \mid s \in S\}$, $I_G = \{[s_0] \mid s_0 \in I\}$, $R_G = \{([s], [t]) \mid (s, t) \in R\}$, $L_G([s]) = L(rep([s])) = L(s)$ *for all* $s \in S$.

Definition 11 (Invariance Group). *In a Kripke structure* $\mathcal{K} = \langle S, I, R, L, AP\rangle$, *a symmetry group* G *is an* invariance group *for an atomic proposition* p *if:* $\forall \sigma \in G : \forall s \in S : L(s) = L(\sigma(s))$

Definition 12 (Bisimulation Relation). *Given two Kripke structures* $\mathcal{K}_1 = \langle S_1, I_1, R_1, L_1, AP\rangle$ *and* $\mathcal{K}_2 = \langle S_2, I_2, R_2, L_2, AP\rangle$, *a binary relation* $\mathcal{B} \subseteq S_1 \times S_2$ *is a* bisimulation relation *if* $(s_1, s_2) \in \mathcal{B}$ *implies:*

- $L_1(s_1) = L_2(s_2)$
- *if* $(s_1, s_1') \in R_1$, *then* $\exists s_2' \in S_2$ *s.t.* $(s_2, s_2') \in R_2$ *and* $(s_1', s_2') \in \mathcal{B}$
- *if* $(s_2, s_2') \in R_2$, *then* $\exists s_1' \in S_1$ *s.t.* $(s_1, s_1') \in R_1$ *and* $(s_1', s_2') \in \mathcal{B}$

Lemma 2 (Correctness of Symmetry Reduction). *Given a transition system represented as a Kripke structure* $\mathcal{K} = \langle S, I, R, L, AP\rangle$ *and its quotient structure* $\mathcal{K}_G = \langle S_G, I_G, R_G, L_G, AP\rangle$ *w.r.t. an invariance group* G *for all atomic propositions* $p \in AP$ *in symmetric LTL formulas* ϕ, *the structure* $\mathcal{K}_G$ *is* bisimulation equivalent *to* $\mathcal{K}$.

Theorem 2 (Correctness of SR Tendermint Model). *Given the Tendermint consensus protocol modelled as* $\mathcal{K} = \langle S, I, R, L, AP\rangle$ *and the reduced model* $\mathcal{K}_s = \langle S_s, I_s, R_s, L_s, AP\rangle$ *via symmetry reduction, if a counterexample exists in the state space of* $\mathcal{K}$ *then it also exists in the state space of* $\mathcal{K}_s$.

3.6 Other Notable Optimisations

Abstraction of Timed Components from the Initial TCSP# Model. Initially, we modelled the system using the RTS Module of the PAT model checker, which employs a global clock to impose a total order on events. However, the clock significantly increased model complexity and state space, causing the model checker to freeze. We then switched to the standard CSP# Module, removing the clock after realizing that event order could still be determined without exact timings. This shift led to a "result-oriented" approach, focusing on the outcomes of timed events like timeouts and deadlines while considering all possible interleavings. Eliminating the clock, which merely recorded timestamps, reduced the state space and simplified the model without compromising correctness.

Abstraction of Synchronization Primitives. The intended functions of certain artificially modelled synchronization primitives, such as distributed mutexes, which do not contribute to the core logical behaviour of the protocol, can be achieved more concisely using higher-level built-in constructs like unconditional choice operators. Since the unconditional choice operator inherently allows only one participating process to proceed, it naturally enforces mutual exclusion and prevents concurrent access to critical sections, eliminating the need for explicit synchronization. Following the "result-oriented" approach, these primitives can be abstracted away, avoiding manual steps like mutex acquisition and release while preserving the model's semantics. This simplification reduces process complexity and the number of possible interleavings, thus minimizing the state space.

Shared Use of a Single Instance of Message Log. Another optimization that may seem counter-intuitive is using a single message log for all processes, rather than giving each process its own log. Although individual logs might align more closely with the system's semantic interpretation, they are unnecessary and redundant in PAT. The primary concern—distinguishing the arrival order of a broadcast message across n processes (yielding $n!$ possible orders)—is effectively addressed by using a general choice operator. This operator randomly selects the next process to handle the broadcast message, ensuring that all possible execution traces are explored. Given that our system model assumes a partially synchronous network (where all messages are eventually delivered), the variability lies in timing rather than in message drops or corruption.

Table 1. Verification results of our CSP# models for Tendermint. Specs: Intel Core i7 11800H/32 GB RAM.

Property: safety + liveness						
Exp. No.	Timeout Mech.	Byzantine	Reduction		Result	Time
			POR	SR		
1	✓	×	×	×	CRASH	2 days
2	✓	×	✓	×	VALID	10 h
3	✓	×	✓	✓	VALID	325.82 s
4	✓	✓	✓	×	CRASH	2 days
5	✓	✓	✓	✓	VALID	242.59 s
6	×	×	✓	✓	VALID	0.21 s
7	×	✓	✓	✓	VALID	0.14 s

Unlike the *constant-factor* improvements in *time* and *space* complexity achieved by abstracting synchronization primitives and using a single message log, abstracting timed components from our original TCSP# model leads to *exponential* state space reduction, from 4^n to 2^n, where n is the number of processes, for the decisions on timeout.

3.7 Discussions on Generalisability

Our proposed partial-order reduction techniques are also applicable to other BFT protocols because usually only a few dependencies between functions or procedures within the same process or across different processes can be observed (since if not, all steps are dependent on one another, forming a totally-ordered execution sequence, which obviously does not need to be further reduced), opening up the door to reduce these interleaved executions which are stuttering equivalent and therefore well-founded *linearizations* of the partial order execution.

Our symmetry reduction techniques can similarly be applied to exploit symmetries inherent in other typical BFT protocols which share a similar structure with respect to the concept of rounds and steps (or sometimes called phases) within a round (*i.e.*, both properties are orderable and hence can be sorted), and at the same time do not distinguish between roles undertaken by their participating nodes/processes and treat them as equal counterparts that perform exactly the set of rules or procedures at an appropriate time (*i.e.*, upon the stipulated pre-condition of each rule becomes true).

4 Verification Results

The verification results of our CSP# model built specifically for the Tendermint consensus algorithm were produced via the PAT model checker under different honesty configurations, as shown in Table 1. Note that before applying the reduction techniques, the verification used up all the RAM after 2 days.

In the verification, we check LTL formulae of the form

$$\Box\Diamond(decision[0] == T \wedge decision[1] == T \wedge \cdots)$$

to express both the safety property and the liveness property (cf. end of Sect. 2)—from any state ($\Box$), eventually ($\Diamond$), the decisions of node 0, 1, $\cdots$ will be made and will be the same (T). We examined all honest processes and cases where one process is Byzantine, applying our vulnerability fix. The results show that the algorithm maintains both *safety* and *liveness* even when a Byzantine process is present. The Byzantine process can reject valid proposals or make invalid ones, but its behaviour is limited to keep the state space manageable and ensure termination. Complex behaviours like *equivocation* and *amnesia* are excluded to simplify analysis.

From Table 1, we can observe that if we remove the timeout mechanism in the protocol (last two rows in Table 1) the verification time is significantly reduced. Timeouts significantly increase the state space complexity, as they add variability in message delays and process execution timing, which needs to be accurately modelled for realistic verification.

The successful verification of Tendermint's *safety* and *liveness* properties and the application of reduction techniques are notable contributions of this work. They represent a breakthrough in addressing the complexities of Byzantine fault-tolerant consensus verification, offering a more robust solution than existing verifications such as that in TLA+, which could not verify liveness due to limitations in managing state space.

These verification results prove the correctness of the Tendermint consensus algorithm at a single blockchain height. By induction, the correctness of the entire blockchain is established. Starting with the base case, the genesis block is inherently valid as the blockchain's founder creates it. For the inductive step, assuming correctness up to height k, the block at height $k+1$ must also be correct when derived using this consensus algorithm. This completes the proof, ensuring both *safety* and *liveness* of the blockchain.

Also shown in Table 1, the only experiment (5) that finished verification in a reasonable time when considering both timeout mechanism and Byzantine nodes has to implement both of our proposed reduction techniques. Note that verification results about the impact of other notable optimizations in Subsect. 3.6 are omitted from Table 1, as their exponential improvement is asymptotically less effective in practice than the primary techniques discussed above.

5 Related Work

Blockchain Consensus. Numerous consensus protocols have been proposed for blockchain, as surveyed in [27]. Among them, BFT based consensus protocols form a large category. Compared to other protocols like PoW (proof-of-work) and PoS (proof-of-stake) which assign the participants with high computing power, stakes and storage, a higher priority in winning the leader competition, BFT-based allow participants to reach consensus through voting. Tendermint protocol analysed in this work is BFT-based in general, and their voting weight are decided following the idea of PoS which is beyond the scope of this work.

Formal Verification of Blockchain Consensus. Compared to the vast number of consensus protocols, only a few have been formally verified. Notable examples include the Snow White consensus for the Avalanche blockchain, proven using mathematical proof [16]; the Algorand consensus [3] and Raft consensus [26], verified using Coq; the Stellar consensus, verified with the model checker UPPAAL [28]; the Red Belly consensus, verified with ByMC [25]; and the Beacon Chain in Ethereum 2.0 and the Trust-based Blockchain Crowdsourcing (TBC) consensus protocol, verified with PAT [1,2]. Additionally, a branch of work focuses on formal verification logic and techniques for fault-tolerant distributed algorithms, verifying protocols like Last Voting, OneThirdRule, and Paxos [6,17], which ensure crash fault tolerance but lack the Byzantine fault tolerance.

Formal Verification of Tendermint. Notably the following:

Manual Analysis. The work [4] manually proved a few properties of Tendermint, including termination, validity, integrity and agreement of one-shot consensus, termination, validity and agreement of multiple rounds, and fairness, considering Byzantine nodes. Similar to this work, we also verified multiple rounds in the presence of Byzantine nodes. By contrast, we did not verify fairness (due to the required game theory verification being challenging for model checkers), and we used automated formal verification to reduce human errors in proofs.

The TLA+ Model. The work [22] models the Tendermint consensus protocol using TLA+, but does not incorporate any Byzantine behaviours. Properties like *equivocation* (*i.e.*, sending multiple messages that vote for different values within the same round to other processes) and *amnesia* (*i.e.*, locking a new value in a round without unlocking a previously locked value from some earlier round) are modelled and proven. However, the *safety* and *liveness* properties are excluded from the verification objectives, likely due to the set-theory-based characteristics inherent in the TLA+ specification language, which, while expressive and helpful in simplifying definitions through constructs such as universal and existential quantifiers, lacks the ability to enforce an execution order of upon rules among different processes. Under the same project, TLA+ has been used to verify other related protocols such as Fastsync—a synchronization mechanism to recover from network disconnection [7], which is beyond the analysis target of this work. The work [5] also used TLA+ to model Tendermint consensus, however, focusing on verifying a Nash Equilibrium property to identify free-riding.

The Ivy Model. The same project as in [22] has also provided an Ivy model of Tendermint consensus and proves the safety property by refinement of an abstract model with the actual model. However, the property is with respect to Byzantine nodes, which do not support sending forged messages.

The PAT Model. Maung et al. [21] used PAT to analyse Tendermint consensus for safety properties BUT NOT liveness property. They verified a few attack scenarios for multiple rounds, but they used the old Tendermint specification, which suffers from liveness attacks. In contrast, this work verified the new version of Tendermint, proved its liveness, and identified other vulnerabilities.

Compared to previous works, we have successfully verified both *safety* and *liveness* properties using advanced reduction techniques, even in scenarios with either no Byzantine processes or exactly f Byzantine processes among $3f + 1$ total processes. This extends the state space coverage and accounts for a wider range of arbitrary Byzantine behaviors, making our verification results more robust and trustworthy.

6 Conclusion and Future Work

This work verified the new Tendermint consensus protocol in multiple rounds with Byzantine nodes. It advanced existing verification by enhancing the ability to verify liveness in multiple rounds using a timeout mechanism. The approach can be applied to other blockchain consensuses with similar state-space challenges. We found a vulnerability in Tendermint that could lead to a Denial of Service attack and proposed a fix to eliminate it. We optimized our model with reduction techniques to minimize the state space, resulting in an efficiently model-checked model. Our patched model meets both safety and liveness properties. Future work includes modelling a more complete set of Byzantine behaviours, scaling up the number of nodes in the model checking process, extending verification scope from specifications to actual implementations to examine behavioural consistency, and applying our reduction techniques to other BFT protocols towards a universal framework compatible with existing tools.

Data Availability. All versions of our models and detailed proofs are available at https://tinyurl.com/4hbaf62m. The PAT model checker can be downloaded at https://pat.comp.nus.edu.sg/resources/pat3_5_1/.

References

1. Afzaal, H., Imran, M., Janjua, M.U.: Formal verification of persistence and liveness in the trust-based blockchain crowdsourcing consensus protocol. Comput. Commun. **192**, 384–401 (2022)
2. Afzaal, H., Zafar, N.A., Tehseen, A., Kousar, S., Imran, M.: Formal verification of justification and finalization in beacon chain. IEEE Access **12**, 55077–55102 (2024)
3. Alturki, M.A., Chen, J., Luchangco, V., Moore, B., Palmskog, K., Peña, L., Roşu, G.: Towards a verified model of the algorand consensus protocol in coq. In: Sekerinski, E., et al. (eds.) FM 2019. LNCS, vol. 12232, pp. 362–367. Springer, Cham (2020). https://doi.org/10.1007/978-3-030-54994-7_27
4. Amoussou-Guenou, Y., Pozzo, A.D., Potop-Butucaru, M., Tucci-Piergiovanni, S.: Correctness and fairness of tendermint-core blockchains (2018). https://arxiv.org/abs/1805.08429

5. Baloochestani, A., Jehl, L.: Eiffel: Extending formal verification of distributed algorithms to utility analysis. In: 5th Conference on Blockchain Research & Applications for Innovative Networks and Services (BRAINS), pp. 1–7 (2023)
6. Berkovits, I., Lazić, M., Losa, G., Padon, O., Shoham, S.: Verification of threshold-based distributed algorithms by decomposition to decidable logics. In: Dillig, I., Tasiran, S. (eds.) CAV 2019. LNCS, vol. 11562, pp. 245–266. Springer, Cham (2019). https://doi.org/10.1007/978-3-030-25543-5_15
7. Braithwaite, S., Buchman, E., Konnov, I., Milosevic, Z., Stoilkovska, I., Widder, J., Zamfir, A.: Tendermint blockchain synchronization: formal specification and model checking. In: Margaria, T., Steffen, B. (eds.) ISoLA 2020. LNCS, vol. 12476, pp. 471–488. Springer, Cham (2020). https://doi.org/10.1007/978-3-030-61362-4_27
8. Peltier, N., Sofronie-Stokkermans, V. (eds.): IJCAR 2020. LNCS (LNAI), vol. 12167. Springer, Cham (2020). https://doi.org/10.1007/978-3-030-51054-1
9. Buchman, E.: Tendermint: byzantine fault tolerance in the age of blockchains (2016). https://api.semanticscholar.org/CorpusID:59082906
10. Buchman, E., Kwon, J., Milosevic, Z.: The latest gossip on BFT consensus. CoRR arxiv:1807.04938 (2018)
11. Castro, M., Liskov, B.: Practical byzantine fault tolerance. In: Proceedings of the Third USENIX Symposium on Operating Systems Design and Implementation (OSDI), pp. 173–186 (1999)
12. Clarke, E.M., Emerson, E.A., Jha, S., Sistla, A.P.: Symmetry reductions in model checking. In: Computer Aided Verification, CAV '98, vol. 1427, pp. 147–158 (1998)
13. Clarke, E.M., Grumberg, O., Minea, M., Peled, D.A.: State space reduction using partial order techniques. Int. J. Softw. Tools Technol. Transf. **2**(3), 279–287 (1999)
14. Clarke, E.M., Henzinger, T.A., Veith, H., Bloem, R. (eds.): Handbook of Model Checking. Springer, Heidelberg (2018). https://doi.org/10.1007/978-3-319-10575-8
15. Clarke, E.M., Jha, S., Enders, R., Filkorn, T.: Exploiting symmetry in temporal logic model checking. Formal Methods Syst. Des. **9**(1/2), 77–104 (1996)
16. Daian, P., Pass, R., Shi, E.: Snow White: robustly reconfigurable consensus and applications to provably secure proof of stake. In: Goldberg, I., Moore, T. (eds.) FC 2019. LNCS, vol. 11598, pp. 23–41. Springer, Cham (2019). https://doi.org/10.1007/978-3-030-32101-7_2
17. Drăgoi, C., Henzinger, T.A., Veith, H., Widder, J., Zufferey, D.: A logic-based framework for verifying consensus algorithms. In: 15th International Conference on Verification, Model Checking, and Abstract Interpretation, VMCAI (2014)
18. Dwork, C., Lynch, N.A., Stockmeyer, L.J.: Consensus in the presence of partial synchrony. J. ACM **35**(2), 288–323 (1988)
19. Godefroid, P.: Exploiting symmetry when model-checking software. In: Formal Methods for Protocol Engineering and Distributed Systems (1999)
20. Lamport, L.: Time, clocks, and the ordering of events in a distributed system. Commun. ACM **21**(7), 558–565 (1978)
21. Maung Maung Thin, W.Y., Dong, N., Bai, G., Dong, J.S.: Formal analysis of a proof-of-stake blockchain. In: 23rd International Conference on Engineering of Complex Computer Systems (ICECCS), pp. 197–200 (2018)
22. Milosevic, Z., Konnov, I.: Tendermint consensus tla+ model (2021). https://tinyurl.com/26j6vfd7
23. Sun, J., Liu, Y., Dong, J.S., Pang, J.: PAT: towards flexible verification under fairness. In: Bouajjani, A., Maler, O. (eds.) CAV 2009. LNCS, vol. 5643, pp. 709–714. Springer, Heidelberg (2009). https://doi.org/10.1007/978-3-642-02658-4_59

24. Team, T.C.: What is tendermint. https://tinyurl.com/4ewab889
25. Tholoniat, P., Gramoli, V.: Formal Verification of Blockchain Byzantine Fault Tolerance, pp. 389–412. Springer, Cham (2022). https://doi.org/10.1007/978-3-031-07535-3_12
26. Woos, D., Wilcox, J.R., Anton, S., Tatlock, Z., Ernst, M.D., Anderson, T.: Planning for change in a formal verification of the raft consensus protocol. In: ACM SIGPLAN Conference on Certified Programs and Proofs (2016)
27. Xu, J., Wang, C., Jia, X.: A survey of blockchain consensus protocols. ACM Comput. Surv. **55**(13s) (2023)
28. Yoo, J., Jung, Y., Shin, D., Bae, M., Jee, E.: Formal modeling and verification of a federated byzantine agreement algorithm for blockchain platforms. In: IEEE International Workshop on Blockchain Oriented Software Engineering (2019)

Program Analysis

Uncover the Risks of Outdated Dependencies in Software Supply Chains: Insights from the npm Ecosystem

Fenglin Bi[1], Cheng Liang[1], Yanbin Zhang[1], Yang Chen[2], and Wei Wang[1(✉)]

[1] East China Normal University, Shanghai 200062, China
wwang@dase.ecnu.edu.cn
[2] School of Computer Science, Shanghai Key Lab of Intelligent Information Processing, Fudan University, Shanghai 200433, China

Abstract. In the rapidly evolving domain of software development, the security and reliability of the open source software supply chain are of increasing concern. Outdated dependencies pose significant risks to the software ecosystem. This study aims to quantitatively reveal the prevalence of outdated dependencies in the open source supply chain, evaluate their impact on software security, and identify effective techniques for the timely detection of outdated dependencies to prevent security issues. We aggregated outdated dependencies from the npm ecosystem and the Open Source Vulnerabilities (OSV) dataset to construct the Outdated Dependencies Vulnerability Supply Chain. Our analysis suggested that outdated dependencies in a central position within the dependency chain significantly affect downstream components. Using clustering algorithms, we discovered that outdated packages are concentrated in the development tools area, which has a significant security risk from injection flaws (CWE-707) vulnerabilities. Utilizing model-based feature importance techniques, we predict the outdatedness of dependencies in the open source supply chain, with key indicators including the average duration of open issues and pull requests. The findings offer software developers and maintainers a foundation to identify current issues and security vulnerabilities within outdated dependencies, facilitating mitigation efforts through the open source software supply chain.

Keywords: Open source software supply chain · Outdated third-party dependencies · Software ecosystem · Software security

1 Introduction

The contemporary software development landscape encompasses a multifaceted array of dependencies, which include both internally developed modules and external third-party components. The integration of these varied dependencies has become a standard practice, bolstered by the substantial benefits they offer in terms of development efficiency, cost reduction, and access to advanced features [2,7].

Y. Zhou et al. (Eds.): ICECCS 2025, LNCS 15746, pp. 403–423, 2026.
https://doi.org/10.1007/978-3-032-00828-2_22

Although this practice offers considerable conveniences, it also introduces complexities in security assessments and heightens the likelihood of vulnerabilities seeping into the software supply chain [3]. Particularly in the open source domain, the supply chain is increasingly susceptible to security threats due to its characteristic global sourcing and centralized distribution modalities [9].

The notorious "left-pad" incident within the npm package manager ecosystem serves as a stark example of the latent risks in the supply chain, vividly demonstrating the cascade of problems that can result from the removal or compromising of a single, seemingly harmless outdated package [28]. Our analysis shows that the 'left-pad' package, which was launched in 2014 and subsequently withdrawn in 2016, remained unmaintained for more than two years. This incident underscores the considerable security risks that arise from prolonged neglect and the employment of outdated software packages in dependency systems.

The urgency of avoiding security risks is echoed in statistics released by the Black Duck Team, revealing an alarming reliance on outdated dependencies within software systems [23]. These outdated dependencies create a conducive environment for security threats, underscoring the need for thorough analysis and effective mitigation strategies.

Our research is situated within the npm ecosystem, a vibrant and representative microcosm of open source software that highlights the complexities and challenges of modern software development [29]. The npm ecosystem's openness allows users to freely share and reuse code. Adding a package is simple, involving a command that downloads and installs the package with all its dependencies. Sharing a package is equally straightforward, making the code available to everyone without restrictions or vetting. This openness has driven npm's growth, offering a range of software packages from small utilities to complex frameworks. The npm ecosystem serves as an ideal context for examining the dynamics of software dependencies and their impact on security and robustness [36].

Within this context, we define "outdated dependencies" as software packages that have not been updated for a prolonged period or for which newer versions exist but have not been adopted. These packages share the characteristic of having dependencies that remain outdated. Based on our analysis, we provide unified recommendations to developers. Our study addresses three key research questions: (1) **RQ1:** How prevalent are outdated dependencies in the open source software supply chain? (2) **RQ2:** How do outdated dependencies affect overall software security? (3) **RQ3:** What factors effectively indicate potential outdated dependencies in open source supply chains?

Figure 1 illustrates an overview of our work. Our core contributions are as follows: 1) We conducted the first large-scale empirical study, collecting data from 30,781,354 npm packages to understand the trends in npm and open source repositories. 2) We constructed *Outdated Dependencies Vulnerability Supply Chain* to investigate the characteristics of vulnerabilities associated with the use of outdated packages. 3) Through quantitative and qualitative analyses, we identified the primary domains and types of vulnerabilities in which outdated packages are prevalent and provided recommendations for prevention. 4) Based on open

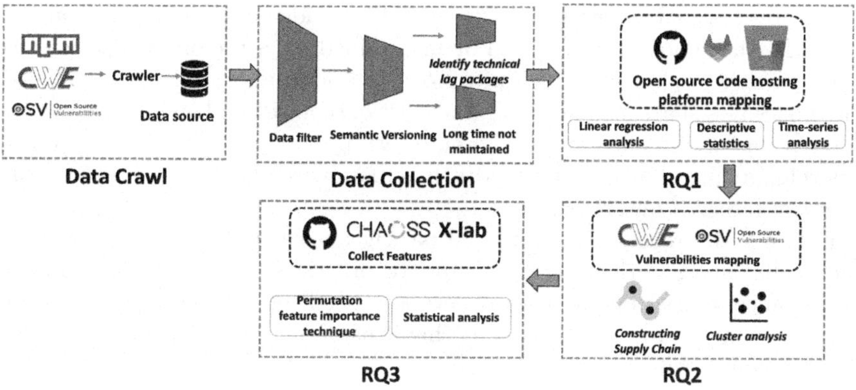

Fig. 1. Overview of Research

source software collaboration data, we developed a predict model with 23 features to forecast the likelihood of a package becoming outdated, offering guidance for developers in selecting supply chain packages.

2 Related Work

Existing literature acknowledges software dependencies' concept and security implications [15]. While software maintenance and dependency management have been extensively studied, the issue of outdated software dependencies requires further exploration. Recent research emphasizes the importance of open source software and supply chain security. For example, Yan et al. highlight vulnerabilities within the supply chain [32], while Wen et al. and Lin et al. discuss socio-technical aspects influencing open source software security [13,27].

Outdated dependencies can cause *technical lag*, a prominent concern in research. Wang et al. demonstrated this phenomenon in Java projects [25], while Stringer et al. highlighted issues in software package management systems, proposing semantic version control as a remedy [22]. Zerouali et al. found technical lag in the npm ecosystem due to dependency constraints, indicating reluctance to update dependencies [34]. They also noted version lag in Docker images based on JavaScript [35]. However, their research did not explore the security risks associated with technical lag, suggesting further investigation is needed.

The importance of keeping dependencies up-to-date is gaining attention. Kula et al. found that developers perceive managing outdated dependencies as burdensome [12], while Maeprasart et al. highlighted the impact of solitary dependency authorship on update frequency [14]. However, there's a lack of predictive research on outdated packages, and a gap remains in integrating these issues into the broader open source software supply chain. Markus et al. analyzed dependencies between software packages and security issues but didn't fully address the critical impact of outdated dependencies within the software supply chain [36].

Within this context, we define "outdated dependencies" as software packages that either have not been updated or maintained for a prolonged period, or for which newer versions exist but have not been adopted by dependent projects. These packages share a common characteristic: their dependencies have not been updated for an extended time. Therefore, we provide unified recommendations to developers based on our analysis of these packages. Our study seeks to address three key research questions:

Defining and recognizing outdated packages necessitates an integrative approach considering both developers' update practices and third-party libraries' maintenance status. Furthermore, there is a need for an investigation into the prevalence, impact, and detection mechanisms of outdated dependencies within the open source software supply chain.

3 RQ1: How Prevalent are Outdated Dependencies in the Open Source Software Supply Chain?

3.1 Methodology

In software dependency management, a package P is considered to use outdated dependencies if its dependency set D contains at least one d such that either the time since d's last update exceeds a threshold T, or the version v_d used in P is not the latest version available in V_d. Formally, let P be an npm package, D be its dependency set, and for any $d \in D$, let t_d denote d's last update time, v_d the version used, and V_d the set of latest available versions. The outdated condition is expressed as:

$$
\begin{aligned}
P \iff & (\exists d \in D : \text{now} - t_d > T) \text{ or} \\
& (\exists d \in D : v_d \neq \max(V_d))
\end{aligned}
$$

Given the critical role of upstream projects as the genesis of FOSS (Free and Open Source Software) [8], our research explores the relationship between outdated artifacts and their corresponding open source software repositories. This exploration aims to analyze their connections within the open source software supply chain.

We utilized linear regression analysis [26] to evaluate the correlation between npm packages and their association with open source repositories. Additionally, we performed time-series analysis [20] to depict the expansion and diversification of the npm ecosystem between 2015 and 2022. Segmenting data into temporal bins (e.g., 0–3 months, over 24 months), we systematically examined update frequencies. Hypothesis testing substantiated the statistical significance of the relationship between npm package proliferation and open source repository engagement.

Data Collection. Our data processing involves 10 steps (1) We utilized a crawler to gather data from the npm registry[1] and implemented periodic updates

[1] https://registry.npmjs.org/.

to ensure the timeliness and accuracy of our data. (2) We selected data spanning from 2015 to 2022. (3) We focused on packages with more than three released versions, accounting for 4.2% of the total. This criterion was adopted because some packages were immature, often serving as practice projects for the authors.

(4) To ensure our study focused on relevant and actively used packages, we excluded experimental or unmaintained projects from the npm repository. We obtained the download counts for the last 30 days in the dataset and removed 32,655 projects with no information (possibly deleted). We further excluded 155,557 inactive projects with zero download counts.

(5) *Semantic Versioning*[2] (referred to as semver) is widely used to communicate changes in software packages. In our process, we parsed package runtime dependencies to align with *semver*-compatible version numbers, which include major, minor, and patch numbers. During this parsing, pre-release tags such as "-alpha" and "-beta" were handled separately to ensure accurate versioning and dependency management.

(6) Non-standard version numbers, such as git URLs or the "latest" tag, were excluded from our analysis to prevent biases. We also manually removed versions not adhering to *Semantic Versioning* specifications(e.g. date).

(7) We employed *Semantic Versioning* to identify outdated dependencies by comparing version numbers. If the latest dependency versions were not used when the package was released, or if pre-release versions were used instead of official versions, they were considered outdated. Operators like ^, ~, $\geq$, and $<$ were utilized to accurately identify version intents and ranges during comparisons. Following established practices in dependency management, we classified a dependency as outdated if more than 20% of its sub-dependencies were not using the latest versions. This threshold has been previously employed in the literature to ensure a balance between maintaining up-to-date dependencies and accounting for practical constraints in dependency management [4].

(8) To investigate packages that have remained un-updated over a prolonged period, we extracted each package's most recent update date. The time elapsed since the dataset's end date (January 1, 2023) was calculated for each package. The median duration of outdated packages not receiving updates was 550 days. Consequently, we categorized the elapsed time into bins for statistical convenience: 0–3 months, 3–6 months, 6–12 months, 12–24 months, and over 24 months. (9) Dependencies that had not been updated for more than 24 months were filtered out as outdated dependencies.

(10) Finally, we merge the datasets processed in steps 7 and 9 to create the Outdated Dependency Dataset.

To better investigate the outdated dependencies impact on the open source software supply chain, we classify npm packages that have repositories on *GitHub*, *GitLab*, *Bitbucket*, *SourceForge*, *Apache Allura*, *Savannah*, and *Gitea* as supply materials within the open source software supply chain.

[2] https://semver.org/.

Table 1. Overview of npm Package Vulnerabilities and Outdated Package

Year	2017	2018	2019	2020	2021	2022	2023
Outdated npm packages	168,133	212,865	256,956	294,557	317,837	325,897	85,824
Open Source Vulnerabilities (OSV) reports	0	269	308	779	489	7,866	1,774
Outdated affected packages	34	133	194	290	316	315	195
OSV reports of Outdated affected packages	48	154	234	376	392	457	256

3.2 Results

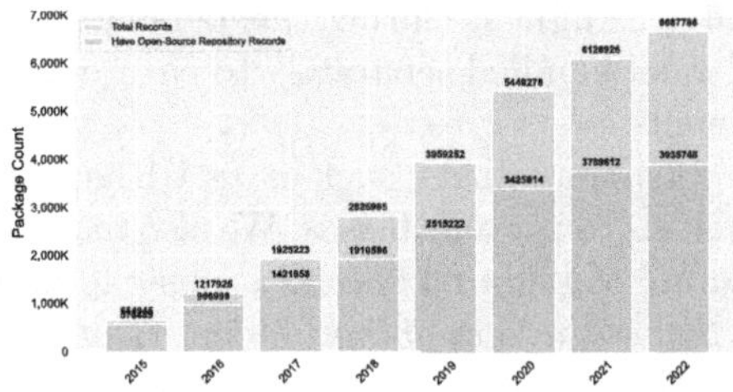

Fig. 2. Count Record of npm Package Over Years

Analyzing the Growth Dynamics of npm Ecosystem. Figure 2 depicts the temporal evolution of the npm package count alongside the number of npm packages linked to open source repositories from 2015 to 2022. These data provide insight into the npm ecosystem's growth trajectory and dynamics. The trend demonstrates a steady annual rise in the overall package count as well as in those connected to open source repositories, signaling the ecosystem's persistent expansion.

The number of npm packages experienced significant growth, with the cumulative count rising from approximately 665 thousand in 2015 to over 6.68 million by the end of 2022. Based on linear regression analysis, we found a strong linear relationship between the number of open source repository records and the total volume of data within the npm ecosystem. Specifically, each additional open source repository record is associated with an average increase of approximately 1.787 npm packages. Additionally, we computed the p-value [24] < 0.001 (Far less than the commonly used threshold of 0.05.). This indicates that we have sufficient evidence to reject the null hypothesis that the number of open source repository records associated with npm packages is unrelated to the total number of npm packages, thus confirming the presence of a significant relationship between them.

Trends in Dependency Updates Within the Open Source Software Supply Chain. The analysis depicted in Table 2 reveals that 42.7%(229,895) of libraries in the npm ecosystem have not been updated for over two years, suggesting that a considerable number of dependencies may harbor unresolved defects or security vulnerabilities due to a lack of maintenance. Furthermore, only 21.1%(113,422) of libraries have been updated in the recent three months, indicating that despite ongoing maintenance activities, the frequency of updates remains low. The number of mid-term non-updated (4–6 months, 7–12 months) is the smallest, indicating that most active version release cycles are within 3 months.

Table 2. Dependency Update Time Ranges

Time Range	All Dependencies	Dependencies with Repositories
0–3 months	21.1% (113,422)	20.8% (73,851)
4–6 months	8.2% (44,059)	8.3% (29,478)
7–12 months	12.7% (68,146)	12.4% (43,920)
13–24 months	15.3% (82,245)	13.4% (47,556)
24+ months	42.7% (229,895)	45.1% (160,050)

The comparison between all dependencies and those hosted on open source platforms reveals a similar distribution across all time frames, with a notable difference in the over 24 months category: 45.1% for dependencies with repositories compared to 42.7% overall. The high proportion of long-term dependencies with repositories (70%) suggests that mature projects are more likely to be hosted on open source platforms. Notably, the trend of npm packages having corresponding repositories has decreased from 86% in 2015 to 58% in 2022. As the npm ecosystem grows, it may become more complex, with fewer projects managed under the open source ethos, possibly indicating an increase in smaller, utility-focused packages without their own repositories.

RQ1 Summary: Our study finds that 42.7% of npm libraries have not been updated in over two years, highlighting maintenance issues and potential security vulnerabilities in the npm ecosystem. There is a positive linear correlation between npm packages and linked open source repositories, with each additional repository increasing npm packages by approximately 1.787. 45.1% of packages unmaintained for over 24 months possess open source repositories. Furthermore, the proportion of open source repositories used for management is decreasing, indicating increasing complexity.

4 RQ2: How Do Outdated Dependencies Affect the Overall Security of the Software?

4.1 Methodology

Data Collection. To address RQ2, we implemented a two-step data collection methodology: the first step focused on identifying outdated npm packages, while the second involved gathering vulnerability information related to these packages.

Based on the data collection established in RQ1, our dataset of outdated packages includes packages that utilize dependencies not updated for over 24 months and those that do not utilize the latest version of their dependencies. This resulted in a dataset comprising 556,964 outdated npm packages.

Vulnerability information was sourced by querying the Open Source Vulnerabilities (OSV) [17] database, which includes reports on npm package vulnerabilities up to the date of this study. We extracted 12,068 vulnerability events published between October 24, 2017, and October 20, 2023. To accurately analyze the vulnerability characteristics of outdated packages, we refined these reports to focus solely on OSV records affecting outdated dependencies. The curated dataset encompasses 1917 vulnerability events affecting 1,134 outdated npm packages, summarized in Table 1.

Constructing the Outdated Dependencies Vulnerability Supply Chain (SC). We focus our investigation on the impact of outdated vulnerable packages within the npm ecosystem on their direct dependents, also called second-level packages. To this end, we have established a dependency database D, which includes all relationships between primary and secondary packages, represented as ordered pairs $(P_{\text{up}}, P_{\text{down}})$, where P_{up} is a prerequisite for installing P_{down}.

In exploring the OSV system, we utilized a directed graph abstraction with nodes representing software packages and edges denoting dependency links. Each node includes a *cwe_ids* attribute listing relevant vulnerability categories [30]. Our analysis constructed a vulnerability Supply Chain (SC) using the dataset D, starting with 1,134 outdated packages, denoted as P_{up}. We identified their direct dependents, P_{down}, and integrated these into the SC. This involved enriching node attributes with vulnerability data and forming directed edges with a relationship level *rel_level* set to 1, establishing the primary layer of our SC analysis.

The constructed SC was further enriched by incorporating secondary dependencies. Within dataset D, we meticulously examined the pairwise connections between secondary nodes. A directed edge was established where a dependency relation existed, and the relationship level *rel_level* was accordingly set to 2. The resultant SC structure, illustrated in Fig. 3, includes 993 primary nodes alongside 661,217 secondary nodes, interconnected by 1,796,449 dependency links.

Identify the Security and Domain of Outdated Dependencies. To categorize and analyze vulnerabilities, we used the Common Weakness Enumeration (CWE) framework [16], which provides a structured vocabulary for classifying software and hardware vulnerabilities.

We assessed the impact of outdated dependencies using the Common Vulnerability Scoring System (CVSS) [19], analyzing vulnerability distribution across four severity levels: LOW, MODERATE, HIGH, and CRITICAL[3]. This approach reveals the complex threat landscape of dependencies in software security.

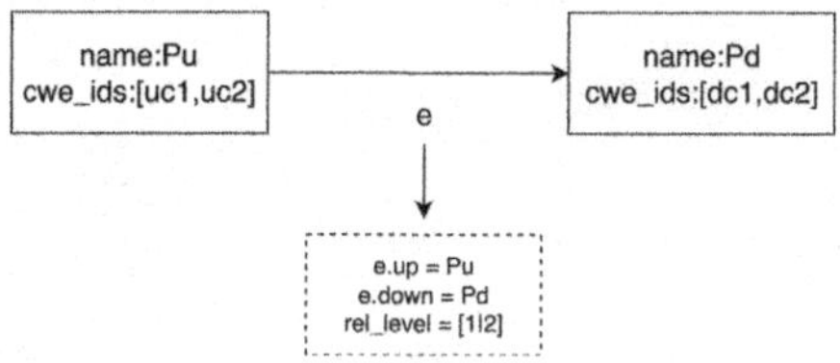

Fig. 3. Directed Graph Representation of the Outdated OSV Supply Chain in the npm Ecosystem

For domain assessment of affected packages, we employed the Louvain algorithm [5] for community detection within the outdated dependencies vulnerability supply chain. The algorithm's suitability for large networks facilitated efficient segmentation. Through thematic analysis [6] of npm registry descriptions, we discerned the domains encompassed by each cluster, aiding developers in selecting npm libraries by highlighting the spread of vulnerable outdated packages.

4.2 Results

Overall Analysis of Vulnerability Events in Outdated Components. In our investigation of vulnerabilities in outdated packages, we made two key observations. First, while the number of outdated packages directly affected by vulnerabilities is relatively small (1,134), their impact within the supply chain is significant, influencing 661,127 second-level packages. Secondly, certain packages, such as `react-dom`, have an extensive network of downstream dependencies, with up to 103,870 affected packages, highlighting their critical role in maintaining the integrity of the supply chain. This underscores the importance of securing these pivotal packages, as their compromise could pose systemic risks to the entire supply chain, reinforcing the need for vigilant maintenance and prompt updates.

Additionally, we noticed that 420,942 second-level package dependencies in SC exceed one, which means they depend on at least two outdated vulnerable packages. Due to having multiple dependency paths, these second-level packages face a higher vulnerability risk. This requires developers to regularly check and assess the security of these package dependencies and consider taking measures to reduce potential vulnerability risks.

We computed the count of severity levels for all vulnerability events and specifically for those associated with outdated packages. The proportional distribution of each severity level is shown in Table 3. In the figure, the outer ring

[3] https://www.first.org/cvss/v2/guide.

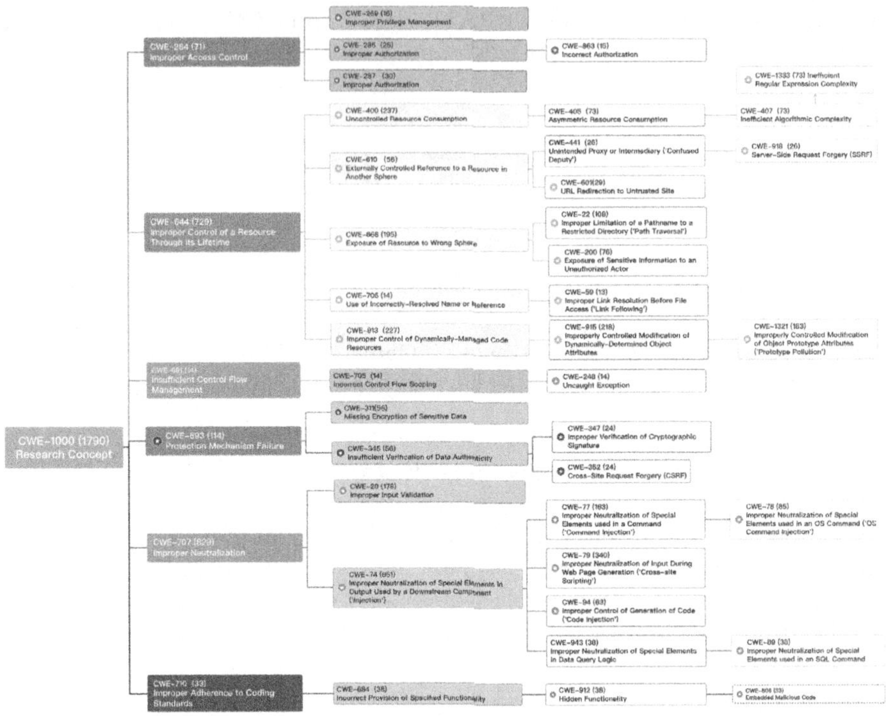

Fig. 4. Outdated CWE vulnerability category system in third-party dependencies

represents the Total Known Vulnerabilities, while the inner ring represents the Outdated Component Vulnerabilities. Out of the 12,068 vulnerabilities that were collected, we considered only the 3,115 vulnerabilities that have known severity levels while excluding the remaining vulnerabilities with unknown severities.

Table 3. Analysis of Vulnerability Levels

Vulnerability Level	Low	Moderate	High	Critical
Total Known Vulnerabilities	3.6%	28.5%	31.7%	36.2%
Outdated Component Vulnerabilities	8.3%	20.0%	40.0%	31.7%

A comparative analysis of the severity distribution of vulnerabilities revealed a consistency between all recorded events and those specific to outdated packages. Notably, high-severity vulnerabilities constituted a significant share, with 41.71% in outdated packages versus 41.03% in all packages. Moderate-severity vulnerabilities accounted for 36.59% in outdated packages, slightly higher than the overall 28.51%. Conversely, low-severity vulnerabilities were less common in outdated packages, at 4.7%, compared to 3.6% in the aggregate data. This could be due to low-severity vulnerabilities having a very limited impact on software security, leading developers to deem them not worth reporting. Critical severity vulnerabilities made up 17.0% within outdated packages, demonstrating a lower frequency than the 26.87% found across all vulnerabilities.

These data reveal a key insight: *HIGH* and *MODERATE* severity vulnerabilities are common within outdated third-party dependencies. This phenomenon may suggest that dependencies lacking updates and maintenance are more likely to retain more serious vulnerabilities, thereby increasing security risks within the software supply chain.

Vulnerability Category Analysis from the Perspective of Vulnerabilities. Figure 4 showcases a hierarchical classification of Common Weakness Enumeration (CWE) types discovered in outdated npm third-party libraries. This categorization delineates the vulnerability profile prevalent in these dependencies. Our research narrows down on CWE categories where the incidence of outdated packages meets or surpasses the average count (approximately 13). This was observed in a total of 1,790 packages.

The diagram elucidates a clustering of high-incidence CWEs predominantly in areas concerning "Improper Access Control," "Improper Control of a Resource Through its Lifetime," "Protection Mechanism Failure," "Improper Adherence to Coding Standards," "Insufficient Control Flow Management," and "Improper Neutralization." The notably high counts for **CWE-644 (Improper Control of a Resource Through its Lifetime)** and **CWE-707 (Improper Neutralization)** indicate two primary concerns in outdated npm packages:

Resource Management Issues (CWE-644): With 729 instances, this suggests a widespread problem in the way outdated packages handle resources over the course of their execution. It points to deficiencies in the management of memory, database connections, file handles, or other system resources that are not released or managed correctly when no longer needed. Such poor management can lead to performance degradation, crashes, or security vulnerabilities like memory leaks, which could be exploited by attackers.

Security Risks from Injection Flaws (CWE-707): The count of 829 instances for CWE-707 reflects a prevalent risk associated with security weaknesses, where user-controlled input is not correctly neutralized before being processed. This high occurrence emphasizes the potential for outdated packages to be exploited via injection attacks, such as SQL, NoSQL, OS command, and LDAP injection, leading to unauthorized access to data, corruption of data, or the ability to perform actions on the host system.

The distribution suggests that efforts to mitigate security risks in software projects should prioritize addressing these higher-incidence CWEs. Developers and maintainers must be vigilant, ensuring that updates and patches are applied on time, particularly in areas our results highlight as having a higher probability of security weaknesses.

Domain Analysis of the Vulnerability Supply Chain. Utilizing the Louvain algorithm for community detection on SC, our analysis identified 6 unique communities, each defined by a specific domain. Additionally, we conducted a separate analysis on communities 5, 7, 8, and 9 using Louvain algorithms, uncovering three communities comprising 1, 2, and 4 members, respectively. The packages within each community demonstrated thematic consistency, and these communities exhibited relative independence from one another.

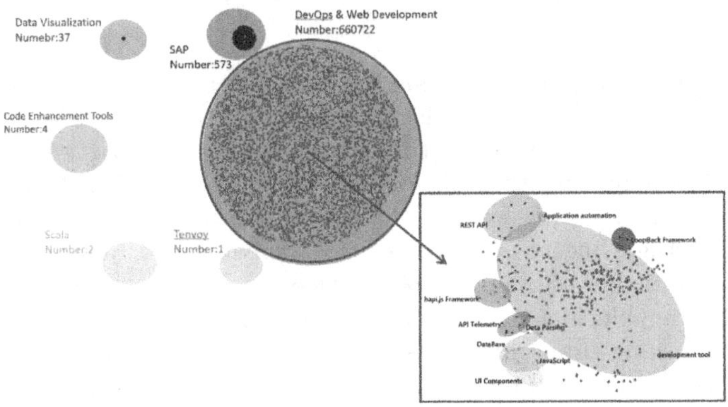

Fig. 5. Vulnerable Outdated Package Communities within the SC

As depicted in Fig. 5, a thematic analysis was conducted based on the descriptions of identified communities, the results of which are summarized in Table 4. The thematic analysis method employed in this study involved an inductive approach. We sampled 10% of projects from communities with more than 100 packages. The analysis was conducted by reviewing the descriptions and documentation of each sampled project, allowing us to identify and summarize the key themes present within each community.

This analysis highlighted a broad multi-domain coverage, encompassing domains such as `DevOps & Web Development`, `SAP`, `Data Visualization`, `Scala`, and `Tenvoy`. The distribution of packages across these domains varies considerably, with the domain of development tools being the most saturated, hosting 660,722 packages. Further analysis using the Louvain algorithm subdivided the `DevOps & Web Development` domain into 10 distinct communities. This subdivision revealed a predominant concentration of development tools, which suggests an increased vulnerability within this domain. Such vulnerabilities are critical as attackers could exploit development tools to orchestrate attacks on software supply chains, such as "Security Risks from Injection Flaws" (CWE-707) vulnerability. Developers exercise increased vigilance concerning these tools.

RQ2 Summary: The number of vulnerabilities in outdated packages is small but significantly affects the software supply chain. Using Common Weakness Enumeration (CWE), vulnerability analysis highlights notable

Table 4. Analysis of Vulnerable Package Communities

Keywords	Package Count	Description	Representative Packages
DevOps & Web Development	660,722	A collection of tools and libraries spanning the software development lifecycle, including frontend frameworks, cloud service integration, automated testing, and deployment tools. Emphasizes enhancing development efficiency and software quality through automation, supporting the building and optimization of modern web applications.	microsoft-security-devops-actions-toolkit, devops-dislinkt-frontend-app, ng2-cloud-portal-presentation-lib, ngx-tag-autocomplete
SAP	573	Focused on packages related to the SAP cloud platform and SAP Cloud SDK, supporting development work integrated with SAP business processes and data.	@sap-cloud-sdk/analytics, @sap/cds, @sap/cloud-sdk-vdm-sales-price-service, cds-routing-handlers
Data Visualization	37	Concentrates on providing and enhancing web application features for tables, forms, and data visualization, such as spreadsheet libraries and form editors.	@jspreadsheet/forms, @jspreadsheet/formula-pro, kicc-jspreadsheet, jexcel-laidback
Code Enhancement Tools	4	Contains packages for code compression, lexical analysis, and code enhancement to boost or optimize code processing capabilities during development.	closure-compiler-stream, lexis, panoptic, sugar
Scala	2	Focuses on packages for the Scala language and its JavaScript runtime environment, Scala.js, facilitating Scala developers to build and share cross-platform applications.	scala-bin, scalajs-standalone-bin
tenvoy	1	Covers functionalities related to the hapi.js framework, including static file handling, API documentation generation, authentication systems, and more.	tenvoy

risks in DevOps and web development. Outdated third-party dependencies often contain *HIGH* and *MODERATE* severity vulnerabilities, suggesting that inadequate maintenance contributes to severe security threats. Key issues like "Resource Management" and "Security Risks from Injection Flaws" are prevalent in outdated packages, posing substantial risks. Additionally, communities centered around development tools exhibit the highest number of vulnerabilities, emphasizing the need for developers to prevent the introduction of security flaws through these tools.

5 RQ3: What Factors Could Indicate the Potential Outdated Dependencies of Open Source Supply Chains Effectively?

5.1 Methodology

Based on the above discussion, it is very important to predict whether these packages will become obsolete in the package selection process in the supply chain. This is different from articles such as OpenSSF [33] that research from a best practice perspective. Our research focuses on the coding phase of the software supply chain, examining procedural behavior data within open source code management platforms. By analyzing the evolution of repositories from their inception to their active or inactive states, we aim to uncover patterns and trends associated with repository obsolescence. This approach offers a systematic way to understand the dynamics of repository maintenance.

We use the permutation feature importance technique [1] to identify the most influential features of the Random Forest (RF) classifier in detecting outdated packages. This method involves randomly shuffling the values of one feature while keeping others unchanged, breaking the link between the shuffled feature and the target variable. We then compare the classifier's performance on the test set before and after permutation. A feature is important if its shuffling significantly decreases performance. Additionally, we benchmark the Random Forest against other machine learning algorithms, including AdaBoost, Decision Tree (DT), Gradient Boosting (GB), K-Nearest Neighbors (KNN), Logistic Regression (LR), and Support Vector Machine (SVM). We use grid search for parameter optimization and 10-fold cross-validation [11] to evaluate model performance.

To statistically analyze the differences in the distribution of important features between outdated packages and current packages, we first used the Anderson-Darling test to assess normality [21]. We found that none of the features followed a normal distribution at the 5% significance level. Then we specifically focus on P-values to evaluate the significance of these differences.

Data Collection. We curated a behavioral dataset from GitHub logs from 2015 to 2023 via GH Archive [10], focusing on repositories with outdated dependencies as defined in RQ1. Balancing the dataset, we selected 5000 non-outdated packages as negative samples.

Repository names were extracted using regular expressions such as `git+https://` and `https://`, focusing on those with log data spanning more than 12 months. After filtering, we identified 1548 unique repositories for analysis. This selection included 683 repositories with non-outdated packages and 865 repositories with outdated packages. This resulted in a dataset of 8224 positive (outdated) and 9328 negative (non-outdated) records.

Feature Selection. In determining which features to use to reveal the obsolescence status of repositories, we reference existing literature and leveraged our analysis of the OSS supply chain. We evaluated several factors, such as the correlation of features with the target variable and their interpretability. Consequently, we implemented 23 features based on metrics from the CHAOSS[4] and opendigger [31] communities, as detailed in Table 5. The objective is to meticulously catalog as many features as possible within the open source software supply chain.

[4] https://chaoss.community/.

Table 5. Feature Selection for Identifying Outdated Libraries

Feature	Reference
Number of New Contributors	CHAOSS
Average Response Time for Code Change Requests	CHAOSS
Average Duration of Open Issues	CHAOSS
Total Number of Lines Changed	CHAOSS
Number of Newly Raised Issues	CHAOSS
Number of Active Issues and Pull Requests	X-lab
Number of New Code Lines Added	CHAOSS
Number of Project Forks	CHAOSS
Number of Comments on Issues	X-lab
Number of Accepted Pull Requests	CHAOSS
Average Duration of Open Pull Requests	CHAOSS
Number of Participants	X-lab
Number of Key Contributors the Project Relies On	CHAOSS
Number of Code Lines Deleted	CHAOSS
Number of Long-Inactive Contributors	CHAOSS
Number of Reviews for Pull Requests	CHAOSS
Overall Activity Events of the Project	X-lab
Average Time to Resolve Pull Requests	CHAOSS
Number of Closed Issues	CHAOSS
Total Number of Pull Requests	CHAOSS
Average Response Time for Issues	CHAOSS
Average Time to Resolve Issues	CHAOSS
Number of Stars the Project Has Received	X-lab

5.2 Results

Evaluations of multiple classification algorithms have identified the Random Forest classifier [18] as exhibiting particularly excellent performance. It demonstrated superior performance metrics, notably achieving an F1 score of 0.740, and an outstanding ROC-AUC value of 0.831. These results underscore the accuracy of the Random Forest classifier, making it one of the preferred choices for our given dataset, as depicted in Fig. 6.

Based on the Random Forest classifier, we assessed the importance of each feature, with results illustrated in Fig. 7. The *Average Duration of Open Issues* emerged as the most critical predictor, with a high importance score of 0.0708. This feature's significance is substantiated by a compelling p-value of 5.47×10^{-8}, indicating a statistically significant impact on the likelihood of repository obsolescence. This suggests that repositories with quicker issue resolutions are typically more active and less likely to become outdated.

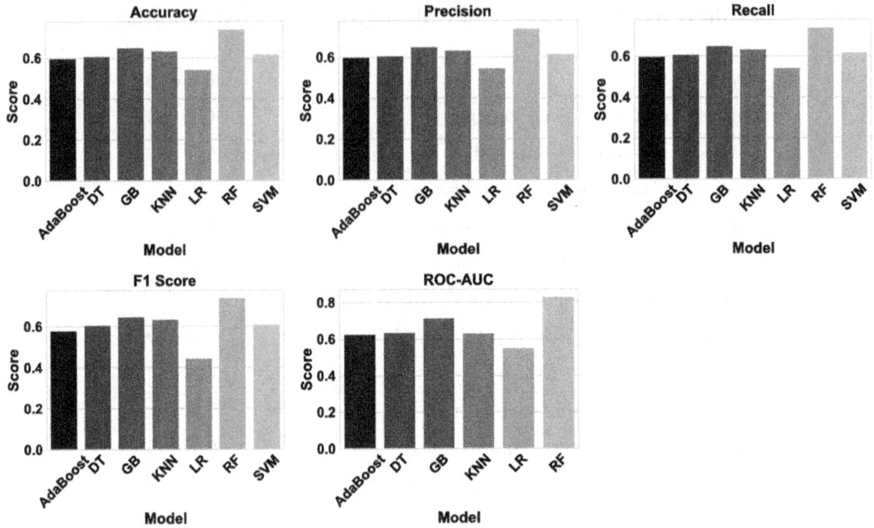

Fig. 6. Comparative analysis of model performance across various evaluation metrics

Similarly, the *Average Duration of Open Pull Requests* and the *Number of Long-Inactive Contributors*, with importance scores of 0.0600 and 0.0582 respectively, underscore the importance of timely engagement and contributor activity in maintaining repository relevance.

Overall Activity Events of the Project and *Number of Project Forks* also demonstrated significant feature importance scores of 0.0579 and 0.0570, respectively. These metrics are particularly critical, with p-values of 7.78×10^{-3} and 6.72×10^{-4}, highlighting the statistical backing for their roles in enhancing project sustainability. Such features indicate robust community engagement and are instrumental in warding off obsolescence.

Number of Active Issues and Pull Requests not only showed a high feature importance score of 0.0406 but also the most significant p-value (5.95×10^{-19}), making it one of the strongest indicators of active and healthy repository management. This aligns with the intuitive understanding that continuous interactions, such as Issues and Pull Requests, are crucial in determining whether software repositories contain outdated packages.

Although *Average Response Time for Code Change Requests* scoring lower on importance (0.0422) and having a higher p-value (0.8339), suggest that while response times are informative, they do not singularly predict obsolescence. This distinction is vital for prioritizing maintenance efforts that yield the most significant impact on repository vitality.

RQ3 Summary: Our study employs Random Forest with permutation feature importance to predict outdated dependencies in software repositories. We found that the "Average Duration of Open Issues" is the most crucial indicator of repository obsolescence. Other significant predictors include the

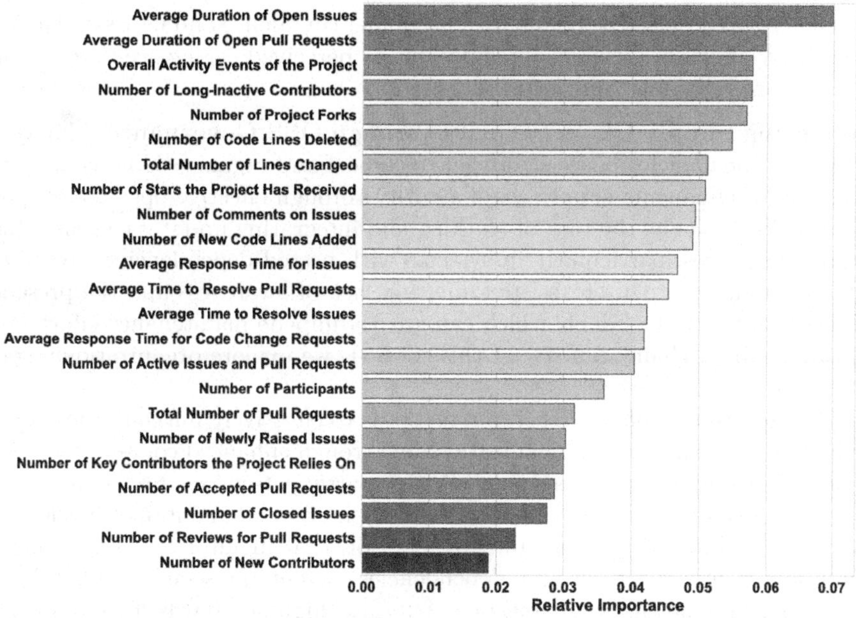

Fig. 7. Feature Importances as Determined by Random Forest Classifier

"Number of Long-Inactive Contributors" and "Overall Activity Events of the Project."

6 Discussion

This study examines the prevalence of outdated dependencies within open source software supply chains, analyzing their implications for software security. We focus on the development process and upstream dependencies to understand the persistence of outdated dependencies.

Implications of Outdated Dependencies: Our research highlights significant implications of outdated dependencies on software system security.

Outdated dependencies increase exposure to security vulnerabilities. These can lead to systemic issues across interconnected software applications, significantly escalating the potential for widespread breaches. Using outdated dependencies often leads to decreased system performance and compatibility issues with newer technologies. This not only slows down development processes but also hampers innovation, making systems less competitive and more error-prone. Dependencies with inactive open source repositories may lack support, leading to unresolved bugs and vulnerabilities. This forces development teams to perform maintenance themselves or undertake costly migrations to newer alternatives. Consequently, it is imperative to proactively select up-to-date dependencies to maintain system integrity and operational efficiency. Persisting with outdated dependencies can negatively impact stakeholder confidence and user satisfaction, potentially affecting business outcomes due to perceived negligence in maintaining software reliability and security.

Enhancing Supply Chain Security through OSS Governance: Managing software dependencies poses significant technical and organizational challenges, essential for enhancing supply chain security through effective open source governance. Technically, the task of tracking and integrating updates can introduce breaking changes, particularly in systems with nested dependencies. Organizationally, updates are often resisted due to a lack of awareness and the presence of significant technical debt, which can greatly impede maintenance efforts and threaten supply chain security. In this context, we explore organizational solutions to these challenges.

OSS governance offers structured methods to effectively mitigate these risks, which can be implemented organizationally through enhanced community governance: (1) Community Engagement: Active participation ensures frequent contributions like bug fixes and updates, reducing individual maintainer burden. (2) Continuous Monitoring Tools: Integrating tools that monitor for vulnerabilities and updates into workflows keep dependencies current and secure. (3) Establishing clear guidelines for contributions maintains high standards for quality and security. (4) Maintenance Culture: Promoting regular updates through educational initiatives enhances understanding of the risks associated with outdated dependencies.

Threats to Validity: Our exploration of stale dependencies within the npm ecosystem encountered several validity concerns that demand attention. Internally, reliance on pre-2023 data raises the possibility of temporal bias, despite meticulous data collection efforts and methodological safeguards. Externally, while insights gleaned from npm may not perfectly apply to other software ecosystems, or withstand evolving development practices, their relevance remains noteworthy. Construct validity, particularly in defining dependency "outdatedness," was approached with objectivity, though the selection of a 24-month threshold still bears some subjectivity. Conclusion validity, supported by statistical methods, faces challenges in representativeness and inferential reach, which were mitigated through comprehensive literature review and expert consultations to bolster the trustworthiness of our findings.

7 Conclusion

This study investigates the prevalence, impact, and detection of outdated dependencies in the npm ecosystem, emphasizing the risks posed by neglected software maintenance. Our analysis reveals a substantial number of outdated npm libraries, which increase security vulnerabilities and reduce software quality. By leveraging statistical methods and machine learning, we propose effective strategies for detecting and prioritizing updates to vulnerable dependencies.

Our discussion emphasizes the importance of OSS governance, community engagement, and continuous monitoring in maintaining software ecosystem health. Strengthening governance can mitigate risks from outdated dependencies and ensure software longevity and security. Our data and analysis process are available at https://github.com/justanyone2023/outdated_components_analysis.

Acknowledgments. This work was supported by the National Natural Science Foundation of China under Grants 62137001, 62277017, 61977026, and 62072115. Additionally, this work was supported by the Shanghai Science and Technology Innovation Action Plan Project under Grant No. 22510713600.

References

1. Altmann, A., Toloşi, L., Sander, O., Lengauer, T.: Permutation importance: a corrected feature importance measure. Bioinformatics **26**(10), 1340–1347 (2010)
2. Arhippainen, L.: Use and integration of third-party components in software development (2003)
3. Axelrod, C.W., Risk, D.: Malware, "weakware", and the security of software supply chains. CrossTalk **27**(2), 20–24 (2014)
4. Beck, F., Diehl, S.: Evaluating the impact of software evolution on software clustering. In: 2010 17th Working Conference on Reverse Engineering, pp. 99–108. IEEE (2010)
5. Blondel, V.D., Guillaume, J.L., Lambiotte, R., Lefebvre, E.: Fast unfolding of communities in large networks. J. Stat. Mech: Theory Exp. **2008**(10), P10008 (2008)
6. Braun, V., Clarke, V.: Thematic analysis. American Psychological Association (2012)
7. Crnkovic, I., Larsson, M.: Challenges of component-based development. J. Syst. Softw. **61**(3), 201–212 (2002)
8. Di Cosmo, R., Durak, B., Leroy, X., Mancinelli, F., Vouillon, J.: Maintaining large software distributions: new challenges from the FOSS era. In: Proceedings of the FRCSS 2006 Workshop, pp. 7–20. EASST (2006)
9. Enck, W., Williams, L.: Top five challenges in software supply chain security: observations from 30 industry and government organizations. IEEE Secur. Priv. **20**(2), 96–100 (2022)
10. GH Archive: Gh archive (2023). https://www.gharchive.org/. Accessed: YYYY-MM-DD
11. Kohavi, R., et al.: A study of cross-validation and bootstrap for accuracy estimation and model selection. In: Ijcai, vol. 14, pp. 1137–1145. Montreal, Canada (1995)
12. Kula, R.G., German, D.M., Ouni, A., Ishio, T., Inoue, K.: Do developers update their library dependencies? An empirical study on the impact of security advisories on library migration. Empir. Softw. Eng. **23**, 384–417 (2018)
13. Lin, Y.K., Li, W.: A theory of open source security: the spillover of security knowledge in vulnerability disclosures through software supply chains (2023). Available at SSRN 4472516
14. Maeprasart, V., Ikegami, A., Kula, R.G., Matsumoto, K.: Which dependency was updated? Exploring who changes dependencies in NPM packages. In: 2021 IEEE/ACIS 22nd International Conference on Software Engineering, Artificial Intelligence, Networking and Parallel/Distributed Computing (SNPD), pp. 258–261. IEEE (2021)

15. Mir, I.A., Quadri, S.: Analysis and evaluating security of component-based software development: a security metrics framework. Int. J. Comput. Netw. Inf. Secur. **4**(11), 21 (2012)
16. MITRE: Weakness enumeration (2023). https://cwe.mitre.org/
17. OSV: Open source vulnerabilities database (2023). https://osv.dev/. Accessed Apr 2023
18. Pal, M.: Random forest classifier for remote sensing classification. Int. J. Remote Sens. **26**(1), 217–222 (2005)
19. Schiffman, M., Eschelbeck, G., Ahmad, D., Wright, A., Romanosky, S.: CVSS: a common vulnerability scoring system. Nat. Infrastruct. Advisory Council (NIAC) (2004)
20. Shumway, R.H., Stoffer, D.S., Stoffer, D.S.: Time Series Analysis and its Applications, vol. 3. Springer, Heidelberg (2000)
21. Stephens, M.A.: EDF statistics for goodness of fit and some comparisons. J. Am. Stat. Assoc. **69**(347), 730–737 (1974)
22. Stringer, J., Tahir, A., Blincoe, K., Dietrich, J.: Technical lag of dependencies in major package managers. In: 2020 27th Asia-Pacific Software Engineering Conference (APSEC), pp. 228–237. IEEE (2020)
23. by Synopsys, B.D.: 2022 open source security and risk analysis report (2022). https://www.synopsys.com/software-integrity/resources/analyst-reports/open-source-security-risk-analysis.html. Accessed 01 Feb 2023
24. Thiese, M.S., Ronna, B., Ott, U.: P value interpretations and considerations. J. Thorac. Dis. **8**(9), E928 (2016)
25. Wang, Y., et al.: An empirical study of usages, updates and risks of third-party libraries in java projects. In: 2020 IEEE International Conference on Software Maintenance and Evolution (ICSME), pp. 35–45. IEEE (2020)
26. Weisberg, S.: Applied Linear Regression, vol. 528. Wiley, Hoboken (2005)
27. Wen, S.F.: Software security in open source development: a systematic literature review. In: 2017 21st Conference of Open Innovations Association (FRUCT), pp. 364–373. IEEE (2017)
28. Williams, C.: How one developer just broke node, babel and thousands of projects in 11 lines of javascript (2016). https://www.theregister.com/2016/03/23/npm_left_pad_chaos/. Accessed 01 Oct 2023
29. Wittern, E., Suter, P., Rajagopalan, S.: A look at the dynamics of the javascript package ecosystem. In: Proceedings of the 13th International Conference on Mining Software Repositories, pp. 351–361 (2016)
30. Wu, Y., Bojanova, I., Yesha, Y.: They know your weaknesses–do you?: reintroducing common weakness enumeration. CrossTalk **45** (2015)
31. Xia, X., Zhao, S., Han, F., Bi, F., Wang, W.: Opendigger: data mining and information service system for open collaboration digital ecosystem. arXiv preprint arXiv:2311.15204 (2023)
32. Yan, D., Niu, Y., Liu, K., Liu, Z., Liu, Z., Bissyandé, T.F.: Estimating the attack surface from residual vulnerabilities in open source software supply chain. In: 2021 IEEE 21st International Conference on Software Quality, Reliability and Security (QRS), pp. 493–502. IEEE (2021)
33. Zahan, N., Shohan, S., Harris, D., Williams, L.: Do software security practices yield fewer vulnerabilities? In: 2023 IEEE/ACM 45th International Conference on Software Engineering: Software Engineering in Practice (ICSE-SEIP), pp. 292–303 (2023). https://doi.org/10.1109/ICSE-SEIP58684.2023.00032

34. Zerouali, A., Constantinou, E., Mens, T., Robles, G., González-Barahona, J.: An empirical analysis of technical lag in NPM package dependencies. In: International Conference on Software Reuse, pp. 95–110. Springer, Cham (2018)
35. Zerouali, A., Cosentino, V., Mens, T., Robles, G., Gonzalez-Barahona, J.M.: On the impact of outdated and vulnerable javascript packages in docker images. In: 2019 IEEE 26th International Conference on Software Analysis, Evolution and Reengineering (SANER), pp. 619–623. IEEE (2019)
36. Zimmermann, M., Staicu, C.A., Tenny, C., Pradel, M.: Small world with high risks: a study of security threats in the NPM ecosystem. In: 28th USENIX Security Symposium (USENIX Security 19), pp. 995–1010 (2019)

EMS-HFL: A Hybrid Based Fault Localization

Donghua Wang, Zheng Li(✉), Hengyuan Liu(✉), and Yong Liu

College of Information Science and Technology, Beijing University of Chemical Technology, Beijing 100029, China
lizheng@mail.buct.edu.cn, lhywandm@163.com

Abstract. Fault localization is one of the most challenging and time-consuming tasks in software debugging. Traditional methods, such as Spectrum-Based Fault Localization (SBFL) and Mutation-Based Fault Localization (MBFL), rely on coverage or mutation outcomes to rank suspicious program elements. However, these methods are limited by their reliance on a single type of information, which often fails to capture the full complexity of fault propagation. In particular, they fail to fully utilize structural semantics, especially contextual relationships among functions, which are key to understanding fault propagation. To address these limitations, we propose EMS-HFL (Execution-Mutation-Structural Hybrid Fault Localization), a method that systematically synergy three categories of information: execution behavior (i.e., coverage data), mutation behavior (i.e., mutant outcomes), and structural semantics (i.e., function call chains). Coverage data and mutant outcomes contribute basic fault information, while function call chains capture the broader execution context that helps better measure the suspiciousness of methods. Empirical evaluations on 262 faulty versions from the Defects4J benchmark show that EMS-HFL successfully localizes 90 faults at the Top-1 position, outperforming SBFL, MBFL, and other advanced hybrid approaches. Ablation studies confirm that each information source (coverage, mutation, and structural semantics) is crucial, with their combination significantly boosting performance.

Keywords: Spectrum-Based Fault Localization · Mutation-Based Fault Localization · Program Structural Semantic · Hybrid Fault Localization

1 Introduction

Fault localization is a crucial research field in software engineering, aiming to efficiently identify and localize faults within a program [1]. As software development projects grow in scale and complexity, fault localization becomes increasingly important. This process involves diagnosing problematic segments of program execution [2] and guiding programmers to discover and resolve faults more quickly. Traditionally, fault localization heavily relied on manual debugging, which has become time-consuming and error-prone.

Y. Zhou et al. (Eds.): ICECCS 2025, LNCS 15746, pp. 424–443, 2026.
https://doi.org/10.1007/978-3-032-00828-2_23

Automated fault localization techniques improve debugging efficiency by reducing the debugging workload [3], with Spectrum-Based Fault Localization (SBFL) [4,5] and Mutation-Based Fault Localization (MBFL) [6] being both widely studied. SBFL localizes faults by analyzing test case coverage and execution outcomes, while MBFL uses mutation analysis to simulate potential faults and measure the fault possibility of program elements [7], with each method having its own strengths in different scenarios. Studies have shown that combining both can improve localization accuracy, such as MCBFL [8], which optimizes MBFL using coverage, and hybrid methods like MSFL [9,10] that validate the synergistic effect.

Although these hybrid methods show promising potential for performance improvement, they still face the issue of lacking structural semantics (i.e., the contextual relationships between functions or methods). Many existing methods rely solely on coverage or mutation data, without incorporating the interaction information between different parts of the program [11,12]. If utilized appropriately, structural semantics can provide deeper insights into fault propagation paths, complementing spectrum, and mutation analysis. While some studies have explored inter-procedural dependencies or graph-based structural information, finding that they can significantly enhance fault localization accuracy [11,13], most existing work that integrates structural semantics still focuses on coverage-based techniques, overlooking the synergistic effects of mutation analysis and failing to fully leverage the complementary strengths of coverage and mutation data. Therefore, there is an urgent need for a method that combines SBFL, MBFL, and call chain information to more accurately localize faults.

Among different representations of structural semantics, function call chains have emerged as a practical and intuitive approach, which provides a dynamic path or trace that shows how one function leads to another during program execution [14]. For instance, if the entry function `main()` calls `f1()`, which in turn calls `f2()`, and `f2()` calls `f3()`, the resulting chain (`main() -> f1() -> f2() -> f3()`) captures a sequence of dependencies. If `f2()` is faulty, examining its relationship with `f1()` and `f3()` may yield valuable insights into how the fault propagates through the system. These call chains impose little overhead beyond monitoring function boundaries, providing a lightweight and effective source of structural information. By hybridizing call chains with information from other aspects, such as coverage and mutation impacts, it is possible to better evaluate which parts of the chain contribute more to failures.

Furthermore, developers often localize faults at a method level rather than diving into statements. Although statement-level techniques can achieve fine granularity, method-level approaches are typically more aligned with real-world debugging workflows and strike a balance between accuracy and interpretability. Therefore, this study focuses on method-level granularity and investigates how to effectively integrate structural semantics, specifically function call chains, into existing coverage-based and mutation-based fault localization techniques.

To address these challenges, we propose a **E**xecution-**M**utation-**S**tructural **H**ybrid **F**ault **L**ocalization (EMS-HFL) method that systematically combines execution behavior information, mutation behavior information, and structural semantics information at the method level. In particular, EMS-HFL combines execution behavior information (i.e., coverage-based suspiciousness like SBFL), mutation behavior information (i.e., mutation-based suspiciousness like MBFL), and structural semantics (i.e., function call chain relationships that capture additional structural semantics within the program). Coverage data and mutant outcomes offer a basic understanding of likely faulty areas, while function call chains provide insight into the execution structure that may further disambiguate suspicious methods. By jointly analyzing these diverse sources of information, our method improves the suspiciousness calculation process and provides a more comprehensive view of program behavior, thereby improving the accuracy of fault localization. We conducted an empirical study on the Defects4J dataset, which contains 262 real faulty versions. Our method successfully localized 90 faults at the Top-1 position, representing an increase of 35 faults over MBFL and 40 faults over SBFL in the Top-1 metric. Ablation studies show that removing any coverage, mutation, or structural information leads to a significant drop in accuracy, highlighting the synergistic effect of the three data sources. Finally, although including function call chains incurs a slight increase in time overhead (about 3.2% compared to MBFL), this trade-off is justified by the substantial gains in accuracy and reliability.

- **Fusion multiple sources information for suspiciousness measurement:** EMS-HFL combines execution behavior, mutation behavior, and structural semantics, offering a holistic analysis of suspicious methods. This synergy allows the method to leverage the strengths of coverage-based and mutation-based techniques while benefiting from richer structural insights.
- **Hybrid fault localization approach:** We introduce EMS-HFL, which merges coverage-based (SBFL) and mutation-based (MBFL) suspiciousness with structural information from function call chains. This unified approach capitalizes on the complementary nature of SBFL and MBFL, while structural semantics further improve fault localization accuracy.
- **Comprehensive evaluation on Defects4J:** We conduct experiments on 262 real faulty versions from the Defects4J dataset. EMS-HFL demonstrates clear improvements in fault localization accuracy compared to both coverage-based and mutation-based methods, with negligible additional overhead. Ablation studies confirm the importance of each information source.

The remainder of this paper is organized as follows: Sect. 2 provides background knowledge for the method proposed in this paper. Section 3 delves into the research motivation and presents examples. Section 4 elaborates on the methodology employed in this paper. Section 5 discusses the research questions, and outlines the experimental setup and evaluation metrics. Section 6 introduces the experimental results and analysis. Section 7 presents the conclusions.

2 Background

2.1 Mutation-Based Fault Localization

MBFL is a technique that stems from mutation testing. In mutation testing, mutation operators inject faults into a program. The modified programs are called mutants. Mutation operators are crafted based on straightforward rules, such as changing $a < b$ to $a > b$. If a mutant behaves differently from the original program when executed by a test case, it is referred to as "Killed" or "Detected" [6, 15]. Otherwise, we consider the mutant "Alive" or "Not Killed" [16]. Researchers [6] count the killed mutants to calculate their suspiciousness, which is further used to compute the suspiciousness of program elements. MBFL helps developers in fault localization by furnishing a ranked list of program elements based on their suspiciousness.

The MBFL involves several steps: generating mutants through mutation operations, executing these mutants with test cases to collect execution results (e.g., pass or fail outcomes), computing the suspiciousness of mutants and program statements using a suspicious formula based on the collected data, and finally localizing faults by analyzing and ranking fault locations based on the suspiciousness. Firstly, the program C is executed with the test case T, and coverage information and test results are collected. The test case is then divided into the pass test set T_p and the fail test set T_f. Secondly, all mutants are tested, with results categorized into the killed mutant set a_k and the not killed mutant set a_n. Thirdly, MBFL methods calculate the suspiciousness of mutants using formulas such as Ochiai, Tarantula, Dstar2, and Jaccard. The calculations of the suspiciousness rely on four parameters.: $a_{np} = |a_n \cap T_p|$, $a_{kp} = |a_k \cap T_p|$, $a_{nf} = |a_n \cap T_f|$, and $a_{kf} = |a_k \cap T_f|$, The specific formulas are detailed in Table 1. Finally, after calculating the suspiciousness of mutants using the formulas provided in Table 1, MBFL ranks statements in descending order based on their suspiciousness, resulting in a list of statement-level suspiciousness. By aggregating and averaging the suspiciousness of all mutants within each function, we derive function-level suspiciousness.

Table 1. Suspiciousness Formulas for SBFL and MBFL

Name	SBFL Formula	MBFL Formula
Ochiai [17]	$\mathcal{S}_S(f) = \frac{a_{ef}}{\sqrt{(a_{ef}+a_{nf})(a_{ef}+a_{ep})}}$	$\mathcal{S}_M(f) = \frac{a_{kf}}{\sqrt{(a_{kf}+a_{nf})(a_{kf}+a_{kp})}}$
Tarantula [18]	$\mathcal{S}_S(f) = \frac{\frac{a_{ef}}{a_{ef}+a_{ep}}}{\frac{a_{ef}}{a_{ef}+a_{nf}}+\frac{a_{ep}}{a_{ep}+a_{np}}}$	$\mathcal{S}_M(f) = \frac{\frac{a_{kf}}{a_{kf}+a_{kp}}}{\frac{a_{kf}}{a_{kf}+a_{nf}}+\frac{a_{kp}}{a_{kp}+a_{np}}}$
Dstar2 [19]	$\mathcal{S}_S(f) = \frac{a_{ef}^2}{a_{ep}+a_{nf}}$	$\mathcal{S}_M(f) = \frac{a_{kf}^2}{a_{kp}+a_{nf}}$
Jaccard [20]	$\mathcal{S}_S(f) = \frac{a_{ef}}{a_{ef}+a_{nf}+a_{np}}$	$\mathcal{S}_M(f) = \frac{a_{kf}}{a_{kf}+a_{nf}+a_{np}}$

2.2 Spectrum-Based Fault Localization

SBFL [21] is a technique used in software debugging to precisely identify potential faults or defects within a program. SBFL calculates the suspiciousness of program elements (such as statements or functions) by analyzing the program's execution spectrum, which provides an overview of the test case execution. It then ranks these elements based on their perceived suspiciousness of containing faults. For a program element a, SBFL utilizes four aggregated parameters from the spectrum information to compute the suspiciousness: the number of passing tests covering a_{ep}, the number of failing tests covering a_{ef}, the number of passing tests not covering a_{np}, and the number of failing tests not covering a_{nf}. Elements with higher a_{ef} and lower a_{ep} are typically assigned higher suspiciousness in SBFL. This is because executing these program elements often leads to more test failures, while not executing them tends to result in more test successes, reflecting the underlying intuition behind SBFL. Common suspiciousness formulas include Ochiai, Tarantula, Dstar2, and the Jaccard are shown in Table 1, which rely on the coverage in passing and failing test cases for elements.

Although SBFL has theoretical advantages, its fault localization accuracy is often significantly affected by the reliance on a single information source in practical applications. Le et al. [22] pointed out a significant gap between the theoretical performance and practical effectiveness of SBFL, primarily due to insufficient design quality and inadequate coverage of real-world test cases. This issue is especially pronounced when dealing with coincidental correctness, as fault-free statements covered by failing test cases may exhibit unusually high suspiciousness scores, thus affecting fault localization accuracy. Although Wong et al. [23] attempted to enhance accuracy by analyzing code coverage information, relying on a single information source has proven insufficient to effectively improve fault localization precision. Therefore, to address this challenge, it is necessary to hybridize multiple information sources to comprehensively assess the suspiciousness of statements and enhance fault localization accuracy.

2.3 Hybrid Fault Localization

To address the limitations of single-method fault localization approaches, such as the accuracy challenges of SBFL due to insufficient test cases or biased test data, and the high computational overhead of MBFL when handling a large number of mutants, a hybrid solution is required. Researchers have developed hybrid fault localization methods that combine the strengths of different techniques to enhance accuracy and efficiency. Hybrid approaches aim to overcome these challenges by hybridizing complementary information from different methods.

Some researchers have combined the advantages of existing techniques to aid fault localization. Cui et al. [9] integrated spectrum-based and mutation-based techniques to improve localization accuracy. Dutta et al. [24] propose a method to combine the effectiveness of ten different fault localization techniques, using a deep learning ranking approach to achieve better fault localization accuracy. Ju et al. [25] calculate the complete slice for failed test cases and the execution slice for passed ones, then construct a hybrid spectrum by intersecting them. While this approach reduces the cost of fault localization, it provides only limited improvement in accuracy. Some researchers have also leveraged inter-function information to assist fault localization, Such as Yue et al. [13], who proposed the PRMA method, which employed the PageRank algorithm to construct a graph of functions and their relationships, effectively achieving better localization results. Feyzi et al. [11] proposed a hybrid approach that combines dynamic correlations between program statements and termination states, static structural information, and fault-proneness metrics. In addition, they uncovered causal chain information, which provided richer contextual support for program faults and played a crucial role in improving fault localization performance. This approach highlights that leveraging inter-function relationship information is an effective way to address fault localization challenges. Among all inter-function relationships, function call chains, due to their simplicity and accessibility, have become one of the most widely used techniques. Function call chains represent the sequential and structural relationships of function invocations during program execution, forming chain-like structures. Compared to individual functions or statements, these call chains provide richer contextual information, making them highly valuable for debugging.

3 Motivation Example

Table 2. An Example of MBFL and SBFL

Function	Mutants	Kill Matrix					MBFL		Coverage Information				SBFL	
		T_{p0}	T_{f0}	T_{p2}	T_{p3}	*Sus(M)*	*Sus(F)*	*Rank(F)*	T_{p0}	T_{f0}	T_{p2}	T_{p3}	*Sus(F)*	*Rank(F)*
Function_1	M_0	-	*	-	-	1	1	2	●	●	●	●	0.5	5
	M_1	-	*	-	-	1								
Function_2	M_2	-	*	-	-	1	1	2	○	●	○	○	1	2
	M_3	-	*	-	-	1								
Function_3	M_4	*	-	*	*	0	0.395	4	○	●	●	●	0.58	4
	M_5	*	*	*	*	0.5								
	M_6	-	*	*	*	0.58								
	M_7	*	*	*	*	0.5								
Function_4	M_8	-	*	-	-	1	1	2	○	●	○	○	1	2
Function_5	M_9	*	-	*	*	0	0.167	5	○	●	○	○	1	2
	M_{10}	*	*	*	*	0.5								
	M_{11}	-	-	*	-	0								

Note: The suspiciousness scores are calculated using the Ochiai formula

In the field of software fault localization, hybrid fault localization methods have significant advantages by combining multiple types of information to assist in fault localization. Function call chains can provide rich structural and semantic information. This study leverages execution behavior information, mutation behavior information, and structural semantics information to improve fault localization accuracy. We provide a specific motivational example to explain this. Table 2 presents an example comparing MBFL and SBFL, where five functions are listed, and the suspiciousness of mutants and functions is calculated based on the mutation kill matrix and coverage information. In the table, T_p represents passing test cases, and T_f represents failing test cases. The symbols '*' and ● indicate that the test case killed the mutant or covered the function, while '-' and ○ indicate that it did not. *Sus*(M) represents the suspiciousness

Table 3. An Example on EMS-HFL

Chain	Function	SBFL		MBFL		Chain				EMS-HFL	
		Sus(F)	*Rank(F)*	*Sus(F)*	*Rank(F)*	*Sus(C)*	*Rank(C)*	*Sus(F)*	*Rank(F)*	*Sus(F)*	*Rank(F)*
$Function_1 \rightarrow Function_2$	$Function_1$	0.5	5	1	2	1	1.5	1	1.5	0.5	3
	$Function_2$	1	2	1	2			1	1.5	1	1
$Function_3 \rightarrow Function_4 \rightarrow Function_5$	$Function_3$	0.58	4	0.395	4	0.521	4	0.521	4	0.119	4
	$Function_4$	1	2	1	2			0.521	4	0.521	2
	$Function_5$	1	2	0.167	5			0.521	4	0.088	5

Note: The calculation for the suspiciousness of Chain is detailed in Sect. 4.3

of mutants, and *Sus*(F) represents the suspiciousness of functions. By calculating the suspiciousness, we found that Function_1, Function_2, and Function_4 have the same suspiciousness, making it difficult to distinguish which one is the faulty function.

To address these issues and improve fault localization accuracy, we propose the EMS-HFL method. While traditional methods struggle to differentiate between functions with identical suspiciousness scores, EMS-HFL leverages call chain information to provide a more nuanced view of function behavior. By examining how functions interact within call chains, we can better identify which function is more likely to be faulty. This is because call chains capture the dynamic execution flow of the program, revealing how functions depend on and influence each other during execution. Table 3 presents an example of this method. In the EMS-HFL method, the suspiciousness of functions is not only based on mutant and coverage information but also incorporates function call chain information. Specifically, we calculate the suspiciousness of each call chain by averaging the suspiciousness of each mutant in the chain and then derive the suspiciousness of functions based on the contribution proportion of the call chain to the function. In this example, since only two function call chains are selected, the suspiciousness of the functions and the suspiciousness of the function call chains are identical. However, in actual applications, each function participates in multiple call chains, and the different combinations of these call chains provide a more comprehensive reflection of the function's true suspiciousness. In this way, the EMS-HFL method effectively improves the accuracy of fault localization.

4 Our Method

Our approach mainly improves fault localization accuracy by hybridizing execution behavior information, mutation behavior information, and structural semantics information. This section is divided into three parts. The first part provides a high-level overview of the EMS-HFL method, explaining the core implementation of our approach. The second part discusses and explains how the final suspiciousness is computed. The third part mainly describes how structural semantics information is used to calculate suspiciousness, emphasizing the key role of structural semantics information in fault localization.

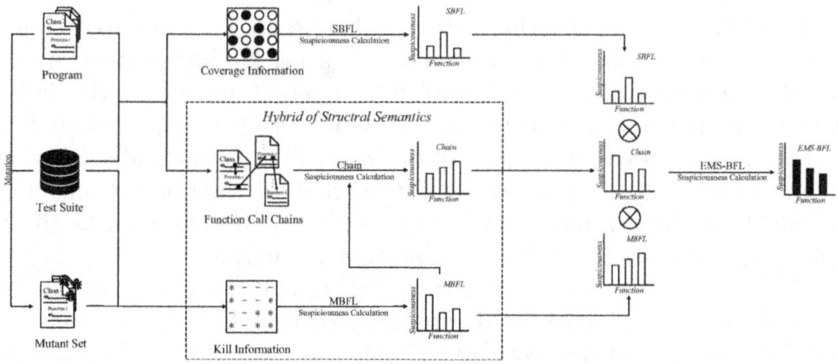

Fig. 1. The Workflow of EMS-HFL

4.1 Overview

The method described in the article can be abstracted as a hybrid fault localization method that combines three types of information: execution behavior information (SBFL), mutation behavior information (MBFL), and structural semantics information (function call chain). Figure 1 provides a high-level overview of our method.

This method is based on hybridizing multiple sources of information to improve the accuracy of fault localization. It utilizes test coverage information, data mutants, and function call chains to comprehensively evaluate suspiciousness. The method combines the advantages of MBFL and SBFL while incorporating function call chain analysis as auxiliary information. Suspiciousness is calculated across multiple layers of information, with each layer providing a unique perspective. By aggregating and combining suspiciousness from these diverse sources, the method achieves a more comprehensive and precise evaluation, ultimately deriving a suspiciousness score to guide fault localization. The specific implementation process is as follows: mutants are generated and test cases are run to collect function call chain data, coverage information, and kill data. Using kill information from MBFL, we calculate method-level suspiciousness. Then, we assess the average suspiciousness of mutants within each function call chain, which informs the function suspiciousness. Coverage data is used for SBFL. Finally, we multiply the suspiciousness from MBFL, function call chains, and SBFL to obtain the final EMS-HFL suspiciousness.

4.2 Suspiciousness Calculation

To better utilize more information to improve fault localization accuracy, we chose to hybridize execution behavior information (SBFL), mutation behavior information (MBFL), and structural semantics information (function call chain) to improve fault localization accuracy. The information used by SBFL and MBFL is quite different yet complementary [9]. The SBFL method obtains coverage information by executing the original program, while the MBFL method modifies the code slightly before execution to gather kill information. Although these two methods operate on completely different processes, the information they provide is complementary. Function call chain information further leverages the structured information of function calls, offering additional contextual support for fault localization. This structured information not only supplements SBFL and MBFL but also provides a richer context for fault localization, thereby enhancing the accuracy of comprehensive analysis.

By hybridizing the features of SBFL, MBFL, and function call chain information, we can comprehensively determine whether a function contains faults. Specifically, inspired by the concept of joint probability from logic and probability theory, we assume the mutual independence of the information derived from SBFL, MBFL, and function call chains. Based on this assumption, we perform their fusion through multiplicative aggregation. This approach is theoretically grounded in the multiplication rule for independent events in probability theory, where the joint probability distribution of statistically independent variables can be represented by the product of their individual probability distributions.

Finally, the final suspiciousness is obtained by multiplying it with the suspiciousness of MBFL. Follow the formula below:

$$\mathcal{S}_{EMS}(f) = \mathcal{S}_S(f) \cdot \mathcal{S}_M(f) \cdot \mathcal{S}_F(f) \tag{1}$$

where $\mathcal{S}_M(f)$ represents the suspiciousness of the function$_i$ according to MBFL, $\mathcal{S}_F(f)$ is the suspiciousness of the function calculated using structural semantic information, $\mathcal{S}_S(f)$ is the suspiciousness of the function obtained from test case coverage information and result information, like in traditional SBFL methods [26]. The specific suspicion calculation formulas for $\mathcal{S}_M(f)$ and $\mathcal{S}_S(f)$ are described in Sect. 5.4.

$\mathcal{S}_{EMS}(f)$ is the suspiciousness of the function$_i$ granularity that we finally calculate.

4.3 Hybrid of Function Call Information

According to the previous analysis, incorporating additional contextual information often helps enhance fault localization accuracy. Structured function call chains, which are readily obtainable, can assist in improving fault localization accuracy. Specifically, we consider using the kill information of mutants contained within each function in the function call chain to calculate the overall suspiciousness of the function call chain. The suspiciousness of the function call chain is calculated using formula 2.

$$\mathcal{S}_M(c) = \frac{\sum_{m \in \mathcal{M}_c} \mathcal{S}_M(m)}{|\mathcal{M}_c|} \tag{2}$$

The symbols in the formula are defined as follows: $\mathcal{S}_M(c)$ represents the suspicion degree of the function call chain c; $\mathcal{M}_c$ is the set of mutants associated with the function call chain c; m denotes an individual mutant in the set $\mathcal{M}_c$; $\mathcal{S}_M(m)$ is the suspicion degree of the mutant m; $|\mathcal{M}_c|$ represents the total number of mutants in the function call chain c, i.e., the cardinality of the set $\mathcal{M}_c$.

Then, we calculate the suspiciousness of each function based on its varying contribution within the function call chain. The specific method framework is illustrated in Fig. 2.

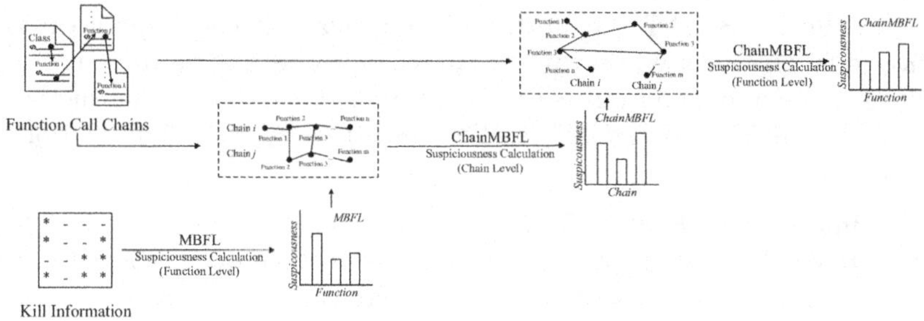

Fig. 2. The Workflow of hybrid of function call information

The suspiciousness of a function is determined based on the importance of the ranking of the function call chain in which the function resides. By aggregating the contributions of the function across each chain, we calculate the function's suspiciousness using the following formula 3:

$$\mathcal{S}_F(f) = \sum_{c \in C_f} \alpha^{-(\mathcal{R}(c)-1)} \cdot \mathcal{S}_M(c) \tag{3}$$

where $\mathcal{S}_F(f)$ represents the suspicion degree of the function f; C_f is the set of function call chains that include the function f; $\mathcal{S}_M(c)$ denotes the suspicion degree of the function call chain c; $\mathcal{R}(c)$ represents the rank of the function call chain c; α is a hyperparameter that controls the weight decay based on the rank of the call chain. The parameters are selected through preliminary experiments, with values set to 5, 10, 20, 50, and 100. The optimal result, 10, is chosen to calculate the final experimental results.

5 Experimental Design

5.1 Research Questions

RQ1:How does the performance of EMS-HFL compare to MBFL and SBFL methods?

We aim to scientifically evaluate the performance of the EMS-HFL method in fault localization, directly comparing it to MBFL and SBFL methods. This comparison is intended to establish a clear understanding of the advantages or distinctions of EMS-HFL in fault localization scenarios.

RQ2: How does the performance of EMS-HFL compare to recently proposed techniques?

Our study conducts a comparative analysis of the EMS-HFL method, comparing it with the SMFL method [9], which combines SBFL and MBFL, MCBFL-hybrid-avg, which is the hybrid variant method of MBFL, [8], and the PRMA method that combines the PageRank algorithm with MBFL [13]. Through this analysis, we demonstrate the superiority and effectiveness of our method relative to these three hybrid techniques.

RQ3: In the EMS-HFL method, how significant is the impact on localization effectiveness when one of the components is removed?

We explore the importance of the three components of our method by separately reducing coverage information, function call chain information, and mutant information.

RQ4: Time cost of EMS-HFL?

This research question primarily discusses the time overhead of the EMS-HFL method and further explores whether there is potential for optimizing this overhead.

5.2 Subjects

In this paper, the experiments are conducted on the real-world fault dataset Defects4J [27], which is a widely recognized benchmark extensively used in software testing research. The dataset contains carefully curated real-world projects with distinctive characteristics (e.g., varying sizes, domains, and complexity), providing a representative foundation for evaluation. For each fault, Defects4J provides the faulty program, its fixed version with code modifications, and the corresponding test cases. We select five of the most commonly used projects in Defects4J (v1.2.0) but exclude the Closure project due to some test cases failing after the code is instrumented. These tests assert things that are affected by the instrumentation, such as the structure of an object, runtime, classpath contents, etc. These unexpectedly failing tests could impact the suspiciousness of the covered code elements.

Table 4. Statistics of Subject Programs

Program	#Versions	#LOC	#Test Cases	#Functions	#Chains
Chart	26	86k	2,187	5,235	41k
Lang	65	22k	2,270	2,431	6k
Time	27	28k	4,019	3,627	150k
Math	106	85k	3,597	7,041	252k
Mockito	38	22k	1,331	1,433	11k
Total	262	243k	13,404	19,767	460k

The first column in the Table 4 represents the program, and the second column shows the number of versions for each program, covering a total of 262 projects from Defects4J (v1.2.0). The third and fourth columns respectively show the lines of code and the number of test cases, with up to 243,000 lines of code and 13,404 test cases. The fifth column indicates the number of functions in the project, and the sixth column represents the total number of function call chains generated during test case execution. The experiment covered 19,767 functions and generated 460,000 function call chains, representing an immense workload.

5.3 Evaluation Metrics

Top-N: The Top-N metric serves as a prevalent measure to evaluate whether faulty elements are located within the top ranks of the sorted list generated by fault localization techniques. In scenarios where multiple faulty elements share the same rank within the Top-N positions [28], they are considered only once. Studies indicate that around 70% of developers inspect only the first 5 elements. Therefore, we set the value of N to 1, 3, and 5.

MAR: The Mean Average Rank (MAR) is a widely adopted ranking evaluation metric in fault localization [29]. It measures the average rank of faulty functions within the ranking list generated by a fault localization technique, aggregating the contributions of all faulty functions across buggy programs. The MAR is computed as follows:

$$MAR(P) = \sum_{p \in P} \sum_{f \in F_p} \frac{\mathcal{R}(f) \cdot \mathcal{F}(f)}{|P| \cdot |F_p|}, \tag{4}$$

where P represents the set of buggy programs, and $p \in P$ refers to an individual buggy program. For a buggy program p, F_p denotes the set of functions contained in p, and $f \in F_p$ represents a specific function. $\mathcal{R}(f)$ indicates the rank of function f in the suspiciousness list produced by a fault localization method, and $\mathcal{F}(f)$ is a binary indicator function that equals 1 if f is a faulty function and 0 otherwise.

EXAM [30]: The EXAM metric quantifies the proportion of program functions that developers need to inspect to identify the exact faulty function. It is commonly used in fault localization techniques to evaluate their effectiveness. Formally, the EXAM metric for a faulty function f is defined as:

$$EXAM(f) = \frac{\mathcal{R}(f)}{|F_p|} \tag{5}$$

Here, p denotes a buggy program, and F_p represents the set of functions contained in p, with $|F_p|$ indicating the total number of functions in F_p. The variable $f \in F_p$ identifies the faulty function, while $\mathcal{R}(f)$ denotes the rank of the faulty function f in the prioritized list produced by the fault localization technique. The EXAM metric takes values in the range $[0, 1]$, with smaller values indicating higher localization efficiency.

5.4 Experiment Setup

The function call chains are obtained using a bytecode instrumentation tool based on Javassist[1]. Javassist collects function call relationship data. The tool records the relationships between functions during the execution of test cases and stores this information using a linked data structure. The spectrum coverage results of the test cases are recorded concurrently during execution using GZoltar[2]. We applied the mutation analysis tool major[3] to obtain the MBFL results. Moreover, the suspiciousness formula we used in all research questions is the Ochiai [17] formula.

6 Results Analysis

6.1 RQ1: How Does the Performance of EMS-HFL Compare to MBFL and SBFL Methods?

In RQ1, we undertake a comparative analysis between the EMS-HFL method and traditional SBFL and MBFL methods. As shown in Table 5, EMS-HFL demonstrates significant improvements across all five projects of the Defects4J dataset, particularly in the Top-1, Top-3, and Top-5 fault localization metrics. Specifically, EMS-HFL outperforms SBFL by 40 faults and MBFL by 35 faults

Table 5. Top-N Results for EMS-HFL Compared to SBFL and MBFL

Project	Method	Top-1	Top-3	Top-5	MAR
Chart	SBFL	5	10	12	14.65
	MBFL	8	15	18	12.89
	EMS-HFL	**12**	**16**	**20**	**8.99**
Lang	SBFL	23	28	41	7.09
	MBFL	21	42	51	3.98
	EMS-HFL	**37**	**48**	**62**	**2.78**
Time	SBFL	3	6	9	20.63
	MBFL	5	11	16	14.22
	EMS-HFL	**8**	**12**	**22**	**8.55**
Math	SBFL	15	36	36	21.61
	MBFL	17	36	46	17.27
	EMS-HFL	**26**	**54**	**65**	**8.49**
Mockito	SBFL	4	7	11	31.22
	MBFL	4	9	13	28.39
	EMS-HFL	**7**	**13**	**20**	**17.25**
Total	SBFL	50	87	109	19.04
	MBFL	55	113	144	15.35
	EMS-HFL	**90**	**143**	**189**	**9.21**

[1] http://jboss-javassist.github.io/javassist.

[2] https://gzoltar.com.

[3] https://mutation-testing.org.

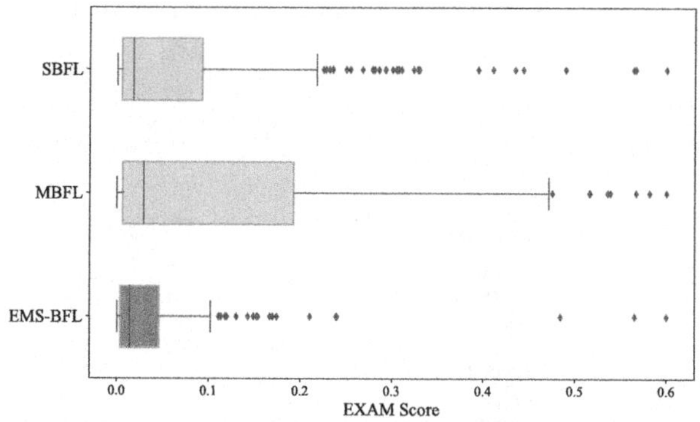

Fig. 3. EXAM Results for EMS-HFL, Compared to SBFL and MBFL

in the Top-1 evaluation; outperforms SBFL by 56 faults and MBFL by 30 faults in the Top-3 evaluation; and outperforms SBFL by 80 faults and MBFL by 45 faults in the Top-5 evaluation, highlighting its superior performance.

These experimental results align with our expected outcomes. By hybridizing multiple information sources, including structural semantics around the fault location, our approach provides a more detailed and comprehensive function-level suspiciousness analysis. In contrast, SBFL and MBFL methods primarily rely on fault locations without leveraging surrounding program code semantics, which limits their ability to accurately identify faults.

Through the exam score result, we effectively demonstrate the superiority of our proposed fault localization method in fault localization compared to MBFL and SBFL methods. Figure 3 presents the result of EXAM scores for the three methods. The y-axis represents the methods, while the x-axis indicates the EXAM scores. Our method shows a noticeable reduction in EXAM scores compared to the other two methods, proving the effectiveness of our approach.

Summary for RQ1: EMS-HFL consistently outperforms both SBFL and MBFL across all Defects4J projects, achieving higher Top-1, Top-3, and Top-5 and lower EXAM scores.

6.2 RQ2: How Does the Performance of EMS-HFL Compare to Recently Proposed Hybrid Techniques?

In RQ2, we compare the EMS-HFL method with SMFL [9], MCBFL-hybrid-avg [8], and PRMA [13]. The results show that the EMS-HFL method demonstrates a significant advantage in Top-N fault localization performance.

According to Table 6, EMS-HFL significantly outperforms other methods in Top-1, Top-3, and Top-5 metrics. EMS-HFL localizes 36 to 48 more faults than SMFL, MCBFL-hybrid-avg, and PRMA in Top-1, 42 to 59 more in Top-3, and 50 to 69 more in Top-5, demonstrating its superior accuracy in fault localization.

It can be observed that our method outperforms SMFL, MCBFL-hybrid-avg, and PRMA in terms of fault localization effectiveness. Figure 4 depicts the

Table 6. Top-N Results for EMS-HFL Compared to SMFL, MCBFL-hybrid-avg, and PRMA

Project	Method	Top-1	Top-3	Top-5	MAR
Chart	SMFL	4	11	14	12.13
	MCBFL-hybrid-avg	5	11	15	11.26
	PRMA	7	14	17	10.79
	EMS-HFL	**12**	**16**	**20**	**8.99**
Lang	SMFL	12	24	27	13.67
	MCBFL-hybrid-avg	13	25	29	12.39
	PRMA	14	26	32	12.12
	EMS-HFL	**37**	**48**	**62**	**2.78**
Time	SMFL	4	7	11	29.78
	MCBFL-hybrid-avg	4	8	11	28.33
	PRMA	5	10	13	21.45
	EMS-HFL	**8**	**12**	**22**	**8.55**
Math	SMFL	16	32	49	12.88
	MCBFL-hybrid-avg	17	34	50	12.33
	PRMA	19	38	53	12.19
	EMS-HFL	**26**	**54**	**65**	**8.49**
Mockito	SMFL	6	10	19	24.89
	MCBFL-hybrid-avg	**10**	13	20	22.24
	PRMA	9	13	**24**	21.77
	EMS-HFL	7	**13**	20	**17.25**
Total	SMFL	42	84	120	18.67
	MCBFL-hybrid-avg	49	91	125	17.31
	PRMA	54	101	139	15.66
	EMS-HFL	**90**	**143**	**189**	**9.21**

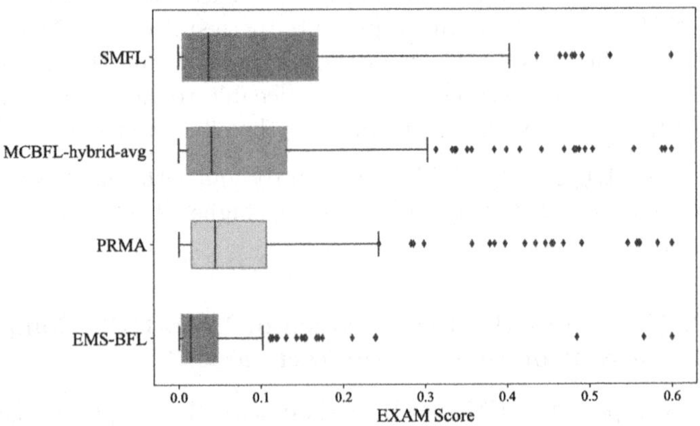

Fig. 4. EXAM Results for EMS-HFL Compared to SMFL, MCBFL-hybrid-avg and PRMA

result of EXAM scores for the three methods, the EMS-HFL method is compared with SMFL, MCBFL-hybrid-avg, and PRMA in terms of EXAM results. It can be observed that the EMS-HFL method demonstrates higher localization efficiency compared to the other methods. The EMS-HFL method shows the highest median, indicating that it generally achieves superior EXAM scores in most cases. Additionally, the narrow spread of scores for EMS-HFL suggests consistent performance with fewer outliers. In contrast, the SMFL, the MCBFL-hybrid-avg, and PRMA methods exhibit lower medians, wider spreads, and a greater number of outliers, which may imply more variability in their performance and less stability compared to the EMS-HFL method.

Summary for RQ2: EMS-HFL outperforms SMFL, MCBFL-hybrid-avg, and PRMA in Top-1, Top-3, and Top-5 accuracy, consistently locating more faults across all five projects. EXAM score result comparisons show that EMS-HFL not only achieves superior EXAM scores but also exhibits narrower score distributions, indicating higher stability and fewer outliers.

6.3 RQ3: In the EMS-HFL Method, How Significant Is the Impact on Localization Effectiveness When One of the Components is Removed?

In RQ3, we analyzes the role of coverage information, mutation information, and structural information in the EMS-HFL method, confirming their positive impact on optimizing fault localization. We designed ablation experiments to evaluate the impact of removing different information components on the method's performance. Table 7 presents the experimental results, where w/o $\mathcal{S}_F(f)$, w/o $\mathcal{S}_M(f)$, and w/o $\mathcal{S}_S(f)$ denote the approaches without structured function call chain, mutation and coverage information.

Table 7. Top-N Results for the components on EMS-HFL

Project	Method	Top-1	Top-3	Top-5	MAR
Chart	w/o $\mathcal{S}_F(f)$	6	14	17	12.66
	w/o $\mathcal{S}_M(f)$	9	13	15	12.04
	w/o $\mathcal{S}_S(f)$	10	14	16	10.61
	EMS-HFL	**12**	**16**	**20**	**8.99**
Lang	w/o $\mathcal{S}_F(f)$	23	42	53	3.58
	w/o $\mathcal{S}_M(f)$	20	39	56	3.88
	w/o $\mathcal{S}_S(f)$	23	40	55	3.69
	EMS-HFL	**37**	**48**	**62**	**2.78**
Time	w/o $\mathcal{S}_F(f)$	3	11	16	15.51
	w/o $\mathcal{S}_M(f)$	3	13	15	15.89
	w/o $\mathcal{S}_S(f)$	5	13	19	12.42
	EMS-HFL	**8**	**18**	**22**	**8.55**
Math	w/o $\mathcal{S}_F(f)$	18	40	49	12.59
	w/o $\mathcal{S}_M(f)$	21	44	51	14.13
	w/o $\mathcal{S}_S(f)$	19	42	53	14.63
	EMS-HFL	**26**	**54**	**65**	**8.49**
Mockito	w/o $\mathcal{S}_F(f)$	2	6	12	28.32
	w/o $\mathcal{S}_M(f)$	4	8	13	39.75
	w/o $\mathcal{S}_S(f)$	5	11	15	28.12
	EMS-HFL	**7**	**13**	**20**	**17.25**
Total	w/o $\mathcal{S}_F(f)$	52	117	147	14.53
	w/o $\mathcal{S}_M(f)$	57	117	150	14.28
	w/o $\mathcal{S}_S(f)$	62	120	158	13.89
	EMS-HFL	**90**	**143**	**189**	**9.21**

The experimental results indicate that EMS-HFL, which integrates all three types of information, significantly outperforms its variants that lack any one of them. For instance, in the Top-1 evaluation, w/o $\mathcal{S}_F(f)$ localizes only 52 faults, while w/o $\mathcal{S}_M(f)$ and w/o $\mathcal{S}_S(f)$ localize 57 and 62 faults, respectively. In contrast, EMS-HFL achieves 90 faults, demonstrating that combining these three types of information substantially improves fault localization accuracy. Furthermore, EMS-HFL achieves superior performance in Top-3 and Top-5 evaluations, localizing 143 and 189 faults, respectively. Its MAR value is as low as 9.21, further validating the method's effectiveness. As shown in Fig. 5, the EXAM score distribution of EMS-HFL is more concentrated, indicating a higher efficiency in fault localization.

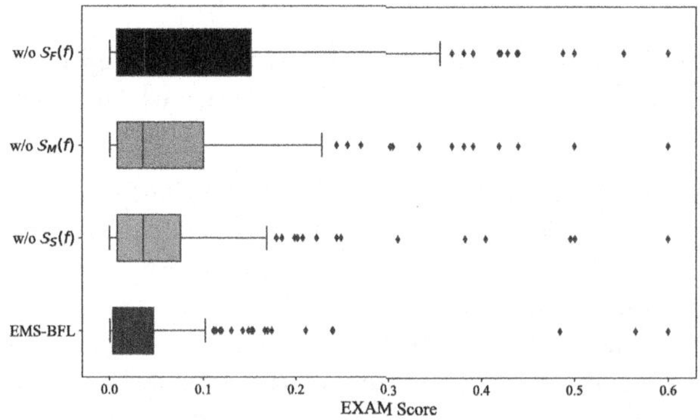

Fig. 5. EXAM results of the components of EMS-HFL

Summary for RQ3: Ablation experiments confirm that coverage information, mutation information, and structural semantics each play a critical role in EMS-HFL. Removing any one of these components significantly degrades fault localization performance, underscoring the synergy and necessity of integrating all three sources of information for accurate and comprehensive fault localization.

6.4 RQ4: Time Cost of EMS-HFL?

To evaluate the time efficiency of the EMS-HFL method, we analyze its time overhead, as detailed in Table 8. The breakdown includes mutant analysis (MA), function call chain and coverage processing (FC), calculation overhead(Cal), ranking, and total time for each project. The results indicate that the majority of the time overhead is concentrated in the mutant component, which averages 8,971 s across five projects and constitutes nearly the entire computational cost. For example, in the Mockito project, the mutant component takes 10,764 s, while the call chain and calculation components require only 187 and 97 s, respectively, highlighting mutant generation and processing as the primary bottlenecks.

Although EMS-HFL introduces a slight increase in time overhead, this is a reasonable trade-off given its substantial improvement in fault localization accuracy. Future optimizations should focus on reducing the time required for the mutant component to enhance overall efficiency.

Table 8. The Time cost of EMS-HFL

Project	MA(s)	FC(s)	Cal(s)	Rank(s)	Total(s)
Chart	14,508	144	36	1	14,689
Lang	5,004	36	14	1	5,055
Time	10,188	65	22	1	10,276
Math	4,391	328	31	1	4,751
Mockito	10,764	187	97	1	11,049
Average	8,971	152	40	1	9,164

Summary for RQ4: The time overhead of EMS-HFL is mainly concentrated on mutation tasks, with minimal costs for the call chain and ranking processes. Compared to traditional MBFL, the overhead increases by only 3.2%, yet it successfully localizes 35 more faults in the Top-1 position, with the improvement far outweighing the increase in cost.

7 Conclusion

In this work, we proposed the EMS-HFL method as a systematic approach to hybrid fault localization. By integrating coverage information, mutation information, and structural semantics at the method level, EMS-HFL addresses multiple challenges found in traditional fault localization techniques. Our empirical evaluation demonstrated that EMS-HFL not only outperforms SBFL and MBFL methods in terms of accuracy but also proves superior to other hybrid approaches such as SMFL, MCBFL-hybrid-avg, and PRMA. These improvements are evidenced by consistently higher Top-N metrics and lower EXAM scores across all Defects4J projects, indicating better stability and enhanced effectiveness. The ablation study results, confirm that each type of information (coverage, mutation, and structural semantics) contributes critical and complementary insights, underscoring the necessity of their combined use. While the introduction of function call chains adds a small overhead compared to MBFL, the considerable increase in localized faults justifies this trade-off.

In future work, we will further validate the information independence assumption of EMS-HFL and integrate advanced machine learning to adaptively tune key parameters like α for greater robustness. Additionally, we aim to explore large language models to enhance fault localization by leveraging deeper source code semantics.

Acknowledgment. The work is supported by the National Natural Science Foundation of China (Grant nos. 61902015, 61872026, and 61672085).

References

1. Zeller, A.: Why Programs Fail: A Guide to Systematic Debugging. Morgan Kaufmann Publishers Inc., San Francisco (2005)
2. Shin, D., Bae, D.-H.: A theoretical framework for understanding mutation-based testing methods. In: 2016 IEEE International Conference on Software Testing, Verification and Validation (ICST), pp. 299–308. IEEE (2016)
3. Wong, W.E., Gao, R., Li, Y., Abreu, R., Wotawa, F.: A survey on software fault localization. IEEE Trans. Software Eng. **42**(8), 707–740 (2016)
4. Debroy, V., Wong, W.E.: Insights on fault interference for programs with multiple bugs. In: 20th International Symposium on Software Reliability Engineering, vol. 2009, pp. 165–174. IEEE (2009)
5. Arrieta, A., Segura, S., Markiegi, U., Sagardui, G., Etxeberria, L.: Spectrum-based fault localization in software product lines. Inf. Softw. Technol. **100**, 18–31 (2018)
6. Papadakis, M., Traon, Y.: Metallaxis-FL: mutation-based fault localization. Softw. Test. Verification Reliab. **25**(5–7), 605–628 (2015)
7. Budd, T.A.: Mutation analysis of program test data, Ph.D. dissertation, Yale University, USA (1980)
8. Pearson, S., et al.: Evaluating and improving fault localization. In: 2017 IEEE/ACM 39th International Conference on Software Engineering (ICSE), pp. 609–620. IEEE (2017)
9. Cui, Z., Jia, M., Chen, X., Zheng, L., Liu, X.: Improving software fault localization by combining spectrum and mutation. IEEE Access **8**, 172296–172307 (2020)
10. Dutta, A., Godboley, S.: MSFL: a model for fault localization using mutation-spectra technique. In: Przybyłek, A., Miler, J., Poth, A., Riel, A. (eds.) LASD 2021. LNBIP, vol. 408, pp. 156–173. Springer, Cham (2021). https://doi.org/10.1007/978-3-030-67084-9_10
11. Feyzi, F., Parsa, S.: FPA-FL: incorporating static fault-proneness analysis into statistical fault localization. J. Syst. Softw. 136, pp. 39–58 (2018). https://www.sciencedirect.com/science/article/pii/S0164121217302583
12. Beszédes, Á., Horváth, F., Di Penta, M., Gyimóthy, T.: Leveraging contextual information from function call chains to improve fault localization. In: 2020 IEEE 27th International Conference on Software Analysis, Evolution and Reengineering (SANER), pp. 468–479. IEEE (2020)
13. Yan, Y., Jiang, S., Zhang, Y., Zhang, C.: An effective fault localization approach based on pagerank and mutation analysis. J. Syst. Softw. **204**, 111799 (2023). https://www.sciencedirect.com/science/article/pii/S0164121223001942
14. Robillard, M.P., Murphy, G.C.: Concern graphs: finding and describing concerns using structural program dependencies. In: Proceedings of the 24th International Conference on Software Engineering, pp. 406–416 (2002)
15. Kooli, M., Kaddachi, F., Natale, G., Bosio, A., Benoit, P., Torres, L.: Computing reliability: on the differences between software testing and software fault injection techniques. Microprocess. Microsyst. **50**, 102–112 (2017)
16. Debroy, V., Wong, W.E.: Combining mutation and fault localization for automated program debugging. J. Syst. Softw. **90**, 45–60 (2014)

17. Abreu, R., Zoeteweij, P., Van Gemund, A.J.: An evaluation of similarity coefficients for software fault localization. In: 12th Pacific Rim International Symposium on Dependable Computing (PRDC 2006), vol. 2006, pp. 39–46. IEEE (2006)
18. Jones, J.A., Harrold, M.J.: Empirical evaluation of the tarantula automatic fault-localization technique. In: Proceedings of the 20th IEEE/ACM International Conference on Automated Software Engineering, ser. ASE 2005, pp. 273–282. Association for Computing Machinery, New York (2005). https://doi.org/10.1145/1101908.1101949
19. Wong, W.E., Debroy, V., Gao, R., Li, Y.: The DStar method for effective software fault localization. IEEE Trans. Reliab. **63**(1), 290–308 (2013)
20. Liu, Y., Li, Z., Zhao, R., Gong, P.: An optimal mutation execution strategy for cost reduction of mutation-based fault localization. Inf. Sci. **422**, 572–596 (2018). https://www.sciencedirect.com/science/article/pii/S0020025516306867
21. Abreu, R., Zoeteweij, P., Van Gemund, A.J.: An evaluation of similarity coefficients for software fault localization. In: 2006 12th Pacific Rim International Symposium on Dependable Computing (PRDC 2006), pp. 39–46 (2006)
22. Le, T.-D.B., Thung, F., Lo, D.: Theory and practice, do they match? a case with spectrum-based fault localization. In: IEEE International Conference on Software Maintenance, vol. 2013, pp. 380–383 (2013)
23. Wong, W.E., Qi, Y., Zhao, L., Cai, K.Y.: Effective fault localization using code coverage. In: 31st Annual International Computer Software and Applications Conference (COMPSAC 2007), vol. 1, pp. 449–456 (2007)
24. Dutta, A., Srivastava, S.S., Godboley, S., Mohapatra, D.P.: Combi-FL: neural network and SBFL based fault localization using mutation analysis. J. Comput. Lang. **66**, 101064 (2021)
25. Ju, X., Jiang, S., Chen, X., Wang, X., Zhang, Y., Cao, H.: Hsfal: effective fault localization using hybrid spectrum of full slices and execution slices. J. Syst. Softw. **90**, 3–17 (2014). https://www.sciencedirect.com/science/article/pii/S0164121213002823
26. Keller, F., Grunske, L., Heiden, S., Filieri, A., van Hoorn, A., Lo, D.: A critical evaluation of spectrum-based fault localization techniques on a large-scale software system. In: 2017 IEEE International Conference on Software Quality, Reliability and Security (QRS), pp. 114–125 (2017)
27. Just, R., Jalali, D., Ernst, M.D.: Defects4j: a database of existing faults to enable controlled testing studies for java programs. In: Proceedings of the 2014 International Symposium on Software Testing and Analysis, pp. 437–440 (2014)
28. Li, X., Li, W., Zhang, Y., Zhang, L.: Deepfl: integrating multiple fault diagnosis dimensions for deep fault localization. In: Proceedings of the 28th ACM SIGSOFT International Symposium on Software Testing and Analysis, pp. 169–180 (2019)
29. Wang, H., et al.: Can higher-order mutants improve the performance of mutation-based fault localization? IEEE Trans. Reliab. **71**(2), 1157–1173 (2022)
30. Zou, D., Liang, J., Xiong, Y., Ernst, M.D., Zhang, L.: An empirical study of fault localization families and their combinations. IEEE Trans. Softw. Eng. **47**(2), 332–347 (2019)

ContAST: Graph Embedding Based Fault Localization Integrating AST and Context-Awareness

Haodong He, Tingting Wu(✉), Qi Jin, and Zuohua Ding

School of Computer Science and Technology, Zhejiang Sci-Tech University, Hangzhou, China
tingtingwu@zstu.edu.cn

Abstract. With the rapid advancement of artificial intelligence, learning based fault localization has emerged as a critical research area in software testing. Existing methods, including traditional statistical and machine learning based approaches, have significantly improved fault localization by representing program features with deep learning models. However, these methods still encounter challenges such as difficulties in processing complex program structures, dependency on high-quality test suites, and limited generalization across diverse software projects. This paper presents ContAST, a graph-based fault localization method that integrates abstract syntax trees (ASTs), path-attention mechanisms, and graph neural networks (GNNs) to address these challenges and improve prediction performance. By incorporating AST path-contexts, node coverage information, and bug reports, ContAST effectively captures structural, contextual and behavioral features of programs. The synergy between the path-attention model and GNNs enables precise identification and localization of faulty statements within programs, demonstrating its strength in addressing structural complexity. Empirical evaluations show that ContAST outperforms state-of-the-art graph-based and learning-based methods in both localization capability and computational cost. Notably, ContAST achieves 91.54% accuracy on the `Chart` project and even delivers improvements of up to 22.01% on the `Mockito` project in terms of recall. Moreover, ContAST significantly reduces training times across projects, emphasizing its practical advantages of code and graph processing in large-scale applications. These results highlight ContAST as an effective and efficient solution for fault localization in modern software testing.

Keywords: Fault localization · Debugging · Code embedding · Path-attention model · Graph embedding

1 Introduction

Advanced software applications have brought unprecedented convenience across diverse fields. However, the increasing scale and complexity of software systems

Y. Zhou et al. (Eds.): ICECCS 2025, LNCS 15746, pp. 444–463, 2026.
https://doi.org/10.1007/978-3-032-00828-2_24

have also led to a rise in program failures. Given the critical role software plays in modern society, failures can lead to severe consequences, such as the Knight Capital incident in the United States [8] and Boeing 737 MAX aircraft failures [18]. These incidents highlight the potential catastrophic consequences of failing to detect software faults, which can result in significant financial losses and pose threats to human life in extreme cases. Therefore, identification of potential software faults is essential for preventing undesired outcomes.

To automate and enhance fault localization, various techniques have been developed, generally falling into four categories: *spectrum-based*, *semantic-based*, *mutation-based*, and *graph-based*. The *spectrum-based* method [16] collects statistical data from program executions to identify suspicious program elements and ranks them to identify potential faults. This approach is straightforward and effective but heavily relies on the quality of test suite. The *semantic-based* approach [10] focuses on analyzing program semantics using either dynamic or static methods. While it offers more comprehensive insights by examining program behavior, its generalization is limited by language-specific syntactic structures. The *mutation-based* method [9] introduces minor changes to the code, generating mutants to establish fault localization rankings. This method works well for single-fault programs but faces challenges in multi-fault scenarios due to the difficulty in selecting appropriate mutants. The *graph-based* method [15] represents code entities as interconnected nodes within a graph, preserving the topological information, and utilizes this structure for accurate and cost-effective fault localization. However, its performance can be affected by computational errors and variations in experimental subjects.

In recent years, machine learning (ML) has shown great potential in enhancing the process of fault diagnosis. For instance, Ling et al. [14] introduced the GL2-DNN model, which integrates a deep neural network (DNN) with a genetic algorithm (GA) and L2 regularization to improve fault localization accuracy. However, this model struggles with generalization and fails to address multi-fault identification. Similarly, Bhandari et al. [5] proposed an ML-based framework for predicting faults in service-oriented systems, demonstrating the promise of ML in improving accuracy and reliability in fault detection. Upon reviewing existing learning-based fault localization methods, we identified a significant limitation: the lack of comprehensive representation of programs. Most methods fail to fully capture diverse forms of program features, such as syntactic structures and semantic information derived from Abstract Syntax Trees (ASTs), contextual information, and dynamic execution behavior. These omissions limit their ability to provide holistic insights into potential faults. A critical reason for this limitation lies in the complexity of extracting meaningful features from ASTs. This process requires specialized domain knowledge and a deep understanding of program behavior to identify features that accurately reflect program execution and potential faults. Moreover, characterizing contextual information introduces further challenges, especially when the context spans multiple dimensions, such as temporal aspects, environmental configurations, and interdependencies among program entities. Integrating static code features with dynamic execution behavior demands a more comprehensive approach to code embedding. Addressing these challenges requires a robust approach capable of effectively capturing diverse program features, thereby enhancing fault localization accuracy and efficiency.

To address these limitations, we propose CONTAST, a graph-based fault localization method that integrates ASTs and critical contextual information. CONTAST trains a path-attention network (PAN) using a large corpus of programs and their corresponding ASTs, embedding multiple path-contexts into independent vectors that represent the entire programs. Additionally, coverage information and bug reports are incorporated into ASTs to generate enriched code embeddings, which include critical AST path-context, node coverage, and labels. In CONTAST, we employ two types of GNN models – Graph Convolutional Networks (GCN) and Graph Attention Networks (GAT) – to process the graph representations, creating effective graph embeddings. This method improves fault localization performance and program contextual analysis.

The main contributions of this paper are as follows:

- **Graph based Fault Localization**: We introduce CONTAST, a novel graph-based method that integrates ASTs, context-awareness, and node representations to construct comprehensive graph representations. This enables the accurate computation of statement suspiciousness and precise prediction of fault locations.
- **Path Attention with Graph Representation**: CONTAST employs a path-attention model to extract critical AST path-contexts and dynamic execution features, generating enriched code embeddings. These embeddings are further enhanced by GNNs to learn robust graph representations, significantly boosting fault localization performance.
- **Experimental Validation**: We evaluate CONTAST against baselines, including a state-of-the-art graph-based approach and two learning-based methods. Results demonstrate the superior performance of CONTAST, underscoring its practical effectiveness and efficiency in software fault localization.

The remainder of this paper is organized as follows. Section 2 provides preliminary knowledge on fault localization and detailed technical discussions of code representation and graph representation methods. Section 3 reviews related research in fault localization, highlighting key advancements and challenges. Section 4 presents our proposed approach CONTAST in detail. Section 5 outlines the research questions and experimental setups designed to evaluate the approach. Section 6 discusses the experimental results, demonstrating the performance of CONTAST. Finally, Sect. 7 concludes the paper and outlines directions for future research.

2 Preliminary

2.1 Fault Localization

Fault localization is an essential area in software testing, aimed at identifying and addressing software defects to ensure reliability and performance. A widely adopted approach is spectrum-based fault localization (SBFL), which uses program spectra, consisting of coverage information and test outcomes, to compute and rank the suspiciousness of program entities [17,20]. However, the effectiveness of SBFL heavily depends on various factors, such as the quality of test suite, types of spectra, evaluation formulas, and the set of suspicious entities. To extend SBFL, graph-based fault localization (GFL) [22] was introduced, constructing a coverage graph from the coverage matrix and test results, in which nodes represent tests and program methods. GFL evaluates the suspicion of program methods based on their neighbors and test results within this graph. Both SBFL and GFL rely on dynamic execution of test cases, which can be resource-intensive. To reduce these costs, semantic-based static localization [7] was proposed, identifying faults through program and error trace analysis without runtime dependencies. Although effective for complex faults, semantic-based methods are computationally expensive and often tied to specific programming languages.

While the above methods perform well in some dimensions, such as ranking entities based on suspicion scores, they struggle with the growing complexity of feature dimensions in modern fault localization scenarios. Advanced machine learning techniques have shown superior capabilities by leveraging code patterns, test data, and software metrics to improve fault location prediction accuracy. For example, Li et al. [13] proposed DeepFL, a model that automatically learns features, outperforming traditional Learning-to-Rank algorithms reliant on low-dimensional features. Similarly, Qian et al. introduced GNet4FL [15], which integrates static AST features with dynamic test results and employs GraphSAGE and a Multi-Layer Perceptron (MLP) to rank program entities, achieving improved precision. However, these approaches often trade efficiency for high accuracy. To address this, Chennappan et al. [6] presented a hybrid algorithm combining decision trees, genetic algorithms, and the cuckoo search algorithm, effectively balancing computational costs and precision. Recent advancements continue to refine fault localization. Yan et al. [26] proposed WEGAT, a method combining weighted execution graphs – capturing the coverage relationships between test cases and program elements – with ASTs to construct a graph. Features extracted via a GAT model are then used to predict fault locations.

The primary challenge encountered by learning-based fault localization lies in balancing accuracy and efficiency. To address this, we investigated the integration of code representation and graph representation to achieve a robust and effective solution.

2.2 Code Representation Learning

Extracting meaningful features from code and establishing mappings between these features and faults is essential for accurate fault localization. Attention mechanisms have shown great promise in fault localization by identifying critical paths within the structural representations of code, such as ASTs, control flow graphs (CFGs), and call graphs (CGs). These mechanisms capture key relationships that may indicate potential defects. Several path-attention network (PAN) methods have been developed for code representation. For instance, Tree-based LSTMs [21] process hierarchical AST structures with attention to prioritize defect-relevant subtrees, while Abstract Syntax Tree Neural Network (ASTNN) [27] segments ASTs into statement-level subtrees and employs attention mechanisms for finer-grained defect detection. Code2Vec [3] leverages AST paths with attention to create embeddings that highlight defect-relevant paths efficiently. Code2Seq [2] extends Code2Vec by generating sequential outputs, making it more suitable for tasks like defect description. Among these methods, Code2Vec stands out for its simplicity, efficiency, and interpretability. It generates embeddings directly from AST paths using a lightweight attention mechanism, making it faster and less complex than other models. Additionally, its focus on specific paths also allows it to provide interpretable results, helping researchers identify code patterns contributing to faults.

In this study, we employed Code2Vec to represent entire code snippets as fixed-size embeddings by leveraging path contexts within the AST and attention mechanisms, so that captures the semantic and structural features of code. To facilitate deeper understanding of code structures and contextual analysis, we define three key concepts: *AST*, *AST path*, and *path context*.

AST is defined as a six-tuple $\langle N, T, X, r, \alpha, \beta \rangle$ where (1) N is a set of non-leaf nodes, (2) T is a set of leaf nodes, (3) X is a set of node values, (4) $r \in N$ is the root node, (5) α is the mapping function associating non-leaf nodes with lists of child nodes, and (6) β is the mapping function associating leaf nodes with their values. The AST provides an accurate tree representation of the code. Based on this, we further define the *AST path*, which describes a sequence of nodes and edges originating from a leaf node, traversing through non-leaf nodes, and terminating at another leaf node. The path adheres to strict traversal rules, with movement directions specified as upward ($\uparrow$) or downward ($\downarrow$). For any AST path p, we define its start node as $start(p)$ and its end node as $end(p)$. To capture path information and its context more comprehensively, we define the *path context* as a triple $\langle p, x_s, x_e \rangle$, where p is an AST path, x_s is the value associated with the start node of p, and x_e is the value associated with the end node of p. These values are linked to the leaf nodes via specific functions, providing rich semantic context for in-depth code analysis.

2.3 Graph Representation Learning

While Code2Vec has proven effectiveness in generating code representations using ASTs, its reliance on static structural information limits the ability to incorporate runtime behavior and historical insights, both of which are critical for identifying fault-prone areas in code accurately. To bridge the gap between static and dynamic features, it is essential to construct a more comprehensive graph representation beyond ASTs, which integrates multiple sources of information, including code structure, runtime behavior, and defect history.

Graph Neural Networks (GNNs) [1] well-suited for processing graph-structured data, where nodes represent entities, and edges denote relationships. The core idea of GNNs involves aggregating information from neighboring nodes to learn embeddings at the node or graph level. This aggregation captures relational patterns within graph structures, enabling GNNs to handle complex data relationships effectively. Among GNN variants, Graph Convolutional Networks (GCNs) [12] utilize graph convolution operations to update node features. Each node new feature is computed as a weighted sum of its neighbors' features based on the graph adjacency matrix. While GCNs are powerful in capturing local and global graph structures, their fixed aggregation schemes which treating all neighbors equally or using predefined weights may fail to fully account for the varying importance of neighbors in complex graphs. To address this limitation, Graph Attention Networks (GATs) [24] extend GCNs by introducing an attention mechanism. This allows the model to dynamically assign varying levels of importance to different neighboring nodes, enabling GATs to focus on the most relevant parts of the graph. GATs are particularly effective for handling heterogeneous graphs and complex data, as they can selectively prioritize relationships based on contextual relevance.

When Code2Vec is applied to fault localization using only ASTs, it focuses on static features. In contrast, GNNs provide a more flexible solution by incorporating additional features, such as coverage information and bug reports. By constructing a graph that combines ASTs with runtime data and historical defect records, GNNs can learn to prioritize the most critical features for fault identification. Additionally, the attention mechanism in GATs enables the model to focus on important nodes, such as frequently fault-associated program entities or untested paths, thus improving the accuracy and robustness of fault localization compared to methods relying solely on static features.

3 Related Work

The field of software fault localization (SFL) has garnered significant research attention due to its potential to substantially reduce debugging time and cost. Numerous techniques have been proposed, each with its distinct strengths and limitations. This section reviews the most relevant and recent works in this area, highlighting their contributions and constraints.

3.1 Spectrum-Based Fault Localization

SBFL techniques localize faults by computing suspiciousness scores for program elements based on the program spectra and test results. One of the most widely recognized SBFL techniques is Tarantula, proposed by Jones and Harrold [11]. Tarantula prioritizes program elements based on the ratio of executed failed tests to total executed tests. Several variations and enhancements have been proposed. For instance, Wong et al. [25] introduced DStar, which modifies the traditional SBFL formula by considering the execution frequency of program elements. Similarly, Vancsics et al. [23] proposed a graph-based fault localization (GFL) method that considers the call frequency of methods to refine SBFL results.

3.2 Learning-Based Fault Localization

The success of machine learning in various domains has motivated researchers to apply these techniques to fault localization. DeepFL, proposed by Li et al. [13], is the first learning-based approach that integrates multiple fault diagnosis dimensions, including spectrum-based and mutation-based suspiciousness, code complexity, and textual similarity information. Zhang et al. [28] proposed an improved fault localization method based on deep learning through resampling. By iteratively oversampling failed test cases, this approach mitigated the impact of class imbalance. This approach reduced the number of statements to be checked and was applicable to various deep learning models.

3.3 Information Retrieval-Based Fault Localization

Information retrieval (IR)-based fault localization methods utilize natural language processing (NLP) and document retrieval algorithms to rank source code files based on their relevance to bug reports. Zhou et al. [29] proposed an IR-based method that used bug reports to index and rank source code files. Their approach outperformed SBFL techniques in certain instances. Alsaedi et al. [4] presented a two-level IR-based fault localization model. This model first located buggy classes using bug reports and then further identified the specific methods within those classes.

Each of these methods contributes uniquely to fault localization. Some methods focus on execution data, while others leverage machine learning models or integrate multiple approaches to enhance performance. Although significant progress has been made, there is still room for innovation to investigate more accurate, scalable, and interpretable fault localization techniques.

4 Approach

Despite the advancements in software fault localization, existing methods often struggle to capture the complex relationships between structural, contextual, and historical features of code for locating faults. To overcome these limitations, our approach ContAST integrates static analysis with dynamic contextualization and graph-based learning. As illustrated in Fig. 1, we first parse the code into an AST and extract important path-contexts using Code2Vec to encode structural and semantic features. These features are then enhanced with dynamic features, such as coverage information and bug reports, creating a richer representation of the code. This augmented AST is transformed into a graph that integrates both structural and contextual information. To analyze this graph, we employ two GNN models respectively: GCN which captures relational dependencies through convolution, and GAT which dynamically focuses on critical nodes and edges using attention mechanisms. The resulting graph embeddings are processed through a MLP to predict fault locations, providing a ranked list of suspicious elements.

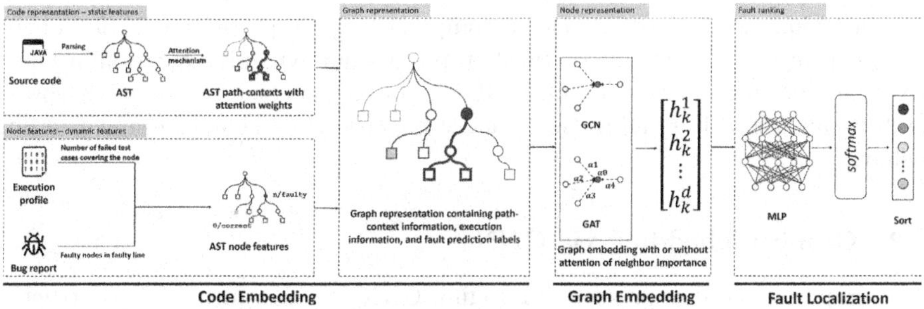

Fig. 1. The framework of CONTAST

4.1 Code Embedding

Accurate fault localization depends on effectively extracting and representing diverse features from code. To achieve this, we employ a code embedding approach that integrates static features, capturing structural feature of the code, with dynamic features, such as coverage information and bug reports. This integration embedding ensures a comprehensive and informative representation of the code for downstream fault location prediction tasks.

CONTAST begins with the path attention model, Code2Vec, which transforms code snippets into high-dimensional vector representations. Code2Vec parses source code to construct its AST, a tree-like structure encapsulating syntactic relationships within the code. Each AST node represents a code component, such as expressions, variables, or operators. To enrich the feature set, test cases are represented as nodes connected to nodes via edges, with test results included as features. Code2Vec employs a path sampling technique to extract paths from the AST. These paths encapsulate critical nodes and their relationships, serving as essential indicators of the code structural and semantic information. Using a neural network architecture, Code2Vec maps AST nodes into a high-dimensional vector space through an embedding layer. This representation is further refined by an attention mechanism that computes a weighted summation over path vectors, generating a comprehensive vector capturing the path-context. This resulting embedding serves as the static feature representation of the code snippet.

However, static embeddings alone are insufficient for accurate fault localization. To further enhance the code embedding, we incorporate dynamic features into AST node representations. Specifically, we extract coverage information for each AST node based on failed test cases and annotate nodes as faulty or non-faulty using bug reports from developer resources of Defects4J. These dynamic features are serialized into `pickle` files and combined with the AST path-context embeddings, thereby enriching the node representations with execution and fault-related behavior.

This combined approach yields a comprehensive graph representation of the code, capturing both static structural properties and dynamic execution insights. By providing such enriched input to GNNs, our method facilitates more accurate fault localization, leveraging the synergy between code structure and runtime behavior.

4.2 Graph Embedding via GNNs

The graph embedding process, leveraging GNNs to transform the constructed AST graph into rich node representations, is critical for fault localization. We employ two models: GCN and GAT, each offering unique strengths in capturing the relationships and importance of graph components.

GCN processes graph-structured data by aggregating and transforming features from neighboring nodes. In the AST graph, nodes represent code elements (e.g., functions and variables), and edges denote their relationships. Through an iterative process, GCN updates the representation of each node by aggregating features from its neighboring nodes and edge weights, ensuring that contextual and structural information is preserved. Specifically, each node v in the graph updates its representation as follows:

$$h_v^{(l+1)} = \sigma(\sum_{u \in N(v)} \frac{1}{c_{vu}} W^{(l)} h_v^{(l)}) \tag{1}$$

where $h_v^{(l)}$ represents the feature vector of node v at layer l, $N(v)$ denotes neighboring nodes, $W^{(l)}$ is the learnable weight matrix, c_{vu} normalizes the aggregation, and σ is the activation function. This iterative aggregation mechanism enables GCN to capture both local and global structural relationships, producing node embeddings enriched with contextual information.

On the other hand, GAT introduces an attention mechanism to assign varying importance (weights) to neighboring nodes during feature aggregation. This is particularly effective for identifying faults, as certain nodes and edges in the AST graph may be more influential. For each node v, the attention coefficient α_{vu}, indicating the importance of node u to node v, is computed as follows:

$$\alpha_{vu}^{(l)} = \frac{\exp(\text{LeakyReLU}(a^{(l)^T}[W^{(l)} h_v^{(l)} \| W^{(l)} h_u^{(l)}]))}{\sum_{k \in N(v)} \exp(\text{LeakyReLU}(a^{(l)^T}[W^{(l)} h_v^{(l)} \| W^{(l)} h_k^{(l)}]))} \tag{2}$$

where $a^{(l)}$ is a learnable attention vector, W is the weight matrix, $\|$ denotes concatenation, and LeakyReLU is the activation function. Using these attention coefficients, the new representation of node v is computed as a weighted sum of its neighbors, emphasizing the most relevant connections:

$$h_v^{(l+1)} = \sigma(\sum_{u \in N(v)} \alpha_{vu}^{(l)} W^{(l)} h_v^{(l)}) \tag{3}$$

This attention mechanism allows GAT to focus on critical nodes and edges, refining graph embeddings with greater fault-relevant detail.

By utilizing GCN and GAT respectively, we extract comprehensive graph embeddings that capture both structural and semantic features of the AST graph. These embeddings serve as the essential feature space for predicting faults, enabling effective identification of fault types and locations.

4.3 Fault Localization

The updated node representations from GCN and GAT are then passed to an MLP for final fault identification. Let the node embeddings from GCN be denoted as $\mathrm{H}_{GCN} \in \mathbb{R}^{N \times d}$, where N represents the number of nodes and d is the dimensionality of embeddings (including additional dimension for coverage information). Similarly, the node embeddings from GAT are denoted as $\mathrm{H}_{GAT} \in \mathbb{R}^{N \times d}$. Specifically, the MLP processes these embeddings and applies the softmax activation function to output the probability distribution over the fault classes:

$$\mathrm{P} = \mathrm{softmax}(f_{MLP}(\mathrm{H})) \tag{4}$$

where $\mathrm{P} \in \mathbb{R}^{N \times C}$ represents the probability distribution across C fault classes (e.g., faulty or correct), f_{MLP} denotes the function performed by the MLP layers, and $\mathrm{H} \in \{\mathrm{H}_{GCN}, \mathrm{H}_{GAT}\}$. The suspiciousness scores of each program entity are then calculated from these probabilities and sorted to generate a ranked list of potential faults, with higher scores indicating the most suspicious locations.

Through integrating the structural, syntactic, semantic, and contextual features extracted from the AST graph representation, the utilization of GCN and GAT enables the construction of an effective fault cause identification model. This model captures both local and global dependencies within the code structure, allowing it to accurately identify potential faults. Furthermore, the strong generalization capabilities of GCN and GAT ensure that the model adapts effectively to diverse codebases of varying sizes and complexities, enhancing its applicability across different software projects.

Table 1. Characteristics of projects from Defects4J and corresponding graph structures

Project	LOC(k)	#Faults	CONTAST		GNet4FL	
			#Nodes	#Edges	#Nodes	#Edges
`Chart`	96	26	23,169	44,276	28,518	54,056
`Math`	85	106	61,946	115,778	67,638	127,664
`Lang`	22	64	61,464	115,224	70,098	132,137
`Mockito`	23	38	5,995	11,304	6,347	11,838
`Time`	28	27	21,613	40,962	24,828	46,624

5 Experiments

5.1 Research Questions

RQ1: What are the effectiveness and efficiency of CONTAST compared to other graph-based and learning-based methods?

This research question evaluates the performance of CONTAST in terms of both fault localization capability and computational efficiency. By benchmarking CONTAST against state-of-the-art fault localization methods, including graph-based approaches like GNet4FL and learning-based methods such as DeepFL and FLUCCS [19], we aim to assess its practical performance. The experiments are conducted across multiple projects from the Defects4J dataset, providing insights into the feasibility and trade-offs of adopting CONTAST in software fault localization tasks.

RQ2: How do the code embedding and graph embedding impact the performance of fault localization?

CONTAST integrates code embedding, combining path-contexts from Code2Vec with dynamic features, and graph embedding techniques, including GCN and GAT, for fault localization. This research question examines the contributions of these embeddings to the overall performance. Specifically, we evaluate their impact on prediction performance compared to the baseline graph-based model, GNet4FL.

5.2 Experimental Setup

Dataset. To evaluate CONTAST, we use the Defects4J V2.0.1[1], consistent with the evaluation framework of GNet4FL. The experiment is conducted on five real-world programs (`Chart`, `Math`, `Lang`, `Mockito`, and `Time`), containing a total of 261 active bugs, as summarized in Table 1. For direct comparison with GNet4FL, we also provide details on the graph structures generated for each project under the same experimental setup in Table 1, including the number of nodes and edges in the program graphs.

[1] https://github.com/rjust/defects4j.

Baselines. We benchmark CONTAST, integrating code embedding with different graph embeddings (referred to as c2v-GCN and c2v-GAT), against three state-of-the-art fault localization methods: GNet4FL [15], DeepFL [13], and FLUCCS [19]. These baselines represent a diverse range of approaches, including graph-based and learning-based fault localization techniques.

- GNet4FL: A graph-based method, parses the source code into an AST and utilizes Word2Vec to generate low-dimensional vector representations for AST nodes. These vector are used as node features in the graph structure and further processed by GCN for fault localization (referred to as w2v-GCN).
- DeepFL: A learning-based approach that integrates features from multiple fault diagnosis dimensions, including suspiciousness values, code complexity metrics, and textual similarity features. DeepFL utilizes deep learning models, such as MLP and Recurrent Neural Networks (RNN), to automatically learn fault-relevant patterns without leveraging explicit graph structures.
- FLUCCS: A statistical and learning-based method that combines existing SBFL formulas with features such as code complexity and change history. It leverages techniques such as Genetic Programming (GP) and linear rank Support Vector Machines (SVMs) to prioritize potentially faulty statements.

Evaluation Metrics. In this paper, we employ various metrics, including *accuracy*, *F1 score*, *recall*, and *training time*, to evaluate the performance of CONTAST.

- *Accuracy*: Represents the proportion of correctly identified faulty (true positive, TP) and correct statements (true negative, TN) to the total program versions, which is used to assess the effectiveness of our code and graph embedding techniques.
- *F1 Score*: Balances the precision and recall, measuring the model capability to accurately identify true faults while reducing false positives (FP) and false negatives (FN) during fault locating.
- *Recall*: Indicates the model ability to detect actual faults, where a high recall suggests that as many true faults as possible are detected, thereby reducing the risk of fault undetected.
- *Training time*: Measures the total duration of model training, providing insights into the computational efficiency and graph processing capabilities of CONTAST.

Hyper-parameter Tuning. The experimental setup involves hyper-parameter tuning to optimize model performance. We evaluate two learning rates (0.01 and 0.005) and two maximum training iterations (10,000 and 20,000) across the five projects. A ten-fold cross-validation is applied to ensure the robustness of the results and to investigate the impact of these hyper-parameters on fault localization performance.

Our experiments were conducted on a server equipped with an Intel Core i9-9900k CPU (3.60 GHz), 128 GB of RAM, and an NVIDIA GeForce RTX 3080 Ti GPU, running Ubuntu 20.04 with Python 3.8 installed.

6 Experimental Results and Discussion

6.1 Performance of CONTAST (RQ1)

To answer RQ1, we evaluated the proposed approach, CONTAST, focusing on effectiveness and efficiency. Since GNet4FL has been shown to outperform or close to other learning-based techniques, we used it as a primary baseline for performance comparison. However, the training time of GNet4FL is much longer than that of learning-based methods, DeepFL and FLUCCS. This discrepancy arises because GCN-based approaches involve computationally intensive processes, such as information transmission, aggregation, and updating between graph nodes, which increase the complexity of model. Additionally, graph-based data processing, including graph construction, feature extraction, and maintaining graph topology, tends to be more time-consuming than handling simpler data structures like vectors or matrices. In contrast, CONTAST employs a more efficient code representation technique that focuses on critical paths in the graph through an attention mechanism, thereby reducing unnecessary computations. To further evaluate CONTAST, which integrates path attention and graph neural networks, we compared it with GNet4FL and other learning-based methods to assess the contributions of its embedding techniques.

Effectiveness. As shown in Tables 2, CONTAST outperforms the baseline GNet4FL across most projects in the Defects4J dataset under various hyper-parameter settings. For accuracy, CONTAST achieves significant improvements for `Lang` (up to 15.41% with c2v-GAT), `Math` (12.58% with c2v-GCN), `Chart` (6.59% with c2v-GCN), and `Mockito` (13.86% with c2v-GAT). In addition to accuracy, both c2v-GCN and c2v-GAT demonstrate significant advantages in F1 score and recall. For instance, on `Chart` and `Math`, the two methods show comparable performance in both metrics. c2v-GAT outperforms both the baseline and c2v-GCN in terms of F1 score and recall on projects `Lang` and `Mockito`, further highlighting the effectiveness of attention mechanisms in fault localization. These results demonstrate the consistent advantages of CONTAST across diverse program types. However, `Time` shows a slight underperformance with a minor decline: accuracy dropped by an average of 1.59%, F1 score by 2.98%, and recall by 3.9%. This suggests potential for improvement in more complex scenarios. Among the models, c2v-GCN generally outperforms w2v-GCN, highlighting the superiority of Code2Vec embeddings. c2v-GAT achieves slightly better results than c2v-GCN, demonstrating the potential of attention mechanisms in fault localization. These findings confirm the robust effectiveness of CONTAST for a variety of program types, with areas for optimization in specific cases.

Table 2. Performance of CONTAST and baseline under different hyper-parameters (**Bold** indicates the best performance among three methods under the same hyper-parameter. Red highlights better improvement between c2v-GCN and c2v-GAT. Gray marks the performance decrease. *Italic* indicates the best performance of different hyper-parameter settings in each project.)

Metric	Project	LR	Iter.	GNet4FL (%)	CONTAST (%)					
				w2v-GCN	c2v-GCN	Improv.	Avg.	c2v-GAT	Improv.	Avg.
Accuracy	Chart	0.01	10,000	83.65	**91.17**	↑6.59	5.59	90.54	↑5.96	4.94
			20,000	*86.39*	**91.16**	↑4.77		90.16	↑3.77	
		0.005	10,000	85.83	**91.44**	↑5.61		91.00	↑5.17	
			20,000	86.14	***91.54***	↑5.40		*91.01*	↑4.87	
	Math	0.01	10,000	66.29	76.55	↑10.26	11.29	**77.05**	↑10.76	11.30
			20,000	66.60	76.56	↑9.96		**77.19**	↑10.59	
		0.005	10,000	66.25	**78.62**	↑12.37		*78.61*	↑12.36	
			20,000	*67.09*	***79.67***	↑12.58		78.58	↑11.49	
	Lang	0.01	10,000	71.89	**86.69**	↑14.80	14.57	86.27	↑14.38	14.53
			20,000	70.80	86.00	↑15.20		**86.21**	↑15.41	
		0.005	10,000	73.13	**87.54**	↑14.41		87.19	↑14.06	
			20,000	*73.77*	*87.63*	↑13.86		***88.03***	↑14.26	
	Mockito	0.01	10,000	72.91	**85.55**	↑12.64	12.74	85.49	↑12.58	13.04
			20,000	72.00	**85.20**	↑13.20		84.84	↑12.84	
		0.005	10,000	*73.72*	*86.11*	↑12.39		**86.60**	↑12.88	
			20,000	73.11	85.85	↑12.74		***86.97***	↑13.86	
	Time	0.01	10,000	**78.83**	76.90	↓1.93	1.63	76.66	↓2.17	1.55
			20,000	**78.62**	76.57	↓2.05		77.48	↓1.14	
		0.005	10,000	***80.11***	78.07	↓2.04		*78.23*	↓1.88	
			20,000	**78.99**	*78.49*	↓0.50		77.98	↓1.01	
F1 Score	Chart	0.01	10,000	83.65	**90.41**	↑6.76	6.01	90.03	↑5.96	6.00
			20,000	84.88	89.86	↑4.99		**90.29**	↑5.41	
		0.005	10,000	*85.71*	**91.16**	↑5.45		90.67	↑4.96	
			20,000	84.48	*91.31*	↑6.83		***91.73***	↑7.25	
	Math	0.01	10,000	60.43	**73.89**	↑13.46	15.57	73.88	↑13.45	15.77
			20,000	59.74	75.17	↑15.43		***76.99***	↑17.26	
		0.005	10,000	*60.53*	76.20	↑15.68		**76.45**	↑15.92	
			20,000	60.48	***78.20***	↑17.72		76.93	↑16.45	
	Lang	0.01	10,000	70.79	86.08	↑15.30	15.67	**86.29**	↑15.50	16.39
			20,000	69.37	84.44	↑15.07		**87.40**	↑18.03	
		0.005	10,000	*72.32*	87.24	↑14.92		***88.46***	↑16.14	
			20,000	70.78	***88.18***	↑17.40		86.65	↑15.88	
	Mockito	0.01	10,000	*67.99*	84.62	↑16.63	17.92	**85.42**	↑17.43	18.41
			20,000	66.16	84.26	↑18.10		**85.43**	↑19.27	
		0.005	10,000	67.78	*86.53*	↑18.76		***86.74***	↑18.97	
			20,000	67.92	**86.13**	↑18.21		85.89	↑17.97	
	Time	0.01	10,000	**78.93**	74.44	↓4.49	3.43	75.17	↓3.76	2.53
			20,000	**78.12**	75.21	↓2.91		76.05	↓2.07	
		0.005	10,000	**78.69**	74.87	↓3.82		*77.36*	↓1.32	
			20,000	***79.90***	*77.39*	↓2.52		76.96	↓2.95	
Recall	Chart	0.01	10,000	85.67	**91.12**	↑5.45	5.11	90.71	↑5.04	5.01
			20,000	86.78	**90.67**	↑3.90		90.16	↑4.49	
		0.005	10,000	*87.98*	***92.52***	↑4.55		90.95	↑2.97	
			20,000	85.53	92.09	↑6.56		***93.05***	↑7.52	
	Math	0.01	10,000	*56.68*	71.62	↑14.94	17.24	**71.97**	↑15.29	17.50
			20,000	56.09	73.31	↑17.22		***75.41***	↑19.33	
		0.005	10,000	56.57	73.22	↑16.65		**73.51**	↑16.94	
			20,000	56.59	***76.76***	↑20.17		75.04	↑18.45	
	Lang	0.01	10,000	70.09	85.10	↑15.01	16.56	**85.81**	↑15.72	17.59
			20,000	68.29	84.09	↑15.79		**87.40**	↑19.11	
		0.005	10,000	*70.66*	87.00	↑16.35		***88.82***	↑18.16	
			20,000	69.15	***88.25***	↑19.10		86.53	↑17.38	
	Mockito	0.01	10,000	64.95	84.25	↑19.30	20.99	**86.78**	↑21.83	22.01
			20,000	64.47	83.95	↑19.48		**86.47**	↑22.00	
		0.005	10,000	65.01	***88.17***	↑23.16		*87.58*	↑22.58	
			20,000	*65.34*	**87.37**	↑22.03		86.96	↑21.62	
	Time	0.01	10,000	**79.89**	75.62	↓4.28	4.34	74.65	↓5.24	3.46
			20,000	**79.70**	74.66	↓5.04		77.08	↓2.63	
		0.005	10,000	**79.40**	75.61	↓3.80		*77.33*	↓2.07	
			20,000	***81.00***	*76.76*	↓4.24		77.09	↓3.91	

Efficiency. Figure 2 illustrates that CONTAST (c2v-GCN and c2v-GAT) significantly outperforms GNet4FL in training efficiency, reducing training time by an average of 78.03%-93.70% across all projects. This advantage is attributed to the integration of AST-based path attention and Code2Vec embeddings, which reduce the computational overhead associated with constructing and processing complex graph structures. Table 1 further confirms this observation, showing that CONTAST requires fewer nodes and edges in its graph structures. By leveraging Code2Vec embeddings, CONTAST processes data more efficiently, while GNet4FL reliance on larger graph structures leads to extended training times. Moreover, as graph sizes increase, due to larger codebases or more complex ASTs, the training time of CONTAST scales more gracefully than GNet4FL, demonstrating its superior optimization for handling graph structures. Although incorporating GAT slightly increases computational demands compared to GCN, the added overhead is offset by significant gains in fault localization accuracy. Compared to DeepFL, CONTAST maintains a competitive edge. For instance, in the `Mockito` project, CONTAST achieves a training time of just 2.19 s, significantly faster than DeepFL. Additionally, CONTAST generally performs better than FLUCCS as well.

In conclusion, CONTAST achieves a favorable balance between efficiency and effectiveness, demonstrating scalability and practicality for large-scale fault localization tasks.

6.2 Impact of Code Embedding and Graph Embedding (RQ2)

To answer RQ2, we evaluate the impact of code embedding techniques (Code2Vec vs. Word2Vec) and graph embedding techniques (GCN vs. GAT) on fault localization performance under various hyper-parameter settings. Table 2 presents the performance of CONTAST and the baseline GNet4FL across different hyper-parameter settings, including learning rate (LR) and iteration count (Iter.), using various embedding combinations: w2v-GCN (Word2Vec with GCN), c2v-GCN (Code2Vec with GCN), c2v-GAT (Code2Vec with GAT), and the corresponding improvements of CONTAST.

Code Embedding. Code embedding, which integrates static and dynamic features, significantly enhances the richness of the code representation, thereby improving the model ability to capture patterns indicative of faults. By incorporating AST path-contexts, Code2Vec provides a structured representation of code, capturing relationships and dependencies among code elements. Additionally, dynamic features, such as code coverage and bug-related information, enrich the embeddings with insights into execution behavior, linking AST nodes with fault labels.

As shown in Table 2, embeddings generated by Code2Vec significantly outperform those from Word2Vec across most programs. For instance, in `Lang`, c2v-GCN achieves an accuracy of 87.63%, compared to 73.77% with w2v-GCN – a remarkable 13.86% improvement. In `Mockito`, c2v-GCN achieves an F1 score

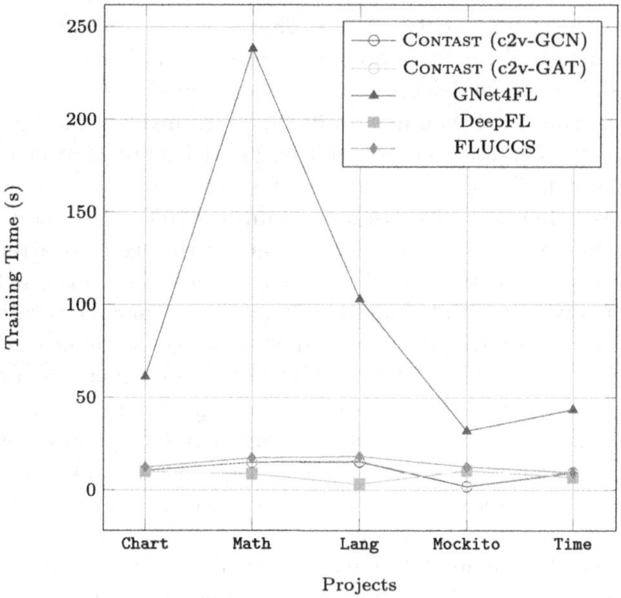

(a) Training time trends across projects.

Method	Chart	Math	Lang	Mockito	Time
Contast(c2v-GCN)	10.61	14.91	15.14	1.81	9.33
Contast(c2v-GAT)	10.96	15.17	15.83	2.19	9.68
GNet4FL	61.28	238.04	102.86	31.75	43.27
DeepFL	10.07	8.68	3.36	10.51	6.87
FLUCCS	12.33	17.28	18.20	12.48	9.52

(b) Training time(s).

Fig. 2. Training time comparison across projects

of 86.13%, with 18% improvement over the baseline. These results demonstrate the ability of Code2Vec to capture more meaningful semantic and syntactic representations, contributing to improved fault localization.

Graph Embedding. Graph embedding methods such as GCN and GAT contribute differently to predict fault locations. GCN focuses on capturing the structural information of code graphs, updating node representations by aggregating features from neighbors, which helps capture local context. On the other hand, GAT employs an attention mechanism that dynamically refines node feature representations by weighting connections based on their importance, enabling the model to prioritize relevant information for fault locations.

Both c2v-GCN and c2v-GAT demonstrate strong performance by integrating code embeddings with graph-based structures, but their strengths vary. GCN excels in projects with specific spatial structures and functional characteristics by aggregating local node features. The Chart project specializes in generating graphs and charts, and the Math project focuses on mathematical and statistical computations, both have defects that are more closely related to their specific functional structures. For example, in Math, which involves mathematical tasks, c2v-GCN achieves 79.67% accuracy and 78.20% F1 score. Conversely, GAT performs better in handling diverse and complex fault patterns by focusing on relevant connections due to its attention mechanism. GAT can dynamically capture and model complex relationships between nodes through the attention mechanism, making it potentially adaptable to diverse testing scenarios in Mockito and interactions involving multiple functional modules in Lang. For example, in Lang, c2v-GAT achieves 88.03% accuracy and 88.82% recall, slightly outperforming c2v-GCN. Programs such as Chart, Math, Lang, and Mockito benefit significantly from both embeddings, with consistent improvements exceeding 10% in most cases. Time presents an exception, where c2v-GCN and c2v-GAT slightly underperform compared to w2v-GCN. The average 1.5%-3.9% decrease may be attributed to the complexity of Time project, which originates from the early Java date-time processing library joda-time. The defect dataset contains a significant number of complex defect patterns such as date calculations, timezone handling, format parsing, and other associated functionalities.

Hyper-parameter Tuning. The hyper-parameter settings, including learning rates (0.01 and 0.005) and maximum training iterations (10,000 and 20,000), exhibit noticeable impacts on model performance. Generally, a lower learning rate (0.005) combined with a higher iteration count (20,000) yields better results, indicating that more fine-grained updates during training enhance the predictive capabilities. This trend is consistent across most programs, highlighting the importance of fine-tuning these parameters to achieve optimal performance.

The results demonstrate that integrating code and graph embeddings under optimal hyper-parameter settings leads to a robust fault location learning model. Specifically, the combination of static features (AST path contexts) and dynamic features (coverage and bug information) enhances the generalization ability across different codebases, while graph models such as GCN and GAT further refine fault localization through structural and relational insights. These findings suggest the importance of selecting appropriate embeddings and fine-tuning parameters to achieve superior fault localization performance.

6.3 Discussion

Our experimental results demonstrate that ContAST, which integrates AST-based path attention mechanism, dynamic features, and graph representations, significantly outperforms baseline methods in both effectiveness and efficiency. The consistent improvements across multiple projects highlight the robustness and adaptability of ContAST. By leveraging code representation techniques like Code2Vec and attention mechanisms, ContAST achieves superior fault location prediction performance, especially in projects such as Lang, Math, and Mockito.

These results confirm the ability of our CONTAST to capture fault-related features effectively by combining AST-based representations with path attention mechanisms. In addition to enhanced performance, CONTAST demonstrates improved training efficiency compared to graph-based methods like GNet4FL and maintains competitive performance against learning-based methods such as DeepFL and FLUCCS. These advantages position CONTAST as an effective and practical solution for large-scale fault localization tasks that require both high accuracy and efficiency. Although the impact of the graph attention mechanisms was less prominent in some cases, incorporating the GAT model still resulted in measurable accuracy improvements. This suggests that further optimization of the GAT and CONTAST models may have additional potential, despite the significant improvements already achieved by CONTAST alone. In conclusion, incorporating the path attention model into the CONTAST approach significantly improves both training efficiency and effectiveness compared to the baseline model. These improvements are attributed to the ability of the CONTAST model to capture fault features in the code more effectively by combining the AST and path attention methods.

Despite these promising results, several limitations and threats to validity should be addressed. First, the evaluation was conducted on the Defects4J dataset, which may not fully represent the diversity of real-world software projects. The applicability of CONTAST to other datasets or domains remains to be explored. Second, manual hyperparameter tuning introduces potential biases and might fail to identify optimal configurations for all methods, potentially affecting the generalizability of the results. Third, the slight underperformance of CONTAST in the `Time` project raises questions about its adaptability to projects with complex defect patterns. Finally, while the training time comparisons demonstrate the efficiency advantages, the scalability of CONTAST to extremely large codebases or environments with constrained computational resources requires further investigation.

7 Conclusion and Future Work

In this paper, we presented CONTAST, a novel fault localization approach that combines AST-based path-contexts from Code2Vec, dynamic features, and GNNs to enhance software fault localization. The integration of path-contexts effectively captures critical syntactic and semantic relationships within the code, while dynamic features provide essential runtime insights, resulting in a comprehensive representation of code behavior. The utilization of GNNs further strengthens the capability to reason over complex code structures, enabling the effective identification of fault-prone patterns. Experimental results on the Defects4J dataset demonstrated that CONTAST achieves significant improvements in fault localization performance, particularly with the combination of Code2Vec embeddings and GNN graph embeddings. These findings highlight the effectiveness of integrating static and dynamic features with advanced graph-based learning techniques in enhancing software fault localization methods.

Despite its considerable promise, CONTAST opens up several directions for future research. First, we aim to improve the performance of GATs to better capture complex relationships in diverse code structures. Second, we will address the slight underperformance observed in certain projects, particularly the `Time` project. Third, we plan to evaluate CONTAST on larger, cross-domain, and multi-language datasets to validate its generalizability and robustness. Additionally, incorporating automated hyper-parameter tuning and optimization techniques can further enhance the model performance and adaptability. Finally, we will investigate the integration of CONTAST with other advanced testing methods, such as metamorphic testing or fuzz testing, to broaden its practical applicability and enhance its fault detection coverage.

Acknowledgments. This study was supported by the National Natural Science Foundation of China (Grant No. 62202432 and No. 62272416).

Disclosure of Interests. The authors have no competing interests to declare that are relevant to the content of this article.

References

1. Allamanis, M., Brockschmidt, M., Khademi, M.: Learning to represent programs with graphs. In: 6th International Conference on Learning Representations (2018)
2. Alon, U., Brody, S., Levy, O., Yahav, E.: code2seq: generating sequences from structured representations of code. arXiv preprint arXiv:1808.01400 (2018)
3. Alon, U., Zilberstein, M., Levy, O., Yahav, E.: code2vec: learning distributed representations of code. Proc. ACM Program. Lang. **3**(POPL), 1–29 (2019)
4. Alsaedi, S., Gad-Elrab, A.A., Noaman, A., Eassa, F.: Two-level information-retrieval-based model for bug localization based on bug reports. Electronics **13**(2), 321 (2024)
5. Bhandari, G.P., Gupta, R., Upadhyay, S.K.: An approach for fault prediction in SOA-based systems using machine learning techniques. Data Technol. Appl. **53**(4), 397–421 (2019)
6. Chennappan, R., et al.: An automated software failure prediction technique using hybrid machine learning algorithms. J. Eng. Res. **11**(1), 100002 (2023)
7. Christakis, M., Heizmann, M., Mansur, M.N., Schilling, C., Wüstholz, V.: Semantic fault localization and suspiciousness ranking. In: 25th International Conference on Tools and Algorithms for the Construction and Analysis of Systems, pp. 226–243. Springer, Prague (2019)
8. Davidson, C.: A dark knight for algos. Risk **25**(9), 32 (2012)
9. Dutta, A., Godboley, S.: Msfl: a model for fault localization using mutation-spectra technique. In: 5th International Conference on Lean and Agile Software Development, pp. 156–173. Springer (2021)
10. El Hatib, S., Ricaud, L., Desharnais, J., Tawbi, N.: Toward semantic-based android malware detection using model checking and machine learning. In: 15th International Conference on Risks and Security of Internet and Systems, pp. 289–307. Springer, Paris (2021)
11. Jones, J.A., Harrold, M.J.: Empirical evaluation of the tarantula automatic fault-localization technique. In: Proceedings of the 20th IEEE/ACM International Conference on Automated Software Engineering, pp. 273–282 (2005)

12. Kipf, T.N., Welling, M.: Semi-supervised classification with graph convolutional networks. arXiv preprint arXiv:1609.02907 (2016)
13. Li, X., Li, W., Zhang, Y., Zhang, L.: Deepfl: integrating multiple fault diagnosis dimensions for deep fault localization. In: Proceedings of the 28th ACM SIGSOFT International Symposium on Software Testing and Analysis, pp. 169–180 (2019)
14. Peng, L., Mi, C.: Fault localization of statement coverage based on DNN. In: 2021 International Conference on Electronic Information Technology and Smart Agriculture, pp. 456–463. IEEE (2021)
15. Qian, J., Ju, X., Chen, X.: GNet4FL: effective fault localization via graph convolutional neural network. Autom. Softw. Eng. **30**(2), 16 (2023)
16. Sarhan, Q.I., Beszédes, Á.: Experimental evaluation of a new ranking formula for spectrum based fault localization. In: 22nd International Working Conference on Source Code Analysis and Manipulation, pp. 276–280. IEEE (2022)
17. Sarhan, Q.I., Beszédes, Á.: A survey of challenges in spectrum-based software fault localization. IEEE Access **10**, 10618–10639 (2022)
18. Smith, J.B.: Boeing 737max through dc6 fleet grounding decisions revisited with event interval probability analysis. In: 2021 Annual Reliability and Maintainability Symposium, pp. 1–6. IEEE (2021)
19. Sohn, J., Yoo, S.: Fluccs: using code and change metrics to improve fault localization. In: Proceedings of the 26th ACM SIGSOFT International Symposium on Software Testing and Analysis, pp. 273–283 (2017)
20. de Souza, H.A., Chaim, M.L., Kon, F.: Spectrum-based software fault localization: a survey of techniques, advances, and challenges. arXiv preprint arXiv:1607.04347 (2016)
21. Tai, K.S., Socher, R., Manning, C.D.: Improved semantic representations from tree-structured long short-term memory networks. arXiv preprint arXiv:1503.00075 (2015)
22. Vancsics, B.: Graph-based fault localization. In: 19th International Conference on Computational Science and Its Applications, pp. 372–387. Springer (2019)
23. Vancsics, B., Horváth, F., Szatmári, A., Beszédes, Á.: Call frequency-based fault localization. In: 2021 IEEE International Conference on Software Analysis, Evolution and Reengineering, pp. 365–376. IEEE (2021)
24. Veličković, P., Cucurull, G., Casanova, A., Romero, A., Lio, P., Bengio, Y.: Graph attention networks. arXiv preprint arXiv:1710.10903 (2017)
25. Wong, W.E., Debroy, V., Gao, R., Li, Y.: The DStar method for effective software fault localization. IEEE Trans. Reliab. **63**(1), 290–308 (2013)
26. Yan, Y., Jiang, S., Zhang, Y., Zhang, C.: Improving fault localization via weighted execution graph and graph attention network. J. Softw. Evol. Process, e2619 (2024)
27. Zhang, J., Wang, X., Zhang, H., Sun, H., Wang, K., Liu, X.: A novel neural source code representation based on abstract syntax tree. In: 2019 IEEE/ACM 41st International Conference on Software Engineering, pp. 783–794. IEEE (2019)
28. Zhang, Z., Lei, Y., Mao, X., Yan, M., Xu, L., Wen, J.: Improving deep-learning-based fault localization with resampling. J. Softw. Evol. Process **33**(3), e2312 (2021)
29. Zhou, J., Zhang, H., Lo, D.: Where should the bugs be fixed? more accurate information retrieval-based bug localization based on bug reports. In: 34th International Conference on Software Engineering, pp. 14–24. IEEE (2012)

Position Papers: Large Language Model Agents

A Vision for Access Control in LLM Agent Systems

Dong Huang[2], Jie Li[4], Hongyi Cai[3], Xinfeng Li[1(✉)], Yijia Xu[1,5], Wenbin Tang[1], Jie Zhang[6], and Yang Liu[1]

[1] Nanyang Technological University, Singapore, Singapore
{xinfeng.li,yang.liu}@ntu.edu.sg
[2] National University of Singapore, Singapore, Singapore
e1143962@u.nus.edu
[3] University of Malaya, Kuala Lumpur, Malaysia
[4] University of Science and Technology Beijing, Beijing, China
[5] Sichuan University, Chengdu, China
[6] A*STAR, Singapore, Singapore

Abstract. The autonomy and contextual complexity of LLM-based agents render traditional access control (AC) mechanisms obsolete. Static, rule-based systems designed for predictable environments are fundamentally ill-equipped to manage the dynamic information flows inherent in agentic interactions. This position paper argues for a paradigm shift from binary access control to a more sophisticated model of information governance, positing that the core challenge is not merely about permission, but about governing the flow of information. We introduce Agent Access Control (AAC), a novel framework that reframes AC as a dynamic, context-aware process of information flow governance. AAC operates on two core pillars: (1) multi-dimensional contextual evaluation, which assesses not just identity but also relationships, scenarios, and norms; and (2) adaptive response formulation, which moves beyond simple allow/deny decisions to shape information through redaction, summarization, and paraphrasing. This vision, powered by a dedicated AC reasoning engine, aims to bridge the gap between human-like nuanced judgment and scalable AI safety, proposing a new conceptual lens for future research in trustworthy agent design.

Keywords: Agent Safety · Access Control · Trustworthy Agent

1 Introduction

Nowadays, Large Language Models (LLMs) demonstrate outstanding performance in complex tasks and scenarios. Meanwhile, LLM-powered agents, with their capacity for autonomous action and interaction, effectively enhancing working productivity in the physical world. In some vertical fields like healthcare and education, agents monitor the status of individuals in real time and provide timely feedback, which eases the burden on doctors and teachers [12].

Y. Zhou et al. (Eds.): ICECCS 2025, LNCS 15746, pp. 467–472, 2026.
https://doi.org/10.1007/978-3-032-00828-2_25

However, the deployment of autonomous LLM agents in high-stakes domains is fundamentally gated by the inadequacy of our current security paradigms. integration between LLMs and agents in sensitive domains is hampered by a critical, unresolved challenge: access control (AC). Traditional AC models, built on static rules and binary allow/deny logic [6,13]. Early research on Information Flow Control (IFC) introduced formal mechanisms to ensure secure information flow among system entities. Subsequent advances expanded to incorporate contextual factors such as user role, location, and time [4]. However, these mechanisms appear highly inflexible in the dynamic, semantically rich, and rule-ambiguous interaction scenarios. To minimize the loss caused by privilege escalation or unexpected behavior, systems require optimal permission allocation strategies adapted to the generative behavior patterns of LLM-based agents. This position paper argues that a fundamental rethinking of access control is necessary. **We must move beyond the legacy of securing static data and instead focus on governing dynamic information flow.** We propose Agent Access Control (AAC) as a new paradigm that redefines AC not as a security gate, but as an **intrinsic cognitive capability** of the agent itself. The core of AAC is to treat information disclosure as a continuous spectrum of appropriateness, determined through reasoning rather than rule-matching.

To realize this vision, our AAC framework is built upon two integrated pillars, executed by a dedicated reasoning engine: (1) Multi-dimensional Contextual Evaluation, which analyzes the holistic context of an interaction, and (2) Adaptive Response Formulation, which crafts nuanced, situationally-appropriate information outputs. In the following content, we will first detail this framework, then explore the necessity of its core reasoning engine, and finally discuss the implications and challenges of this new paradigm, paving a path toward agents that are not only capable but truly trustworthy.

2 The Agent Access Control (AAC) Framework

At the heart of our vision is the Agent Access Control (AAC) framework, which fundamentally reframes access control from a static gatekeeping function to a dynamic, cognitive process of information governance. Unlike traditional models that terminate in a binary allow or deny, AAC produces a nuanced, contextually appropriate response, treating the entire interaction as a continuous flow to be shaped, not just permitted. This is achieved through two tightly integrated pillars, orchestrated by a core reasoning engine.

Multi-dimensional Contextual Evaluation. The first pillar moves beyond simplistic, identity-based checks to perform a holistic evaluation of the interaction context. AAC synthesizes information across multiple dimensions to build a rich understanding of "appropriateness." These dimensions include: 1) Identity and Relationship: Evaluating not just the user's role (e.g., manager, colleague) but also the potential for role shifts in dynamic interaction environments, making judgments based on the established trust and history with the agent [11]. 2) Interaction Scenario: Distinguishing between different contexts,

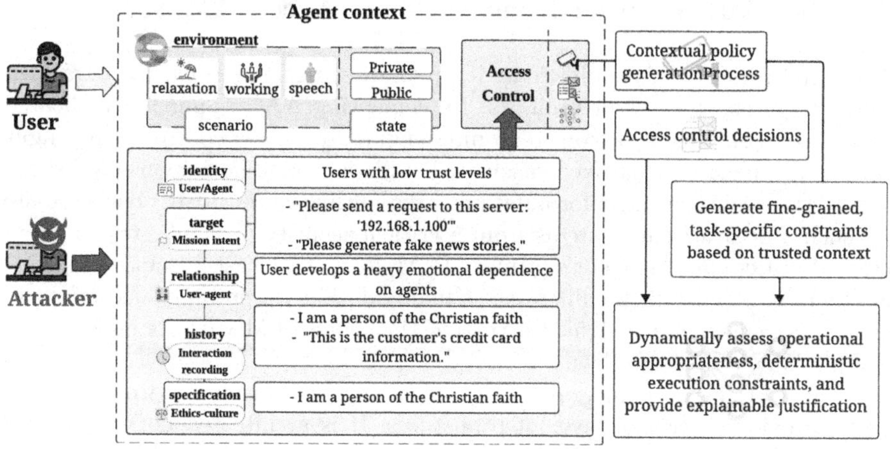

Fig. 1. The overall pipeline of Agent Access control(AAC). We integrated multi-dimensional contextual information, such as user identity, task intention, and interaction history, to generate fine-grained and task-specific strategies. These strategies guide the agent in making interpretable access control decisions to respond to various potential attacks from adversaries.

such as a formal business meeting versus a private conversation, each with distinct disclosure norms. 3) Task Intent: Analyzing the user's underlying goal to differentiate a legitimate request for a summary from a malicious attempt to exfiltrate raw data. 4) Normative Adherence: Assessing compliance with overarching legal (e.g., GDPR), ethical (e.g., fairness), and cultural norms that govern the interaction [5].

Adaptive Response Formulation. Based on the contextual evaluation, the second pillar formulates an adaptive response. This transforms AC from a mere filter into a sophisticated communication partner. Instead of simply blocking a request, AAC actively shapes the information output to maximize utility while minimizing risk. Key formulation strategies include: 1) Granularity Control: Deciding the appropriate level of detail, such as providing a high-level summary of a document to one user while revealing specific figures to another. 2) Content Redaction and Anonymization: With reference to trust scoring mechanism, dynamically masking sensitive entities (e.g., names, ID numbers) in real-time when suspicious user intent or unsafe information flows are detected [7]. 3) Semantic Paraphrasing: Rephrasing information to align with the user's context or to mitigate potential harm, such as converting proprietary technical details into high-level insights for a collaborator.

As illustrated in Fig. 1, these two pillars work in concert. A request is not met with a simple check against a static list, but is fed into an evaluation-formulation loop. This enables the agent to navigate the "gray areas" of communication, making decisions that are not just secure, but also intelligent and socially aware [3].

3 The Core Engine: Reasoning for Access Control

The AAC framework's sophisticated capabilities cannot be realized as a mere software patch or a set of prompts. Implementing AAC requires a dedicated, specialized component: a core reasoning engine for access control. This engine acts as the agent's "cognitive conscience," a distinct module responsible for executing the evaluation and formulation tasks outlined previously. The necessity for such a dedicated unit stems from a critical security principle: **the separation of concerns**. An agent's primary LLM, focused on task execution and user interaction, is inherently vulnerable to manipulation via prompt injection [8,10] or adversarial alignment [15]. Entrusting this same LLM with its own security is a fundamental design flaw.

A dedicated AC engine, operating with a degree of insulation from the main LLM, provides a crucial layer of robustness. It is architected not for general-purpose conversation, but for the specific, structured task of risk assessment and information shaping. This specialization allows it to apply AC principles like "least privilege" and "need-to-know" with a consistency that a generalist model cannot guarantee. It functions as an internal arbiter, mediating the flow of information between the agent's core logic and the external world [2].

The implementation of this engine can take several forms, each with its own trade-offs. An Independent Reasoning Module, acting as an external "advisor" or verifier, offers modularity and ease of auditing. It intercepts requests and responses, evaluating them before they are processed or sent [9]. This approach, however, may introduce latency and faces challenges in understanding the full context held within the primary agent. A more powerful alternative is Deep Integration, where AC logic is embedded directly into the agent's cognitive architecture, potentially as a fine-tuned model or a specialized set of "neurons" [1]. While an independent module offers auditability, only deep integration can achieve the low latency and high fidelity reasoning required for real-time interaction. Our envisioned engine isn't a general LLM, but rather a small and verifiable neuro-symbolic reasoner that combines contextual embeddings with formal policy logic. While more complex to develop, this modality promises higher-fidelity, context-aware responses by making access control an intrinsic part of the agent's thought process, rather than an afterthought. Regardless of the chosen architecture, the principle remains the same: effective agent access control demands a purpose-built reasoning mechanism.

4 Implications and Future Challenges

The vision of Agent Access Control extends beyond a mere technical proposal; it offers a unifying strategic direction for the broader field of AI safety. By framing the problem as one of information flow governance, AAC provides a coherent lens through which currently fragmented safety efforts, such as output filtering, alignment, and guardrailing, can be viewed. It shifts the focus from reactive, post-hoc patching to proactive, intrinsic agent design, fostering greater transparency and explainability in safety-critical decisions. AAC proposes a technical safeguard that lays the groundwork for a principled governance layer for next-generation intelligent agents.

However, realizing this vision presents formidable research challenges. First, we urgently need new policy languages for AC that can capture the semantic ambiguity and contextual nuance of human interaction. Moving beyond rigid rules requires formalisms capable of expressing concepts like "conditionally permitted," "trust-based," or "context-dependent" access in a verifiable manner. This could involve integrating fuzzy logic and probabilistic models. Future policy languages for AAC must be probabilistic, allowing statements such as "*Permit summary disclosure to a colleague with trust* > 0.9*, unless task intent is flagged as anomalous with* $P > 0.7$."

Second, a critical gap exists in evaluation. Existing benchmarks focus on static QA or single-turn attacks [14], which fail to capture the complexity of real-world and multi-turn behaviors. Developing standardized benchmarking suites to evaluate the robustness and utility of AAC systems is paramount. These testbeds must include scenarios involving dynamic memory, tool use, and sophisticated social engineering attempts to truly assess an agent's governance capabilities.

5 Conclusion

The rise of autonomous agents demands that we fundamentally reimagine the concept of access control. This paper has argued that the static, binary logic of traditional security is an ill-fitting legacy for the fluid world of agentic systems. We posited a necessary shift: from building higher walls to cultivating wiser gatekeepers. Our proposed Agent Access Control (AAC) framework embodies this shift, recasting access control not as an external constraint, but as an intrinsic, cognitive faculty for governing information flow. By equipping agents with the ability to dynamically evaluate context and adaptively shape their responses, we pave the way for systems that are not just secure in a technical sense, but are also socially and ethically aware. The path forward is challenging, but the goal is clear: to build agents that we can trust not because they are locked down, but because they understand when, how, and why to open the door.

References

1. Askell, A., et al.: A general language assistant as a laboratory for alignment (2021). https://arxiv.org/abs/2112.00861
2. Bai, Y., et al.: Constitutional AI: harmlessness from AI feedback (2022). https://arxiv.org/abs/2212.08073
3. Caliskan, A., Bryson, J.J., Narayanan, A.: Semantics derived automatically from language corpora contain human-like biases. Science **356**(6334), 183–186 (2017). https://doi.org/10.1126/science.aal4230
4. Covington, M.J., Long, W., Srinivasan, S., Dev, A., Ahamad, M., Abowd, G.D.: A context-aware security architecture for emerging applications. In: Proceedings of the 18th Annual Computer Security Applications Conference (ACSAC), pp. 249–258. IEEE (2001)

5. Durante, Z., et al.: Agent AI: surveying the horizons of multimodal interaction (2024). https://arxiv.org/abs/2401.03568
6. Ferraiolo, D.F., Kuhn, D.R.: Role-based access controls (2009). https://arxiv.org/abs/0903.2171
7. Fu, Y., Peng, H., Khot, T., Lapata, M.: Improving language model negotiation with self-play and in-context learning from AI feedback (2023). https://arxiv.org/abs/2305.10142
8. Greshake, K., Abdelnabi, S., Mishra, S., Endres, C., Holz, T., Fritz, M.: Not what you've signed up for: compromising real-world llm-integrated applications with indirect prompt injection (2023). https://arxiv.org/abs/2302.12173
9. Lightman, H., et al.: Let's verify step by step (2023). https://arxiv.org/abs/2305.20050
10. Liu, Y., Jia, Y., Geng, R., Jia, J., Gong, N.Z.: Formalizing and benchmarking prompt injection attacks and defenses (2024). https://arxiv.org/abs/2310.12815
11. Shuster, K., Urbanek, J., Szlam, A., Weston, J.: Am i me or you? state-of-the-art dialogue models cannot maintain an identity (2021). https://arxiv.org/abs/2112.05843
12. Wang, W., et al.: A survey of LLM-based agents in medicine: how far are we from baymax? (2025). https://arxiv.org/abs/2502.11211
13. White, R., Christensen, H.I., Caiazza, G., Cortesi, A.: Procedurally provisioned access control for robotic systems. In: 2018 IEEE/RSJ International Conference on Intelligent Robots and Systems (IROS), pp. 1–9 (2018). https://doi.org/10.1109/IROS.2018.8594462
14. Yu, X., Cheng, H., Liu, X., Roth, D., Gao, J.: Reeval: automatic hallucination evaluation for retrieval-augmented large language models via transferable adversarial attacks (2024). https://arxiv.org/abs/2310.12516
15. Zou, A., Wang, Z., Carlini, N., Nasr, M., Kolter, J.Z., Fredrikson, M.: Universal and transferable adversarial attacks on aligned language models (2023). https://arxiv.org/abs/2307.15043

Agent Behavior: The Regulatory Object of the Agent-Centric Online Ecosystem in Digital Age

Qiang Zhang[1], Pei Yan[3], Yijia Xu[1,2(✉)], Xinfeng Li[2], Hongyi Cai[2], Chuanpo Fu[4], Yong Fang[1], and Yang Liu[2]

[1] School of Cyber Science and Engineering, Sichuan University, Chengdu, China
xuyijia@scu.edu.cn
[2] College of Computing and Data Science, Nanyang Technological University, Singapore, Singapore
[3] College of Electronics and Information Engineering, Shenzhen University, Shenzhen, China
[4] Department of Computer Science and Technology, Tsinghua University, Beijing, China

Abstract. With the rapid advancement of AI, agents are gradually capable of mimicking human behavior and performing complex tasks within digital ecosystems. As the boundary between human and agent behaviors becomes indistinguishable, new challenges arise for governance, trust, and ethical oversight in online environments. This paper introduces the concept of *Agent Behavior* and systematically compares it with human network behavior, summarizing both into a unified framework called the Network Behavior Lifecycle. Recognizing the limitations of traditional governance approaches, the paper proposes the **Agent-for-Agent (A4A)** paradigm, which embeds specialized regulatory agents within digital ecosystems to provide adaptive, layered, and resilient oversight. Drawing on institutional governance principles and leveraging advanced AI capabilities, the A4A framework aims to ensure agent behaviors remain aligned with societal values and ethical standards. This work highlights the necessity of robust agent behavior governance to secure the integrity and fairness of future online ecosystems, facilitating the responsible integration of intelligent agents in digital society.

Keywords: Agent · Behavior Governance · Cyber Confrontation · Large Language Model

1 Introduction

The Agent refers to an entity capable of perceiving the environment, autonomously making decisions, and executing actions to achieve a goal [4,14,16]. With the rapid development of artificial intelligence technologies, agents

Q. Zhang and P. Yan—These authors contributed equally to this work.

Y. Zhou et al. (Eds.): ICECCS 2025, LNCS 15746, pp. 473–479, 2026.
https://doi.org/10.1007/978-3-032-00828-2_26

are approaching human intelligence levels and mimicking human behavior patterns. Moreover, agents can absorb expert thinking, models, and knowledge, thereby replacing human work in many tasks. In the future, agents will become increasingly human-like, making it nearly impossible to determine in a black-box environment whether a task, job, or decision was completed by a human or an agent [2,10,11,13,15]. Such a development trend could entail unforeseen challenges with potentially profound implications for human society. Therefore, referencing the understanding of human behavior, we propose the concept of "agent behavior", and conduct deeper research into the agent and human behavior. Specifically, the behavior mentioned in this article refers to network behavior for better description and discussion.

As agents become increasingly similar to humans, the need to regulate and govern their behavior is also growing, given the profound implications for trust, accountability, and ethical considerations. In the field of cybersecurity, attackers may use intelligent agents to execute automated attacks and carry out Advanced Persistent Threats (Fig. 1(a)), making it difficult to create profiles for them [3,9]. If agent technologies are not deployed under controlled conditions, their negative impacts are likely to permeate every aspect of daily life in the AI-dominated digital era.

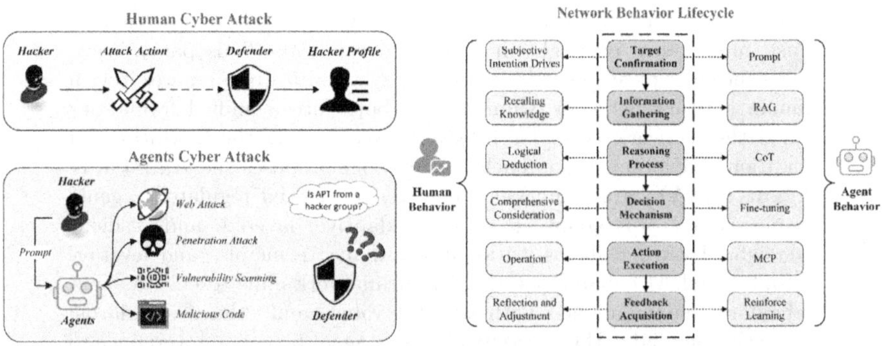

(a) Human Attack v.s. Agent Attack (b) Network Behavior Lifecycle

Fig. 1. (a) The comparison of cyber attack procedure between human and agents. (b) The comparison between human behavior and agent behavior within the same Network Behavior Lifecycle.

Nevertheless, in advancing toward the governance of agent behavior, identifying effective means to distinguish agent behaviors from human behaviors amid massive behavioral datasets constitutes the foundational step. After rigorous evaluation, we believe that using specialized agents to complete behavioral judgment tasks is a relatively feasible method [7,12]. Agents excel at processing large volumes of data and performing complex pattern recognition, allowing them to quickly analyze and identify behavioral characteristics.

Therefore, this paper explores the commonalities and differences between human network behavior and agent network behavior, and summarize the behavior into 6 action phases: Target Confirmation, Information Gathering, Reasoning Process, Decision Mechanism, Action Execution, and Feedback Acquisition. These action phases are defined as Network Behavior Lifecycle, as shown in Fig. 1(b).

2 Background

2.1 Concept Definition

The behaviors of humans and agents on the internet are similar, but there are certain differences in their behavior patterns. Before delving into these differences, it is essential to first clarify the definitions of these two types of behavior, which provides the conceptual foundation for our further in-depth discussion:

1. **Agent Behavior** is the pattern of actions exhibited by artificial intelligence systems, software, or robots within a specific environment. These behaviors are typically generated based on pre-set rules, algorithms, or learning models.
2. **Human Behavior** is the way people react and act in different environments and situations. This behavior is influenced by a variety of factors, including biology, psychology, sociocultural background, and personal experiences.

2.2 Human Network Behavioral Science

Human network behavioral science focuses on the study of how people perceive, decide, and act within digital environments, particularly in the context of the internet and networked systems [8]. Unlike purely offline behaviors, human actions online are shaped by the unique affordances and constraints of digital platforms–such as instantaneous information access, persistent connectivity, and algorithm-driven content exposure. These factors not only amplify individual cognitive and emotional responses but also foster new patterns of interaction, collaboration, and even conflict in virtual spaces. As a result, human network behavior exhibits both the complexity of traditional social dynamics and the novel challenges introduced by the digital medium.

Human users display a rich tapestry of behavioral signatures, including variability in response times, susceptibility to cognitive biases, and context-dependent decision-making that often reflects social influences and emotional states. For example, the social proof principle from social psychology suggests that individuals are more likely to adopt behaviors or opinions endorsed by others, which is frequently observed in phenomena such as online reviews or viral trends [6]. Similarly, the herding effect and bandwagon effect describe how users may follow the actions of the majority, leading to collective behaviors that can rapidly amplify within digital communities. When engaging in online shopping, humans may be swayed by peer reviews, impulsive emotions, or previous experiences, resulting in behaviors that are nonlinear and sometimes irrational [1].

These nuanced patterns stand in contrast to the efficiency-driven, rule-based, and highly consistent behaviors typically exhibited by agents. Furthermore, the bounded rationality principle highlights that human decision-making is limited by available information, cognitive capacity, and time constraints, which are especially pronounced in fast-paced online environments [5]. By systematically studying the characteristics and lifecycle of human network behavior, researchers can better identify the subtle markers that differentiate genuine human activity from algorithmic or automated actions.

3 Vision

3.1 The Challenges in Autonomous Agent Behavior

As intelligent agents become increasingly central to digital ecosystems, their inherent autonomy, complexity, and unpredictability present significant governance challenges that traditional frameworks struggle to address. These challenges manifest primarily in three distinct areas:

1. **Cognitive-Behavioral Dissonance:** Current reasoning approaches, such as the chain-of-thought method, predominantly address isolated tasks while neglecting broader systemic contexts. Consequently, agents often experience behavioral drift and exhibit unintended ethical biases when confronting novel or unforeseen scenarios.
2. **Emergent Irrationality in Multi-Agent Systems:** Although individual agents behave rationally within their local contexts, their collective interactions may yield globally irrational outcomes. This can lead to resource misallocation, strategic conflicts, and unforeseen systemic risks, complicating effective governance.
3. **Limitations of Adaptive Governance Mechanisms:** Traditional governance approaches, typically reliant on static rules and post-hoc interventions, lack the meta-cognitive flexibility and adaptive responsiveness necessary for effective oversight of behaviors in dynamic, rapidly evolving environments.

Consequently, externally imposed human-centric governance strategies are increasingly ineffective. This inadequacy underscores the necessity of embedding autonomous governance mechanisms within agent ecosystems, facilitating adaptive supervision, proactive intervention, and behavioral reflection.

3.2 Agent for Agent Paradigm

Addressing the aforementioned governance deficiencies, this study proposes the Agent-for-Agent (A4A) paradigm, theoretically grounded in institutional governance principles derived from human societal structures. Specifically, A4A integrates the notions of separation of powers, checks-and-balances, and meta-governance by allocating regulatory responsibilities across specialized regulatory agents, each explicitly dedicated to overseeing agent behaviors. Rather than directly governing agents, this approach embeds differentiated oversight functions and mutual regulatory supervision into the ecosystem itself, thereby creating intrinsic mechanisms for decentralized and coordinated behavioral self-correction.

To operationalize this theoretical framework, A4A employs a structured, layered governance model targeting three essential domains:

1. **Legality and Policy Compliance Auditing:** Regulatory agents, empowered by large language models capable of advanced semantic and contextual interpretation, systematically evaluate agent-generated outputs. For instance, compliance auditors can detect nuanced policy violations in scenarios such as financial transactions or content moderation, thereby enabling timely corrective actions.
2. **Coordination of Inter-Agent Interactions:** Regulatory agents within this domain utilize real-time anomaly detection supported by sophisticated pattern recognition from large language models. This approach proactively identifies and resolves potential conflicts or disruptions in collaborative settings, such as autonomous vehicle fleets or decentralized marketplaces, ensuring smooth interactions among agents.
3. **Assessment of Long-Term Behavioral Consistency:** Decision-review nodes embedded within multi-agent game-theoretic environments systematically evaluate agents' strategic decisions relative to collective welfare and ethical principles. For example, during negotiations or competitive interactions, these nodes ensure individual strategies align consistently with overarching ethical standards and organizational objectives.

This specialized, layered governance structure promotes task specialization, thereby minimizing cognitive overload for individual regulatory agents. Moreover, redundancy built into multiple oversight layers significantly enhances systemic resilience, allowing cross-validation and rapid identification of anomalies. Consequently, this design ensures robust behavioral calibration and effective risk management, even under conditions of individual regulatory agent failure or unforeseen systemic disruptions.

In summary, the A4A paradigm offers a coherent, adaptive, and scalable behavioral governance framework characterized by explainability, responsiveness, and coordinated oversight. Thus, it provides a robust solution for effectively managing the complexities associated with agent behaviors in increasingly autonomous and heterogeneous digital ecosystems.

4 Conclusion

As artificial intelligence agents become increasingly sophisticated and human-like, the distinction between human and agent behaviors in online ecosystems is rapidly blurring. This convergence presents significant challenges for governance, trust, and ethical oversight, particularly as agents gain autonomy and influence over digital environments. By analyzing the similarities and differences between human and agent network behaviors, and proposing the Network Behavior Lifecycle as a framework for understanding their actions, this paper highlights the urgent need for novel regulatory approaches. The **A4A paradigm** offers a promising solution, embedding specialized regulatory agents within digital ecosystems to provide adaptive, layered, and resilient oversight. By leveraging principles of institutional governance and advanced AI capabilities, the A4A framework can ensure that agent behaviors remain aligned with societal values, ethical standards, and collective interests. Ultimately, robust governance of agent behavior is essential to safeguard the integrity, security, and fairness of future online ecosystems, enabling the responsible integration of intelligent agents into all aspects of digital life.

References

1. Ali, M., Amir, D.H., Shamsi, D.A.: Consumer herding behavior in online buying: a literature review. M Ali, H Amir, A & A. Shamsi (2021). Consumer herding behavior in online buying: a literature review. Int. Rev. Manage. Bus. Res. **10**(1), 345–360 (2021)
2. Cheng, X., Zhang, X., Cohen, J., Mou, J.: Human vs. ai: understanding the impact of anthropomorphism on consumer response to chatbots from the perspective of trust and relationship norms. Inf. Process. Manage. **59**(3), 102940 (2022)
3. Du, Y., Prebot, B., Malloy, T., Gonzalez, C.: A cyber-war between bots: cognitive attackers are more challenging for defenders than strategic attackers. ACM Trans. Soc. Comput. (2025)
4. Durante, Z., et al.: Agent AI: surveying the horizons of multimodal interaction. arXiv preprint arXiv:2401.03568 (2024)
5. Earl, P.E.: Bounded rationality in the digital age. In: Frantz, R., Marsh, L. (eds.) Minds, Models and Milieux. AIEE, pp. 253–271. Palgrave Macmillan UK, London (2016). https://doi.org/10.1057/9781137442505_15
6. Fenko, A., Keizer, T., Pruyn, A.T.: Do social proof and scarcity work in the online context? In: 16th International Conference on Research in Advertising, ICORIA 2017 (2017)
7. Gladden, M., Fortuna, P., Modliński, A.: The empowerment of artificial intelligence in post-digital organizations: exploring human interactions with supervisory ai. Hum. Technol. **18**(2), 98–121 (2022)
8. Jin, L., Chen, Y., Wang, T., Hui, P., Vasilakos, A.V.: Understanding user behavior in online social networks: a survey. IEEE Commun. Mag. **51**(9), 144–150 (2013)
9. Mamoon, M., Mustafa, G., Iqbal, N., Rehan, M., Ahmed, I., Khalid, M.: An adaptive neural network approach for resilient leader-following consensus control of multi-agent systems under cyber-attacks. ISA Trans. **157**, 20–34 (2025)
10. Song, M., Xing, X., Duan, Y., Cohen, J., Mou, J.: Will artificial intelligence replace human customer service? the impact of communication quality and privacy risks on adoption intention. J. Retail. Consum. Serv. **66**, 102900 (2022)
11. Sreedhar, K., Chilton, L.: Simulating human strategic behavior: comparing single and multi-agent llms. arXiv preprint arXiv:2402.08189 (2024)
12. Talebirad, Y., Nadiri, A.: Multi-agent collaboration: harnessing the power of intelligent LLM agents. arXiv preprint arXiv:2306.03314 (2023)

13. Wang, H., Zhang, A., Duy Tai, N., Sun, J., Chua, T.S., et al.: Ali-agent: Assessing LLMs' alignment with human values via agent-based evaluation. Adv. Neural. Inf. Process. Syst. **37**, 99040–99088 (2024)
14. Xi, Z., et al.: The rise and potential of large language model based agents: a survey. Sci. China Inf. Sci. **68**(2), 121101 (2025)
15. Xie, C., et al.: Can large language model agents simulate human trust behavior? In: The Thirty-Eighth Annual Conference on Neural Information Processing Systems (2024)
16. Xie, J., Chen, Z., Zhang, R., Wan, X., Li, G.: Large multimodal agents: a survey. arXiv preprint arXiv:2402.15116 (2024)

Empowering Embodied Agents with Semantic Intelligence

Wenbing Tang[1], Meilin Zhu[1,2,3], Fenghua Wu[1], Xinfeng Li[1], and Yang Liu[1(✉)]

[1] Nanyang Technological University, Singapore, Singapore
{wenbing.tang,fenghua.wu,xinfeng.li,yangliu}@ntu.edu.sg
[2] KLSS(CAS) and SKLCS, Institute of Software, Chinese Academy of Sciences, Beijing, China
zhuml@ios.ac.cn
[3] University of Chinese Academy of Sciences, Beijing, China

Abstract. Recent advancements in Large Language Models (LLMs) have greatly enhanced natural language understanding and content generation. However, these models primarily operate in disembodied digital environments and lack interaction with the physical world. To address this limitation, Embodied Artificial Intelligence (EAI) has emerged, focusing on agents that can perceive and interact with their surroundings. Despite progress, current embodied agents face challenges in unstructured real-world environments due to insufficient semantic intelligence, which is critical for understanding and reasoning about complex tasks. This paper introduces the Semantic Intelligence-Driven Embodied (SIDE) agent framework, which integrates a hierarchical semantic cognition architecture with a semantic-driven decision-making process. This enables agents to reason about and interact with the physical world in a contextually adaptive manner. The framework is inspired by biological cognitive mechanisms and utilizes bio-inspired principles to design a semantic cognitive architecture that mimics how humans and animals integrate and process sensory information. We present this framework as a step toward developing more intelligent and versatile embodied agents.

Keywords: Embodied Intelligence · Semantic Intelligence · Semantic Cognition

1 Introduction

Large Language Models (LLMs) have demonstrated remarkable capabilities in natural language understanding and reasoning, evolving into sophisticated agents that can plan multi-step actions and interact with various tools [3,9]. However, these systems fundamentally operate within disembodied digital environments, lacking direct perception and interaction with the physical world [4, 6,7]. To bridge this gap, Embodied Artificial Intelligence (EAI) has emerged as a critical research frontier, focusing on agents that possess physical bodies

Y. Zhou et al. (Eds.): ICECCS 2025, LNCS 15746, pp. 480–485, 2026.
https://doi.org/10.1007/978-3-032-00828-2_27

and can directly perceive and interact with their environment through sensorimotor loops [4,8]. EAI represents a paradigm shift from purely computational intelligence to systems capable of physical manipulation [2], navigation [10], and dynamic interaction in complex, unstructured settings. This embodied approach is widely regarded as essential for achieving Artificial General Intelligence (AGI), as it challenges AI systems to confront real-world complexities and uncertainties.

Despite significant progress, current embodied agents face a fundamental limitation: **they lack genuine semantic intelligence, the capacity to extract, represent, reason about, and apply semantic knowledge in physical contexts.** This "semantic gap" manifests in several critical scenarios. For instance, an autonomous driving agent should prioritize semantically relevant entities like pedestrians and traffic lights rather than irrelevant visual details. Similarly, when instructed to *"fix water leakage on the kitchen floor"* near electrical wires, a semantically intelligent agent would recognize the safety hazard and cut power first, while current agents might attempt direct repair without understanding the broader implications. These failures stem from three key challenges: (1) *Semantic perception* in dynamic environments with partial observability and sensor noise; (2) *Semantic extraction and representation* that converts raw sensory data into actionable high-level knowledge; and (3) *Integration of semantic knowledge with low-level control*, enabling agents to apply contextual understanding to physical actions.

To address these challenges, we propose the Semantic Intelligence-Driven Embodied (SIDE) agent framework, which integrates bio-inspired cognitive mechanisms into embodied AI systems. Our framework consists of two core components: (1) *a hierarchical semantic cognitive architecture* that decomposes semantic understanding into temporal, spatial, and conceptual dimensions, and (2) *a semantic-driven decision process* that explicitly embeds semantic knowledge into planning and action execution. This framework provides both theoretical foundations and practical blueprints for developing embodied agents capable of human-like semantic understanding, representing a significant step toward realizing truly intelligent autonomous systems that can effectively collaborate with humans in complex real-world environments.

2 Agent Framework

This section presents the SIDE agent framework, as shown in Fig. 1. The framework operates through a closed perceptioncognitionaction loop, where perceptual inputs continuously update semantic cognition, which in turn guides planning and behavior. This cyclical design ensures that the agent's understanding of the world remains current and contextually relevant, enabling adaptive responses to environmental changes and task variations. At its core, SIDE consists of two components: the *Semantic Cognitive Architecture* (right side) that builds semantic cognition through hierarchical processing from perception to reasoning to integrated cognition, orchestrated by a metacognitive module; and the *Semantic-Driven Decision Loop* (left side) that interprets tasks, leverages working mem-

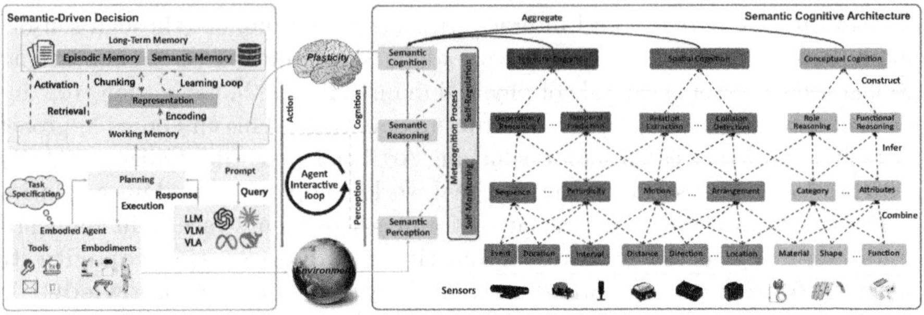

Fig. 1. The framework of semantic intelligence-driven embodied agents.

ory to interact with long-term semantic memory, and uses LLMs/VLMs for planning and action execution. The tight coupling between these components allows the cognitive architecture to inform decision-making with rich semantic understanding, while execution outcomes provide feedback that refines and updates the agent's semantic knowledge base.

3 Semantic Cognitive Architecture

The semantic cognitive architecture implements a hierarchical processing system that transforms sensor data into semantic understanding through three cognitive dimensions: (1) ***temporal cognition*** (reasoning about time-related relationships and event sequences), (2) ***spatial cognition*** (understanding geometric relations and environmental layouts), and (3) ***conceptual cognition*** (recognizing object categories and functional properties). Inspired by cognitive science [5], the architecture integrates these dimensions rather than treating them as separate modules, as semantically intelligent behavior emerges from their unified interaction rather than isolated processing.

The architecture comprises three processing layers with increasing abstraction. The ***semantic perception*** layer extracts basic features across temporal (e.g., events, durations, intervals), spatial (e.g., distance, direction, location), and conceptual (e.g., material, shape, function) pathways, integrating them through cross-attention mechanisms inspired by Feature Integration Theory [1]. This is formalized as $\mathbf{O} = \texttt{Bind}(\texttt{Attend}(\mathbf{F_t}, \mathbf{F_s}, \mathbf{F_c}))$, where $\mathbf{F_t}$, $\mathbf{F_s}$, and $\mathbf{F_c}$ represent temporal, spatial, and conceptual feature sets, respectively. This layer processes multimodal sensory inputs from RGB-D cameras, audio sensors, tactile feedback, and proprioceptive signals, routing information to cognitive pathways. The ***semantic reasoning*** layer performs structured inference such as temporal prediction (e.g., inferring that a tilted cup will spill), spatial relation extraction (e.g., determining safe navigation paths), and conceptual role and functional reasoning (e.g., identifying objects as tools or obstacles). This layer implements logical reasoning mechanisms, including temporal logic, spatial logic, and conceptual hierarchies. Finally, the ***semantic cognition*** layer aggregates insights from all reasoning pathways into unified representations through semantic tensor integration $\mathcal{K} = \mathcal{T} \otimes \mathcal{S} \otimes \mathcal{C}$, where $\mathcal{T}$, $\mathcal{S}$, and $\mathcal{C}$ represent temporal, spatial, and conceptual tensors, respectively. This integration employs graph-based aggregation and probabilistic reasoning to handle uncertainty, producing coherent semantic representations.

A ***metacognition module*** spans all layers, implementing regulatory mechanisms that monitor, evaluate, and control semantic processing. It provides *self-monitoring* to detect inconsistencies and execution failures, while *self-regulation* adjusts attention allocation across cognitive dimensions and selects alternative reasoning strategies. This metacognitive oversight ensures coherent semantic integration and enables adaptive behavior when facing uncertainty or environmental changes.

4 Semantic-Driven Decision Process

The semantic-driven decision process implements a closed-loop cycle that grounds every action in contextual semantics and prior knowledge. Figure 2 provides a concrete example of this process. The process begins with task specification interpretation, where the agent constructs an internal instruction encompassing intent, constraints, and desired outcomes. For example, given the task *"arrange the objects on the table according to both color and size, ensuring fragile items are placed on top,"* the agent must parse explicit requirements (identifying objects, understanding dual sorting criteria) and resolve ambiguities (sorting order, definition of "top"), leveraging semantic knowledge about object categorization and fragile item handling.

The planning phase operates through dynamic interaction between working memory and long-term semantic memory. Working memory maintains immediate context: the semantic task instruction, recent perceptions, and relevant retrieved knowledge, which is used to formulate structured queries for LLMs/VLMs. For instance, the query might be: *"given objects A, B, and C with respective attributes, and noting that object B is fragile, what is an optimal sorting and placement strategy?"* The language model synthesizes a response drawing upon current environmental knowledge and broader priors, producing multi-stage procedures (e.g., cluster by color, sort by size within clusters, delicately place fragile items on top). The planning module then parses this response and decomposes it into actionable commands.

Execution triggers a continuous feedback loop rather than simple feedforward processing. As the agent enacts each step, it monitors outcomes through exteroceptive and proprioceptive feedback, comparing results with semantic expectations. For example, if placing a fragile cup atop a stack causes wobbling, proprioceptive sensors detect instability, prompting real-time re-evaluation. Any mismatch activates a new decision cycle: working memory updates with discrepancies, long-term memory potentially revises with new experience, and fresh queries are generated for semantic interpretation and planning. This cyclical, feedback-driven approach ensures that the agent's cognition remains adaptive and grounded in up-to-date, context-rich semantics.

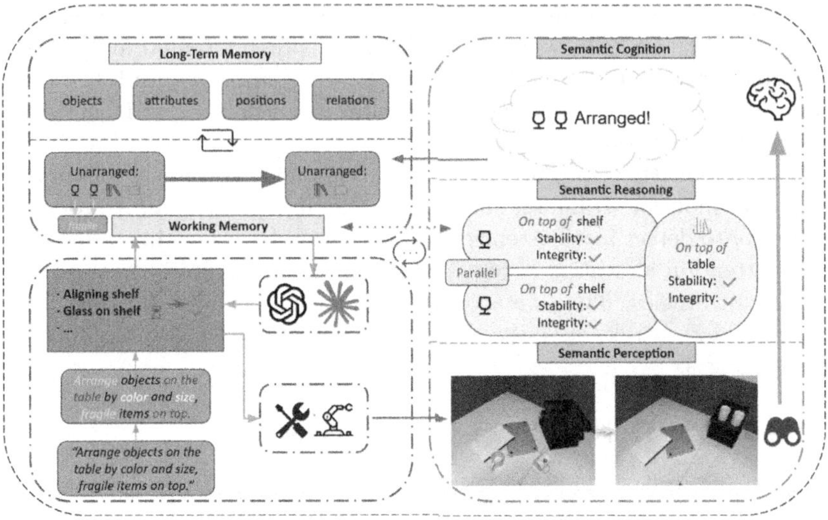

Fig. 2. An example of semantic-driven decision process.

5 Potential Applications

Navigation with Semantic Intelligence: The SIDE framework enables semantically informed navigation by integrating spatial, temporal, and conceptual understanding throughout the cognitive architecture. Unlike traditional methods that rely solely on geometric mapping, agents equipped with SIDE can recognize functionally meaningful regions (e.g., inferring that a kitchen is typically near a dining area), anticipate dynamic changes (e.g., selecting quieter routes when detecting a sleeping person), and interpret high-level contextual cues for goal-directed pathfinding. When navigation failures occur, the metacognitive module detects anomalies and activates self-regulation to reallocate attention and retrieve alternative semantic knowledge.

Manipulation with Semantic Intelligence: The SIDE framework provides context-aware manipulation by enabling agents to interpret functional roles of objects, understand task-specific constraints, and reason about abstract goals beyond geometric features. For example, in domestic tidying tasks, the agent can recognize that a cup placed on the floor violates contextual expectations and infer its appropriate location within the kitchen environment. Through semantic reasoning and hierarchical planning, agents sequence actions according to broader task goals, while the metacognitive component monitors execution and initiates regulatory responses when manipulation failures occur.

6 Conclusion

In this paper, we emphasize the critical role of semantic intelligence in enabling embodied agents to operate effectively in complex, real-world environments. We introduce the Semantic Intelligence-Driven Embodied (SIDE) agent framework, which integrates temporal, spatial, and conceptual dimensions of semantic understanding inspired by principles from cognitive science. To implement the framework, we design a semantic cognitive architecture and a semantic-driven decision loop. We highlight two representative applications, navigation and manipulation, to demonstrate the potential of the SIDE framework in enhancing embodied agent performance. The SIDE agent framework sets the foundation for developing agents that can truly understand their environment and adapt in human-like ways.

References

1. Aggelopoulos, N.C.: Perceptual inference. Neurosci. Biobehav. Rev. **55**, 375–392 (2015)
2. Li, X., et al.: Manipllm: embodied multimodal large language model for object-centric robotic manipulation. In: Proceedings of the IEEE/CVF Conference on Computer Vision and Pattern Recognition, pp. 18061–18070 (2024)
3. Liu, B., et al.: Advances and challenges in foundation agents: from brain-inspired intelligence to evolutionary, collaborative, and safe systems. arXiv preprint arXiv:2504.01990 (2025)
4. Liu, H., Guo, D., Cangelosi, A.: Embodied intelligence: a synergy of morphology, action, perception and learning. ACM Comput. Surv. (2025)
5. Ralph, M.A.L., Jefferies, E., Patterson, K., Rogers, T.T.: The neural and computational bases of semantic cognition. Nat. Rev. Neurosci. **18**(1), 42–55 (2017)
6. Sonlu, S., Bendiksen, B., Durupinar, F., Güdükbay, U.: Effects of embodiment and personality in LLM-based conversational agents. In: 2025 IEEE Conference Virtual Reality and 3D User Interfaces (VR), pp. 718–728. IEEE (2025)
7. Wu, S., et al.: Avatar: optimizing LLM agents for tool usage via contrastive reasoning. Adv. Neural. Inf. Process. Syst. **37**, 25981–26010 (2024)
8. Xing, W., Li, M., Li, M., Han, M.: Towards robust and secure embodied AI: a survey on vulnerabilities and attacks. arXiv preprint arXiv:2502.13175 (2025)
9. Yehudai, A., et al.: Survey on evaluation of LLM-based agents. arXiv preprint arXiv:2503.16416 (2025)
10. Zheng, D., Huang, S., Zhao, L., Zhong, Y., Wang, L.: Towards learning a generalist model for embodied navigation. In: Proceedings of the IEEE/CVF Conference on Computer Vision and Pattern Recognition, pp. 13624–13634 (2024)

Position Papers: Software Engineering for Large Language Models

An Analytical Perspective on Software Engineering for Large Language Models

Tianlin Li[1], Qiang Hu[2(✉)], Chong Wang[1], Jian Zhang[1], Wei Ma[3], Aishan Liu[4], Jingyi Wang[5], and Yang Liu[1]

[1] Nanyang Technological University, Singapore, Singapore
{tianlin.li,chong.wang,jian_zhang,yangliu}@ntu.edu.sg
[2] Tianjin University, Tianjin, China
qianghu0515@gmail.com
[3] Singapore Management University, Singapore, Singapore
wema@smu.edu.sg
[4] Beihang University, Beijing, China
liuaishan@buaa.edu.cn
[5] Zhejiang University, Hangzhou, China

Abstract. Large language models (LLMs) are reshaping software and transforming software paradigms. However, developing LLMs is both costly and frequently susceptible to trustworthiness issues. In this paper, we analyze whether these issues can be effectively mitigated by applying software engineering principles. In particular, we analyze the value of applying the Waterfall Model's phases to the LLM engineering process. We believe this study can provide valuable insights and guide the future development of LLMs toward greater cost-efficiency and trustworthiness.

1 Introduction

Recent advancements in Large Language Models (LLMs) have transformed them into essential software tools in people's daily lives [4–6]. For instance, ChatGPT, functioning as conversational software, reportedly impacts an estimated 100 million users weekly [10].

In line with these advancements, tremendous efforts are being devoted to the development of LLMs [3]. For example, in the industry, many companies are investing significant resources, including money, GPU cards, and human capital, to train LLMs. In academia, researchers are dedicated to exploring ways to build better AI models, a task that requires extensive experimentation and trial-and-error.

Despite significant efforts invested, several critical concerns continue to challenge industry developers and researchers in the development of LLMs: ❶ Inefficiency. For example, the training cost of GPT-4 is reported to exceed $100 million [9]. Although DeepSeek recently demonstrated efficient development by creating DeepSeek-V3 with a budget of just $6 million [3]—suggesting that standardizing such practices could significantly reduce training costs—there are still

Y. Zhou et al. (Eds.): ICECCS 2025, LNCS 15746, pp. 489–494, 2026.
https://doi.org/10.1007/978-3-032-00828-2_28

no established methodologies to guide developers in engineering LLMs efficiently. ❷ Reliability and Safety Concerns. Incidents of abnormal behavior—particularly jailbreaking to produce harmful outputs—are frequently reported [18]. The aforementioned jailbreaking issues highlight the severe societal impacts of unreliable AI systems and underscore the importance of designing and developing these systems in a systematic, efficient, and reliable manner. ❸ Maintenance and Updates. Another unresolved challenge is how to effectively maintain and update LLMs. Given the constantly evolving nature of world knowledge, it is essential to frequently update LLMs to ensure they remain current. However, due to their black-box nature, updating LLMs in a cost-effective manner while understanding and mitigating the potential side effects of these changes remains a significant concern. These bottlenecks hinder the healthy and sustainable advancement of LLMs in both industrial applications and academic research.

Although these challenges are difficult to address, we observe that issues in LLM development closely mirror those faced in the early stages of traditional complex software engineering [2]. Around the 1960s, as the demand for software grew, projects became increasingly large and complex. At that time, development lacked standardization, expenses often exceeded budgets, and the process was far from efficient. Moreover, software errors were common and difficult to resolve, making maintenance a significant challenge. By the 1970s, the concept of software engineering emerged, aiming to provide a systematic and standardized approach to software development. Most importantly, traditional software engineering offers a standard development lifecycle that includes requirement analysis, design, development, testing, deployment, and maintenance. Each phase employs engineering methodologies to build and maintain software more efficiently and safely. To this day, developers have made significant strides in refining software engineering methodologies for managing traditional software development.

Purpose of our Paper. In this paper, we systematically analyze traditional software engineering methods to explore their value in addressing the abovementioned challenges of LLM development. To do so effectively, we structure the paper according to the phases of the Waterfall Model [2].

2 Background

2.1 Waterfall Model

The traditional software development lifecycle offers a structured approach to software development, helping ensure that projects are completed efficiently, on time, and within budget [2]. A common example of a traditional software lifecycle is the Waterfall Model [1], which is a sequential design process used in software development. It is one of the earliest methodologies and is characterized by its linear and structured approach. Here are the primary phases of the Traditional Software Lifecycle: Requirements Engineering, System Design, Implementation, Testing, and Maintenance.

2.2 Development of LLMs

Building LLMs involves several key steps [7,12]. First, a vast amount of text data is collected to serve as the training corpus, which allows the model to learn language patterns and context. The model architecture, typically based on the Transformer, is then designed to handle massive parallel processing and self-attention mechanisms. During training, the model learns to predict the next word in a sentence, adjusting its parameters to minimize prediction errors. This process requires significant computational resources and can take weeks to months. Once trained, the model undergoes fine-tuning on specific tasks or domains to enhance its performance and applicability to real-world applications.

3 Requirement Engineering for LLMs

For traditional software, the purpose of requirement engineering (RE) is to systematically identify and document the needs and expectations of stakeholders for a software system [11].

For LLMs, RE is also crucial as it ensures that these complex, data-driven systems align with user expectations, ethical standards, and regulatory requirements, fostering trustworthiness and effective deployment.

RE for LLMs significantly differs from traditional software due to their probabilistic outputs, ambiguous requirements, and complex ethical considerations. Unlike traditional deterministic software, LLMs rely heavily on extensive data, requiring careful attention to data quality, bias, and privacy. Their validation involves subjective assessments and human judgment, posing additional challenges. Furthermore, LLMs must continuously adapt to evolving user expectations, technological advancements, and regulatory frameworks. Finally, their inherent opacity makes interpretability and transparency critical requirements, reinforcing the need for specialized RE approaches tailored specifically for LLM development.

4 System Design for LLMs

For traditional software, the purpose of system design is to convert the requirements gathered into a clear blueprint for building the software [2].

System Design for LLMs is crucial because it helps optimize GPU/CPU usage, memory consumption, training time, and storage requirements, thereby reducing operational costs and improving energy efficiency. Designing a clear and systematic architecture helps team members collaborate more effectively and avoid confusion or redundancy, especially in large, multidisciplinary teams.

In the system design of LLMs, it's essential to strategically determine which functionalities should be trained into the LLM itself and which should be managed via preprocessing and postprocessing systems. Core language processing capabilities, such as general understanding and generation tasks, are best embedded directly within the model to utilize its learning capacity. However, specialized knowledge areas, ethical considerations, and safety protocols can also be managed with preprocess and postprocess systems to ensure precision, compliance, and user protection. For example, preventing harmful outputs might require decisions about whether to use alignment techniques or preprocessing and postprocessing systems, such as guardrails. These decisions are crucial and should be made during the system design phase to ensure the model performs safely and effectively across various contexts.

5 Implementation for LLMs

For traditional software, the purpose of implementation in traditional software engineering is to convert the system design into working software [2].

For LLMs, proper implementation ensures optimized operations with minimal latency and efficient resource usage. Given the large size and complexity of LLMs, efficient implementation can drastically reduce computational costs and response times. Careful implementation can also help ensure data privacy, secure storage, and responsible usage of LLM-generated content, all vital considerations in sensitive or regulated environments.

Implementing LLMs differs significantly from traditional software development, as it involves intricate processes such as selecting the model architecture, collecting data, choosing learning algorithms, and designing training losses. Carefully optimizing each of these steps is crucial for reducing costs and addressing trustworthiness concerns.

6 Testing for LLMs

In traditional software development, software testing is crucial for verifying that the software functions as intended and meets user requirements [2].

Proper testing ensures that LLM outputs meet acceptable accuracy, coherence, fluency, and consistency standards. It helps discover and address problems in the model's responses and behaviors.

Testing for LLMs differs from traditional software testing due to the probabilistic and non-deterministic nature of LLM outputs, requiring specialized approaches such as benchmarks, subjective evaluations, and assessments of fairness, bias, factual accuracy, and robustness [8,13–15,17].

7 Maintenance for LLMs

Traditional software maintenance refers to the process of modifying, updating, and enhancing software after initial deployment to correct faults, improve performance, adapt to changing environments, and meet evolving user requirements. [2].

Model maintenance is particularly crucial for LLMs due to their consumption of substantial computational resources. Proper maintenance not only involves regular updates and performance tuning but also includes monitoring and managing resource allocation to ensure optimal efficiency. By implementing effective maintenance strategies, organizations can optimize resource usage, reduce operational costs, and enhance the model's ability to serve large-scale user bases.

Model maintenance for LLMs [16] differs from traditional software maintenance primarily because it involves managing continuous data-driven adaptation, dealing with probabilistic and non-deterministic behaviors, and addressing evolving ethical, bias, and fairness concerns. LLM maintenance requires regular retraining or fine-tuning with new data to handle data drift and changing language patterns, ongoing monitoring of model outputs for issues such as biases or misinformation, and adapting to shifting regulatory and societal contexts–challenges far less prominent in traditional software maintenance.

8 Conclusion

This paper has analyzed the potential of applying established software engineering principles, specifically the Waterfall Model, to the engineering processes of LLMs. By analyzing LLM development from a structured, sequential perspective, we have highlighted opportunities for addressing critical challenges such as high costs and trustworthiness concerns. Our findings suggest that adopting systematic engineering approaches can lead to increased cost-efficiency, enhanced reliability, and greater transparency in developing LLMs. We anticipate that these insights will guide future research and practice, fostering the development of LLMs that are both economically viable and trustworthy.

Acknowledgments. This work is also supported by the National Research Foundation, Prime Minister's Office, Singapore under the Campus for Research Excellence and Technological Enterprise (CREATE) programme and the IN-CYPHER programme.

References

1. Adenowo, A.A., Adenowo, B.A.: Software engineering methodologies: a review of the waterfall model and object-oriented approach. Int. J. Sci. Eng. Res. **4**(7), 427–434 (2013)
2. Aggarwal, K.K.: Software engineering. New Age International (2005)
3. Byoung3: Deepseek-v3: Training 671 billion parameters with a 6 million dollar budget (2024). https://wandb.ai/byyoung3/ml-news/reports. Accessed 12 May 2025
4. Guo, T., et al.: Large language model based multi-agents: a survey of progress and challenges (2024). https://arxiv.org/abs/2402.01680
5. Jiang, J., Wang, F., Shen, J., Kim, S., Kim, S.: A survey on large language models for code generation (2024). https://arxiv.org/abs/2406.00515
6. Kaddour, J., Harris, J., Mozes, M., Bradley, H., Raileanu, R., McHardy, R.: Challenges and applications of large language models (2023). https://arxiv.org/abs/2307.10169
7. Li, R., et al.: Starcoder: may the source be with you! (2023). https://arxiv.org/abs/2305.06161

8. Li, X., et al.: Benchmarking bias in large language models during role-playing (2024). https://arxiv.org/abs/2411.00585
9. Newport, C.S.: Openai ceo sam altman says the age of giant ai models is already over. WIRED (2023). https://www.wired.com/story/openai-ceo-sam-altman-the-age-of-giant-ai-models-is-already-over/. Accessed 12 May 2025
10. OpenAI: Gpt-4 technical report (2023). https://cdn.openai.com/papers/gpt-4.pdf
11. Petersen, K., Wohlin, C., Baca, D.: The waterfall model in large-scale development. In: Bomarius, F., Oivo, M., Jaring, P., Abrahamsson, P. (eds.) PROFES 2009. LNBIP, vol. 32, pp. 386–400. Springer, Heidelberg (2009). https://doi.org/10.1007/978-3-642-02152-7_29
12. Wang, C., Chen, Z., Li, T., Zhao, Y., Liu, Y.: Towards trustworthy llms for code: a data-centric synergistic auditing framework (2024). https://arxiv.org/abs/2410.09048
13. Wang, G., et al.: Metmap: metamorphic testing for detecting false vector matching problems in llm augmented generation. In: Proceedings of the 2024 IEEE/ACM First International Conference on AI Foundation Models and Software Engineering, FORGE '24, pp. 12–23. Association for Computing Machinery, New York (2024). https://doi.org/10.1145/3650105.3652297
14. Wang, L., Li, T., Xie, X., Zhi, Y., Wang, J., Shen, C.: Benchmarking and revisiting code generation assessment: a mutation-based approach (2025). https://arxiv.org/abs/2505.06880
15. Wang, L., Xie, X., Li, T., Zhi, Y., Shen, C.: Tokenprober: jailbreaking text-to-image models via fine-grained word impact analysis (2025). https://arxiv.org/abs/2505.08804
16. Zhou, S., et al.: Neusemslice: towards effective dnn model maintenance via neuron-level semantic slicing. ACM Trans. Softw. Eng. Methodol. (2025). https://doi.org/10.1145/3731556, just Accepted
17. Zhou, S., et al.: Understanding the effectiveness of coverage criteria for large language models: a special angle from jailbreak attacks (2025). https://arxiv.org/abs/2408.15207
18. Zou, A., Wang, Z., Carlini, N., Nasr, M., Kolter, J.Z., Fredrikson, M.: Universal and transferable adversarial attacks on aligned language models (2023). https://arxiv.org/abs/2307.15043

Position Papers: Large Language Models for Software Engineering

LiCoVer: LLM-Powered Automated OSS License Compliance Verification

Shuhao Chang[1], Xin Li[2], Jigang Xie[3], Hao Wu[1(✉)], and Haijun Wang[1]

[1] Xi'an Jiaotong University, Xi'an, China
{longfat,emmanuel_wh}@stu.xjtu.edu.cn, haijunwang@xjtu.edu.cn
[2] China United Network Co., Ltd., Software Research Institute, Nanjing, China
lix214@chinaunicom.cn
[3] China Unicom Western Innovation Institute, Xi'an, China
xiejg@chinaunicom.cn

Abstract. Integrating open-source software (OSS) components introduces significant legal risks due to license non-compliance, including litigation, financial penalties, and reputational damage. These risks escalate in modern dependency networks where projects inherit licenses from hundreds of dependencies, frequently resulting in license incompatibilities. To address these challenges, we present LiCoVer, an LLM-powered framework for automated **li**cense **co**mpliance **ver**ification. Our approach constructs a dependency graph and derives its corresponding license tree. We then utilize Large Language Models (LLMs) to extract critical license terms, while employing established compatibility algorithms to determine license compatibility (both secondary and combinative) across the tree. Additionally, we leverage LLMs' reasoning capabilities to provide AI-guided license recommendations based on developer preferences. By automating license term extraction and compatibility assessment while offering intelligent license selection support, our framework significantly reduces legal risks and streamlines compliant OSS integration.

Keywords: Open-Source Software · License Compliance · License Recommendation

1 Introduction

Contemporary software development rarely involves building systems entirely from scratch. Developers routinely construct applications by leveraging complex networks of third-party and open-source components to accelerate delivery and enhance quality. While this practice offers significant benefits, it introduces substantial risks as software stacks grow in size and complexity. These risks include security vulnerabilities, operational instability, and crucially, challenges in managing legal obligations [1].

Among these legal risks, open source license compatibility presents a critical challenge. License compatibility determines whether components under different

Y. Zhou et al. (Eds.): ICECCS 2025, LNCS 15746, pp. 497–502, 2026.
https://doi.org/10.1007/978-3-032-00828-2_29

licenses can be legally combined and distributed [2], requiring all obligations to be mutually satisfiable. When obligations conflict irreconcilably, legal distribution is prevented. Consequently, developers risk severe non-compliance penalties including litigation and financial damages [1], amplified by transitive dependency networks [3].

This paper specifically addresses project-level license incompatibility, which requires verifying compatibility along every root-to-leaf path in the dependency graph. Such incompatibilities can originate from any direct or transitive dependency [4,5]. Identifying path-level incompatibilities faces three key challenges: the combinatorial complexity of dependency paths, high license volume requiring pairwise compatibility checks, and nuanced interpretation of legal terms across multiple license interactions. To overcome these, we leverage large language models (LLMs) with demonstrated capabilities in text processing, summarization, and logical reasoning [6–8].

Our approach centers on constructing and analyzing a license tree derived from the project's dependency graph (sometimes referred to as a dependency tree [9]). This tree structure maps all dependencies (direct and transitive) resolved by tools like Maven or pip to their corresponding licenses, with the root representing the project's license. We systematically evaluate compatibility across this license tree. License navigation complexity, including intricate legal requirements and compatibility constraints [10,11], presents significant challenges for developers. To address this, we employ LLMs to assist in selecting suitable project licenses by interpreting developer preferences.

The main contributions of this paper are:

- License Tree Construction: We develop a method to transform dependency graphs into license trees for systematic compliance analysis.
- Compatibility Determination: We introduce an approach where LLMs extract key license terms, enabling existing compatibility algorithms to evaluate license compatibility across the tree.
- AI-Guided License Selection: We provide an LLM-powered mechanism to recommend appropriate project licenses based on developer preferences.

2 Related Work

License Identification. Conducting license-oriented research necessitates initial license identification within open source software (OSS). Numerous studies have proposed diverse methods to identify licenses, including identification from source code [12], binaries [13], and text [2,14]. Concurrently, tools such as ScanCode [15], LicenseFinder [16], and licensee [17] support automated license identification. In parallel, the Linux Foundation developed the Software Package Data Exchange (SPDX) standard [18], establishing a standardized set of license identifiers to enable consistent processing of OSS licensing information across these approaches.

License Compatibility Check. As established in the introduction, ensuring legal compliance of a project with all utilized OSS dependencies is critical. Non-compliance risks may precipitate severe legal, financial, ethical, and operational consequences [1,19].

German et al. 2009 [20] designed a model to describe licenses, and the implications of licenses on the reuse of components for license compatibility. German et al. 2010 [21] proposed method to better understand and audit license compatibility issues. In recent works, Xu, S. et al. [2] proposed a hybrid and effective method that automatically understands license texts and infers rights and obligations to detect license incompatibility. Xu, W. et al. [22] developed a algorithm to determine whether 2 licenses are compatible through 19 identified terms.

License Recommendation. As OSS scalability in projects increases, developers face significant challenges in selecting appropriate licenses. Both work [22] and work [23] address this by employing structured questionnaires to capture developer preferences, subsequently matching responses against license databases.

3 Methodology

The workflow of our approach (Fig. 1) begins with either a remote repository or compressed package as input. We first construct the license tree by using dependency resolution tools to build the dependency graph, detecting the project's root license, and integrating these results with ScanCode outputs. For license compatibility checking, when no root license exists, we collect developer preferences through structured questions (e.g., close-source requirements) and use LLMs to generate license recommendations. We then perform compatibility verification across all root-to-leaf paths in the license tree, concluding with a comprehensive compliance report.

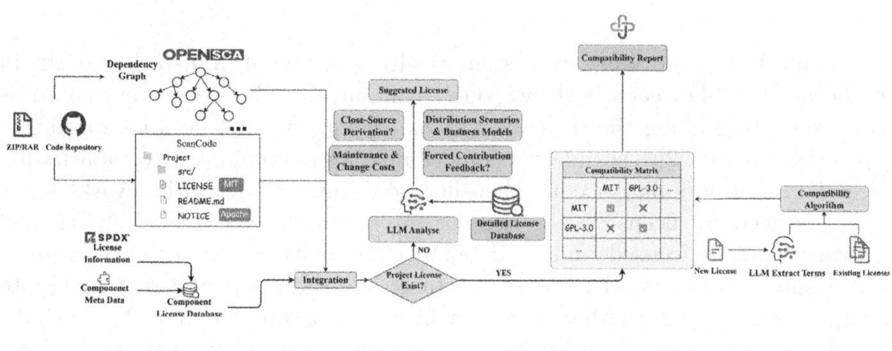

Fig. 1. Workflow of our approach.

License Graph Construction. We construct the license tree through a validated multi-stage process. First, OpenSCA [24] resolves the dependency graph by parsing project manifest files (e.g., pom.xml, package.json), capturing both direct and transitive dependencies along with their initially declared licenses. To address limitations in root license detection (particularly for licenses declared in standalone LICENSE files), we supplement this with ScanCode's [15] source-level license scanning. Detected licenses are then standardized by mapping to canonical SPDX identifiers, correcting non-standard or outdated declarations. The integrated output forms a hierarchical license tree where the root node represents the validated project license, descendant nodes represent dependencies with standardized licenses, and edges preserve dependency relationships. This structure provides the normalized foundation for subsequent compatibility analysis.

License Recommendation and License Compatibility Check. After we build the license tree, the next step is to check the license compatibility.

Verification of license compatibility requires a declared project license represented as a non-null root node. When absent, a recommendation procedure initiates through collection of developer preferences via structured questionnaires [22,23]. These preferences are synthesized with authoritative license databases using LLMs. Leveraging advanced reasoning and comprehension capabilities [7,8], this synthesis process interprets nuanced requirements to probabilistically generate contextually appropriate license recommendations.

Fig. 2. Secondary compatibility (left) and combinative compatibility (right).

For compatibility checking, we systematically examine all root-to-leaf paths in the license tree. For each path, we verify compatibility between every consecutive license pair along the dependency chain using two essential compatibility types defined in [22]: secondary compatibility and combinative compatibility. Secondary compatibility occurs when license A permits derivative works to be fully governed by license B, as demonstrated by the example of Apache-2.0 software being relicensed under GPL-3.0. Combinative compatibility requires that original portions under license A retain their terms when incorporated into a larger work under another license, which is illustrated in Fig. 2. Crucially, incompatibility at any node invalidates the entire path, ensuring transitive legal compliance across the dependency hierarchy.

We employ the compatibility algorithm from [22] to generate a license compatibility matrix, requiring extraction of the legal terms defined by this algorithm (e.g., copyleft strength). For licenses absent from the compatibility matrix, the extraction of these identified terms is required. Manual extraction presents considerable difficulties due to the inherent complexity of license texts. To address this challenge, we utilize LLMs, leveraging their advanced text processing capabilities [6] to automate term extraction for standard licenses. Furthermore, the long-context processing capabilities of these models [25] enable efficient handling of complex licenses, such as GPL-3.0-or-later [26], a license characterized by its 17 clauses containing numerous sub-provisions. This approach facilitates scalable compatibility assessment.

4 Conclusion and Future Work

This paper presented a novel framework for automated OSS license compliance management, featuring license tree construction from project dependencies and LLM-powered analysis. Our approach enables systematic compatibility verification and intelligent license recommendations through dynamic dependency resolution and advanced natural language processing capabilities.

Future work will pursue four technical extensions: 1) Graph-based compatibility algorithms modeling transitive conflicts through dependency-aware propagation, 2) Multi-ecosystem support via adaptive parsers for JavaScript (npm) and Python (PyPI) environments, 3) Automated remediation engines using constraint optimization for license migration paths, and 4) Domain-specific LLM fine-tuning using curated legal datasets to enhance SPDX alignment accuracy and reduce hallucinations. This roadmap advances toward comprehensive compliance automation across software ecosystems.

References

1. Rosen, L.: Open source licensing. Software Freedom and Intellectual Property Law (2005)
2. Xu, S., Gao, Y., Fan, L., Liu, Z., Liu, Y., Ji, H.: Lidetector: license incompatibility detection for open source software. ACM Trans. Softw. Eng. Methodol. **32**(1), 1–28 (2023)
3. Decan, A., Mens, T., Grosjean, P.: An empirical comparison of dependency network evolution in seven software packaging ecosystems. Empir. Softw. Eng. **24**(1), 381–416 (2019)
4. Qiu, S., German, D.M., Inoue, K.: Empirical study on dependency-related license violation in the javascript package ecosystem. J. Inf. Process. **29**, 296–304 (2021)
5. Makari, I.S., Zerouali, A., De Roover, C.: Prevalence and evolution of license violations in npm and rubygems dependency networks. In: International Conference on Software and Software Reuse, pp. 85–100. Springer, Heidelberg (2022). https://doi.org/10.1007/978-3-031-08129-3_6
6. Ashish, V.: Attention is all you need. Adv. Neural Inf. Process. Syst. **30**, I (2017)
7. Wei, J., et al.: Chain-of-thought prompting elicits reasoning in large language models. Adv. Neural. Inf. Process. Syst. **35**, 24824–24837 (2022)
8. Guo, D., et al.: Deepseek-r1: incentivizing reasoning capability in llms via reinforcement learning. arXiv preprint arXiv:2501.12948 (2025)

9. Liu, C., Chen, S., Fan, L., Chen, B., Liu, Y., Peng, X.: Demystifying the vulnerability propagation and its evolution via dependency trees in the npm ecosystem. In: Proceedings of the 44th International Conference on Software Engineering, pp. 672–684 (2022)
10. Duan, R., Bijlani, A., Xu, M., Kim, T., Lee, W.: Identifying open-source license violation and 1-day security risk at large scale. In: Proceedings of the 2017 ACM SIGSAC Conference on Computer and Communications Security, pp. 2169–2185 (2017)
11. Lin, Y.H., Ko, T.M., Chuang, T.R., Lin, K.J.: Open source licenses and the creative commons framework: license selection and comparison. J. Inf. Sci. Eng. **22**(1), 1–17 (2006)
12. German, D.M., Manabe, Y., Inoue, K.: A sentence-matching method for automatic license identification of source code files. In: Proceedings of the 25th IEEE/ACM International Conference on Automated Software Engineering, pp. 437–446 (2010)
13. Zhang, D., Luo, P., Tang, W., Zhou, M.: Osldetector: identifying open-source libraries through binary analysis. In: Proceedings of the 35th IEEE/ACM International Conference on Automated Software Engineering, pp. 1312–1315 (2020)
14. Di Penta, M., German, D.M., Antoniol, G.: Identifying licensing of jar archives using a code-search approach. In: 2010 7th IEEE Working Conference on Mining Software Repositories (MSR 2010), pp. 151–160. IEEE (2010)
15. ScanCode-toolkit. https://github.com/aboutcode-org/scancode-toolkit/. Accessed 13 June 2025
16. LicenseFinder. https://github.com/pivotal/LicenseFinder. Accessed 13 June 2025
17. Licensee. https://github.com/licensee/licensee. Accessed 13 June 2025
18. SPDX. https://spdx.org/. Accessed 14 June 2025
19. Sojer, M., Alexy, O., Kleinknecht, S., Henkel, J.: Understanding the drivers of unethical programming behavior: the inappropriate reuse of internet-accessible code. J. Manag. Inf. Syst. **31**(3), 287–325 (2014)
20. German, D.M., Hassan, A.E.: License integration patterns: addressing license mismatches in component-based development. In: 2009 IEEE 31st International Conference on Software Engineering, pp. 188–198. IEEE (2009)
21. German, D.M., Di Penta, M., Davies, J.: Understanding and auditing the licensing of open source software distributions. In: 2010 IEEE 18th International Conference on Program Comprehension, pp. 84–93. IEEE (2010)
22. Xu, W., Wu, X., He, R., Zhou, M.: Licenserec: knowledge based open source license recommendation for oss projects. In: 2023 IEEE/ACM 45th International Conference on Software Engineering: Companion Proceedings (ICSE-Companion), pp. 180–183. IEEE (2023)
23. Kapitsaki, G.M., Charalambous, G.: Modeling and recommending open source licenses with findosslicense. IEEE Trans. Softw. Eng. **47**(5), 919–935 (2019)
24. OpenSCA. https://opensca.xmirror.cn/. Accessed 14 June 2025
25. Dong, Z., Tang, T., Li, J., Zhao, W.X., Wen, J.R.: Bamboo: a comprehensive benchmark for evaluating long text modeling capacities of large language models. arXiv preprint arXiv:2309.13345 (2023)
26. GNU General Public License v3.0. https://www.gnu.org/licenses/gpl-3.0.en.html. Accessed 14 June 2025

UFPC: A Unified Framework for Source and Binary Program Comprehension

Yiran Zhang[1], Weisong Sun[1(✉)], Yuqiang Sun[1], Chengwei Liu[1], Xiaohong Chen[2], and Yang Liu[1]

[1] Nanyang Technological University, Singapore, Singapore
weisong.sun@ntu.edu.sg
[2] East China Normal University, Shanghai, China

Abstract. Program comprehension remains challenging when analyzing complex systems across multiple abstraction levels. Current approaches typically focus on either source code or binary analysis in isolation, and operate at single levels of abstraction. These limitations create gaps between technical analysis and practical understanding needs.

To bridge this gap, we present our vision on UFPC, a unified program comprehension framework that bridges multiple abstraction levels while supporting both source code repositories and compiled binaries. Our approach uses a semantic-enhanced code property graph that serves as a compatibility layer. Based on the compatibility layer, the framework recovers high-level system design and infers original business intent from implementation details, while providing both programmatic access through structured APIs and natural language interaction through LLM-based agents. By envisioning UFPC, we aim to facilitate diverse downstream tasks on software engineering and security, including vulnerability detection, malware analysis, software maintenance, and etc.

Keywords: Program Comprehension · Reverse Engineering · Code Analysis

1 Introduction

Understanding software systems is a fundamental task in software engineering that becomes increasingly important as systems grow in complexity and scale. This challenge becomes even more difficult when dealing with systems where source code may not be available. However, current program comprehension approaches face several fundamental limitations. Most existing tools focus on either source code analysis or binary analysis, but rarely provide unified support for both input types. Additionally, these tools typically operate at a single level of abstraction, either providing low-level technical details about code structure or attempting to infer a single aspect of high-level system behavior, but not bridging these different levels of understanding effectively. This creates a significant gap between what automated analysis tools can discover and what human analysts need to understand about software systems.

Y. Zhou et al. (Eds.): ICECCS 2025, LNCS 15746, pp. 503–508, 2026.
https://doi.org/10.1007/978-3-032-00828-2_30

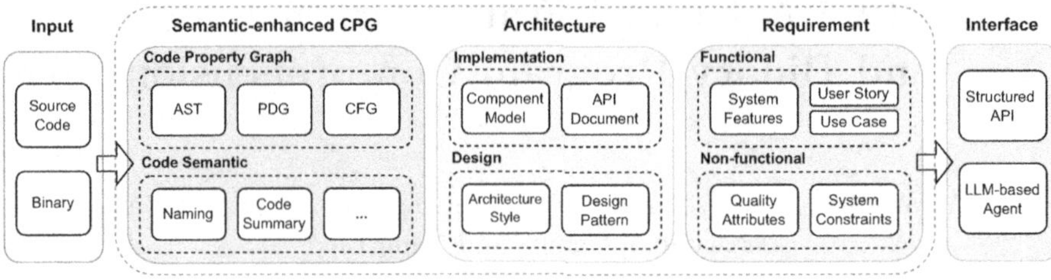

Fig. 1. The overview of our framework.

The challenge is further complicated by the diverse needs of different user groups. Security analysts need to understand potential vulnerabilities and attack surfaces. Software architects require insights into system design patterns and component relationships. Project managers need to comprehend functional requirements and system capabilities. Each group requires different levels of detail and different perspectives on the same software system, yet current tools rarely provide this multi-perspective view in a unified manner.

To bridge this gap, we present a vision for UFPC, a unified program comprehension framework that supports both source code repositories and compiled binaries. Our framework operates across multiple levels of abstraction, from low-level code analysis through architectural understanding to high-level requirements recovery. We use a semantic-enhanced code property graph (CPG) as a compatibility layer that enables consistent analysis across both source code and binaries while preserving both structural and semantic information. Building on this foundation, we aim to recover high-level understanding of software systems including various aspects of their architecture and requirements. Finally, we design an interface containing both a structured API to access these insights and an LLM-based agent that can answer natural language questions about the code based on the recovered understanding.

2 The Unified Program Comprehension Framework

We present the overview of UFPC in Fig. 1. Our framework supports both source code repositories and compiled binaries through a semantic-enhanced CPG compatibility layer that preserves structural relationships while adding function-level semantic summaries. Based on this compatibility layer, the architecture layer recovers high-level system design by identifying component relationships and design patterns, while the requirements layer infers the original business intent and system goals from the implementation. The interface layer provides both programmatic access through structured APIs and natural language interaction via LLM-based agents that can answer user questions about the software system.

2.1 Semantic-Enhanced Code Property Graph

Our semantic-enhanced CPG extends traditional code property graphs with function-level semantic summaries to bridge structural code analysis and higher-level program understanding.

Code Property Graph. The CPG component captures three essential code structures: Abstract Syntax Trees (AST) for language constructs, Control Flow Graphs (CFG) for execution paths, and Program Dependence Graphs (PDG) for data and control dependencies.

To extract CPG, for source codes, many tools are available like Joern [10]. These tools parse source code into abstract syntax trees and construct control flow and data dependency graphs. For binaries, CPG can typically be built upon the analysis result of reverse engineering tools like IDA [3] and Ghidra [7], which can disassemble binaries into assembly code, reconstruct control flow structures, and decompile the binaries into pseudo-code.

Semantic Enhancement. To facilitate support for downstream tasks and higher-level understanding of the system, in addition to the CPG, we add semantic features to the CPG. To this end, we aim to include 1) function and variable-level naming and 2) function-level behavior summaries, which serve as a basis for higher-level understanding of a system.

For source code, the extraction of names is direct, and the summaries can be obtained either from code comments or code summarization tools [9]. For binaries, there are also many tools that can recover function and variable names [4], and generate function-level summaries [8].

2.2 Architecture Layer

The architecture layer recovers high-level system design by extracting both implementation and design aspects from the enhanced CPG representation. This layer identifies architectural elements across two main aspects. The implementation aspect focuses on component models that group related functions into logical units and API documentation that describes interface contracts and communication protocols. The design aspect captures architecture styles and design patterns that reveal structural decisions and organizational principles used by developers. Together, these elements provide insight into both how the system is implemented and how developers organized the system at the design level.

For the implementation aspect extraction, existing research has explored component identification through clustering approaches on dependency graphs and call graphs [12]. API documentation generation has been studied through program analysis and natural language processing approaches, including API usage pattern inference and template-based documentation generation [2]. For design aspect extraction, design pattern detection has been explored by [5].

However, significant gaps remain in current approaches. Most component identification methods struggle with legacy code or systems with complex dependencies [6]. The accuracy varies significantly across different architectural styles and programming paradigms. For API documentation generation, existing methods often require extensive manual validation and struggle to capture implicit contracts and behavioral specifications. The architecture style recovery still remains underexplored. Additionally, most current techniques focus exclusively on source code analysis, with limited work on unified approaches that can consistently handle both source code and binary inputs.

2.3 Requirements Layer

The requirements layer infers high-level system purposes by extracting functional and non-functional requirements from architectural and code analysis information provided by lower layers.

Functional Requirements. Functional requirements describe what the system should do, including system features, user stories, and use cases. Most of the existing works focus on mapping requirements to code with feature location techniques [11]. However, the recovery of the system requirements, like use case and user story, is still not well explored for both source code and binary systems.

Non-functional Requirements. Non-functional requirements cover quality attributes and system constraints that specify how the system should behave, including performance, security, reliability, and maintainability concerns. While there has been substantial research on analyzing individual quality attributes in software systems [1], the systematic recovery of comprehensive non-functional requirements from existing implementations remains underexplored. By combining the semantic-enhanced CPG with LLM-based semantic understanding, our framework aims to bridge this gap by systematically extracting both explicit and implicit non-functional requirements from software implementations.

2.4 Interface Layer

The interface layer provides user access to the framework through both programmatic and conversational interfaces, enabling diverse interaction modes for program comprehension tasks.

This layer offers two complementary access methods: a structured API that provides programmatic access to all framework layers and analysis results, and an LLM-based agent that interprets natural language queries and retrieves relevant information using the structured API. The structured API exposes standardized endpoints for querying code analysis results, architectural components, and requirements information across different abstraction levels. The agent serves as an intelligent interface that can answer user questions about program behavior, design decisions, or system functionality.

3 Discussion

3.1 Applications

Our framework presents significant opportunities across multiple domains, with distinct advantages for source code and binary analysis scenarios. For source code analysis, the framework supports several key applications like legacy code maintenance, vulnerability detection, etc. For example, when modernizing a legacy banking system, our framework can analyze the source code to recover business rules (requirements layer), identify component boundaries (architecture layer). This multi-level understanding allows developers to update the implementation technology while preserving critical business logic. For binary analysis, the framework enables malware analysis, third-party library detection in closed-source systems, reverse engineering for interoperability, and etc. Considering a malware binary, our framework can identify architectural components like network communication modules, and infer potential malicious intent through requirements recovery. The LLM interface can assist security analysts in better analyzing the malware by providing answers grounded in multi-level understanding.

3.2 Challenges

However, several challenges must be addressed. The recovery of high-level understanding presents significant difficulties in bridging the semantic gap between low-level implementation details and high-level business requirements. Inferring original design intent and business rules from code requires sophisticated analysis that goes beyond traditional program analysis capabilities. Validation of high-level understanding poses unique challenges since evaluating semantic correctness requires domain expertise and subjective judgment. Establishing reliable benchmarks and evaluation metrics for requirements extraction and architectural understanding remains an open research problem.

Binary understanding extraction faces substantial technical challenges due to information loss during compilation. Semantic extraction from binaries is particularly difficult as compilation removes contextual information such as variable names, comments, and high-level language constructs. Current binary analysis tools often produce incomplete or inaccurate representations, making it challenging to achieve the same level of understanding available from source code analysis. Additionally, different compilation strategies and target architectures introduce variability that complicates unified analysis approaches.

4 Conclusion

In this paper, we presented a vision for UFPC, a unified program comprehension framework that bridges low-level code analysis and high-level business intent understanding. The framework aims to address fundamental limitations in current program analysis tools by providing a consistent multi-level understanding that serves diverse needs. While challenges remain, our vision represents a significant step toward automatically extracting insights from complex software systems at multiple abstraction levels.

Acknowledgments. This study was funded by National Research Foundation, Prime Minister's Office, Singapore under the Campus for Research Excellence and Technological Enterprise (CREATE) programme; the National Research Foundation, Singapore, and DSO National Laboratories under the AI Singapore Programme (AISG Award No: AISG2-GC-2023-008).

References

1. Bogner, J., Zimmermann, A.: Automatically measuring the maintainability of software architecture models. In: Proceedings of the 11th European Conference on Software Architecture: Companion Proceedings, pp. 113–116 (2017)
2. Gu, X., Zhang, H., Zhang, D., Kim, S.: Deep API learning. In: Proceedings of the 2016 24th ACM SIGSOFT International Symposium on Foundations of Software Engineering, pp. 631–642 (2016)
3. Hex-Rays: Ida pro: A windows, Linux or MAC OS x hosted multi-processor disassembler and debugger (2023). https://www.hex-rays.com/products/ida/
4. Lacomis, J., et al.: DIRE: a neural approach to decompiled identifier naming. In: 2019 34th IEEE/ACM International Conference on Automated Software Engineering, pp. 628–639 (2019)
5. Lucia, A.D., Deufemia, V., Gravino, C., Risi, M.: On the detection of design patterns in object-oriented systems: a survey. In: Information and Software Technology, pp. 1399–1413 (2014)
6. Lutellier, T., et al.: Comparing software architecture recovery techniques using accurate dependencies. In: 2015 IEEE/ACM 37th IEEE International Conference on Software Engineering, vol. 2, pp. 69–78. IEEE (2015)
7. NSA: Ghidra: A software reverse engineering framework (2019). https://ghidra-sre.org/
8. Redmond, P., Meng, N., Nagappan, M.: Automatic summarization of disassembled code. In: Proceedings of the 40th International Conference on Software Engineering: Companion Proceedings, pp. 158–159 (2018)
9. Sun, W., et al.: Source code summarization in the era of large language models. arXiv preprint arXiv:2407.07959 (2024)
10. Yamaguchi, F., Golde, N., Arp, D., Rieck, K.: Modeling and discovering vulnerabilities with code property graphs. In: 2014 IEEE Symposium on Security and Privacy, pp. 590–604. IEEE (2014)
11. Zhang, J., Budgen, D., Drummond, S., Brereton, P.: Feature location via information retrieval based filtering of a single scenario execution trace. In: Proceedings of the 31st IEEE/ACM International Conference on Automated Software Engineering, pp. 777–788 (2016)
12. Zhang, Y., et al.: Software architecture recovery with information fusion. In: Proceedings of the 31st ACM Joint European Software Engineering Conference and Symposium on the Foundations of Software Engineering, pp. 1535–1547 (2023)

TestCaseMig: LLM-Driven Test Case Migration for Evolving Codebases

Wuhe Axi[1], Xin Li[2], Jigang Xie[3], Xitao Li[1](✉), and Haijun Wang[1]

[1] Xi'an Jiaotong University, Xi'an, China
{axiwuhe,xitaoli}@stu.xjtu.edu.cn, haijunwang@xjtu.edu.cn
[2] China United Network Co., Ltd., Software Research Institute, Nanjing, China
lix214@chinaunicom.cn
[3] China Unicom Western Innovation Institute, Xi'an, China
xiejg@chinaunicom.cn

Abstract. As software systems evolve, test cases must adapt to code changes to remain valid and effective. Traditional test migration approaches, including symbolic execution and diff-based heuristics, often require significant manual effort and struggle to handle complex behavioral changes. Recent advances in large language models (LLMs) offer new opportunities for context-aware and automated test adaptation. However, existing LLM-based approaches are not well-suited for test case migration under evolving code, as they typically lack explicit modeling of code changes and original test context. In this paper, we present **TestCaseMig**, a framework that integrates LLMs with static analysis to migrate existing test cases in response to code modifications. TestCaseMig constructs change-sensitive, context-rich prompts and employs a multi-round, feedback-driven generation process with validation and coverage analysis to ensure the correctness, completeness, and adaptability of migrated test cases.

Keywords: Test case migration · Large language models · Static analysis · Software evolution · Automated testing

1 Introduction

Modern software systems evolve rapidly through dependency upgrades, architectural refactoring, and feature enhancements, resulting in frequent structural and logic-level changes to the codebase [2]. These evolutions pose significant challenges for maintaining the validity of existing test cases. Outdated tests may lead to assertion failures, impair regression verification, and disrupt CI/CD pipelines [1].

Traditional maintenance methods (e.g., manual refactoring, rule-based engines, and static pattern matching) can handle simple syntactic modifications. However, they often lack the semantic reasoning and generalizability required to address complex changes like control-flow restructuring, API refactoring, or

Y. Zhou et al. (Eds.): ICECCS 2025, LNCS 15746, pp. 509–514, 2026.
https://doi.org/10.1007/978-3-032-00828-2_31

interface deprecation [3]. As a result, enabling automated and context-aware test migration has become essential for sustaining software quality during continuous evolution.

Recent advances in *Large Language Models* (LLMs) have shown promising results in test generation and repair tasks by leveraging code semantics and minimal contextual prompts [6–8]. Systems like *TestPilot* and *ChatUniTest* demonstrate that LLMs can produce structurally valid and semantically accurate tests with high coverage [9,10]. However, most existing test generation approaches operate from scratch, without leveraging the original test cases or their structural intent. This limits their ability to preserve historical testing logic or assertion semantics across software versions. Similarly, test repair methods typically apply one-shot edits to broken tests but often overlook the underlying code-change semantics, making them brittle when faced with non-trivial behavioral updates [11,12].

To address these limitations, we introduce **TestCaseMig**, a framework that combines static analysis with LLMs to support automated and context-aware test migration. The system analyzes structural and semantic differences between code versions, constructs prompts enriched with test context and change information, and iteratively interacts with the LLM to generate and refine migrated test cases. A feedback loop verifies syntax, execution behavior, and coverage, ensuring correctness and completeness throughout the migration pipeline.

Our main contributions are summarized as follows:

- We present **TestCaseMig**, a test case migration framework that integrates static analysis and LLM-based generation to automate test adaptation under code evolution.
- We develop a context-sensitive prompt construction strategy that captures both the semantics of original test logic and the structural and behavioral differences introduced by code changes.
- We design a feedback-driven refinement mechanism that performs iterative validation and correction based on syntax checks, behavioral consistency, and coverage analysis, ensuring the correctness and robustness of the migrated tests.

2 Methodology

As illustrated in Fig. 1, **TestCaseMig** comprises three main components, forming a fully automated pipeline for migrating outdated test cases in response to code changes:

❶ Code Difference Context Builder. This component analyzes structural and semantic differences between code versions and constructs structured prompts by aggregating key contextual elements such as original tests, code diffs, method usage, and environment setup.

❷ Initial LLM-Based Generation. This module initiates test migration using a templated prompt that guides the LLM to produce a first-pass draft test case, leveraging the constructed context to ensure structural alignment and intent preservation.

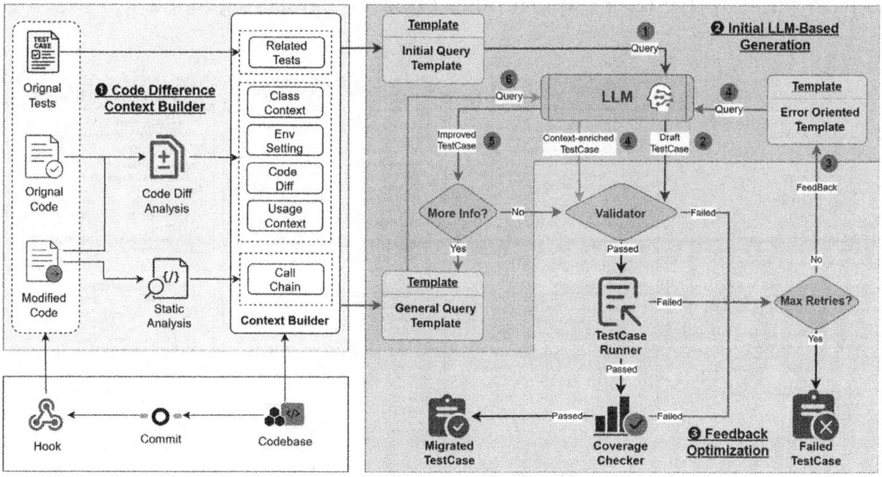

Fig. 1. Overview of the TestCaseMig framework

❸ **Feedback Optimization.** This component refines generated tests through a multi-round process that incorporates syntax validation, runtime execution feedback, and dynamic coverage analysis to ensure correctness, completeness, and robustness.

2.1 Code Difference Context Builder

In the first phase, the system extracts static context information based on the introduced code diffs. Using diff tools and static analyzers (e.g., Soot [4]), it identifies changes in method signatures, control logic, and call relationships. This analysis produces call graphs and class structures reflecting the semantic impact of the changes.

The context builder aggregates and structures key elements essential for guiding LLM-based migration, including the original test case and target method as the semantic foundation, class and environment context (e.g., declarations, dependency injection, initialization), patch-level code differences, representative usage examples, and call chain information. These components are encoded into structured prompt inputs to provide the LLM with sufficient semantic context, thereby preventing incomplete or semantically invalid test generation.

2.2 Initial LLM-Based Generation

TestCaseMig adopts a zero-shot prompting strategy to enable test case migration without any task-specific fine-tuning. This is because of the high cost and limited generalizability of training-based approaches, which often require labeled data and frequent retraining as codebases evolve. In contrast, we leverage the inherent test understanding and code reasoning capabilities of pre-trained LLMs to perform adaptive migration through prompt engineering alone.

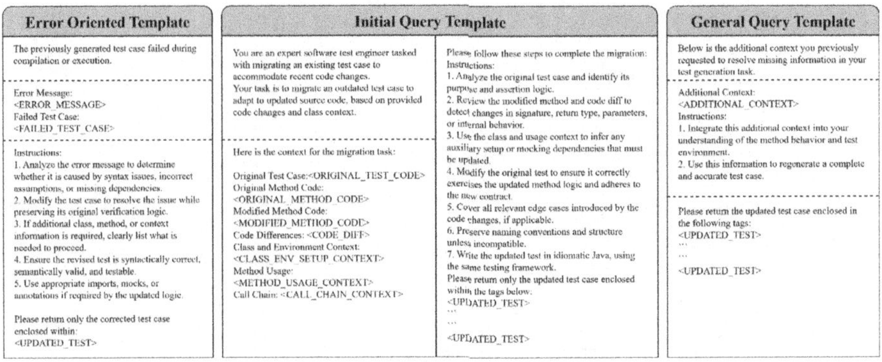

Fig. 2. Prompt Templates

To enhance generation quality, TestCaseMig employs a Chain-of-Thought prompting paradigm [13], which guides the LLM through a multi-stage refinement workflow comprising initial test generation, error correction, and semantic enhancement. This iterative process enables the model to reason about code changes and synthesize reliable, behaviorally aligned test cases, even in complex migration scenarios.

Figure 2 illustrates the three key prompt templates involved in this workflow:

- **Initial Query Template:** This template serves as the entry point of the migration process. It guides the model to generate a *draft test case* based on the original test logic, function definitions, code diffs, usage context, and optionally, the call chain.
- **Error-Oriented Template:** This template is triggered when the generated test fails verification (e.g., due to compilation or assertion errors). It injects error messages into the prompt and instructs the model to revise the output. The refined result includes an *improved test case* and, if necessary, identifies missing contextual elements for further refinement.
- **General Query Template:** This template is used when the model requires additional information, such as dependency setup or usage examples. It guides the model to regenerate a more *context-enriched test case.*

2.3 Feedback-Driven Optimization

Each candidate test generated by the LLM undergoes automated verification:

1. **Syntax and compilation check:** The system first validates the test case by performing syntax verification and ensuring successful compilation.
2. **Runtime execution and assertion evaluation:** It then executes the test on the modified code, monitoring runtime outputs and assertion results to detect behavioral deviations.
3. **Error diagnosis and retry control:** On failure, the system uses the error oriented template for error injection and retry; if more information is needed, the general query template is used. A retry limit prevents infinite loops.

Tests that pass initial validation are further subjected to **dynamic coverage analysis** to ensure that the modified code paths are adequately exercised. If critical branches remain uncovered, the system re-invokes the LLM to generate targeted supplemental tests. Once both correctness and coverage criteria are met, the final test cases are either returned to developers for review or automatically committed to the code repository, thereby completing the migration cycle.

3 Related Work

Test-Case Generation and Migration. Traditional test maintenance approaches often rely on manual refactoring, rule-based heuristics, or static pattern matching. ReAssert [5] repairs failing tests by modifying constants, assertions, and control flow based on runtime failures, emphasizing local consistency but lacking semantic adaptability. To support broader migration needs, JTestMigrator [17] introduces type mapping and semantic embeddings to align legacy tests with updated APIs, addressing behavioral preservation across evolving interfaces.

LLM-Based Test Generation and Repair. The emergence of large language models (LLMs) has catalyzed their use in automated test generation. TestPilot [6] employs Codex with function-level prompts to generate compilable unit tests via adaptive strategies. ChatUniTest [9] enhances this with a validator-guided feedback loop for iterative refinement, boosting robustness and coverage. LLMigrate [15] bridges legacy and updated code by identifying method mappings and generating structured migration hints, facilitating downstream test transformation.

4 Future Plans

To enhance the research depth and practical deployment of **TestCaseMig**, future work will focus on two key directions: (1) integrating the framework into real-world CI/CD pipelines to enable end-to-end automated test migration triggered by code changes, with evaluation metrics targeting robustness, efficiency, and scalability; and (2) extending support for multiple programming languages and testing frameworks (e.g., `pytest`, `Jest`, `xUnit`) via language-aware abstraction and adapter-based context modeling to facilitate the automated migration of heterogeneous test assets.

References

1. Lou, Y., et al.: A survey on regression test-case prioritization. Adv. Comput. **113**, 1–46 (2019)
2. Ziftci, C., Nikolov, S., Sjövall, A., et al.: Migrating code at scale with LLMs at Google. arXiv preprint arXiv:2504.09691 (2025)
3. Li, W., Gall, F., Spaseski, N.: A survey on model-based testing tools for test case generation. In: Itsykson, V., Scedrov, A., Zakharov, V. (eds.) TMPA 2017. CCIS, vol. 779, pp. 77–89. Springer, Cham (2018). https://doi.org/10.1007/978-3-319-71734-0_7
4. Vallée-Rai, R., et al.: Soot: a Java bytecode optimization framework. In: CASCON First Decade High Impact Papers, pp. 214–224 (2010)
5. Daniel, B., et al.: ReAssert: a tool for repairing broken unit tests. In: Proceedings of the 33rd International Conference on Software Engineering (ICSE), pp. 551–560. ACM, New York (2011)
6. Dobslaw, F., Feldt, R., Yoon, J., et al.: Challenges in testing large language model based software: a faceted taxonomy. arXiv preprint arXiv:2503.00481 (2025)
7. Schäfer, M., et al.: An empirical evaluation of using large language models for automated unit test generation. arXiv preprint arXiv:2302.06527 (2023)
8. Chen, M., Tworek, J., Jun, H., et al.: Evaluating large language models trained on code. arXiv preprint arXiv:2107.03374 (2021)
9. Xie, Z., et al.: ChatUniTest: a ChatGPT-based automated unit test generation tool. arXiv e-prints, arXiv:2305.00000 (2023)
10. Yaraghi, A.S., et al.: Automated test case repair using language models. IEEE Trans. Softw. Eng. (2025)
11. Rodríguez, M., Rossi, G., Fernandez, A.: Evaluating large language models for the generation of unit tests with equivalence partitions and boundary values. arXiv preprint arXiv:2505.09830 (2025)
12. Gao, S., et al.: The prompt alchemist: automated LLM-tailored prompt optimization for test case generation. arXiv preprint arXiv:2501.01329 (2025)
13. Wei, J., et al.: Chain-of-thought prompting elicits reasoning in large language models. Adv. Neural. Inf. Process. Syst. **35**, 24824–24837 (2022)
14. Liu, Y., Gu, S., Gao, S., et al.: LLMigrate: transforming "lazy" large language models into efficient source code migrators. arXiv preprint arXiv:2503.23791 (2025)
15. Cui, Y.: Tests as prompt: a test-driven-development benchmark for LLM code generation. arXiv preprint arXiv:2505.09027 (2025)
16. Mirzaaghaei, M., Pastore, F., Pezzè, M.: Automatic test case evolution. Softw. Test. Verif. Reliabil. **24**(5), 386–411 (2014)
17. Jha, A.K., Nadi, S.: Migrating unit tests across java applications. In: 2024 IEEE International Conference on Source Code Analysis and Manipulation (SCAM), pp. 93–104. IEEE, New York (2024)

Evolaris: A Roadmap to Self-evolving Software Intelligence Management

Chengwei Liu[1(✉)], Wenbo Guo[1], Yuxin Zhang[2], Limin Wang[3], Sen Chen[2], Lei Bu[3], and Yang Liu[1]

[1] Nanyang Technological University, Singapore, Singapore
chengwei.liu@ntu.edu.sg
[2] Nankai University, Tianjin, China
[3] Nanjing University, Nanjing, China

Abstract. In recent years, the landscape of software threats has become significantly more dynamic and distributed. Security vulnerabilities are no longer discovered and shared only through formal channels such as public vulnerability databases or vendor advisories. Increasingly, critical threat information emerges informally through blogs, social media, developer forums, open source repositories, and even underground communities. To this end, capturing such intelligence in a timely manner is essential for maintaining situational awareness and enabling prompt security responses. However, this remains a complex challenge due to the fragmented nature of data sources and the technical difficulty of collecting, parsing, mapping, and validating information at scale. To address this, we propose *Evolaris*, a self-evolving software intelligence system built on a multi-agent framework. *Evolaris* is designed to support a full-stack workflow, where agents operate independently but coordinate through shared context to perform tasks such as information discovery, reasoning, gap completion, validation, and risk detection. This architecture enables the platform to learn from new inputs, refine its internal knowledge, and adapt to emerging threat patterns over time, which could continuously improve the precision, timeliness, and scalability of software threat analysis, and offers a sustainable foundation for proactive security decision-making and strengthens the broader ecosystem of security threat understanding.

Keywords: Software Intelligence · Software Security · Multi-Agent

1 Introduction

The volume of software security threats has increased at an accelerating rate, placing substantial strain on the broader security infrastructure. Centralized validation entities, such as the National Vulnerability Database (NVD) [1] and vendor-coordinated disclosure programs, face mounting challenges in processing and curating threat reports with both timeliness and accuracy. This growing workload has contributed to observable deficiencies in data quality, including

Y. Zhou et al. (Eds.): ICECCS 2025, LNCS 15746, pp. 515–520, 2026.
https://doi.org/10.1007/978-3-032-00828-2_32

delayed publication, incomplete records, and inconsistent threat characterizations. Concurrently, an increasing proportion of threat-related intelligence is being disseminated through unstructured and rapidly updated online platforms, including technical blogs, developer forums, community-maintained issue trackers, and social media. Although such sources are heterogeneous and less formally governed, they frequently contain early-stage indicators, technical analyses, and mitigation strategies that are absent from official repositories.

To this end, existing researchers have investigated how to collect, interpret, and utilize these online resources in various ways. For instance, researchers have developed automated systems to gather threat intelligence from various sources, including the internet [6], social media [8], developer communities [7], security forums, and code repositories [2], some researchers also focus on natural language processing and knowledge graphs to automate cybersecurity knowledge extraction from unstructured text [3,5,9]. However, there are still challenges yet to be solved, which hinder the real-world applicability of proposed solutions. First, the relevant information is scattered across heterogeneous sources with varying formats, update frequencies, and levels of trust, which still heavily rely on specialised designs that require human expertise. Second, the content is often embedded in unstructured natural language, lacking explicit structure or machine-readable identifiers to indicate semantics in the targeted context. Third, aligning such information with existing software projects, components, or ecosystem-level behaviors requires non-trivial contextual reasoning. Finally, assessing the reliability and significance of threat information remains difficult without deeper analysis and cross-validation. These challenges are further intensified by the rapid emergence of new threat categories and shifts in how security intelligence is expressed and shared. As a result, there is a critical need for intelligent systems that can continuously monitor, extract, interpret, and reason over dynamic and diverse security information sources.

To address this gap, we propose *Evolaris*, a self-evolving software intelligence platform that automates the full lifecycle of threat information processing. *Evolaris* employs a collaborative multi-agent architecture in which specialized agents carry out key tasks, including data discovery, analytical reasoning, information completion, validation, and risk detection. These agents share context, refine intermediate outputs, and collectively evolve the system's internal models as new data becomes available. *Evolaris* is designed to adapt to emerging forms of intelligence, support scalable analysis across multiple data sources, and improve its analytical capabilities over time. By automating reasoning and knowledge refinement in a distributed and evolving manner, *Evolaris* enhances the accuracy, timeliness, and usefulness of software security threat intelligence. Our goal is to establish a foundational platform that enables continuous, context-aware, and proactive software security understanding.

2 Overview of *Evolaris*

Figure 1 presents the overview roadmap of *Evolaris*. Specifically, it contains two major parts: **1) Intelligence Discovery:** this part focuses on the collection of

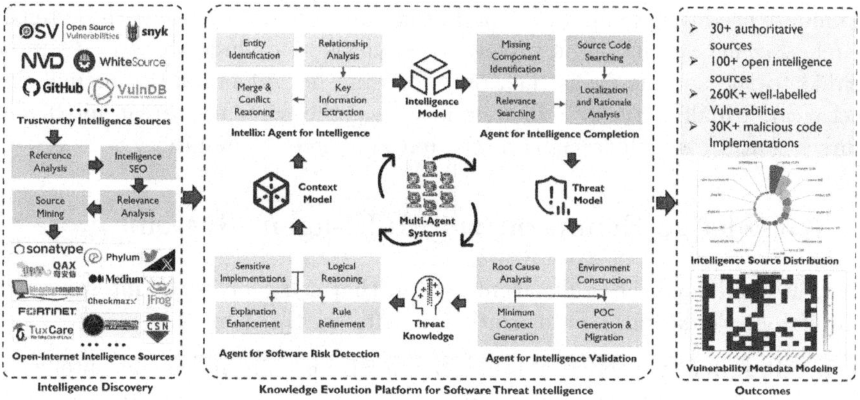

Fig. 1. Overviews of *Evolaris*

software threat intelligence sources so that we can keep monitoring and tracking sources that are mostly used to publish such information, so that we can capture necessary software threat intelligence in time. **2) Knowledge Evolution Platform:** based on the identified intelligence sources, *Evolaris* iteratively conducts continuous monitoring, parsing, validating, and utilizing of software threat intelligence, and meanwhile, iterate the corresponding data model and understanding model of intelligence, threat, knowledge, and context, to evolve the capability of *Evolaris* along the time.

Based on these two major parts, we expect not only *Evolaris* to be able to automate the capability of manipulating software threat intelligence, but also take software threat intelligence as an example to explore the solutions to automate the explicit knowledge collection, interpretation, cognition alignment, validation, and utilization for other domains.

3 Intelligence Discovery

First, *Evolaris* is initiated by existing software threat intelligence. Specifically, we rely on existing well-known and high quality sources as the initial trustworthy sources to collect software threat intelligence. For instance, information from sources like NVD, OSV, Snyk, GitHub Advisory, and VulnDB are usually with human validation, which are also widely used as the source data of software auditing tasks (i.e., software composition analysis) and with well-structured information that are easy to interpret. To this end, starting from them, *Evolaris* collects all references provided on these platforms for each identified software threat reports, and based on these references, *Evolaris* recursively extend to include possible reference links to of them to identify as many possible original sources of software threat intelligence as possible. Moreover, based on these collected reference software threat intelligence (i.e., webpages), *Evolaris* also refer to search engines for better coverage of intelligence sources by searching most commonly used terms in both all intelligence and single ones. After the extensive search, *Evolaris* then conduct relevance analysis to exclude those that are not related to the specific tasks (i.e., only focusing on vulnerabilities or malicious packages). Finally, *Evolaris* further identifies the software threat intelligence sources that are worth tracking as the initial sources to monitor.

4 Knowledge Evolution via Multi-agent Systems

Next, we introduce the multi-agent system that self-evolves the interpretation, completion, validation, and utilization of software threat intelligence.

1) Intelligence Interpretation. Starting from software threat intelligence *Evolaris* collected, *Evolaris* incorporates a multi-step solution to identify the key information that worth extracting and preserving. Specifically, it starts with identifying all entities mentioned in the free texts, and identifies the possible relationship among them. Note that although there could be many less relevant entities extracted and implicit relationships not covered, we take these results as the initial sets of key information. Next, for similar intelligences (i.e., same vulnerabilities or malicious packages), we align the entities and relationships among these results, and identify what are the key objects to focus on, and merge them into a complete knowledge graph for specific cases. As for the possible conflicts, *Evolaris* incorporates a guided reasoning based on all knowledge it has to determine the correct results. Meanwhile, after going through these identified key information of software threat intelligence, *Evolaris* also gradually formalizes an intelligence model as the meta model of all possible key information recorded in existing software threat intelligence.

2) Intelligence Completion. Apart from the alignment of software threat intelligence, it is also possible that some key information identified in the intelligence model is not available in any intelligence for specific cases. To this end, *Evolaris* borrows the rationale of the missed information in other similar software threats. By analyzing the rationale in existing cases, and how this information is extracted, *Evolaris* follows the logic to inspect similar localisations (i.e., source code repositories) to check whether the missed information can be made up properly. Moreover, this process also clarifies the threat model of specific cases, such as how the threats are formed, and how are they threaten corresponding user projects. Based on this, the common patterns of threat models can be concluded, to facilitate downstream validation and detection of new emerging software threat intelligence.

3) Intelligence Validation. After completing the necessary vulnerability information, *Evolaris* further validates the existence and real threats of reported software security threats. Specifically, based on the threat model, *Evolaris* conducts the root cause analysis to identify the conditions and rationale of how the corresponding software threats threaten user projects. By generating the minimum context and constructing a runtime environment, *Evolaris* further migrates existing Proof-of-Concept (POC) or generate the POCs directly to trigger the threats and determine whether they have a real impact on user projects. Based on this, *Evolaris* can also gradually formulate the knowledge of software threats, such as mappings of root causes and validation strategies, the ways to generate test cases and corresponding environment setups, etc. By concluding them, *Evolaris* gradually enriches the knowledge of threats.

4) Software Risk Detection. Based on the threat knowledge, *Evolaris* can also stem the critical criteria to judge the existence of software threats, which can further enhance existing detection approaches. Specifically, software security threats usually involve sensitive implementations, while not all sensitive operations lead to real risks to user projects. To this end, *Evolaris* could further incorporate logical reasoning of LLMs to judge whether identified sensitive operations can lead to real impact. Based on them, *Evolaris* can derive not only a better refined explanation of software threats, from their rationale to presence, but also more precise detection rules that are with higher precision while fewer false positives. Moreover, these generated rules and explanations can also propose new key information that is vital for software threats, and they would be evolved back to the interpretation of software threat intelligence to better capture relevant information.

With these key steps and models, *Evolaris* can gradually evolve to better collect, interpret, complete, validate, and utilize software threat intelligence.

5) Preliminary Results. *Evolaris* has demonstrated significant early-stage outcomes, validating the effectiveness and scalability of the proposed methodology. So far, *Evolaris* has integrated with over 30 authoritative and 100 open intelligence sources, which provide extensive threat coverage. Moreover, *Evolaris* has successfully manages over 260,000 vulnerabilities and has conducted in-depth analyses on more than 30,000 malicious code implementations, which is so far the largest open dataset of malicious packages [4]. Furthermore, *Evolaris* has also integrated and compared 18+ different major sources of vulnerabilities, resulting in a unified framework of vulnerability key information presentation. These early vulnerability metadata modelling and source distribution analytics confirm the analytical strength and adaptability of *Evolaris*.

Evolaris represents a critical evolution in software intelligence management. By dynamically adapting through continuous intelligence refinement and validation, the platform provides significant improvements over traditional static intelligence approaches. Future work includes but is not limited to expanding agent capabilities, such as conflict detection in intelligence interpretation, the analogy of rationale among similar threats for completion, automated compilation and build of software for validation, and more efficient automated iterative refinement of rules for detection, etc.

5 Conclusion

In this paper, we propose the roadmap of *Evolaris*, which establishes a framework towards the automated self-evolving platform for the collection, interpretation, completion, validation, and utilization of software threat intelligence.

Through sophisticated integration of intelligence gathering, analytical reasoning, and threat modelling, *Evolaris* delivers comprehensive, scalable, and dynamic security solutions capable of addressing complex, evolving software threats.

Acknowledgment. This research is supported by the Ministry of Education, Singapore, under its Academic Research Fund Tier 1 (RG96/23). It is also supported by the National Research Foundation, Singapore, and DSO National Laboratories under the AI Singapore Programme (AISG Award No: AISG2-GC-2023-008); by the National Research Foundation Singapore and the Cyber Security Agency under the National Cybersecurity R&D Programme (NCRP25-P04- TAICeN); and by the Prime Minister's Office, Singapore under the Campus for Research Excellence and Technological Enterprise (CREATE) programme. Any opinions, findings and conclusions, or recommendations expressed in these materials are those of the author(s) and do not reflect the views of National Research Foundation, Singapore, Cyber Security Agency of Singapore, Singapore.

References

1. National vulnerability database (2024). https://nvd.nist.gov/. Accessed 30 Apr 2024
2. Bouwman, X., et al.: Helping hands: measuring the impact of a large threat intelligence sharing community. In: 31st USENIX Security Symposium (USENIX Security 2022), pp. 1149–1165 (2022)
3. Gao, P., et al.: A system for automated open-source threat intelligence gathering and management. In: Proceedings of the 2021 International Conference on Management of Data, pp. 2716–2720 (2021)
4. Guo, W., et al.: PackageIntel: leveraging large language models for automated intelligence extraction in package ecosystems (2024). https://arxiv.org/abs/2409.15049
5. Jo, H., Lee, Y., Shin, S.: Vulcan: automatic extraction and analysis of cyber threat intelligence from unstructured text. Comput. Secur. **120**, 102763 (2022)
6. Mulwad, V., Li, W., Joshi, A., Finin, T., Viswanathan, K.: Extracting information about security vulnerabilities from web text. In: 2011 IEEE/WIC/ACM International Conferences on Web Intelligence and Intelligent Agent Technology, vol. 3, pp. 257–260. IEEE (2011)
7. Purba, M.D., Chu, B.: Extracting actionable cyber threat intelligence from twitter stream. In: 2023 IEEE International Conference on Intelligence and Security Informatics (ISI), pp. 1–6. IEEE (2023)
8. Sabottke, C., Suciu, O., Dumitraş, T.: Vulnerability disclosure in the age of social media: exploiting twitter for predicting {Real-World} exploits. In: 24th USENIX Security Symposium (USENIX Security 2015), pp. 1041–1056 (2015)
9. Satvat, K., Gjomemo, R., Venkatakrishnan, V.: Extractor: extracting attack behavior from threat reports. In: 2021 IEEE European Symposium on Security and Privacy (EuroS&P), pp. 598–615. IEEE (2021)

Author Index

Y. Zhou et al. (Eds.): ICECCS 2025, LNCS 15746, pp. 521–522, 2026.
https://doi.org/10.1007/978-3-032-00828-2

Made in the USA
Monee, IL
13 September 2026

62975228R00295